Jason
Balai

MCSE Guide to Microsoft® Windows® 2000 Server

Michael J. Palmer

COURSE
TECHNOLOGY

Thomson Learning™

ONE MAIN STREET, CAMBRIDGE, MA 02142

Australia • Canada • Denmark • Japan • Mexico • New Zealand • Philippines
Puerto Rico • Singapore • South Africa • Spain • United Kingdom • United States

MCSE Guide to Microsoft® Windows® 2000 Server is published by Course Technology.

Associate Publisher	Kristen Duerr
Senior Acquisitions Editor	Stephen Solomon
Product Manager	David George
Production Editor	Christine Spillett
Developmental Editor	Deb Kaufmann
Quality Assurance Manager	John Bosco
Associate Product Manager	Laura Hildebrand
Marketing Manager	Susan Ogar
Text Designer	GEX, Inc.
Composition House	GEX, Inc.
Cover Designer	Efrat Reis

Disclaimer

Course Technology reserves the right to revise this publication and make changes from time to time in its content without notice.

The Web addresses in this book are subject to change from time to time as necessary without notice.

For more information, contact Course Technology, One Main Street, Cambridge, MA 02142;

or find us on the World Wide Web at *www.course.com*.

For permission to use material from this text or product, contact us by

- Web: www.thomsonrights.com
- Phone: 1-800-730-2214
- Fax: 1-800-730-2215

ISBN 0-619-01517-9
Printed in Canada
3 4 5 CODE 03 02 01

CHAPTER THREE
Planning Network Protocols and Compatibility   79

APPENDIX A
Exam Objectives Tracking for MCSE Certification Exam #70-215:
Installing, Configuring, Administering Windows® 2000 Server   715

GLOSSARY   727

INDEX   737

Preface

Career opportunities abound for well-prepared server administrators, which is one of the fastest growing fields in information technology. This book is designed to provide you with a thorough grounding in Windows 2000 Server, the powerful server operating system of the new millennium. If you are new to Windows 2000 Server or server administration, this is your ticket to an exciting future. If you are preparing for certification as a Microsoft Certified Professional (MCP) or as a Microsoft Certified Systems Engineer (MCSE), this book provides the knowledge you need as preparation for certification exam # 70-215, *Installing, Configuring, and Administering Microsoft Windows 2000 Server.* Others who have prior experience with Windows NT Server or Windows 2000 Server will find that the book adds depth and breadth to that experience.

The book is filled with all kinds of features to help you prepare for the exam and to help you develop as a confident server administrator. You learn, step-by-step, how to accomplish the Windows 2000 Server tasks, from the easiest to the most complex. Your learning is supplemented by realistic examples, insightful tips, thought-provoking review questions, hands-on projects, and case projects that simulate those you'll experience in real life.

Windows 2000 Server ushers in a new and mature server network operating system well positioned to meet the needs of the smallest to the largest organizations. It provides the cornerstone on which to build a business, an Internet Web site, or access information-rich data sources. Windows NT Server has been one of the most successful server network operating systems ever offered and Windows 2000 Server builds on that success with new and extensive networking features.

When you complete this book, you will have a solid foundation on which to build as a sophisticated and experienced Windows 2000 Server administrator. This book provides you with knowledge that you can apply right away and other knowledge you can apply in the future. As part of your preparations, the book gives you plenty of direct experience and a wide range of planning, installation, configuration, management, and troubleshooting scenarios.

Each chapter in the book is filled with hands-on projects that cover many aspects of installing and managing Windows 2000 Server. The projects are designed to make what you learn come alive through actually performing the tasks. Besides the hands-on projects, each chapter gives you experience through realistic case projects that put you in the shoes of a Windows 2000 Server consultant who works in all kinds of situations fulfilling the needs of clients. Also, every chapter includes review questions to drive home your knowledge while preparing you for the Microsoft certification exam. All of these features are offered to reinforce your learning so you feel confident in the knowledge you have gained from each chapter and so you develop as a resourceful server administrator.

Chapter 1, "Networking with Microsoft Windows 2000 Server," helps you plan the general networking model to use for Windows 2000 Server. This chapter explains the Windows 2000 Server capabilities as an operating system, presents new features in Windows 2000 Server, and helps you plan which file system to implement when you set up a server. In **Chapter 2**, "Planning for Server Hardware," you learn the hardware requirements for Windows 2000 Server and how to develop specifications for a server that include choosing the right processor, the right amount of memory, and the right amount of disk storage. You also learn how to plan for optimum disk performance and fault tolerance. **Chapter 3**, "Planning Network Protocols and Compatibility," provides background in networking and network protocols. It helps you to understand the many protocols used by Windows 2000 Server and how to select the best protocol for your organization's needs. You also learn how to install and configure protocols for different applications and types of networks.

Chapter 4, "Planning the Active Directory and Security," gives you a solid introduction to the Active Directory, which is a new feature to Windows 2000 Server. Knowledge of the Active Directory enables you to take command of your organization's server and manage network resources that include workstations, printers, and shared data. Part of your learning includes hands-on experience with installing the Active Directory. Chapter 4 also gives you an opportunity to learn how to secure a server and network resources.

In **Chapter 5**, "Server Installation," you learn how to plan a server installation so that it goes smoothly from step 1. Next, you learn the step-by-step process of installing Windows 2000 Server using different methods such as installing the operating system via CD-ROM and installing it through the network. In **Chapter 6**, "Server Configuration," you discover how to configure the server for specialized monitors, keyboards, network communications, and many other needs. You also learn to use the Device Manager to analyze hardware properties and troubleshoot problems. **Chapter 7**, "Configuring Server Storage, Backup, and Performance Options," continues with configuration issues for server disk storage, backups, and performance enhancements. It also shows you how to protect against lost data and equipment power failures. In **Chapter 8**, "Managing Accounts and Client Connectivity," you learn how to configure client accounts, account security policies, and how to set up client operating systems to access a Windows 2000 Server network. As part of the client operating system setup, you learn how to implement Remote Installation Services. **Chapter 9**, "Managing Groups, Folders, Files, and Object Security," gives you grounding in how to manage the server and security through groups and how to securely set up shared folders and files for access by clients.

In **Chapter 10**, "Managing Dfs, Disk Quotas, and Software Installation," you learn more about sharing folder and file resources by setting up the Distributed File System (Dfs). You also learn how to establish disk quotas and how to install server software. **Chapter 11**, "Installing and Managing Printers," shows how Windows 2000 Server takes much of the headache out of managing network printing. In this chapter you learn how to set up and manage all types of printers. In **Chapter 12**, "Remote Access and Virtual Private Networks," you learn about turning a Windows 2000 Server into a tool that can be accessed from home by telecommuters or by users who travel from city to city. You also learn how to set up a Windows 2000 Server as a secure virtual private network (VPN), which capitalizes on a popular trend in networking. **Chapter 13**, "Managing Internet and Network Interoperability," shows you how to make a Windows 2000 server function as a full-featured Web server. You also learn how to set up critical network communication features such as Domain Name Service and terminal services.

The last three chapters in the book show you how to monitor and tune a server and the network to which it is connected, and you learn to troubleshoot problems. In **Chapter 14**, "Server Monitoring and Optimization," you learn how to use Windows 2000 Server tools to track server performance. You also learn techniques for improving server performance in all kinds of ways. **Chapter 15**, "Network Monitoring and Tuning," shows you how to use Windows 2000 Server monitoring tools to measure network performance and determine how to improve that performance. Both Chapters 14 and 15 give you solid grounding in tuning server and network elements such as memory, file system cache, disk storage, and network communications. Finally, in **Chapter 16**, "Troubleshooting," you learn how to troubleshoot a full range of problems that can emerge including software, hardware, and network problems.

FEATURES

To aid you in fully understanding Windows 2000 concepts, there are many features in this book designed to match the ways in which you learn.

- ♦ **Chapter Objectives.** Each chapter in this book begins with a detailed list of the concepts to be mastered within that chapter. This list provides you with a quick reference to the contents of that chapter, as well as a useful study aid.

- ♦ **Illustrations and Tables.** Numerous illustrations of server screens and components aid you in the visualization of common setup steps, theories, and concepts. In addition, many tables provide details and comparisons of both practical and theoretical information and can be used for a quick review of topics.

- ♦ **Chapter Summaries.** Each chapter's text is followed by a summary of the concepts it has introduced. These summaries provide a helpful way to recap and revisit the ideas covered in each chapter.

- ♦ **Review Questions.** The end-of-chapter assessments begin with a set of review questions that reinforce the ideas introduced in each chapter. These questions not only ensure that you have mastered the concepts, but are written to help you become familiar with the types of questions used in Microsoft certification examinations.

- ♦ **Hands-on Projects.** Although it is important to understand the theory behind server and networking technology, nothing can improve upon real-world experience. To this end, along with theoretical explanations, each chapter provides numerous hands-on projects aimed at providing you with real-world implementation experience.

- ♦ **Case Project.** Located at the end of each chapter is a multipart case project. In this extensive case example, as a consultant at the fictitious Aspen Consulting, you implement the skills and knowledge gained in the chapter through real-world server setup and administration scenarios.

♦ **Team Case Projects.** Each chapter concludes with two optional team case projects that enable you to work in a small group of students to solve a real-world problem or to extensively research a topic. These projects give you experience working as a team member, which is a common format used by many businesses and corporations.

TEXT AND GRAPHIC CONVENTIONS

Wherever appropriate, additional information and exercises have been added to this book to help you better understand what is being discussed in the chapter. Icons throughout the text alert you to additional materials. The icons used in this textbook are as follows.

 Tips are included from the author's experience that provide extra information about how to attack a problem, how to set up Windows 2000 Server for a particular need, or what to do to in certain real-world situations.

 The Note icon is used to present additional helpful material related to the subject being described.

 The cautions are included to help you anticipate potential mistakes or problems so you can prevent them from happening.

 Each Hands-on Project in this book is preceded by the Hands-On icon and a description of the exercise that follows.

 Case Project icons mark the case project. These are more involved, scenario-based assignments. In this extensive case example, you are asked to implement independently what you have learned.

 Optional Case Project icons indicate special projects that students can tackle as a group and that often require extra research and group decision making, which simulates the team environment stressed in many organizations.

INSTRUCTOR'S MATERIALS

The following supplemental materials are available when this book is used in a classroom setting. All of the supplements available with this book are provided to the instructor on a single CD-ROM.

Electronic Instructor's Manual. The Instructor's Manual that accompanies this textbook includes:

♦ Additional instructional material to assist in class preparation, including suggestions for lecture topics, suggested lab activities, tips on setting up a lab for the hands-on assignments, and alternative lab setup ideas in situations where lab resources are limited.

♦ Solutions to all end-of-chapter materials, including the Review Questions, Hands-on Projects, Case Projects and Optional Team Case Projects assignments.

Course Test Manager 1.3. Accompanying this book is a powerful assessment tool known as the Course Test Manager. Designed by Course Technology, this cutting-edge Windows-based testing software helps instructors design and administer tests and pre-tests. In addition to being able to generate tests that can be printed and administered, this full-featured program also has an online testing component that allows students to take tests at the computer and have their exams automatically graded.

PowerPoint presentations. This book comes with Microsoft PowerPoint slides for each chapter. These are included as a teaching aid for classroom presentation, to make available to students on the network for chapter review, or to be printed for classroom distribution. Instructors, please feel at liberty to add your own slides for additional topics you introduce to the class.

STUDENT'S MATERIALS

Student case assignment files. The instructor's CD-ROM comes with student case assignment files for each chapter. These files contain the end-of-chapter Case and Optional Team Case assignments in electronic format so that students can enter their answers and submit them through e-mail, to a shared network folder, or print them for submission to the instructor.

Electronic glossary. An electronic glossary with hyperlinks is provided on the instructor's CD-ROM for distribution to each student, such as through a Web page or a shared network folder.

Windows 2000 Server command summary. A summary of the Windows 2000 Server Command Prompt window commands is provided for distribution to students in electronic format.

ACKNOWLEDGMENTS

Writing and sharing ideas is truly a privilege, as is working with the many fine people who are behind the scenes of every page in this book. I want to thank senior acquisitions editor Stephen Solomon and associate publisher Kristen Duerr for making this project possible. I am also very grateful to have the opportunity to work with Deb Kaufmann who is the development editor for the book. Her careful and wise influence are reflected on each page and she is always a vital source of encouragement each step of the way. Dave George is the product manager who is responsible for bringing what starts as a concept to fruition as a bound book. Laura Hildebrand, the associate product manager, provides help and guidance in producing the highest quality instructors and students materials. Christine Spillett has provided great expertise in the copy editing and production editing services for all chapters in the book.

John Bosco, the quality assurance team leader, and the quality assurance team members, Alex White, Burt LaFountain, John Freitas, Matthew Carroll, and Nicole Ashton, have contributed immensely by carefully making sure each chapter, each hands-on assignment, each review question, and each case project is fully tested for accuracy. I am also indebted to the technical reviewers for the book and to many other remarkable people at Course Technology who include publisher Marjorie Hunt, marketing manager Susan Ogar, manufacturing coordinator Denise Widjeskog, and editorial assistant Elizabeth Wessen.

DEDICATION

To my parents Helen and Edward Palmer

READ THIS BEFORE YOU BEGIN

To the Student

This book offers a beginning from which to understand the power and resources of Windows 2000 Server. Every chapter is designed to present you with easy-to-understand information about Windows 2000 Server to help you plan and implement this operating system in different networking contexts. Each chapter of the book ends with review questions, hands-on projects, case assignments, and team case assignments that are written to be as realistic as the work you will soon be performing. Your instructor can provide you with answers to the review questions and additional information about the hands-on projects. When you complete the case and optional team case assignments, you can submit them electronically or in written form. The student project files provided by your instructor consist of Microsoft Word files for each end of chapter case and optional team case project. You can enter your answers in the space provided within the file and submit them to your instructor by disk, by printing out your answers, through the network, or through e-mail.

To the Instructor (Refer to the Instructor's Resource Kit that accompanies this text for more details.)

Setting up the classroom or lab file server. To complete the projects and assignments in the book, the students will need access to a computer running Windows 2000 Server. To maximize the learning experience, it is recommended that you have one or more servers that can be dedicated for classroom use. Each server need not be an expensive model, but should be on Microsoft's Hardware Compatibility List. There is an advantage in having several servers for student projects so that the students have more flexibility in their practice. Every server should be equipped with Microsoft Windows 2000 Server and have licenses as appropriate for your laboratory or practice setup. The Instructor's Resource Kit contains many suggestions about how to set up a lab, including how to equip and manage a lab in which there are limited resources. It also contains alternative projects and assignments for students.

The Hands-on Projects in the text require that students have Administrator privileges or accounts with Administrator privileges.

Internet assignments. A few projects require Internet access for information searches. These projects are not mandatory; however, the projects will help train the student in using this resource as a prospective server administrator.

Accepting assignments electronically. The case assignment files included on the instructor's CD-ROM are for distribution to your students and are in Microsoft Word format. This enables you to accept assignments electronically, if appropriate to your classroom setting. For more details, please refer to the Instructor's Manual.

System requirements. The recommended software and hardware configurations are as follows:

Workstation Clients

- Windows 3.11 or higher (Windows 95, Windows 98, Windows NT Workstation, or Windows 2000 Professional are preferred)
- 386 or higher processor with 4 MB of RAM (486 or higher with 8+ MB of RAM preferred)
- VGA monitor
- Mouse or pointing device
- Network interface card connected to the classroom, lab, or school network
- Hard disk drive
- At least one high density 3.5-inch floppy disk drive
- Internet access and a browser (recommended but not required for selected research assignments)

Windows 2000 Server Hardware

- Listed in Microsoft's Hardware Compatibility List
- Pentium 166 MHz or faster
- 64 MB of RAM or more
- VGA or better resolution monitor
- Mouse or pointing device
- High density 3.5-inch floppy disk drive
- 12X or faster CD-ROM drive
- One or more hard disks with at least 1 GB or more of disk storage
- Network interface card for network communications
- Tape system (recommended but not required)
- Modem (recommended but not required)
- Printer (to practice setting up a network printer)

NETWORKING WITH MICROSOFT WINDOWS 2000 SERVER

After reading this chapter and completing the exercises you will be able to:

♦ Plan what network model to apply to your network

♦ Compare the differences between Windows 2000 Professional, Server, Advanced Server, and Datacenter

♦ Explain Windows 2000 capabilities as a server operating system

♦ Explain the new features in Windows 2000

♦ Describe the file systems that are compatible with Windows 2000 and choose the file system that is right for your server

Microsoft Windows servers reach millions of people each day in mundane and dramatic ways. When you use the Internet to check stock quotes, purchase a music CD, or access your favorite news Web site to play local or national news clips, chances are that you are linking into a Microsoft Windows NT or Windows 2000 server. On-call physicians are paged for emergencies, organ donors are located, and new medical procedures are taught through the help of Microsoft Windows servers. The next time you apply for a job, send an e-mail, develop a budget, or take a class, the facilitator in the background may be a Microsoft Windows server. The audio, video, or game entertainment on your next airline flight may be brought to you by a Microsoft Windows server, and you may arrange where to stay at your destination through the same server.

All of these technologies exist now, and new ones are available nearly every day. As a new or experienced Microsoft Windows 2000 Server professional, you have a ground-floor opportunity to participate in a technology that is pushing the boundaries of information sharing. This chapter introduces you to peer-to-peer and server-based networking, and to the new features and capabilities of Windows 2000. You also learn about the role of Microsoft file systems and how to plan which file system to implement.

PLANNING A NETWORKING MODEL

Microsoft Windows 2000 Server is a server **network operating system** (**NOS**). It is used to coordinate the ways our computers access resources available to them on the network. A **network** is a communications system enabling computer users to share computer equipment, application software, and data, voice, and video transmissions. Physically, a network contains computers joined by communications cable or sometimes by wireless devices. Networks can link users who are in the same office or building, in a different state, or as far away as on a different continent (see Figure 1-1).

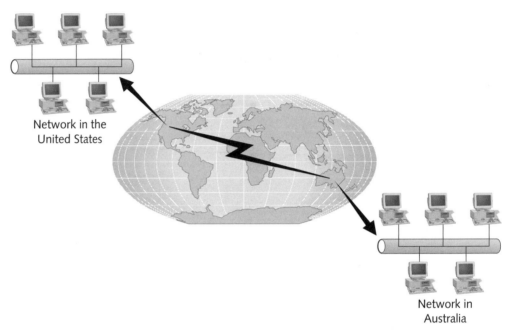

Network in the
United States

Network in
Australia

Figure 1-1   Networking across continents

A workstation or client NOS is one that enables individual computers to access a network, and in some cases to share resources on a limited basis. A **workstation** is a computer that has its own central processing unit (CPU) and may be used as a standalone or network computer for word processing, spreadsheet creation, or other software applications. A **client** is a computer that accesses resources on another computer through a network or by a direct connection.

Microsoft Windows 2000 Server can be implemented using either of two models for networking, or a combination of both: peer-to-peer networking and server-based networking. **Peer-to-peer networking** focuses on spreading network resource administration among server and nonserver members of a network, while **server-based networking** locates administration on one or more servers. Often small organizations use the peer-to-peer networking model, while middle-sized and large networks use the server-based model—although Windows 2000 Server enables flexibility in using either model.

Using Peer-to-Peer Networking

A peer-to-peer network is one of the simplest ways to network. On a peer-to-peer network, workstations communicate with one another through their own operating systems. Windows 98 is an example of an operating system that can be used for peer-to-peer network communication. Files, folders, printers, and the contents of entire disk drives can be made available on one computer for others to access. No special computer, such as a mainframe computer or server, is needed to enable workstations to communicate and share resources (see Figure 1-2).

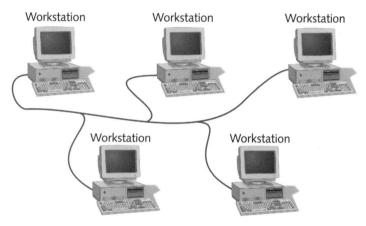

Figure 1-2   A simple peer-to-peer network without a server

 TIP   Although a server can be used as a powerful workstation in a peer-to-peer context, generally this is not an effective use of its management capabilities.

Using Windows 98 alone, a group of computer users can set up workgroups to help them share information and work as a team. A **workgroup** is a grouping of computer users who share one or more resources, for example files and printers, in a decentralized way. Consider a small tax accounting firm that employs seven people, each with her or his own computer that is connected to a simple network. The most recent tax rules can be placed in a folder on one computer that is shared with all others. Blank electronic tax forms can be placed in a folder on another computer, and a third computer might house a database of customer information. In this case, spreading the information among the three computers enables it to be housed with the workgroup member who is responsible for maintaining it. Also, the firm can save money by purchasing only one or two printers to share on the network, instead of purchasing one for each computer.

Strict peer-to-peer networking can be effective for very small networks, but there are problems when resource management is totally decentralized. In our accounting office example, if workgroup members turn off their computers, no one can access their shared resources. Another problem is that a workstation operating system is not designed to handle a growing load of clients in the same way as a server operating system.

As a general rule, when a workgroup grows to over 10 members, peer-to-peer networking is much less effective for several reasons:

- It offers only moderate network security. Access to information can be limited to a certain drive or folder, but not to individual files. Also, access to financial data cannot be audited.

- There is no centralized storage or account management. As the number of network users grows, so does the need to have a central place to store and manage information. It is much easier to manage files by locating them on a central file server for all to access.

- Network management becomes more difficult because there is no point of centralized administrative control from which to manage users and critical files, including backing up important files.

- Peer-to-peer networks can soon experience slow response because this model is not optimized for heavy multiple access to one computer. If many workgroup members decide to access one shared drive or other shared resources at the same time, all are likely to experience slow computer response from the load.

Using Server-based Networking

Microsoft Windows 2000 Server is a more robust network operating system than Windows 98 or Windows 95. Like Windows 98 and Windows 95, you can run programs on Windows 2000 Server and use desktop features such as My Computer to view folders and the Start button to launch programs (try Hands-on Projects 1-1 and 1-2.) But Windows 2000 Server offers much more because it is a multipurpose server that enables full-scale network resource management. A **server** is a single computer that provides extensive multiuser access to network resources. For example, a single Windows 2000 Server can act as a file and print server, a Web server, a network administration server, a database server, an e-mail server, or a combination of any of these. Depending on the hardware capabilities, the server is designed to handle hundreds of users at once, resulting in faster response when delivering the shared resource, and less network congestion as multiple workstations access that resource. Figure 1-3 illustrates a network with a file server (try Hands-on Project 1-3 to view computers on a network).

The server-based model offers a wide array of options for modern networking. For instance, implementing Windows 2000 Server can provide the following advantages:

- All members can share computer files.

- Printers and other resources can be shared; they can also be located in a central place for convenience.

- Access to resources can be centrally controlled and administered.

- All members can have electronic mail (e-mail) and send messages to other office members through the network and file server.

- Members can share software applications, such as an accounting package or word processing software. This provides an opportunity to have everyone using the same software (and the benefits of common support for one software package).

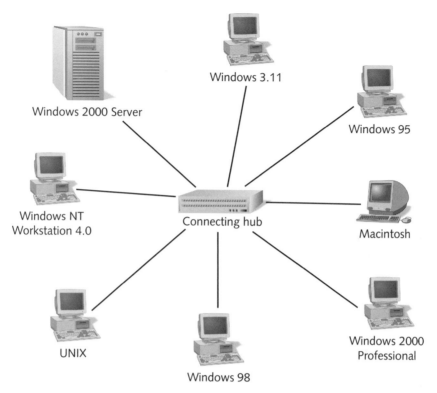

Windows 3.11

Windows 95

Windows 2000 Server

Windows NT
Workstation 4.0

Connecting hub

Macintosh

UNIX

Windows 98

Windows 2000
Professional

Figure 1-3   A server-based network

- All computers can be backed up more easily. With a network and file server, the backups can be done from one location and regularly scheduled to run from the server. The server can be backed up, too.

- The sharing of computer resources can be arranged to reflect the work patterns of groups within an organization. For example, managing partners in a firm can be one group for the purpose of sharing management and financial information on the server.

- The server administrator can save time when installing software upgrades. For example, to implement the latest version of Microsoft Word, the administrator will upgrade only the software at the server. Microsoft Word users on the network can upgrade their versions from the server.

WINDOWS 2000 SERVER AND WINDOWS 2000 PROFESSIONAL COMPARED

Microsoft offers versions of Windows 2000 designed for server and workstation implementations. The basic server version is called Windows 2000 Server, and Windows 2000 Professional is designed for workstations. Microsoft's overall goal is to combine Windows 2000 Server and Windows 2000 Professional on a server-based network to achieve a lower **total cost of**

ownership (**TCO**). The TCO is the total cost of owning a network, including hardware, software, training, maintenance, and user support costs. Windows 2000 Professional is intended as a reliable, easy-to-configure workstation operating system to be used in a business or professional environment. Also, recognizing that professionals are highly mobile, Windows 2000 Professional is designed to work equally well on a desktop computer or a laptop. Windows 2000 Server is intended to play a key management role on the network by administering the **Active Directory**—a database of computers, users, groups, shared printers, shared folders, and other network resources—and a multitude of network services. Also, by combining Windows 2000 Professional workstations and Windows 2000 Server on the same network, it is possible to centralize software updates and workstation configuration via a server.

Microsoft's long-term objective is to encourage users to convert all workstation operating systems on a network to Windows 2000 Professional, because the TCO for Windows 2000 Professional is less than for other workstation NOSs such as Windows 95 and Windows 98. The TCO is less because Windows 2000 Professional is able to use automated configuration and software features designed for it in Windows 2000 Server. Network connectivity, desktop setup, and fast installation of standardized software can be automated from Windows 2000 Server to Windows 2000 Professional, so that the user can set up a workstation with practically no technical knowledge or assistance.

 A study conducted by International Data Corporation and reported by Kathleen Ohlson in *Network World* ("Managed Environments Lower Costs, Analysts Say," February 2, 1998) shows that the yearly TCO of a workstation on an average network is $10,400. This cost can be reduced by two-thirds or more when centralized server services are used to reduce configuration, support, and maintenance costs.

Windows 2000 Professional and Windows 2000 Server share the same hardware memory capability to support up to 4 GB of RAM. Both also share the same new interface and desktop features. Beyond these similarities, Windows 2000 Server supports up to four processors, while Windows Professional supports up to two. Windows 2000 Server also offers more services and user connectivity options that are appropriate for a server instead of a workstation. These services include the following:

- The capability of handling virtually unlimited numbers of users simultaneously (depending on the hardware platform). Windows 2000 Professional is designed optimally for 10 simultaneous users
- Active Directory management
- Network management
- Web-based management services
- Network-wide security management
- Network storage management
- Remote network access, network-wide communications services, and high-speed network connectivity
- Application services management
- Network printer management through the Active Directory

WINDOWS 2000 SERVER, ADVANCED SERVER, AND DATACENTER COMPARED

Windows 2000 Server is divided into three different products to match the network application: Windows 2000 Server, Windows 2000 Advanced Server, and Windows 2000 Datacenter. Windows 2000 Server provides a comprehensive set of server and Web services for up to four-processor systems and supports up to 4 GB of RAM. Windows 2000 Advanced Server is intended for high-end enterprise networks that require up to eight-processor servers, clustered servers, or both. **Clustering** is a technique in which two or more servers are linked to equally share the server processor load, server storage, and other server resources (see Figure 1-4). Windows 2000 Advanced Server also has the ability to handle up to 8 GB of RAM. Windows 2000 Datacenter is targeted for large database and data manipulation services. The Datacenter version supports 64 GB of RAM, clustering, and individual servers with up to 32 processors.

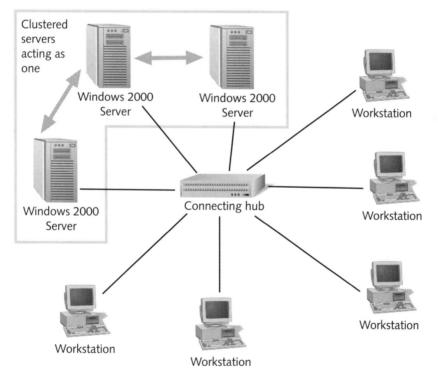

Figure 1-4 Server clustering

WINDOWS 2000 SERVER CAPABILITIES

Like its Windows NT Server predecessor, Microsoft Windows 2000 Server is equipped with a range of capabilities that makes it a versatile server NOS. These capabilities make it at home as a file server, a Web server, or a center for client/server applications. The Windows 2000 Server capabilities include the following:

- Sharing resources
- Managing resources
- Security
- Scalability and compatibility
- Reliability
- Distributability
- Fault tolerance
- Internet integration and electronic commerce

 Windows 2000 Server has been in development since 1994 and contains about 45 million lines of computer code, compared to Windows NT Server 4.0, which has about 15 million lines of code.

Sharing Resources

Data files, software, and print services are examples of resources that a file server can make available on a network. Before file servers, PC users carried files on disk from office to office (a method sometimes called the "sneakernet"). At one university, a budget officer created disks of budget information, which were then distributed to each department. Every department would review the disk files, make changes, and send its disk back to the budget officer to be incorporated in the calculations for the next budget. Creating a university-wide budget involved lots of work since over a hundred disks were carried back and forth to distribute original data, and make corrections or additions.

The implementation of a network and a server changed the effort to create a new budget each year. With a network, the budget officer could put data files on the server. Each department could access its own budget information, share it with others in the department, adjust the data, and return it, all without asking anyone to leave his or her office.

A Windows 2000 file server enables files that need to be used by several people to be stored at one location for all to access. Those who have accounts or authorized access to the file server can quickly obtain shared files. By storing information in one place, controls can be set up to ensure everyone obtains the same, consistent, data. It is easier to back up data, too, because of its central location.

Windows 2000 servers provide options to share files by creating a shared folder. When a shared folder is available through the network, a user with the right authorization can map that folder as though it were a drive on his or her computer (see Figure 1-5). A **mapped folder** or **drive** is shared on the network by a file server or workstation. It gives designated network workstations access to the files and data in its shared volume or folder. The workstation, via software, determines a drive letter for the shared volume, which is the workstation's map to the data (try Hands-on Project 1-10).

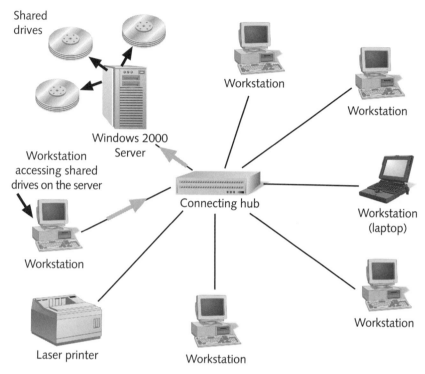

Figure 1-5   Accessing shared server drives

Windows 2000 Server print services enable many kinds of printers to be shared on a network. For example, a printer connected to the server can be shared with all network users or only with a designated group of users. Print services to other shared network printers also can be managed from the server.

Many offices find network print services save on making a substantial investment in printing equipment. For example, in an office with six people working in close proximity, all can share a single network printer instead of purchasing six printers, one for each employee. In another example, an architectural firm can save by sharing one expensive plotter for printing building drawings, instead of purchasing lower-quality plotters for each architect.

Another advantage of Windows 2000 Server is the ability to load or run software applications on workstations across the network. A site license can be purchased to have one shared copy of a word processor or one shared copy of an entire suite of programs, such as Microsoft Office, installed on the server. For example, if the site license is for 400 users, then that many users have the option to install it from the file server to their workstations over the network. Another option is to run a network version of the software, which means that only a few utility files are permanently loaded at the workstations, while the main program files are always loaded from the server each time the program is started. The advantage of this method is that it saves workstation disk space. A disadvantage is that it may create an excessive load on the server and the network, if there are several hundred users who have network installations.

Using application services on a network can save the network administrator or client support people hours of work. When a software upgrade is released, the network administrator loads one copy on the server that can be shared by all users. This represents hours of savings when compared to purchasing individual licenses and loading the software at each workstation, such as in our example of 400 users. Also, by using the file server as the central application program source, it is easier to ensure that all users have the same software and version level. This saves many hours for client support people by reducing the need to support an extensive range of software and different software versions.

Managing Resources

A server-based network consists of **resources** that can be managed through Windows 2000 Server. Windows 2000 Server offers a way to centralize management of network resources in order to simplify network management tasks. The network resources are file servers, workstations, shared printers, and shared folders. With Windows 2000 Server, the network administrator can manage access to software, the Internet, print services, data files, and other network services.

One way in which a Windows 2000 server helps manage a network is through the Active Directory and container objects such as domains, organizational units, trees, forests, and sites. These objects are explained in Chapter 4. They offer a way to manage resources, workstations, software, and the network from one central location. For the network administrator, they offer a way to manage the network resources with minimum confusion and time expenditure.

Security

At one time computer security was given little attention. Today, security is an important issue. File servers house sensitive data that must be protected from intruders accessing it through a local network or via the Internet. Windows 2000 Server is compatible with a C2 top-secret security rating from the United States government. The C2 rating means that a server NOS provides security at many levels through the following:

- File and folder protection
- Account and network access passwords
- File, folder, and account auditing
- Server access protection on a network
- Server management controls

Scalability and Compatibility

Most users want a system that can grow as their organization's needs grow. **Scalability** is the ability of a computer operating system to function on a range of computers from small to large. For example, you might start out with a single-processor Pentium server and 100 users. In a year, you grow to 400 users and find you need a more powerful server, such as a four-processor computer. When you move from the single-processor to the four-processor computer, you want to also move the operating system, in order to keep your investment in software.

Windows 2000 Server can be scaled to handle substantial growth. The operating system can support from 1 to 15,000 user connections. It works on both single-processor and multi-processor computers, including 80486s, Pentiums, and **symmetric multiprocessor** (**SMP**) computers. Windows 2000 Server (Datacenter) can run on computers that have up to 32 processors, depending on the capability of the hardware, and it runs on thousands of different computers.

Windows 2000 Server also can handle small and large databases. Microsoft Access is an example of a small database system that works with Windows 2000 Server. Larger database capabilities are fulfilled by relational database systems such as Microsoft SQL Server and Oracle. A single database on a Windows 2000 server can hold more than 200 GB of information and have more than 5,000 users accessing it at the same time.

Another area of advancement is the ability to communicate with a wider range of computers and networks. Windows 2000 Server communicates with IBM, Novell, UNIX, Banyan, DEC, and other network operating systems. Also, it can be accessed by workstations with any of the following operating systems (try Hands-on Project 1-4):

- MS-DOS
- Windows 3.x
- Windows 95 and Windows 98
- Windows NT and Windows 2000
- Macintosh
- UNIX

Reliability

Several features of Windows 2000 Server make it reliable and powerful. One feature is that the Windows 2000 Server operating system kernel runs in privileged mode, which protects it from problems created by a malfunctioning program or process. The **kernel** consists of the core programs and computer code of the operating system. The **privileged mode** gives the operating system kernel an extra level of security from intruders and prevents system crashes due to out-of-control applications.

When a user runs an MS-DOS program on Windows 2000 Server, the operating system uses the **virtual DOS machine** component. The virtual DOS machine tricks the MS-DOS application into responding as though it were the only application running. Each virtual DOS machine session runs in a separate memory space, and several MS-DOS programs can be running at once, each within a different virtual DOS machine session. If a program attempts to make a direct call to memory or to a hardware component, and the operating system detects an error condition or an exception to security, the program may be stopped by Windows 2000.

 The virtual DOS machine consists of two processes, which are Ntvdm.exe and Wow.exe ("Wow" stands for Windows on Windows). It also employs two system files that consist of virtual device drivers, Ntio.sys and Ntdos.sys.

Windows 2000 Server also runs 16-bit Windows applications by using the virtual DOS machine. When the 16-bit program is started, Windows 2000 starts a virtual DOS machine session and then starts a 16-bit version of Windows within that session (try Hands-on Project 1-7). If an error occurs when you run a 16-bit Windows program, Windows 2000 Server can terminate the program without affecting another program or process that is active.

Another powerful feature of Windows 2000 is that it takes full advantage of the multitasking and multithreading capabilities of modern Pentium computers. **Multitasking** is the ability to run two or more programs at the same time. For example, Microsoft Word prints a document at the same time that a Microsoft Excel spreadsheet is calculating the sum of a column of numbers. **Multithreading** is the capability of programs written in 32-bit code to run several program code blocks, or "threads," at the same time. For instance, a Microsoft Access database query runs a thread to pull data out of the database, while another thread generates a subtotal of data already obtained.

The multitasking in Windows 2000 is called preemptive multitasking. That means each program runs in an area of memory separate from areas used by other programs. Early versions of Windows used cooperative multitasking, in which programs shared the same memory area. The advantage of preemptive multitasking is that it reduces the risk of one program interfering with the smooth running of another program.

Distributability

There are many software applications written to distribute functions among computers. For example, a sales analysis program might use programs at one computer, databases from two other computers, and special information display screens at a user's computer. The process of dividing computer functions across many computers is called **distributability**.

Windows 2000 Server handles software distributability through the **Distributed Component Object Model** (**DCOM**), a capability designed for client/server networks so that software applications can be integrated across several computers. For example, DCOM makes it possible to integrate a payroll system for a company with multiple locations, housing Windows 2000 servers and workstations at each location. The payroll applications and database information can be maintained at and coordinated among all locations.

Fault Tolerance

Computer software and hardware sometimes fail for many reasons. Protection from these failures is called **fault tolerance**. Windows 2000 Server comes with many fault-tolerance capabilities. Some of those fault-tolerance options are as follows:

- Recovery from hard disk failures

- Recovery from lost data in a file

- Recovery from system configuration errors

- Protection from power outages

- Advanced warning about system and hardware problems (try Hands-on Project 1-5)

Internet Integration and Electronic Commerce

Many organizations are interested in offering information or services on the **World Wide Web** (**Web** or **WWW**) through the Internet. Windows 2000 Server is designed as a home for Microsoft's Web server software called Internet Information Services (IIS). IIS gives organizations the ability to take advantage of intranet software as well as Internet software. The **Internet** is a collection of thousands of smaller networks tied together around the globe by a vast array of network equipment and communications links; an **intranet** is a private network within an organization. Like the Internet, an intranet uses Web-based software and the TCP/IP communications protocols, but intranets are highly restricted from public access. Intranets are currently used to enable managers to run high-level reports, to enable staff members to update human resources information, and to provide access to other forms of private data.

Windows 2000 Server has a service, called the Indexing Service, that automatically indexes the content of information created for Internet and intranet access within a company. Index information is created for **Hypertext Markup Language** (**HTML**), text files, or Microsoft Office documents, such as Microsoft Word. The Indexing Service enables quick searches for the indexed topics, while using low network overhead.

Microsoft has a strong commitment to Web development. It offers the IIS for Windows NT Server and Windows 2000 Server, and Peer Web Services for Windows 2000 Professional, Windows NT Workstation, Windows 98, and Windows 95. Microsoft also offers FrontPage for Web development, and HTML-formatting options are built into Microsoft Office.

NEW FEATURES INTRODUCED IN WINDOWS 2000 SERVER

Windows 2000 Server incorporates a wide range of new features that are designed to make it more flexible for existing and future network technologies. The new features that are of particular interest to network and server administrators include:

- *Active Directory*: The Active Directory is a database that is used to store information about resources such as user accounts, computers, and printers; it groups resources at different levels (hierarchies) for local and universal management.

These groupings are called containers, because they are like storage bins that can hold network resources and other lower level bins. The Active Directory also provides a centralized means to quickly find a specific resource through indexing.

The Active Directory is an example of a directory service, similar to Novell Directory Service (NDS), which is a design concept that enables network resources to be centralized for easier management. A directory service is often compared to a telephone book because it provides a way to easily find one or more resources, including specific attributes of those resources. In a directory service, each object has associated attributes that are appropriate to that object. The attributes of a user account, for instance, include the account name, the user's full name, the resources that the user shares on the network, security restrictions, and groups to which the user belongs. Significantly, a directory service goes beyond a telephone book in that it provides a way to manage resources.

- *Distributed network architecture (DNA)*: Windows 2000 Server offers new ways to distribute network and management resources, to match the needs of all types of networks. One important change from Windows NT Server 4.0 is that there is no longer one server, called the primary domain controller, that maintains the master copy of account and security information plus one or more servers, called backup domain controllers, that keep copies of this information as a backup. In Windows 2000 Server, multiple servers can be designated as domain controllers, each containing a copy of the Active Directory and able to verify a user who wants to log onto the network. Windows 2000 Server supports the Distributed File System (Dfs), which enables users to employ the Active Directory and Windows Explorer to consolidate files, folders, and resources from various servers and computers into a single tree structure for easier access.

- *Kerberos security*: **Kerberos** is a security system that enables two parties on an open network to communicate without interception from an intruder. Kerberos works through a special communications protocol that enables a client to initiate contact with a server and request secure communication. The server responds by providing an encryption key that is unique to that communication session, and it does so by using a protected communication called a ticket.

- *Flexible server and network management*: One of the most flexible and powerful management tools, offering a huge range of capabilities, is the Microsoft Management Console (MMC). The MMC is a management tool that you customize by choosing among "snap-in" modules, which can be installed or removed at will. One advantage of this approach is that all management functions can be accessed from one place, instead of having to be accessed from several places, as in Windows NT 4.0 (try Hands-on Project 1-6 to view the MMC snap-ins).

- *IntelliMirror*: IntelliMirror is a concept built into the combined use of Windows 2000 Server and Windows 2000 Professional. It is intended to enable Windows 2000 Professional clients to access the same desktop settings, applications, and data regardless of the location from which they access the network or even if they are not on the network. IntelliMirror also uses information in the

Active Directory to ensure that consistent security and group policies apply to the client and that the client's software is upgraded or removed on the basis of a central management scheme.

- *Web-based Enterprise Management (WBEM)*: Web-based Enterprise Management is intended as a means to make life easier for network and server administrators. WBEM is an attempt to standardize the tools and interfaces used by administrators to gain a total picture of the relationship between their networks and the physical devices connected to their networks, servers, and workstations. WBEM uses the Common Information Model (CIM), which is a proposed standard, to obtain consistent tracking and management information about a network and its attached devices.

- *Hierarchical Storage Management (HSM)*: Through **Hierarchical Storage Management** (**HSM**), information is stored on the basis of policies set up by the server administrator, so that users can access all kinds of information no matter where it is stored, and that the information is stored economically. It is expensive and unnecessary to attempt to store all information on hard disks, when less expensive removable media such as Zip disks, tapes, CD/ROMs, and read/write CD-ROMs are available. HSM enables the administrator to decide which medium is most appropriate for information storage.

- *Zero Administration for Windows (ZAW)*: **Zero Administration for Windows** (**ZAW**) is a combination of management techniques and tools that enable an organization to reduce TCO. Most of the new features already described for Windows 2000 Server are part of ZAW—Active Directory, distributed network architecture, improved security, expanded management capabilities, IntelliMirror, WBEM, and HSM.

- *Power management*: Power management is handled through OnNow, which is similar to power management in Windows 95 and Windows 98, enabling portions of a system, such as hard disks and the monitor, to "sleep" when they are not in use for a specific period of time.

- *International language compatibility*: Windows 2000 supports more languages and language capabilities than previous versions of Windows, including Hindi, Chinese, and multiple versions of English. This is an important feature, because servers are used all over the world.

FILE SYSTEM COMPATIBILITY

Windows 2000 Server primarily supports two file systems: the File Allocation Table (FAT) file system and NT File System (NTFS). It also supports conversion of the OS/2 High-Performance File System (HPFS) to NTFS.

FAT

The **File Allocation Table** (**FAT**) **file system** is an older file system that was initially designed for computers with small disk systems, such as early computers with 20, 40, 100,

250, or 500 MB of disk storage. Most computers sold today come with much larger disk storage, such as 4, 8, or 10 GB, or more. Because today's applications and data files quickly consume disk space, many computer owners are purchasing additional disk drives.

FAT was developed to use with MS-DOS and is compatible with Windows NT and Windows 2000, Windows 95, Windows 98, OS/2, and various UNIX computer operating systems. The early version of FAT has become known as FAT16, because it was designed for 16-bit systems. FAT32 is a later version of FAT that was introduced in Windows 95 operating system release 2 (Windows 95 OSR2).

FAT16 disk drives are set up in a series of allocation units (previously called clusters) to form a partition. An allocation unit may consist of 2, 4, or 8 sectors on a disk. Files are created from one or more allocation units. The operating system keeps track of used and unused allocation units in a disk area called the file allocation table, which is kept in the beginning allocation units of the partition. The file allocation table has one of four types of entries for each allocation unit, indicating:

- That the unit is available to be used
- A number showing the next allocation unit occupied by a file
- An end-of-file mark showing the last allocation unit for a file using several allocation units
- A mark indicating that the allocation unit is damaged or cannot be read

A FAT system also contains lists of associated files that form a directory. A directory tracks the following information or attributes about its files:

- Name
- Time and date of creation or last update
- Attributes, such as read-only
- Size
- Number of the first allocation unit it occupies

FAT16 has several advantages:

- It is a simple file system that is supported by many small computer operating systems.
- It has a low operating system overhead.
- It can support partitions up to 4 GB.
- It can support file sizes up to 2 GB.

Some important disadvantages of FAT16 are:

- It becomes corrupted over time as files are spread among disjointed allocation units and pointers to each unit are lost.
- FAT does not offer many file or directory security or auditing options.
- It does not support long filenames; filenames are limited to 11 characters, 8 for the main name and 3 for an extension.

The FAT32 system is supported only by Windows 95 OSR2, Windows 98, and Windows 2000. In Windows 95 and Windows 98, it enables smaller allocation units than FAT16 and can support partitions of from 2 GB to 2 TB (terabytes). In Windows 2000 it also allows smaller allocation units than FAT16, but the largest FAT32 partition is limited to 32 GB or smaller. In all three operating systems, the largest FAT32 file size is 4 GB. FAT32 does include support for long filenames.

NTFS

The **NT File System** (**NTFS**) is the native Windows NT and Windows 2000 file system, a modern system designed for the needs of a network server environment. Windows NT 4.0 uses NTFS version 4 (NTFS 4) and Windows 2000 uses NTFS 5. The Windows NT Service Pack 4 update for Windows NT 4.0 provides an add-on that enables that operating system to access partitions that are formatted for NTFS 5.

As a full-featured network file system, NTFS is equipped with security features designed to meet the U.S. government's C2 security specifications. C2 security refers to high-level "top-secret" standards for data protection, system auditing, and system access, which are required by some government agencies. NTFS also incorporates such features as:

- Long filenames
- File compression
- Large file capacity
- File activity tracking
- POSIX support
- Volume striping and volume extensions

NTFS enables the use of filenames of up to 256 characters. This is an advantage over the FAT16 system, because files can more easily be named to reflect their contents.

NTFS security accomplishes several goals. One is to create security measures to determine what type of access is allowed for users of folders and of files within folders. The file and folder access can be tailored to the particular requirements of an organization. For example, the system files on a server can be protected so that only the server administrator has access. A folder of databases can be protected with read access, but no access to change data; and a public folder can give users in a designated group access to read and update files, but not to delete files.

File compression is a process that significantly reduces the size of a file by techniques such as removing unused space within a file or using compression algorithms. Some files can be compressed by more than 40 percent, saving important disk space for other storage needs. This is particularly useful for files that are accessed infrequently. NTFS provides the ability to compress files as needed.

File compression can be used on specified files after the server is generated (explore this capability via Hands-on Project 1-8). A disadvantage is that compressed files take longer to access, because they must be decompressed when retrieved.

NTFS can be scaled to accommodate very large files, particularly for database applications. A Microsoft SQL Server database file might be 20 GB or larger. This means an organization can store pictures, scanned images, and sound clips in a single database. The NTFS system can support files up to 16 exabytes (in theory).

Another NTFS feature is that it keeps a log or journal of file system activity. This is a critical process should there be a power outage or hard disk failure. Important information can be retrieved and restored in these situations. FAT does not have this capability.

NTFS provides support for the **portable operating system interface (POSIX)**. POSIX is a set of standards designed to enable portability of applications from one computer system to another and has been used particularly for UNIX systems. Windows 2000 follows the POSIX 1 standard, which includes case-sensitive filenames and the use of multiple filenames (called hard links). For example, the files Myfile.doc and MYFile.doc are considered different files (except when using Explorer or the Command Prompt window).

Two important volume-handling features of NTFS are the ability to create extensions on an existing volume (such as when new disk storage is added) and the ability to stripe volumes, which is a process that equally divides the contents of each file across two or more volumes as a way to extend disk life, enable fault-tolerance features, and balance the disk load for better performance.

In addition to the NTFS 4 features already described, NTFS 5 adds several new features:

- Ability to encrypt files
- No system reboot after creating an extended or spanned volume
- Ability to reduce drive designations
- Indexing for fast access
- Ability to retain shortcuts and other file information when files and folders are placed on other volumes
- Ability to establish disk quotas

With NTFS 5, files can be encrypted so that their contents are available only to those granted access. Also, volume extensions can be set up without the need to reboot the system (in NTFS 4 you have to reboot after adding an extension onto an existing volume). Volume mount points can be created as a way to reduce the number of drive designations for multiple volumes, instead of designating a new drive per each new volume. NTFS 5 incorporates fast indexing in conjunction with the Active Directory to make file searching and retrieval faster than in NTFS 4. A new technique called Distributed Link Tracking is available in NTFS 5, so that shortcuts you have created are not lost when you move files to another volume. Finally, NTFS 5 enables you to set up disk quotas to control how much disk space users can occupy. Disk quotas are a vital tool for disk capacity planning and to ensure that there is enough disk space for all server operations and critical files.

 NTFS 4 does not have built-in disk quota capabilities, but third-party software is available to set up disk quotas.

A limitation of NTFS is that it is designed for Windows NT and Windows 2000 systems. For example, if you set up a computer to run both Windows 2000 and Windows 98 (called a dual-boot system), Windows 98 will not recognize the NTFS files when it is running. (Try Hands-on Project 1-9 to view the properties of an NTFS folder.)

 Third-party utilities are available to enable Windows 95 and Windows 98 to view NTFS-formatted files on a dual-boot computer.

CDFS and UDF

Windows 2000 recognizes two additional file systems used by peripheral storage technologies. The **compact disc file system** (**CDFS**) is supported so that Windows 2000 can read and write files to **compact disc** (**CD-ROM**) disk drives. CD-ROM capability is important for loading the Windows 2000 operating system and for sharing CD-ROM drives on a network. The **Universal Disk Format** (**UDF**) file system is also used on CD-ROM and large-capacity **digital video disc** (**DVD-ROM**) media, which are used for huge file storage to accommodate movies and games.

Choosing a File System

If Windows 2000 Server is intended for a computer with only one disk drive that has less than 2 GB of disk storage, then the FAT file system may be sufficient. It can also be used when the disk is under 2 GB and you have MS-DOS, Windows 3.1x, or Windows 95 OSR1 also loaded on the same computer, using FAT16 (a dual-boot system). Also, you may need to use FAT32 for a dual-boot system in which Windows 95 OSR2 or Windows 98 accompany Windows 2000 on the same computer and you are using a 2 GB or larger disk.

On most modern Windows 2000 servers, NTFS is preferred over FAT16 or FAT 32 because it has so many more capabilities that you need for a network, particularly for security. Also, most servers have the type of users who need a system that can handle demanding applications with high memory and disk requirements. Particularly for systems with 2 GB or more of disk storage or more than one hard drive, NTFS is the best choice. NTFS is better at handling file operations on large disks and can combine multiple drives so that they are recognized under one drive letter, such as one logical drive C. Also, for users who anticipate extremely large disk requirements, NTFS supports a much larger total volume size.

Security is another important consideration in the selection of a file system on a server. FAT has limited security capabilities, such as setting an attribute to make a file read-only or hidden. NTFS has extensive security based on permissions. Permissions are a security property that can be placed on a drive, folder, or file. For example, access to a folder can be restricted to a certain group of users so that any group member has authority to read a file and add new files to the folder. Non-group members can be prevented from accessing the folder entirely. Also, the NTFS system enables a folder or file to be audited, so there is a record of the number of times that a file is successfully opened.

Another advantage of NTFS, which many administrators prefer, is transaction logging. If a disk error occurs while a file is being updated, the data is recovered in an instant. FAT uses file caching, which also enables it to recover data after a disk problem. But the FAT recovery may not be as quick or as accurate if there have been many updates recorded in cache.

A disadvantage of using NTFS is that the server contents cannot be converted back to FAT16 or FAT32, should there be a need. However, a FAT16 or FAT32 partition can be converted to NTFS on a one-time basis. Table 1-1 compares the FAT16, FAT32, and NTFS file systems.

Table 1-1   FAT and NTFS compared

Feature	FAT16	FAT32	NTFS
Total volume size	4 GB	2 GB to 2 TB	2 TB
Maximum file size	2 GB	4 GB	Theoretical limit of 16 exabytes
Compatible with floppy disks	Yes	Yes	No
Filename length	11 characters	256 characters	256 characters
Security	Limited security based on attributes and shares	Limited security based on attributes and shares	C2-compatible extensive security and auditing options
File compression	Supported with extra utilities	Supported with extra utilities	Supported as part of NTFS
File activity tracking	None	None	Tracking via a log
POSIX support	None	Limited	POSIX.1 support
Hot fix	Limited	Limited	Supports hot fix
Large database support	Limited	Yes	Yes
Multiple disk drives in one volume	No	No	Yes

CHAPTER SUMMARY

❑ Network servers are used in familiar and unexpected places. They provide a foundation for the Internet, but are also used to distribute new movies to theaters, provide banking services, and help your local auto repair shop to order parts. The constantly growing use of servers has spurred the need for innovative server operating systems, such as Windows 2000 Server, which can match the demands of the millennium. The use of server-based networks is outpacing peer-to-peer networks because networking everywhere is growing more complex, so there is more need for network management.

❑ Windows 2000 Server offers traditional server capabilities such as file and printer sharing, and it offers advanced C2-compatible security, Web and network communications, and network management capabilities. One of the most important new features of Windows 2000 Server is the Active Directory. Zero Administration for Windows initiatives are also important as a way to drastically reduce the total cost of ownership of a network.

❑ The NTFS file system is a central feature of Windows 2000 because it offers strong security, fault tolerance, the ability to compress files, indexing, disk quotas, and encryption. However, Windows 2000 still retains backward compatibility with the FAT16 and FAT32 file systems. This compatibility makes it well suited for small to large server implementations on all kinds of networks.

In the next chapter, you learn about planning for the hardware used in a computer that runs Windows 2000 Server. Key issues are introduced such as CPU size, memory, disk storage, and tape storage.

KEY TERMS

Active Directory — A Windows 2000 database of computers, users, shared printers, shared folders, and other network resources, and resource groupings that is used to manage a network and enable users to quickly find a particular resource.

client — A computer that accesses resources on another computer via a network or by a direct connection.

clustering — The ability to share the computing load and resources by linking two or more discrete computer systems together to function as though they were one.

compact disc (CD-ROM) — A ROM medium that typically holds up to 1 GB of information.

compact disc file system (CDFS) — A 32-bit file system used on standard capacity CD-ROMs.

Component Object Model (COM) — Standards that enable a software object, such as a graphic, to be linked from one software component into another one. COM is the foundation that makes object linking and embedding (OLE) possible.

digital video disc (DVD-ROM) — Also called digital versatile disk, a ROM medium that can hold from 4.7 to 17 GB of information.

distributability — Dividing complex application program tasks among two or more computers.

Distributed Component Object Model (DCOM) — A standard built upon COM to enable object linking to take place over a network. COM is a standard that allows a software object, such as a graphic, to be linked from one software component to another (such as copying a picture from Microsoft Paint and pasting it in Microsoft Word).

fault tolerance — Techniques that employ hardware and software to provide assurance against equipment failures, computer service interruptions, and data loss.

File Allocation Table (FAT) file system — A file system based on the use of a file allocation table, a flat table that records the clusters used to store the data contained in each file stored on disk. FAT is used by several operating systems, including MS-DOS, Windows 95, Windows 98, and Windows 2000.

Hierarchical Storage Management (HSM) — A storage management system that enables administrators to establish storage policies, archiving techniques, and disk capacity planning through automated procedures and the coordinated use of different media, including tapes, CD-ROMs, hard drives, and Zip drives.

Hypertext Markup Language (HTML) — A formatting language that is used to enable documents and graphic images to be read on the World Wide Web. HTML also provides for fast links to other documents, to graphics, and to Web sites. The World Wide Web is a series of file servers with software such as Microsoft's Internet Information Services (IIS), which make HTML and other Web documents available for workstations to access.

Internet — A global network of diverse Web and information servers offering voice, video, and text data to millions of users.

intranet — A private network within an organization. It uses the same Web-based software as the Internet, but is highly restricted from public access. Intranets are currently used to enable managers to run high-level reports, to enable staff members to update human resources information, and to provide access to other forms of private data.

Kerberos — A security system developed by the Massachusetts Institute of Technology to enable two parties on an open network to communicate without interception from an intruder, by creating a unique encryption key for each communication session.

kernel — An essential set of programs and computer code that allows a computer operating system to control processor, disk, memory, and other functions central to its basic operation.

mapped folder or drive — A disk volume or folder that is shared on the network by a file server or workstation. It gives designated network workstations access to the files and data in its shared volume or folder. The workstation, via software, determines a drive letter for the shared volume, which is the workstation's map to the data.

multitasking — The capability of a computer to run two or more programs at the same time.

multithreading — Running several program processes or parts (threads) at the same time.

network — A communications system that enables computer users to share computer equipment, software, and data, voice, and video transmissions.

network operating system (NOS) — Software that enables computers on a network to communicate and to share resources and files.

NT File System (NTFS) — The native Windows 2000 file system, which has a more detailed directory structure than FAT and supports security measures not found in FAT. It also supports large disks, long filenames, and file compression.

peer-to-peer network — A network on which any computer can communicate with other networked computers on an equal or peerlike basis without going through an intermediary, such as a server or host.

Portable Operating System Interface (POSIX) — Standards set by the Institute of Electrical and Electronics Engineers (IEEE) for portability of applications.

privileged mode — A protected memory space allocated for the Windows 2000 kernel that cannot be directly accessed by software applications.

resource — On a Windows 2000 Server network, a server, shared printer, or shared directory that can be accessed by users. On workstations as well as servers, a resource is an IRQ, I/O address, or memory that is allocated to a computer component, such as a disk drive or communications port.

scalable — A computer operating system that can be used on small to large computers with a single Intel-based processor and on larger computers, such as those with multiple processors.

server — A single computer that provides extensive multiuser access to network resources.

server-based network — A model in which access to the network, and resources, and the management of resources, is accomplished through one or more servers.

symmetric multiprocessor (SMP) — A type of computer with two or more CPUs that share the processing load.

total cost of ownership (TCO) — The cost of installing and maintaining computers and equipment on a network, which includes hardware, software, maintenance, and support costs.

Universal Disk Format (UDF) — A removable-disk formatting standard used for large capacity CD-ROMs and DVD-ROMs.

virtual DOS machine — In Windows 2000, a process that emulates an MS-DOS window in which to run MS-DOS or 16-bit Windows programs in a designated area of memory.

workgroup — As used in Microsoft networks, a number of users who share drive and printer resources in an independent peer-to-peer relationship.

workstation — A computer that has its own CPU and may be used as a standalone computer for word processing, spreadsheet creation, or other software applications. It also may be used to access another computer such as a mainframe computer or file server, as long as the necessary network hardware and software are installed.

World Wide Web (Web or WWW) — A vast network of servers throughout the world that provide access to voice, text, video, and data files.

Zero Administration for Windows (ZAW) — A combination of management options and tools that enable an organization to reduce the total cost of ownership (TCO).

REVIEW QUESTIONS

1. Which file system has the ability to encrypt files?

   a. FAT32

   b. FAT16

   c. NTFS 4

   d. NTFS 5

   e. all of the above

   f. only a, c, and d

2. You have two computers that can be used as servers for the databases in a client/server application. What technique can you use to enable the load to be spread between both servers for good performance and fast access to the databases?

   a. clustering

   b. hot fixing

   c. direct linking

   d. Create a client/server algorithm that causes the first user to access one server, the second user to access the other server, the third user to access the first server, and so on for all users who log on.

3. What capability enables you to run 16-bit Windows programs in Windows 2000?

   a. Create a dual-boot system and log on to the non-Windows-2000 operating system, then log on to Windows 2000.

   b. the virtual DOS machine

   c. drive mapping

   d. none of the above because Windows 2000 cannot run 16-bit applications

4. An Active Directory element that consists of accounts, computers, and printers is a(n):

   a. container

   b. media

   c. box

   d. attribute

5. You are setting up a small network for a three-person investment firm. Each member will have a Windows 98 computer and only occasionally shares files with the other members. However, they do want you to set up a shared printer. What network model is most appropriate in this situation?

   a. server-based

   b. peer-to-peer

   c. print-based

   d. open-system

6. Which of the following operating systems can be clients of Windows 2000 Server?

   a. Windows 3.11

   b. Windows 95

   c. Windows NT Workstation 3.51

   d. Windows 98

   e. all of the above

   f. only b, c, and d

7. DVD-ROM uses which file system?

   a. NTFS 4

   b. FAT32

   c. FAT16

   d. UDF

   e. all of the above

   f. only a and b

   g. only a and d

8. You have a Pentium II 300 MHz single processor computer that is currently running Windows 2000 Server. Your server monitoring shows that you need more horsepower because the number of users has grown dramatically in just six months. Which of the following types of computers can you use to replace your existing server?

   a. a two-processor Pentium II computer

   b. a four-processor Pentium III computer

   c. an IBM ES9000 mainframe computer

   d. all of the above

   e. only a and b

   f. only b and c

9. The Social Security office in your city has accepted your bid to install Windows 2000 Server on their local network. One of the requirements of the bid is to have C2-type security. Which file system would you use on the server?

   a. NTFS 5

   b. FAT32

   c. HPFS

   d. UDF

10. When several 32-bit programs run at the same time in Windows 2000:

    a. they are limited to using only 10 percent of the CPU

    b. they each run in their own memory space

    c. they run in a special FAT-enabled partition for better performance

    d. there is a risk that if one program "crashes" it will cause the others to crash as well

11. Which of the following runs in privileged mode in Windows 2000?

    a. the kernel

    b. the command line window

    c. programs written for MS-DOS

    d. My Computer

12. Which of the following is an example of a difference between Windows 2000 Server and Windows 2000 Professional?

    a. Windows 2000 Server can use up to 4 GB of RAM, but the maximum for Windows 2000 Professional is 2 GB.

    b. Windows 2000 Professional does not support NTFS 5.

    c. Windows 2000 Server supports more user connectivity and more network services.

    d. Windows 2000 Professional can run on a single-processor computer only.

13. On which system can you use NTFS to format floppy disks?

    a. Windows NT 4.0

    b. Windows 2000

    c. Windows 98

    d. all of the above

    e. none of the above

14. You are working to set up computers and a network for a firm that processes payrolls for small and large companies. It is imperative that the computers used by each employee have an operating system that is reliable for the sensitive work performed. Which operating system would you set up on each employee's computer?

    a. Windows 98

    b. Windows 2000 Server

    c. Windows 2000 Professional

    d. Windows 2000 Server Datacenter

15. A university's finance division, which handles the administrative business end of the campus, has asked you to draft a plan to reduce the total cost of ownership for networked computers over the next two years. Which of the following would you recommend?

    a. Upgrade existing Windows NT 3.51 and Windows NT 4.0 servers to Windows 2000 servers.

    b. Upgrade Windows 3.11 and Windows 95 workstations to Windows 98.

   c. Upgrade Windows 3.11 and Windows 95 workstations to Windows 2000 Professional.

   d. all of the above

   e. only a and c

16. The ability to recover data on a hard disk after an unexpected hardware problem is called

   a. rebooting

   b. fault tolerance

   c. auditing

   d. data dumping

17. A physician's group is just implementing Windows 2000 Server on a computer that already has Windows 98, a 4 GB drive, and is formatted for FAT32. Their plan is to make this a dual-boot system for the first six months, so they have ready access to all files via Windows 2000 or Windows 98. When they install Windows 2000 Server, what file system should they use for this operating system?

   a. NTFS 5

   b. NTFS 4

   c. FAT32

   d. FAT16

18. Which of the following operating systems support power management?

   a. Windows 95

   b. Windows 98

   c. Windows NT 4.0

   d. Windows 2000

   e. all of the above

   f. only b and d

   g. only a, b, and d

19. Which of the following is true?

   a. FAT32 can be converted to NTFS 5, but NTFS 5 cannot be converted to FAT32.

   b. FAT32 can be converted to NTFS 5 and NTFS 5 can be converted to FAT32.

   c. FAT32 can be converted to FAT16, but not to NTFS 5.

   d. FAT16 can be converted to FAT32, but not to NTFS 5.

20. What is Kerberos?

   a. a form of security

   b. a type of shared drive

   c. a Web server

   d. a form of multithreading

21. Long filenames can consist of up to how many characters?

    a. 8

    b. 11

    c. 128

    d. 256

22. The alumni office at your school is planning to implement a server that will hold a 40 GB database. Which of the following file systems can handle a single database file of this size?

    a. NTFS 5

    b. NTFS 4

    c. FAT32

    d. all of the above

    e. only a and b

23. Which of the following languages is (are) supported by Windows 2000?

    a. Hindi

    b. Chinese

    c. English

    d. all of the above

    e. only b and c

24. The ability to install a variety of drivers for modems, monitors, keyboards, disk adapters, and pointing devices in Windows 2000 is an example of:

    a. testability

    b. extensibility

    c. distributability

    d. resource sharing

25. Which of the following is new to Windows 2000 Server?

    a. Active Directory

    b. Web-based Enterprise Management (WBEM)

    c. NTFS security

    d. all of the above

    e. only a and b

    f. only a and c

HANDS-ON PROJECTS

Project 1-1

In this hands-on activity you try out My Computer in Windows 2000. You will need access to a computer running Windows 2000 Server or Windows 2000 Professional, and an account provided by your instructor.

To use My Computer:

1. Log on to Windows 2000 by pressing **Ctrl+Alt+Del**.
2. Enter the user name and password in the Log on to Windows dialog box and then click **OK** (you may also need to enter the domain name).
3. Double-click **My Computer** on the desktop to open the My Computer window. Click a drive such as C: to view how the display changes (see Figure 1-6)
4. Maximize the window by clicking the maximize button on the right side of the title bar.
5. Click the **View** menu, highlight **Toolbars**, and notice the toolbar options. Make sure that a checkmark appears in front of **Standard Buttons** and **Address Bar**. If one of these options is not checked, click it now. If you need to check the other option, click the **View** menu, point to **Toolbars**, and click **Address Bar** and/or **Standard Buttons**.
6. Click the **View** menu one more time, highlight **Explorer Bar**, and notice the options. Click **Search** and observe the search panel that is displayed in the left side of the window. This tool enables you to search for a specific file or folder in Windows 2000.
7. Move the cursor to point to a disk drive. What information is displayed about the drive? Record your observations in a lab journal or in a word processed document.
8. Click the **Close** button on the right side of the title bar to close My Computer.

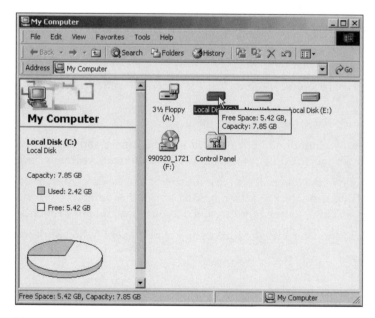

Figure 1-6   My Computer

Project 1-2

In this hands-on activity, you briefly experiment with the Start button to practice starting a program in Windows 2000.

To start a program:

1. Log on to Windows 2000, if you logged off after Hands-on Project 1-1.

2. Click the **Start** button on the desktop.

3. Highlight **Programs** and then highlight **Accessories**. (If Accessories and other menus are not displayed, click the double up or down arrows to view the Program menu's contents.)

4. Notice the accessory options that are installed in Windows 2000. Move the cursor to each option to display its menu contents or a brief explanation of its function. Record the options in your lab journal or in a word-processed document.

5. Click **WordPad** or **Calculator** to practice starting an application.

6. How would you open Windows Explorer?

7. Close the application that you opened in Step 5, when you are finished viewing it.

Project 1-3

This hands-on activity enables you to view workstations connected to the network through the My Network Places icon on the Windows 2000 desktop. You will need access to a computer running Windows 2000 Server or Windows 2000 Professional, and an account provided by your instructor.

To view the networked workstations:

1. Log on to Windows 2000.

2. Double-click **My Network Places** on the desktop (see Figure 1-7).

3. Click the **View** menu, highlight **Toolbars**, and click **Standard Buttons** (do not click it if it is already checked).

4. Double-click **Entire Network** and click the hyperlink to **Search for computers** (see Figure 1-8).

5. Click the **Search Now** button to look for all computers.

6. Notice how many computers are connected to the network and record four or five names in your lab journal or in a word-processed document. Are any printers listed?

7. Double-click one of the computers to determine if it has resources to share. If it does not, click the Back arrow on the button bar and try another computer. When you find a computer that is sharing resources, notice if the resources are folders, printers, or both.

8. Close the screen showing shared resources and close the entire Network screen.

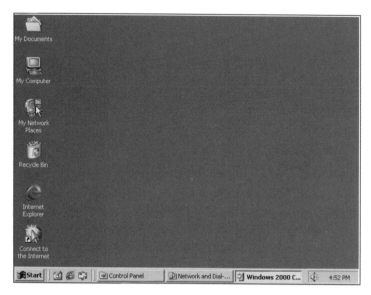

Figure 1-7   Selecting My Network Places

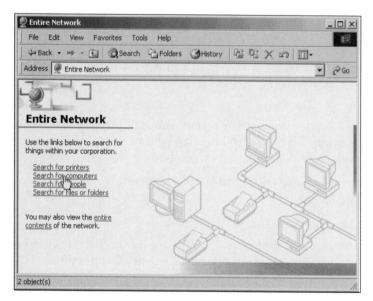

Figure 1-8   Searching for network computers

Project 1-4

In this hands-on activity, you determine the operating systems used by four computers on your network.

To determine the operating systems in use:

1. Log on to Windows 2000.
2. Double-click **My Network Places** on the desktop.
3. Double-click **Entire Network**.
4. Click the **entire contents** hyperlink on the left side of the screen.
5. Double-click **Microsoft Windows Network**.
6. Double-click a domain (one of the icon(s) representing connected computers), such as **TheFirm**.
7. Right-click a computer and click **Properties**.
8. Notice the name of the domain or workgroup to which the computer belongs, as shown in the Comment section of the Properties dialog box.
9. Notice the operating system type, as shown in the Type section, and then close the dialog box.
10. Repeat Steps 7, 8, and 9 three more times on different computers and record the information that you obtain in your lab journal or in a word-processed document.
11. Close My Network Places or the domain screen when you are finished.

Project 1-5

My Network Places has many new options that are not available in its predecessor, Network Neighborhood. For example, it enables you to verify your network connection and the speed of the network. This activity shows you how to do both.

To verify the network connection and network speed:

1. Log on to Windows 2000.
2. Double-click **My Network Places** on the desktop.
3. In the My Network Places information text on the left side of the window, click the underlined hyperlink that says **Network and Dial-up Connections**.
4. Double-click **Local Area Connection**.
5. In the connection section of the Local Area Connection Status dialog box, determine the status and the speed of the connection (see Figure 1-9).
6. Determine how long you have been connected and the number of packets sent and received.
7. Record the information you have gathered in your lab journal or in a word-processed document.
8. Click Close on the Local Area Connection Status dialog box and close the Network and Dial-up Connections window.

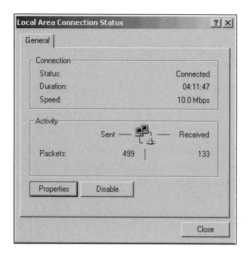

Figure 1-9   Network connection status

Project 1-6

In this project, you open the Microsoft Management Console (MMC) and view the available snap-ins for Windows 2000 Server. Before you start, find out from your instructor what account to use so that you have privileges to access the MMC.

To access the MMC:

1. Log on to Windows 2000 Server.

2. Click **Start**, click **Run**, and enter **mmc** in the Run box. Click **OK**. Maximize the console screens, if necesary.

3. Click the **Console** menu.

4. Click **Add/Remove Snap-in** or press **Ctrl+M**.

5. Notice which snap-ins are already set up in the MMC.

6. Click the **Add button** in the Add/Remove Snap-in dialog box.

7. Scroll through the options in the Add Standalone Snap-in dialog box. How would you add a snap-in to the console?

8. Do you find any snap-ins that are from a vendor other than Microsoft? If so, what are they?

9. Record your observations about the snap-ins and vendors in your lab journal or in a word-processed document.

10. Click **Close** in the Add Standalone Snap-in dialog box, click **Cancel** in the Add/Remove Snap-in dialog box, and close the MMC. (Click **Cancel** if you are asked to save console settings.)

Project 1-7

In this project, you view the virtual DOS machine process in action. Before you start, find out the location of a 16-bit application from your instructor.

To view the virtual DOS machine process:

1. Log on to Windows 2000 Server.
2. Click **Start** and click **Run**.
3. Enter the path and name of the 16-bit application and click **OK**, or use the Browse button to find it. If you use the Browse button, find the appropriate drive in the Look in box and then click through the appropriate folders and subfolders. Double-click the application in the Browse window, and then click **OK**.
4. Press **Ctl+Alt+Del** (don't worry, you won't reboot the computer).
5. Click **Task Manager**.
6. Once the Task Manager starts, click the **Processes** tab (if it is not displayed already).
7. Use the scroll bar to locate ntvdm.exe.
8. Notice the name of your 16-bit process listed under the ntvdm.exe process.
9. What other process(es) is (are) running under ntvdm.exe? Record your observations in your lab journal or in a word-processed document. Close Task Manager and then close the 16-bit application.

Project 1-8

In this project, you practice compressing all files in an NTFS 5 folder. Before you start, ask your instructor about which folder to use for this project.

To compress the files in the folder:

1. Log on to Windows 2000 Server.
2. Click **Start**, point to **Programs**, point to **Accessories**, and then click **Windows Explorer**.
3. Scroll or browse to find the folder that your instructor has designated for this assignment and right-click it.
4. Click **Properties**.
5. Click the **Advanced** button.
6. Click the check box, **Compress contents to save disk space**. Click **OK**.
7. Click **OK**.
8. Close Windows Explorer.

Project 1-9

In this hands-on activity, you use Windows 2000 Explorer to view files and then to view the properties of a folder created in NTFS. Make sure that you log on to a computer running Windows 2000 Server or Windows 2000 Professional that is using the NTFS.

To use Explorer:

1. Click the **Start** button, point to **Programs**, point to **Accessories**, and then click **Windows Explorer**.

2. Notice there are two scroll panels or panes of information, one containing Folders on the left, and one that is untitled on the right.

3. Scroll down to view folders and files in both panels, or click My Computer in the left panel and double-click the drive containing Windows 2000 system files in the right panel, such as drive C.

4. Scroll to the WINNT folder. If the folder is not displayed, look for it on drive D (or another drive) in the desktop under the Folders pane. Every folder created in NTFS contains properties, such as information about the folder size, sharing, and security options. Right-click the **WINNT** folder and then click the **Properties** option on the shortcut menu.

5. Click each tab to view its contents and make notes about its purpose in your lab journal or in a word-processed document.

6. If you have access to Windows 95 or Windows 98, compare the tabs and properties of a Windows 2000 NTFS folder with a FAT16 or FAT32 folder in Windows 95 or Windows 98. Record your comparisons.

7. Click **Cancel** to close the Properties dialog box.

8. Close Windows Explorer.

Project 1-10

In this hands-on activity, you use My Network Places to find out how to map a network drive. Before you start, ask your instructor for the name of a network computer that is set up to share a folder.

To use My Network Places to map a drive:

1. Double-click **My Network Places** on the desktop.

2. Double-click **Entire Network** and then click the hyperlink to **Search for computers**.

3. Click the **Search Now** button to look for all computers.

4. Double-click the computer specified by your instructor or continue to double-click computers until you find one with a shared folder.

5. Right-click the shared folder and then click **Map Network Drive**.

6. Select a drive letter for the mapped drive or use the default drive letter (see Figure 1-10).

7. Click **Finish** to map the drive.

8. In the resulting drive or domain window, examine the files and subfolders that you can access, and double-click a text file to view its contents, if one is available.

9. Close the drive window and the other windows you have opened.

10. How would you access the drive you mapped in Windows Explorer or My Computer? Record your answer in your lab journal or in a word-proccessed document.

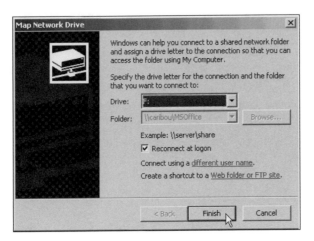

Figure 1-10 Mapping a network drive

CASE PROJECT

Aspen Consulting Project: Planning a Server Implementation

In this and the chapters that follow, you will work on an extensive range of projects as a Windows 2000 Server consultant for Aspen Consulting, a computer consulting firm that operates from offices on the East and West Coasts in the United States and from Vancouver and Montreal in Canada. Your boss is Mark Arnez, one of the managing partners of Aspen Consulting. Aspen Consulting has over 100 consultants who specialize in networking, server operating systems implementation, and support of Microsoft computer operating systems. Your company has clients throughout the United States and Canada. The work is challenging because your clients are very diverse, including accounting firms, manufacturing companies, colleges, universities, law firms, mail-order houses, and publishing companies.

Today Mark asks you to plan a server installation for a small hospital in a rural area near Vancouver. The hospital has 32 computers running Windows 95 and Windows 98 that are just now being networked. They also have an old IBM System 38 minicomputer that has handled patient records and accounting. The company that supports their patient records and accounting systems has gone out of business, and the hospital is considering two new software systems that run on Windows 98, Windows NT, and Windows 2000. They also want to develop a software system that enables doctors, patients, and members of the community to look up health information from a 500 MB database that the hospital has just purchased, but not yet implemented.

1. What networking model do you recommend for this hospital and why?

2. The hospital administrator does not fully understand what a server can do. Explain the features that servers offer.

3. Prior to hearing your answer in question 2, the hospital administrator was thinking about using Windows 98, Windows 2000 Professional, or Windows 2000 Server to replace the IBM System 38. Now she asks how your response about servers might be clarified through a comparison of what these operating systems can provide. Prepare a table or a report that compares these operating systems to one another in a network setting.

4. Next she asks that you make a recommendation for the 500 MB database they have purchased. Should this be put on a full-featured server or made available as a shared drive from a Windows 98 computer? Fully explain your answer.

5. Because patient records and patient/doctor information must be kept confidential, which file system would you recommend for the computer that houses the patient records and accounting systems? Why do you recommend this file system and what other advantages does it offer in the context of information sharing for the hospital?

6. As a rural hospital, they have to be conscious of the budget as they move into the future. What are some factors that they can consider in this implementation to help reduce computer and networking costs over the next few years?

7. Last, as she is considering server and workstation options, the administrator remembers that they use an old 16-bit Windows purchase-order system. Can this run in Windows 2000?

OPTIONAL CASE PROJECTS FOR TEAMS

Team Case One

Your boss, Mark Arnez, wants to compile a list of ways in which Windows 2000 Server is used in small, medium-sized, and large organizations. He asks you to form a small group of consultants to compile the most comprehensive list possible. Use the library, the Internet, and any other resources to compile a list, and report back to Mark.

Team Case Two

You are in the lunchroom discussing an assignment with two of your colleagues. You are working with a small tax preparation firm that consists of five people—four tax accountants and one administrative assistant. Their office is networked, and they each have computers running Windows 95. The administrative assistant's computer is used as a server in that it stores the tax-accounting software and each client's records in a database—all made available through a shared drive. Unfortunately, there are times when all four accountants access the shared drive simultaneously, resulting in delays when they need to quickly access information because they have clients in their offices. Your debate is whether to upgrade all computers to Windows 98 or to install a server, even though this is just a small office. Poll your colleagues and create a report summarizing your group's conclusions.

2

PLANNING FOR SERVER HARDWARE

After reading this chapter and completing the exercises you will be able to:

♦ Explain the hardware requirements for Windows 2000 Server

♦ Explain the importance of using Microsoft's hardware compatibility list

♦ Determine specifications for your server in terms of the right processor type, bus type, and advanced bus features

♦ Select the right network interface card (NIC) for your server

♦ Calculate the amount of memory needed for your server

♦ Plan disk capacity, disk architecture, and fault tolerance

♦ Plan a backup system and CD-ROM specifications

The server hardware provides an essential foundation for building a Windows 2000 server, because you can only fully take advantage of the operating system's capabilities when the hardware meets operating system specifications. At one time, network server operating systems were rudimentary and could not take advantage of all the features available even in basic personal computers. That situation has changed dramatically as server hardware manufacturers now struggle to keep up with the new capabilities built into server operating systems, with Windows 2000 Server as a prime example. Windows 2000 Server is capable of implementing advanced features that make it possible to outfit a server for high-speed networking, sophisticated disk storage, and multiple-processor computing. With features like these, a server that fits on your desktop can rival a mainframe computer that occupies the space of a small house.

In this chapter, you look at the vital elements required to fully outfit a server for different kinds of situations. You begin by looking at the minimum hardware requirements for Windows 2000 Server and the different processor options, which include Pentium and Pentium Xeon. You learn about bus architectures and new options such as the I_2O architecture and server clustering. Two other important areas are the selection of the right NIC for your server and choosing the proper amount of memory. Server storage, tape backup capabilities, and CD-ROM drives will be discussed last to round out your journey in outfitting a server. The discussion in each area is focused on helping you determine the right fit for the smallest to the largest implementations.

SYSTEM REQUIREMENTS

The most basic step in selecting a server is to review the minimum system requirements for Microsoft Windows 2000 Server. In the past, the requirements for Windows NT Server and Windows NT Workstation have been very similar, but that is not the case with Windows 2000 Server and Windows 2000 Professional. Windows 2000 Server includes many more service options and more robust connectivity, which means it requires more resources than Windows 2000 Professional does—which is not surprising because one is a server network operating system, and the other is a client/workstation network operating system. Tables 2-1 and 2-2 give the minimum requirements for Intel and RISC-based computers for Windows 2000 Server and Windows 2000 Professional, respectively.

 Keep in mind that these are *minimum* requirements for installation. Additional hard disk space is required for application and data files, and additional memory may be required for some applications and to increase performance. To maintain backward compatibility so you do not lose your current investment in hardware, Microsoft has worked to keep down the minimum CPU requirements, stressing RAM and hard disk resources instead.

With these requirements in mind, you need to plan hardware that exceeds the minimums to accommodate the clients that will access the server, extra software besides the operating system, and data stored on the server. You will need to plan a server with enough CPU horsepower, disk storage, RAM, and backup resources for a system fully loaded to match the intended use and positioned to grow as your organization grows.

Table 2-1   Minimum Hardware Requirements to Install Windows 2000 Server

Component	Intel-type Computer Requirements
Processor	Pentium 133 MHz or faster
Display	VGA or better
Memory (RAM)	64 MB for five or fewer clients and 128 MB for larger networks
Hard disk space	685 MB for system files (2 GB recommended)
Floppy disk drive	High-density 3.5-inch
CD-ROM drive	Required for installations not performed over the network (12X or faster)
Network interface card (NIC)	Required to connect to the network
Mouse or pointing device and keyboard	Required

Table 2-2   Minimum Hardware Requirements to Install Windows 2000 Professional

Component	Intel-type Computer Requirements
Processor	133 MHz or faster (Pentium recommended for better performance)
Display	VGA or better
Memory (RAM)	32 MB (64 MB is recommended for better performance)
Hard disk space	500 MB for system files (1 GB recommended for better performance)
Floppy disk drive	High-density 3.5-inch
CD-ROM drive	Required for installations not performed over the network (12X or faster)
Network interface card (NIC)	Required to connect to the network
Mouse or pointing device and keyboard	Required

WINDOWS 2000 SERVER COMPATIBILITY

Your first stop in selecting hardware should be to check Microsoft's **hardware compatibility list (HCL)** for Windows 2000 Server, a document that comes with the Windows 2000 Server software and is located in the \Support folder on the Windows 2000 Server CD-ROM. The most up-to-date version is available on the Microsoft Web site, *http://www.microsoft.com/*. (You can practice accessing the HCL in Hands-on Project 2-1).

Microsoft reviews all types of hardware to determine whether they will work with Windows 2000 Server and other Microsoft operating systems, Windows 2000 Professional and Windows 98, for example. There is an HCL for each operating system, which includes information on the following hardware:

- Single-processor computers
- Multiprocessor computers
- Processor upgrades
- PCMCIA hardware
- SCSI adapters and drives
- Video adapters
- Network adapters
- Audio adapters
- Modems
- Printers
- Tape devices
- Uninterruptible power supplies (UPSs)

The best steps you can take to avoid Windows 2000 Server installation difficulties are to select well-known brand names from the HCL and to avoid hardware from small companies that build individual computers from generic parts. Most established computer manufacturers have products compatible with Windows 2000 Server, although their prices may be somewhat higher than those of the smaller companies. Cutting expenses when buying server hardware could prove to be costly later on if it results in unreliable equipment and difficult software installations.

CPU SIZING

Most Intel-based servers sold as of this writing are Pentium III and Pentium III Xeon computers with a CPU clock speed of 500 megahertz (MHz) or faster. The **clock speed** is the rate at which the CPU sends data through the **buses**, or data pathways, inside the computer. A high clock speed helps ensure the CPU does not become bottlenecked with more processing requests than it can handle. Buses come in different capacities, measured in terms of bits. For example, Pentium computers can send data in 32-bit streams. A typical character, such as the letter *r* or the number *5*, is packaged as 8 bits (1 byte). Thus, a 32-bit bus can carry 4 characters in each clock cycle.

 At this writing, Intel is completing work on a new 64-bit processor called Merced, which is likely to displace the Xeon processor in server applications that require a powerful CPU, such as in heavily used Web sites and client/server computing.

Pentium Computers

Windows 2000 Server will work using an Intel-based Pentium with a 166 MHz or higher clock speed. Many organizations have implemented small Pentium servers, 166–233 MHz for example, with positive results. But the limitations of a smaller Pentium computer become apparent as the server demand grows. The slower clock speed puts these servers at a disadvantage compared to Pentium-II- or Pentium-III-based computers.

Windows 2000 Server takes advantage of the Pentium's fast clock speeds and 32-bit bus to provide better server response. Windows 2000 also uses Pentium-enabled features such as multithreading and multitasking (see Chapter 1). A high clock speed is recommended because this increases the speed at which the computer can internally transfer data, such as between the CPU and a disk or tape drive.

Another important factor is processor caching. Processors use specifically allocated workspaces, called registers, to complete tasks. One way to increase the speed at which the processor works is by providing extra storage space on a chip, so that processor operations and instructions can be queued and quickly swapped in and out of the processor's registers. The extra storage is called **processor cache**. A processor uses two levels of cache. Level 1 (L1) cache is built into every processor, but is very small, at 8 KB to 64 KB. Level 2 (L2) cache is a technique for implementing more processor cache in addition to L1, but is often slower, depending on the design. The basic Pentium processor uses a static RAM (SRAM) chip for L2 cache that is plugged into a socket or directly soldered into the main board.

Whereas the Pentium processor uses an SRAM chip plugged into the main board for cache, the Pentium Pro processor integrates cache on the same chip as the processor. The L2 cache built into the Pentium Pro chip is either 256 KB, 512 KB, or 1 MB, with 512 KB as the most common implementation.

L2 caching architecture has been changed in the Pentium II and Pentium III processors by placing processor cache on a separate "daughter" board that attaches to the main computer board. This architecture is less expensive than the Pentium Pro, but not as fast. Pentium II and Pentium III caching, however, is faster than the early Pentium and SRAM chip combination, because access to the daughter board is designed to be faster than access to an SRAM chip plugged into the main board. Besides L2 caching, another difference introduced with the Pentium II is a faster external operating bus speed than is used in the Pentium and Pentium Pro computers.

There are differences between the Pentium II and the Pentium III: The Pentium II processors have been manufactured at 350, 400, and 450 MHz, while Pentium III processors are over 500 MHz. The Pentium III also includes special support for faster Web caching and better TCP/IP performance.

Intel's Celeron processor is an option intended for users who want a processor that costs less than a Pentium. One way in which the cost is reduced is that the Celeron does not implement L2 caching. For this reason, the Celeron and similar processors made by other manufacturers are not recommended for Windows 2000 Server.

Pentium II and Pentium III computers can be purchased with the Xeon architecture, which employs an L2 daughter board caching technique that is over twice as fast as a non-Xeon. Xeon processors are usually sold with 512 KB of L2 cache that can be expanded to over 1 MB. At this writing, a Pentium III Xeon processor is typically two to four times the cost of a non-Xeon Pentium III. Server applications that benefit from fast L2 cache, such as busy Web servers, are one place in which Xeons are used.

When you purchase a processor for a server, consider how cache can improve performance. Cache is particularly important for servers on which clients perform work, such as a Web server or a database server. For example, cache can improve processor response on a database server that processes involved queries on a large database to generate reports. One poorly designed query can slow down the server for all other users. Purchasing a fast processor with 512 KB to 1 MB of cache can significantly improve performance. For a 1-GB or larger database or for a Web server that is accessed by several hundred simultaneous users, consider a Xeon chip with 1 MB of cache.

Multiprocessor Computers

Windows 2000 Server is designed to fully exploit the capabilities of multiprocessor computers. Many computer vendors make Pentium-based multiprocessor computers to be used specifically as servers. These **symmetric multiprocessor** (**SMP**) computers have two, three, four, eight, or more processors to share the processing load.

 If you purchase an SMP computer, make sure you understand the requirements for adding CPUs. Some use an architecture that requires CPUs to be added in multiple numbers, such as in pairs, making CPU upgrades expensive.

Clustering Computers

Clustered computers are computers that operate together as one shared resource. They are linked together by two elements: the operating system, such as Windows 2000, and high-speed links between the computers, such as 100 megabits per second Fast Ethernet. To the user or server manager who logs onto the cluster, the computers appear as one server. A cluster is often composed of identical types of computers, all Intel-based SMP computers, for example. Clustered computers are frequently used to provide uninterrupted service when one computer fails and to provide a means to expand processing power, storage, and RAM when an existing system is heavily overloaded.

Microsoft defines two models for clustering: shared disk and shared nothing. The **shared disk model** is one in which all servers equally share resources that include disks, CD-ROM, and tape storage (Figure 2-1). The **shared nothing model** is one in which each server owns and accesses a particular resource, a disk drive, for example (Figure 2-2). In the shared nothing model, if one computer fails, the resources that it owns can be taken over by a different computer in the cluster that is still operational.

At this writing, clustering is supported in Windows 2000 Advanced Server and Windows 2000 Datacenter. The shared disk model is supported in the framework of what Microsoft calls a failover solution. In this solution, two servers share disk resources and if one server fails, the other clustered server fills the gap. Microsoft's goal in the near future is to implement a second sharing option, called the multiple node solution. In this solution, up to 16 servers can be added to a cluster, with the Windows 2000 operating system allocating CPU load equally among the clustered servers on the basis of current need.

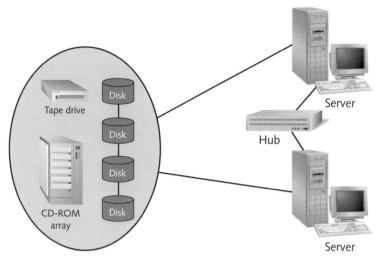

Figure 2-1 Shared disk clustering model

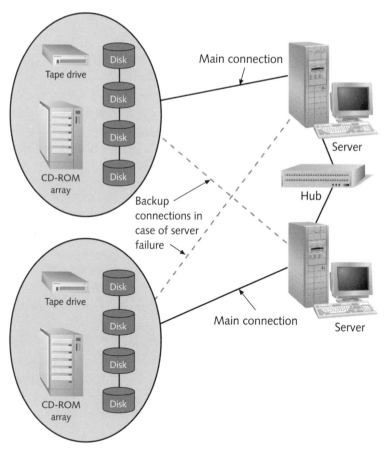

Figure 2-2 Shared nothing clustering model

Bus Architectures

Computers have two buses. The internal bus carries instructions about computer operations to the CPU. The external bus carries data to be processed, such as for mathematical operations. The server's speed is influenced by the size of the bus. Pentium servers have a 32-bit bus (with the exception of the Merced processor, which is 64-bit) and RISC servers have a 64-bit bus.

Windows 2000 Server is a 32-bit operating system, which means it can take advantage of a 32-bit or larger bus design. With this in mind, Windows 2000 supports the following bus types:

- **Industry Standard Architecture (ISA)**: 8-bit and 16-bit bus architecture dating to the early 1980s
- **Extended Industry Standard Architecture (EISA)**: 32-bit bus built on the ISA architecture with faster throughput by means of **bus mastering**, which enables some processing activities to take place on interface card processors instead of on the CPU
- **Micro Channel Architecture (MCA)**: 32-bit bus proprietary to IBM computers and having a slightly faster transfer rate than EISA
- **Peripheral Computer Interface (PCI)**: 32-bit and 64-bit bus with the fastest data transfer rate and local bus capability

Modern servers contain primarily PCI buses for fast transport of information via heavily used components such as disk drives and NICs. They also contain a few ISA or EISA buses for backward compatibility with older components (try Hands-on Project 2-2, which uses the Add/Remove Hardware Wizard to view the buses set up on your computer).

I_2O Architecture

Intelligent input/output (I_2O) architecture is a communications architecture that is new to network servers, although it has been used for years in mainframe computers. I_2O removes some of the I/O processing activities from the main processor to I_2O processors on peripherals designed for I_2O architectures, such as hard disks. I_2O also involves using one general device driver for all I_2O-compliant devices, instead of a separate device driver for each manufacturer's device that uses I_2O. The purpose of I_2O is to increase the speed of operations involving peripherals, while reducing the need for the main processor to handle I/O processes. A driver is software that allows a computer to communicate with devices such as hard disks, printers, monitors, and network interface cards.

I_2O involves two software components: the OS Services Module and the Hardware Device Module (Figure 2-3). The OS Services Module is software that is linked into the Windows 2000 Server operating system to interact with the kernel. The Hardware Device Module is software located on the peripheral controller or adapter that operates independently of the operating system. Communication between the OS Services Module and the Hardware Device Module is accomplished through protocols designed for the I_2O architecture. Windows 2000 Server supports I_2O.

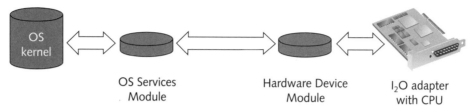

Figure 2-3   I₂O communications architecture

PLUG AND PLAY

One important advance in computer hardware and operating system software is the ability to automatically detect and configure new hardware devices, such as in the addition of a disk or tape drive. This ability is called **Plug and Play** (**PnP**) and must be:

- Built into the device in the computer

- Enabled in the computer's basic input output system (BIOS)

- Built into the computer's operating system kernel

Windows 2000 has even better PnP support than Windows 95 or Windows 98, a feature that was lacking in the previous versions of Windows NT. As you configure hardware, choose a server that has a BIOS that can interface with the Windows 2000 PnP capability. Also, when you add hardware to a server, a NIC for example, purchase one that is PnP-compatible. PnP can help you easily install hardware without struggling to configure it and without conflicts with other devices that use the computer's internal hardware and memory resources. One way to determine if the computer's BIOS supports PnP is to check the documentation for that computer and then verify the capability in the computer's BIOS setup options, as shown in Hands-on Project 2-3.

USB

As you plan the server hardware, plan to purchase a computer that has a **universal serial bus** (**USB**) and external ports. A USB is a relatively new bus standard that improves on the concept of serial and parallel communications, such as the EIA/TIA-232 (formerly RS-232) serial communications approach. When your computer has a USB, you can plug in devices without powering off the computer. USB supports up to 127 separate devices on a single port, including pointing devices, CD-ROM drives, tape drives, cameras, scanners, telephones, and audio equipment. The USB implementation in Windows 2000 also supports PnP, so that each new device is automatically detected when it is installed. The data transfer rate of a USB can be up to 12 Mbps.

CHOOSING NICs

A **network interface card** (NIC) is used to enable a network device, such as a computer or network equipment, to connect to a network. The network connection provided through a NIC involves four components:

- An appropriate connector for the network medium

- A transceiver

- A controller to support media access control (MAC) protocol communications and addressing (see Chapter 3)

- Protocol control firmware

The connector and its associated circuits are designed for a specific type of medium, such as coax, twisted-pair, or fiber-optic cable. Some combination NICs are made with multiple 1.1 connectors so they can be used with different media, such as combination coax and twisted-pair NICs, which are the most common examples of this option. When a combination NIC is used, it comes with software drivers or firmware to match the media options. **Firmware** is software that is stored on a chip, such as a ROM. Also, some NIC drivers are able to detect the medium attached to the NIC and then automatically set up the correct driver for the medium. (Try Hands-on Project 2-4 to find the location of a NIC driver in Windows 2000.)

The cable connector is attached to the transceiver, which may be external to the NIC or built into it. For most computers, servers, and network equipment, the transceiver is built into the interface card.

The MAC controller unit and the firmware work together to correctly encapsulate network source and destination address information, the data to be transported, and error-detection information into frames sent out to the network.

For a typical network, purchase a NIC that can transmit at either 10 Mbps or 100 Mbps. On a heavily loaded network or for a server that is used for multimedia, consider using a high-speed 1-Gbps (gigabit per second) NIC (if your network equipment supports 1 Gbps). Also, many NICs are able to handle both half duplex and full duplex transmissions. **Half duplex** means that the NIC and network equipment are set up so they cannot send and receive at the same time. **Full duplex** is the capacity to send and receive simultaneously (which is possible because of buffering at the NIC). Choose a NIC that can be set for half duplex or full duplex, so you have flexibility. Figure 2-4 illustrates a NIC set in full duplex mode. (Try Hands-on Project 2-5 to learn about duplex and other NIC settings.)

A NIC is customized for a specific type of bus, such as EISA or PCI. When you develop specifications for a server, as mentioned earlier, plan to purchase one with PCI expansion slots and a 32-bit PCI NIC. A NIC with fast throughput is critical to your server.

Purchase a NIC from a brand-name vendor in the Microsoft HCL. If the NIC is preinstalled in the computer, make sure in advance that it is compatible with Windows 2000 and the type of network in which the server will be used, such as Ethernet or token ring.

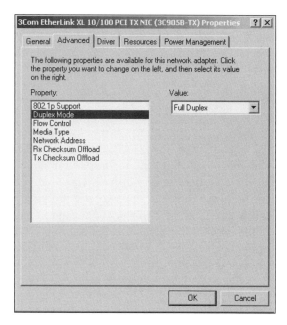

Figure 2-4 NIC Duplex Mode setting

Although Microsoft Windows 2000 Server includes drivers for many brands of NICs, make sure you obtain the most recent driver from the NIC manufacturer. Enhancements are made to NICs for which the latest driver is necessary. Also, an old NIC driver may contain software "bugs" that are corrected by a newer version. Most NIC vendors provide regular updates to their drivers to ensure against transmission problems, and many distribute these updates through the Internet (try Hands-on Project 2-6). The ability to receive frequent updates from a quick, online source is very important, because network drivers are historically problematic.

MEMORY SIZING

Another factor that influences how well a server performs is the amount of memory available to the server. Table 2-3 shows memory guidelines for different versions of Windows 2000 Server on Intel-based computers.

Table 2-3 Memory Guidelines

Operating system	Processor type	Memory
Windows 2000 Server for five or fewer users	Intel	64 MB
Windows 2000 Server for over five users	Intel	128 MB to 4GB
Windows 2000 Advanced Server	Intel	128 MB to 64 GB
Windows 2000 Datacenter	Intel	128 MB to 64 GB

TIP   Microsoft recommends a minimum of 128 MB on all versions of Windows 2000 Server, however, they also recommend that you use at least 256 MB or more for best performance.

Memory is one of the most critical components of a server. An inexpensive way to boost server performance is to install extra RAM. Estimating the amount of RAM needed is not an exact science, but some basic rules still apply. First, start at the minimum amount of memory needed for the operating system kernel (64 MB). Next, determine the number of people who will be accessing the system at the same time and the memory requirements of server software that runs all of the time. Finally, determine the average software requests per user and the amount of memory required for the requests. For example, consider a system with 100 maximum simultaneous users who need an average of 2 MB per connection to access word-processing, spreadsheet, and program files. Also, assume that you are running Domain Name Service (DNS), Windows Internet Naming Service (WINs), and Simple Network Management Protocol (SNMP) services that require 2.3 MB, 2.7 MB, and 2.7 MB, respectively. (These protocols are discussed in Chapter 3.) The calculation of memory is as follows:

64 MB for the operating system + (100 users * 2 MB average memory use) + (7.7 MB for DNS, WINs, and SNMP) = 271.7 MB of memory

 TIP   You can use the Windows 2000 Task Manager to determine the amount of memory used by a process, such as the DNS server process, Dns.exe. (Try Hands-on Project 2-7 to determine the amount of memory that is used by a process.)

In this case, you want at least 272 MB of memory and will likely want to allow for growth by adding an extra margin of 32–64 MB for a total of over 304 MB. The exact amount, of course, will depend on the memory chip combinations that the computer will allow, as determined by its manufactured specifications. Also, when purchasing memory, it is safest to purchase **error checking and correcting** (**ECC**) memory chips. That type of chip keeps some memory in reserve for when problems occur. It also makes an automatic correction if a parity error is detected, preventing the file server from crashing in the event of a memory parity error.

Disk Storage

Choosing the right hard disk drive is just as important as selecting the right bus. Hard disk access on a file server is far more frequent than on a typical workstation. This constant activity leads to congested data paths and the malfunctioning of overused disk drive parts. In choosing a server hard drive, you will need to make decisions about capacity, contention, and fault tolerance.

Disk Capacity

Estimating hard disk capacity is based on calculating space for the following:

- Operating system files
- Software files
- Data and database files
- User files
- General public files
- Utility files
- Server management files

Most server administrators calculate a general figure based on the total number of bytes needed. Table 2-4 illustrates how the number of bytes might be calculated for a law office consisting of 22 users.

Table 2-4   Calculating Disk Capacity

Operating System Files	Estimated Size
Microsoft 2000 Server (depending on the accessories and services installed)	685 MB
Subtotal	685 MB
Application Software	**Estimated Size**
Microsoft Office	150 MB
Microsoft Exchange	150 MB
Paradox database software	70 MB
Accounting software	250 MB
Legal time-accounting software	200 MB
Client databases	275 MB
Court forms	52 MB
Contracts forms	42 MB
Tax law forms	41 MB
Will legal forms	45 MB
Bankruptcy legal forms	35 MB
Database query software	72 MB
Subtotal	1382 MB
User Directories	**Estimated Size**
Each user 100 MB * 22	2200 MB
Subtotal	2200 MB

Table 2-4   Calculating Disk Capacity (continued)

Public Directories	Estimated Size
Shared directories containing word-processing files, spreadsheets, and data	590 MB
Utility directories	50 MB
Subtotal	640 MB
Server Management Software	**Estimated Size**
Extra utilities for server and network management	175 MB
Subtotal	175 MB
Total	5082 MB

Table 2-4 shows a total of 5.082 GB required in estimated disk space. An additional amount should be added to accommodate anticipated growth such as extra space needed by users and for new software that will be installed. Also, in this situation the law firm should take into account expected growth in the databases, accounting data, and legal time-accounting software. Each time the firm bills a client or records information about a new client, data in these areas will grow. Also, some users may need larger allocations for user directories. A margin of growth in this situation might be calculated at 50 percent for the next two years. Adjusting the capacity requirements for growth yields the following estimate:

$$5.082 \text{ GB} + (5.082 \text{ GB} \times 0.5) = 7.623 \text{ GB}$$

Disk Contention

Disk contention is the number of simultaneous requests to read or write data from or to a disk. The number of requests processed by a server can be quite large when there are many users, such as 100 or more. Disk contention can be reduced through the design of the server disk storage. The primary design issues are:

- Speed of the individual disks
- Speed of the disk controllers
- Speed of the data pathway to the disks
- Number of disk pathways
- Disk caching

The speed of the disk is called **disk access time**, measured in milliseconds (ms). This is the time it takes for the read/write heads on the disk to reach the data for reads or updates. A fast disk access time can reduce disk contention. Disk drives manufactured today have fast access times of 10 ms or less. Access time is important, but because most disks are built to be fast, it is not as important as how quickly the data reaches the disk.

The speed of the data pathway or channel is called the **data transfer rate**, and is measured in megabytes per second (Mbps), ranging from about 16.6 Mbps to about 1 Gbps. The data transfer rate is determined by the type of disk controller used in the server and the data pathway. The disk controller is the board that acts as the interface between the disk drives and the computer. Figure 2-5 shows a disk controller. Many computer systems come with **Integrated Device Electronics (IDE)** or **Enhanced Small Device Interface (ESDI)** disk controllers. These controllers provide average data transfer rates and traditionally have been a viable choice for older servers.

Server   Disk controller   Disk drive

Figure 2-5   Disk controller connecting a disk drive

One good choice for a modern server is to implement a **Small Computer System Interface (SCSI)**, which takes advantage of the 32-bit bus architecture of Pentium computers. SCSI interfaces rely less on the main system CPU than IDE and ESDI controllers do, freeing the CPU for other work. Data transfer rate enhancements continue to be implemented for SCSI devices. The standard SCSI-1 interface has a data transfer rate of 5 MBps, which is many times that of IDE or ESDI. The second generation SCSI-2 interfaces come with narrow and wide bus options. The wide interfaces have about twice the data transfer speed, 20 MBps, as the narrow ones, at 10 MBps. Today Ultra SCSI and wide Ultra SCSI adapters are used on Pentium-based servers because they transfer data at 20 MBps and 40 MBps, respectively. Some servers are equipped with Ultra2 SCSI adapters that are relatively new on the market, offering 80 MBps data transfer. SCSI-3 adapters are made for **Reduced Instruction Set Computers (RISC)** computers and have speeds up to 100 MBps. RISCs have CPUs that require fewer instructions for typical operations, which enables their processors to work faster. Table 2-5 summarizes the SCSI interface speeds.

Wide Ultra SCSI adapters for Intel-based computers are called SCSI-3 by some manufacturers.

Several disk drives or other devices, such as a tape drive or CD-ROM drive, can be daisy-chained on the cable of a SCSI adapter. Wide Ultra SCSI or Ultra2 SCSI provides the best performance when devices are daisy-chained. Also, it is important to make sure each device connected to the interface has a unique address, with the first device addressed as 0. Problems occur if two devices have the same address. The SCSI cable must be terminated with a SCSI terminator at the last device that is connected.

Table 2-5   SCSI Interface Data Transfer Rates

Interface	Data Transfer Rate
SCSI-1	Up to 5 MBps
Narrow SCSI-2	Up to 10 MBps
Wide SCSI-2	Up to 20 MBps
Ultra SCSI	Up to 20 MBps
Wide Ultra SCSI	Up to 40 MBps
Ultra2 SCSI	Up to 80 MBps
SCSI-3 (RISC)	Up to 100 MBps

 TIP Omitting the cable terminator is a common cause of problems when connecting several devices to one SCSI adapter. If you experience difficulty recognizing hard disk storage during the Windows 2000 Server installation, check to make sure that the terminator is connected to the last device on the SCSI cable.

Computers designed as servers generally come equipped with SCSI-2 adapters or higher. Watch for new developments with SCSI adapters, particularly in extending data transfer rates over 100 MBps for Pentium-based computers.

The controller of a SCSI device is directly attached to the device. This design makes it possible to mix different devices on the same interface. The SCSI interface plugs into one of the computer's open expansion slots on the main board. A cable is run in daisy–chain fashion from the adapter to the controller card for each device, with a terminator at the last device. Several disk drives, a tape drive, and other SCSI devices can be attached to one adapter, as shown in Figure 2-6.

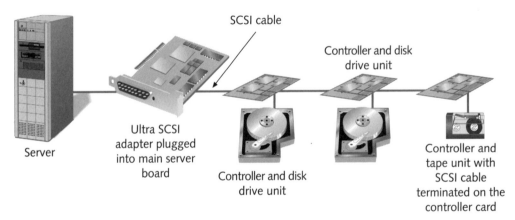

Figure 2-6   Ultra SCSI adapter connected to two disk drives and a tape drive

When you configure a server, be cautious about placing too much demand on access to hard disk storage. If you purchase only one drive, all the users will contend for data on that drive.

If you purchase two drives to place on one SCSI adapter, the data contention on the single pathway may be excessive. One solution is to purchase a server with an Ultra SCSI or Ultra2 SCSI interface and put both drives on the same pathway. A better solution is to create two separate pathways with two adapters, as shown in Figure 2-7 (a technique that can also be used for attaching RAID drives, which are discussed later in this chapter).

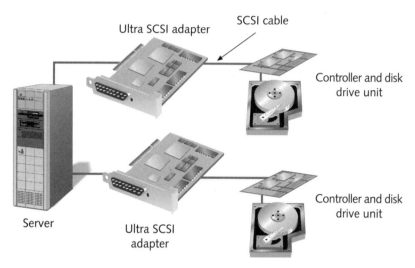

Figure 2-7   Using two SCSI adapters to create separate data paths for hard disk drives

 One method to significantly increase performance on a server is to purchase two or more hard disk drives and divide the flow of data between two or more data pathways by placing the drives on different adapters.

Using Fibre Channel

A newer alternative to SCSI is **Fibre Channel**, a high-speed communications method used to connect disk storage devices to computers. You can purchase a Fibre Channel Host Bus Adapter (HBA) to install in a PCI, EISA, MCA, or SBUS (Sun Microsystems SPARC bus) expansion slot in a server and attach Fibre-Channel-compatible disk drives (including RAID) to the HBA. This adaptation is compatible with both the SCSI, and IP protocols (see Chapter 3). Two important advantages of Fibre Channel in a server are that it is fast (from 100 Mbps to 1 Gbps) and that it enables peripherals to be attached further away (up to 10 kilometers) than other peripheral connection methods. Windows 2000 Server currently supports Fibre Channel using SCSI-based protocol communications. Server hardware applications of Fibre Channel use the Fibre Channel Arbitrated Loop (FC-AL) standard. This standard enables connection of up to 126 devices (host computers and peripherals), up to 1 Gbps data transfer, and hot-pluggable adapters and devices. ("Hot-pluggable" means that you can plug an adapter into a server or attach a new disk drive without shutting down the server.) Unlike SCSI, FC-AL requires no terminators, which makes adding a new device easier.

DISK STORAGE FAULT TOLERANCE

Because hard disk drives are prone to failure, one of the best data security measures is to plan for disk redundancy in servers and host computers. This is accomplished in two ways: by installing backup disks and by installing RAID drives.

One fault-tolerance option common to many server and host computer operating systems is **disk mirroring** to store redundant data. With disk mirroring, there are two separate drives for each disk volume of data. One is the main drive used to handle all of the user's requests to access or write data. The second drive contains a mirror image of the data on the first. Each time there is an update or deletion, it is made on the main drive and replicated on the second. If the main drive fails, the mirror drive takes over with no data loss. In disk mirroring, both drives are attached to the same disk controller or SCSI adapter. For example, one SCSI adapter plugged into a slot on the computer's main board might have two disk drives, the primary drive and a mirrored drive (Figure 2-8).

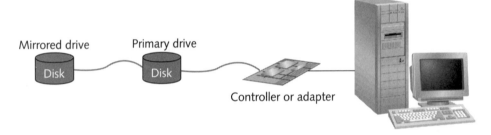

Figure 2-8   Disk mirroring

Disk mirroring has a weakness: it leaves the data inaccessible if the controller or adapter fails. To compensate for that weakness, you can use **disk duplexing**, another fault-tolerance method, combining disk mirroring with redundant adapters or controllers. Each disk is still mirrored by using a second backup disk, but the backup disk is placed on a controller or adapter that is separate from the one used by the main disk (Figure 2-9). If the primary disk, controller, or adapter fails, users may continue their work on the redundant one. Some operating systems can switch from the primary to the backup disk without interruption in service to the users, while others require that the server or host computer be rebooted to use the mirror drive instead of the failed main drive.

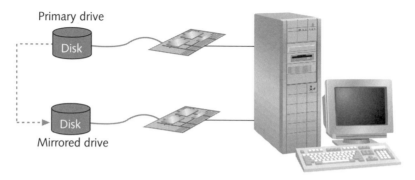

Figure 2-9   Disk duplexing

Another approach to disk redundancy is the use of a **redundant array of inexpensive** (or **independent**) **disks** (**RAID**). RAID is a set of standards for lengthening disk life and preventing data loss. There are eight levels of RAID, beginning with the use of disk striping. **Striping** is the ability to spread data over multiple disk volumes. For example, part of a large file may be written to one volume and part to another. The goal is to spread disk activity equally across all volumes, preventing wear from being focused on a single volume in a set. The six essential RAID levels are as follows:

- *RAID level 0*: Striping with no other redundancy features is RAID level 0. Striping is used to extend disk life and to improve performance. Data access on striped volumes is fast because of the way the data is divided into blocks that are quickly accessed through multiple disk reads and data paths. A significant disadvantage to using level 0 striping is that if one disk fails, you can expect a large data loss on all volumes. RAID level 0 is supported in Windows 2000, using 2 to 32 disks in a set. In Windows 2000 Server, this is called striped volumes, whereas in Windows NT 4.0 it is called stripe sets.

- *RAID level 1*: This level employs simple disk mirroring and is used on smaller networks, in situations in which fast read access is more important than fast disk writing, and as a means to duplicate the operating system files in the event of a disk failure. Windows 2000 Server supports level 1, but includes disk duplexing as well as mirroring through the fault-tolerance driver Ftdisk.sys. If there are three or more volumes to be mirrored or duplexed, this solution is more expensive than the other RAID levels. When you plan for disk mirroring, remember that write access is slower than read access, because information must be written twice, once on the primary disk and once on the secondary disk. Many server administrators consider disk mirroring and disk duplexing to offer the best guarantee of data recovery when there is a disk failure.

- *RAID level 2*: This uses an array of disks whereby the data is striped across all disks in the array. Also, in this method all disks store error-correction information that enables the array to reconstruct data from a failed disk. The advantages of level 2 are that disk wear is reduced and data can be reconstructed if a disk fails.

- *RAID level 3*: Like level 2, RAID level 3 uses disk striping and stores error-correcting information, but the information is only written to one disk in the array. If that disk fails, the array cannot rebuild its contents.

- *RAID level 4*: This level stripes data and stores error-correcting information on all drives, in a manner similar to level 2. An added feature is its ability to perform checksum verification. The checksum is a sum of bits in a file. When a file is recreated after a disk failure, the checksum previously stored for that file is checked against the actual file after it is reconstructed. If the two do not match, you will know that the file may be corrupted. RAID levels 2 through 4 are not supported by Windows 2000 Server because they do not offer the full protection found in level 5.

- *RAID level 5*: Level 5 combines the best features of RAID, including striping, error correction, and checksum verification. Windows 2000 Server supports level 5, calling it "stripe set with parity on basic disks" or a RAID-5 volume, depending on the disk architecture. Whereas level 4 stores checksum data on only one disk, level 5 spreads both error-correction and checksum data over all of the disks, so there is no single point of failure. This level uses more memory than other RAID levels, with at least 16 MB recommended as additional memory for system functions. In addition, level 5 requires at least three disks in the RAID array. Recovery from a failed disk provides roughly the same guarantee as with disk mirroring, but takes longer with level 5. However, if more than one disk fails in the array, you may not be able to recover some or all of the data in the entire array of disks, in which case you will have to restore data from a tape backup.

Windows 2000 Server supports only RAID levels 0, 1, and 5 for disk fault tolerance, with levels 1 and 5 recommended. RAID level 0 is not recommended in most situations because it does not really provide fault tolerance, except to help extend the life of disks. All three RAID levels support FAT- and NTFS- formatted disks. RAID fault-tolerance methods are not supported in Windows 2000 Professional. When you decide upon using RAID level 1 or RAID level 5, consider the following:

- The boot and system files can be placed on RAID level 1, but not on RAID level 5. Thus, if you use RAID level 5, these files must be on a separate disk or a separate RAID level 1 disk set (except for hardware RAID, which is discussed in the next section).

- RAID level 1 uses two hard disks, and RAID level 5 uses from 3 to 32.

- RAID level 1 is more expensive to implement than RAID level 5, when you consider the cost on the basis of each megabyte of storage. Keep in mind that in RAID level 1, half of your total disk space is used for redundancy, whereas that value is one-third or less for RAID level 5. The amount of RAID level 5 used for parity is $1/n$ where n is the number of disk drives in the array.

- RAID level 5 requires more memory than RAID level 1.

- Disk read access is faster in RAID level 1 and RAID level 5 than is write access, with read access for RAID level 1 identical to that of a disk that does not have RAID.

- Because RAID level 5 involves more disks (and more spindles) and because the read/write heads can acquire data simultaneously across striped volumes, it has much faster read access than RAID level 1.

On a Windows 2000 server, mirrored/duplexed and RAID disks are set up using the Disk Management snap-in in the Microsoft Management Console (MMC), a central tool for managing the server disk and CD-ROM drives. The Disk Management snap-in (Figure 2-10) replaces the Disk Manager used in Windows NT 4.0, but offers similar disk management options, as follows:

- Viewing status information about drives, including file system information
- Creating an NTFS partition on a new disk drive
- Combining two physical drives into one logical drive
- Changing drive letter assignments
- Partitioning and formatting drives
- Extending a partitioned drive or a volume to include any free space not already allocated
- Creating a mirrored volume
- Creating a striped or RAID-5 volume
- Creating a spanned or extended volume

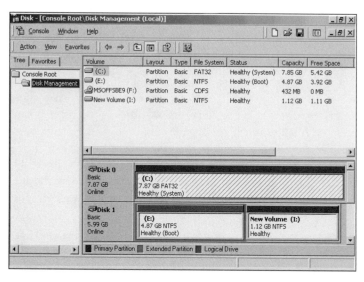

Figure 2-10   Windows 2000 Disk Management snap-in

SELECTING DISK STORAGE FAULT TOLERANCE

The disk storage fault tolerance-method you use depends on factors such as:

- The importance of the data stored on the server
- How soon a server must be working after a disk problem
- The amount of data stored on the server
- How fast the data must be accessed
- Budget constraints

Consider three different situations for planning fault tolerance. In the first, you are planning a server to be used by a team of 10 software developers for a full-featured human resources hiring system used by large department stores. None of the software on this server is used in a live environment, because the server is strictly for testing and development. Also, the developers only work with limited test data instead of a large human resources database. However, the application developers are under rigid deadlines for completing each phase of the software. In this situation, the disk storage requirements are not large and a disk crash is unlikely to cause them to lose data that cannot be replaced. The main concern is to have the server quickly working again after a disk failure, so the developers can keep up with their deadlines. In this situation, disk mirroring or RAID level 1 is likely to meet their needs. If the main disk drive is lost, the mirrored disk can quickly take over so they do not lose precious time. Disk duplexing is another alternative, if there is a concern that they may lose an adapter or disk controller and sacrifice time due to this type of failure.

In another example, a Windows 2000 server is used by tellers and loan officers in a small bank with 15 employees. The bank cannot afford to risk loss of data or downtime because of a failed disk drive or controller. Also, during certain peak periods, they experience heavy disk read and write activity. The bank is likely to benefit from dividing data among two disk drives on different SCSI adapters, with a mirrored drive for each main drive. The disk load is spread between two drives for faster access during peak times at the bank. If one disk drive fails, the mirrored drive can take over. If an adapter fails, both of the drives on that adapter can be switched to the remaining adapter until the failed adapter is replaced. An even better option is to connect two small RAID level 5 arrays to two different adapters. This provides two paths for better disk response and the advantage of disk redundancy should one of the RAID drives fail. Also, if an adapter fails, its RAID drive can be switched temporarily to the working adapter.

A third scenario is a mail-order company that sells collectibles, stamps, and plates. This company has 55 customer service representatives, who take telephone orders and enter the data in an interactive order- entry database on a Windows 2000 server. Customer service representatives work around the clock, and any server downtime costs hundreds of dollars a minute. Also, the company cannot afford to lose any data due to a failed drive, because it could mean a loss of thousands of dollars. This is a good application for multiple data paths and large RAID level 5 arrays. The multiple data paths will help the server respond to aggressive disk demands, and the RAID level 5 arrays prevent data loss if a drive in an array fails.

2

Also, this setup prevents downtime, because the disk array continues working even though a drive has crashed.

SOFTWARE RAID COMPARED TO HARDWARE RAID

Two approaches to RAID can be implemented on a server: software RAID and hardware RAID. Software RAID implements fault tolerance through the server's operating system, such as using RAID levels 1 or 5 through the Windows 2000 Disk Management snap-in. Hardware RAID is implemented through the server hardware and is independent of the operating system. Many manufacturers implement hardware RAID on the adapter, such as a SCSI adapter, to which the disk drives are connected. The RAID logic is contained in a chip on the adapter. Also, there often is a battery connected to the chip that ensures that the chip never loses power and has fault tolerance to retain the RAID setup even when there is a power outage. Hardware RAID is more expensive than software RAID, but offers many advantages over software RAID:

- Faster read and write response

- The ability to place boot and system files on different RAID levels, such as RAID levels 1 and 5

- The ability to "hot-swap" a failed disk with one that works or is new, thus replacing the disk without shutting down the server (this option can vary by manufacturer)

- More setup options to retrieve damaged data and to combine different RAID levels within one array of disks, such as mirroring two disks using RAID level 1 and setting up five disks for RAID level 5 in a seven-disk array (the RAID options depend on what the manufacturer offers)

| CAUTION |

> One limitation of hardware RAID is that with some vendors you might be required to purchase all components from the same vendor—adapter, cable, and disk drives, for example. When you purchase hardware RAID, find out first if you have the option to use disk drives from other vendors and if the drives can be upgraded to larger sizes. For instance, if you purchase five 9 MB drives to start, can you replace them with larger drives (20 MB for example), as your needs grow?

When you purchase RAID, look for options that give you better management capabilities. One important option is the ability to set up and manage RAID from within Windows 2000 Server, instead of having to access setup from a control key combination before the operating system is loaded when you boot. Another option is to have lights or an LED display on the front of the server to tell you the status of the RAID, such as when a disk has failed.

BACKUP MEDIA

Another form of redundancy to protect data is equipping a server with backup capabilities. Windows 2000 Server supports backup to different kinds of removable media that include tape, Zip/Jaz disks, and CD-ROMs. Tape backup is used for large backup needs, because a single tape can hold over 40 GB. Byte for byte, tape backup is usually the least expensive and most convenient way to back up an entire server. When you have smaller backup needs, such as backing up a specific set of files, then Zip/Jaz disks or rewriteable CD-ROMs are likely to be more convenient and faster than tape. For example, a 100 MB or 1 GB Zip/Jaz disk may be all that is necessary to back up key accounting files each evening and when your organization performs the monthly accounting system maintenance. The Zip/Jaz disk is convenient and will be faster than using tape in this situation.

When you outfit a system with tape, Zip, and/or CD-ROM drives, consider using SCSI technology for each and do not connect a drive used for backups to a SCSI adapter used for hard disk drives. For example, a tape drive used to back up Windows 2000 servers on a network can be mounted inside a server or it can be an external unit; either way it should be attached as the only device on an adapter (Figure 2-11).

If hard disks also are on the same adapter as the tape drive, for example, server access to the disks may be slowed due to the high traffic through that adapter during backups.

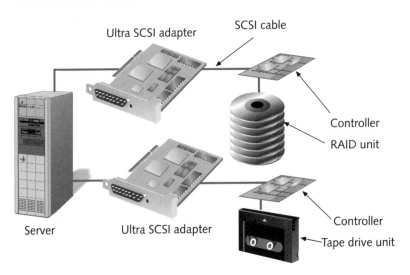

Figure 2-11   Connecting a tape drive to a separate adapter

 Reliable backup systems and media are one of the best investments you can make. When data is lost, the expense of backup equipment and media is small compared to the cost of the human resources needed to reconstruct data

Choosing a CD-ROM Drive

A CD-ROM drive is necessary to load the Windows 2000 Server operating system, unless you choose to load the system over the network. Another good reason for having the drive is to run software that is only available on CD-ROM. In the law office example used earlier, the CD-ROM drive might be used to make legal forms software available to all attorneys and paralegals connected to the server. On school lab servers, CD-ROM drives can be used to make study resources available, such as dictionaries, encyclopedias, and writing aids.

Another way to implement CD-ROM access is to purchase a CD-ROM "jukebox" or server that can be connected to the Windows 2000 server by using a SCSI adapter or Fibre Channel (Figure 2-12). CD-Technology, DEC/Compaq, NEC, Plextor, Sony, and Toshiba are examples of CD-ROM vendors on Microsoft's HCL. CD-ROMs come in various speeds ranging up to 48X and faster. Windows 2000 requires that you have a 12X or faster CD-ROM drive. If you plan to use multiple CD-ROMs for sharing through a server, investigate the many options for CD-ROM arrays. The arrays offer throughput that can match Ultra SCSI speeds. CD-ROM arrays come in various configurations, such as 7, 10, 14, and 32 CD-ROM drives in a single tower array. One user can be connected to one or more CD-ROMs in the array through a Windows 2000 server.

Figure 2-12   CD-ROM "jukebox"

 Windows NT 4.0 does not support Digital Video Discs (DVD), but Windows 2000 does. It is not necessary to have a DVD drive on a server, unless you plan to use it for network access to movies, for example.

Setting Up and Testing the Server

There are several steps you can take once your new server arrives, which will help you be ready for Windows 2000 Server installation. A first step is to boot the computer to make sure it works. As the server boots, it is likely to go through a test of the banks of RAM.

If you need to install the NIC, turn off the computer, unplug it from the wall outlet, and remove the monitor, mouse, and keyboard. Next, remove the cover, according to the manufacturer's instructions. Locate an empty slot for the NIC. The circuit board slots are usually located at the rear of the main circuit board or on a separate board that connects to the main board. At the end of each slot, there is a slot cover on the frame of the server. Remove the slot cover before installing the NIC. Consult the manual to be certain which are 32-bit EISA and PCI slots. Make sure you plug the NIC into the appropriate type of slot, depending on the type of NIC (EISA or PCI).

After removing the slot cover, check to make sure your wrist grounding strap is on securely. Remove the NIC from its antistatic protective bag and firmly install it into a slot. You may hear a slight click as the card goes into place against the bottom of the slot.

Plan to execute a fast test of the NIC to be certain that the NIC is installed properly. Reattach the monitor, mouse, keyboard, and power cord. Once the computer is on, run the test software included with the NIC. The test program should indicate the NIC is installed correctly and is ready to be used.

Repeat the same type of procedures if you also need to install one or more SCSI adapters. Install SCSI adapters in the appropriate EISA or PCI expansion slots. If possible, leave space between boards inside the server (empty slots between occupied slots). This allows for better air circulation and reduces the impact of heat generated by the computer. It also helps to prolong the life of the boards.

After the SCSI adapters are installed, boot the computer again to make sure it boots properly. If the adapter manufacturer has included test software, make sure you use it to test the installation. Once you are certain that the newly installed components are working, let the computer run for several days as a "burn-in" period. Any defective components are likely to fail after you run the computer for several days. If there is a defective component, such as a monitor or floppy disk drive, you will have the opportunity to replace it before starting the Windows 2000 Server installation. This is much easier than puzzling over Windows 2000 Server installation problems caused by defective hardware.

CHAPTER SUMMARY

- The hardware used for servers are not just PCs anymore. There is a wide range of sophisticated options from fast processors to fault-tolerant disk drives. The challenge for you is putting together server specifications that match your organization's needs.

- When you plan the hardware, begin with specifications that match the role the server will play on the network. It is better to start with too much server than with too little. A server that begins its job undersized will quickly be a source of problems. At first an undersized server may appear to be a network problem because of slow response and delays at the server. You may spend hours locating the problem, and your users quickly will lose confidence in the installation. Well-planned server hardware enables you to get a fast start, so you can proceed with the next steps in managing the server. Also, the server will quickly spawn confidence, enabling users to immediately enjoy productivity gains.

2

❑ The first step in selecting hardware is to check the Microsoft hardware compatibility list (HCL) to make sure that all components will work with Windows 2000 Server. One reason for taking this step is to ensure that drivers are available for each hardware component and that they are compatible with the operating system installation. The CPU you select from the list depends on the anticipated server load. In many cases a Pentium-based CPU is a good selection for small and medium-sized installations (a few users to several hundred). If the installation is for a demanding client/server system, a multimedia server, or a large Web server, a Xeon, SMP, or RISC-based computer is likely to be needed.

❑ Computers use different types of bus architectures, such as ISA, EISA, MCA, and PCI. For most installations a PCI-based computer works best, with perhaps one or two EISA expansion slots. The EISA slots are compatible with older adapters, while the predominant PCI slots provide high throughput for critical components, such as the NIC. The selection of the NIC depends on network and computer requirements. If the network is 100 Mbps using twisted-pair cable, the NIC will need to match those requirements. Also, modern servers should be equipped with one or more USB ports and Plug and Play compatibility. I_2O architecture is an added feature that can significantly improve a server's performance.

❑ The selection of disk storage depends on the requirements for factors such as capacity, speed, and data transfer rate. SCSI adapters are generally used to connect hard disks to the computer because of their fast throughput. Fibre Channel is an even faster and more flexible option for servers that experience heavy disk access by a large number of users. Fault-tolerance options also need to be considered when disk storage is selected. Disk mirroring, disk duplexing, and RAID are fault- tolerance methods supported by Windows 2000 Server. Installing removable backup systems is another way to implement fault tolerance so that data on hard disks can be backed up regularly.

❑ Most servers have at least one CD-ROM drive. Options are available to connect an array of CD-ROM drives for situations in which the server makes multiple CD-ROMs available to users. Windows 2000 is compatible with regular CD-ROM and DVD drives, with at least a 12X drive recommended.

❑ The last stage in preparing the server hardware is to install components such as NICs, SCSI adapters, RAM, and tape drives (if they are not preinstalled by the manufacturer). Each device should be tested after it is installed. The server and components should have a burn-in period of several days to make sure that all parts are functional before the Windows 2000 Server operating system is loaded.

In the next chapter, you learn about Windows 2000 protocol options to meet nearly every networking possibility, including Internet communications and communications with other server operating systems, such as NetWare. You also continue to learn about the planning process involved in making preparations to implement Windows 2000 Server in different kinds of situations.

KEY TERMS

bus — A pathway in a computer used to transmit information. This pathway is used to send CPU instructions and other data being transferred within the computer.

bus mastering — A process that reduces the reliance on the CPU for input/output activities on a computer's bus. Interface cards that have bus mastering can take control of the bus for faster data flow.

clock speed — Rate at which the CPU sends bursts of data through a computer's buses.

data transfer rate — Speed at which data moves through the disk controller along the data channel to a disk drive.

disk access time — Amount of time it takes for a disk drive to read or write data by moving a read/write head to the location of the data.

disk duplexing — A fault-tolerance method similar to disk mirroring in that it prevents data loss by duplicating data from a main disk to a backup disk; but disk duplexing places the backup disk on a different controller or adapter than is used by the main disk.

disk mirroring — A fault-tolerance method that prevents data loss by duplicating data from a main disk to a backup disk. Some operating systems also refer to this as disk shadowing.

driver — Software that enables a computer to communicate with devices like network interface cards, printers, monitors, and hard disk drives. Each driver has a specific purpose, such as to handle network communications.

Enhanced Small Device Interface (ESDI) — An early device interface for computer peripherals and hard disk drives.

error checking and correcting memory (ECC) — Memory that can correct some types of memory problems without causing computer operations to halt.

Extended Industry Standard Architecture (EISA) — A computer bus design that incorporates 32-bit communications within a computer. It is an industry standard used by several computer manufacturers.

Fibre Channel — A high-speed method for connecting computer peripherals, such as disk drives, to servers and other host computers through copper and fiber-optic cable. Current implementations of Fibre Channel in Windows 2000 servers provide data transfer rates of up to 1 Gbps.

firmware — Software that is stored on a chip in a device, such as in a ROM chip, and that is used to control basic functions of the device such as communication with a disk drive.

full duplex — The capacity to send and receive signals at the same time.

half duplex — The ability to send or receive signals, but not simultaneously.

hardware compatibility list (HCL) — A list of computer hardware tested by Microsoft and determined to be compatible with Windows 2000 Server.

Industry Standard Architecture (ISA) — An older expansion bus design dating back to the 1980s, supporting 8-bit and 16-bit cards and with a data transfer rate of 8 MB per second.

Integrated Device Electronics (IDE) — An inexpensive hard disk interface that is used on Intel-based computers from the 80286 to Pentium computers.

intelligent input/output (I₂O) — A computer communications architecture that removes some of the I/O processing activities from the main processor to I₂O processors on peripherals designed for I₂O architectures, such as hard disks. I₂O devices use one general device driver for all I₂O-compliant devices.

Micro Channel Architecture (MCA) — A bus architecture that is used in older IBM Intel-based computers. It provides 32-bit communications within the computer.

network interface card (NIC) — An adapter board designed to connect a workstation, server, or other network equipment to a network medium.

Peripheral Computer Interface (PCI) — A computer bus design that supports 32-bit and 64-bit bus communication for high-speed operations.

Plug and Play (PnP) — Ability of added computer hardware, such as an adapter or modem, to identify itself to the computer operating system for installation.

processor cache — A special data storage area used only by the system processor and located on either the processor chip or a chip separate from the processor.

Reduced Instruction Set Computer (RISC) — A computer that has a CPU that requires fewer instructions for common operations. The processor works faster because the commands to the CPU are reduced.

redundant array of inexpensive (or **independent**) **disks (RAID)** — A set of standards designed to extend the life of hard disk drives and to prevent data loss from a hard disk failure.

shared disk model — Linking two or more servers to operate as one and to equally share resources that include disk, CD-ROM, and tape storage.

shared nothing model — Linking two or more servers to operate as one, but with each owning particular disk, CD-ROM, and tape resources.

Small Computer System Interface (SCSI) — A 32- or 64-bit computer adapter that transports data between one or more attached devices, such as hard disks, and the computer. There are several types of SCSI adapters, including SCSI, SCSI-2, SCSI-3, wide SCSI, narrow SCSI, wide Ultra SCSI, and Ultra2 SCSI. All are used to provide high-speed data transfer to reduce bottlenecks within the computer.

striping — A data storage method that breaks up data files across all volumes of a disk set to minimize wear on a single volume.

symmetric multiprocessor (SMP) — A type of computer with two or more CPUs that share the processing load.

universal serial bus (USB) — A bus standard that enables you to attach all types of devices—keyboards, cameras, pointing devices, telephones, and tape drives, for example—to one bus port on a computer. Up to 127 devices can be attached to one port, and it is not necessary to power off the computer when you attach a device. USB was developed to replace the traditional serial and parallel bus technologies on computers.

REVIEW QUESTIONS

1. You are planning a server for a company that wants to implement hard disk fault tolerance. The company is not worried about expense, but does want a server that has very good read and write performance. Which of the following would you implement?

    a. software RAID level 1

    b. hardware RAID level 5

    c. IDE controllers

    d. a bus extender

2. Which type of NIC is likely to provide the fastest performance?

    a. PCI

    b. MCA

    c. ISA

    d. EISA

3. Your assistant is installing a NIC in a Windows 2000 Server that is connected to a full-duplex switch port. How should the NIC be set up?

    a. for 10 Mbps communication

    b. for ATM communication

    c. for half-duplex communication

    d. for full-duplex communication

4. Which of the following are features of a USB port on a computer running Windows 2000 Server?

    a. Plug and Play

    b. ability to connect a device without shutting down the computer

    c. connectivity for up to 180 devices

    d. all of the above

    e. only a and b

    f. only b and c

5. Which type of SCSI interface is fastest?

    a. narrow SCSI-2

    b. wide Ultra SCSI

    c. Ultra2 SCSI

    d. wide SCSI-2

6. You have installed a SCSI adapter and connected three hard drives to it. When you start the computer, it does not recognize any of the hard drives. Which of the following might you do to troubleshoot?

a. Check the addresses for the drives.

b. Check the battery on the SCSI adapter.

c. Check the terminator on the last drive.

d. all of the above

e. only a and b

f. only a and c

7. Which type of adapter reduces reliance on the CPU for I/O processing?

a. L2

b. bus mastering

c. parity leveling

d. dual channel

8. You are looking at disk drive and adapter specifications because you want to ensure fast access to data. Which of the following is most important, when you consider the types of equipment on the market today?

a. head rotation

b. disk access time

c. data transfer rate

d. disk braking method

9. You have a small Windows 2000 Server implementation in which you need 2.2 GB of space for data, and there are two 5 GB disk drives already installed. Which of the following would be your best bet in terms of providing protection for your data and the operating system files?

a. RAID level 0

b. disk mirroring

c. RAID level 5

d. Just install the disks on a SCSI adapter.

10. You need to perform a nightly backup of a server that holds 72 GB of data. Which removable medium is your best choice??

a. Zip disk

b. CD-ROM

c. tape

d. high-density floppy disk

11. Which of the following is compatible with 32-bit and 64-bit bus architecture?

    a. EISA

    b. MCA

    c. PCI

    d. all of the above

    e. none of the above

12. You are setting up two clustered servers so that each has equal access to disk storage. Which model is this?

    a. shared disk

    b. shared CPU

    c. shared nothing

    d. shared master

13. What is the minimum amount of hard disk space necessary to install Windows 2000 Server on an Intel-based computer?

    a. 685 MB

    b. 742 MB

    c. 522 MB

    d. 367 MB

14. You are working on specifications for memory for your server. Your boss, who is very conscious of the budget, says you only need memory for the operating system. Is he right? As you consider the options, keep in mind that there will be 45 users of the server, which will be set up for TCP/IP and DNS Services.

    a. Yes, you only really need memory for the operating system.

    b. No, you need memory for the operating system and to run TCP/IP.

    c. No, you need memory for operating system, users who access the server, and services such as DNS.

    d. No, because all servers should be outfitted with at least 512 MB regardless of the operating system needs.

15. Which of the following are characteristics of Fibre Channel?

    a. Up to 126 devices can be connected.

    b. It does not use a terminator at the end.

    c. Its maximum reach is limited to 9 feet.

    d. all of the above

    e. only a and b

    f. only a and c

16. Which of the following gives you protection against a hard drive adapter failure?

    a. mirroring

    b. sectoring

    c. channel diversion

    d. duplexing

2

17. Your server seems to be experiencing memory errors that will not self-correct. One problem is that it might not have what type of memory?

    a. 70 nanosecond

    b. RAM_2

    c. ECC

    d. 72-pin

18. One difference between Windows 2000 Server and Windows 2000 Professional is that:

    a. Windows 2000 Professional does not support disk fault tolerance.

    b. Windows 2000 Server has fewer NIC drivers that can be adapted for it because it supports more connections.

    c. Windows 2000 Professional runs software faster.

    d. Windows 2000 Server requires less memory.

19. Which processor does not use Level 2 caching?

    a. Pentium II

    b. Pentium Pro

    c. Pentium III

    d. Celeron

20. You are working with your boss to develop specifications for a server, and she asks how much disk space is actually available for data in RAID level 5 when there are four disks. Which of the following the appropriate answer?

    a. 90%

    b. 75%

    c. 65%

    d. 50%

21. Your community college is working to replace a Pentium 233 MHz Web server because it is extremely slow and its use is growing geometrically. Which of the following would give you the best performance in terms of processor caching?

    a. Pentium Pro

    b. Pentium II

    c. Pentium III

    d. Pentium III Xeon

22. You have set up RAID 5 via SCSI connectivity on your server. In the middle of the afternoon, the server diagnostic lights show that two drives have failed. What is your most likely recourse?

    a. You have no problems because up to two drives can fail without loss of data.

    b. Replace the terminators on both disk controllers.

    c. Perform a restore from your most recent tape backup.

    d. Use the Windows 2000 Server Disk Management snap-in to reinitialize each drive.

23. What is the minimum CD-ROM drive that can be used with Windows 2000 Server?

    a. 48X

    b. 32X

    c. 24X

    d. 12X

24. Your boss has found a bargain in a Pentium II computer for a server. What step(s) is (are) most important in making certain that you can install Windows 2000 Server on it?

    a. Check to make sure it matches the minimum hardware requirements.

    b. Check to see if it is listed in the HCL.

    c. Make sure that it has a USB port.

    d. all of the above

    e. only a and b

    f. only a and c

25. Which of the following differentiates hardware RAID from software RAID?

    a. Hardware RAID is usually more expensive.

    b. You cannot put boot and system files on hardware RAID.

    c. You can only implement RAID level 1 on software RAID.

    d. all of the above

    e. only a and b

    f. only a and c

HANDS-ON PROJECTS

Project 2-1

In this hands-on activity, you view the HCL for Windows 2000 Server. You will need the Windows 2000 Server CD-ROM.

To access the HCL:

1. Log on to Windows 2000 Server (or Professional).

2. Insert the Windows 2000 Server CD-ROM.

2

3. Double-click **My Computer** on the desktop.

4. Double-click the drive that contains the CD-ROM, such as drive D.

5. Click **Browse This CD**, if the Microsoft Windows 2000 CD dialog box is displayed.

6. Double-click the **Support** folder.

7. Double-click the **Hcl.txt** file (or **HCL**, depending on your settings for viewing files) in the Support folder and scroll through its contents. Maximize the Notepad window, if necessary.

8. Find four manufacturers of display monitors on the list and record them in your lab journal or in a word-processed document.

9. Find four manufacturers of pointing devices and two manufacturers of USB controllers. Record this information in your lab journal or word-processed document.

10. Close Notepad when you are finished.

11. Close the Support, Microsoft Windows 2000 CD-ROM, and My Computer windows.

Project 2-2

In this project, you view the hardware components set up in your computer.

To view the components:

1. Log on to Windows 2000.

2. Click **Start**, point to **Settings**, and then click **Control Panel**.

3. Double-click the **Add/Remove Hardware** icon.

4. When the Add/Remove Hardware Wizard starts, click **Next**.

5. Select **Add/Troubleshoot a device** and then click **Next**.

6. Wait a few moments as the Wizard searches for new devices.

7. Scroll through the devices text box.

8. Is there a PCI bus in the computer? What other buses are there?

9. What type of processor is installed? If there is a tape drive, what kind is it?

10. Record your observations in your lab journal or in a word-processed document.

11. Click **Cancel** to exit the Wizard and then close the Control Panel.

Project 2-3

In this hands-on activity you check the BIOS setup screen on a computer to determine if it has an option to enable Plug and Play.

To check the Plug and Play option in the BIOS setup:

1. Find out how to access the computer's BIOS from your instructor or lab assistant. On most computers you access the BIOS setup screen by typing a specific key right after turning on the computer's power. For example, some computers use the F1 or Del keys.

2. Follow the on-screen instructions to view or access the BIOS setup menu(s).

3. If there are two or more menus, such as Main, Advanced, Security, and so on, use the right and left arrow keys (or the keys mentioned on-screen) to view the different menus and their options.

4. Look for a reference to Plug and Play, such as one that says Plug and Play O/S [Yes]. In this example, Yes means it is enabled, and No means it is not.

5. Make sure that you exit the BIOS setup without making any changes. On some computers, you can exit by pressing Esc and typing no to the query about saving your changes.

6. Record your findings in your lab journal or in a word-processed document.

Project 2-4

In this project, you find the location of the NIC driver in a computer running Windows 2000 Server. Log onto an account with Administrator privileges for this project.

To find the driver location:

1. Log on to Windows 2000.
2. Click **Start**, point to **Settings**, and then click **Control Panel**.
3. Double-click the **System** icon.
4. Click the **Hardware** tab and the **Device Manager** button.
5. Double-click **Network Adapters** and then double-click the actual network adapter that appears under Network Adapters.
6. Click the **Driver** tab.
7. Click the **Driver Details** button.
8. In the Driver files text box, notice the location of the driver and its filename. Record both.
9. Click **OK** and then click **Cancel**.
10. Close the Device Manager and then click **Cancel**.
11. Close the Control Panel.

Project 2-5

In this project, you view the properties and capabilities of a NIC in a server. You will need access to a computer running Windows 2000 Server (or Windows 2000 Professional) and to an account with Administrator privileges.

To view the NIC properties and capabilities:

1. Log on to Windows 2000 Server.
2. Click **Start**, point to **Settings**, and then click **Network and Dial-Up Connections**.
3. Right-click **Local Area Connection** and then click **Properties**.
4. Make sure the General tab is displayed and then click the **Configure** button for the NIC.

2

5. Click the **Advanced** tab and notice the properties available through the NIC, such as Duplex Mode and Media Type. Record the available properties in your lab journal or in a word-processed document.

6. Click the **Duplex Mode** property and determine the current duplex setting in the Value: box. Click the list arrow in the Value: box to determine which other duplex settings are available.

7. Click the **Media Type** property and determine the media options in the Value: box.

8. Select other properties and view their associated options.

9. Click the other tabs available for the NIC, which can include Driver, Resources, and Power Management (depending on the NIC's capabilities and driver).

10. Record your observations in your lab journal or in a word-processed document before exiting.

11. Click **Cancel** on the NIC properties dialog box and **Cancel** on the Local Area Connection Properties dialog box.

12. Close the Network and Dial-up Connections dialog box, if it is displayed.

In this and in other projects that involve NICs, the NIC properties and tabs that you view in the NIC properties dialog box may vary slightly depending on the type of NIC installed, because these are influenced by the manufacturer and the NIC driver written by the manufacturer.

Project 2-6

In this hands-on assignment, you practice obtaining a NIC driver from a vendor's Web site. You need access to Microsoft Internet Explorer on a workstation or server and Internet access.

To find a NIC driver:

1. Open Internet Explorer, for example by doubling-clicking it on the desktop of Windows 95, Windows 98, Windows NT, or Windows 2000.

2. Enter **www.3com.com** in the address line.

3. Find the link for support and click it.

4. Click the link for network interface cards.

5. Select a technology, such as Ethernet, or a card type, such as Etherlink III, or a product number, such as 3C590. Click **Go There** or the hyperlink to search for your selection.

6. Choose a card, such as the EtherLink III PCI and then click its hyperlink. If you selected the product number in Step 5, skip this step and go to Step 7.

7. Find the Windows 2000 driver or lastest Windows NDIS driver on the list of drivers.

8. What other drivers are available?

9. How would you download a driver?

10. Record your answers to Steps 8–9 and any other observations on this project in your lab journal or in a word-processed document.

11. Close Internet Explorer.

> The Web site page options may change over time. If the Web page has changed since this writing, use the Support option and search to find drivers or network interface cards.

Project 2-7

In this hands-on activity, you use Task Manager to determine the amount of memory used while running the IIS service in Windows 2000 Server. IIS must already be installed on the server before you start.

To determine the amount of memory used by IIS:

1. Log on to Windows 2000 Server.

2. Type **Ctl+Alt+Del**.

3. Click the **Task Manager** button on the Windows Security dialog box

4. Click the **Processes** tab, if it is not already displayed.

5. Use the scroll bar to find the IIssrv.exe service,. Next, find Mstask.exe. For each service find the amount of memory that it uses under the Mem Usage column.

6. Record the memory usage in your lab journal or in a word-processed document.

7. Close Windows Task Manager.

CASE PROJECT

Aspen Consulting Project: Planning Server Specifications

Moose Jaw Outfitters is a "mail-order" company that sells outdoor clothing in Canada and the U.S. Although they are known as a mail-order company, Moose Jaw Outfitters does most of its business via telephone and an Internet Web site. Actual orders sent through the mail represent their third largest source of sales. The company also has two large outlet stores, one in Winnipeg, Canada and another in St. Cloud, Minnesota, which represent the fourth largest source of income.

The Winnipeg store is the location of the main headquarters for Moose Jaw Outfitters, where the company maintains customer service representatives to take telephone orders, has a Web site for Internet orders, processes mail orders, keeps its main inventory of products, and handles its general business and accounting functions. There are clothing factories in both Winnipeg and St. Cloud. The St. Cloud location also maintains customer service representatives for telephone orders. The company has hired you to help their IT Department implement new servers. Most of the IT Department members are located in Winnipeg, but the St. Cloud site also has some IT staff. Both sites have computer resources and are net-worked via LANs, which are linked together through a WAN. IT operations go 24 hours a day, seven days a week, because the Customer Service Department takes telephone orders around the clock.

1. The Customer Service, Business, and Inventory Departments currently use separate customer service, business, and inventory programs on two large minicomputers, one located in Winnipeg and one in St. Cloud. Their plan is to purchase a new client/server system that will integrate all three areas into one software system. The new client/server system requires that they purchase three new Windows 2000 servers for the Winnipeg site and two servers for the St. Cloud site:

   ❐ One server at each site will be used for application programs, customer service pro-grams, and utility software.

   ❐ One server at the Winnipeg site will house the main, large, integrated database requiring over 15 GB of disk space.

   ❐ One server at each site will be used for generating business and inventory reports and to provide customer service information. These servers will contain a copy of the main integrated database at the Winnipeg site, each updated from the Winnipeg main database server four times each day.

   The IT Department has asked you to provide specifications for the servers at both sites. What questions would you ask the company to help you create specifications?

2. The Customer Service Department currently has a problem with slow access to their information on the minicomputers. How might you generate your specifications to help ensure fast access for them?

3. Another problem faced by Customer Service is that the minicomputers are aging, and a disk drive seems to fail about once every month or two. Usually this means that a computer is down for two to three hours while a new drive is installed and the data is recovered through a tape backup. Also, sometimes information from recently placed orders is lost. What type of fault tolerance is available through Windows 2000 Server that can help in this area should you consider as you create the server specifications?

4. What tape back up specifications do you recommend, particularly since you already know that the LANs in both locations are busy around the clock?

5. A Web server, which is not part of the client/server system, but which will feed infor-mation to that new system, is maintained by the Customer Service Department. The Web server is used to advertise over the Internet and to take orders; it has been in place for almost three years, and is a Pentium 133 computer with two mirrored drives. Growth in the accessing of the Web server has nearly quadrupled over the three years of its existence, and the company views it as an important competitive strategy. What specifications would you create to help them in their planning to upgrade that server?

6. The Business Department has 18 employees, 14 full-time and 4 part-time, who want to set up a new server from which to install Microsoft Office software and to centrally store Excel spreadsheets and Word documents. That server will also provide network print services for their department. They estimate that they will need about 8 GB of disk space now and that this will grow about 2 GB per year. What type of processor and disk storage do you recommend for this server?

7. What tape backup do you recommend for the Business Department's new server?

OPTIONAL CASE ASSIGNMENTS FOR TEAMS

Team Case One

Mark Arnez wants to develop some in-house research about different manufacturers' options for hardware RAID that is compatible with Windows 2000 Server and the computers on which the operating system runs. Form a group to research as many hardware RAID options as you can find, for example through the Internet.

Team Case Two

Mark also wants some information about what computer is the fastest Web server available on the market right now. Form a team to research Web server test results from different publications and testing groups, and provide a report about the components used in the fastest Web server.

3

PLANNING NETWORK PROTOCOLS AND COMPATIBILITY

After reading this chapter and completing the exercises you will be able to:

♦ Explain basic network concepts, including network terms, types of networks, and network interface cards

♦ Explain the NDIS and ODI network driver specifications

♦ Explain the communications protocols used in Windows 2000 Server, including TCP/IP, NWLink, NetBEUI, DLC, and AppleTalk

♦ Plan network binding order, change the binding order, and bind and unbind protocols

♦ Plan how to implement protocols on different types of networks

Networking with Windows 2000 Server is about communication. Network communication takes place in many forms, including communicating with computers and printers, communicating with software applications, transporting e-mail, and providing Internet and intranet information exchange. The ability to communicate is made possible by using techniques that servers, workstations, and printers can agree upon. As you learned in the Chapter 1, Windows 2000 Server has a vast range of capabilities that enable networking on a small, medium, and large scale. Many of these capabilities are related to providing a common network language and enabling the translation of information between different kinds of networks and network operating systems.

When you set up a Windows 2000 Server, the first step is understanding the role of that server on the network and planning how to set up the server to meet that role. In this chapter, you will learn about the network communication services available through Windows 2000 Server and how to plan their optimal use in different situations. The chapter begins by providing you with networking basics that explain how communication occurs on a network. Next, you learn about network communications issues and about the communication languages, called protocols, that are used to address specific needs. You also learn how to plan network protocol implementations on different kinds of networks and how to improve network performance by setting the protocol binding order.

BASIC NETWORK CONCEPTS

A computer or networking device communicates through a set of communications guidelines, in a way that is similar to using a language, but the language used by computers is in a binary format of zeros and ones that is sent through network communications cable. The communication languages of computers are called **protocols**. A protocol consists of guidelines for the following:

- How data is formatted into discrete units called packets and frames
- How packets and frames are transmitted across one or more networks
- How packets and frames are interpreted at the receiving end

Packets and **frames** are units of data transmitted from a sending computer to a receiving computer. These units might be compared to words in a language. In a language, people communicate by using words to compose sentences and paragraphs in order to convey a thought. The words by themselves do not convey the full thought until they are placed in the context of a sentence or paragraph. Like words, packets and frames usually do not convey their full meaning until the complete stream of information is received; and just as words must be properly placed in sentences and paragraphs, packets and frames must be received in the proper order to be understood.

Sometimes the terms *packet* and *frame* are used as if they have the same meaning. However, there is a difference between these terms, which is that a packet operates at a higher level of communication than does a frame. The higher level of communication associated with a packet enables it to contain routing information so that it can be forwarded from one network to another.

Packets and frames are divided into three general sections: a header, data, and a trailer. The header contains information that controls how the packet is transmitted, the data section contains the actual data that is transported, such as part of a Word file, and the footer is used to detect transmission errors. One of the most important functions of the header section is to house the addresses of the sender and receiver, called the source and destination addresses. Packets and frames use addressing, which is similar to the concept of addressing an envelope in the U.S. mail. Everyone is familiar with completing a surface mail envelope by providing the unique home or business address of the recipient and a return address. Network communications work in the same way, because the sender and receiver each have unique addresses and both addresses are included in the packet or frame so that there is a known destination and a way to return the communication in case the destination cannot be found or there is a delivery error. Also, in some protocols, the header and footer are used to indicate the beginning and end of a packet or frame. Figure 3-1 illustrates the basic packet or frame format.

| Header with source, destination, and routing information | Variable-length data | Footer with error data |

Figure 3-1   Basic packet and frame format

Protocol, packet, and frame communication guidelines are established by standards organizations, such as the Institute of Electrical and Electronics Engineers (IEEE), which represents over 140 countries. Two other standards organizations are the International Organization for Standardization (ISO), which has over 100 member countries, and the American National Standards Institute (ANSI), a United States organization that influences over 11,000 product standards and is an ISO member.

Types of Networks

The design of a network is its **topology**, which represents the overall layout of the network communications cable and the way in which packets and frames travel along the network. One or more network topologies are configured to form small, medium, and large-sized networks. A network that covers a relatively small distance, such as one that joins computers in the same office area or that links computers on different floors in a building is called a **local area network** (**LAN**). A LAN joins computers, printers, and other computer equipment within a limited service area and generally employs only one topology (see Figure 3-2).

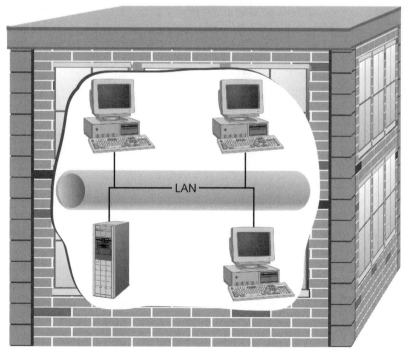

Figure 3-2   A LAN in a building

When multiple LANs are joined within a city or metropolitan region, the full network is called a **metropolitan area network** (**MAN**). A state university in one city is a MAN when it links several research centers and other facilities throughout the same city. In this example, there might be a veterinary lab on the edge of the city, an outreach branch in the center of the city, an observatory in another part of the city, a medical research facility in a hospital, and a main campus near the city center. A large business campus might have LANs used for administrative processing connected to LANs used for scientific research. Both of these also are examples of **enterprise networks** because they link a large array of resources for networked computers to use. The resources in an enterprise network may include mainframes, minicomputers, servers, printers, plotters, fax equipment, access to multiple networks, Internet access, intranets, and a vast range of software accessibility (see Figure 3-3).

Figure 3-3   Resources in an enterprise network

A network that extends across cities, states, or continents is called a **wide area network** (**WAN**). For example, a multinational corporation with branch sites in New York, Toronto, London, and Stockholm can join the LANs at each site into a WAN that connects them all together. Another example of WAN communications is using the Internet to download new software from a company in Vancouver to your workstation in Los Angeles.

Network Interface Cards

The device used to connect a workstation, file server, or other network equipment to the communications cable is called its network interface card (NIC). The NIC contains a transmitter/receiver, or transceiver, for sending and receiving data signals on the cable. Each NIC comes with a set of software drivers to encode and decode the data so that it can be formatted to send on the cable and received data can be read by a workstation or server. NICs also have built-in memory chips to provide temporary storage while the data is waiting to be transmitted or to be sent to the computer's CPU for processing.

NICs are designed for the four main types of network communication media: coaxial cable, twisted-pair cable, fiber-optic cable, and wireless communications (such as radio waves). Some NICs come with adapters for both coaxial and twisted-pair cable. Figure 3-4 shows a NIC with the capability to connect to twisted-pair or coax cable (although you should not connect both at the same time). Many vendors sell computers with the NIC already installed, for college and business customers. (Try Hands-on Project 3-1 to experiment with a NIC.)

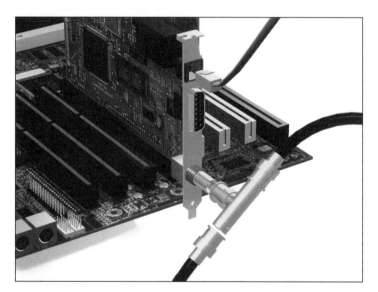

Figure 3-4   Connecting cable to a NIC

Each workstation and server has a unique address associated with its NIC, which is called the **physical address** or **device address** and is burned into a Programmable Read-only Memory chip (PROM) in the NIC. (Try Hands-on Projects 3-2 and 3-3 to view the physical address of a NIC.) To prevent confusion on the network, it is important that no two network cards have the same address. If this should happen and both NICs are active, network communications become unreliable, because it is difficult for the network to determine if packets are being sent or received by a single, distinguishable node.

Network administrators often refer to the physical address as the media access control (MAC) address, which is a more technical reference to the **media access control sublayer** of the data-link layer (Layer 2) in the Open Systems Interconnection (OSI) model. The OSI model was developed for network communications by the ISO and ANSI. The MAC sublayer examines physical address information in frames and controls the way devices share communication on a network.

NETWORK DRIVER SPECIFICATIONS

Windows 2000 network communication is accomplished through three elements:

- A network driver specification built into Windows 2000
- The NIC
- A NIC software driver that interfaces the NIC with Windows 2000

The network driver specification might be thought of as a door into a portion of the operating system, providing a means to link the computer to the network. In a sense, the network driver specification is a set of rules that represents a lock, and the NIC driver provides a key to open the lock so that the operating system can communicate on the network through the NIC. The network driver specification includes guidelines for **Ethernet** or **token ring** communications, and guidelines for specific communication protocols used within Ethernet and token ring. It also provides a way to encapsulate and transport multiple protocols on the same network. Each NIC manufacturer provides a driver for their NIC that conforms to the network driver specification used by an operating system, such as Windows 2000 Server. Microsoft also provides NIC drivers on the Windows 2000 Server CD-ROM.

Windows 2000 Server uses the Network Driver Interface Specification (NDIS). Another specification, which is used on Novell NetWare networks, is the Open DataLink Interface (ODI).

NDIS

Created by Microsoft and 3COM, the **Network Driver Interface Specification** (**NDIS**) is a network software driver specification that enables Microsoft network protocols to communicate with a NIC. When you bind a protocol to a NIC, this is accomplished through the NDIS driver. **Network binding** is a process that identifies a computer's NIC with one or more network protocols to achieve optimum communications with network services. For Microsoft operating systems, each protocol that is installed is bound to the NIC during the installation process (Figure 3-5).

NDIS can bind one or more protocols to a single NIC, allowing each protocol to send information on the same network. For example, you may have one process sending information using the TCP/IP protocol while another process is sending information using the NWLink (IPX/SPX) protocol to communicate with a Novell NetWare server (you learn about these protocols later in this chapter).

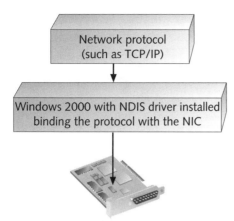

Network interface card

Figure 3-5   Binding a protocol to a NIC

ODI

Another driver that is used to transport multiple protocols is the **Open Datalink Interface (ODI)** driver. This driver is used on Novell NetWare networks to support communications with NetWare file servers, mainframes and minicomputers, and the Internet, similarly to NDIS.

 ODI communications can be used on older Microsoft networks, such as networks that use Windows NT 3.5x and 4.0 Server, but this is not advised. The best preparation for upgrading to Windows 2000 Server is to convert Windows NT 3.5x and 4.0 Server versions to use the 32-bit NDIS driver for network communications, if they are not already using NDIS.

COMMUNICATIONS PROTOCOLS

Windows 2000 Server supports several communications protocols to provide network services over LANs and WANs: TCP/IP, NWLink (IPX/SPX), NetBIOS/NetBEUI, DLC, and AppleTalk. Any or all of these protocols can be bound to a Windows 2000 server's NIC via NDIS. The communications protocols are summarized in Table 3-1 and described in detail in the following sections.

Table 3-1   Microsoft-supported Communications Protocols

Protocol	Function
TCP/IP (Transmission Control Protocol/Internet Protocol)	Software drivers for TCP/IP communications with servers, workstations, mainframes, UNIX computers, and Internet and intranet servers
NWLink (NetWare Link)	Microsoft developed drivers for communications with Novell NetWare networks
NetBIOS (Network Basic Input/Output System)	A link to programs that use the NetBIOS interface
NetBEUI (NetBIOS Extended User Interface)	Software drivers for a data transport protocol used on small Microsoft-based networks
DLC (Data Link Control protocol)	Software drivers for communication with IBM mainframe and minicomputers and with specific peripherals such as some types of printers
AppleTalk	Software drivers for communication with Apple Macintosh computers

TCP/IP

One important difference between Windows 2000 Server and earlier versions of Windows NT Server is that TCP/IP takes center stage in Windows 2000 as the protocol of choice. Small and large networks increasingly need TCP/IP for Internet, World Wide Web (Web), and intranet connectivity. Also, as more LANs grow into enterprise networks and connect to WANs, TCP/IP is needed because it is ideal for communications that go over dissimilar networks. Further, many networks require connectivity to a host computer, such as a mainframe running IBM's Multiple Virtual Storage (MVS) operating system or a minicomputer with UNIX. The protocol for all of these jobs is **Transmission Control Protocol/Internet Protocol (TCP/IP)**. TCP/IP is used around the globe for reliable network communications. TCP/IP is many protocols wrapped into one, all working together to establish the most error-free communications possible. The TCP portion was originally developed to ensure reliable connections on government, military, and educational networks. TCP provides for reliable end-to-end delivery of data by controlling data flow. Nodes agree upon a "window" for data transmission that includes the number of bytes that will be sent. The transmission window is constantly adjusted to account for existing network traffic. TCP/IP monitors for requests to start a communications session, establishes sessions with other TCP nodes, handles transmitting and receiving data, and closes transmission sessions when they are finished. TCP is also considered a **connection-oriented communication** because it ensures that packets are delivered, that they are delivered in the right sequence, and that their contents are accurate.

Some applications use the **User Datagram Protocol (UDP)** with IP instead of using TCP. These are typically applications in which the reliability of the communication is not a major concern, such as for information used to boot diskless workstations over a network. UDP is a **connectionless communication** because it does not provide checking to make sure that a connection is reliable and that data is sent accurately. The advantage of UDP is that it has less overhead than TCP.

The IP portion of the TCP/IP protocol provides network addressing to ensure that data packets and frames quickly reach the correct destination. It uses a system of addressing that consists of four numbers separated by periods, such as 129.77.15.182. IP provides for routing data over different networks, so that data sent from one network only goes to the appropriate destination network instead of to all networks that are linked together. IP also handles fragmenting packets, because the packet sizes may vary from one network to another. IP is connectionless communication because it relies on TCP to provide connection-oriented communications.

The combination TCP/IP protocol is particularly well suited for medium and large networks, but it is important on any enterprise network or on a LAN that connects to a WAN.

 Before upgrading Windows NT 3.5x and 4.0 servers to Windows 2000, Microsoft recommends that you convert them and their client workstations to TCP/IP, if it is not already implemented (you can practice converting Windows NT Server 4.0 to TCP/IP in Hands-on Project 3-4). Also, work to eliminate the use of any other protocols, such as NetBEUI or NWLink, unless these are required to support connectivity to older servers and printers, such as to NetWare version 4 or earlier servers.

IP Addressing

The IP address format is called the **dotted decimal notation** address. It is 32 bits long and contains four fields, consisting of decimal values representing 8-bit binary octets. An IP address in binary octet format looks like this: 10000001.00000101.00001010.1100100, which converts to 129.5.10.100 in decimal format. Part of the address is the network identifier (NET_ID), and another part is the host identifier (HOST_ID), the way the parts are designated depends on the size of the LAN, how the LAN is divided into smaller networks, and if the packet or frame is unicast or multicast. A unicast is a transmission in which one packet is sent from a server to each client that requests a file or application, a video presentation for example. Thus, if five clients request the video presentation, the server sends five packets per each transmission to the five clients. In the same example, a multicast means that the server is able to treat all five clients as a group and send one packet per transmission that reaches all five clients (see Figure 3-6). Multicasts can be used to significantly reduce network traffic when transmitting multimedia applications.

In a unicast on a typical medium-sized LAN of up to 65,536 connections, the first two octets are normally the network ID, and the last two are the host ID. In a multicast transmission on the same network the four octets are used to specify a group of nodes to receive the multicast, which consists of those nodes that are multicast subscription members.

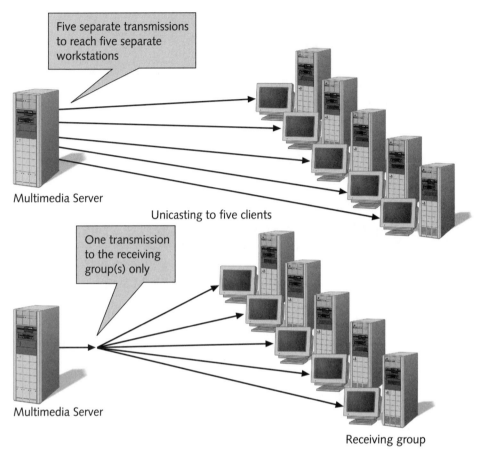

Figure 3-6   Unicasting compared to multicasting

Another special-purpose form of addressing is the **subnet mask**. A subnet mask is used for two purposes: to show the class of addressing used, and to divide a network into subnetworks to control network traffic. In the first instance, the subnet mask enables an application to determine which part of the address is for the network ID and which is for the host ID. For example, a subnet mask for a Class A network is all binary 1s in the first octet and all binary 0s in remaining octets: 11111111.00000000.00000000.00000000 (255.0.0.0 in decimal). Figure 3-7 shows the IP address and subnet mask setup dialog box in Windows 2000.

To divide the network into subnetworks, the subnet mask consists of a subnet ID within the network and host IDs, which are determined by the network administrator. For example, the entire third octet in a Class B address could be designated to indicate the subnet ID, which would be an octet of 11111111.11111111.11111111.00000000 (255.255.255.0). Another option would be to designate only the first 5 bits in the third octet as the subnet ID and the last 3 bits (and last octet as well) for the host ID, which would be 11111111.11111111.11111000.00000000 (255.255.248.0).

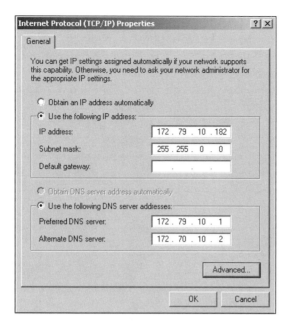

Figure 3-7   IP address and subnet mask setup

 TIP   Many server administrators use TCP/IP because the ability to create subnets provides important versatility in controlling network congestion and in setting up security so that only authorized users can reach specific parts of a network or specific intranets.

Static and Dynamic Addressing

Each server and workstation needs a unique IP address, either specified at the computer or obtained from a server that assigns temporary IP addresses. Before setting up TCP/IP, you need to make some decisions about how to set up IP addressing on the network. The options are to use what Microsoft calls static addressing or dynamic addressing. **Static addressing** involves assigning a dotted decimal address that is each workstation's permanent, unique IP address. This method is used on many networks, large and small, when the network administrator wants direct control over the assigned addresses. Direct control may be necessary when network management software is used to track all network nodes and the software depends on each node having a permanent, known IP address. Permanent addresses give consistency to monitoring network statistics and to keeping historical network performance information. The disadvantage is that IP address administration can be a laborious task on a large network. Most network administrators have an IP database to keep track of currently assigned addresses and unused addresses to assign, as new people are connected to the network.

Dynamic addressing automatically assigns an IP address to a computer each time it is logged on. An IP address is leased to a particular computer for a defined period of time. This addressing method uses the **Dynamic Host Configuration Protocol** (**DHCP**), which is supported by Windows 2000 Server for dynamic addressing. The protocol is used to enable a Windows 2000 server with DHCP services set up to detect the presence of a new workstation and assign an IP address to that workstation. On your network, this would require you to load DHCP services onto a Microsoft 2000 server and configure it to be a DHCP server. It would still act as a regular server for other activities, but with the added ability to automatically assign IP addresses to workstations. A Windows 2000 DHCP server leases IP addresses for a specified period of time, which might be one week, one month, one year, or a permanent lease. When the lease is up, the IP address is returned to a pool of available IP addresses maintained by the server. On Windows 2000 servers that provide Internet communication, when one is configured as a DHCP server, **Windows Internet Naming Service** (**WINS**) is also installed so that the Windows 2000 Server is both a DHCP and a WINS server. A WINS server is able to translate a workstation name to an IP address for Internet communication, for example translating the workstation name, Palmer, to its IP address, such as 129.77.15.182.

CAUTION
When you use DHCP, plan to apply it to client workstations and not to servers, or to make each server's IP address permanent. It is important for server IP addresses to always remain the same so there is no doubt about how to access a server. For example, consider how hard a Web server would be to find on the Internet if its IP address changed periodically.

TCP/IP Advantages and Disadvantages

There are several advantages that TCP/IP offers:

- It is very well suited for medium to large networks, for enterprise networks, and for any network that has Internet connectivity or uses intranets.

- It is designed for routing and has a high degree of reliability.

- It is used worldwide for connecting to the Internet and for using intranets.

- It is key to Microsoft's strategy to accomplish a lower Total Cost of Ownership (TCO), and to many of the new features of Windows 2000 Server such as application services management, Zero Administration for Windows (ZAW), and Distributed Network Architecture (DNA; see Chapter 1).

- It is compatible with standard tools for analyzing network performance.

- It enables the use of DHCP and WINS through a Microsoft 2000 Server.

- It provides the ability for diverse networks and network operating systems to communicate via LANs and WANs, and scales easily from small to large networks.

- It is compatible with Microsoft Windows Sockets, which is used by software applications, for example for client/server and telecommunications connectivity.

Windows Sockets (WinSock) interfaces software applications that use "sockets" with network protocols such as TCP/IP and IPX. Created by the University of California at Berkeley, WinSock is an open specification in Windows operating systems for different network protocol functions that use different addressing methods (sockets). Windows 2000 DHCP Server is one example of an application that uses WinSock.

3

TCP/IP does have some disadvantages as well:

- It is more difficult to set up and maintain than other protocols.

- It is somewhat slower than IPX/SPX and NetBEUI on networks with light to medium traffic. (However, it may be faster on heavy volume networks, where there is a high frequency of routing frames.)

One situation in which you would use TCP/IP would be on a large enterprise network, such as on a college or business campus, where there is extensive use of routers and connectivity to mainframe or UNIX computers. A **router** is a device that connects networks, is able to read IP addresses, and can route packets to designated networks, because it reads routing information in packets (OSI Layer 3) and keeps tables of information about the fastest route from one network to another (see Figure 3-8). You also would use it in a smaller network situation, in which 100–200 Windows-based workstations access intranet or Internet services through a Windows 2000 server offering Web services, using Microsoft's Internet Information Server.

Protocols in the TCP/IP Suite

Complementing the main TCP/IP protocols are several application protocols and services that help make up the TCP/IP "protocol suite":

- **Telnet:** This is an application protocol within TCP/IP that provides support for terminal emulation, for example for an IBM 3270 terminal or a DEC VT220 terminal. Telnet enables a user to connect to a host computer so that the host responds as though it were connected to a terminal.

- **File Transfer Protocol (FTP):** This is a protocol that enables the transfer of data from one remote device to another, using the TCP and Telnet protocols. Through FTP, a user in England can use the Internet to log on to a host computer in California and download one or more data files from the host.

- **Simple Mail Transfer Protocol (SMTP):** This protocol is designed for the exchange of electronic mail between networked systems. Windows 2000, UNIX, NetWare and other computer operating systems can exchange messages if they have TCP/IP accompanied by SMTP. SMTP is particularly useful for electronic mail that goes over the Internet.

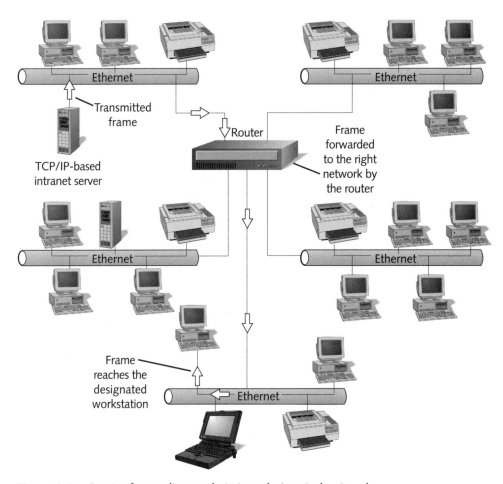

Figure 3-8   Router forwarding packets to a designated network

- **Domain Name Service (DNS):** This service is particularly important to Windows 2000 Server when the Active Directory is installed. DNS is used to translate domain and computer names, such as *microsoft.com*, to an IP address (and vice versa). The DNS software runs on one computer that acts as a network zserver for the address translations. The process of translating names to addresses is called resolution, a process you have already used if you access the Internet. Windows 2000 Server can be set up to act as a DNS server on a network. Often there are at least two DNS servers set up on a network, one to act as the primary server and one to act as a secondary, or backup, server in case the primary DNS server cannot be reached. Windows 2000 Server offers dynamic DNS services, which means that a new network client can discover the DNS server and add its own DNS entry without you manually entering it. Plan to implement dynamic DNS services to reduce your administrative tasks.

- **Address Resolution Protocol (ARP):** This protocol enables a sending node to obtain the IP and MAC addresses of the intended recipient before packets are sent. ARP is used by network management software and by DHCP servers to help determine the actual location of a client workstation.

- **Simple Network Management Protocol (SNMP)**: This protocol is used by network managers and network management software to gather statistics on network performance and to locate network problems. SNMP's ability to quickly help identify server and network problems is one important reason why TCP/IP is popularly used on networks. It is also critical to Windows 2000 servers that use network monitoring software, such as Microsoft's Network Monitor.

- **Internet Group Management Protocol (IGMP)**: This protocol is used when an application employs multicasting. Both the server and client workstations must be configured for multicast operations, and so are configured to use IGMP. The routers in between the server and workstations also are configured for multicasts. One important function of IGMP is to keep routers informed of which workstations belong to which multicast groups to make sure that multicast packets reach the right workstations.

- **Internet Control Message Protocol (ICMP)**: This protocol is used for network error reporting, particularly through routing devices. ICMP enables network administrators to locate and determine network problems. For example, ICMP enables a network administrator to poll a device to determine if it is connected to the network (try Hands-on Project 3-5).

- **Routing Information Protocol (RIP)**: This protocol is used by routing devices to share network information with one another. For example, it is used by routers to share tables in which they keep information about the location of specific computers on the network (stored in a routing table). RIP also enables routing devices to determine the shortest path from one network location to another, and share that information with other routing devices.

- **Open Shortest Path First (OSPF) protocol**: Designed to be more efficient than RIP, OSPF is a routing protocol that shares routing table information and that can set up routes to match the type of transmission, such as data or video.

- **Hypertext Transfer Protocol (HTTP)**: This protocol enables the transport of Hypertext Markup Language (HTML) documents over the Internet. These are the documents that you read through an HTTP-compliant browser, such as Microsoft Internet Explorer and Netscape Communicator, providing access to text and embedded audio, video, and graphics files.

- **Resource Reservation Protocol (RSVP)**: This protocol enables network resources to be reserved for specific kinds of high-demand uses, such as for multimedia applications that combine audio and video in a news clip, movie, or instructional application. RSVP enables an application to reserve the resources it needs, such as network paths with higher speeds. By implementing RSVP, network-hungry multimedia applications can coexist with less demanding simple data applications, but they can be given a higher delivery priority because they are more time-sensitive.

- **Quality of Service** (**QoS**): Often used with RSVP, this service consists of network transmission techniques that are used to help guarantee the transmission quality, throughput, and reliability of a network system. The overall goals of QoS are to ensure that the proper network resources are assigned to specific applications and to reduce the likelihood that valuable network resources are underutilized. QoS is used for multimedia, telephony, and mission-critical applications to help guarantee they have appropriate resources, such as time-sensitive communications. In Windows 2000 Server, the Active Directory verifies that an application or user has authority to use QoS and to assign a high priority for a transmission. The QoS capabilities that can be accessed in Windows 2000 Server via TCP/IP with RSVP are:

    - Admission Control Service (ACS), which enables you to reserve network resources through policies that you establish in the Windows 2000 Active Directory

    - Differentiated Quality of Service, which provides utilities to allocate resources to applications, such as allocating high-speed network routes to multimedia or client/server applications

    - Prioritized LANs (based on the IEEE 802.1p standard) to give specific applications, such as audio e-mail high priority, and other applications, games for example, lower priority

Table 3-2 provides a summary of the applications and protocols in the TCP/IP suite that are discussed in this chapter and supported by Windows 2000 Server.

Table 3-2   Protocols and Applications in the TCP/IP Suite

Protocol or Application	Function
TCP	A connection-oriented protocol that is used with IP for reliable end-to-end communications
UDP	Used with IP as an alternative to TCP in situations requiring low overhead and in which connectionless communications are appropriate
IP	Used with TCP or UDP, a connectionless protocol that handles addressing and routing
Telnet	Provides terminal emulation
File Transfer Protocol (FTP)	Used to transfer files
Simple Mail Transfer Protocol (SMTP)	Provides electronic mail services
Domain Name Service (DNS)	Resolves computer names to IP addresses, and IP addresses to computer names
Address Resolution Protocol (ARP)	Enables the sending node to determine the MAC or physical address of another node
Simple Network Management Protocol (SNMP)	Enables computers and network devices to gather network performance information so that a network administrator can analyze performance and locate problem areas

Table 3-2   Protocols and Applications in the TCP/IP Suite (continued)

Protocol or Application	Function
Internet Group Management Protocol (IGMP)	Enables multicast packets to reach their recipients, and routers to determine which workstations belong to a multicast group
Internet Control Message Protocol (ICMP)	Used for network error reporting, particularly via routing devices
Routing Information Protocol (RIP)	Used by routing devices to communicate the contents of routing tables with one another
Open Shortest Path First (OSPF)	Used by routing devices to share routing table information and to evaluate network paths to match a type of transmission to the appropriate path
Hypertext Transfer Protocol (HTTP)	Used to transport HTML documents over the Internet or via an intranet
Resource Reservation Protocol (RSVP)	Used to enable a network application to reserve the resources it needs, such as bandwidth, service class, and priority
Quality of Service (QoS)	Provides mechanisms to measure and allocate network resources on the basis of transmission speed, quality, priority, and reliability.

NWLink and IPX/SPX

Some Novell NetWare servers use a connectionless protocol called the **Internet Packet Exchange** (**IPX**) protocol. IPX is used mainly on NetWare version 4.x and earlier servers. NetWare version 5.x servers typically use TCP/IP instead of IPX.

IPX, like TCP/IP, has routing capabilities, so data is transported over multiple networks in an enterprise. Along with IPX, Novell implements a companion protocol called **Sequence Packet Exchange** (**SPX**). SPX enables the exchange of application-specific data with greater reliability than IPX because it is a connection-oriented communication, whereas IPX is connectionless. One use of SPX is for the exchange of database data on the network. Novell's remote console utility and print services also take advantage of SPX. This utility enables a workstation to display the same information that appears on a NetWare server monitor. With the remote console software, the workstation user can execute server console commands without having to be at the server keyboard.

IPX/SPX can be deployed on a Microsoft network in one of two ways. One way is to install the ODI driver instead of NDIS at workstations and on pre-Windows 2000 servers. Because this offers limited 16-bit support, the better way is to use NetWare Link (NWLink). **NWLink** is a network protocol used on Microsoft networks via NDIS to emulate IPX/SPX.

The best way to install NWLink is to install it as part of Client Service for NetWare (CSNW), which installs three elements as follows (Figure 3-9 shows two of the three elements installed):

- Client Service for NetWare
- NWLink IPX/SPX/NetBIOS Compatible Transport
- NWLink NetBIOS

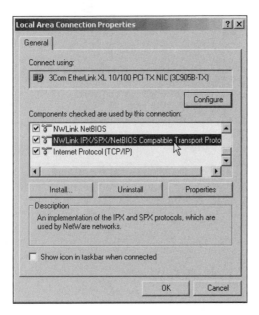

Figure 3-9   Windows 2000 with CSNW components installed

 When you set up NWLink, you need to configure three elements in the process: the frame type, network number, and internal network number. In many situations, Windows 2000 automatically configures the frame type to match what is already in use by NetWare servers. The frame type determines how frames are formatted for NetWare communications. Windows 2000 also automatically configures the network number, or you can configure it by checking with the NetWare administrator. NetWare uses the network number, such as 1, to identify the network to which it is connected.

The internal network number is used to create a direct network route between a Windows 2000 server and a NetWare server in the following situations:

- When there are two or more frame types associated with the NetWare server you are accessing
- When your computer running Windows 2000 has two or more NICs, and NWLink is bound to more than one of these NICs
- When an application, such as a database, implements NetWare's Service Advertising Protocol (SAP) to identify a specific server

NWLink offers several advantages, such as routing over enterprise networks and the ability for Microsoft Windows-based operating systems to access NetWare servers as clients. NetWare clients, such as those that use NetWare Client32, can also access Windows 2000 servers. It is easy to install and provides more effective communication with NetWare file servers than does the ODI driver. NWLink supports WinSock and NetBIOS over IPX. NWLink also supports Microsoft's File and Print Services for NetWare (FPNW). When FPNW is installed in Windows 2000 Server, NetWare clients can access files, printers, and applications via the Windows 2000 Server. NWLink's disadvantages are that it is not as universal as TCP/IP and it is not transported as fast as NetBEUI. Also, IPX/SPX and the NWLink emulation are really designed as proprietary protocols used mainly on NetWare networks. Another disadvantage is that IPX/SPX is a "chatty" protocol in that each packet transmitted must be acknowledged by the receiving node.

The most common situations for using Microsoft's NWLink to emulate IPX/SPX are as follows:

- To enable a workstation running Microsoft Windows 95, Windows 98, Windows NT, or Windows 2000 to communicate with one or more NetWare servers (pre-version 5)

- To set up a Microsoft Windows NT or a Windows 2000 server as a gateway to one or more NetWare servers

- To enable NetWare clients to access a Windows 2000 server.

For example, assume that you are configuring workstations running Windows 98 for a network with five Novell NetWare servers and no other host computers. In this situation, you would configure all workstations to use NWLink. However, consider another situation where there is one NetWare 5.0 server and four Windows 2000 servers on a network, and some print services are to be handled through the Windows 2000 servers. One solution would be to configure all Windows-based workstations for NWLink and TCP/IP. Depending on the need for access to the NetWare server, a better solution would be to configure one of the Windows 2000 servers for NWLink and set it up to act as a gateway to NetWare by installing Microsoft's Gateway Service for NetWare. Now the workstations would only need to use TCP/IP, because they would access the NetWare server through the Windows 2000 Server gateway. In this instance, the gateway functions to make the NetWare directories appear as a shared folder on the Windows 2000 Server.

NetBIOS and NetBEUI

NetBIOS Extended User Interface (**NetBEUI**) is a communications protocol that is native to Microsoft network communication; however, with the release of Windows 2000, NetBEUI is not recommended over TCP/IP in most situations. First developed by IBM in 1985, it is an enhancement of **Network Basic Input/Output System** (**NetBIOS**). NetBIOS, which is not a protocol, is a method for interfacing software with network services. It also provides a naming convention.

NetBIOS

When a software application is written for compatibility with the NetBIOS interface, it calls the NetBIOS.dll file, which links the software to the transport driver. The transport driver communicates with NetBEUI for network transmissions. The transport driver used to interface with TCP/IP is called NetBIOS for TCP/IP (NetBT) and is contained in the file Netbt.sys. The driver that interfaces with NetBEUI and NetBIOS over IPX is NetBIOS.sys. Microsoft Windows 3.1; 3.11, 95, and 98 are most compatible with older programs requiring the NetBIOS interface. Windows NT and Windows 2000 use a NetBIOS emulator (a program that simulates NetBIOS) for communication between NetBIOS and NetBEUI. Figure 3-10 illustrates the communication flow from NetBIOS applications to NetBEUI, in order to transport data over a network.

 You can find the Netbt.sys and NetBIOS.sys files in *Winnt**System32**Drivers*. Also, depending on which services are installed that use NetBIOS, you can find NetBIOS.dll in other system folders, such as \\Winnt\\System32\\dllcache and \\Winnt\\System32\\Netmon\\Parsers.

NetBIOS names are used to name objects on a network, such as a workstation, server, or printer. For example, your workstation might use your favorite nickname for identification to other network users, the network printer you access might be named HPLaser, and the server you access might be named Netserver. These names make it easy for human beings to identify a particular network resource. They are translated into an address for network communications by the NetBIOS Name Query services.

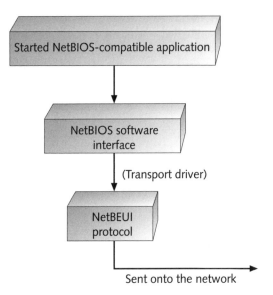

Figure 3-10 NetBIOS/NetBEUI communication

There are two important elements to remember about NetBIOS names. First, each name must be unique. No network object can have the same name as another object. If it could, there would be great confusion about how to communicate with objects having the same name. Second, names are no more than 16 characters. The first 15 characters are used by a user to assign a name, and the last character is used to identify the type of network resource, such as a server or printer, which the operating system handles using a hexadecimal number.

NetBEUI

NetBEUI was developed when computer networking primarily meant local area networking for a relatively small number of computers (generally, from a couple of computers to about 200). It was not developed to take into account enterprise networks, in which packets are directed from one network to another through routing and routers. For this reason, NetBEUI is suited for small LANs using older Microsoft or IBM server operating systems such as Microsoft LAN Manager and IBM LAN Server.

Advantages and Disadvantages of NetBEUI

NetBEUI is a good choice on small Microsoft networks running only Windows-based clients and a combination of Windows 2000 and Windows NT servers, for several reasons. First, it is simple to install, and it is very compatible with Microsoft workstation and server operating systems. Second, it can handle nearly limitless communication sessions on one network, because the 254-session limitation of earlier versions is removed. Microsoft specifications, for example, show that a Windows server can support 1000 sessions on one NIC. Third, NetBEUI has low memory requirements and can be quickly transported over small networks. Fourth, it has solid error detection and recovery. Fifth, it is self-configuring and self-tuning. Last, it can provide both connection-oriented and connectionless communications.

The inability to route NetBEUI is a major disadvantage for medium and large networks, including enterprise networks. This means a NetBEUI frame cannot be forwarded by a router from one network to another, because there is not enough information in the NetBEUI frame to identify specific networks. When NetBEUI is used over two or more LANs that are connected together, the LANs must be connected by **bridge** devices, which operate at a lower communication level (OSI Layer 2) than routers (OSI Layer 3) and do not look for routing information. Or, routers that can be set to route or bridge (called brouters) must be set in bridge mode to forward NetBEUI frames from one network to another, resulting in extra total network traffic. Another disadvantage is that there are fewer network analysis tools for it than for other protocols. NetBEUI also is not widely supported by computers running non-Microsoft operating systems and it is limited to small LANs. Last, NetBEUI is chatty, because it sends out more broadcast traffic than TCP/IP (but not more than IPX/SPX).

Consider two different networking situations. In the first situation, you are responsible for setting a up network for a credit union that has 52 workstations, four network printers, no routers, no outside connections to other networks, and one Microsoft NT server. This is a good context for using NetBEUI as the sole protocol. In a second situation, you are setting up communication on a busy college network with 520 nodes, including an IBM mainframe, 10 Windows 2000 servers, and Internet access. That network has four routers linking different LANs across campus. NetBEUI is not a good choice in this situation because it cannot route. TCP/IP is the best alternative because it has routing capabilities and IP addressing for Internet access.

DLC

When it is not possible to connect to an IBM mainframe using TCP/IP, another way to connect is to use the **Data Link Control (DLC) protocol**. Microsoft Windows NT, Windows 2000, Windows 95, and Windows 98 offer a DLC driver that can be installed. DLC provides the ability to connect to IBM's older network communications system, called Systems Network Architecture (SNA). Another use for DLC is to communicate with printers directly connected to the network, such as a Hewlett Packard 4Si laser printer equipped with print services and network connectivity.

The main advantage to using DLC is that it is an alternative to TCP/IP when TCP/IP is not available. The disadvantages are that the protocol is not routable. Also, DLC is not truly designed for peer-to-peer communication between workstations, but only for connectivity to a computer such as an older IBM ES9000 mainframe or AS/400 minicomputer, or connectivity to a peripheral device that uses DLC.

AppleTalk

Macintosh computer networks use a peer-to-peer network protocol called **AppleTalk**. AppleTalk is only supported in very limited ways on non-Macintosh networks. On a Microsoft network, Macintosh computers are linked in by setting up the Windows 2000 Server Services for Macintosh, which include the following components:

- File Server for Macintosh (MacFile)
- Print Server for Macintosh (MacPrint)
- AppleTalk protocol

Using MacFile, the Windows 2000 Server becomes a file server for Macintosh computers as well as for computers running Microsoft operating systems. Through MacPrint and AppleTalk, Macintosh clients can print documents on network printers that are managed by a Windows 2000 server, and non-Macintosh clients can print files on printers shared by Macintosh computers. The Services for Macintosh also include the ability to route AppleTalk and to set up remote access for Macintosh computers via modem and telephone lines.

PROTOCOL BINDING ORDER

When a network uses multiple protocols for communication among servers, workstations, and printers, some network operating systems, Windows NT and Windows 2000 for example, have the ability to establish an order in which protocols are bound to a NIC. Setting the binding order for file and print services is one way to inexpensively improve network performance. The binding order is most important on workstations when they attempt to connect to a server. For example, your network might contain 20 Windows 2000 servers configured for TCP/IP and two NetWare 4.0 servers configured for IPX/SPX. On this network there are over 1000 Windows NT and Windows 2000 workstations that access the servers and are configured to use both TCP/IP and NWLink. The workstations primarily access the Windows 2000 servers and network printers using TCP/IP. In this situation you can dramatically improve network performance by setting up each workstation so that TCP/IP is first in the binding order, and NWLink is second. This means that each workstation will first use TCP/IP when it attempts to connect to a server, instead of first attempting to connect through NWLink and then sending another connection attempt using TCP/IP. On a busy network with over 1000 workstations and on which all of the users start to log on to servers at 8 a.m. when they come to work, this simple adjustment can reduce the morning network traffic by half. (You can practice setting the binding order in Hands-on Projects 3-6 and 3-7. Also, try Hands-on Project 3-8 to unbind a protocol.)

It is helpful to set the binding order on Windows NT and Windows 2000 servers, but the gain is not as dramatic in terms of network performance as it is for workstations. This is because there are fewer servers than workstations, and generally the servers remain logged on to the network.

In Windows NT and Windows 2000, the binding order can be set for both file services and print services; in some cases, the binding order will not be the same for both. For example, TCP/IP may be used for file services on Windows 2000 servers, and IPX/SPX may be used for print services managed through a NetWare server. In this case, you would set TCP/IP to have the first binding order for file services, and NWLink to be first for print services.

PLANNING A NETWORK

Before you begin implementing Windows 2000 Server and deciding upon which protocols are needed, analyze your network requirements and develop a network plan. The first step in network planning is to assess the business or organizational needs for which the network is to be used. These include the following:

- Size and purpose of the organization
- Potential growth of the organization in terms of people and services
- Number of mission-critical applications on the network
- Important cycles for the business or organization
- Relationship of the network resources to the mission of the business or organization
- Security needs
- Amount budgeted for network and computer resources

- Internet and intranet requirements

- Interconnectivity needed to other computers, such as IBM mainframes, Macintosh computers, and NetWare servers

There are many other considerations, but these provide a good start. For example, if you are working with a large organization that is likely to grow, there will be a particular emphasis on planning how to implement TCP/IP and its associated protocols. For a small network, such as a 15-person dental office, the network design needs to be reliable, and easy to manage on a small budget. NetBEUI may be a good choice for this network, if there are no routers and no plans for Internet connectivity.

Some organizations, such as accounting and payroll departments or banks, work with very sensitive financial information, requiring a high degree of reliability, security, and fault tolerance. Also, those organizations have especially urgent cycles of business activity, including daily electronic transmissions of money, daily account balancing, month-end and year-end accounting cycles, income tax reporting, and regular audits from independent financial auditors. Your network planning and management must always take into account those important business cycles. For example, you do not want to convert from NetBEUI to TCP/IP in the middle of year-end processing or just before an electronic transmission to the Federal Reserve.

In many cases, the network and computing resources are a cornerstone in the business strategy of an organization. A president of a subscription company that markets collectible items regards the computer capabilities of his company as the key reason the company stays ahead of the competition. Computing resources enable that company to provide the fastest customer service and delivery of products. When a customer places an order, a series of inventory, billing, customer profiling, promotional, manufacturing, and product-shipping events occurs automatically through the computer systems. For colleges, computer systems play an important role in attracting and retaining students, for example recruiting, admitting, and registering students, and providing grade and degree progress information. In these situations the versatility of TCP/IP and QoS may be important. Also, on a college campus that has Macintosh labs, the ability to configure AppleTalk is vital.

At one time, security was not a priority on many computers and networks, because few people knew how to intrude into systems. Times have changed, and responsible network planning always includes a blueprint for security. Besides guarding against intrusions, security also includes backing up data, planning for computer failures, and having a plan for disaster recovery. If security is important in your implementation, consider the ability to set up subnets and routers.

 From the start, learn how the network is related to the needs of its users, determine what resources already exist, and plan a secure network positioned for growth. A given in networking is that once a network is successfully implemented and managed, the requests to expand its capabilities start immediately.

Selecting the Right Protocol

The protocols you employ on a network depend on several factors:

- Do packets need to be routed?

- Is the network small (20 or so connections), medium (100 to 500 connections), or large (over 500 connections)?

- Are there Microsoft 2000 servers?

- Are there mainframe host computers, and do they use SNA?

- Are there NetWare servers?

- Is there direct access to the Internet or to Web-based intranet applications?

- Are there mission-critical or multimedia applications?

If there is a need to route packets, such as on an enterprise network, your best choice is likely to be TCP/IP because it is designed for routing and it is used on many types of networks. For a small nonrouted network with only Microsoft servers and workstations, NetBEUI can be a good choice as long as there is no Internet or intranet activity. A network with a combination of NetWare (pre-version 5) and Windows 2000 servers will need to employ TCP/IP and NWLink, whereas a network with only NetWare 5.x servers and Windows 2000 servers can use TCP/IP as the sole protocol.

Connectivity to Internet or Web-based services requires that TCP/IP be implemented and that FTP services be used to transfer files. TCP/IP also is the first choice for connectivity to mainframe and UNIX computers. The Telnet terminal emulation available through TCP/IP may be needed to connect to the mainframe. DLC is another option for IBM mainframe and minicomputer communications, if TCP/IP cannot be used.

TCP/IP is the protocol of preference for medium to large-sized networks. It can be routed, is reliable for mission-critical applications, and has solid error checking. Network monitoring and analysis becomes very important on these networks, and TCP/IP has associated protocols to accomplish these activities, too. Also, any network that uses multimedia applications and multicasting should employ TCP/IP.

 In many cases it is necessary to use a combination of protocols to accommodate different types of network applications. Modern networks often use combinations of the major protocols, TCP/IP, NetBEUI, and IPX/SPX. However, remember that it is best to use only those protocols that are required, because the more protocols that are transported, the more drain there is on network performance.

Sample Planning Scenarios

Consider that you are selecting a protocol for a college network that uses Windows 2000 Server, uses routing to several buildings, employs multimedia applications, has Internet connectivity, and uses Windows 98 for 700 clients. In this situation, TCP/IP can be used alone. TCP/IP offers several advantages, including the ability to route packets and use of RSVP and QoS to allocate resources for multimedia. In this situation, TCP/IP also provides Internet accessibility for research and e-mail, and supports HTTP for Web browser use.

In another scenario, you are planning a network for a company that has five NetWare 3.0 and 4.0 servers and eight Windows 2000 servers. Also, you want to set up a Windows 2000 gateway to one of the NetWare servers, and there is an IBM mainframe that is set up only for SNA connectivity. In this situation, you will likely need to set up NWLink on the Windows 2000 servers for connectivity to NetWare, DLC to connect to the IBM mainframe, and TCP/IP for connectivity between the Windows 2000 servers and their clients. As part of the planning, you will need to determine which resources are used most frequently by which Windows NT Workstation and Windows 2000 Professional clients. For example, the business office workstations may access the Windows 2000 servers most, the mainframe next most frequently, and the NetWare servers least. Their workstations should be set up to have a binding order of TCP/IP, DLC, and NWLink. Or, if they will only access the one NetWare server via the Windows 2000 gateway, then those workstations only need TCP/IP and DLC, bound in that order.

In a third scenario, you have a network that contains four NetWare 4.0 servers set up for IPX/SPX communication. The decision is made to upgrade the NetWare servers to version 5.0. Also, your organization has purchased a new client/server system that requires three Windows 2000 servers. To reduce the number of protocols needed on the network, you should plan to convert the NetWare servers and clients to TCP/IP and to set up TCP/IP on the new Windows 2000 servers.

In a last scenario, there is an office of 22 tax accountants, who have a small network without routers. Each accountant has a Windows 98 computer, and there is one Windows 2000 server. Also, one of the accountants has Internet access through a modem on her workstation. This is a situation in which NetBEUI is effective and easy to manage. Only the workstation that has Internet connectivity needs to be configured for TCP/IP. However, if there is a plan to have Internet connectivity for all network users via the server, then TCP/IP can be used instead of NetBEUI for all workstations and the server.

CHAPTER SUMMARY

❑ Protocols are the heart of network communications. Just as life would be silent without language, networks would be silent without protocols. Because protocols are vital to network communication, your first step in setting up a network that uses Windows 2000 is to plan how to set up the network and implement the right protocols. Different protocols are used for different kinds of networks such as LANs and WANs. Protocols also influence how you set up a network interface card and network client workstations.

❑ Network operating system vendors establish specifications for network drivers to enable protocol transport on a network. Microsoft uses the NDIS driver, which is fundamental to communication on Microsoft networks. Through the NDIS driver, Microsoft supports single to multiple protocol communications for TCP/IP, IPX/SPX, NetBEUI, DCL, and AppleTalk. Because so many networks use Internet and intranet connectivity, TCP/IP is generally the protocol of choice when you set up Windows 2000 Server.

TCP/IP is preferred because it provides reliable communication, IP addressing, and a suite of associated protocols that support many kinds of network functions.

❑ As you plan a network, carefully plan which protocols are needed to match what your organization wants to accomplish through the network. Also, keep two goals in mind: to use only those protocols that are necessary and to tune network performance through the protocol access order. Your thorough planning before setting up Windows 2000 Server and its associated network can be the cornerstone for having a successful and efficient network within a reasonable budget.

In the next chapter you are introduced to the Active Directory and learn how to plan its use for different types of situations.

KEY TERMS

Address Resolution Protocol (ARP) — A protocol in the TCP/IP suite that enables a sending station to determine the MAC address of another station on a network.

AppleTalk — A peer-to-peer protocol used in network communication between Macintosh computers.

bridge — A network transmission device that connects together different LAN segments using the same access method, for example connecting an Ethernet LAN to another Ethernet LAN or a token ring LAN to another token ring LAN. Bridge devices look at MAC addresses (OSI Layer 2) but do not look at routing information (Layer 3) in a frame.

connectionless communication — Also called a connectionless service, a communication service that provides no checks (or minimal checks) to make sure that data accurately reaches the destination node.

connection-oriented communication — Also called a connection-oriented service, this service provides several ways to ensure that data is successfully received at the destination, such as requiring an acknowledgement of receipt and using a checksum to make sure the packet or frame contents are accurate.

Data Link Control protocol (DLC) — Available through Microsoft Windows 2000, Windows NT, Windows 95, and Windows 98, this protocol enables communication with an IBM mainframe or minicomputer.

device address — Same as *physical address.*

Domain Name Service (DNS) — A TCP/IP application protocol that resolves domain and computer names to IP addresses, or IP addresses to domain and computer names.

dotted decimal notation — An addressing technique that uses four octets, such as 100000110.11011110.1100101.00000101, converted to decimal (For example, 134.22.101.005), to differentiate individual servers, workstations, and other network devices.

dynamic addressing — An addressing method whereby an Internet Protocol (IP) address is assigned to a workstation without the need for the network administrator to manually set it up at a workstation.

Dynamic Host Configuration Protocol (DHCP) — A network protocol that provides a way for a server to automatically assign an IP address to a workstation on its network.

enterprise network — A network that often reaches throughout a large area, such as a college campus, a city, or across several states. The main distinguishing factor of an enterprise network is that it brings together an array of network resources such as many kinds of servers, mainframes, intranets, printers, and the Internet.

Ethernet — A network transport system that uses a carrier sensing and collision detection method to regulate data transmissions.

File Transfer Protocol (FTP) — Available through the TCP/IP protocol, FTP enables files to be transferred across a network or the Internet between computers or servers.

frame — A unit of data that is transmitted on a network; it contains control and address information, but not routing information.

Hypertext Transfer Protocol (HTTP) — A protocol in the TCP/IP suite that transports HTML documents over the Internet (and through intranets) for access by Web-compliant browsers.

Internet Control Message Protocol (ICMP) — A TCP/IP-based protocol that is used for network error reporting, particularly through routing devices.

Internet Group Management Protocol (IGMP) — Part of the TCP/IP protocol suite, the protocol that is used in multicasting and which contains addresses of clients. It is used by the server to tell a router which clients belong to the multicast group.

Internet Packet Exchange (IPX) — A protocol developed by Novell for use with its NetWare Server operating system (see Sequence Packet Exchange).

local area network (LAN) — A series of interconnected computers, printers, and other computer equipment that share hardware and software resources. The service area is usually limited to a given floor, office area, or building.

media access control (MAC) sublayer — A network communications function that examines physical address information in frames and controls the way devices share communications on a network.

metropolitan area network (MAN) — A network that links multiple LANs within a large city or metropolitan region.

NetBIOS Extended User Interface (NetBEUI) — A communication protocol native to Microsoft network communications. It is an enhancement of NetBIOS, and was developed for network peer-to-peer communication among workstations with Microsoft operating systems installed on a local area network.

NetWare Link (NWLink) — A network protocol that simulates the IPX/SPX protocol for Microsoft Windows 95, Windows 98, Windows NT, and Windows 2000 communication with Novell NetWare file servers and compatible devices.

Network Basic Input/Output System (NetBIOS) — A combination software interface and a network naming convention. It is available in Microsoft operating systems through the file, NetBIOS.dll.

network binding — A process that links a computer's network interface card or a dial-up connection with one or more network protocols to achieve optimum communication with network services. For Microsoft operating systems, you should always bind a protocol to each NIC that is installed.

Network Driver Interface Specification (NDIS) — A set of standards developed by Microsoft and 3COM for network drivers that enables communication between a NIC and a protocol, and that enables the use of multiple protocols on the same network.

Open Datalink Interface (ODI) — A driver that is used by Novell NetWare networks to transport multiple protocols on the same network.

Open Shortest Path First (OSPF) protocol — A TCP/IP-based routing protocol that can evaluate network paths and match a type of transmission, such as data or video, to the appropriate network path.

packet — A unit of data that is transmitted on a network, and contains control and address information as well routing information.

physical address — Also called a device address, a unique hexadecimal number associated with a device's network interface card.

protocol — A strictly defined set of rules for communication across a network that specifies how networked data is formatted for transmission, how it is transmitted, and how it is interpreted at the receiving end.

Quality of Service (QoS) — Mechanisms used to measure and allocate network resources on the basis of transmission speed, quality, throughput, and reliability.

Resource Reservation Protocol (RSVP) — Enables an application to reserve the network resources it needs, such as network paths with higher speeds.

router — A device that connects networks, that can read IP addresses, and that can route packets to designated networks, because it reads routing information in packets (Layer 3) and keeps tables of information about the fastest route from one network to another.

Routing Information Protocol (RIP) — A TCP/IP-based protocol that enables routing devices to share information about a network.

Sequence Packet Exchange (SPX) — A Novell connection-oriented protocol used for network transport when there is a particular need for data reliability (see Internet Packet Exchange).

Simple Mail Transfer Protocol (SMTP) — An e-mail protocol used by systems having TCP/IP network communications.

Simple Network Management Protocol (SNMP) — A TCP/IP-based protocol that enables servers, workstations, and network devices to gather standardized data about network performance and identify problems.

static addressing — An IP (Internet Protocol) addressing method that requires the network administrator to manually assign and set up a unique network address on each workstation connected to a network.

subnet mask — A designated portion of an IP address that is used to indicate the class of addressing on a network and to divide a network into subnetworks as a way to control traffic and enforce security.

Telnet — A TCP/IP application protocol that provides terminal emulation services.

token ring — Using a ring topology, a network transport method that passes a token from node to node. The token is used to coordinate transmission of data, because only the node possessing the token can send data.

topology — The physical layout of the cable and the logical path followed by network packets and frames sent on the cable.

Transmission Control Protocol/Internet Protocol (TCP/IP) — A protocol that is particularly well suited for medium and large networks. The TCP portion was originally developed to ensure reliable connections on government, military, and educational networks. It performs extensive error checking to ensure data is delivered successfully. The IP portion consists of rules for packaging data and ensuring it reaches the correct destination address.

User Datagram Protocol (UDP) — A protocol used with IP as an alternative to TCP and that offers low-overhead connectionless communications.

wide area network (WAN) — A far-reaching system of networks that can extend across state lines and across continents.

Windows Internet Naming Service (WINS) — A Windows 2000 Server service that enables the server to convert workstation names to IP addresses for Internet communication.

REVIEW QUESTIONS

1. You are setting up a bridged network between two floors in a small office building that has one Windows 2000 server and 42 users who run Windows 95 and Windows 98. Can you implement NetBEUI as a protocol on this network?

   a. Yes

   b. No

   c. NetBEUI can be implemented as long as you use NWLink for network print services.

   d. NetBEUI can be implemented, but you must use DLC for any workstation that connects to the Internet.

2. What protocol enables a DHCP server to determine the IP and physical addresses of a client that has just joined the network?

   a. NetBIOS

   b. RIP

   c. ARP

   d. all of the above

   e. only a and b

   f. only a and c

3. Which of the following network driver specifications enable(s) you to transport two or more protocols on the same network?

   a. NDIS

   b. ODI

   c. ARP

   d. all of the above

e. only a and b

f. only a and c

4. You work for a news organization that offers multimedia news clips over the Internet via a Windows 2000 Web server. You have several Internet network connections, some of which are high-speed and some of which are not. Which of the following TCP/IP capabilities might be useful to you?

3

a. RSVP

b. multicasting

c. QoS

d. all of the above

e. only a and b

f. only b and c

5. You are setting up a new network that uses two Windows 2000 servers for a business and accounting system that will be available for administrative use at a community college. Only 20 users will access the system in the first two months. Gradually more users will go onto the system, until there are 322 within 12 months. All of the client workstations are Windows 2000 Professional and Windows 98. What protocol will you set up?

a. NetBEUI for the first year and then convert to TCP/IP when you know the system is working properly

b. TCP/IP from the beginning

c. UDP/IP for fastest response

d. UDP for the first two months and then convert to TCP when you know the system is working properly

6. Which of the following is (are) available through AppleTalk?

a. file services

b. print services

c. peer-to-peer networking

d. all of the above

e. only a and b

f. only a and c

7. You are manually setting up TCP/IP on your Windows 2000 server. Which configuration elements must you establish to communicate on the network?

a. a WINS server address

b. an IP address

c. a subnet mask

d. all of the above

e. only a and b

f. only b and c

8. You have a network that contains both Windows 2000 servers and NetWare 5.0 servers as the main host computers accessed by Windows 95, Windows 98, and Windows 2000 workstations. Which of the following protocols do you need to set up?

   a. NetBEUI

   b. NWLink

   c. TCP/IP

   d. all of the above

   e. only a and c

   f. only b and c

9. One important difference between TCP and UDP is that

   a. TCP contains source and destination addresses and UDP does not.

   b. TCP is connection-oriented and UDP is not.

   c. UDP is connection-oriented and TCP is not.

   d. UDP cannot be routed, but TCP can.

10. A NIC contains which of the following?

    a. transmitter

    b. serial bus

    c. power supply

    d. all of the above

    e. only a and b

    f. only a and c

11. Which of the following is (are) part of the QoS implementation in Windows 2000?

    a. Prioritized LANs

    b. Address Resolution Protocol

    c. Admission Control Service

    d. all of the above

    e. only a and b

    f. only b and c

12. 155.242.1.299 is an example of what type of address?

    a. MAC

    b. dotted decimal

    c. physical

    d. subaddress

13. Your TCP/IP-based network seems to have some problems with slowdowns. Which of the following protocols might help you gather information about network performance and locate the problem?

    a. SNMP

    b. DNS

    c. DHCP

    d. all of the above

    e. only a and b

    f. only b and c

14. Your network consists of four Windows 2000 servers, a mainframe, 20 networked Hewlett Packard 4Si printers, and 122 workstations that run Windows 2000 Professional. The workstations primarily access the Windows 2000 servers and are configured for TCP/IP, NetBEUI, DLC, and NWLink. Communication with the servers is via TCP/IP and communication with the mainframe and network printers is through DLC. Network performance does not seem to be as fast as you would like it. What simple step(s) might you take to improve network performance?

    a. Convert all communications to NetBEUI.

    b. Eliminate the use of NWLink and NetBEUI.

    c. Check the network access order at the workstations.

    d. Convert all communication to DLC because it has low overhead.

    e. only a and c

    f. only b and c

15. Which of the following protocols cannot be routed?

    a. IPX/SPX

    b. NWLink

    c. NetBEUI

    d. TCP/IP

16. As you are planning the setup of Windows 2000 servers on a routed network using TCP/IP, you realize that setting up TCP/IP on all 272 workstation clients will require lots of manual labor. What can you do to reduce your workload?

    a. turn off routing

    b. use DHCP and set up one of the Windows 2000 servers as a DHCP server

    c. set up one of the Windows 2000 servers as a DNS server

    d. use RIP at the routers instead of SMTP

17. What type of address is burned into a NIC?

    a. MAC

    b. IP

    c. NetBEUI

    d. HTTP

18. Which type of packet can be used to send fewer network transmissions for a multimedia presentation over a network?

    a. unicast

    b. multicast

    c. broadcast

    d. frame

19. Which of the following contains routing information?

    a. frame

    b. packet

    c. bus

    d. MAC sublayer

20. When you bind a protocol, you bind it to

    a. a driver

    b. a computer bus

    c. a NIC

    d. a WINS server

21. Which TCP/IP-based protocol is needed for Web communications that involve HTML?

    a. Telnet

    b. SMTP

    c. HTTP

    d. WWW

22. 255.255.0.0 is an example of

    a. a device address

    b. a binding number

    c. a DNS server address

    d. a subnet designation

23. NetBIOS is

    a. an interface

    b. a protocol

    c. a socket

    d. a topology

24. You are configuring routers to communicate with one another. Which of the following TCP/IP-based protocols might you use?

    a. RIP

    b. FTP

    c. SMTP

    d. all of the above

    e. only a and b

    f. only a and c

25. Originally your network was small and relied on a network service provider to provide translation of IP addresses to computer names. Now you have a larger operation and want to place this function on your own network. Which Windows 2000 capability enables you to do this?

    a. DLC server

    b. DNS server

    c. Active Directory

    d. bridging

HANDS-ON PROJECTS

Project 3-1

In this project, you check to make sure that the NIC in a computer running Windows 2000 is working properly. You will need an account with Administrator privileges.

To check on the NIC:

1. Log on to Windows 2000 Server.

2. Click **Start**, point to **Settings**, and then click **Network and Dial-up Connections**.

3. Right-click **Local Area Connection** and then click **Properties**. Make sure you are viewing the General tab.

4. What type of NIC is installed in your computer?

5. Click the **Configure** button.

6. Click the **General** tab.

7. What does the Device status text box say about how the NIC is working?

8. Record the information that you obtain in your lab journal or in a word-processed document.

9. Click **Cancel** to close the NIC's Properties dialog box.

10. Click **Cancel** to close the Local Area Connection Properties dialog box.

11. Close the Network and Dial-up Connections dialog box, if it has remained open.

Project 3-2

In this hands-on activity you determine the physical (MAC) address of the NIC in a Windows 2000 server. (This project will also work using Windows 2000 Professional).

To determine the physical address:

1. Log on to Windows 2000.

2. Click **Start**, point to **Programs**, point to **Accessories**, and then click **Command Prompt**.

3. Type **ipconfig /all** and press **Enter** at the command prompt (see Figure 3-11).

4. Notice the physical address of the NIC.

5. Is there an IP address assigned?

6. What is the description of the NIC?

7. Is there a DNS server on your network? If so, what is its IP address?

8. What other information is available from using Ipconfig?

9. Record the information that you obtain in your lab journal or in a word-processed document.

10. Close the Command Prompt window.

```
Command Prompt                                                      _|□|x|

E:\>ipconfig /all

Windows 2000 IP Configuration

        Host Name . . . . . . . . . . . . : LAWYER
        Primary DNS Suffix  . . . . . . . : TheFirm.com
        Node Type . . . . . . . . . . . . : Broadcast
        IP Routing Enabled. . . . . . . . : No
        WINS Proxy Enabled. . . . . . . . : No
        DNS Suffix Search List. . . . . . : TheFirm.com

Ethernet adapter Local Area Connection:

        Connection-specific DNS Suffix  . :
        Description . . . . . . . . . . . : 3Com EtherLink XL 10/100 PCI TX
<3C905B-TX>
        Physical Address. . . . . . . . . : 00-10-5A-CE-76-0E
        DHCP Enabled. . . . . . . . . . . : No
        IP Address. . . . . . . . . . . . : 129.70.10.1
        Subnet Mask . . . . . . . . . . . : 255.255.0.0
        Default Gateway . . . . . . . . . :
        DNS Servers . . . . . . . . . . . : 129.70.10.1

E:\>
```

Figure 3-11   Using Ipconfig

Project 3-3

In this project, you practice another way to view a physical address in Windows 2000 Server.

To view the physical address:

1. Log on to Windows 2000, if you logged off after Hands-on Project 3-2.
2. Click **Start**, point to **Programs**, point to **Administrative Tools**, and click **Computer Management**.
3. Click **System Information** in the left pane under **System Tools**.
4. Double-click **Components** in the right pane.
5. Double-click **Network** in the right pane and double-click **Adapter**.
6. Notice the value of the MAC address and compare it with the MAC address you obtained in Hands-on Project 3-2. What other information is available on this screen?
7. Close the Computer Management tool.

Project 3-4

This hands-on activity enables you to practice converting a server running Windows NT 4.0 to TCP/IP as preparation for upgrading to Windows 2000 Server. You will need an account with Administrator privileges. Also, obtain an IP address and subnet mask to use from your instructor.

To set up TCP/IP in Windows NT 4.0 before converting to Windows 2000:

1. Click **Start**, point to **Settings**, and then click **Control Panel**.
2. Double-click the **Network** icon.
3. Click the **Protocols** tab in the Network dialog box, then click **Add**.
4. Highlight the **TCP/IP Protocol** option and then click **OK**.
5. Determine if there is a Windows NT DHCP server on the network. If there is one, click Yes, otherwise click No. For this practice session, click **No**.
6. Insert the Windows NT Server CD-ROM as requested, enter the path to the CD-ROM drive and \I386, and click **Continue**. (If Remote Access Service is installed, there is a dialog box that enables you to click Yes or OK, depending on your service pack level, to configure for this service).
7. The installation program returns to the Protocols tab after the files are loaded. Click the **Bindings** tab to automatically configure the NIC for TCP/IP.
8. Click the **Protocols** tab, point to **TCP/IP Protocol**, and then click the **Properties** button.
9. Click the **IP Address** tab and then enter the IP address and the network subnet mask.
10. If there is a DNS server, click the **DNS** tab and complete the Host Name and Domain text boxes. Click **Add** under DNS Service Search Order, enter the address of the DNS Server (obtain this from your instructor), and click **Add**. Click **Apply** and then **OK**.

11. If there is a WINS server, click the **WINS Address** tab and then enter the addresses of the primary and secondary WINS servers. Also, if you specified a DNS server, click the box, **Enable DNS for Windows Resolution**. Click **Apply** and then **OK**.

12. Click **Close** in the Network dialog box.

13. Windows NT will perform a binding review.

14. If necessary, save any open work, then click **Yes** to restart the computer to have the new protocol take effect.

Project 3-5

In this hands-on activity, you experiment with the Ping utility, which uses ICMP. Before you start, obtain from your instructor two addresses to Ping, one that is an IP address on your local network and the other an IP address on a distant network connected to your campus or on the Internet. You can use either Windows 2000 Server or Windows 2000 Professional for this assignment.

To use Ping:

1. Click **Start**, point to **Programs**, point to **Accessories**, and then click **Command Prompt**.

2. Type **Ping** and the IP address of the local network node (or type the address of your node if you found one in Hands-on Project 3-1). What information is produced from using Ping?

3. Type **Ping** and the IP address of the distant node. Is the node responding? What information do you see?

4. If you obtained a DNS server address from Hands-on Project 3-1, Ping it to see if it is responding.

5. Record the information that you obtain in your lab journal or in a word-processed document.

6. Close the Command Prompt window.

Project 3-6

In this hands-on activity, you set the binding order in Windows NT 4.0 (you do the same thing for Windows 2000 in the next project). You will need a computer running Windows NT 4.0 Workstation or Server that is configured for at least two network providers (protocols) and two print providers, and access to an account with Administrator privileges.

To set the binding order in Windows NT 4.0:

1. Log on to Windows NT.

2. Click **Start**, point to **Settings**, and then click **Control Panel**.

3. Double-click the **Network** icon and then click the **Services** tab.

4. Click the **Network Access Order** button.

5. Under Network Providers, click the network type or protocol listed second and then click **Move Up**.

6. Under Print Providers, click the network type or protocol listed second and then click **Move Up**.

7. Click **OK** and then click **Close**.

8. Click **Yes** to restart the computer (save any open work first).

Project 3-7

In this project, you change the network access order in Windows 2000 Server or Windows 2000 Professional. The operating system should already be configured for two network and print providers and you will need access to an account with Administrator privileges.

To change the network access order in Windows 2000 Server or Professional:

1. Log on to Windows 2000.

2. Right-click **My Network Places** on the desktop and then click **Properties** on the menu.

3. Click the network connection that you want to change — ask your instructor which connection to use or click **Local Area Connection**.

4. Click **Advanced** on the menu bar in the Network and Dial-up Connections dialog box.

5. Click **Advanced Settings** on the Advanced menu.

6. Click the **Adapters and Bindings** tab to view the current bindings (see Figure 3-12). What bindings exist on your computer?

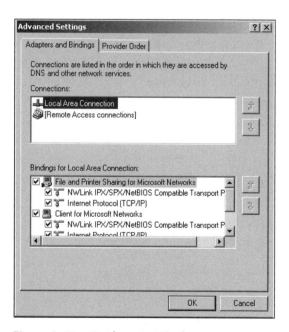

Figure 3-12   Bindings in Windows 2000

7. Click the **Provider Order** tab.

8. Under Network Providers, click the network type or protocol listed second and then click the up arrow button.

9. Under Print Providers, click the network type or protocol listed second and then click the up arrow button.

10. Click **OK**.

11. Close the Network and Dial-up Connections dialog box.

12. If you are keeping a lab journal, note that you do not have to restart Windows 2000 to change the access order, whereas you did have to restart Windows NT in the previous hands-on project. Also, make a note of the differences between what is displayed for network bindings and access order between Windows NT 4.0 and Windows 2000. In addition, note how you accessed the Network and Dial-Up Connections dialog box in this project compared to how you accessed it in Hands-on Project 3-1.

Project 3-8

In this project, you practice removing NWLink from the access order in Windows 2000 by unbinding it. You will need a Windows 2000 server or workstation that has NWLink installed before you start.

To unbind NWLink:

1. Log on to Windows 2000.

2. Right-click **My Network Places** on the desktop and then click **Properties** on the menu.

3. Click the network connection that you want to change — ask your instructor which connection to use or click **Local Area Connection**.

4. Click **Advanced** on the menu bar in the Network and Dial-up Connections dialog box.

5. Click **Advanced Settings** on the Advanced menu.

6. Click the **Adapters and Bindings** tab to view the current bindings.

7. Under File and Printer Sharing for Microsoft Networks, click the check box to the left of NWLink IPX/SPX/NetBIOS Compatible Transport Protocol to remove the check.

8. Under Client for Microsoft Networks, also click the check box to the left of NWLink IPX/SPX/NetBIOS Compatible Transport Protocol to remove the check.

9. Click **OK**.

10. Close the Network and Dial-up Connections dialog box.

11. Make a note in your lab journal that it is not necessary to reboot Windows 2000 to unbind a protocol.

CASE PROJECT

Aspen Consulting Project: Protocol Planning and Implementation

3

Batesberg College is a liberal arts college that has 742 students, 51 faculty, and a staff of 43. There are eight buildings on campus that serve as classrooms and offices. Three additional buildings are dorms. All buildings are networked via Ethernet and connected by brouters (routers that can be set up to bridge or route) in each building. There is a computer machine room in the basement of the Administration Building that houses the following:

❑ A UNIX computer that is used for administrative computing, including registration

❑ Seven Novell NetWare 3.11 servers that support the faculty, which are used by student labs throughout campus, and which are set up for IPX/SPX

❑ Two Windows NT 4.0 servers set up to use NetBEUI and TCP/IP — one server is used for a client/server system for the Development Office, and one is a Web server

Five of the classroom buildings house student labs, with one lab in each. Four of the labs consist of computers running Windows 95 and Windows 98. The fifth lab consists of Macintosh computers that do not connect to any server, but use peer-to-peer networking. All of the student dorms provide Ethernet network access. The Development Office has just completed a fund-raising campaign to upgrade computer facilities. The campus computer planning committee has mandated that four of the NetWare servers will be converted to Windows 2000 Server, and the remaining three will be upgraded to NetWare 5.0. Also, the Windows NT 4.0 servers will be upgraded to Windows 2000 Server.

1. What preparations do you recommend to the Batesberg College Information Technology Department in terms of preparing the Windows NT 4.0 servers for the upgrade to Windows 2000? Why?

2. The Windows 2000 workstations in the Registrar's Office are set up to use TCP/IP, NWLink, and AppleTalk. These workstations are used to access the UNIX computer and the Web server only. Which of these protocols is really needed for the workstations, and should the workstations be set up to take advantage of access order? Explain your answer.

3. The Journalism Department uses the Macintosh lab to teach students about different types of publication software. They want students to be able to connect to one of the new Windows 2000 servers for lab use. What are their options for connecting to one of these servers?

4. The Chemistry, Math, Sociology, and Zoology departments want to use simulated multimedia lab presentations that will run to the labs and dorms from two of the new Windows 2000 servers. What server capabilities will help make multimedia use a reality?

5. After all of the server upgrades are made, and considering the requests presented in Questions 3 and 4, what protocols do you recommend for the entire campus network? Note that the IT director likes NetBEUI for Windows 2000 servers because he believes it creates the lowest overhead, and he wants to set up all brouters to bridge. How would you make your recommendations address the IT director's interest in NetBEUI?

6. Also, after the upgrades have been completed and adjustments have been made to the campus workstations, the business office has discovered that four of their Windows 98 computers can no longer access their networked Hewlett Packard 4Si printers. What do you suggest?

7. The IT director is new because he was the Development Office's database manager who was recently promoted. He has heard about connectionless and connection-oriented services, but is not sure how these apply to protocols. Prepare an explanation of how they apply to TCP/IP and IPX/SPX.

OPTIONAL CASE PROJECTS FOR TEAMS

Team Case One

Mark Arnez has been hearing about the new version of IP, called IPv6 or IP Next Generation, which is under development. He asks that you form a team to research this developing protocol and to explain its advantages. How might the protocol affect the use of Windows 2000? Consider using the Internet to help in your research.

Team Case Two

Mark wants you to form a team to give a presentation about why TCP/IP has become the protocol of the Internet. Research the Internet — past, present, and future — and explain the full story of this relationship.

4

PLANNING THE ACTIVE DIRECTORY AND SECURITY

After reading this chapter and completing the exercises you will be able to:

♦ Explain the contents of the Active Directory

♦ Plan how to set up Active Directory elements such as organizational units, domains, trees, forests, and sites

♦ Plan which Windows 2000 security features to use in an organization, including interactive logon, object security, and services security

♦ Plan how to use groups, group policies, and security templates

♦ Plan IP security measures

Early networks existed in a realm of trust, similar to small communities in which people never locked their doors. Today, life is more complex, and security is as much an issue for networks as it is for large and small communities. One profound effect that you can have on your organization through server and network planning is to provide a blueprint for security that enables your organization to accomplish work in a secure but flexible context. Some organizations impose such tight security that it not only exceeds what is necessary, but limits what people can accomplish through their network. Security that is poorly planned or excessive can reduce the ability of your network and servers to help people reach their productivity goals. Other organizations ignore security until it is too late, and critical information is stolen or compromised.

In this chapter, you learn the capabilities available in Windows 2000 Server that enable you to build a network to exactly fit the security needs of your organization. Windows 2000 Server offers the Active Directory and an extensive range of security tools to help you manage network resources. The Active Directory provides a way to track all of your network resources, including servers, printers, and users. You learn how to structure the Active Directory for different types of situations from small offices to large multisite organizations. You also learn about the security tools in Windows 2000, which include logon security, rights and permissions, group policies, security templates, and IP security.

DEFINING THE ACTIVE DIRECTORY

In Chapter 1 you learned that the Active Directory houses information about all network resources such as servers, printers, user accounts, groups of user accounts, security policies, and other information. You might think of it as the central nervous system of your Windows 2000 Server network because it has such a far-reaching impact on a network, from the smallest print request to the largest management activity.

In previous versions of Windows NT Server, some of the information now contained in the Windows 2000 Active Directory, such as information about user accounts, groups, and privileges, is stored in the Security Accounts Manager database (SAM). The SAM is kept on a main server, called the primary domain controller (PDC), and is regularly backed up on other servers called backup domain controllers (BDCs), as Figure 4-1 shows. Every Windows NT Server network can have only one PDC, but many BDCs. If the PDC fails, you manually promote a BDC to become the new PDC.

Domain resources

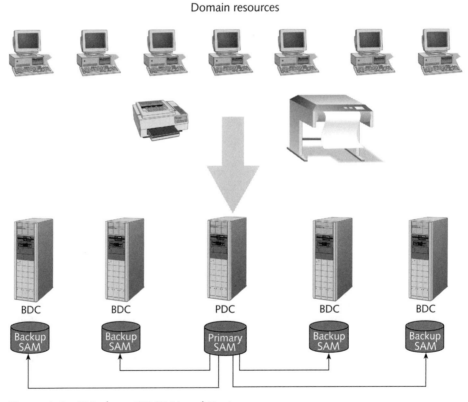

Figure 4-1   Windows NT SAM architecture

Windows 2000 Server retires the SAM and implements a broad range of directory services through the Active Directory. If you are a Windows NT Server administrator, one of the first changes you will notice is that there are no PDCs and BDCs; instead, all Windows 2000 Servers participate in tracking network resource information via the Active Directory, and are simply called **domain controllers (DCs)**. In the Active Directory, a **domain** is a fundamental component or container that holds information about all network resources that are grouped within it—servers, printers and other physical resources, users, and user groups. Every resource is called an **object** and is associated with a domain (see Figure 4-2). When you set up a new user account or a network printer, for instance, it becomes an object within a domain.

Domain objects

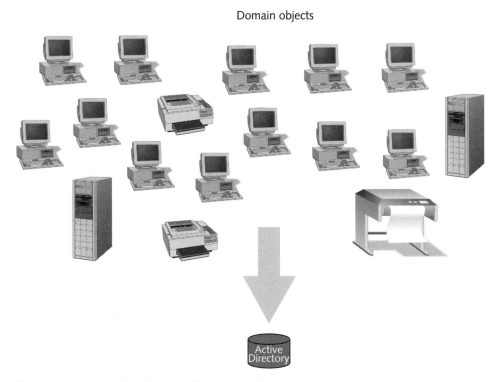

Figure 4-2 Domain objects in the Active Directory

In Windows 2000 Server, each DC is equal to every other DC in that it contains the full range of information that composes the Active Directory (see Figure 4-3). For example, when you create a new user account the information associated with that account can be created on any Windows 2000 Server DC, as opposed to the old Windows NT Server method of creating accounts only on the PDC. The Windows 2000 Server implementation of DCs is called **multimaster replication**. When an account is created, the full information about that account is replicated on every other DC. The advantage of this approach is that if one DC fails, the Active Directory is fully intact on all other DCs, and there is no visible network interruption, because you do not have to pause to manually promote a server to take over as the master database.

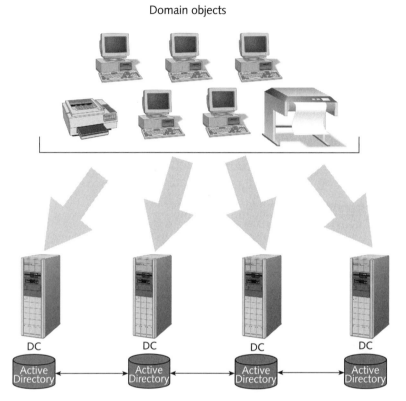

Figure 4-3 Windows 2000 Active Directory architecture

In Windows 2000 Server, you can set replication of Active Directory information to occur at a preset interval instead of as soon as an update occurs. Also, you can determine how much of the Active Directory is replicated each time it is copied from one DC to another.

In Windows NT 4.0, the process of replicating the PDC to one or more BDCs could create significant network traffic, particularly over a slow WAN link. This problem has been addressed in Windows 2000 Server in two ways: (1) Windows 2000 Server can replicate individual properties instead of entire accounts (as in Windows NT 4.0), which means that a single property can be changed without replicating information for the whole account, and (2) Windows 2000 Server can replicate the Active Directory on the basis of the speed of the network link, such as replicating more frequently over a LAN link than over a WAN link.

Two general concepts are important as a starting place for understanding the Active Directory: schema and namespace. These concepts are described in the next sections. (Try Hands-on Project 4-1 to practice installing the Active Directory.)

Schema

Each kind of object in the Active Directory is defined through a **schema**, which is like a small database of information associated with that object, including the object class and its attributes. To help you understand a schema, consider the characteristics associated with a vehicle. First, there are different classes of vehicles, including automobiles, trucks, tractors, and motorcycles. Further, each class has a set of attributes. For automobiles those attributes include engine, headlights, seats, steering wheel, dashboard, wheels, windshield, CD player, cup holder, and many others. Some of those attributes must be present in every automobile, such as an engine and wheels. Other attributes are optional—whether there is a CD player or cup holder, for instance.

A user account is one class of object in the Active Directory that is defined through schema elements unique to that class. The user account class as a whole has the following schema characteristics (see Figure 4-4):

- A unique object name
- A **globally unique identifier** (**GUID**), which is a unique number associated with the object name
- Required attributes (those that must be defined with each object)
- Optional attributes (those that are optionally defined)
- A syntax (format) to determine how attributes are defined
- Pointers to parent entities, such as to a parent domain

Examples of required user account attributes that must be defined for each account are:

- Username
- User's full name
- Password

Providing an account description or specifying if the account is enabled for remote access over a telephone line are examples of optional attributes that do not have to be completed when you create an account. In some instances, the attributes that are required and those that are optional can be influenced by the security policies that the server administrator sets in the Active Directory for a class of objects. This is true, for example, with account passwords because it is possible (but not recommended) for you to have a security policy that does not require account passwords.

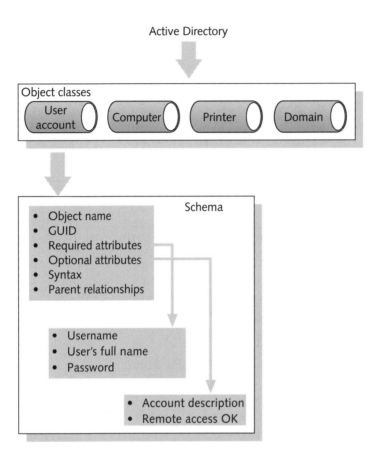

Figure 4-4   Sample schema information for user accounts

 Each attribute is automatically given a version number and date when it is created or changed. This information enables the Active Directory to know when an attribute value, such as a password, is changed, and update only that value on all DCs.

When you install Windows 2000 Server for the first time on a network server, designating it as a domain controller, you also create several object classes automatically. The default object classes include:

- Domain
- User account
- Group
- Shared drive

- Shared folder
- Computer
- Printer

You can supplement the schema contents by using the Schema Manager snap-in for the Microsoft Management Console (MMC). Schema extensions can be added without rebooting Windows 2000 Server, which means that they can be used right after you add them.

4

Schema information for objects in a domain are replicated on every DC. Each object has a **common name** (**CN**) and a **distinguished name** (**DN**). The CN is the most basic and unique name for an object, which may be HPLaserMain for a printer, or the combination first-name and lastname for a user account, RobBrown for example. The DN of an object gives more information; it contains the name of the object, the object class name, and the name of any higher-level entities to which the object belongs, such as a domain. When an Active Directory client needs to access an object, such as a user account or printer, that client can use the DN for unmistakable identification of the object. In the example of RobBrown who belongs to the domain *tracksport.org*, the DN would be:

/DC=ORG/DC=tracksport/CN=Users/CN=RobBrown

Notice in this example, that there are two CNs—one is Users, which identifies the user account object class, and the other is RobBrown, which identifies one of the users within the Users class. Also, there are two DCs that equate to the namespace, *tracksport.org*.

This DN is also an example of a **relative distinguished name** (**RDN**), a DN in which part of the name is a reference to another part of the name. In this case, Users is a higher-level, or parent, object (accounts in a domain), and RobBrown is an attribute (one username) of that parent object. Both are linked in a two-way relationship. If you search for RobBrown as an account, your search route would follow the database structure from domain (tracksport.org), through Users, to RobBrown. If you are the user RobBrown and you want to change your password, you would go from account RobBrown through the parent object Users to update that information associated with the RobBrown account. The RDN relationship enables users to quickly find an object, such as a specific account, by going from the domain level to the accounts object level, and finally to the specific account. Consider how much longer it would take to perform a search for an account in a structure that did not divide objects into groupings, so that you would have to search every object (printers, domains, group names, accounts, etc.) until you found the single account you wanted to locate. This might be like trying to locate a city on a map that did not show states, provinces, countries, and continents.

Besides the DN, each object can be identified through its globally unique identifier (GUID), which is a hexadecimal number, such as 8112AF88BC42 to identify a specific computer, created by the Active Directory for an object. A GUID is never reused when you delete an object. You can, however, change the name of the object, but retain the same GUID, such as when you rename a user account.

Namespace

The Active Directory is also essential in providing Domain Name Service (DNS). As you learned in Chapter 3, DNS is a TCP/IP-based utility that converts dotted decimal addresses to computer and domain names and vice versa, through a process called **name resolution**. A computer running Windows 2000 Server can be set up to act as a DNS server on a network. For example, when you send a TCP/IP request to connect with *microsoft.com*, the DNS server at Microsoft's site resolves that domain name to the address, 207.46.130.150. The DNS services are configured so that *microsoft.com* is a parent, or root, domain. Within that domain there are child objects, such as the Microsoft developers network (*msdn.microsoft.com*), which resolves to 207.46.130.161.

The ability to resolve names takes place in a designated logical area of a network, called a **namespace**, that is set up for this purpose. The namespace contains a domain name, such as *microsoft.com*. On a network consisting of Windows 2000 servers, namespace logic is composed of two key elements: (1) the Active Directory, which contains named objects and (2) one or more DNS servers that can resolve names. These services can be on a single computer, such as a Windows 2000 server in a small network that is set up as a DC and a DNS server. Or, they can be distributed across several servers on a large network, which might have two servers set up as DNS servers and 22 set up as DCs.

Microsoft recognizes two kinds of namespaces: contiguous and disjointed. A **contiguous namespace** is one in which every child object contains the name of the parent object, such as in the example of the child object *msdn.microsoft.com* and its parent object *microsoft.com*. When the child name does not resemble the name of its parent object, this is called a **disjointed namespace**, such as when the parent for a university is *uni.edu*, and a child is *bio.ethicsresearch.com*.

 TIP If you are an e-mail user, you may already be familiar with another type of name that enables you to quickly identify the account name and domain of someone with whom you communicate. That name is called the **user principle name (UPN)** and is in the format *username@domain*, such as *RobBrown@tracksport.org*.

ELEMENTS IN THE ACTIVE DIRECTORY

The Active Directory has a tree-like structure that is similar to the hierarchy of folders and subfolders in a directory structure. For example, in a directory structure information is stored in a root folder, which is at the highest level. The root folder may contain several main folders, 15 or 20, for instance. Under each folder there exist subfolders, and within subfolders there can be more subfolders. Subfolders can have a nearly infinite depth, but typically do not go more than five or ten layers deep. Just as files are the basic elements that are grouped in a hierarchy of folders and subfolders, objects are the basic elements of the Active Directory and are grouped in a hierarchy of larger containers. Also, just as the folder structure affects how you can set up security on a server, the Active Directory structure creates boundaries for security in a network enterprise. The hierarchical elements, or containers, of the Active Directory are the following (see Figure 4-5):

- Domains
- Organizational units (OUs)
- Trees
- Forests
- Sites

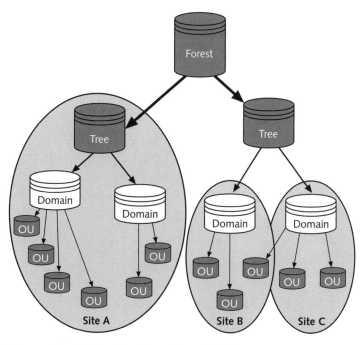

4

Figure 4-5   Active Directory hierarchical containers

Domain

A domain is a grouping of objects that typically exists as a primary container within the Active Directory. The basic functions of a domain are as follows:

- To provide a security boundary around objects that have a common relationship
- To establish a set of information to be replicated from one DC to another
- To expedite management of a set of objects

Domains can also be set up in Windows NT Server, but without the use of hierarchical containers or the Active Directory.

When you are migrating from Windows NT Server to Windows 2000 Server, an additional function of a Windows 2000 Server domain is to provide an easy migration path from an existing Windows NT Server domain.

When you use the server-based networking model (see Chapter 1) to verify users who log on to the network, there is at least one domain. For example, if you are planning the Active Directory for a small business of 34 employees, who have workstations connected to a network that has one or two Windows 2000 servers, then one domain is sufficient for that business (see Figure 4-6). The domain functions as a security boundary within which to group all of the network resource objects consisting of servers, user accounts, shared printers, and shared folders and files. If there is Internet connectivity and one or more intranets, then the domain provides a security boundary to keep information within intranets secure from outside access via the Internet. The boundary establishes the capability to manage what information comes into the network from the Internet and what information goes out.

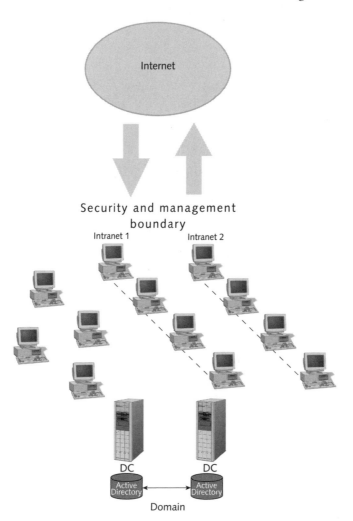

Figure 4-6   Single domain

In a medium or large business you might use more than one domain—for instance when business units are separated by long distances and you want to limit the amount of DC replication over expensive WAN links as well as establish tight security boundaries for each location. For example, consider a company that builds tractors in South Carolina and that has a parts manufacturing division in Japan. Each site has a large enterprise network of Windows 2000 servers, and the sites are linked together in a WAN by an expensive satellite connection. When you calculate the cost of replicating DCs over the satellite WAN link, you cannot justify it in terms of the increased traffic that will delay other vital daily business communications. In this situation, it makes sense to create two separate domains, one for each site, as shown in Figure 4-7.

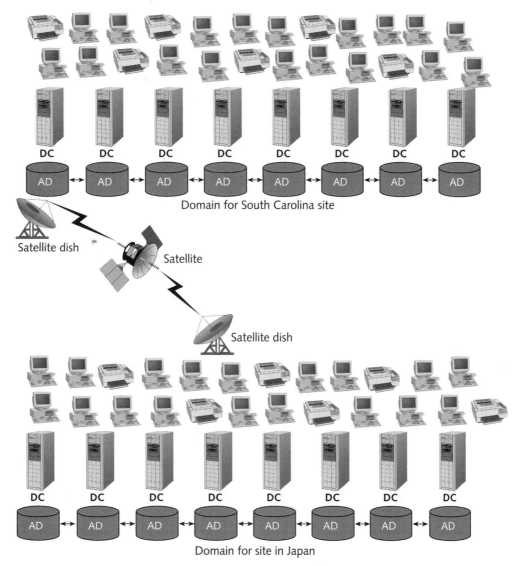

Figure 4-7   Using multiple domains

Microsoft has general guidelines for when to use a domain and when not to, as shown in Table 4-1, but keep in mind that when you set up the Active Directory there is at least one domain.

Table 4-1 Domain Creation Dos and Don'ts

Dos	Don'ts
Create a domain in circumstances that require special security measures between organizational groupings, such as departments, units, or divisions	Create domains that represent the organizational structure, because frequent reorganizations result in major restructuring of domains and the Active Directory
Create a domain for specialized management of particular resources (often also related to the security and network architecture)	Create domains along business process divisions, which are often political divisions within an organization, because new management may redefine business process activities, resulting in a major restructuring of domains and the Active Directory
Create a domain to migrate Windows NT servers to Windows 2000	
Create a domain when geography or WAN links make it difficult to replicate DCs between organizational groupings, such as departments, units, or divisions	

The guidelines in Table 4-1 are not set in stone, and you may find that a particular business process or unique set of requirements causes you to ignore them. For example, a research organization might have separate units, all of which work on different and highly classified projects. For the sake of security, each unit might be a separate domain, causing your domain structure to completely reflect the structure of the organization. As you plan in this type of situation, just remember that if there is a major restructuring of the organization, you will face equally major work in restructuring domains and resources in the Active Directory. For this reason, the Active Directory provides another alternative, called an organizational unit. (Try Hands-on Projects 4-2 and 4-3 to practice managing a domain and objects in a domain.)

Organizational Unit

An **organizational unit** (**OU**) offers a way to achieve more flexibility in managing the resources associated with a business unit, department, or division than is possible through domain administration alone. An OU is a grouping of related objects within a domain, similar to the idea of having subfolders within a folder. OUs can be used to reflect the structure of the organization without having to completely restructure the domain(s) when that structure changes.

OUs allow the grouping of objects so that they can be administered using the same group policies, such as security and desktop setup. OUs also make it possible for server administration to be delegated or decentralized. For example, in a software company in which the employees are divided into 15 project teams, the user accounts, shared files, shared printers, and other shared resources of each team can be defined as objects in separate OUs. There would be one domain for the entire company and 15 OUs within that domain, all defined in the Active Directory. With this arrangement, file and folder objects can be defined to specific

OUs for security, and the management of user accounts, account setup policies, and file and folder permissions can be delegated to each group leader (OU administrator).

Consider another example of a larger network and organization, which is a grocery chain that has three separate divisions: manufacturing, distribution, and retail. In this scenario, the manufacturing unit consists of five sites that are networked into a WAN, and the computer resources of that unit are managed by their own IT group of server administrators and programmers. The manufacturing unit provides prepared foods, which include canned items, frozen foods, bakery goods, soft drinks, and other foods. The distribution unit transports all food items to the retail stores and has its own independent IT group and network. Finally, the retail unit provides central management of hundreds of grocery stores throughout 20 states, and it networks each store into a central site through a WAN with computer resources managed by a third independent IT group. In this situation, there are three separate administrative units, each with its own IT group and unique management policies. Each administrative group can be incorporated into an individual OU, as in Figure 4-8.

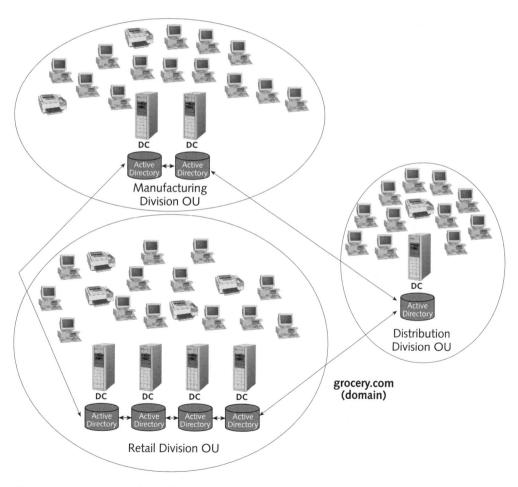

Figure 4-8   OUs used to reflect the divisional structure of a company

OUs can be nested within OUs, as subfolders are nested in subfolders, so that you can create them several layers deep. In the grocery chain example, you might have one OU under the Retail OU for the Accounting Department, an OU under the Accounting OU for the Accounts Receivable Group, and an OU under Accounts Receivable for the cashiers—creating four layers of OUs. The problem with this approach is that creating OUs many layers deep can get as confusing as creating subfolders several layers deep. It is confusing for the server administrator to track layered OUs, and it is laborious for the Active Directory to search through each layer.

When you plan to create OUs, keep three concerns in mind:

- Microsoft recommends that you limit OUs to 10 levels or fewer.

- The Active Directory works more efficiently (using less CPU resources) when OUs are set up horizontally instead of vertically. Using the grocery chain example, it is more efficient to create the Accounting, Accounts Receivable, and Cashier OUs directly under the Retail OU, resulting in two levels instead of four.

- The creation of OUs involves more processing resources because each request through an OU (for example to determine a permission on a folder) requires CPU time. When that request must go several layers deep through nested OUs, even more CPU time is needed.

Microsoft has several guidelines, which are presented in Table 4-2, to help you plan for OUs. Compare this table with Table 4-1 to assess when you might create an OU and when to create a domain.

Table 4-2   OU Creation Dos and Don'ts

Dos	Don'ts
Create OUs, as needed, to represent the organizational structure of departments, units, and divisions for different policies and to delegate administration	Create OUs more than 10 layers deep
Create OUs, as needed, to represent objects in the Active Directory that have similar policies, security, or other characteristics, such as shared printers or shared disk drives	Create more OUs than absolutely necessary
Create OUs, as needed, to represent specific project areas, such as for employees who are temporarily helping with the installation of a new client/server system	Create OUs for major security boundaries when this can be handled by a domain or by sites (discussed later), such as for IP traffic control
Create OUs, as needed, to represent the business process or political functions in an organization, such as an OU for the president's office, one for the Business Office, and one for each research group in a health research organization	Create OUs for DC replication

Tree

A **tree** contains one or more domains that are in a common relationship, and has the following characteristics:

- Domains are represented in a contiguous namespace and can be in a hierarchy.

- Two-way trust relationships exist between domains in which each domain can access the resources of the other.

- Member domains use the same schema for all types of common objects.

- Member domains use the same global catalog (a global catalog is something like an encyclopedia of information about objects and their attributes in all domains).

The domains in a tree typically have a hierarchical structure, such as a root domain at the top and other domains under the root. In the *tracksport.org* example, *tracksport.org* might be the root domain and have four domains under the root to form one tree: *east.tracksport.org*, *west.tracksport.org*, *north.tracksport.org*, and *south.tracksport.org,* as shown in Figure 4-9. These domains use the contiguous namespace format in that the child domains each contain the name of the parent domain.

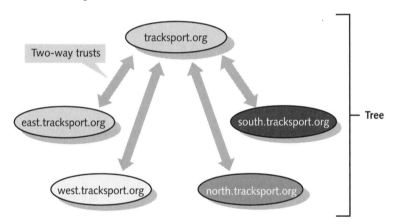

Figure 4-9   Tree with hierarchical domains

The domains within a tree are in what is called a Kerberos **transitive trust** relationship, which consists of two-way trusts between all domains (see Figure 4-9). This is similar to the universal trust relationship among domains in Windows NT Server. In a **two-way trust**, each domain is trusting and trusted. A **trusted domain** is one that is granted access to resources, whereas a **trusting domain** is the one granting access. In a two-way trust, members of each domain can have access to the resources of the other.

Because all domains have a two-way trust relationship, any one domain can have access to the resources of all others. The security in the two-way trust relationships is based on Kerberos techniques (see Chapter 1), using a combination of protocol-based and encryption-based security techniques between clients and servers. A new domain joining a tree has an instant trust relationship with all other member domains, which makes all objects in the other domains available to the new one.

All domains in a tree share the same schema, which means that they share the same object classes and attributes. One important advantage of this arrangement is the way it affects security. For example, if the first domain in the tree requires password restrictions, such as a minimum password length, then all others will have the same restriction.

All member domains share the same global catalog. The **global catalog** is a subset of the Active Directory; it contains information about all objects in the domain where it resides and partial information (only selected schema elements) about objects on other domains. The first DC created in a domain is also set up by default as a global catalog server. The value of the global catalog is that DCs in one domain do not have to replicate their information to DCs in another domain. The global catalog serves the following purposes:

- Authenticating users when they log on

- Providing lookup and access to all resources in all domains

- Providing replication of key Active Directory elements

- Keeping a copy of the most used attributes for each object for quick access

Each tree must have at least one DC that is also configured to operate as a global catalog server. When you plan a tree, also plan the location of global catalog servers so that users are quickly authenticated for access in the tree. In the *tracksport.org* example, consider that each domain is separated by many miles, for example when the parent domain is in Washington, D.C., and the child domains are located in Boston, Los Angeles, Chicago, and Atlanta. In this situation, it makes sense to have a global catalog server in each location because authentication over WAN links is likely to be slow. If there is only one global catalog server in Washington, then users in the other four cities will have to wait longer to log on than users in Washington. If there is a global catalog server in each of the five cities, then logon response will be faster, and the WAN links will be free to give priority to other types of communications.

Table 4-3 lists the dos and don'ts for creating trees.

Table 4-3 Tree Creation Dos and Don'ts

Dos	Don'ts
Define main domains before defining a tree	Define a tree prior to creating the first domain
Plan the hierarchy of domains and use of OUs before creating a tree	Define a tree if you can use a single domain structure (a better alternative than using trees, if possible)
Define a tree when you have domains in different countries so that you can set up each domain to use a language native to the country where it resides	Define a tree if you must use a disjointed namespace

Table 4-3   Tree Creation Dos and Don'ts (continued)

Dos	Don'ts
Define a tree if you are planning multiple domains that will be administered at different sites by different people	
Create a tree and multiple domains when WAN connectivity is slow between distant sites, because global catalog replication transfers less information and requires less bandwidth than DC replication	

Forest

A **forest** consists of one or more trees that are in a common relationship and that have the following characteristics:

- The trees use a disjointed namespace

- All trees use the same schema

- All trees use the same global catalog

A forest provides a means to relate trees that use a contiguous namespace in domains within each tree but that have disjointed namespaces in relationship to each other. Consider, for example, an international automotive parts company that is really a conglomerate of separate companies, each having a different brand name. The parent company is PartsPlus located in Toronto. PartsPlus manufactures alternators, coils, and other electrical parts at plants in Toronto, Montreal, and Detroit and has a tree structure for domains that are part of *partsplus.com*. Another company that they own, Marty and Mike's (*2m.com*), makes radiators in two South Carolina cities, Florence and Greenville, and radiator fluid in Atlanta. A third member company, Chelos (*chelos.com*), makes engine parts and starters in Mexico City, Oaxaca, Monterrey, and Puebla, all in Mexico—and also has a manufacturing site in Valencia, Venezuela. In this situation, it makes sense to have a contiguous tree structure for each of the three related companies and to join the trees in a forest of disjointed name spaces, as in Figure 4-10.

The advantage of joining trees into a forest is that all domains share the same schema and global catalog. A schema is set up in the root domain, which is *partsplus.com* in our example, and the root domain is home to the master schema server. At least one DC functions as a global catalog server, but in our example, it is likely that you would plan to have a global catalog server located at each geographic site (domain).

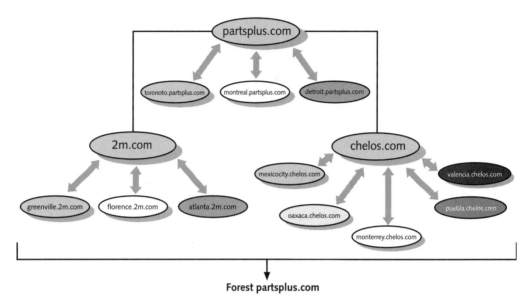

Figure 4-10   A forest

Kerberos trusts are transitive between trees in a forest, but they cannot be transitive between two or more forests. The Active Directory structure in Figure 4–10 is also called a **single forest** model by Microsoft. It is possible to join two or more forests for common communication in a model that Microsoft calls a **separate forest** (see Figure 4-11). In a separate forest, there cannot be transitive trusts between forests, which is a critical consideration when you plan the Active Directory. Establishing a separate forest means that replication cannot take place between forests, that there are different schema and different global catalogs, and that the forests cannot be blended into a single forest in the future. Table 4-4 lists guidelines for creating forests.

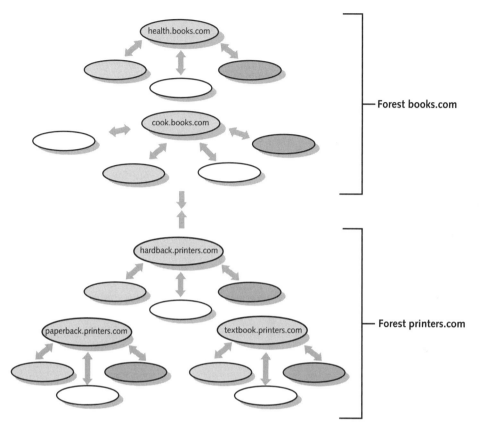

Figure 4-11   Separate forest model

Table 4-4   Forest Creation Dos and Don'ts

Dos	Don'ts
Create a forest to join trees/domains that can share schemas and global catalogs	Create forests when the member trees have little in common or cannot share the same schema
Create a single forest when there is no need to separate internal and external DNS resources between trees	Create a single or separate forest until you understand the security needs of all domains, trees, and potential forests
Create separate forests when the internal and external DNS resources must be keep separate between two or more forests	Create a separate forest when there is a possibility that the forests may merge into a single forest in the future
Establish a forest's name by using the name of the root domain or first domain in the first tree	Create a separate forest when the member forests must have a Kerberos transitive trust between them

Site

A **site** is a TCP/IP-based concept within the Active Directory that is linked to IP subnets and has the following functions:

- Reflects one or more interconnected subnets (see Chapter 3), usually connected at 512 Kbps or faster
- Reflects the same boundaries as the LAN it represents
- Is used for DC replication
- Is used to enable a client to access the DC that is physically closest
- Is composed of only two types of objects, servers, and configuration objects

Sites are based on connectivity and replication functions; therefore, they do not have a visible entry in the Active Directory or a namespace name. You might think of sites as a way of grouping Active Directory objects by physical location so the Active Directory can identify the fastest communications paths between clients and servers and between DCs. The physical representation of the network to the Active Directory is accomplished by defining subnets that are interconnected. For this reason, one site may be contained within a single OU or a single domain, or a site may span multiple OUs and domains, depending on how subnets are set up. The most typical boundary for a site consists of the LAN topology and subnet boundaries rather than the OU and domain boundaries.

There are two important reasons to define a site. First, by defining site locations based on IP subnets, you enable a client to access network servers using the most efficient physical route. In the PartsPlus example, it is faster for a client in Toronto to be authenticated by a Toronto global catalog server than for the client to go through Detroit or Mexico City. Second, DC replication is most efficient when the Active Directory has information about which DCs are in which locations.

Within a site, each DC replicates forest, tree, domain, and OU naming structures, configuration naming elements, such as computers and printers, and schema information. One advantage of creating a site is that it sets up redundant paths between DCs so that if one path is down, there is a second path that can be used for replication. This redundancy is in a logical ring format, which means that replication goes from DC to DC around a ring until each DC is replicated. If a DC is down along the main route, then the Active Directory uses site information to send replication information in the opposite direction around the ring. Whenever a new DC is added or an old one removed, the Active Directory reconfigures the ring to make sure there are two replication paths available from each DC.

 The Windows 2000 Server feature that automatically adds or removes DCs is called the Knowledge Consistency Checker (KCC).

When information is replicated within a site, the information is sent from DC to DC uncompressed so there is less demand placed on each DC's CPU. Replication information that is sent between different sites is compressed so that it goes over WAN links more quickly and creates less interference with other WAN communications. Intersite compression is in a ratio of up to 10 to1.

Two different sites are connected via a **site link object**, which is defined to the Active Directory. The schema of a site link object contains information that enables it to determine the cost of using different routes between sites. For example, there may be three network routes between two sites: one 1.2 Gbps ATM link, one 44.736 Mbps telecommunications link, and one 1.544 Mbps telecommunications link. A cost can be assigned to each link so that the Active Directory can determine their relative speeds and which route to use under which circumstances. The schema also contains information to show when one site link object connects to multiple sites, such as might be true for a satellite-based route. Last, there may be information to show when a particular link is available, because some links purchased over telecommunications lines may be available only during working hours, for example.

Two or more site link objects can be joined in a **site link bridge** object so that all member site links can communicate with one another. For example, if Site A is connected to Site B by site link object 1 and Site B is connected to Site C by site link object 2, then both site link objects can be combined by a site link bridge. The site link bridge enables communication between Site A and Site C. Normally, a site link bridge is really an IP router, as shown in Figure 4-12.

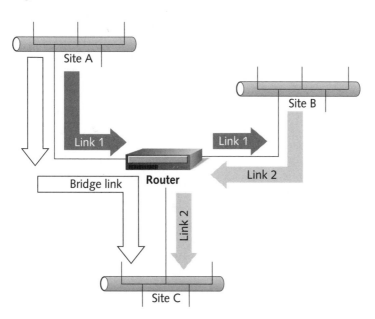

Figure 4-12   Site link bridge

Table 4-5 lists general site creation recommendations.

Table 4-5   Site Creation Dos and Don'ts

Dos	Don'ts
Create sites to reflect interconnected high-speed IP subnets	Create sites for small networks that have no IP subnets
Create sites on medium-sized and large networks to enable fast connectivity for users and for DCs	Create sites for IP links that have less than 128 Kbps of available bandwidth
Create additional sites on medium-sized and large networks when user connectivity and DC replication experiences slow response	Create extra sites to improve network performance without first determining what network congestion factors are causing poor performance
Create sites to enable ring-based DC fault tolerance	
Create one or more sites for a domain that encompasses two or more far-reaching geographic locations	

TIP   If you are new to IP communication, the concept of sites may at first be confusing. As you plan for a site keep in mind two factors. First, a site is simply a grouping of subnets and is really a concept that is independent of OUs, domains, trees, and forests (although one site might contain multiple OUs or domains). Second, the purpose of creating a site is to enable network traffic to go along the most efficient route on a medium-sized or large network. Whereas OUs, domains, trees, and forests are used to manage computer, printer, and user resources, sites are used to speed communication between resources.

Consider a state university's network that might take advantage of sites. The university has three domains, *students.uni.edu*, *faculty.uni.edu*, and *staffadmin.uni.edu*, organized into a single tree. Also, there are three campuses that are in different cities. The domains span each campus location. Thus *students.uni.edu* contains accounts and printers on DCs at all locations, for example. Each domain contains OUs that are appropriate to that domain, for instance *students.uni.edu* has an OU for students at each campus for a total of three OUs all at the same level. The campuses are relatively large with 7000 students, 10,000 students, and 18,000 students, and have networks that are physically divided into subnets. In this situation, you can designate each campus network as a site in the Active Directory, which enables it to find the fastest routes for traffic that is on-campus and for traffic that goes between campuses. For example, when a student logs on to *students.uni.edu*, the Active Directory can help that student find the nearest DC and avoid the chance that the logon authentication is performed over a WAN link at a different campus location. Another advantage is that the DC replication for each domain between sites (over WAN links) can be set to occur less frequently than replication within a site.

ACTIVE DIRECTORY GUIDELINES

The many components available in the Active Directory make its planning a potentially complex process. The following guidelines summarize the most important aspects of the Active Directory planning process covered so far in this chapter. Following them will simplify the process and help you to plan the best setup for your situation:

- Above all, keep the Active Directory as simple as possible and plan its structure *before* you implement it.

- Implement the least number of domains possible, with one domain being the ideal and building from there.

- Implement only one domain on most small networks.

- When you are planning for an organization that is likely to reorganize in the future, use OUs to reflect the organization's structure.

- Create OUs horizontally and not vertically within a domain.

- Create only the number of OUs that are absolutely necessary.

- Do not build an Active Directory with more than 10 levels of OUs (and hopefully no more than one or two levels).

- Use domains for natural security boundaries.

- Implement trees and forests only as necessary.

- Use trees for domains that have a contiguous namespace.

- Use forests for multiple trees that have disjointed namespaces between them.

- Use sites in situations where there are multiple IP subnets and multiple geographic locations, as a means to improve logon and DC replication performance.

SECURITY BASICS

Windows 2000 Server has several levels of security, which include the following:

- Account or interactive logon security
- Object security
- Services security (network authentication)

Account logon security involves making sure that each computer that accesses network servers has authorization through a preestablished account. Object security includes providing a list of which accounts can access a particular object, such as a shared folder or printer, and what type of access is permitted for each account. Network services security is determined by providing access to specific accounts and defining the extent of that access. Each of these options is discussed in the following sections.

Interactive Logon Security

Whenever a user accesses one or more Windows 2000 servers, he or she logs on to an account that is defined on a domain controller (DC) and is part of the Active Directory information. The DC checks to make certain that the user account is already defined and also authenticates the logon by checking the exact account name and password that the user provides from his or her workstation.

 It is possible to set up a Windows 2000 server on a small network to act as a local computer that does not run the Active Directory service. In this case, the Windows 2000 server acts as a simple server that authenticates accounts only on that server. This use of Windows 2000 Server makes the computer act as just another local computer on the network, similar to a Windows 2000 Professional computer, but capable of handling far more accounts. This use of Windows 2000 Server is not recommended unless you have a small network of perhaps 10 to 20 users, and you have minimum security requirements and no connections to other networks.

Windows 2000 Server performs authentication using three approaches.

1. The default authentication is through Kerberos using a password or a **smart card**, a card about the size of a credit card that contains access information and can be plugged into a computer. To use this method, you must set up each Windows 2000 DC to authenticate via Kerberos and each workstation must also be set up as a Kerberos client.

2. Another option is to use Windows NT LAN Manager, which is an earlier method of authentication used by Windows NT servers and their clients. This method is used on a network that contains both Windows 2000 servers and Windows NT servers or when Windows NT server domain authenticates to a domain that has Windows 2000 servers.

3. A third authentication method is **Secure Socket Layer/Transport Layer Security** (**SSL/TLS**), which is used to authenticate a secure Windows 2000 Web server, for example. SSL/TLS uses **certificates** to authenticate a connection; the certificate is an encrypted set of information associated with a workstation, equivalent to a unique digital fingerprint. When a workstation requests access to the Web server, it sends its certificate, and the server responds by sending back a certificate to complete the authentication. To use this kind of authentication, you must first enable the **Extensible Authentication Protocol** (**EAP**) at the Web server.

Object Security

Each object in the Active Directory has a set of **security descriptors** that define how that object may be accessed. For example, a server will have a set of accounts and information about the type of access each account is allowed. Another example is a folder that has security descriptors to show which users can access that folder and what type of access they are allowed. A set of security descriptors is called an **access control list** (**ACL**), and it contains all information about access to a particular object. A shared folder on a server called Payroll with an ACL that specifies only the accounts RBrown, LMason, AGonzales, and MKlein can have full access in an organization of 275 employees, while another folder called Paypolicies has an ACL that includes read-only access for everyone in the organization.

Each ACL for an object typically contains three categories of information:

- The user accounts (or account groups) that can access the object

- The permissions that determine the type of access

- The ownership of the object (the default owner of an object is its creator; ownership can be taken by another user account if that account has sufficient permission)

4

Each user account or group of accounts is assigned a type of access to an object, called a **permission**. There are standard permissions and special permissions. A standard permission is most frequently used and consists of the object permissions that are available by default. The types of permissions available are related to the nature of the object and appropriate security that applies to the object. The typical standard permissions that are available for objects in the Active Directory are as follows:

- *Deny*: No permission to access the object or a restriction on certain types of access

- *Read*: Permission for viewing an object, reading its contents (for folders and files), and determining properties or attributes of the object

- *Write*: Permission to change object properties or the contents of an object (for folders and files)

- *Delete All Child Objects*: Permission to remove an object, for example from an OU or domain

- *Create All Child Objects*: Permission to add an object, such as to an OU or domain

- *Full Control*: Permission to access the object for nearly any purpose, including to take ownership of the object or to change the permissions associated with that object

A special permission is used in situations in which a standard permission must be more finely tuned for a particular kind of access. For example, you may need to give applications developers in the organization Full Control to a folder but want to modify access so that some elements of Full Control are not available, such as the ability to change permissions. Figure 4-13 shows how you can set special permissions for the folder WINNT (see Chapter 9 for information about how to access and configure this dialog box).

CAUTION

When you belong to one user group that has limited permissions, such as Read, and one group that has more permissions, such as Full Control, then your access defaults to the highest level of permissions (Full Control in this example). The exception to the rule is Deny, which supercedes other permissions. For instance, if you belong to a group that has Deny Access to an object, and another group that has Full Control, then you have no access to that object. The exception to the last example is the group with Administrator privileges, because administrators must always have access to manage all server resources.

All objects have an owner who is by default the user account that created the object. The object owner has Full Control permission when the object is first created. An owner cannot transfer ownership to another account, but instead the new owner must take ownership, which means that the new owner must first have the right permission level to take ownership.

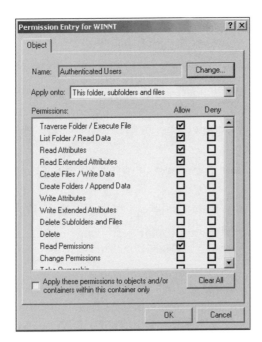

Figure 4-13   Special permissions for a folder

Services Security

Access to services offered by Windows 2000 Server can be controlled through a security feature called network authentication. A Windows 2000 server may offer many different kinds of services to clients, such as DHCP or WINS (see Chapter 3). When you configure one of these services, you can specify which users and groups have read access to enable them to view and use the service (Figure 4-14). Another example is the ability to run services that perform specific tasks on a Windows 2000 Server, which include the logon service, the backup service, and others. These abilities are **rights** and are usually associated with a group of users, such as administrators, backup operators, or all users. The security that is available for a service depends on the type of service and its purpose. When you install a service (see Chapter 6), make sure that you plan in advance who should have access to it and what type of access is needed.

> Only give all users default access to an object or a service when it is installed. In most situations this type of access is inappropriate. You should always check the security, make the necessary adjustments, and test the security before you make an object or service available network-wide following its installation.

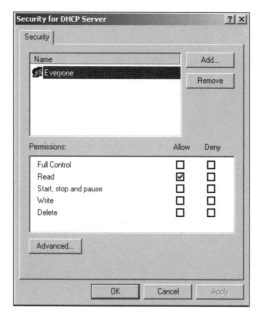

Figure 4-14   DHCP security

USING GROUPS

Windows 2000 Server employs two general types of groups, those used for security and those used for e-mail lists. **Security groups** are groups of users that are created as a way of reducing the amount of work you have to do when administering security. For example, if you are managing an Active Directory in which there are 700 users, it is much easier to divide the users into logical groupings on the basis of the type of security they will need and then assign security to each group. It is much faster to assign security to 10 or 15 groups than to assign security individually to 700 users. This principle still holds true even if you have far fewer users, so that you can spend more of your time on tasks other than setting up security.

Security groups appear in ACLs, but can also be used as e-mail distribution lists, which are lists of users created so that an e-mail message can be sent one time to all users on the list. Figure 4-15 shows the members of the Windows 2000 Server security group called DHCP Administrators, who have access to manage the DHCP server service.

The other type of group is called a **distribution group** and is intended strictly for use as an e-mail distribution list, for example for Microsoft Exchange. Distribution groups do not appear in ACLs.

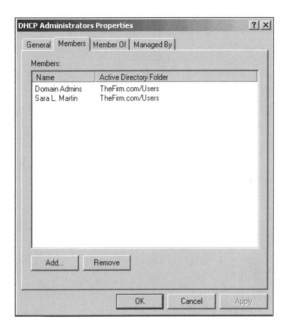

Figure 4-15   DHCP Administrators security group

Group Policies

When sites, domains, OUs, and groups are created, it is possible to establish group policies that apply to those Active Directory elements. For example, in your organization there might be a need to limit access to network resources in a specific OU by limiting what options appear on the desktop of the client workstations, such as eliminating the My Network Places icon in Windows 2000 Professional. Network access by these users might be limited to a menu that automatically appears when they log on to the network. In another situation, you might decide to eliminate a group's access to the Control Panel or you might remove the Run option from the Start button. Group policies are set up by installing the Group Policy snap-in in the Microsoft Management Console (MMC).

Security Templates

In Windows NT 4.0 and earlier, security that applies to groups is set by using several differ-ent tools, such as User Manager for Domains, Event Viewer, My Computer, and others.

Windows 2000 Server manages security policies from one location, the Security Templates snap-in for the MMC (Figure 4-16, in which the MMC setup has previously been saved as the file, security.msc). This snap-in enables you to set up security that governs the following (try Hands-on Projects 4-4 and 4-5):

- Account policies
- Local server or domain policies
- Event log tracking policies
- Group restrictions

- Service access security
- Registry security
- File system security

4

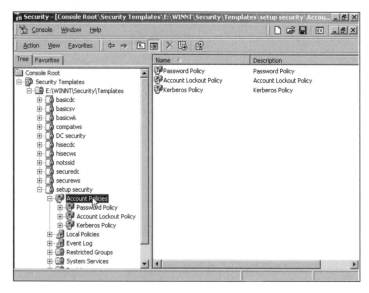

Figure 4-16   Security Templates snap-in

Before you create a security template, develop a plan to match your security needs. Your plan should address the following questions:

- What password restrictions should apply to accounts?
- What security restrictions are needed for folders and files, and how should those restrictions be inherited by subfolders within folders?
- What elements of the Registry should be secured?
- What restrictions should apply to individual server services, such as access to the Event logging service or to printing services?
- Should account activity be tracked through auditing?
- Which accounts should be allowed to log on to the server locally and which should be able to log on through the network?
- Which accounts should be allowed to schedule tasks to automatically run on the server?

When you are ready to create a security template, use these general steps:

1. Make sure there is no default security template that already matches what you want to do.

2. Make sure that the Group Policy and Security Templates snap-ins are installed in the MMC.

3. Create a security template by clicking the main folder under Security Templates in the MMC (such as \WINNT\Security\Templates), Action, and New Template.

4. Enter a name for the template and a description, and then click OK.

5. Double-click the new template in the right pane and configure the appropriate elements, such as System Services.

6. Import your newly created template to an existing group policy by installing the Security Configuration and Analysis snap-in, right-click that snap-in, open a database or create a new one, double-click the template configuration file (.inf f.6) you created (only if you created a new database), right-click the Security Configuration and Analysis snap-in again, and then click Configure Computer Now.

You can change security directly for a specific Active Directory grouping, such as an OU, by modifying the group policy settings in the properties for for that OU. However, it is more effective planning to create a security template for different Active Directory groupings and then import the template. For example, if you have 20 OUs set up in a domain and wanted to use one security policy for 10 OUs and a different one for the other 10 OUs, then you would create two security templates and import the appropriate template for each OU to the MMC Group Policy snap-in.

IP SECURITY POLICIES

Windows 2000 supports the implementation of **IP security** (**IPSec**), which is a set of IP-based secure communications and encryption standards created through the Internet Engineering Task Force (IETF). When an IPSec communication begins between two computers, the computers first exchange certificates to authenticate the receiver and sender. Next, data is encrypted at the NIC of the sending computer as it is formatted into an IP packet which consists of a header containing transmission control information, the actual data, and a footer with error-correction information (see Chapter 3). IPSec can provide security for all TCP/IP-based application and communications protocols, including FTP and HTTP, which are used in Internet transmissions (see Chapter 3). IPSec policies are managed through the IP Security Policy Management snap-in in the MMC. A computer that is configured to use IPSec communication can function in any of three roles:

- *Client (Respond Only):* When Windows 2000 Server is contacted by a client using IPSec, it will respond by using IPSec communication. This mode is also called responder.

- *Server (Request Security)*: When Windows 2000 Server is first contacted or when it initiates a communication, it will use IPSec by default. If the responding client does not support IPSec, Windows 2000 Server will switch to the clear mode, which does not employ IPSec. This role is also called the initiator.

- *Secure Server (Require Security)*: Also called the lockdown role; Windows 2000 Server will only respond using IPSec communication, which means that communication via any account and with any client is secured through strict IPSec enforcement.

4

 TIP When you use the Secure Server setup and also plan to set up Windows 2000 Server for SNMP communication, for example to monitor the network through the Windows 2000 Network Monitoring tool, you should consider omitting SNMP communication from IPSec. You can do this by establishing a filter in the IP Security Policy Management snap-in. The advantage of omitting SNMP communication is that you can still monitor activity from non-IPSec capable computers in order to track network problems.

IPSec security policies can be established through the IP Security Policies snap-in so that specific security standards apply to all computers that log on to a domain in the Active Directory. When you right-click IP Security Policies in the MMC and click Create IP Security Policy, Windows 2000 Server starts the IP Security Policy Wizard (see Figure 4-17) to help guide you through the steps in creating a security policy. A security policy consists of your specifications for what security methods to use for client and server communication, what IP filters to apply to communications, and which domain or domains are affected by the policy.

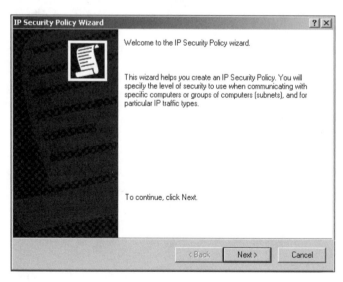

Figure 4-17   IP Security Policy Wizard

CHAPTER SUMMARY

❑ The Active Directory and security are closely related in Windows 2000 server, and the best step you can take before setting up a server is to plan these elements thoroughly. The Active Directory is a set of directory services that enable you to manage a server, multiple servers, and an enterprise network. The most basic component of the Active Directory is an object. Each object is defined through an information set called a schema.

❑ In most cases, you will define one or more domains in the Active Directory, consisting of user accounts, printers, and other network resources. Because domains are difficult to restructure, for management purposes you have the option to divide a domain into smaller containers called organizational units, which can reflect your organization's structure. For large organizations, domains can be organized into trees and multiple trees, can be organized into forests. Keep in mind that an Active Directory can quickly become complex as you populate it with combinations of organizational units, domains, trees, and forests. Often the best rule when implementing the Active Directory is to keep it as simple and manageable as possible.

❑ For organizations that use TCP/IP communication and subnets, the Active Directory offers the ability to configure sites, which are often related to geographic locations or clusters of subnets. Sites enable you to configure physical network communications components for the best performance on a medium-sized to large network, taking advantage of existing subnets.

❑ By grouping objects in containers, such as OUs and domains, you have the ability to control and customize security in Windows 2000. Security can be attached to user accounts and other objects as well as to services. For example, you can require that all users in a domain have a password that is at least eight characters long. Some of the tools that you can use to configure security for Active Directory containers include group policies, security templates, and IPSec.

In the next chapter, you begin to put your advance planning to work as you learn how to install Windows 2000 Server. You find that the installation process is relatively simple because of your preparations through planning.

KEY TERMS

access control list (ACL) — A list of all security descriptors that have been set up for a particular object, such as for a shared folder or a shared printer.

certificate — An encrypted set of information associated with a workstation that is equivalent to a unique digital fingerprint and that is used to authenticate logon to a server, such as a Web server.

common name (CN) — The most basic name of an object in the Active Directory, such as the name of a printer.

contiguous namespace — A namespace in which every child object contains the name of its parent object.

disjointed namespace — A namespace in which the child object name does not resemble the name of its parent object.

distinguished name (DN) — A name in the Active Directory that contains all hierarchical components of an object, such as that object's organizational unit and domain, in addition to the object's common name. The distinguished name is used by an Active Directory client to access a particular object, such as a printer.

distribution group — A list of Windows 2000 Server users that enables one e-mail message to be sent to all users on the list. A distribution group is not used for security and thus cannot appear in an ACL.

domain — A grouping of resource objects, for example, servers and user accounts, that is one element of the Active Directory in Windows 2000 Server. A domain usually is a higher-level representation of how a business, government, or school is organized, for example reflecting a geographical site or major division of that organization.

domain controller (DC) — A Windows 2000 server that contains a full copy of the Active Directory information, that is used to add a new object to the Active Directory, and that replicates all changes made to it so those changes are updated on every DC in the same domain.

Extensible Authentication Protocol (EAP) — A protocol used to provide a range of security services for different manufacturer's security devices, such as smart cards. EAP is used with other remote access protocols, for example for security through the Internet.

forest — A grouping of trees that each have contiguous namespaces within their own domain structure, but that have disjointed namespaces between trees. The trees and their domains use the same schema and global catalog.

global catalog — A grand repository for all objects and the most frequently used attributes for each object in all domains. Each tree has one global catalog.

globally unique identifier (GUID) — A unique number, up to 16 characters long, that is associated with an Active Directory object.

IP security (IPSec) — A set of IP-based secure communications and encryption standards created through the Internet Engineering Task Force (IETF).

Kerberos transitive trust relationship — A set of two-way trusts between two or more domains in which Kerberos security is used.

multimaster replication — In Windows 2000 Server, there can be multiple servers, called DCs that store the Active Directory and replicate it to each other. Because each DC acts as a master, replication does not stop when one is down, and updates to the Active Directory continue, for example creating a new account.

name resolution — A process used to translate a computer's domain name into the object that it represents, such as to a dotted decimal address associated with a computer, and vice versa.

namespace — A logical area on a network that contains directory services and named objects, and that has the ability to perform name resolution.

object — A network resource, such as a server or a user account, which has distinct attributes or properties, which is usually defined to a domain, and which exists in the Windows 2000 Active Directory.

organizational unit (OU) — A grouping of objects, usually within a domain, that provides a means to establish specific policies for governing those objects and that enables object management to be delegated.

permission — In Windows 2000, privilege to access an object, such as to view the object or to change it.

relative distinguished name (RDN) — An object name in the Active Directory that has two or more related components, such as the RDN of a user account name that consists of User and the first and last name of the actual user.

right — In Windows 2000, access privileges for high-level activities such as logging on to a server from the network, shutting down a server, and logging on locally.

schema — Elements used in the definition of each object contained in the Active Directory, including the object class and its attributes.

Secure Sockets Layer/Transport Layer Security (SSL/TLS) — An authentication method that uses certificates to verify users' right to access a remote server, such as a Web server.

security descriptor — An individual security property associated with a Windows 2000 Server object, for example to enable the account MGardner (the security descriptor) to access the folder, Databases.

security group — A group of Windows 2000 Server users that assign access privileges to objects and services. Security groups appear in ACLs.

separate forest — An Active Directory model that links two or more forests in a partnership; however, the forests cannot have Kerberos transitive trusts or use the same schema.

single forest — An Active Directory model in which there is only one forest, with interconnected trees and domains that use the same schema and global catalog.

site — An option in the Active Directory to interconnect IP subnets so that the server can determine the fastest route to connect clients for authentication and to connect DCs for replication of the Active Directory. Site information also enables the Active Directory to create redundant routes for DC replication.

site link bridge — An Active Directory object that combines individual site link objects to create faster routes, when there are three or more site links.

site link object — An object created in the Active Directory to indicate one or more physical links between two different sites.

smart card — A security device that contains information such as access keys, passwords, and a personal identification number (PIN). The smart card is about the size of a credit card and can be plugged into a computer.

transitive trust — A trust relationship between two or more domains in a tree in which each domain has access to objects in the others.

tree — Related domains that use a contiguous namespace, share the same schema, and have two-way, transitive trust relationships.

trusted domain — A domain that has been granted security access to resources in another domain.

trusting domain — A domain that allows another domain security access to its resources and objects, such as servers.

two-way trust — A domain relationship in which both domains are trusted and trusting, enabling one to have access to objects in the other.

user principle name (UPN) — A name that combines an account name with the domain name, such as *RobBrown@tracksport.org*, for easy identification, such as in e-mail.

REVIEW QUESTIONS

4

1. You are in a meeting to plan the Active Directory at a college, and a colleague suggests that your organization create a top-level OU for all academic departments and then sequentially create one OU under the next for each of the 22 academic departments so that the OUs are 23 layers deep. Which of the following best matches your response?

   a. You endorse the plan.

   b. You recommend using 23 trees instead of OUs.

   c. You recommend creating the top-level department's OU and then creating the other 22 OUs directly under it so that the OUs are only two layers deep.

   d. You endorse the plan, but add that an OU should be created for each faculty member.

2. Members of the business division in your organization have the ability to view the contents of files in a shared server folder called Vendors and to create new files. This is an example of a

   a. permission.

   b. right.

   c. trust.

   d. transitive trust.

3. Your organization has a root domain called *consult.com* and other child domains called *web.cs.com* and *products.conslt.com*. This is an example of a

   a. disjointed namespace.

   b. contiguous namespace.

   c. commercial namespace.

   d. nonreciprocal namespace.

4. Which of the following would most likely be required in the schema for a user account?

   a. username

   b. user's full name

   c. user's room number or address

   d. all of the above

   e. only a and b

   f. only b and c

5. When an IPSec communication begins, it starts by

   a. encrypting data.

   b. checking the end-to-end network route for intruders.

   c. sending certificates.

   d. verifying the client's operating system license.

6. When a domain joins a tree,

   a. it is trusted but not trusting to other domains in the tree.

   b. it immediately forms a transitive trust relationship with other domains in the tree.

   c. it has a trust relationship only with the OUs under it.

   d. it gains Full Control permission of all objects in the other domains within that tree.

7. You are planning to migrate objects in a Windows NT 4.0 Server domain to a new set of Windows 2000 servers and then retire Windows NT 4.0. How might you prepare for the migration?

   a. First, create a tree in the Windows 2000 Active Directory.

   b. Create OUs in the Windows 2000 Active Directory, and migrate the Windows NT domain to each OU.

   c. Designate a distribution group in the Windows 2000 Active Directory to first test the migration.

   d. Create an equivalent domain in the Windows 2000 Active Directory, and migrate the Windows NT domain to the Windows 2000 domain.

8. What is the minimum number of domain controllers (DCs) that must exist in a domain?

   a. 1

   b. 2

   c. 3

   d. one for each OU

9. A global catalog server is also a

   a. router.

   b. WAN link.

   c. domain controller.

   d. DNS server.

10. Your boss has won a NASA contract to develop a new satellite guidance system that must be kept top-secret. Which of the following IP security measures would you recommend in planning for the new server purchased for this project?

    a. Client (Respond Only)

    b. Secure Server (Require Security)

    c. Server (Request Security)

    d. Certificate (Responder Security)

11. A group of 25 physicians is implementing a new network that uses two Windows 2000 servers and that will have Internet access. Besides the physicians, there is 1 bookkeeper, a business manager, 5 billing clerks, 28 nurses, and 5 nurse practitioners. Each will have a connection to the network. How many domains are needed when the Active Directory is configured?

    a. 1

    b. 2, one for access within the building, and one for physicians who dial in remotely from home

    c. 3, one for the physicians, one for the nurse practitioners and nurses, and one for the remaining staff

    d. 4, one for the physicians, one for the nurse practitioners, one for the nurses, and one for the remaining staff

12. You have just created a new security template. What is the last step you should perform in the process?

    a. Turn off sharing violation so that the template does not interfere with other templates that have similar names.

    b. Import the template to a group policy.

    c. Delete the existing group policy for the domain so that the template can go into effect.

    d. Remove the Security Templates snap-in from the MMC.

13. In a forest, all trees

    a. use the same global catalog.

    b. use the same schema.

    c. use a disjointed namespace between trees.

    d. all of the above

    e. only a and c

    f. only b and c

14. A set of security descriptors associated with an object compose that object's

    a. unique ID.

    b. access control list.

    c. schema.

    d. security template.

15. The employees in the research group of your organization have decided to use the same desktop setup so that it is easy to go from one computer to another in the labs. Which tool enables you to provide this service for them?

    a. User Manager

    b. Computer Manager

    c. Group Policy snap-in

    d. Security Configuration snap-in

4

16. Which of the following are objects in the Active Directory?

    a. shared printers

    b. domains

    c. shared folders

    d. all of the above

    e. only a and c

    f. only a and b

17. Your community college has a main campus and two large branch locations in a city of over 2 million persons. The main campus and branch locations consist of routed networks that have multiple subnets. What Active Directory component could make DC replication over the LAN and WAN links most efficient?

    a. setting up sites

    b. setting up domains

    c. setting up OUs

    d. setting up trees

18. When a DNS server converts a computer name to a dotted decimal address, this is called

    a. name recognition.

    b. name resolution.

    c. pinging.

    d. piping.

19. Which OU structure in the Active Directory is likely to result in the most CPU resource use?

    a. OUs nested 5 layers deep

    b. OUs nested 15 layers deep

    c. 5 OUs on the same level

    d. 15 OUs on the same level

20. A site link bridge is most likely to be a(n)

    a. Active Directory in an untrusted domain.

    b. telecommunications link.

    c. router.

    d. dial-up access line.

21. Your organization has domains in Canada, France, and Norway, wants to unite these domains in one container, but also wants to set up each domain to use the language native in its country. What Active Directory container would be appropriate in this situation?

    a. a site

    b. a forest

    c. a parent domain

    d. a tree

22. By default an object is owned by

    a. the account that created it.

    b. the server administrator.

    c. the domain in which it was created.

    d. the OU in which it was created.

23. You have just installed Windows 2000 Server and created accounts. By default, the security for access to these accounts is via

    a. LAN Manager.

    b. Secure Socket Layer/Transport Layer Security (SSL/TLS).

    c. Kerberos.

    d. all of the above

    e. only a and c

    f. only a and b

24. What Active Directory model links two forests?

    a. joined forests

    b. separate forests

    c. single forests

    d. forests cannot be linked in any way

25. Network authentication in Windows 2000 Server as a security technique involves

    a. authorization via an account.

    b. authorization via a smart card.

    c. authorization via a one-way trust.

    d. all of the above

    e. only a and b

    f. only a and c

HANDS-ON PROJECTS

Project 4-1

In this hands-on activity, you practice installing the Active Directory to convert a standalone computer to a domain controller.

To install the Active Directory:

1. Log on to Windows 2000 Server as Administrator.

2. Click **Start**, point to **Programs**, point to **Administrative Tools**, and then click **Configure Your Server**.

3. Click **Active Directory** in the left window pane.

4. Scroll down in the right window pane and then click **Start the Active Directory Wizard**.

5. Click **Next** in the Active Directory Installation Wizard.

6. Click **Domain controller for a new domain** (notice that if this were an additional domain controller in an existing domain, you could also set it up through the Active Directory Installation Wizard by using the other option in this dialog box). Click **Next**.

7. Click **Create a new domain tree**. Click **Next**.

8. Click **Create a new forest of domain trees**. Click **Next**.

9. Enter a practice domain name, such as **mycompany.com**, or enter a name provided by your instructor. Click **Next** (at this point the wizard will take a few moments to check that a domain does not already exist and to set up the domain).

10. Leave MYCOMPANY (or the name you entered in Step 9, if it is different) as the domain NetBIOS name (for users of other versions of Windows) and click **Next**.

11. Leave C:\WINNT\NTDS as the database location and C:\WINNT\NTDS as the log location (your system may use a different drive location by default, depending on the location of the \WINNT folder). Click **Next**.

12. Leave the shared system volume location as the default, C:\WINNT\SYSVOL (again the drive will depend on the location of the \WINNT folder). Notice that the wizard warns that the Sysvol folder must be on a volume formatted with NTFS version 5. Click **Next**. (At this point, if a DNS server is not already installed or available on the network, the wizard provides an option to install it as part of the setup process.)

13. The Permissions dialog box gives you the option to use permissions compatible with pre-Windows 2000 servers, such as Windows NT Server 4.0—or to use permissions compatible only with Windows 2000 servers. Click **Permissions compatible with pre-Windows 2000 servers** for this project. (Note that this is also a good choice if there are Web servers in the domain, because they may interact with non-Windows 2000 servers.) Click **Next**.

14. Enter an Administrator password and confirm it for use in the Directory Services Restore Mode. Click **Next**.

15. Review in the summary scroll box the selections you have made and note them in your lab journal or in a word-processed document. Is there an option to retrace your steps in case you want to change a parameter? Click **Next** to proceed. (If you do not have permission from your instructor to install the Active Directory, click Cancel at this point to exit setup.)

16. Wait a few minutes as the wizard configures the Active Directory. Notice the line near the bottom of the dialog box that shows each configuration activity.

17. Click **Finish**.

18. Make sure you have saved any open work, and then click **Restart Now**.

Project 4-2

In this assignment, you view the tool used to manage domains and trust relationships.

To view the domain management tool:

1. Click **Start**, point to **Programs**, and point to **Administrative Tools**.

2. Click **Active Directory Domains and Trusts**.

3. In the left window pane, right-click the domain you created in the last project (or an existing domain).

4. Click **Properties**.

5. Click each of the **General**, **Trusts**, and **Managed By** tabs to view their contents. Make notes about their contents in your lab journal or in a word-processed document.

6. Click **Cancel**.

7. Close the Active Directory Domains and Trusts manager.

Project 4-3

In this assignment, you view the tool used to manage Active Directory users and computers.

To view the user and computer management tool:

1. Click **Start**, point to **Programs**, and point to **Administrative Tools**.

2. Click **Active Directory Users and Computers**.

3. In the left window pane, right-click the domain you created (or an existing domain).

4. Click **Properties**.

5. Click each of the **General**, **Managed By**, and **Group Policy** tabs to view their contents. Make notes about their contents in your lab journal or in a word-processed document.

6. On the Group Policy tab, click the **Default Domain Policy**, and then click **Properties**.

7. Click the **Security** tab.

8. Click each of the groups listed in the Name box and watch to see what permissions are granted to each (record your observations).

9. How can you add another group to the list?

10. Click **Cancel** in the Default Domain Policies Properties dialog box.

11. Click **Cancel** in the domain properties dialog box.

12. Close the Active Directory Users and Computers management tool for the domain.

Project 4-4

In this hands-on activity you install the Security Templates snap-in and find out where to view the security set up in the default template for services.

To install the Security Template:

1. Click **Start** and **Run**.

2. Click the **Browse** button to find the MMC at \WINNT\system32\mmc.exe.

3. Once you find mmc.exe, double-click it and click **OK** to start it in the Run dialog box. Maximize the MMC windows, if necessary.

4. Click the **Console** menu and then click **Add/Remove Snap-in**.

5. Click **Add** in the Add/Remove Snap-in dialog box.

6. Use the scroll bar to find **Security Templates**, click this option, and then click **Add**.

7. Click **Close**, and then click **OK**.

To view the default security for services:

1. Double-click **Security Templates** in the left pane of the MMC and then double-click C:\WINNT\Security\Templates (your drive and directory location may be different).

2. Double-click the **setup security** template (in the left or right pane) and then click **System Services** under it.

3. Scroll through the services listed and make a note of 5 or 10 services.

4. Double-click the **Computer Browser** service and notice which startup mode it uses.

5. Click the **Edit Security** button.

6. Notice which groups have access to this service.

7. What permissions are given to these groups?

8. Record your observations in your lab journal or in a word-processed document.

9. Click **Cancel** and click **Cancel** again.

10. Leave the MMC open for the next project.

Project 4-5

In this project, you view the default account policies in Windows 2000 Server.

To view the default account policies:

1. Go back to the MMC that you left open in Hands-on Project 4-4.

2. Find the setup security template in the left pane and click **Account Policies** under it.

3. Double-click **Password Policy** in the right window pane.

4. What attributes are available for the password policy and how are they set? Record this information in your lab journal or in a word-processed document.

5. Double-click **Maximum Password Age**.

6. Notice that you can change the expiration period for passwords in the template (however this only changes the template, which would have to be imported again to a group policy).

7. Click **Cancel**.

8. Close the MMC (if you are asked whether to save the console settings, click No).

CASE PROJECT

Aspen Consulting Project: Planning the Active Directory and Security

Moose Jaw Outfitters, the company with which you worked in the last chapter, is contacting you again to help them plan the Active Directory and security for their networks in Winnipeg, Canada and St. Cloud, Minnesota. The Winnipeg site has a medium sized-network of 170 users, and 5 subnets using TCP/IP. That site also has Internet connectivity and maintains a Web server. Both sites have Customer Service, Business, Inventory, and IT Department members. The Winnipeg site houses most of the management team, but St. Cloud has a vice president in charge of that location, an operations manager, and supervisors for the Customer Service, Business, Inventory, and IT groups at that location. Winnipeg also has a Marketing Department.

1. The IT Department is very inexperienced with the Active Directory. Create a brief presentation for them about the Active Directory, including its purpose, Active Directory elements, how it is backed up, and the information contained in the Active Directory.

2. Prepare a list of questions for the company that would help you in planning their Active Directory implementation.

3. Before you have a chance to complete your research, the company asks for your preliminary evaluation of how the Active Directory might be implemented. On the basis of what you already know about this company, explain how you would use the following Active Directory elements and why:

   - OUs

   - Domains

   - Trees

   - Forests

   - Sites

4. Where would you place DCs and global catalog servers in this implementation?

5. Create a presentation of the Windows 2000 Security options that will be useful for Moose Jaw Outfitters.

6. Explain for the IT Department how IPSec might be an advantage for the company as a way to secure communications in sensitive areas, such as for the Business and Marketing Departments.

7. What type of security do you recommend for the Web server? Why?

OPTIONAL CASE PROJECTS FOR TEAMS

Team Case One

The consultants at your company are interested in how the Windows 2000 Active Directory compares to directory services in Windows NT 4.0 Server. Create a team to research the similarities and differences and present your findings.

Team Case Two

The consultants are also interested in the emerging Kerberos developments and how they can be of benefit to Windows 2000 Server users. Form a team to research Kerberos to explain how it works, its benefits, and which new Kerberos implementations are emerging.

5

SERVER INSTALLATION

After reading this chapter and completing the exercises you will be able to:

♦ Make installation, hardware, and site-specific preparations to install Windows 2000 Server

♦ Install Windows 2000 Server using different methods, including from a CD-ROM, from the installation disks, over a network, unattended and from another operating system

♦ Go through a Windows 2000 server installation step by step, and test the installation

♦ Upgrade a Windows NT server and domain

♦ Create an emergency repair disk

♦ Install a service pack

♦ Troubleshoot installation problems and uninstall Windows 2000 Server

Windows 2000 Server is designed to install easily, as long as you have made the advance preparations described in the planning chapters of this book. Planning the file system, hardware implementation, network protocols, and Active Directory has a large payoff when you install Windows 2000 Server. To complement your advance planning, the installation follows a logical step-by-step process using a wizard to guide you from screen to screen. In most places, if you need to retrace one or more steps, there is an option to go back. Features of the installation wizard include automatic detection of hardware, drivers for a wide range of equipment, recommendations about what services to install, and the ability to customize the installation as needed.

In this chapter, you go through the advance preparations that apply directly to the installation process, including driver preparations, selecting a file system, selecting a protocol, partitioning disk storage, and other preparations. You learn about different installation approaches, for example over the network, from a CD-ROM, and using a floppy boot disk. You also install networking and optional server service software.

INSTALLATION PREPARATIONS

As is true for any important undertaking, the Windows 2000 Server installation goes most successfully if you have made a few preparations. For example, the installation requires the following:

- Information about what hardware components are installed

- A determination of which file system to use

- Creation of an Administrator account

- The name of the server

- An installed NIC

- A determination of which protocols to install

Before you begin the installation, review the preparations in the sections that follow that affect your circumstances and consider recording preparation information and having it at your side for the installation.

SERVER HARDWARE COMPONENTS

The most important step that you can take in preparing the hardware for installation is to carefully select the server components for your organization's needs and choose components that are on Microsoft's hardware compatibility list (HCL; see Chapter 2). Also, make sure your prospective server meets or exceeds the hardware system requirements provided in Chapter 2. After your hardware arrives, compile a list of hardware components such as computer type, monitor and adapter, SCSI adapters, keyboard type, hard disk drive capacity, CD-ROM drive and adapter, tape drive and adapter, and NIC information. Table 5-1 is an example of how you might prepare this information to have it available during the installation.

Table 5-1   Server Hardware Component Information Form

Hardware Component	Description
CPU type (Pentium, Pentium II, Pentium III, SMP, Xeon)	
Type of buses (ISA, PCI)	
Amount of RAM	
Hard disk and adapter type (manufacturer and model information)	
Hard disk capacity	
CD-ROM drive and adapter type (manufacturer and model information)	

Table 5-1 Server Hardware Component Information Form (continued)

Hardware Component	Description
Mouse or pointing device	
Monitor and monitor adapter (manufacturer and model information)	
Keyboard type	
Floppy drive type	
Tape drive and adapter (manufacturer and model information)	
NIC (manufacturer, model, specifications)	

In addition to making a hardware list, check and record the **basic input/output system (BIOS)** configuration settings on the computer. The BIOS is a program on a read-only or flash memory chip that establishes basic communication with components such as the monitor and disk drives. The BIOS setup is accessed differently on each computer, for example by pressing F1, Delete, or some other key combination when the computer is booted. Most BIOS setup menus are character-based screens holding information about the BIOS version and manufacturer, hardware components, which drive to boot from first, drive statistics such as the size and number of cylinders per disk, floppy drive type, and so on. The main reason to check the BIOS setup prior to installing Windows 2000 is to check the boot drive order, because the BIOS setup program usually has an option to specify the order. This is the order in which the computer checks drives for an operating system boot sector. Most server administrators have the BIOS check drives in the following order: floppy drive, hard drive, and CD-ROM drive. If the floppy drives are empty, the computer boots from a hard drive, and if there is no hard drive, it boots from a CD-ROM drive. If you use the installation setup floppy disks and CD-ROM to install Windows 2000, then set the BIOS to boot first from the floppy. If you plan to install Windows 2000 Server directly from CD-ROM (if your computer supports a CD-ROM boot), change the order to boot from the CD-ROM drive first.

Also, it is possible for a computer to lose its setup information due to a defective battery or some other system problem. You can quickly restore the setup information if you have a record of the settings. Figure 5-1 is an example BIOS setup screen. Notice that the First Boot Device, "Removable Devices" on this particular screen, refers to the floppy drive, and the boot order is floppy drive, hard drive, CD-ROM drive, and network boot.

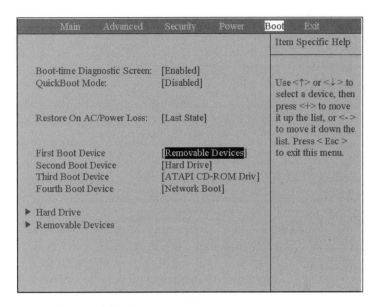

Figure 5-1   BIOS setup screen

The key combination needed to start the BIOS setup is often displayed when the computer first boots up. After the installation is complete, make sure the boot drive order is set for floppy, hard, and CD-ROM drive, which provides more alternatives for using diagnostic tools later.

Another hardware preparation task is to make sure you have the most up-to-date drivers for hardware such as SCSI adapters, RAID drives, the NIC, and CD-ROM drives. The drivers usually are included on a floppy disk or CD-ROM that accompanies the hardware. If the drivers are not with the hardware, contact the manufacturer or obtain the drivers from a Web page. Place driver files on a floppy disk for easiest use during installation or obtain a CD-ROM from the hardware vendor. Microsoft includes many drivers on the Windows 2000 Server CD-ROM, but drivers for some hardware are not included or may not be the most current.

 Even when these drivers are included on the Windows 2000 Server CD-ROM, it is prudent to obtain the latest drivers from the hardware manufacturers and use them during the installation or install them later (see Chapter 6) so that your server is working at its optimum when you let users on.

If you are installing on an SMP computer, obtain the most recent copy of the **hardware abstraction layer** (**HAL**) driver from the manufacturer. The HAL is a set of program routines used to control a specific hardware component from within the operating system kernel. Special HAL drivers may be needed to install Windows 2000 Server on a multiprocessor SMP computer.

CAUTION
If you have a problem installing Windows 2000 Server after carefully selecting and preparing the server computer, it most likely will be related to a missing or out-of-date driver. Obtaining current drivers before you start the installation enables you to address this problem on the spot.

5

MAKING DECISIONS BEFORE STARTING

There are several decisions you need to make before starting the installation. If you wait to make the decisions until you are doing the installation, you may have to undo your choices later. The decisions you make in advance will save you time and make the installation go faster. Also, some decisions, such as the name of the server, may require input from a supervisor or management committee. The decisions you need to consider are the following:

- How to partition the disk
- What file system(s) to use
- What the server name will be
- What the password for the Administrator account will be
- What protocol(s) will be selected
- What licensing method will be used
- If the server will be a DC and what the domain name will be (or what the name is of an existing domain or workgroup the server will join)

Disk Partition Selection

You have the option to partition the server hard disks for Windows 2000 Server only or for a combination of operating systems, such as MS-DOS and Windows 2000. **Partitioning** is a process in which a hard disk section or a complete hard disk is set up for use by an operating system. A disk can be formatted after it is partitioned. **Formatting** is an operation that divides a disk into small sections called tracks and sectors for the storage of files.

When you install Windows 2000, you can make decisions about how to partition the disk storage. Depending on what partitions exist already, you can:

- Use an existing partition
- Delete an existing partition and create a new one
- Create a new partition, if one does not exist

If you create a partition, you will need to specify its size to the setup program. Plan to make the partition for the system files no smaller than 685 MB for an Intel-based computer, and keep in mind that Microsoft recommends 2 GB as the minimum size.

Some server administrators like to create a **dual-boot system**, partitioning a few megabytes of disk space for MS-DOS (FAT). The reason for having an MS-DOS partition is to provide a way to boot the server and run diagnostic and repair utilities in case one or more Windows 2000 boot files are damaged due to a power problem or some other difficulty.

 A Windows 2000 Server installation allows you to leave another operating system on the server to create a dual-boot system. Compatible operating systems are MS-DOS, Windows 3.x, Windows 95, and Windows 98. You can run only one operating system at a time. Also, FAT16 and FAT32 operating systems, such as MS-DOS and Windows 98, cannot view NTFS-formatted files without installing a special third-party utility for this purpose. In most cases, you will allocate only a few megabytes for FAT16 or FAT32, just enough for the operating system and to perform minimum functions.

If you select to partition for FAT16/FAT32 and NTFS, plan to partition the FAT portion before starting the Windows 2000 installation. Use the MS-DOS FDISK utility to partition a FAT area and then use the MS-DOS FORMAT command to format the partition. Size the partition so that it will be large enough to hold the utility programs you need plus the MS-DOS or Windows 95/98 operating system files.

On a dual-boot system, the Windows 2000 boot loader is placed by the setup program on the system partition of the computer, such as drive C. The boot loader recognizes that there are two or more operating systems on that computer. When you boot, it displays a character-based screen that enables you to select which operating system you want to start. For example, if you have a dual-boot system using Windows 2000 Server and MS-DOS, then the menu on the screen shows both options.

 Windows 2000 Server has a flexible disk management tool you can use after the system is installed. During installation, partition only what you need to for the Windows 2000 operating system files (and for a dual-boot system, if you use this alternative). You can use the Disk Management snap-in for the MMC to fully customize disk storage after Windows 2000 is installed.

The contents of the Windows 2000 boot loader menu are specified in the Boot.ini text file (see Figure 5-2), which is located in the root folder on the disk used to boot the computer, such as Drive C. The file is marked as read-only and may be hidden if Windows Explorer or My Computer is not set to view operating system files (change this property using the Tools menu, Folder Options, and View tab). To remove an operating system from the boot loader or edit its entry in the menu, you can edit Boot.ini manually, using Notepad or WordPad. Before you edit the file, remove its read-only designation (right-click the file, click Properties, and uncheck Read-only on the General tab). The file contains two sections: [boot loader] and [operating systems]. The [boot loader] section specifies a timeout value in seconds for selecting an operating system; the default operating system is booted if a selection is not made before the timeout value is reached. The [operating systems] section lists the operating systems that can be started, such as Windows 2000 Server and Windows 98.

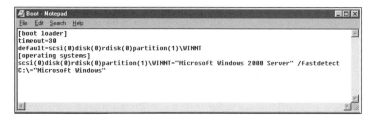

Figure 5-2 Boot.ini file

The operating system location for Windows 2000 Server is specified in terms of the Advanced RISC Computing (ARC) pathname. In Figure 5-2, the scsi() value shows that a SCSI drive (with BIOS disabled) is installed; the value inside the parentheses is determined by the SCSI driver. On a SCSI disk, the disk() value is the ID of the disk in the chain of devices connected to the SCSI adapter (counting from 0). The rdisk() value is usually for SCSI disks. Partition() is the number of the partition, which is 1 to 4 (counting from 1). If the ARC path starts with multi() instead of scsi(), this shows that a non-SCSI drive is installed (or a SCSI drive with BIOS enabled), which always has the value 0. The disk() value also is always 0 for non-SCSI drives, but reflects the ID for a SCSI drive with the BIOS enabled. For non-SCSI disks, the rdisk() value is always 0 or 1 (counting from 0) for single-channel controllers, which can have up to two disks; or it can be 0 to 3 for dual-channel controllers, which can have up to four disks attached. For example, the line:

```
multi(0)disk(0)rdisk(1)partition(1)\WINNT
```

would mean that the operating system is in folder \WINNT on a non-SCSI disk, multi(0)disk(0); on the second disk in the channel path, rdisk(1); and on the first partition of that disk, partition(1). The line:

```
scsi(1)disk(2)rdisk(0)partition(1)\WINNT
```

would mean that the operating system is in folder \WINNT on a SCSI disk designated as 1 by its driver, scsi(1); on the third disk in the SCSI chain, disk(2) (counting from 0); and on the first partition, partition(1) (counting from 1).

Windows 2000 Server File Systems

In Chapter 1 you learned the differences between the FAT16, FAT32, and NTFS file systems. In nearly all installations, it is recommended that you install the more robust NTFS because it is meant for networking. NTFS offers the best security, performance, and file handling for network users. This is particularly true if you anticipate that the server will need to handle large files, such as databases. NTFS also has features such as encryption and file compression, which are not included with FAT16 or FAT32.

 TIP If a partition is set up for FAT and is 2 GB or smaller, Windows 2000 will format it as FAT16, and if it is over 2 GB, Windows 2000 will format it as FAT32.

Server Name

Because the server name affects everyone who uses the server, consider soliciting input from a supervisor or management team. This helps ensure their support of the project, and it ensures that an appropriate name is selected. The server name is seen in Network Neighborhood and My Network Places on Windows 95/98 and Windows 2000, and in other network utilities. There are some general guidelines to consider when selecting a name:

- Use a name that is relatively short so it is easy to type.

- Make the name descriptive of the server's function or reflective of the organization that uses it.

- Select a name that is easy for everyone to remember and use.

- Make sure the name is not used already by another network computer.

If there are several servers on a network, develop a naming scheme, such as one that identifies servers by department, function, or location. For example, if one server is used by the accounting department, one by marketing, and another for research, you might name them ACCOUNT, MARKET, and RESEARCH. This is easier for users than if you name them SERVER1, SERVER2, and SERVER3. In a school with lab servers in the library, student union, and fine arts building, you might name them LIBRARY, UNION, and ARTS. These types of naming schemes are important to network administrators as well as to users. They make it easier to identify and manage servers on a network that may have 10, 20, or more servers.

Administrator Account Password

At the time of installation, Windows 2000 Server creates a master account called the Administrator account. This account has access to all areas of the server, including security administration, file administration, and control of user accounts. The Administrator account also has permission to take ownership of any server resource. Entry into the Administrator account is controlled by a password that is established at the time the server is created. The password can be changed later, but it saves time to have a password ready before starting the installation. Select a password that is difficult to guess and avoid using information that can be identified with you, such as your nickname, favorite car, favorite food, or the name of a family member. A long password, for example 10 characters or more, is appropriate for this sensitive account. Windows 2000 Server accepts passwords up to 14 characters, and passwords are case-sensitive. Make sure you remember the password, because you will need it to log on to the Administrator account as soon as the operating system is installed.

 Microsoft recommends that all users have a "strong password," which has the following characteristics: (1) is over seven characters long, (2) has a combination of letters, numbers, and symbols, and (3) includes at least one symbol in characters 2 through 6.

Protocol Selection

As you learned in Chapter 3, you need to select a protocol to use for communicating on the network. NetBEUI is appropriate for small networks of 20 or 30 users that do not have routing or Internet connectivity. In most cases, plan to use TCP/IP, not NetBEUI. If the server will be used as a gateway to NetWare, you need to install Client Service for NetWare (CSNW) and NWLink for communication. Also, you will need to install Gateway Service for NetWare (GSNW) to set up and manage the gateway.

GSNW can be set up in Windows 2000 Server to link to any NetWare version, but if the corresponding NetWare server is version 5.x and uses TCP/IP, then the NetWare administrator will need to set up the IPX/SPX gateway software in NetWare.

Fortunately you do not need to make all of these decisions from the start. You can configure additional protocols after the server is set up. If you use the default protocol setup, Windows 2000 Server assumes that there is a DHCP server, which means you do not have to provide configuration information for TCP/IP. However, if you customize the TCP/IP setup, you will need an IP dotted decimal address for the server and a subnet mask. Obtain this from a network administrator. If you are the network administrator, you may keep a database that shows the next available address. If you are just starting out, contact a network professional or an Internet service provider for more information.

Some network administrators install Windows 2000 Server using the default TCP/IP setup with DCHP for convenience. Just after the installation, they disable DHCP and manually configure TCP/IP with permanent address information. By providing permanent information, they ensure that users can always access the server at the same address.

Licensing Method

Windows 2000 offers two licensing methods: per server and per seat. In **per server licensing**, each server is granted a limited number of **client access licenses** (**CALs**), which specify the number of clients that can be logged on at the same time. **Per seat licensing** involves purchasing a separate license for each client that will access the server. In larger settings, such as a company or university, where there are many servers, it may be more cost-effective to purchase a license for each workstation. This way, the licensed workstation is billed only for access to those servers where it has security authorization. However, in most smaller office settings where there is only one server, a server license for a set number of workstations makes more sense. By default, Windows 2000 Server usually includes five per server or per seat licenses out of the box.

Network Access

When you install Windows 2000 Server, you can install it to be a new workgroup server, to join an existing workgroup, or to join an existing domain. As you learned in Chapter 1, you can use peer-to-peer or server-based networking. In the peer-to-peer network model, you designate a new workgroup via the server or you designate that the server will join an existing workgroup. In this type of installation, Windows 2000 Server is a **standalone server**. You might use this selection on a very small network or when you are bringing Windows 2000 Server into an existing Windows NT Server 4.0 network in a context where it will not act as a domain controller (DC) and where you are not ready to implement the Active Directory. Another situation in which you would set up a standalone server is when there is no existing domain and you want to promote the server to be the first DC by installing the Active Directory services after the server is installed (see Chapter 4).

In the server-based model, you designate that the server will join an existing domain. The server can assume two roles in an existing domain: DC or member server. A **member server** belongs to a domain, but does not contain a copy of the Active Directory, does not replicate the Active Directory, and does not authenticate logons. A typical use of a member server is in a client/server operation where one server is used strictly to store the databases. The database server does not need to handle logon checking because the information it houses is accessed indirectly through software applications on a DC. A member server could also be dedicated to handling print, CD-ROM, or fax services. If you choose to join a domain as a DC or member server, make sure you have the domain name, a DC and DNS server connected to the network, and an account already created in the domain for the new server.

INSTALLATION OPTIONS

There are several ways to install Windows 2000 Server. The method you choose depends on the resources at your computer. For example, if the computer is not equipped with a CD-ROM drive, you can perform an installation over a network. No matter what method you select, you must have software licenses for the server and the number of users who will access the server. The primary installation methods are as follows:

- CD-ROM only
- Floppy disk and CD-ROM
- Network installation
- Installation from an existing operating system
- Unattended installation

The installation methods are described in the sections that follow. Each of the installation methods consists of techniques to boot the computer and to enable you to load the installation files. Even though the startup techniques vary, such as performing the installation from CD-ROM or over the network, in every case you start the setup by running either Winnt.exe (Winnt) or Winnt32.exe (Winnt 32). Winnt and Winnt32 perform the same function, but Winnt32 runs in the 32-bit Windows environment.

Winnt is used if your computer is already running MS-DOS, Windows 3.1, or Windows 3.11. Use Winnt32 if the computer is already loaded with Windows 95, Windows 98, Windows NT Server, Windows NT Workstation, or Windows 2000 (for an upgrade). There are several switches that can be used with either Winnt or Winnt32, as shown in Tables 5-2 and 5-3. Notice that the switches for Winnt are different from those used for Winnt32 (try Hands-on Project 5-1 to view Winnt32 switches).

For example, using Winnt, if you want to specify a location for the installation files that is different from the directory from which you start Winnt.exe, use the /s switch and specify the drive and directory after the switch, for example *Winnt /S:E:\I386*. When using Winnt32, you may want to check the computer to make sure is it compatible with Windows 2000 by using the */checkupgradeonly* switch, or if you have trouble during the installation use the */debug* switch to record errors in a file.

5

Table 5-2 Command-line Switches for Winnt

Switch	Purpose
/?	Lists the switches for Winnt
/a	Initiates the accessibility options for those who have visual, hearing, or movement disabilities
/e:command	Executes a command after the Windows portion of the setup, for example to start a program or open the Control Panel
/i:initialization filename	Specifies that you are using an initialization file other than the default, Dosnet.inf (This initialization file shows where installation files are located)
/r:foldername	Creates an optional folder of files copied from the Windows 2000 Server CD-ROM (The folder remains after the installation is completed)
/rx:folder	Creates an optional folder of files copied from the Windows 2000 Server CD-ROM (the folder is deleted after the installation is completed)
/s:drive:\folder /s:\\ server\share\folder	Uses a path for the installation files other than the current path
/t:drive\folder	Copies the temporary files used by the installation to a specified location (otherwise, they are copied to the target drive of the installation)
/u:script file	Used in an unattended installation to specify the name of the script or answer file containing installation commands and should be used with the /s command
udf:id	Enables a uniqueness database file to be used with an unattended installation as a way to ensure that particular information in the script can be changed, such as the name of the server ("id" specifies the name of the database file, for example udf:install.dbf)

Table 5-3 Command-line Switches for Winnt32

Switch	Purpose
/?	Lists the switches for Winnt32
/checkupgradeonly	Creates only a report to tell you if the computer is compatible with Windows 2000 (the report is called Upgrade.txt for computers running Windows 95/98, and Winnt32.log for computers running Windows NT 3.51 or 4.0)
/cmd:command	Executes a command before the Windows portion of the setup is completed and just after you have provided configuration information
/comdcons	Adds a Recovery Console option to the Boot.ini file so that you can fix problems with an installation
/copydir:folder	Creates a special subfolder in the final Winnt directory, usually implemented for information specific to that installation, for example to store specialized drivers for use only during the installation (the folder is retained after the installation is completed)
/copysource:folder	Creates a special subfolder in the final Winnt directory, usually implemented for information specific to that installation, for example to store specialized drivers for use during the installation or to store for later use (the folder is deleted after the installation is completed)
/debug level:file	Creates a file to help you debug installation problems, on the basis of the level you specify (Winnt32.log is the default if no file is specified; levels are 0 = major errors, 1 = errors, 2 = warnings, 3 = information, 4 = detailed information)
/m:folder	Enables you to install files from the default installation folders on the CD-ROM and from a folder you specify with the /m command — (if the installation finds two files of the same name, it uses the file in the folder specified by /m)
/makelocalsource	Copies the CD-ROM source files to the same disk that is designated for the Winnt folder (enabling you to later install additional services or components from your local hard disk)
/noreboot	Does not automatically reboot after files are copied to the hard disk, enabling you to run a command in the interim, for example to check the dates on driver files for the most current versions
/s:*drive:\folder* /s:\\ *server\share\folder*	Uses a path for the installation files other than the current path — also enables you to copy files from two or more sources by specifying multiple /s commands
/syspart:drive	Enables you to copy the files used by setup to a hard drive, remove the hard drive, and install it in another computer (can be used by computer manufacturers, who install the first phase, but leave the second phase of the installation to the purchaser to specify parameters unique to her or his site such as the server name; must be used with /tempdrive)

Table 5-3   Command-line Switches for Winnt32 (continued)

Switch	Purpose
/tempdrive:drive	Temporary files and the final Windows 2000 system files are copied to the drive specified, for example to drive D: in /tempdrive:D
/unattend	Enables you to upgrade a version of Windows 2000 to a later version, using the parameters already in place for your current version
/unattend [seconds]:script file	Used in an unattended installation to specify the name of the script file containing installation commands (the seconds parameter is used to create an interval between the time that the setup files are copied and the time that the computer reboots, so you can interrupt to enter a command)
udf:id	Enables a uniqueness database file to be used with an unattended installation so that particular information in the script can be changed, such as the name of the server (id specifies the name of the database file, for example udf:install.dbf)

5

The Windows 2000 Server CD-ROM contains installation files in the \I386 folder for Pentium, Pentium Pro, Pentium II, and Pentium III computers using Intel, Cyrix, or AMD processors.

CD-ROM Installation

If your computer supports booting from the CD-ROM drive, this method is the easiest because you only need the Windows 2000 Server CD-ROM to start the installation, and it is faster than the other methods. To start the installation from CD-ROM:

1. Make sure the computer's BIOS is set to boot first from the CD-ROM drive.

2. Insert the Windows 2000 Server CD-ROM in the CD-ROM drive.

3. Power off the computer.

4. Turn on the computer, allowing it to boot from the CD-ROM. On some computers you may be prompted to press Enter to boot from CD-ROM.

5. This method automatically starts Winnt.exe, and you follow the instructions on the screen.

Try Hands-on Project 5-2 to practice a CD-ROM installation.

Floppy Disk and CD-ROM Installation

Another way to start the Windows 2000 Server setup is by using the four floppy setup disks and the Windows 2000 Server CD-ROM that accompany your purchase of Windows 2000 Server. This method is for those computers that cannot boot from CD-ROM. The steps to use this method are as follows:

1. Make sure the computer's BIOS is set to boot first from floppy drive A:.

2. Power off the computer.

3. Insert Setup Disk #1 into drive A and the CD-ROM into the CD-ROM drive.

4. Turn on the computer, allowing it to boot from Setup Disk #1.

5. This method automatically starts Winnt.exe, and you follow the instructions on the screen, such as inserting Setup Disk #2 next.

 TIP   You can make copies of the floppy setup disks by: (1) formatting four floppy disks, (2) inserting the Windows 2000 Server CD-ROM, (3) clicking Start, Run, and entering the drive letter of the CD-ROM, plus the path \bootdisk\makeboot.exe or \bootdisk\makebt32.exe, (4) clicking OK, and (5) following the on-screen instructions.

Network Installation

Network installation enables you to perform the Windows 2000 Server installation from a shared network directory on another computer. This method is useful if you have a diskless workstation or one that does not have a CD-ROM drive. Also, the method is useful if you operate a large network and plan to implement many Windows 2000 servers. The network installation can be fast (but usually not as fast as the CD-ROM installation), and you can arrange to install all of the servers in the same way.

Before you start, make sure you have an appropriate number of software licenses for the servers you create.

The network method requires a prospective server computer that is connected to the network and can access a shared drive, such as one running Windows 3.11, Windows 95, Windows 98, or Windows NT.

Follow these general steps to start a network installation:

1. Copy the installation files to the host computer that will offer the shared folder, such as an existing Windows 2000 server. To copy the files, first create the folder on the host computer, calling it, for example, \I386. Insert the Windows 2000 Server CD-ROM in the host computer and copy the files from the I386 folder on the CD-ROM.

2. Share the host's folder, giving it Read or Change share permissions.

3. To start the installation, map the prospective server computer to the shared folder. Run the Winnt.exe or Winnt32.exe program (depending on the operating system you used to boot the prospective server), using the switches that match your needs (see Tables 5-2 and 5-3).

4. Follow the instructions on the screen.

Hands-on Projects 5-3 and 5-4 enable you to practice a network installation.

Installation from an Existing Operating System

You can run the Windows 2000 Server installation on a computer that already has a Microsoft-based operating system (MS-DOS or Windows 3.1 or higher) installed, such as one running Windows 98 or Windows NT. You might use this method to upgrade to Windows 2000 Server only or to have a dual-boot system. If you are upgrading to Windows 2000 Server only, simply delete the Windows 98 partition and create an NTFS partition as part of the installation process. If you want to have a dual-boot system, leave the Windows 98 FAT16 or FAT32 partition and create another partition for NTFS (make sure you have plenty of disk storage for NTFS first, for example by adding more disks). Use these steps to start this type of installation:

1. Boot the computer to use its current operating system, such as Windows 98.

2. Insert the Windows 2000 Server CD-ROM.

3. Click Start, click Run, and enter the drive letter of the CD-ROM followed by the appropriate installation command and switches, such as *D:\i386\winnt32 /debug4:debug.log*.

4. Follow the instructions on the screen. (If you originally booted the computer using Windows 95, Windows 98, Windows NT, or Windows 2000 Professional, the screens will all be in GUI format from the start.) The first dialog box asks you if you want to upgrade Windows 2000 or to install a new copy of Windows 2000. Use the upgrade option to replace the current operating system, but keep your existing settings and applications. Use the install new copy (clean install) option if you plan to have a dual-boot system or to install from scratch.

 TIP If you install Windows 2000 Server from MS-DOS, start the SMARTDRIVE utility before running Winnt.exe to enable the process to go faster.

Unattended Installation

An unattended installation is usually performed via a network installation, but you specify a set of unattended parameters before the Windows 2000 Server installation begins. The parameters enable you to provide a script or **answer file**, which gives responses to questions that come up in the installation. No license agreement is presented during the unattended installation, because it is assumed that you have already read the license information and that you have the appropriate number of licenses for the total number of unattended installations.

You can perform an unattended installation using Winnt or Winnt32 and a combination of the /S switch and /U switch, as in the following example:

```
Winnt32 /s:\\mainserver\I386 \unattend:unattend.txt
```

The /S: switch indicates where to find the installation files, such as on a network computer (/S:*server\share\folder*) or in a local folder (/S:*drive:\folder*). The /unattend: switch provides the name of the answer file, Unattend.txt for example, for the unattended installation.

Unattend.txt is an actual answer file that is provided as an example, and is found in the \I386 folder on the Windows 2000 CD-ROM. You can use a text editor, such as Notepad, to edit the answer file or use the Setup Manager, which is the file Setupmgr.exe on the Windows 2000 CD-ROM or in the Windows 2000 Server Resource Kit available from Microsoft. Use the Start button Run option to start Setupmgr.exe, which initiates the Windows 2000 Server Setup Manager Wizard. Follow the steps in the Wizard to create an answer file. This file contains predetermined answers to questions asked by Windows 2000 Setup, including information about what file system to use, where to install the operating system files, and the name for the server. The following is an example of several answers that can be provided in the answer file (see the i386 unattend.txt file for more examples):

```
[Unattended]
Unattendmode = Fullunattended
OemPreinstall = No
TargetPath = WINNT
Filesystem = NTFS

[UserData]
Fullname = "Sara Martin"
Orgname = "Nishida and McGuire"
Computername = "Lawyer"
```

To further customize an unattended installation, you can create a **uniqueness database file (UDF)**. The UDF works in conjunction with the answer file, allowing you to create a unique answer set for each server setup. For example, the UDF might contain the server name. Each server would have a uniqueness ID in the database associated with its information. The uniqueness ID is specified by the /UDF<*uniqueness id*> command used with the Winnt or Winnt32 command.

An alternative to performing an unattended installation over the network is to use an answer file along with booting from CD-ROM. The answer file is created in the same way as the example Unattend.txt file, but after you create the file, name it Winnt.sif (an .sif file is called an image file) and copy it to a floppy disk. Also, the contents of the Winnt.sif answer file must have a section heading that starts with [Data] and under that section you specify the key code on the Windows 2000 Server CD-ROM case. Using this method, you follow these steps:

1. Set up the computer's BIOS to boot first from CD-ROM.

2. Insert the Windows 2000 CD-ROM and turn on the computer.

3. Immediately insert the floppy disk containing the Winnt.sif file as soon as you see the first text-based setup screen.

4. The Winnt.sif file controls how the setup runs from the CD-ROM in the unattended mode.

Yet another unattended option is to specify which Windows 2000 Server components, such as Management and Monitoring Tools, are to be installed during the graphical portion of the installation described later in the section, "Installation Part 2". You specify which components to install by creating a Cmdlines.txt file, which is used in conjunction with an answer file and that contains a series of command lines to be executed. The Cmdlines.txt file must be located in a folder that you create, called \\$OEM\$ that is placed on the shared network drive containing the installation files or on the floppy disk containing Winnt.sif. The command sequence in the Cmdlines.txt file begins with [Commands] and underneath that heading are placed the individual commands, one to each line, surrounded by quotes. The command lines are interrupted by a utility program, usually Sysdiff.exe, that comes with Windows 2000 Server. Consult the documentation for Sysdiff.exe or the command interrupter that you use to determine the exact command line syntax.

If you plan to duplicate multiple servers, so each is exactly like the other, Windows 2000 supports the Sysprep.exe program which is used to clone Windows 2000 on computers that have the same hardware characteristics. Sysprep.exe is available in the Windows 2000 Server Resource Kit, which can be obtained from Microsoft. This program is run from the Start button and Run option. Another utility in the Resource Kit is called Syspart.exe, which is intended for cloning computers that have different hardware configurations. When you use Syspart.exe, the target computer must already have Windows NT 4.0 installed so it can be upgraded to Windows 2000 Server.

STEPPING THROUGH AN INSTALLATION

Once you have gathered all your information and determined which options you will use to install Windows 2000 Server, you can proceed with the installation. The next sections outline an installation using the CD-ROM only method, but installations are nearly the same for all methods. The installation steps are divided into two parts. In the first part, text-based Setup screens are presented (these screens are graphical if you start by using Winnt32 when a 32-bit operating system is already loaded on the computer). This part primarily focuses on detecting the hardware and loading installation files onto the computer. The second part is a graphical display that uses Windows-based dialog boxes that enable you to configure information specific to the server, such as the Administrator account password, the server name, and network access.

Installation Part 1

After you start Winnt, as detailed earlier in the section "CD-ROM Installation," Setup goes through the following stages:

1. Setup inspects the hardware configuration and loads the drivers and other files to get started. Next, Windows 2000 Server Setup provides a screen with three options: to set up Windows 2000, to repair an existing Windows 2000 installation, and to quit Setup (see Figure 5-3). Press Enter to begin the installation, but also make a note that you can later access the repair option at any time. The repair option enables you to access diagnostic and repair functions on the emergency repair disk (discussed later in this chapter).

2. Setup presents the licensing agreement for Windows 2000 Server. Use the Page Down key to read the agreement and when you are finished reading, press F8 to indicate that you agree.

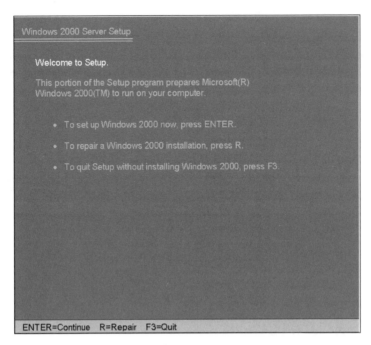

Figure 5-3 Beginning setup options

 Setup provides a way to install a special mass storage driver or HAL, in case the Windows 2000 Server CD-ROM does not contain the driver, or in case Setup cannot find storage devices when it inspects the computer. Press F6 as soon as possible when Setup begins inspecting the hardware. Setup provides a special screen that enables you to install new drivers. Press S, insert the driver disk, and press Enter. Also, if Setup does not recognize the type of computer because it is an SMP computer, obtain a HAL driver from the vendor, press F5 as soon as possible when Setup starts, select Other in the menu, and install the HAL driver from a floppy disk or CD-ROM.

3. Setup scans the hard drive(s) to determine if there are any previous versions of Windows 2000 Server. If it finds one, you have the choice to repair it if it is damaged or to install a new copy of Windows 2000 over the current version. If you see this screen, press Esc to install a new copy.

4. The hard drive scan also determines if any FAT16, FAT32, or NTFS partitions are already in place. Use the up and down arrow keys to select the unpartitioned space or an existing partition on which to install Windows 2000 and press Enter. Figure 5-4 illustrates this screen on a two-disk system that already has a FAT32 partition. If you highlight an unpartitioned space, the control key options change and you should press C to create the partition. Setup displays another screen to confirm the selection and enables you to specify the size of the partition. If you choose to write over an existing partition, press Enter, and Setup displays a warning screen on which you can enter C to continue. If you choose to delete

an existing partition, press D. If the partition you are deleting is the one from which the computer boots, Setup displays another screen from which you press Enter to delete the partition. If the partition is not one from which your computer boots, press L on the next screen to delete it. The original screen reappears, showing the drive is now unpartitioned.

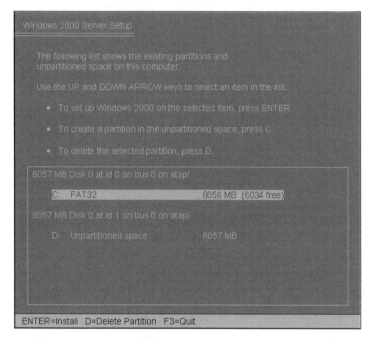

Figure 5-4   Detecting partitions

5. Use the up and down arrow keys to select a file system, NTFS or FAT (a third option is to leave the existing file system, if the drive is already formatted) and then press Enter. On the next screen, Setup warns that files will be deleted, if you are formatting over an existing partition (on some systems the warning notice may appear on the format selection screen). Press F to format the partition. Or, if you change your mind at this point, press Esc to go back and select a different partition. After you start the format, a screen is displayed to show the progress of the format.

6. After the disk is formatted, Setup automatically checks the disks, copies files, and reboots into the Windows 2000 graphical mode. If your computer is set up to boot first from CD-ROM, depending on the computer, you may need to remove the Windows 2000 Server CD-ROM before it reboots and then put the CD-ROM back in after it reboots.

Installation Part 2

Once the computer reboots, you make selections with a mouse or pointing device by click-ing buttons, such as Back and Next, at the bottom of dialog boxes. The Back button enables you to go to previous screens to change your selections, and the Next button is used to move to the next step in the installation process.

The steps of the setup from this point are as follows:

1. The first dialog box is used to gather information about the computer, which includes the keyboard, and pointing device. Click Next. An action bar in the next dialog box shows you the progress of the detection process and automatically goes to the following dialog box when it finishes.

2. In the next dialog box, you have options to change regional and keyboard settings, for instance to customize the server to use a specific language or to customize a language for your locale. For example, you may set up to use English, but want to use the United Kingdom locale English. Complementing the language you can customize number, currency, time, and date formats. Use the Customize bottoms to make adjustments, and then click Next.

3. Enter your name and the name of your organization in the Personalize Your Software dialog box (see Figure 5-5). Click Next.

4. Enter the Product Key. You can find the key on a sticker attached to the reverse side of the Windows 2000 Server CD-ROM jewel case.

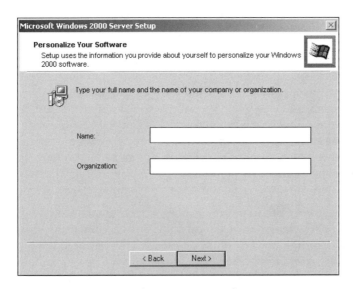

Figure 5-5   Name and organization information

5. In the Licensing Modes dialog box, select the licensing mode (per server or per seat) and enter the number of licenses. You can add licenses later as needed, so only add the number of licenses you have now. Click Next.

6. Enter the name of the computer and provide a password for the Administrator account. Confirm the password and click Next.

7. Enter checks in the boxes of the components that you want to install (Figure 5-6), such as Accessories and Utilities, Management and Monitoring Tools, Message Queuing Services, and Other Network File and Print Services (for UNIX and Macintosh). When you first install Windows 2000 it is recommended that you select only the services you need immediately and install others later, to minimize configuration difficulties. For example, you might install Management and Monitoring Tools and Message Queuing Services now, because you will likely use these right away. To view information about a particular component, click the component name and then click Details. Click Next after you have made the selections.

5

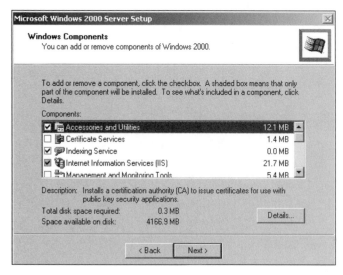

Figure 5-6 Windows 2000 components

8. If there is a modem installed in the server, the Modem Dialing Information dialog box is displayed. Provide your region and country information, telephone area code, number you dial for an outside line (optional), and telephone line type (tone or pulse) in the Modem Dialing Information dialog box. This information is used to establish dial-up networking. Click Next.

9. Verify the accuracy of the date and time in the Date and Time Settings dialog box and make any needed changes. Also, make sure the time zone is correctly set, for example for Mountain Time. Click Next.

10. Setup next displays a dialog box to show that it is configuring your network settings, and then enables you to select typical or custom settings. Click Typical settings if you want to use Client for Microsoft Networks, File and Print Sharing for Microsoft Networks, and TCP/IP. Otherwise click Custom settings to establish a different setup, for example to install NWLink for NetWare connectivity. To keep the installation simple, it is recommended that you use the typical settings and make adjustments later. Click Next after you have made your selection.

11. If the computer is not currently on a network or if you want to specify a workgroup for the computer, click the No radio button, or click Yes if the computer will join a domain. Enter the workgroup or domain name in the text box. Click Next. If you join a domain, you will need to enter the domain account and the password of the account you already created to enable the server to join the domain.

12. Setup now installs the components you have specified (see Figure 5-7), sets up Start menu items, and removes the temporary files created by the installation process.

13. Remove the Windows 2000 Server CD-ROM, click Finish, and restart the computer.

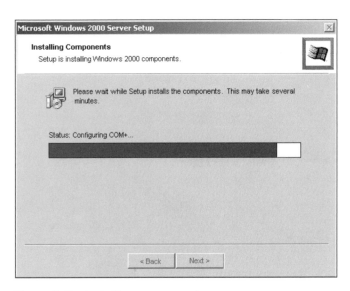

Figure 5-7   Installing components

Testing the New Server

When the new server restarts, a logon screen appears with a message to press the Ctrl+Alt+Del keys at the same time. The Ctrl+Alt+Del combination is used to start the logon screen and does not reboot the server. Press the keys, enter Administrator as the account name and enter the password you supplied during the installation. A dialog box is displayed to enable you to configure the server (see Figure 5-8). Minimize the dialog box when you first log on, because you will learn how to configure the server in the next chapter. The Windows 2000 Server desktop appears, as shown in Figure 5-9.

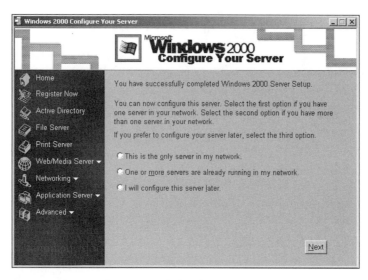

Figure 5-8   Configuration dialog box

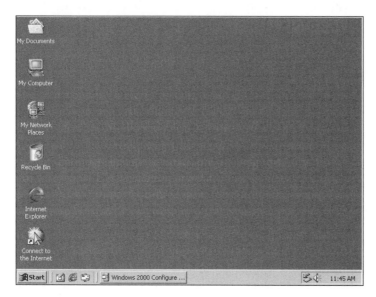

Figure 5-9   Windows 2000 desktop

UPGRADING A WINDOWS NT 4.0 SERVER AND DOMAIN

You can use steps similar to those described in the previous sections to upgrade a Windows NT 4.0 Server to Windows 2000 Server, with the option of retaining security settings, account information, group information, and the domain. Use the following guidelines to upgrade the Windows NT server and the corresponding Windows NT domain:

1. Coordinate a time when you can upgrade the server and domain when no one is accessing it but you.

2. Back up each Windows NT 4.0 server that will be upgraded, including its Registry, before you start an upgrade. Also, make an emergency repair disk before you start and again just after you finish (see the next section to learn how to create an emergency repair disk for Windows 2000 Server).

3. If you are upgrading more than one server in a domain, start by upgrading the Windows NT 4.0 primary domain controller (PDC; see Chapter 4) to be converted to the first Windows 2000 domain controller (DC). Next, and one at a time, upgrade each Windows NT 4.0 backup domain controller (BDC) to be a Windows 2000 domain controller (or some can be upgraded to member servers, but plan to have at least two domain controllers).

4. If TCP/IP is not already implemented, consider upgrading the servers to TCP/IP before you start; or consider setting up the first upgraded server (the former PDC) as a DHCP server (see Chapter 3) and use the default TCP/IP configuration for each upgraded server. Also, set up the first upgraded server to work as a DNS server (see Chapter 3), if one does not already exist on the network, such as via a UNIX server.

5. To begin the upgrade, use the Winnt32 program on the Windows 2000 Server CD-ROM as described in the section, "Installation from an Existing Operating System."

6. Select Upgrade to Windows 2000 (Recommended) on the first screen in setup (see Figure 5-10) so that you can retain existing settings, including the Windows NT Security Accounts Manager (SAM) database information about accounts and groups, and software.

7. Follow the directions in the Windows 2000 Setup (see the section, "Stepping Through an Installation").

8. During the upgrade, the Active Directory Wizard starts and provides the opportunity for you to specify if you want to join an existing domain tree or forest, or start a new one. Specify that you want to start a new one if you are upgrading the PDC; or join an existing one if you are upgrading a BDC — and provide the name of the domain.

Figure 5-10   Selecting the upgrade option

9. The Active Directory Installation Wizard will upgrade the PDC or BDC to have Windows 2000 Server directory services and Kerberos authentication services. Also, it will convert the SAM in the Windows NT Registry to the database used by the Active Directory so that accounts, groups, and security information is retained. If you are upgrading a BDC that is to be set up as a child domain, then a Kerberos transitive trust is automatically created with the parent domain.

10. After you upgrade a PDC, it is still recognized by any Windows NT BDCs as the domain master and can synchronize with live BDCs until they are upgraded. Leave a BDC running until all servers are upgraded (except for the last server to be upgraded, of course), because this gives you a backup alternative if there is a problem. (If you are concerned about upgrade problems, create an extra BDC to match the last BDC before it is converted. Remove the backup BDC from the network and store it in a safe place until you feel assured the upgrade process is fully successful.)

11. Establish a Group Policy for the domain via the Active Directory (see Chapters 4 and 6), including logon restrictions.

12. After all servers are upgraded and there are no Windows NT servers connected to the domain, convert the domain (or all domains) to native mode, which reflects that there are no longer any Windows NT PDCs or BDCs on the network. You can do this by clicking the Start button, pointing to Programs, pointing to Administrative Tools, and clicking Active Directory Domains and Trusts. Right-click the domain you want to convert and click Properties. Click the Change Mode button on the General tab.

CREATING AN EMERGENCY REPAIR DISK

After Windows 2000 Server is installed, you can choose to create an **emergency repair disk** (**ERD**), which enables you to fix problems that may arise with the server. Plan to create a new ERD each time you install software, make a server configuration change, install a new adapter, add a NIC, restructure a partition, or upgrade the operating system. You can create or update the ERD at any time after Windows 2000 Server is installed by starting the Backup Wizard and clicking the Emergency Repair Disk button (try Hands-on Project 5-5).

TROUBLESHOOTING INSTALLATION PROBLEMS

In most cases the installation goes smoothly, but installers sometimes experience problems. Often, difficulties are prevented by making the advance preparations explained earlier in this chapter and in Chapter 2, which include:

- Ensure you purchase a processor and hardware components that are on the Microsoft HCL.

- Test all hardware before installing Windows 2000 Server.

- Run the computer manufacturer's diagnostics before installing Windows 2000 Server.

- Run a comprehensive test of the hard disk to ensure it is functioning properly.

Sometimes prevention is not enough and installation problems occur. Most problems are related to hardware drivers or to the actual hardware. For example, the computer may contain a CD-ROM drive or display adapter that is newly marketed and not contained in the installation selection list. If Windows 2000 Setup does not contain the driver or it is not included on a disk with the hardware, it is necessary to contact the computer vendor for a new driver. Sometimes an adapter card, such as a NIC or hard disk adapter, is loosened when the computer is moved and the card simply needs to be reseated.

If SCSI adapters are used, the SCSI cable may be loose or it may not be properly terminated. A network interface card or sound card driver may be needed, since new models are often introduced to the market. Table 5-4 provides a list of problem descriptions and steps to take to solve the problems.

Table 5-4   Troubleshooting a Windows 2000 Server Setup

Problem Description	Solution Steps
Installation fails when connecting to the domain controller	Make sure you have previously created an account in the domain and provided the right domain name. Also, make sure the computer is connected to the network, that the domain controller and DNS server are working, and that you are using the right protocol.
Setup did not find any mass storage devices on the computer. There is an Inaccessible Boot Device message.	The most common cause is that Setup does not have a driver for a SCSI device or is detecting storage devices in the wrong order, such as the CD-ROM drive first. Press F6 when setup first starts and provide a driver for the mass storage device that will hold the Windows 2000 files. Check to make sure all adapters and controllers are working properly. Check power to all devices. Reseat adapters and controllers. For SCSI devices ensure: (1) The SCSI cabling is properly installed, (2) SCSI devices are terminated, (3) SCSI devices are correctly addressed, and (4) the BIOS correctly recognizes all SCSI adapters. Also, be sure the SCSI boot drive is addressed as 0. Check the manufacturer's recommendations for configuring SCSI adapters and hard disk drives. Try replacing the adapter before replacing the drive(s). For EIDE drives: (1) Check the controller, (2) ensure file I/O and disk access are set to standard, and (3) ensure the system drive is the first device recognized by the controller. For IDE and ESDI drives: (1) Check the cabling and controller, (2) check the drive setup in the BIOS for master/slave relationships, (3) ensure the drive is properly recognized in the BIOS.
You see the STOP Message "øxøøøøøøøø IRQL Not Less or Equal," or you see a message that there is a problem with the HAL.DLL.	Restart the installation and press F5 as soon as possible. Select the appropriate computer type for a single processor or select Other for an SMP computer and load the HAL.DLL that is available from the computer vendor.

5

Table 5-4   Troubleshooting a Windows 2000 Server Setup (continued)

Problem Description	Solution Steps
The installation fails when installing the network components.	Go back to configure network settings. Make sure you have installed a protocol that is appropriate for your network and that you have provided all the information needed to set up the protocol. Check the network interface card to ensure it is working. Reseat or replace the card and start Setup again. Use the diagnostic software provided with the card to test for problems. If this does not work, try a card from a different manufacturer, in case there is a hardware incompatibility.
A problem is reported with NTOSKRNL.EXE or in finding NTLDR.	The Boot.ini file needs to be changed to indicate where to find Windows 2000 (if other than on the primary system drive) or NTLDR is not on the drive used to boot (called the system drive).
A device driver is not available in Setup for a given component, such as a NIC, sound card, video card, or other adapter.	Obtain the most recent driver from the manufacturer.
A STOP message appears during the installation.	Start the installation again. If the STOP message appears a second time, record the message and consult a Microsoft technician. (Also, see Chapter 16 For STOP message solutions.)
Computer locks up	Check the IRQ and I/O settings for conflicts among hardware components and cards (check the NIC and any specialized cards in particular).

INSTALLING SERVICE PACKS

Service packs are used to provide additional capabilities, update the operating system, and to fix reported problems in Windows 2000 Server. When a service pack is issued, it is prudent to obtain the service pack and install it. Typically service packs are issued in version sequences, such as Service Pack 1, Service Pack 2, and so on. When a later version service pack is installed, it is necessary to have the first versions installed as well. Microsoft takes the work out of remembering by including earlier service pack versions in the latest version. For example, when you install Service Pack 3, you are also installing Service Packs 1 and 2, so you can miss an early service pack and still make sure all versions are installed via a later one. If you have installed a service pack and afterward make a change in Windows 2000 Server, you should reinstall all or a portion of the service pack. For example, if you remove and reinstall TCP/IP, then you should reinstall the portion of the latest service pack that affects TCP/IP, which is an installation process called **slip streaming**. You can order service packs online through

Microsoft's Web site at *www.microsoft.com*; and often Microsoft makes service packs available as a free download from its Web site. The general steps for installing a service pack are:

1. Back up the server and make an ERD before you start, as a precaution.

2. Download the service pack contents to a folder on the server or obtain the service pack CD-ROM and insert it. Make sure that you have the 128-bit encryption version for Windows 2000 Server systems for purchased in the United States and Canada.

3. Read the instructions for using the service pack. For example, they may ask that you temporarily deactivate certain third-party drivers (you learn this in Chapter 6). Also, the instructions will tell you how much disk space is needed for the installation.

4. Close all active windows.

5. Start the service pack upgrade by clicking Start and Run. Enter the path to the service pack files and Setup.exe or SpSetup.bat in the Run dialog box, such as D:\Setup.exe. (You can also install a service pack over a network, which requires accessing a shared folder and using the command, Update.exe.)

6. Follow the on-screen instructions in the Setup program to install all of the service pack or to slip stream only a specific element of the service pack.

When you install a service pack, it is possible to uninstall it and go back to the system as it was before the install. If you want the ability to uninstall the service pack, make sure you have twice the required disk space before you start the installation (for the installation files and to save your old files). Perform the installation using the Update.exe program instead of Setup.exe or SpSetup.exe. Table 5-5 shows the typical switches for the Update program. If a problem occurs and you want to uninstall the service pack, use the Control Panel Add/Remove Programs icon (see Chapter 6). Should the installation fail prematurely, because of a power failure for example, and before the service pack is registered in Add/Remove Programs, you can uninstall it by running Spuninst.exe from the temporary folder that the Update program creates on the server's hard drive.

Table 5-5   Windows Service Pack Update Switches

Switch	Purpose
- f	Close all programs when the operating system shuts down prior to rebooting
-n	Disable the backup of old files used to uninstall the service pack
-o	Automatically copy new files over the old OEM files
-q	Install using the quiet mode so that the user does not have to respond to prompts during the installation
-u	Install using the unattended mode
/?	List the available switches

TIP Some Windows 2000 Server updates are available online, using the Windows Update option. Click Start and then click the Windows Update option. If you have not already configured an Internet connection, click Connect Me to the Internet. If you have previously configured a connection, the tool automatically connects to the Microsoft Web site and performs the upgrade. Consult the web site at *www.microsoft.com* for information on the latest updates and service packs for Windows 2000 Server.

UNINSTALLING WINDOWS 2000 SERVER

Sometimes it is necessary to uninstall Windows 2000 Server, for instance when new server hardware is purchased and you want to pass along the old hardware to someone else. For example, to remove Windows 2000 Server and install Windows 98 you might do the following steps:

1. Purchase a new copy of Windows 98 or use the disks from a licensed copy not presently used by someone else.
2. Perform a complete backup of all files on the server computer.
3. If the computer is not set to boot from drive A first, start the BIOS setup program and set it to boot from drive A before trying to boot from drive C (consult the computer documentation on how to use its BIOS setup program).
4. Power off the server and insert the Windows 98 boot disk or CD-ROM, or boot from a Windows 98 Startup disk that you have made previously.
5. Boot the computer from the Windows 98 boot disk or Startup disk.
6. Use the FDISK and FORMAT utilities on the boot disk to delete the NTFS partition and to partition the workstation drive(s) for FAT16 or FAT32 and to format the drive(s).
7. Use the Windows 98 CD-ROM to install the operating system.
8. Install the appropriate applications software and data files on the computer.

If your version of FDISK cannot delete the NTFS partition, an alternative is to insert the Windows 2000 Server CD-ROM or Setup Disk #1 and start an installation. When Setup identifies the existing NTFS partition, highlight the partition and type *D* to delete it. Next, exit the installation, use the Windows 98 CD-ROM (or the installation disks for another operating system) to install the operating system.

CHAPTER SUMMARY

❑ Planning is often the best preparation for any task, and this rule holds true for installing Windows 2000 Server. The best planning steps that you can take are to select a computer and components from the Microsoft HCL that are equipped to handle the anticipated server load in your organization. Also, your preparations should include decisions about how to partition the disk storage, which file system to use, what to name the server, what protocol to set up, which licensing method to use, and how to access the network.

❐ Windows 2000 Server can be installed using any of several methods, which include: using the CD-ROM only, using the installation floppy disks and CD-ROM, installing over a network, or installing from an existing operating system. Fortunately, the installation follows a logical step-by-step process that automates many activities—detection of the disk storage and NIC, for example. Although you may need to troubleshoot a specific installation problem, the likelihood of having to deal with a problem is reduced in proportion to how well you have planned in advance.

❐ One important task after you have completed the installation is to make an emergency repair disk that you update each time you change the server configuration. Also, watch for service packs issued by Microsoft and plan to install them.

Other setup tasks are ahead as you set up a server to match your organization's needs. These tasks begin in the next chapter, which focuses on configuring additional server elements, particularly through the Control Panel.

KEY TERMS

answer file — A text file that contains a complete set of instructions for installing Windows 2000 in the unattended mode.

basic input/output system (BIOS) — A program on a read-only or flash memory chip that establishes basic communication with components such as the monitor and disk drives. The advantage of a flash chip is that you can update the BIOS.

client access license (CAL) — A license to enable a workstation to connect to Windows 2000 Server as a client.

dual-boot system — A computer set up to boot from two or more different operating systems, such as Windows 2000 Server and MS-DOS.

emergency repair disk (ERD) — A disk that contains repair, diagnostic, and backup information for use in case there is a problem with Windows 2000.

format — An operation that divides a disk into small sections called tracks and sectors for the storage of files.

hardware abstraction layer (HAL) — A set of program routines that enables an operating system to control a hardware component, such as the processor, from within the operating system kernel.

member server — A server that is a member of an existing Windows 2000 domain, but that does not function as a domain controller.

partition — A process in which a hard disk section or a complete hard disk is set up for use by an operating system. A disk can be formatted after it is partitioned.

per seat licensing — A server software license that requires that there be enough licenses for all network client workstations.

per server licensing — A server software license based on the maximum number of clients that log on to the server at one time.

slip streaming — Installing only a specific portion of a service pack instead of the entire update.

standalone server — A server that is not a member of a domain, but that is a member of an existing workgroup or that establishes its own workgroup, such as in peer-to-peer networking.

uniqueness database file (UDF) — A text file that contains an answer set of unique instructions for installing Windows 2000 in the unattended mode and that is used with an answer file.

REVIEW QUESTIONS

1. You are installing Windows 2000 Server and get a message that it cannot log on to the domain. Which of the following should you check?

   a. that there is an active domain controller on the network

   b. that you have configured the new server to use the same protocol as is used by the DNS server on the network

   c. that NetBEUI is configured for 802.2 frames on the new server

   d. all of the above

   e. only a and b

   f. only a and c

2. You are installing Windows 2000 Server on a computer that already has Windows 98 installed. What setup command can you use to install Windows 2000 Server and which command option enables you to create a log of any installation errors?

   a. Winnt with the /e option

   b. Winnt with the /log option

   c. Winnt32 with the /debug option

   d. Winnt32 with the /cmd:error.log option

3. In what file would you find the ARC path used to boot Windows 2000 Server?

   a. Boot.ini

   b. Io.sys

   c. Command.com

   d. NTLDR

4. What disk and partition on that disk contain the operating system files when the ARC path is scsi(1)disk(1)rdisk(0)partition(2)?

   a. third disk and third partition on that disk

   b. second disk and first partition on that disk

   c. second disk and second partition on that disk

   d. third disk and second partition

5. When you install Windows 2000 Server you must join
    a. a domain
    b. a workgroup
    c. an account group
    d. all of the above
    e. either a or b
    f. either a or c

6. When you set up Windows 2000 Server for network communication, what protocol(s) is (are) used by Setup as part of the default, or typical, installation?
    a. TCP/IP
    b. NetBEUI
    c. NWLink
    d. all of the above
    e. only a and b
    f. only a and c

7. What element is needed to perform an unattended installation for Windows 2000?
    a. at least 125 MB of RAM
    b. an answer file
    c. 10 client access licenses, instead of 5
    d. a RAM disk installed to store unattended database information

8. You are installing Windows 2000 Server on a dual-processor system, but the installation is having trouble recognizing the mass storage. What might be the problem?
    a. The processors are operating at different speeds.
    b. Setup does not have a driver for the SCSI adapter used for the mass storage.
    c. You need to start the processor service before completing the installation.
    d. Windows 2000 Server can only be used on a system that has just one SCSI adapter, and this system has two.

9. Which of the following is (are) installation options used with Windows 2000 Server?
    a. CD-ROM installation
    b. over the network installation
    c. floppy disk only installation
    d. all of the above
    e. only a and b
    f. only a and c

10. You have installed a dual-boot system consisting of Windows 98 using a FAT32 partition and Windows 2000 Server using an NTFS partition. You have checked your Windows 2000 installation and it looks good. However, when you boot Windows 98, you cannot see the files on the NTFS partition. What might be the source of the problem?

    a. Windows 98 is not compatible with NTFS; thus, this result is normal.

    b. You have not switched on Windows 98 file sharing.

    c. You must run NTLDR just after starting Windows 98 in order to view the NTFS partition.

    d. all of the above

    e. only a and c

    f. only b and c

11. You have chosen to use the Windows 2000 Setup process to partition a 6 GB disk for FAT. Which file system version will be used by Setup?

    a. Setup can only partition disks over 2 GB using NTFS, not FAT.

    b. Setup will partition using FAT16.

    c. Setup will partition using FAT32.

    d. Setup will partition the first 2 GB for FAT32 and the remaining 4 GB for NTFS.

12. When you run Windows 2000 Setup in attended mode, which of the following are true in the initial stages of the process?

    a. You must accept the licensing agreement to proceed.

    b. Setup only detects unpartitioned space on hard disks attached to the computer.

    c. Setup automatically deletes any operating systems already on the computer.

    d. all of the above

    e. only a and b

    f. only b and c

13. Which of the following are components that can be installed by Windows 2000 setup?

    a. Other Network File and Print Services

    b. Management and Monitoring Tools

    c. Message Queuing Services

    d. all of the above

    e. only a and c

    f. only b and c

14. As you are installing Windows 2000 Server, the computer locks up. When you reboot, the installation process starts for a short time and then the computer locks up again. What can you do to resolve the problem?

    a. Check for a conflict in the IRQ settings of the hardware installed in the computer.

    b. Press F10 when you reboot the computer and temporarily remove the NIC driver.

c. Press F7 to have Setup reconfigure the hardware to the lowest common denominator.

d. Make sure that you have at least 8 MB of RAM installed in the computer.

15. An emergency repair disk (ERD) can be created

a. only when you install Windows 2000.

b. by using the Backup Wizard.

c. by using the edisk utility.

d. by using the ERD utility on the Administrative Tools menu.

16. A friend of yours is trying to set up Windows 2000 Server on a computer that he purchased from a local dealer, who builds them from various parts available through mail-order catalogs and the Internet. Unfortunately, Windows 2000 Server is having trouble installing on this computer during the text-based portion of the setup. What advice would you give?

a. Use only generic drivers for hard disk storage.

b. Use the custom components setup in Windows 2000 Server.

c. Replace the computer with one that is on the HCL.

d. Call Microsoft to obtain new Windows 2000 drivers.

17. You have installed Windows 2000 Server, and after the installation you discover that you have lost the floppy setup disks. What is the best option for replacing the disks as soon as possible?

a. Call Microsoft for replacement disks.

b. Run Winnt /O from the Windows 2000 Server CD-ROM.

c. Run Makeboot from the Windows 2000 Server CD-ROM.

d. Don't worry, you will never need these disks again.

18. You are setting up Windows 2000 server for an investment firm that has 14 network clients. What licensing method would you use?

a. per server

b. per seat

c. per network segment

d. per process

19. A standalone server is one that

a. belongs to a domain.

b. acts as a DC.

c. authenticates logons in a single domain.

d. all of the above

e. none of the above

f. only b and c

20. When you install Windows 2000 what must you do to the disk that will hold the operating system files?

   a. Partition and format the disk.

   b. Select the disk spindle, since there are two.

   c. Determine the number of sectors to use on the disk.

   d. all of the above

   e. none of the above

   f. only a and b

21. Which of the following operating systems can coexist on the same computer with Windows 2000 Server?

   a. Windows 95

   b. MS-DOS

   c. Windows 98

   d. all of the above

   e. none of the above

   f. only a and c

22. The Windows 2000 Server operating system files are located on a SCSI disk with the BIOS enabled and are on the third partition of that disk. This disk is the third disk on the SCSI adapter. Which of the following is its ARC path?

   a. scsi(0)disk(2)rdisk(3)partition(2)

   b. multi(0)disk(4)rdisk(0)partition(2)

   c. multi(0)disk(2)rdisk(0)partition(3)

   d. scsi(1)disk(3)rdisk(3)partition(2)

23. You have installed Windows 2000 Server and later decide to change the NIC and install another disk drive. Which of the following should you do after these devices are installed?

   a. Reinstall Windows 2000 Server from the CD-ROM.

   b. Reset the security access to the NIC.

   c. Make a new emergency repair disk.

   d. Bind the NIC to the hard drive so both are recognized by Windows 2000 Server.

24. Which of the following is the most useful password recommendation for when you configure the Administrator account during the Windows 2000 setup?

   a. Do not enter a password at this time because you might forget it and be unable to access the new server.

   b. Do not confirm the password because confirmation causes it to be copied to the Guest account.

   c. Use a relatively long password that is hard to guess.

   d. Use a password that is entirely numeric like a combination lock. This is required by Windows 2000 Server to keep the Administrator account more secure than others.

25. You insert the Windows 2000 CD-ROM to install the operating system on a computer; however, when you power off the computer and reboot, the computer tries to boot from the hard drive, which has no files. Which is your best option?

    a. Set the BIOS boot order to start with the CD-ROM drive.

    b. Temporarily unplug the hard drive from its controller before starting the installation.

    c. Boot from Setup Disk #2 in drive A, which is designed to start the CD-ROM setup programs.

    d. Change the CD-ROM drive speed to at least 24X.

5

HANDS-ON PROJECTS

Project 5-1

In this hands-on activity you view the switches that can be used with the Winnt32 installation program. You will need the Windows 2000 Server CD-ROM.

To view the switches:

1. Start any one of the following computer operating systems: Windows 95, Windows 98, Windows NT 4.0, or Windows 2000.

2. Insert the Windows 2000 Server CD-ROM in the CD-ROM drive.

3. Click **Start** and then **Run**.

4. Enter the drive letter and path of the winnt32 file in the Open box and enter /? after the command as in: **D:\i386\winnt32.exe /?** (winnt32 is located on the Windows 2000 Server CD-ROM in the \i386 folder for Intel-based computers). Click **OK**.

5. What switch would you use to have a Recovery Console option? What switch enables you to create an error log to review installation errors? Record your observations in a lab journal or in a word-processed document.

6. Close the Windows Help dialog box.

Project 5-2

In this activity you practice installing Windows 2000 Server using the CD-ROM only method.

To practice the installation:

1. Go back to the section in this chapter entitled "CD-ROM Installation" and follow those steps.

2. Skip to the section in this chapter entitled "Installation Part 1" and follow the steps.

3. Continue by following the steps in the section entitled "Installation Part 2."

4. Log on to Windows 2000 Server to test your work.

Project 5-3

In this hands-on activity, you practice creating a shared folder from which to load Windows 2000 Server over the network. You need a computer running Windows 2000 Server or Professional, and the Windows 2000 Server CD-ROM.

To create a shared folder from which to install Windows 2000 Server over the network:

1. Log on to Windows 2000 Server as Administrator.

2. Insert the Windows 2000 Server CD-ROM in the computer.

3. Click **Start**, point to **Programs**, point to **Accessories**, and then click **Windows Explorer**.

4. Use Windows Explorer to create a new folder on drive C (or another drive) called Win2000 by clicking the **File** menu, pointing to **New**, and then clicking **Folder**. Enter **Win2000** as the name of the new folder.

5. Click the CD-ROM drive in Windows Explorer, right-click the **I386** folder and drag it to the Win2000 folder. Click **Copy Here** on the shortcut menu.

6. Right-click the **Win2000** folder and then click **Sharing**.

7. Click the **Share this folder** radio button and, enter a share name, such as **Win2000**.

8. Click the **Permissions** button and give the Everyone group **Read** permission only (remove the checks from the other permissions). Click **OK** and then click **OK** again.

Project 5-4

In this activity you practice the steps to run an installation over the network from the shared folder you created in Project 5-3. Access the shared folder from a computer running Windows 95, Windows 98, or Windows NT.

To practice the installation:

1. Double-click **Network Neighborhood**.

2. Locate the Windows 2000 server that is sharing the Win2000 folder, and double-click it.

3. Right-click the **Win2000** folder and then click **Map Network Drive** (see Figure 5-11). (Make sure Windows 95 and Windows 98 are set up for User-level access control.)

Figure 5-11   Mapping a drive

4. In the Map Network Drive dialog box, enter the letter of a drive that is not already mapped, and then click **OK**.

5. Click **Start**, click **Run**, and the click the **Browse** button.

6. Find the Win2000 shared folder.

7. Find and click **Winnt32** so that it appears in the File name text box and then click **Open**.

8. Click **Cancel** so that you do not actually start the installation.

Project 5-5

In this project, you create an emergency repair disk. Have a FAT-formatted floppy disk ready in advance.

5

To create the ERD:

1. Click **Start**, point to **Programs**, point to **Accessories**, point to **System Tools**, and then click **Backup**.

2. Insert the floppy disk.

3. Click **Emergency Repair Disk** and then click **OK** (see Figure 5-12).

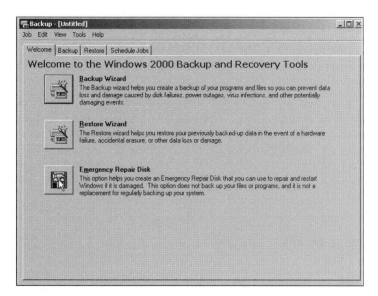

Figure 5-12   Backup Wizard

4. Click **OK** again and close the Backup utility.

5. Click **Start**, point to **Programs**, point to **Accessories**, and then click **Windows Explorer**.

6. Use Windows Explorer to view the files created on the ERD in drive A. Open the Setup.log file using Notepad and examine its contents. Record your findings in a lab journal or in a word-processed document.

7. Close Notepad and close Windows Explorer.

CASE PROJECT

Aspen Consulting Project: Installing Windows 2000

Internal Medicine Associates is a physicians group that has contacted you to install Windows 2000 on their new server. This physicians group consists of 55 doctors, nurses, and staff members who each have a computer that will soon be networked. They also have purchased a dual-processor Pentium III server that has two 20-GB drives on a new state-of-the-art SCSI adapter, 512 MB of RAM, a NIC, and an ISDN (telecommunications) adapter for high-speed Internet connectivity. One reason for the Internet connectivity is to access research databases and medical school sites that provide multimedia physician education services. The server will be used to store patient records, billing information, and application software. It also will serve as a central location from which to load and upgrade software at each client, such as Microsoft Office updates.

1. Before you install Windows 2000 Server, what preparations and decisions will you make?

2. When you install Windows 2000 Server, will you join an existing domain or a workgroup? Why?

3. What installation method will you use? Why? What other installation methods might be appropriate in this situation?

4. When you start the installation, Windows 2000 Server does not recognize the SCSI adapter and the disk storage attached to the adapter. What steps can you take to solve the problem?

5. After you have completed the installation, you accidentally drop one of the setup disks, and the plastic disk cover breaks. You decide to make a new set of the floppy installation disks and to show the group's office manager how to make them. Explain how you can make the new disks. Also, explain why it can be important to have these disks.

6. Once the new installation disks are made, you realize that you should show the office manager how to make an ERD. Explain how this is done and if there is any reason to make other ERDs in the future.

OPTIONAL CASE PROJECTS FOR TEAMS

Team Case One

Mark Arnez asks you to form a group to create documentation for the other consultants about installing Windows 2000 Server. In the documentation, he wants you to explain a scenario for installing Windows 2000 Server in a small office environment like Internal Medicine Associates, and another scenario for an organization that is much larger, such as a corporation or college. From these scenarios, he wants your group to make some general guidelines explaining how to prepare for an installation in a small context as compared to a large context.

Team Case Two

Your documentation for Team Case One has impressed Mark. Now he wants you to supplement it with a detailed list of do's and don'ts for installing Windows 2000 Server.

6

SERVER CONFIGURATION

After reading this chapter and completing the exercises you will be able to:

♦ Explain how to use the tools in the Control Panel

♦ Install and configure the display, pointing devices, keyboard, computer hardware, recovery options, protocols, and additional Windows 2000 Server components

♦ Use the Device Manager to view hardware properties and troubleshoot problems

Successfully installing Windows 2000 Server provides an important foundation on which to build and customize a server for your organization. The next phase in the process is to customize Windows 2000 Server, using the tools that are now installed and ready to use. There are hundreds of ways to customize your server to match specific hardware and software needs. You might start with small steps, configuring a screen saver or new trackball, for example, and move on to more ambitious configuration tasks that include installing more disk storage and configuring additional protocols. If the server is destined for Internet and intranet services, then one of your configuration steps will involve installing the Internet Information Services component, which is updated from the one included with Windows NT 4.0.

You start with small steps in this chapter by learning Control Panel options that include setting up display and pointing devices and configuring protocols and other network options. You learn about tools that can help make server configuration easy, such as the Add/Remove Hardware Wizard and the Network and Dial-up Connections tool. Configuration tasks that may at first sound daunting are greatly simplified by the tools included in Windows 2000.

SETTING UP THE SERVER ENVIRONMENT

Windows 2000 Server offers one place for you to get an immediate start in configuring the server, the Control Panel. Because you may need to immediately set up the server for a particular monitor, pointing device, or keyboard, the Control Panel is often the first place to start configuring. The Control Panel is similar to a control center where you can customize Windows 2000 Server for devices, network connectivity, dial-up capabilities, and many other functions. In the sections that follow, you gain an overview of the Control Panel tools and next you learn how to use them. Plan to thoroughly learn the Control Panel options because they are vital to the role of a server administrator.

CONTROL PANEL OVERVIEW

The Control Panel is accessed by clicking the Start button, highlighting the Settings option, and then clicking Control Panel. Two other ways to access the Control Panel are from My Computer on the Windows 2000 desktop and from the My Computer option in Windows Explorer. Each tool in the Control Panel is represented by an icon or folder. To customize the display, click the View menu, which has options similar to the ones in Windows Explorer. From the View menu, you can customize the toolbars and Explorer bars, the size of the icons, the display of details, and the arrangement of icons. For example, some users like to activate the Standard Buttons and Address Bar for fast access to utilities. Figure 6-1 illustrates the Control Panel with both of these options enabled by placing checks in front of each one.

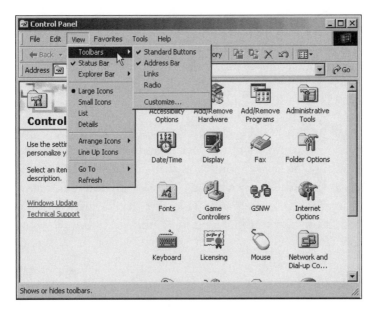

Figure 6-1   Control Panel toolbars

The content and purpose of the Control Panel is changed in Windows 2000 as compared to Windows NT because the focus in Windows 2000 is on server configuration, instead of on combined management and configuration tools. For example, the management of server services and logged on users is part of the Computer Management snap-in in Windows 2000 and not part of the Control Panel as in Windows NT. Some of the icons that appear in the Windows 2000 Control Panel are determined by what applications you have installed, particularly third-party applications that use the Control Panel for configuration.

The sections that follow provide summaries of the Control Panel tools that are typically installed when you install Windows 2000.

Accessibility Options

The Accessibility Options tool enables a computer to accommodate the particular visual, audio, and sensory needs of the user. Keyboard and mouse button options can be used to set up the workstation for easier access. Special SerialKey devices can be installed to provide alternatives to keyboard and mouse use. Table 6-1 lists the options and their purpose.

Table 6-1   Accessibility Options

Accessibility Option	Purpose
Display	Enables the display to be set to use colors and contrast for easier viewing
General	Sets alternative keyboard and mouse access features and provides notification when an accessibility feature is turned off
Keyboard	Provides alternate touch and sound options for keyboard functions
Mouse	Enables the keyboard keypad to act as a pointing device
Sound	Displays visual warnings and captions for sounds

Add/Remove Hardware

Hardware installation and troubleshooting is made easier by clicking this icon to start the Add/Remove Hardware Wizard. Use the icon when you add a new SCSI adapter or install a second NIC, for example. Because Windows 2000 Server supports Plug and Play (PnP), the wizard can detect the device and automatically configure the IRQ and I/O settings.

You can also use the wizard to troubleshoot a problem with a device or to uninstall or unplug a device (see Figure 6-2). For example, you might uninstall a NIC before you replace it with another one, or temporarily unplug a PCMCIA card before removing it from the computer.

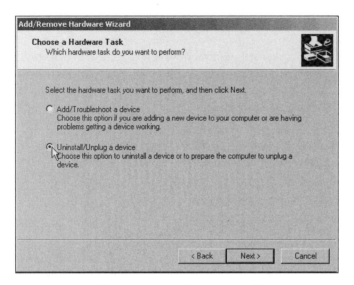

Figure 6-2 Add/Remove Hardware Wizard

 # Add/Remove Programs

Software applications are installed and uninstalled using the Add/Remove Programs tool. For example, click the Add/Remove Windows Components option after starting the tool, to install an application that was not installed at the time of the Windows 2000 Server setup. The components that you can install are listed in Table 6-2. Also, you can install any new software, such as Microsoft Office, by clicking the Add New Programs option or remove an installed application by clicking Change or Remove Programs.

> **TIP** Pre-Windows software or "legacy" MS-DOS software cannot be loaded with the Add/Remove Programs tool. To load legacy software, use the Run option from the Start menu.

Table 6-2 Windows Components

Component	Description
Accessories and Utilities	Installs components that include a wizard to config-ure accessibility options, accessories such as Notepad, communications tools, games, and multimedia tools
Certificate Services	Used for certification authority for security through certificates
Indexing Service	Used to quickly search file contents for specific words or strings of words
Internet Information Services (IIS)	Installs Internet Information Services for a Web site and for FTP-based file transfers through TCP/IP

Table 6-2   Windows Components (continued)

Component	Description
Management and Monitoring Tools	Used to manage and monitor the server and the network
Message Queuing Services	Services for network-based messaging
Networking Services	Installs protocols for specialized services that include DNS, QoS, DHCP, and other services
Other Network File and Print Services	Enables print services for UNIX and Macintosh computers
Remote Installation Services	Enables the installation of Windows 2000 Professional on remote computers that can be booted remotely
Remote Storage	Used to enable Windows 2000 to write files to remote devices, such as tape drives
Script Debugger	Enables debugging of ActiveX script tools, VB script for example
Terminal Services	Enables clients to run programs located on the server, as though they were terminals
Terminal Services Licensing	Controls licensing for terminal services
Windows Media Services	Used to "stream" multimedia from the server to the clients, so that an audio/video file starts playing before it is fully received

Administrative Tools

This folder is added to the Control Panel as a convenience to quickly access shortcuts to administrative tools, such as the Computer Management tool or the Internet Services Manager tool. One reason for having an Administrative Tools folder in the Control Panel is that NT Server 4.0 users may be used to open the Control Panel to access management tools. The other way to access these tools is by clicking Start, pointing to Programs, and pointing to Administrative Tools.

Date/Time

With the Date/Time tool, you can set the calendar date, time, and time zone. This is an important tool for date-stamping files to track software versions, updates to financial information, and logon and access history data on a server or a workstation. Documents, files, and other important information are permanently imprinted with a **date stamp** to record their creation date and time and to record modification dates and times.

Display

The Display tool is used to set video characteristics, including the desktop background, display colors and resolution, the appearance of the title bar, screen-saver parameters, and other options.

There also are settings to help accommodate a user's visual impairments. Table 6-3 lists the Display options.

Table 6-3 Display Options

Display Option	Purpose
Appearance	Sets the appearance of desktop entities such as title bars, application background, window borders, and icons
Background	Sets the display pattern and wallpaper
Effects	Sets visual parameters for icons and which icons to associate with desktop functions
Screen Saver	Sets up a screen saver, controls screen saver parameters, and controls the energy-saving features of your display (if the display is energy-saver-compatible)
Settings	Sets up the color palette and pixel desktop area and is used to troubleshoot problems with display settings
Web	Sets the properties of Web page displays

Fax

When you have fax-capable hardware installed, Windows 2000 provides built-in fax services that you can configure from the Control Panel. There are options to configure user information, including the fax user's name, the fax telephone number, user e-mail address, and other descriptive information. You can also set up a cover page for the entire organization or cover pages for specific individuals or departments. Fax monitoring preferences are configured that include how you are notified when a fax is received.

Folder Options

In previous versions of Windows, you customize folder options from My Computer or Windows Explorer. In Windows 2000 you can customize folder options from the Control Panel as well as from My Computer and Windows Explorer. The folder options enable you to customize the desktop, customize how you browse folders, customize how files are viewed, associate file types with programs, and determine if files set up for network access can be used when you are not logged on to the network. For example, the Folder Options icon enables you to set the desktop to allow you to browse folders by using the same interface as is used for Internet Explorer, or you can use the classic Windows desktop interface. You can also set Windows 2000 to automatically start a program, such as Notepad when you open a file that has a specific extension, for example, starting Notepad when you open files with a .txt extension, such as Netlog.txt. There are four tabs full of options that you can set: General, View, File Types, and Offline Files (see Figure 6-3). Table 6-4 summarizes the options.

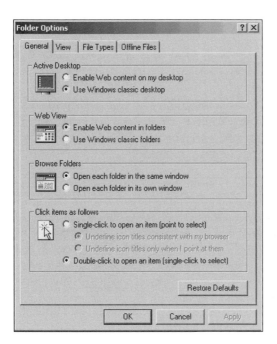

Figure 6-3   Folder Options dialog box

Table 6-4   Folder Options

Folder Option	Purpose
General	Sets up the active desktop and Web views, customizes how folders are opened, and determines if items are opened through a single or double click
View	Determines how files and folders are viewed, such as whether hidden files and folders are displayed and if certain file extensions are displayed
File Types	Enables you to associate a file type, such as an HTTP file (.htp), with a program that runs when you open the file, Internet Explorer for example
Offline Files	Enables you to set up network files shared by other computers so that you can access them offline by storing the files on the server and synchronizing the files between the server and network before logging off

Fonts

Windows 2000 Server supports a huge number of fonts and point sizes, and software vendors offer additional fonts for Windows. Fonts are installed or removed with the Fonts tool. Installed fonts are contained in the \Winnt\Fonts folder.

Game Controllers

This Control Panel option is included primarily for parallel development with Windows 2000 Professional, because you are not likely to attach a game controller to a server. Game controllers in Windows 2000 are connected either to a USB port, to a serial port, or as a card in an expansion slot. If the controller is connected to a USB port, Windows 2000 automatically detects it, as long as the computer is turned on when the controller is installed. If the controller is connected to a serial port or in an expansion slot, then you can configure the controller by using the Game Controllers icon in Control Panel.

GSNW

The GSNW (Gateway Service for NetWare) icon is used to configure Windows 2000 Server to act as a gateway for one or more NetWare file servers. Users running Windows 3.11, Windows 95, Windows 98, Windows NT, and Windows 2000 can access NetWare folders and files as a Windows 2000 Server shared folder instead of logging on to a NetWare server. This tool provides a way to manage the gateway services, which must first be installed, started, and running before they are available to clients.

Internet Options

The Internet Options icon is used to customize Internet access to the server. The properties that you can set up include the location of the home page to access first, the location of temporary Internet files, security parameters, content and certificate management, dial-up connectivity, programs for e-mail access, and advanced options. The advanced options are for browsing, Java access, multimedia access, printing, and security. Windows 2000 offers a wide range of Internet security parameters.

Keyboard

With the Keyboard tool, you can customize the keyboard setup for key repeat rate, cursor blink rate, language, and keyboard type. Also, you can install a new keyboard driver by using this tool.

Licensing

After you install Windows 2000 Server, you may decide to purchase additional licenses to match the growth in network use. The Licensing tool enables you to add new licenses and to remove licenses. It also lets you change the licensing mode from per server to per seat, or vice versa.

Mouse

With the Mouse tool, left-handed users, those who want a different scheme of mouse pointer symbols, and those who want to slow down the mouse response can customize the mouse. The tool is used to install or upgrade a mouse driver, if you change from a mouse to a trackball for example.

Network and Dial-up Connections

The connectivity features in previous Windows versions are united into the Network and Dial-up Connections folder, which can be accessed from the Control Panel and from the Start button Settings menu. This tool is used any time you need to create a new connection to a network, to another computer, to a WAN, or to a dial-up network. There is a Network Connection Wizard that steps you through setting up a new connection. Also, the tool enables you to change the parameters for an existing connection, such as adding a new protocol to connect to the network. Another option is to load network services using the Network and Dial-up Connections tool.

6

 TIP An important new feature in Windows 2000 is the ability to disable a network connection via the Network and Dial-up Connections folder (see Figure 6-4). Use this feature when you need to take the server offline for maintenance, such as when you make changes to protocols or install a new driver.

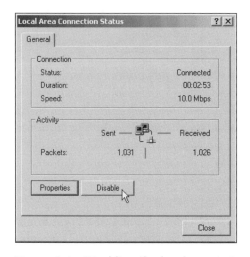

Figure 6-4   Disabling the local area network connection

 ## Phone and Modem Options

Modems work using telecommunications lines or cable TV lines, and modems connected to telecommunications lines may have voice and telephone capabilities. The Phone & Modem Options tool enables you to configure a modem for data and voice communication. You can use the tool to upgrade a current modem driver or to start the Add/Remove Hardware Wizard when you add a new modem.

You use the Phone and Modem tool to check that installed modems are set to their maximum speed and that communications parameters, such as data bits, parity, and stop bits, are set correctly. Usually data bits are set to 8, parity is none, and stop bits equal 1.

Data bits are the number of bits used to represent one character, such as the letter "a." Parity is a method to check for errors, and the stop bit is a character used to indicate that the transmission of a byte of data is complete. Also, by using the Phone and Modem Options tool you can set up the data protocol and compression used in modem communications. On voice- and fax-capable modems, you can set up parameters, such as different ring sequences, for data only, voice, or fax calls, as they are received.

Power Options

Because Windows 2000 supports power management, it enables you to configure these options through the Power Options icon in the Control Panel. For example, you can set management options to turn off the monitor or hard disks after a specified period that they have not been in use. Another option is to have the computer automatically shut down when the off button is pressed. Also, the computer can be set to go into "hibernation" when it is not in use, automatically saving to disk what is in memory.

> **TIP** Some server administrators only use power management to turn off the monitor, or they do not use any power management, depending how a server is being used.

Printers

This is the same Printers folder that can be accessed from the Start button Settings option. It contains the Add Printer Wizard for installing a new printer, plus controls for managing one already set up. (Printer management is covered in Chapter 11.)

Regional Options

Users who prefer to view time in 24-hour notation use this tool to customize the display. The Regional Options tool also enables international customization of numbers, the date and time formats, currency, and language. For the new millenium, there is an option to interpret a two-digit year format to a four-digit format.

Scanners and Cameras

Windows 2000 supports the attachment of scanners and cameras. If you install a scanner card or attach a digital camera, use the Scanners and Cameras icon to install and set up the drivers for these devices.

Scheduled Tasks

In Windows NT there is an AT command available through the Command Prompt window that enables you to run a specific task, command, or script at a specified time. Windows 2000 adds the Scheduled Tasks folder so that you have more flexibility in scheduling tasks from a GUI environment. The addition of the folder enables you to run the Scheduled Task Wizard, which offers a list of programs to schedule, such as Disk Cleanup or Synchronize (for DCs). You can run the task one time only or at regular intervals, such as once a day or once a week at a specified time. For example, you might run Synchronize each evening before starting to back up all servers on a network. Also, you can specify that a task be run from a specific account that has permissions to execute that task.

When you create a scheduled task, a file is created in \Winnt\Tasks that works in conjunction with the AT scheduling command and the Task Scheduler service. The advantages of this addition to Windows 2000 are that scheduled tasks are easier to set up, and they can be ported to any Windows 2000 server by copying the appropriate file.

6

 TIP Use the Computer Management tool to make sure that the Task Scheduler service is set to start automatically before you set up scheduled tasks.

Sounds and Multimedia

Special sound effects are provided with Windows 2000 Server, such as musical chords, dinging bells, "tada!," and others. New sounds can be purchased and added. The Sounds tool enables the server administrator to associate a sound with a specific event, such as receiving a new mail message or shutting down the computer. Of course, to use sounds, the computer needs a sound card and speakers.

Windows 2000 Server supports a wide range of audio, music, and speech capabilities, including multimedia compression, MIDI, and other devices. These devices, including drivers, are added and removed through the Sounds and Multimedia tool. The tool also has playback and recording controls.

System

The server environment and performance are managed from the System tool (see Figure 6-5). Windows 2000 Server has advanced capabilities to set up hardware and user profiles, which is useful when the server functions as a means to provide a common desktop to some or all server users. Desktop settings can be customized so users see the same desktop no matter which computer they use to log on to the server. Also, different hardware profiles can be set up to match changing situations, such as when the server sometimes uses a remote monitor and keyboard and sometimes uses its own monitor and keyboard. Remote setups are used in machine rooms in which there are 10, 20, or more servers, all connected through a switch box to be accessed from a single monitor and keyboard. You can also use the System tool to change the name of the computer or the domain, and to tune the server for better performance.

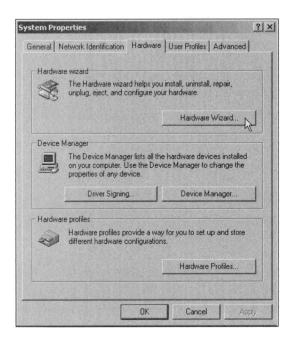

Figure 6-5   System options

CONFIGURING THE SERVER ENVIRONMENT

The immediate configuration tasks involving Control Panel icons often include configuring the display, a pointing device, a keyboard, and startup and power management parameters; installing hardware; configuring protocols; and installing additional software components. The sections that follow describe how to install and configure all of these. However, before discussing the installation of new hardware or how to configure a protocol, it is important to introduce a new feature in Windows 2000 called driver signing.

Configuring Driver Signing

When you install a device such as a pointing device or a NIC, you have the option to make sure that the driver for that device has been verified by Microsoft. When a driver is verified by Microsoft, a unique digital signature is incorporated into that driver, in a process called **driver signing**. When you set up Windows 2000 Server you can choose to be warned that a driver is not signed, to ignore whether or not a driver is signed, or to have the operating system prevent you from installing a driver that is not signed. To set your preference:

1. Log on as Administrator or with Administrator privileges.

2. Open the System icon in the Control Panel.

3. Click the Hardware tab and click Driver Signing (refer to Figure 6-5).

4. Click one of the three options under File signature verification: Ignore – Install all files, regardless of the file signature, Warn – Display a message before installing an unsigned file, or Block – Prevent installation of unsigned files. (The Warn option is set as the default.)

5. Check or remove the check from the option, Apply setting as system default. If you check this option, this means that Windows 2000 Server will apply signature verification to users who log on to the server and attempt to install any software (which gives you a measure of assurance that a virus will not be introduced and that the software is Windows 2000 compatible).

6. Click OK to save your settings in the Driver Signing Options dialog box.

7. Click OK to exit the System Properties dialog box.

When you configure driver signing, you configure it to apply to all new software installations, as well as device drivers. Each time you install a word processor or spreadsheet application, the drivers used in that application are also verified. If you have selected the Block option, this means that drivers and operating system files cannot be modified or overwritten by files that do not have the appropriate digital signature. No software installation can inadvertently install a driver or system file that is inappropriate for your version of Windows 2000 Server.

If you do not have the Block option set and you copy an inappropriate file over a system or driver file, for example a .dll, .exe, or .sys file, Windows 2000 Server automatically runs the System File Checker when the operating system boots. The System File Checker locates the original system file in the Winnt\system32\dllcache folder and then copies it over the inappropriate file. You also have the option to run the System File Checker from the command prompt to check files without rebooting by using these steps:

1. Click Start, point to Programs, point to Accessories, and then click Command Prompt.

2. Enter sfc /? in the Command Prompt window, to view the switch options you can use to check and replace files.

3. Use either the Start button, Run option or the Command Prompt window to run the scan that is appropriate to your situation, such as *sfc /scannow* to begin scanning all system files and overwrite any inappropriate files that it finds. Keep in mind that it is safest to have users off the system when you check files and you still may need to reboot before a replaced file goes into effect.

4. In some cases, the checker may request that you insert the Windows 2000 Server CD-ROM to obtain a file.

5. The checker displays an information box to show its progress. If it finds a file that needs to be replaced, it prompts you (unless you run the utility in quiet mode).

Windows 2000 Server includes another tool, called Sigverif, that verifies system and critical files to determine if they have a signature. This tool only scans files and does not overwrite inappropriate files, enabling you to use the tool while users are logged on. To use Sigverif, click the Start button, click Run, enter Sigverif in the Run dialog box, and click OK. Click the Advanced button in the first dialog box to set the verification options and then click Start to begin verifying files.

Configuring the Display

One of the first server components that you may need to configure is the display. For example, you might decide to replace the existing monitor with one that is smaller or larger, or to use a specialized monitor, any of which requires installing a new driver. Also, you likely will install a screen saver for the display. A new display driver is installed from the Settings tab after opening the Display tool (see Figure 6-6). Click the Advanced button, the Monitor tab, the Properties button, and the Driver tab. Click Uninstall to remove a driver or click Update Driver to put in another one. You will need a driver disk from the monitor manufacturer, or you can use a driver from the Windows 2000 Server CD-ROM. You can also adjust the color and pixel settings of the screen from the Settings tab in the Display Properties dialog box. For example, if your screen supports 32-bit True Color but is set for 256 Colors, you would click the Colors box, select True Color (32 bit), click Apply, and click OK to have the screen go into a temporary test mode using the new setting. You would click Yes if the test looked good, or click No to go back to the original setting (try Hands-on Project 6-1).

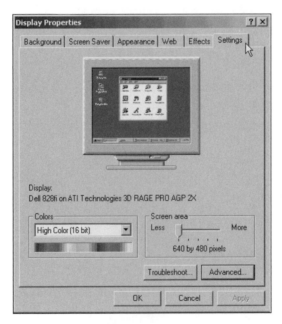

Figure 6-6 Configuring the display

Another way to install or uninstall a driver for any device is to use the Device Manager. Click the System icon in the Control Panel, click the Hardware tab, click the Device Manager button, and double-click the device, such as display adapter. Click the specific device name, such as ATI Technologies Inc. 3D Rage Pro, and click the Driver tab. You can also access the Device Manager from the Computer Management tool.

Installing a screen saver has two important advantages: it extends the life of the display monitor, and it provides security when you step away from the server after logging on. Screen savers are especially important for extending the life of a typical monitor, which functions much like a television screen. The monitor contains a cathode-ray tube with a gun that shoots electrons at a phosphorus-based screen inside the tube. The electrons are fired in patterns to form images on the screen. When the same screen image is displayed continuously for hours, such as on a word-processing screen, the repeated shooting of the electrons to the same areas can "burn" that image into the screen. A screen saver produces constant change on the screen, causing the electron gun to fire at more random screen locations, instead of at the same spot.

Equally important, a screen saver can provide security when you are away from the server, but have not logged off from an account, such as Administrator, which has extensive access to the entire network and its resources. With security enabled, you must enter a password to close the screen saver and return to the work screen. That prevents anyone without the password from accessing the server.

Windows 2000 Server supports **OpenGL**, which is a standard for multidimensional graphics. Several interesting OpenGL-based screen savers are available for Windows 2000, including a few already bundled with the operating system, 3D Flowerbox, 3D Flying Objects, and 3D Pipes, for example. These graphics add a pleasing touch to screen savers.

Choose a screen saver carefully. Some screen savers are CPU-intensive, which means they can slow down user and background processes on a server. This is especially a problem with OpenGL screen savers, including 3D Maze and 3D Pipes. For low system resource use and simplicity, some network administrators use the Logon Screen Saver, which is a moving Windows 2000 box.

To set up a screen saver with a password, double-click the Display icon in the Control Panel and click the Screen Saver tab. Select a screen saver in the Screen Saver box and place a check in the Password protected box, as shown in Figure 6-7. Enter the amount of time that the screen can be inactive before the screen saver is started, such as 10 minutes. Click the Apply button to have the change go into effect immediately and click OK.

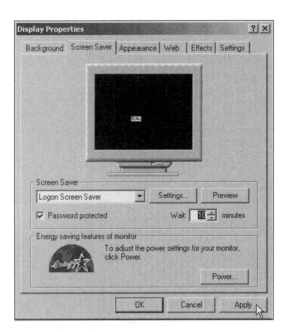

Figure 6-7   Screen saver setup

Configuring the Mouse and Pointing Devices

The Mouse icon in the Control Panel provides a way to customize mouse features and to install a driver for a particular type of pointing device, such as a trackball. The customization options are shown in Table 6-5.

Table 6-5   Mouse Setup Options

Option	Purpose
Buttons	Sets right-handed and left-handed options, single-click and double-click options, plus the double-click speed
Hardware	Sets up a new mouse and driver and hardware resources, such as the IRQ
Motion	Controls the mouse speed and acceleration, and sets the default "snap to" option
Pointers	Customizes the pointer icons displayed with specific functions such as busy or text select

To change the mouse speed, click the Motion tab and adjust the pointer speed bar between slow and fast. If you are installing a new mouse driver, click the Hardware tab, the Properties button, and then the Driver tab (see Figure 6-8). Click Uninstall to remove a driver or click Update driver to update an existing driver or to have the Upgrade Device Driver Wizard detect another pointing device and install the driver. Insert the pointing device manufacturer's disk containing the driver and click Have Disk to install the driver. Provide the path to the driver disk and click OK.

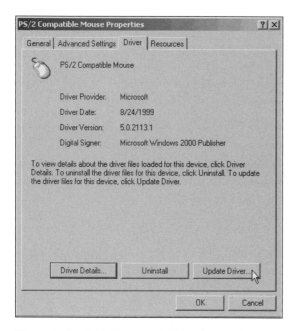

Figure 6-8   Installing a pointing device driver

Configuring the Keyboard

The Keyboard icon in the Control Panel provides a way to change keyboard characteristics or to install a driver for a specialized keyboard. For example, if you find the key repeat rate is too fast, click the Speed tab and move the repeat rate bar to a slower setting. If you are using a specialized keyboard and there is an updated driver for it, click the Hardware tab, the Properties button, and the Driver tab. Click Update Driver to start the Upgrade Device Driver Wizard. Make sure you have the manufacturer's driver disk with the new driver. Table 6-6 summarizes the keyboard configuration options.

Table 6-6   Keyboard Setup Options

Option	Purpose
Hardware	Displays keyboard properties, installs a keyboard driver, and troubleshoots problems
Input Locales	Sets up language and other keyboard properties for locales that use different languages, such as English and Swedish
Speed	Sets up keyboard characteristics such as repeat delay, repeat rate, and cursor blink rate

Adding, Removing, and Testing Hardware

The easiest way to add new hardware is to use the Add/Remove Hardware tool in Control Panel. It is common to add hardware after you have installed Windows 2000 Server, such as a new SCSI adapter, a different monitor adapter, a different keyboard, a tape drive, or a RAID array. The Add/Remove Hardware Wizard can detect the new device as long as you have the Plug and Play service started in advance. When you install a device, make sure you have the most recent copy of the manufacturer's driver for that device, obtaining it via the Internet for instance. For example, if you install a new SCSI adapter card:

1. Turn off the computer and install the card according to the manufacturer's instructions.

2. Turn on and boot the computer, then open the Control Panel and double-click the Add/Remove Hardware icon to start the Add/Remove Hardware Wizard.

3. Click Next.

4. Click Add/Troubleshoot a device.

5. Wait for the wizard to detect and configure the device. Have the manufacturer's device driver available in case you need it for the installation.

If the Add/Remove Hardware Wizard cannot detect the device, check the Plug and Play service by clicking Start, pointing to Programs, pointing to Administrative Tools, and clicking Computer Management (or open Computer Management from the Administrative Tools icon in Control Panel). Click Services and Applications in the left or right pane and double-click Services in the left or right pane. Scroll the right pane until you see Plug and Play, then make sure that the status shows Started (you may need to double-click Plug and Play to view the status). If it does not, double-click Plug and Play, display the General tab, and click Start.

Also, you can use the Add/Remove Hardware Wizard to remove or unplug a device, which you can do from the Choose a Hardware Task dialog box by clicking Uninstall/Unplug a device (try Hands-on Project 6-2). For example, consider a situation in which the original NIC in the server is a 10/100-Mbps NIC and you want to install a 1-Gbps NIC, in order to connect the server directly to a high-speed backbone switch for faster throughput. The general steps you would follow are:

1. Open the Control Panel Network and Dial-up Connections icon, double-click Local Area Connection, click Disable, and close the Network and Dial-up Connections tool.

2. Open the Control Panel Add/Remove Hardware icon, click Next, click Uninstall/Unplug a device (see Figure 6-2), click Next, and click Uninstall a device in the Choose a Removal Task dialog box. Click Next. Select to uninstall the 10/100-Mbps NIC that you want to replace (see Figure 6-9). Click Next and complete the Uninstall steps.

3. Shut down and turn off the computer. Remove the old NIC and install the new one. Turn on the computer to reboot.

4. The Add/Remove Wizard will start when you reboot so that you can configure the new NIC; or you can start the Wizard from the Control Panel. Install and configure the new NIC.

5. Use the Network and Dial-up Connections tool in Control Panel to make sure that the NIC is connected to the network by double-clicking Local Area Connection as you did in Step 1. Also, check the NIC's configuration by clicking Properties in the Local Area Connection Status dialog box, and then click Configure on the General tab. For example, you can configure transmission media type and duplex settings by clicking the Advanced tab (depending on the driver included with your NIC), and you can check for a resource conflict by clicking the Resources tab (resource conflicts are discussed later in this chapter).

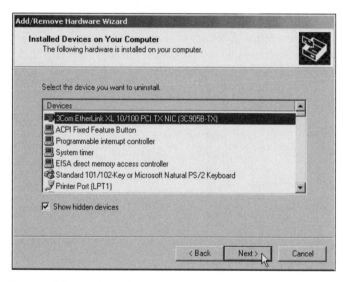

Figure 6-9   Uninstalling a NIC

Because you have just installed the server, you may want to check one or more devices, such as a disk or tape drive, to make certain they are working properly. To check a device, start the Add/Remove Hardware Wizard from the Control Panel, click Next, click Add/Troubleshoot a device, click Next, select the device you want to test, click Next, and view the results. Click Finish to end or click Back to go back and test another device (try Hands-on Project 6-3).

Configuring Startup and Recovery

Windows 2000 Server enables you to configure parameters that govern the startup sequence and how the system recovers from errors. Check theses settings shortly after you install the operating system to make sure they match your needs. The startup parameters enable you to modify the Boot.ini file for a dual-boot system in order to specify which operating system to boot by default and how long to wait in seconds before starting the operating system.

The recovery parameters enable you to provide instructions about how to recover in the event of a system failure. For example, you can have the system create a log to help you locate the source of the failure after the computer reboots, and you can instruct the computer to reboot automatically upon failure. The options are as follows:

- Record the system failure as an event in the system log.

- Transmit an alert message to designated system administrators.

- Write debug information to the default file, \Winnt\Memory.dmp, or to a file you specify.

- Have the computer reboot automatically immediately after the failure.

You can configure the Startup and Recovery options from the Control Panel by double-clicking the System icon, clicking the Advanced tab, and clicking Startup and Recovery. Make the appropriate selections in the Startup and Recovery dialog box (see Figure 6-10) click OK, and then click OK again to acknowledge that you must reboot. Click OK in the System Properties dialog box and click Yes to restart the server (try Hands-on Project 6-4).

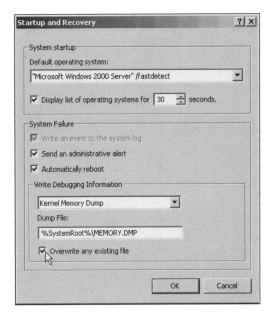

Figure 6-10   Configuring startup and recovery options

Configuring Power Management

After you have installed Windows 2000 Server, check the power management options to make sure that they are set appropriately for the computer and the way you are using the computer on the network. The default power scheme is set at Always On, which means that it will turn the monitor off after 20 minutes, never turn off the hard disks, and never put the system in the standby mode. Also, the default setup is to run the shutdown procedure when you press the power off button, instead of placing the computer in standby mode. **Standby** is a mode in which the computer components are shut down and information in memory is cleared without automatically saving it to disk. The power supply and CPU remain active, waiting to start up all components when you press a key or move the mouse.

Configure the power options by opening Control Panel and double-clicking the Power Options icon. Access the Power Schemes tab first to establish the power settings, which include settings for desktop, laptop, and server computers. The settings change on the basis of the power scheme that you select, Portable/Laptop or Minimal Power Management, for example. In most situations, you will likely select Always On or Minimal Power Management, which are options that primarily involve display monitor power management. Another option is to create your own settings by specifying how soon to turn off the monitor, whether to turn off the hard disks, and whether to use standby mode. For example, you might set up a customized option called Server by following these steps:

1. Open the Power Options icon and access the Power Schemes tab.

2. Click the Turn off monitor list arrow and select After 1 hour.

3. Make sure that the Turn off hard disks list box displays Never.

4. Make sure that the System standby list box displays Never.

5. Click Save As, enter Server in the Save Scheme dialog box, and click OK. Click Apply and then OK to save your work (see Figure 6-11).

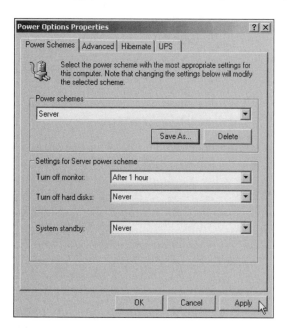

Figure 6-11   Configuring power management

Also check the Advanced tab to determine whether the computer will power off or go into standby mode, which is determined by what you enter in the "When I press the power button on my computer" box. Because you will likely be working on the computer hardware or want to perform a cold boot when you power it off, the default is set to power off. If you select standby mode, consider checking the box titled, "Prompt for password when computer goes off standby," so that only an authorized server administrator can access the server.

The third tab, Hibernate, enables you to set up the computer to hibernate when it is not in use. **Hibernate mode** is similar to standby, but with two important differences: the memory contents are saved before shutting down the disks, and it takes longer to restart all components to resume where you left off.

The fourth tab enables you to configure an uninterruptible power supply (UPS), which is a battery backup device that temporarily supplies power to the server when the main power goes out. You can set up communications between the UPS and the Windows 2000 Server through a serial connection so that the UPS notifies the server when there is a power outage and the server sends you an alert.

Configuring Protocols

The Windows 2000 Server installation steps in Chapter 5 have already illustrated how to install the default protocol configuration. However, you may need to add other protocols or to modify the existing configuration to customize the server for your network. Use the Network and Dial-up Connections folder from the Control Panel (or access the folder from the Start button Settings menu) to set up the server to communicate using other protocols, such as IPX/SPX and NetBEUI, or to configure TCP/IP. For example, you might use IPX/SPX to communicate with a particular network printer, such as an older Hewlett-Packard laser printer; or you might need to set up Windows 2000 Server to communicate as a client or gateway with a Novell NetWare server. If you are adding Windows 2000 Server to an older small network that uses only NetBEUI, then you can install this protocol as well.

Installing NWLink IPX/SPX Compatible Transport

NWLink IPX/SPX/NetBIOS Compatible Transport is installed from the Network and Dial-up Connections folder by opening the folder, double-clicking Local Area Connection, and then clicking the Properties button. Click the Install button, click Protocol, and click Add (see Figure 6-12). Select NWLink IPX/SPX/NetBIOS Compatible Transport, and click OK. As with other installations, you may need to insert the Windows 2000 Server CD-ROM, provide its path, and click to continue.

After installing the protocol, make sure that the right network number and frame type are implemented to work with the NetWare server or IPX/SPX printer to which you will connect.

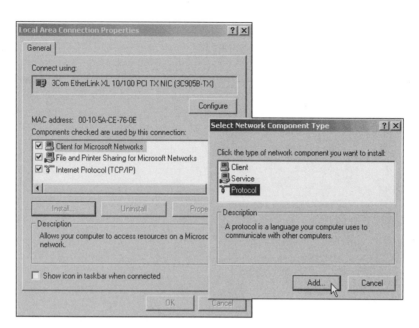

Figure 6-12   Installing a protocol

Depending on the version, NetWare may be using Ethernet frame types 802.2 or 802.3, Ethernet II, or Ethernet SNAP. The Windows 2000 server should be using the same frame type as the NetWare servers or other IPX/SPX-compatible devices already on the network. To check this information, open the Network and Dial-up Connections folder, double-click Local Area Connection, click Properties, and double-click NWLink IPX/SPX/NetBIOS Compatible Transport Protocol in the scroll box. Leave the internal network number as 00000000, if you only plan to connect to a NetWare server as a client or to connect to a printer using IPX/SPX. If you are connecting to a NetWare server to use File and Print Services for NetWare, IPX routing, or a NetWare service that uses **Service Advertising Protocol (SAP)**, then designate an internal network number, such as 00000001 (see Chapter 3). SAP is used by NetWare clients to identify servers and the network services provided by each server. An internal network is mainly used for IPX routing to create the equivalent of a private virtual network between a NetWare server and the Windows 2000 server.

If the servers or printers to which you are connecting only use one frame type, Windows 2000 will automatically determine which frame type is in use so that you do not need to configure it. If more than one frame type is used, Windows 2000 defaults to the Ethernet 802.2 frame, and you will need to manually configure the other frame types and network number (see Chapter 3). To configure additional frame types, click the Manual frame type detection radio button and then click Add (see Figure 6-13). Select the frame type, such as Ethernet 802.3,

Ethernet II, or Ethernet SNAP, and provide the network number. Click OK to add the frame type, and repeat the process for each frame type that you need to use. Click OK in the NWLink IPX/SPX/NetBIOS Compatible Transport Protocol dialog box when you are finished. Click OK on the Local Area Connection Properties dialog box and close all remaining dialog boxes to complete the process. (Practice installing NWLink in Hands-on Project 6-5.)

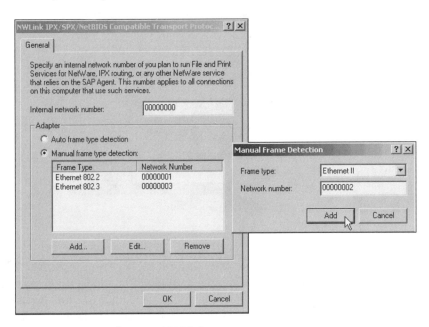

Figure 6-13   Configuring NWLink

Configuring TCP/IP

Configuring TCP/IP also is performed from the Network and Dial-up Connections folder. However, installing TCP/IP can be more complex than installing NWLink, depending on whether dynamic or static addressing is used on the network. As you learned in Chapter 3, static addressing is used on many networks, large and small, when the network administrator wants direct control over the assigned addresses. Direct control might be necessary when network management software is used to track all network nodes, and the software depends on each node having a permanent, known IP address. As you learned, an IP address uses the dotted decimal notation system of addressing, which consists of four numbers separated by periods, such as 129.77.15.182. Permanent addresses provide consistency for monitoring network statistics and for keeping historical network performance information. The disadvantage is that IP address administration can be a laborious task on a large network. Most network administrators who use static addressing have an IP database to keep track of currently assigned addresses and unused addresses to assign as new people are connected to the network.

With dynamic addressing, an IP address is leased to a particular computer for a defined period of time. This addressing method uses the Dynamic Host Configuration Protocol (DHCP), which is a standard supported by Microsoft for dynamic addressing (see Chapter 3). The protocol is used to enable a server with DHCP services to detect the presence of a new workstation and assign addressing data to that workstation.

The sample installation in Chapter 5 used the default TCP/IP setup, which employs DHCP and automatically configures the server. Some server administrators prefer to manually configure TCP/IP on each server, as a way to guarantee that the server addresses never change and so that users are never confused about how to access a server. When you use static addressing on a server, you need to determine the following information before configuring TCP/IP:

6

- *IP address:* The server needs a unique IP address that is compatible with your network and not assigned to any other network computer.

- *Subnet mask:* A subnet mask is a method for showing which part of the IP address is a unique identifier for the network and which part uniquely identifies the workstation (see Chapter 3). On a simple network that does not connect with many other networks, the subnet mask is likely to be 255.255.0.0 or 255.255.255.0. If you use 255.255.0.0, this means the first two sets of digits (the 255s) are the network identification for the computers on that network, and the third and fourth sets of digits (the 0s) are used as the workstation identification. For example, your network might have a network identification of 122.44. All workstations and servers on your network will have IP addresses that start with 122.44 (and usually a 0 in the third place), such as 122.44.0.1, 122.44.0.2, and so on. If your network is composed of several networks combined into one, such as on a college campus, the subnet mask might be 255.255.255.0. In this case, the 255 in the third position is used to identify each smaller network or subnetwork. On a college campus that might mean there is a subnetwork for the administration buildings (122.44.1), one for the classroom buildings (122.44.2), and another for the dorms (122.44.3). In the dorms, your IP address might be 122.44.3.20, and your neighbor across the hall might be 122.44.3.21. Your professor in a classroom building might have the address, 122.44.2.54, and the academic dean in the administration building might have 122.44.1.23.

- *Default gateway:* A **default gateway** is a computer or router that forwards a network communication from one network to another. By specifying the IP address of the default gateway, you enable the server to communicate with workstations on another network. Transmitted data goes from your server to the gateway. The gateway then routes the data to the network it is intended to reach, where it is forwarded to the destination computer.

- *Domain name service (DNS) server:* As you learned in Chapter 3, this is a network server that converts names to IP addresses. For example, if your network has a mainframe called ADMIN, that mainframe also has an IP address, such as 122.44.1.5.

When you send e-mail or some other communication to mainframe ADMIN, a DNS network server converts that name to 122.44.1.5, enabling the communication to be transferred along the network in a format that computers and network devices understand. A DNS server also can convert the IP address back to the name for the sake of human users. The DNS server on a Windows 2000 Server network is usually a DC that also has DNS services installed. Many networks have a primary DNS server and one or more alternate DNS servers as backup in case the primary server is down or busy.

If TCP/IP is not already installed, you can install it using the same steps as are used to install NWLink, described in the last section, but select TCP/IP as the protocol to install instead of NWLink. You will need to configure TCP/IP after you install it. If TCP/IP is already installed, open the Network and Dial-up Connections folder and double-click Local Area Connection. Click the Properties button and double-click Internet Protocol (TCP/IP) in the components scroll box. Click the "Use the following IP address" radio button and enter the IP address, subnet mask, default gateway, and DNS information (see Figure 6-14). (Try Hands-on Project 6-6 to practice configuring TCP/IP.)

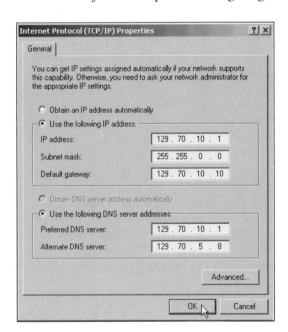

Figure 6-14   Configuring TCP/IP

The Advanced button, shown in Figure 6-14, enables you to configure additional parameters, such as the address of a WINS server and IP security (IPSec). As you learned in Chapter 3, a WINS server translates a workstation name to an IP address for communication between the Internet and Microsoft networks, and may be installed on the same network as a DNS server. When IPSec is enabled, you can specify the security policies explained in Chapter 4: Client

(Respond Only), Secure Server (Require Security), or Server (Request Security). WINS parameters are configured from the WINS tab, and IPsec is set up from the Options tab after you click the Advanced button (see Figure 6-15).

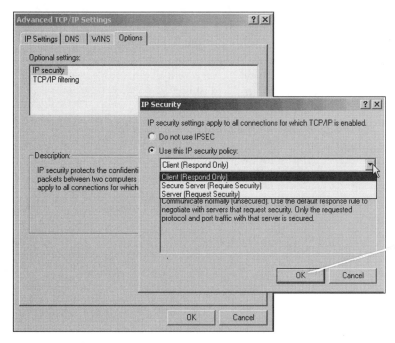

6

Figure 6-15 Configuring IPSec

Installing NetBEUI, DLC, and AppleTalk

NetBEUI, DLC, and AppleTalk are all installed using the Network and Dial-up Connections folder and by following the same steps that are described for installing NWLink. The main difference is that when the Select Network Protocol dialog box is displayed, select NetBEUI, DLC, or AppleTalk instead of NWLink. (Hands-on Project 6-5 provides an opportunity to practice installing NetBEUI.)

Installing Additional Windows 2000 Components

The additional components and software that you did not install initially in Windows 2000 Server can be installed in one of two places: the Network and Dial-up Connections folder and the Add/Remove Programs tool. Additional network components are installed using the Network and Dial-up Connections folder. To install one or more of these components, open the Network and Dial-up Connections folder in the Control Panel or click Start, point to Settings, and click Network and Dial-up Connections. Double-click Local Area Connection, click Properties, click Install, and double-click Service. From here you can install services such as QoS Packet Scheduler and the SAP agent.

To install Gateway (and client) services for NetWare, double-click Client instead of Service after you click the Install button in the Local Area Connection Properties dialog box.

Other Windows 2000 components, such as Internet Information Services, Networking Services, and Indexing Service (see Table 6-2) are installed using the Control Panel's Add/Remove Programs icon. After you open the Add/Remove Programs dialog box, click Add/Remove Windows Components (see Figure 6-16) to view the components that can be installed. Also, a component that is already installed but that has not been configured can be set up by clicking the Configure button that is displayed in the Add/Remove Programs window.

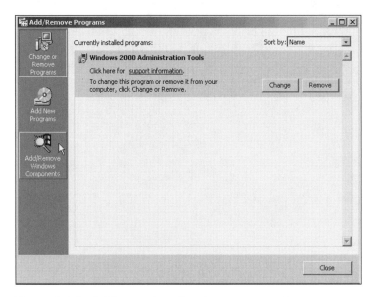

Figure 6-16   Adding and configuring components

MANAGING DEVICES AND RESOURCES

The Add/Remove Hardware Wizard is very effective in automatically setting up hardware parameters, such as resources. A server's **resources** include the **interrupt request (IRQ) line** (which is a channel for communication with the CPU) and other elements such as the **I/O address** and reserved memory range. For example, a computer contains a limited number of IRQ lines, such as 01–15. The video display, each disk drive, each serial and parallel port, and the sound card use a dedicated IRQ to communicate with the processor. Each also needs reserved memory addresses for I/O operations. Sometimes there are resource conflicts when a network adapter, a new SCSI adapter, or some other hardware is automatically configured. Besides using the Add/Remove Hardware Wizard, you can use the Device Manager to check for a resource conflict and to examine other properties associated with a device. For example, consider a situation in which there is an IRQ conflict between the NIC and another device. To check the NIC, click Start, point to Programs, point to Administrative Tools, and click Computer Management. Click System Tools in the left pane, double-click Device Manager in the right pane, and double-click Network adapters. Right-click the specific adapter that is displayed under Network adapters and click Properties. The properties dialog box displays tabs that you can use to fine-tune a device's configuration. To check for a resource conflict, click the Resources tab and look for a conflict message in the Conflicting device list box (see Figure 6-17). If there is a conflict, the Change Setting button will be active, and you can use it to select different resources (try Hands-on Project 6-7 to check for resource conflicts).

Another way to look for resource conflicts is through the Computer Management tool: double-click System Tools, double-click System Information, and then click Hardware Resources and Conflicts/Sharing.

6

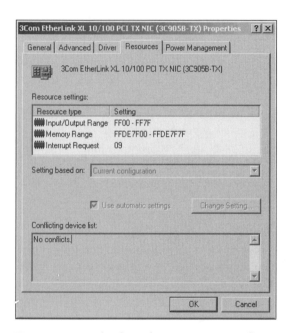

Figure 6-17   Checking for a resource conflict

You can also start Device Manager from the System icon in the Control Panel by displaying the Hardware tab.

CHAPTER SUMMARY

- Windows 2000 Server can be customized in hundreds of ways to match your particular implementation. After you install the server, one of the first stops that you will make to customize the installation is the Control Panel. Using tools in the Control Panel, you can add and remove hardware and software components. The Add/Remove Hardware

Wizard, for example, uses the Windows 2000 Plug and Play capability to significantly automate the installation of SCSI adapters, NIC, hard drives, and a wide range of other hardware. Also, the Control Panel offers tools to configure the display, keyboard, pointing device, folder options, startup and recovery procedures, network services, and protocols. You will use some Control Panel tools frequently, such as the Add/Remove Hardware Wizard and the Network and Dial-up Connections tool. You may use others shortly after installing Windows 2000 Server, but use them infrequently later on, such as the keyboard and mouse configuration tools.

In the next chapter you learn about powerful storage management capabilities in Windows 2000 Server, including fault-tolerant disk configurations and the ability to back up information. You also learn how to configure an uninterruptible power supply.

KEY TERMS

date stamp — Documents, files, and other important information are permanently imprinted by a date stamp to record their creation date and time, and to record modification dates and times.

default gateway — A computer or router that forwards a network communication from one network to another, acting as a gateway between networks.

driver signing — A digital signature that Microsoft incorporates into driver and system files as a way to verify the files and to ensure that they are not inappropriately overwritten.

hibernate — A mode in which the computer components are shut down, and information in memory is automatically saved to disk before the disk is powered off. The power supply and CPU remain active, monitoring in order to startup all components when you press a key or move the mouse.

interrupt request (IRQ) line — A hardware line that a computer component, such as a disk drive or serial port, uses to communicate to the processor that it is ready to send or receive information. Intel-based computers have 16 IRQ lines, with 15 of those available for computer components to use.

I/O address — The address in memory through which data is transferred between a computer component and the processor.

OpenGL — A standard for multidimensional graphics used in Microsoft's 3-D screen savers.

resource — On a workstation or server, an IRQ, I/O address, or memory that is allocated to a computer component, such as a disk drive or communications port. On a Windows 2000 Server network, a resource is a file server, shared printer, or shared directory that can be accessed by users.

Service Advertising Protocol (SAP) — An IPX/SPX-compatible protocol that is used by NetWare clients to identify servers and the network services provided by each server.

standby — A mode in which the computer components are shut down and information in memory is cleared without automatically saving it to disk. The power supply and CPU remain active, waiting to start up all components when you press a key or move the mouse.

REVIEW QUESTIONS

1. You are left-handed, but your mouse is set up for a right-handed person. What tool can you use to change the mouse configuration?

   a. Display tool in the Control Panel

   b. Mouse tool in the Control Panel

   c. Mouse, Keyboard, and Display snap-in for the MMC

   d. all of the above

   e. only a and b

   f. only b and c

2. For which protocol might you configure information about the default gateway?

   a. TCP/IP

   b. DLC

   c. NWLink

   d. AppleTalk

3. Your boss is concerned because some of the company's part-time night shift employees have access to the room where the server is located, and they like to play games on the server. Which option is the easiest to implement to provide more security?

   a. Remove the games.

   b. Set a time limit on the games.

   c. Create a special game account.

   d. Install a screen saver that requires a password.

4. Your Windows 2000 server needs to communicate with a NetWare server that uses IPX routing and applications that use SAP services. What protocol should you configure and how should you configure it?

   a. NWLink configured with an internal network number

   b. TCP/IP configured with an external network number

   c. NWLink configured for IP routing

   d. TCP/IP configured for WINs

5. What is the difference between the hibernate and standby modes?

   a. The BIOS setup contents are written to memory in hibernate mode, but not in standby mode.

   b. Standby mode only shuts down the monitor, whereas hibernate shuts down all server components except the NIC.

   c. The page file is moved to memory in standby mode, but not in hibernate mode.

   d. The memory contents are not written to disk in standby mode, but they are in hibernate mode.

6

6. When you open Windows Explorer and double-click a file that has a .log extension, you want to start Notepad to view that file. What tool enables you to associate this file type with running the Notepad application?

   a. Control Panel Display tool

   b. MMC Services tool

   c. Control Panel Folder Options tool

   d. Computer Manager Devices tool

7. You want to replace an older SCSI adapter with one that is newer. What tool enables you to uninstall the old adapter?

   a. Add/Remove Hardware Wizard

   b. SCSI Adapters tool in Control Panel

   c. Disconnect tool in Control Panel

   d. Add/Remove Windows 2000 Components Wizard

8. You are planning to update software on your company's Windows 2000 server and want to make sure that users cannot access the server temporarily. After you notify users that the server will be unavailable, how can you make sure they cannot access it while you are upgrading software?

   a. Shut down the server and reboot in MS-DOS from a floppy boot disk.

   b. Remove the network cable while the computer is still running.

   c. Put the computer in standby mode.

   d. Disable the NIC.

9. When you install NWLink, which of the following protocols and network services can it simulate?

   a. UDP

   b. SPX

   c. NetBIOS

   d. all of the above

   e. only a and b

   f. only b and c

10. When you set up TCP/IP to use DHCP, what other parameters do you need to configure manually?

    a. IP address

    b. IRQ

    c. DNS server address

    d. all of the above

    e. none of the above

    f. only a and c

11. You have set up NWLink so that your Windows 2000 server can communicate with several older NetWare 3.x and 4.x servers in your enterprise. In the process of configuring NWLink, you let it automatically determine the frame type, however now that it is set up you have problems communicating with some of the NetWare servers. What might you try?

   a. Set up DLC to communicate with the servers.

   b. Use FAT16 as the file system for the Windows 2000 server instead of NTFS.

   c. Find out if the NetWare servers and server applications communicate using more than one frame type.

   d. Make sure that none of the NetWare servers is using a network number that is over four digits.

12. Your company has primarily international clients and the customer relations group wants printed orders, invoices, and letters to show the date in date-month-year (dd-MMM-yy) format and the time in 24-hour format. Which of the following tools enables you to configure these as the defaults for your server?

   a. Control Panel Date/Time tool

   b. Control Panel Regional Options tool

   c. Control Panel Display tool

   d. all of the above

   e. only a and b

   f. only a and c

13. You notice that server response is sometimes slow when the screen saver is running and this is especially a problem when many users are accessing the server in the morning. The screen saver that you have set up is 3D Pipes. Also, you have the colors set at 256 Colors even though your monitor supports High Color (16 bit). Which of the following would you try first to fix the problem?

   a. Change to a non-OpenGL screen saver, such as Beziers.

   b. Use the High Color (16 bit) setting instead of 256 colors.

   c. Upgrade the monitor adapter to go into an ISA expansion slot instead of a PCI slot.

   d. Ask the users to distribute their workload more evenly between morning and afternoon.

14. You decide to assign a new server the same IP address that your department head is using, because she has the address 244.80.1.1 and you realize this is the best address for the server. Since it is late in the evening, you configure the server, leave it connected to the network, and plan to change your boss's address when you come to work tomorrow afternoon. What will happen when your boss logs on in the morning?

   a. She will not experience any problems.

   b. The Ethernet network will give her workstation priority over the server, because she had the IP address first.

    c. She will experience a conflict with the server and may not be able to use her computer on the network.

    d. Only her Internet access will be affected until the Internet negotiates a different IP address for her.

15. From where can you set up different hardware and user profiles?

    a. Control Panel Folder Options tool

    b. Add/Remove Hardware Wizard

    c. Control Panel Multimedia tool

    d. Control Panel System tool

16. You plan to use certificates and need to install the Certificate Services. Which tool do you use?

    a. Add/Remove Windows Components option in the Add/Remove Programs tool

    b. Change or Remove Programs option in the Add/Remove Programs tool

    c. Configure Windows Components option in the Add/Remove Hardware Wizard

    d. Change or Remove Programs option in the Folders tool

17. Your college campus has just decided to enable Macintosh computers to access your Windows 2000 servers. How can this be accomplished?

    a. Use the Network and Dial-up Connections tool to install NWLink with the AppleTalk extension.

    b. Use the Network and Dial-up Connections tool to install AppleTalk.

    c. Use the Add/Remove Programs tool to install TCP/IP with the AppleTalk extension.

    d. Windows 2000 Server does not support AppleTalk; thus, you cannot provide this service.

18. Your server did not originally come with a modem, but after you install Windows 2000 you decide to purchase and install a modem. Which of the following tools enable you to install the modem?

    a. Add/Remove Hardware Wizard

    b. Control Panel Phone and Modem Options tool

    c. Control Panel Accessibility Options tool

    d. all of the above

    e. none of the above because you must use the Computer Management tool

    f. only a and b

19. When you set up a scheduled task, which of the following does that tool work with to run the task?

    a. DNS client service

    b. COM+

    c. AT command

    d. all of the above

e. none of the above

f. only b and c

20. As you run a new server, you notice that the monitor sometimes seems to lock up and that this happens when the LED on the new NIC that you installed shows that the NIC is particularly active. What might be the problem?

a. You do not have enough server memory.

b. There is EMI interference between the NIC and the monitor.

c. The NIC needs to be reseated in its expansion slot.

d. There is a resource-sharing problem between the NIC and the monitor.

21. Your server is about two weeks old and has Windows 2000 Server installed; you are now experiencing problems with the floppy disk drive because there are times when it does not seem to communicate with the server. Which tool can help you test the floppy drive controller?

a. Control Panel Controllers tool

b. Add/Remove Hardware Wizard

c. Network and Dial-up Connections Wizard

d. all of the above

e. none of the above

f. only a and b

22. From where can you start the Device Manager?

a. Control Panel System tool

b. Event Viewer on the Administrative Tools menu

c. Computer Management tool

d. all of the above

e. only a and b

f. only a and c

23. Which of the following is not a Windows 2000 component that you can install?

a. Indexing Service

b. Script Debugger

c. Remote Installation Services

d. File and Print Services for IBM MVS

24. One of the new server operators in your organization has a hearing disability and needs to have visual warnings and captions set up. How can you configure the Windows 2000 servers for these visual displays?

a. Control Panel Accessibility tool using the Sound tab

b. Control Panel Accessibility tool using the Display tab

c. Control Panel Display tool using the Appearance tab

d. Control Panel Display tool using the Settings tab

6

25. Your Windows 2000 Server installation is two days old when the system crashes before you can configure the recovery options. Where might you find information to help you or a Microsoft technician diagnose the source of the crash?

a. in the Applications log

b. in the Memory.dmp file

c. in the file \Winnt\System32\Crash.log

d. in the Device Manager

HANDS-ON PROJECTS

Project 6-1

In this project, you practice configuring the display to use a different pixel setting. For this and the projects that follow, you will need to log on as Administrator or from an account that has Administrator privileges.

To use a different pixel setting:

1. Click **Start**, point to **Settings**, and click **Control Panel**.

2. Double-click the **Display** icon and then click the **Settings** tab.

3. Point the Screen area sliding bar to a different selection. For example, if it is at 640 by 480 pixels, move it to 800 by 600 pixels.

4. Click **Apply** and then click **OK**.

5. When the display changes, notice the new appearance and then click **No** so the change is not made permanent.

6. Record your observations of the display change in a lab journal or word-processed document.

7. While you are in the Settings tab, click **Advanced**. Record the options available to you from the Advanced button and then click **Cancel**.

8. Click **Cancel** to leave the Display Properties dialog box.

Project 6-2

In this activity you practice uninstalling a NIC.

To uninstall the NIC:

1. Click **Start**, point to **Settings**, and then click **Network and Dial-up Connections**.

2. Double-click **Local Area Connection**.

3. Click **Disable** and then close the Network and Dial-up Connections dialog box.

4. Click **Start**, point to **Settings**, and then click **Control Panel**.

5. Double-click the **Add/Remove Hardware** icon and then click **Next**.

6. Click **Uninstall/Unplug a device** (see Figure 6-2) and then click **Next**.

7. Click **Uninstall a device** and then click **Next**.

8. Locate the NIC, such as **3COM EtherLink Xl 10/100 PCI TX NIC** in the Devices box and notice that it has a red "X" through it because you already disconnected it in Step 3. Where is the NIC displayed in the Devices box?

9. Click the NIC so that it is highlighted and then click **Next**.

10. Click **Cancel** in the confirmation dialog box so that you do not really uninstall the NIC.

11. At this point, how can you go back and reconnect the NIC to the network?

12. Record your observations in a lab journal or word-processed document.

6

Project 6-3

In this hands-on activity you troubleshoot a device, using the Add/Remove Hardware Wizard.

To troubleshoot the device:

1. Click **Start**, point to **Settings**, and then click **Control Panel**.

2. Double-click **Add/Remove Hardware**. Click **Next**.

3. Click the **Add/Troubleshoot a device** radio button. Click **Next**.

4. Wait a moment as the wizard checks for new hardware.

5. Use the scroll bar to view the devices that can be tested and note the types of devices in your lab journal or in a word-processed document.

6. Double-click a device to troubleshoot, such as **Printer Port (LPT1)**.

7. Record the results and then click **Back**.

8. Double-click another device to test, such as the NIC or floppy disk drive.

9. Record the results of this test and then click **Finish** to close the wizard.

Project 6-4

In this hands-on activity, you set up Windows 2000 so that it does not start up automatically after there is a system failure.

To configure startup:

1. Click **Start**, point to **Settings**, and then click **Control Panel**.

2. Double-click the **System** icon and then click the **Advanced** tab.

3. Notice the buttons on this tab and record your observations in a lab journal or word-processed document.

4. Click the **Startup and Recovery** button.

5. At the bottom of the Startup and Recovery dialog box, remove the check in front of **Automatically reboot**, or check it if there is no check.

6. Review the other options on this screen and record your observations.

7. Click **OK** in the Startup and Recovery dialog box and then click **OK** to acknowledge that you have to reboot.

8. Briefly look at each tab on the System Properties dialog box and note your observations. What is each tab for? Click **OK** in the System Properties dialog box, and click **Yes** to reboot (save any open work first). Make a note that this activity results in the need to reboot.

Project 6-5

In this activity you practice installing NWLink or NetBEUI (whichever protocol is not already installed in your computer running Windows 2000).

To practice the installation:

1. Click **Start**, point to **Settings**, and then click **Network and Dial-up Connections**.

2. Double-click **Local Area Connection** and then click **Properties**.

3. Click the **Install** button and then double-click **Protocol**.

4. What protocols do you see listed? Are these only protocols that are not already installed? Record your observations.

5. Click **NWLink IPX/SPX/NetBIOS Compatible Transport** or **NetBEUI**, and then click **OK**.

6. If you install NWLink, go back to the section "Installing NWLink IPX/SPX Compatible Transport" and follow the steps described there to configure NWLink after Windows 2000 reboots.

7. Close the Local Area Connection Properties dialog box. Close the Local Area Connection dialog box, and then close the Network and Dial-up Connections tool.

Project 6-6

In this activity you practice configuring TCP/IP. Before you start, obtain an IP address, subnet mask, gateway address, and primary DNS server address from your instructor. Also, TCP/IP must be installed before you begin. If it is not installed, use the steps outlined in the last project to install TCP/IP.

To practice the installation:

1. Click **Start**, point to **Settings**, and click **Network and Dial-up Connections**.

2. Double-click **Local Area Connection** and then click **Properties**.

3. Find **Internet Protocol (TCP/IP)** in the scroll box and double-click it.

4. Click **Use the following IP address:**.

5. Enter the IP address, subnet mask, default gateway address, and preferred DNS server address provided by your instructor. Note that within each entry box, you move from number to number by pressing the period key. For example, to enter the IP address, 129.70.10.1, you would type: **129 [period key] 70 [period key] 10 [period key] 1**.

6. After you have entered the information, click the **Advanced** button and examine each tab. What are the tabs and what information do they enable you to configure? Record your findings in your lab journal or a word-processed document, and then click **Cancel**.

7. Click **OK** if you have permission to save your configuration changes or click **Cancel** so the changes are not saved.

8. Click **OK** in the Local Area Connection Properties dialog box. Click **Close**. Finally, close the Network and Dial-up Connections window.

Project 6-7

6

Sometimes a resource conflict is subtle, such as a NIC locking up intermittently because it uses a portion of an I/O address range that is also used by another device. In this project, you learn how to check for a resource conflict.

To check for a resource conflict:

1. Click **Start**, point to **Programs**, point to **Administrative Tools**, click **Computer Management**, and then double-click **System Tools**.

2. Double-click **Device Manager** and then double-click **Network adapters**.

3. Right-click the adapter installed in your computer and then click **Properties**.

4. What tabs appear in the properties dialog box? Check out each tab to see what it is for.

5. Select the **Resources** tab. What resource settings are used for the NIC?

6. Are there any resource conflicts reported? How would you solve a resource conflict?

7. Record your findings in your lab journal or a word-processed document.

8. Click **Cancel** on the NIC properties dialog box.

9. Before you exit Device Manager, find out what resources are used by another device, such as a communications port or the display adapter.

10. Close the Computer Management tool.

CASE PROJECT

Aspen Consulting Project: Configuring Windows 2000

Health-Wise is a company that makes vitamin supplements sold in grocery and drug stores. This company has a network that connects users to a mainframe computer and to eight older NetWare servers configured to use IPX. The company has an Internet site and already uses TCP/IP for connectivity to the mainframe. DHCP is not used on this network, and there is a network administrator, who keeps a database of IP addresses. The company has purchased a new client/server manufacturing and distribution system that will run on two Windows 2000 servers. Since they have no Windows 2000 experts, they are using Aspen

Consulting to install and configure the new servers. You have just installed the servers and now need to configure them.

1. When you installed Windows 2000 Server, you used DHCP as the default, and now you need to go back and manually configure both servers for TCP/IP. Explain how to configure the protocol, including the tool that you would use to configure it.

2. IPX is not set up as a protocol in the Windows 2000 servers, and you need to set it up so that both servers can communicate with the NetWare servers, which use the Ethernet II and Ethernet SNAP frame types. Explain how you would set up the Windows 2000 servers to be able to communicate with the NetWare servers.

3. As you are configuring protocols, you discover that the NIC on one of the servers is not communicating with the network. What steps can you take to troubleshoot the NIC?

4. Health-Wise is planning to connect one of the new Windows 2000 servers to the Internet by installing an ISDN adapter in an expansion slot. Explain in general how you would install the adapter in Windows 2000 Server.

5. During the Windows 2000 Server installations you omitted installing the Management and Monitoring tools. Explain how you can install them now on both servers.

6. The IT director for Health-Wise asks you to set up a screen saver on each server and to create an immediate way to protect the servers so that people nearby do not access them, in case she forgets to log off the Administrator account when she steps away from the servers. How would you accomplish these tasks?

OPTIONAL CASE PROJECTS FOR TEAMS

Team Case One

Mark Arnez has hired several new and inexperienced consultants. To help orient the new consultants, he asks you to form a team and write a set of general guidelines for installing and configuring protocols in Windows 2000 Server.

Team Case Two

While you are in the break room, you get into a discussion with a group of other consultants about accessibility options for computers. As a group you decide to research the accessibility options in Windows 2000 Server. What are the options? What additional options would your group add to Windows 2000?

7

CONFIGURING SERVER STORAGE, BACKUP, AND PERFORMANCE OPTIONS

After reading this chapter and completing the exercises you will be able to:

♦ Explain basic and dynamic disks

♦ Partition, format, and manage basic disks and convert them to dynamic disks

♦ Create and manage simple, spanned, striped, RAID-5, and mirrored dynamic disks

♦ Mount a drive

♦ Manage removable storage and set up media pools

♦ Perform disk backups

♦ Tune server performance

♦ Configure Windows 2000 Server for an uninterruptible power supply (UPS)

When Intel-based servers first appeared on the scene, disk storage options were limited because disk sizes were relatively small at 20–40 MB. At 20 GB and beyond, disk storage has come a long way and is arguably one of the most important server elements that you will configure and maintain. The lifeblood activities of a server are typically related to providing files, databases, and applications to clients—and all of these require disk storage. Windows 2000 Server crosses an important threshold from Windows NT Server because it offers new ways to integrate and manage storage, such as through removable storage. The implementation of removable storage allows the appropriate kind of storage to be matched to specific types of data. These new disk storage and removable storage capabilities enable you to apply lower total cost of ownership (TCO) through better storage management.

In this chapter, you learn how to use disk storage options that include disk mirroring, disk striping, and RAID level 5 fault tolerance. You will learn removable storage management techniques and how to perform server backups as security against losing important data. Finally, you will learn the basics of optimizing server performance (see Chapter 14 for more advanced optimizing techniques).

BASIC AND DYNAMIC DISKS

Windows 2000 treats disk storage according to two classifications: basic disks and dynamic disks. A **basic disk** is one that uses traditional disk management techniques, such as partitioning, and provides capabilities similar to those available in Windows NT 4.0. A **dynamic disk** is one that does not use traditional partitioning, which means that there is virtually no restriction to the number of volumes that can be set up on one disk. Dynamic disk architecture provides new flexibility for handling large disk storage.

Basic Disks

Because a basic disk uses traditional disk management techniques, it is partitioned and formatted, and can be set up to employ disk sets. It recognizes primary and extended partitions, disk striping (RAID level 0), disk mirroring (RAID level 1), and disk striping with parity (RAID level 5). When you first install Windows 2000 Server, it uses the basic disk structure. Also, if you upgrade any of the Windows NT Server 4.0, 3.51, or 3.5 operating systems to Windows 2000 Server, disk storage is converted to basic disks.

 Basic disks are incorporated in Windows 2000 to provide backward compatibility with earlier versions of Windows and with MS-DOS. For example, you would set up basic disks if you choose to have a dual-boot system consisting of MS-DOS or Windows 98 and Windows 2000 Server (see Chapters 1 and 5). If you later remove all operating systems except Windows 2000 from the computer, then you have the option to convert basic disks to dynamic disks You can manage Windows NT 4.0 disks from a Windows 2000 server, but remember that when you connect to the Windows NT computer you must use tools for managing basic disks.

Disk Partitioning

A hard disk that is low-level formatted can be set up for one or more file systems, such as FAT or NTFS. The process of marking or "blocking" a group of tracks and sectors in preparation for a file system is called **partitioning**. Each partition appears as a logical drive, for example partitioning a single disk into drive C for FAT and drive D for NTFS. A partition is made out of free or unallocated space on the disk—that is, space not yet partitioned for use by any file or operating system.

When a drive is partitioned, a **master boot record (MBR)** and a **partition table** are created in the beginning track and sectors on the disk. The MBR is located in the first sector and track of the hard disk and has startup information about partitions and how to access the disk. The partition table contains information about each partition created, such as the type of partition, size, and location. Also, the partition table provides information to the computer about which partition to access first.

 TIP When you partition a disk, leave 1 MB or more of the disk space free. This is the amount of workspace that Windows 2000 Server needs to convert a basic disk to a dynamic disk, in case you want to upgrade later.

A partition is created by the Disk Management tool, which is an MMC snap-in (see Figure 7-1) and is also accessed from the Computer Management tool. (The Computer Management tool is opened by clicking Start, pointing to Programs, pointing to Administrative Tools, and clicking Computer Management. Click Storage in the Computer Management tool to access Disk Management.) When you install this MMC snap-in, consider installing the Disk Defragmenter snap-in at the same time so that both disk tools are available in one MMC configuration.

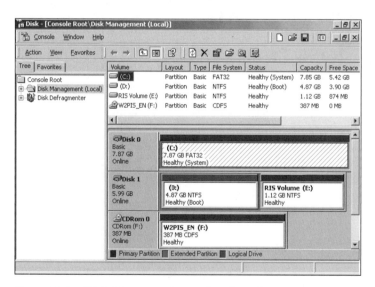

Figure 7-1   Disk Management and Disk Defragmenter snap-ins installed in the MMC

To create a partition in the Disk Management tool, right-click the unallocated disk space that is displayed in the Disk Management snap-in and click Create Partition (or click the disk space, click Action, point to All Tasks, and click Create Partition). The Create Partition Wizard steps you through the process. Try Hands-on Project 7-1 to practice creating a partition and formatting it.

You can use the View menu to customize the display of the snap-in. For example, the View menu Settings option enables you to customize the legend and the scaling. Also, you can access the properties of any disk by right-clicking the disk and clicking Properties. The Properties dialog box gives you access to repair tools, hardware information and drivers, disk-sharing parameters, and Web-sharing parameters.

You can delete a partition from the Disk Management snap-in as well. To delete a partition, right-click the partition you want to delete. The partition will have a dark gray border and shading to indicate that you have selected it. Click Delete Partition on the shortcut menu. The Disk Management snap-in gives you a warning that data will be lost. Click Yes to continue the delete process. After the partition is deleted, the Disk Management snap-in displays a box showing the partition with a black bar on top and indicating that the disk space is unallocated.

When you make a change to the disk configuration and it is not automatically updated in Disk Management, rescan the disks by clicking the Disk Management Action menu and clicking Rescan Disks.

Primary and Extended Partitions

A partition may be set up as primary or extended. A **primary partition** is one from which you can boot an operating system, such as MS-DOS or Windows 2000 Server. Or it may simply hold files in a different file system format. When you boot from a primary partition, it contains the operating system startup files in a location at the beginning of the partition. For example, the startup files for Windows 98 include Io.sys and Msdos.sys. For Windows 2000, those files include Boot.ini, Ntldr (treated as a .sys file), and Ntdetect.com. A partition containing the startup files is called a **system partition**. A single disk must have one primary partition, and can have up to four.

Removable media, such as Zip or Jaz disks, can only be set up as a basic disk primary partition.

An **extended partition** is created from space that is not yet partitioned and is added onto a primary partition. The purpose of an extended partition is to enable you to exceed the four-partition limit of a hard disk. On some computers, an extended partition is not bootable (cannot be a system partition). However, either a primary or an extended partition can hold the Windows 2000 operating system files, which are the files you loaded into the \Winnt folder during the installation (see Chapter 5). There can be only one extended partition on a single basic disk. The partition containing the operating system files is called the **boot partition** by Microsoft. When you work with the terms boot partition and system partition, it helps to remember that their contents are the opposite of what is intuitive—the boot files are on the system partition, and the system files are on the boot partition.

Creating an extended partition is similar to creating a primary partition. In the Disk Management snap-in, right-click unallocated space and click Create Partition. The Create Partition Wizard is started and displays a dialog box that enables you to specify a primary or extended partition (see Figure 7-2). After you specify the type of partition, there is a dialog box to specify the partition's size and another that enables you to review your selections before creating the partition.

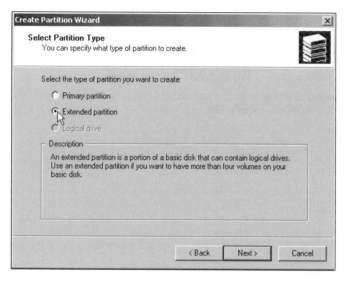

Figure 7-2 Creating an extended partition

A computer with multiple partitions boots from the partition that is designated as the **active partition**, which must also be the system partition containing the startup files. To determine which partition is designated as active, look for the "(System)" designation in the Disk Management pane that gives information about the disk's size and file system (see Figure 7-3). For example, the active (system) partition in Figure 7-3 is the one designated as drive C:. Also notice that the boot partition holding the \Winnt folder is shown as drive D:. Hands-on Project 7-2 shows how to use the Disk Management snap-in to mark a partition as the active partition.

Formatting

If you do not format a partition when it is created, it still needs to be formatted for a particular file system. As you learned in Chapter 1, Windows 2000 supports the FAT16, FAT32, and NTFS file-system formats. **Formatting** is a process that creates a table containing file and folder information for a specific file system in a partition. The process also creates a root directory (folder) and a volume label. Once a partition is formatted, it is called a **volume** and can be assigned a drive letter. Assigning a drive letter makes it easier to refer to the volume, for example assigning it drive letter C.

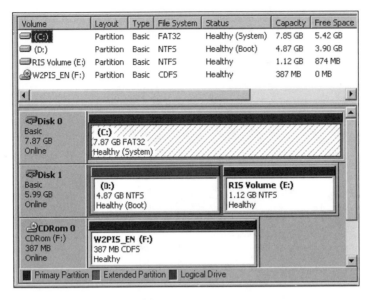

Figure 7-3 System and boot partitions

 By Microsoft's definition, a basic disk volume is any of the following: primary partition, drive in an extended partition, volume set, stripe set with parity, and mirror set.

To format a partition that is not already formatted, open the Disk Management snap-in, right-click the partition to be formatted, and click Format. You will need to specify a volume label, the file system to use, and the allocation unit size (see Figure 7-4). Also, you can select to use the quick format option and to enable file and folder compression.

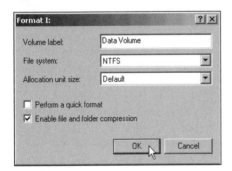

Figure 7-4 Formatting a partition

When you format a partition, avoid using the quick format option, because it does not check for bad sectors during the format.

You can assign a different drive letter to a partition by right-clicking the partition in the Disk Management snap-in, clicking Change Drive Letter and Path, and clicking Edit to change the letter. You also have the option of changing the drive path. Hands-on Project 7-3 enables you to practice changing a drive letter.

Whenever you make a change in the Disk Administrator, for example to partition a drive, format a partition, or assign a new drive letter, update the emergency repair disk (ERD) to reflect the change (see Chapter 5).

Volume and Stripe Sets

Volume sets and stripe sets are disk management concepts that are used in Windows NT Server 4.0 and earlier. A **volume set** consists of two or more partitions that are combined to look like one volume with a single drive letter. A **stripe set** is two or more disks that are combined like a volume set, but that are striped for RAID level 0 or RAID level 5 (see Chapter 2). Windows 2000 Server provides backward compatibility with volume and stripe sets that have previously been created through Windows NT. Windows 2000 Server enables you to use an existing volume or stripe set carried over from a Windows NT upgrade until one or more disks in a set fail. For this reason, it is important that you regularly back up a volume or stripe set until you convert it to a dynamic disk structure. Also, if there is a disk failure before you have an opportunity to convert, you can use the Disk Management snap-in to delete a basic disk volume or stripe set and create a dynamic disk spanned volume or stripe set (see the section on Dynamic Disks that follows).

Converting Disks

Converting a basic disk to a dynamic disk is accomplished from the Disk Management snap-in. When you convert a disk, the process does not damage data in any way, but dynamic disks are not compatible with dual-boot systems. Right-click the basic disk that you want to convert, and click Upgrade to Dynamic Disk (make sure that the disk has 1 MB or more free space).

Make sure that you right-click the disk, for example Disk 0 (see Figure 7-3), and not the volume, for example (C:), or else the upgrade option will not be displayed.

There are circumstances when you may need to change a dynamic disk back to a basic disk, such as when you want to implement a dual-boot setup, or when you want to remove Windows 2000 Server from the computer so that a different operating system—such as Windows 98—can be loaded. If you need to revert back to a basic disk, it is necessary to delete the dynamic volume and destroy its data in the process. A dynamic disk can be converted back to a basic disk by using the following steps:

1. Back up all data on the dynamic disk volume before you start.

2. Delete the dynamic disk volume, using the Disk Management snap-in, by right-clicking the volume and clicking Delete Volume.

3. Click the disk, click the Action menu, and click Restore Basic Disk Configuration.

4. Use the Disk Management snap-in to partition and format the disk, for example for FAT32.

Dynamic Disks

A dynamic disk does not use traditional partitioning, which makes it possible to set up a large number of volumes on one disk and provides the ability to extend volumes onto additional physical disks. There is an upward limit of 32 disks that can be incorporated into one spanned volume. Besides volume extensions and spanned volumes, dynamic disks support RAID levels 0, 1, and 5. Dynamic disks can be formatted for FAT16, FAT32, or NTFS and are used when you do not implement a dual-boot system. Also, dynamic disks can be reactivated, should they go offline because they have been powered down or disconnected.

 If a disk is reported as offline or missing in the Disk Management tool, reactivate it with care if you did not intentionally power it down or disconnect it, because the disk may be corrupted. When you reactivate a corrupted disk, Windows 2000 runs a "checkdisk" utility (described later) to repair files and folders. To reactivate a disk via the Disk Management tool, right-click the disk and click Reactivate Disk.

Basic disks can be converted to dynamic disks after you install Windows 2000 so that you can take advantage of the richer set of options associated with dynamic disks. There are five types of dynamic disk configurations: simple volumes, spanned volumes, mirrored volumes, striped volumes, and RAID-5 volumes. The functional concepts of these disk configurations are similar to those used for Windows NT 4.0 compatible basic disks, but the Windows 2000 dynamic disks have better disk management options and do not use partitioning. For example, the dynamic disk equivalent of a basic disk volume set is called **spanned volumes**, and the equivalent of a basic disk stripe set is called **striped volumes.**

 On dynamic disks, instead of using the basic disk terminology of boot partition and system partition, the volume that contains the \Winnt folder of system files is called the boot volume, and the volume that contains the files used to boot the computer is called the system volume.

Simple Volume

A **simple volume** is a portion of a disk or an entire disk that is set up as a dynamic disk. If you do not allocate all of a disk as a simple volume, you have the option to later take all or a portion of the unallocated space and add it to an existing simple volume, which is called extending the volume. A simple volume does not provide fault tolerance, because it cannot be set up for any RAID level (see Chapter 2).

You might create a simple volume when you have only one disk drive on the server. Another situation in which you might set up a simple volume is when you first set up a server on one basic disk, convert the disk to a simple volume, and later add a second disk to mirror the first (see Chapter 2). Hands-on Project 7-4 enables you to practice setting up a simple volume using the Disk Management snap-in. To extend a simple volume via the Disk Management snap-in, right-click the volume that you want to extend and click Extend Volume.

Spanned Volume

A spanned volume contains 2 to 32 dynamic disks that are treated as one volume (see Figure 7-5). For example, you might create a spanned volume if you have three small hard disks, 1 GB, 1.5 GB, and 2 GB. Another reason to use a spanned volume is if you have several small free portions of disk space scattered throughout the server's disk drives. You might have 600 MB of free space on one drive, 150 MB on another, and 70 MB on a third. All of these free areas can be combined into a single 820 MB spanned volume with its own drive letter, with the advantage that you reduce the number of drive letters needed to make use of the space.

Figure 7-5   Spanned volume

As you add new disks, the spanned volume can be extended to include each disk. Volumes formatted for NTFS can be extended, but those formatted for FAT16 and FAT32 cannot. The advantage of creating spanned volumes is the ability to more easily manage several small disk drives or to maximize the use of scattered pockets of disk space across several disks.

CAUTION

The disadvantage of using a spanned volume is that if one disk fails, the entire volume is inaccessible. Also, if a portion of a spanned volume is deleted, the entire disk set is deleted. For these reasons, avoid placing mission-critical data and applications on a spanned volume.

The spanned volume might be used to store data that is already backed up on another medium, such as tape. For instance, the previous year's accounting data might be stored on a spanned volume. The data is already saved on tape, but a copy is left on disk for fast lookup and retrieval.

Creating a spanned volume involves selecting unallocated space on the disk that is to be in the volume, clicking the Action menu, pointing to All Tasks, and clicking Create Volume. In the Create Volume Wizard, specify Spanned volume. To extend a spanned volume, right-click the volume and click Extend Volume.

Striped Volume

As you learned in Chapter 2, RAID level 0 is disk striping. The main purpose for striping disks in a volume is to extend the life of hard disk drives by spreading data equally over two or more drives. Spreading the data divides the drive load so that one drive is not working more than any other. Another advantage of striping is that it increases disk performance. Contention among disks is equalized and data is accessed faster for both reads and writes than when it is on a single drive, because Windows 2000 can write to all drives at the same time. Striping has been used successfully on mainframes and minicomputers for years as a way to enhance disk performance.

In Windows 2000 Server, striping requires at least two disks and can be performed over as many as 32. The total of striped disks is called a striped volume. Equal portions of data are written in 64 KB blocks in rows or stripes on each disk. For example, consider that you have set up striping across five hard disks and are working with a 720 KB data file. The first 64 KB portion of the file is written to disk 1, the next 64 KB portion is written to disk 2, the third portion is written to disk 3, and so on. After 320 KB are spread in the first data row across disks 1 through 5, the next 320 KB are written in 64 KB blocks in the second row across the disks. Finally, there will be 64 KB in the third row on disk 1 and 16 KB in the third row on disk 2 (see Figure 7-6).

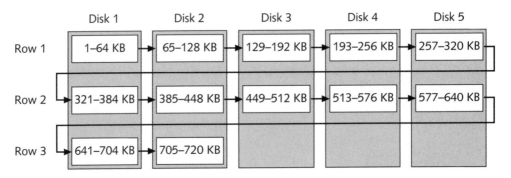

	Disk 1	Disk 2	Disk 3	Disk 4	Disk 5
Row 1	1–64 KB	65–128 KB	129–192 KB	193–256 KB	257–320 KB
Row 2	321–384 KB	385–448 KB	449–512 KB	513–576 KB	577–640 KB
Row 3	641–704 KB	705–720 KB			

Figure 7-6 Disks in a striped volume

> **TIP** Because of its high performance, striping is useful for volumes that store large databases or for data replication from one volume to another. Striping is not a benefit when most of the data files on a server are very small, such as under 64 KB.

Data can be lost when one or more disks in the striped volume fail, because the system has no automated way to rebuild data. If you use striping to increase disk performance for a critical database, consider frequently backing up that database on tape (see later in this chapter) or through the Microsoft File Replication service (see Chapter 10).

A striped volume is created through the Disk Management snap-in. To create a striped volume, select free space on one disk, click Create Volume, and use the Striped volume option in the Create Volume Wizard.

RAID-5 Volume

Fault tolerance is better for a RAID-5 volume than for a simple striped volume. A **RAID-5 volume** requires a minimum of three disk drives. Parity information is distributed on each disk so that if one disk fails, the information on that disk can be reconstructed. The parity used by Microsoft is Boolean (true/false, one/zero) logic, with information about the data contained in each row of 64 KB data blocks on the striped disks. Using the example of storing a 720 KB file across five disks, one 64 KB parity block is written on each disk. The first parity block is always written in row 1 of disk 1, the second is in row 2 of disk 2, and so on, as illustrated in Figure 7-7.

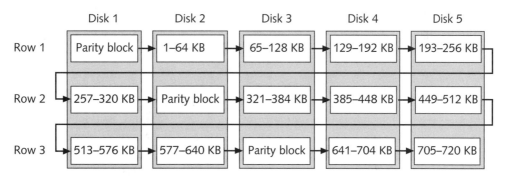

Figure 7-7   Disks in a RAID-5 volume

When you set up a RAID-5 volume, the performance is not as fast as with a striped volume, because it takes longer to write the data and calculate the parity block for each row. However, accessing data through disk reads is as fast as for a striped volume. RAID-5 is a viable fault tolerance choice for mission-critical data and for applications when full mirroring is not feasible due to the expense. It works well with disk arrays that are compatible with RAID-5. A RAID-5 volume is particularly useful in a client/server system that uses a separate database for queries and creating reports, because disk read performance is fast for obtaining data. In applications such as a customer service database that is constantly updated with new orders, disk read performance will be slower than with striping without parity.

 If you create a RAID-5 volume, consider adding 12 MB or more of RAM, because RAID-5 uses more memory than mirroring or simple striping. Also, RAID-5 takes up disk space for the parity information.

The amount of storage space used is based on the formula $1/n$ where n is the number of physical disks in the volume. For example, if there are four disks, the amount of space taken for parity information is $1/4$ of the total space of all disk drives in the volume. This means you get more usable disk storage if there are more disks in the volume. A set of eight 2 MB disks yields more usable storage than a set of four 4 MB disks in RAID-5.

Use the Disk Management snap-in to create a RAID-5 volume. To start, right-click the free space on a disk that is to be part of the volume, click Create Volume, and select the RAID-5 volume option in the Create Volume Wizard.

Mirrored Volume

As you learned in Chapter 2, disk mirroring involves creating a shadow copy of data on a backup disk and is RAID level 1. Only dynamic disks can be set up as a **mirrored volume** in Windows 2000 Server. It is the most guaranteed form of disk fault tolerance because the data on a failed drive is instantly recovered from the mirrored drive. Also, disk read performance is the same as reading data from any single disk drive. The disadvantage of mirroring is that the time to create or update information is doubled because it is written twice, once on the main disk and once on the shadow disk. However, a disk write in mirroring is normally faster than writing to disk when you use RAID-5. A mirrored volume cannot be striped and requires two dynamic disks.

A mirrored volume is particularly well suited for situations in which data is mission-critical and must not be lost under any circumstances, for example customer files at a bank. It also is valuable for situations in which computer systems must not be down for long, such as for medical applications or in 24-hour manufacturing. The somewhat slower update time is offset by the assurance that data will not be lost and that the system will quickly be back on line after a disk failure. However, if fast disk updating is the most important criterion for disk storage, such as when copying files or taking orders over a telephone, then a striped volume may be a better choice than a mirrored volume.

CAUTION

The Windows 2000 Server system and boot partitions can be in a mirrored volume, but they cannot be in a striped or RAID-5 volume.

A mirrored volume is created through the Disk Management snap-in. To create the volume, right-click free space on one disk, click Create Volume, and choose the Mirrored volume option in the Create Volume Wizard.

DISK PERFORMANCE AND REPAIR

Disk drives that are over 80 percent full also are subject to increased mechanical wear. When a disk drive failure occurs, it is most likely to be a read head that has physically touched the disk platter. In all cases this causes damage to the platter, sometimes resulting in the release of metal fragments within the sealed module of the disk unit. One way to increase disk performance and extend the life of hard disks is to make sure that one disk is not accessed and working harder than other disks in a multiple-disk server. Creating striped volumes and

RAID-5 volumes are two ways to equalize the disk load. If neither of these methods is employed, then you should consider monitoring disk usage and manually relocating files on a periodic schedule. By relocating files you can distribute disk access more evenly. Also, dividing disks onto different adapters enables you to increase performance (see Chapter 2).

Extensive fragmentation of files on a disk is another cause of extra wear. **Disk fragmentation** exists when the files on a disk gradually become spread throughout the hard drive, with empty pockets of space scattered throughout. Fragmentation occurs normally over time, the result of creating new files and deleting files. Full and fragmented drives cause the read head to move across the disk more extensively than in situations where disks are maintained regularly. **Defragmenting** a disk is a process used to reorganize files to reduce the number of empty spaces between files. Windows 2000 Server includes the Disk Defragmenter as an MMC snap-in. The Disk Defragmenter includes a tool to analyze a disk to determine the amount of fragmentation (see Figure 7-8) and another tool to defragment a disk. Try Hands-on Project 7-5 to practice using both tools.

7

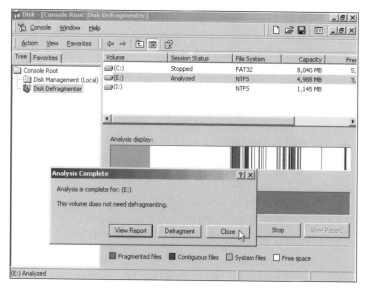

Figure 7-8   Analyzing a disk's fragmentation

 TIP   On a busy server, drives should be defragmented every week to two weeks. On less busy servers, defragment the drives at least once a month.

Sometimes disk performance is affected by files that are corrupted or when the file allocation table has lost pointers to certain files. You can correct these problems and maintain the integrity of the data by periodically running the "checkdisk" utility, called chkdsk, from the Start button, Run option. Chkdsk also starts automatically when you boot Windows 2000 Server and the boot process detects file allocation table or file corruption, for instance in the system files. The chkdsk utility is much more robust in Windows 2000 and Windows NT than it is in other versions of Windows. In Windows 2000 Server it can be used to check FAT, NTFS, or both file systems (on a dual-boot computer). When the file system is FAT, the utility checks the file allocation table, folders, files, disk sectors, and disk allocation units. In NTFS it checks files, folders, indexes, security descriptors, user files, and disk allocation units.

Plan to run chkdsk when there are no users on the server, and lock the disk from use until the process is finished. Also, run chkdsk using the /f switch, which causes it to lock the disk and fix errors that it finds. If you do not use the /f switch, chkdsk may incorrectly identify and fix bogus errors in open files.

If you suspect there is physical damage on a disk, use chkdsk with the /r switch to identify bad sectors. A disk that has a high number of bad sectors, such as several hundred thousand, may need to be replaced. You can use the Recover command in the Command Prompt window to attempt to recover files in a physically damaged area, but use Recover on one file at a time. The format of the Recover command is: Recover [drive and path] *filename*. You cannot use wildcard designations, such as *, with Recover. Table 7-1 shows the switches associated with chkdsk.

CAUTION

Allow plenty of time for chkdsk to run on large disk systems, such as a system having over 5 or 10 GB. If you have multiple disks, you may want to stagger running chkdsk, on different disks for each week. Also, the presence of some bad sectors is normal. Many disks have a few bad sectors that are marked by the manufacturer during the low-level format and on which data cannot be written.

When chkdsk finds lost allocation units or chains, it prompts you with the Yes or No question: Convert lost chains to files? Answer Yes to the question so that you can save the lost information to files. The files that chkdsk creates for each lost chain are labeled Filexxx.chk and can be edited with a text editor to determine their contents.

Table 7-1 Chkdsk Switch and Parameter Options

Switch/Parameter	Purpose
[*volume*] (such as C:)	Specifies that chkdsk only check the designated volume
[*filename*] (such as *.dll)	Enables a check of the specified file or files only
/c	For NTFS only, chkdsk uses an abbreviated check of the folder structure
/f	Instructs chkdsk to fix errors that it finds and locks the disk while checking
/i	For NTFS only, chkdsk uses an abbreviated check of indexes
/L:*size*	For NTFS only, enables you to specify the size of the log file created by the disk check
/r	Searches for bad sectors, fixes problems, and recovers information (when not possible; use the Recover command on separate files)
/v	On FAT shows the entire path name of files; on NTFS shows cleanup messages associated with errors
/x	Dismounts or locks a volume before starting (/f also dismounts or locks a volume)

7

MOUNTING A DRIVE

Windows 2000 enables you to mount a drive as an alternative to giving it a drive letter. A **mounted drive** is one that appears as a folder and that is accessed through a path like any other folder. You can mount a basic or dynamic disk drive, a CD-ROM, or a Zip drive. Only an empty folder on a volume formatted for NTFS can be used for mounting a drive. Once a drive is mounted, other drives can be added to the same folder to appear as one drive. There are several reasons for using mounted drives. The most evident reason is that Windows operating systems are limited to 26 drive letters; mounting drives enables you to reduce the number of drive letters in use, because mounted drives are not associated with letters. Another reason for creating a mounted drive is for user home folders that are stored on the server. A **home directory** or **home folder** is a server folder that is associated with a user's account and that is a designated workspace for the user to store files. As server administrator, you might allocate one drive for all user home folders and mount that drive in a folder called Users. The path to the drive might be C:\Home or C:\Users. In another situation, you might have a database that you want to manage as a mounted drive so that it is easier for users to access. Also, by mounting the drive, you can set up special backups for that database by simply backing up its folder. Try Hands-on Project 7-6 to mount a drive.

MANAGING REMOVABLE STORAGE

Removable storage media (tapes, CD-ROMs, CD-RWs, and magnetic disks such as Zip or Jaz disks) are used to access data in real time, for data archiving, and for data backups. The selection of what media to use is related to factors that include how often the data must be accessed, how much data must be stored, and how fast the data must be available. For example, for full system backups and for many forms of archiving that require large storage but that are accessed infrequently, you will most likely use tapes. Many organizations use tape archives to store large system accounting and tax information for seven years or more, for example. In a small or medium-sized organization, you might archive data to CD or to a Zip disk because the storage needs are smaller. If your organization uses removable media for real-time data access, then CD or Zip media provide faster access than tape.

Understanding Libraries

A media **library** is storage media and the drive (or drives) used by the media. Windows 2000 Server supports two types of media libraries: robotic and stand-alone drive. A **robotic library** is one in which multiple removable media can be mounted and dismounted automatically. For example, in an organization, a complete backup of one or more servers might require the use of multiple tapes. A robotic tape changer can be set up to mount the first tape, dismount it when it is full, and mount the next tape until the backup is completed. A CD-ROM or CD-RW jukebox (see Chapter 2) can be used in the same way to automatically make multiple CD-ROMs or CD-RWs available. A **stand-alone drive library** is one in which the removable media are manually inserted one at a time as needed.

Understanding Media Pools

The media within each type of library are managed by using media pools. A **media pool** consists of media that are used for the same purpose and that are managed in the same way. The backup tapes used by an organization are one example of a media pool. Another media pool might consist of CD-ROMs that are used to provide real-time access in a robotic library, for example to provide reference information at a school's library or to provide access to book catalogs from other libraries. Windows 2000 Server classifies media pools into two broad categories: application media pools and system media pools. An application media pool is one that is automatically created by a software application, for example by a client/server application. Windows 2000 Server includes two applications that create application media pools, the Windows 2000 Server Backup tool (discussed later in this chapter) and the Windows 2000 Server Removable Storage Manager. For example, when you create backups for your organization's server, the Backup tool automatically creates an application media pool called Backup.

A system media pool consists of all other media that are created in some other way, such as when you manually create a CD-ROM or CD-RW through a copying process. There are three types of system media pools: import, free, and unrecognized. An import media pool is one or more media that were created through one media pool and are now being imported into another pool, such as tapes in a media pool used for server backups that are now being imported into a different media pool that is used for long-term archiving in a vault. A free media pool contains media that have been used previously in the same or different media pool, but that are free to be copied over because they no longer contain useful information. Free media also consist of unrecognized media that have been initialized for use in the free media pool. An unrecognized media pool is simply new media that have not been used, such as new tapes.

Understanding Media Classification

Removable media can be classified as either physical or logical, depending on the management properties and the application that is managing the media. *Physical media* are media you can touch, such as tapes or Zip disks, and they are linked to a library. This is the most common classification with which you will work. The *logical media* classification is used when one medium can hold information from two different media pools. For example, if your organization is very small and has a limited budget, you might put backup and archive information on the same tape, such as a 20 GB Travan tape. Another possibility is to use a magnetic disk (or perhaps an optical disc one day) that can store information on two sides, where information on one side is in one media pool and information on the other side is in a different media pool.

7

Creating a Media Pool

A media pool is created by using the Removable Storage snap-in in the MMC. This snap-in enables you to create new media pools, manage media pools, and specify the physical location of a library. It also offers a window from which to view operator requests. For example, if a user requests data from a CD-ROM that is not mounted, a request is issued in the console window to notify the server operator that he or she needs to insert the CD-ROM.

The following general steps illustrate how to create a new media pool:

1. Install the Removable Storage snap-in in the MMC or access it from the Computer Management tool.

2. Double-click Removable Storage in the left pane's tree. Right-click Media Pools in the left pane and click Create Media Pool.

3. Make sure the General tab is displayed (see Figure 7-9).

4. Enter a name for the media pool, enter a description, specify the type of media, and specify how media are allocated (for example, obtaining media from the free media pool).

5. Click the Security tab to specify which groups of users can access and manage the media pool, such as Administrators and Backup Operators.

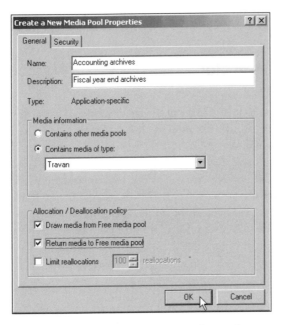

Figure 7-9   Setting up a new media pool

DISK SECURITY THROUGH BACKUP

One of the best ways to make sure you do not lose valuable information on a hard disk is to fully back up information, using backup tapes. In Chapter 2, you learned how to select and install a tape drive and SCSI adapter. Tape backups can be performed from the server or from a workstation connected to the server. There are several advantages to performing backups from a tape drive installed in the server:

- There is no extra load on the network from traffic caused by transferring files from the server to a tape drive on a workstation.

- Equipping each server with its own tape drive gives you a way to perform backups on a multiple server network even if one of the tape drives fails on a server. Backups can be performed from the tape drive on one of the other servers.

- Backing up from a tape drive on a server provides more assurance that the Registry is backed up, since access to the Registry is limited to backups performed at the server. The **Registry** contains vital information about a server's setup.

The advantage of performing backups from a workstation connected to the server is that you can perform all backups from one place, instead of walking to each server to start backups. Besides the extra network load, a disadvantage is that there is a possibility that an intruder can tap into the network and obtain backup data going from the server to the workstation.

Backup Options

The Windows 2000 Server backup software recognizes five backup options, which are variations of full or incremental backups. A **full backup** is a backup of an entire system, including all system files, programs, and data files. A full backup in Windows 2000 Server is called the *normal* backup, which is the same as a full file-by-file backup. A normal backup is a backup of all files that you have selected, usually an entire partition or volume. The normal backup changes each file's archive bit to show that it has been backed up. The advantage of performing full backups each night is that all files are on one tape or tape set.

An **incremental backup** only backs up files that are new or that have been updated. Windows 2000 Server has an *incremental* option that backs up only files that have the archive attribute. When it backs up a file, the incremental backup removes the archive attribute to show that the file has been backed up. A *differential* backup is the same as an incremental backup, but it does not remove the archive attribute. Incremental or differential backups are often mixed with full backups. The advantage of the differential backup is that only the most recent full backup and the most recent differential backup are required to restore data. That saves time over incremental restores, that require a full backup and all the incremental backups back to the last full backup.

Another Windows 2000 Server option is the *copy* backup, which backs up only the files or directories selected. The archive attribute, showing that a file is new or updated, is left unchanged. For example, if the archive attribute is present on a file, the copy backup does not remove it. Copy backups are used in exceptional cases where a backup is performed on certain files, but the regular backup routines are unaffected because the copy backup does not alter the archive bit.

The *daily* backup option backs up only files that have been changed or updated on the day the backup is performed. It leaves the archive attribute unchanged, so regular backups are not affected. A daily backup is valuable, for example, when there is a failing hard disk and little time to save the day's work to that point. It enables the administrator to save only that day's work, instead of all changed files, which may span more than a day.

To perform a tape backup of all files on drive C, for example, you need to have the tape system installed, and you need enough formatted blank tapes to hold the information you plan to back up from the server. Before starting a backup it may be necessary to format a new tape or retension new and used tapes.

Both tasks are performed from the Microsoft Backup tool's Restore tab in one of two ways. One way is to click the medium in the Name box, click the Tools menu, point to Media Tools, and select Format or Re-tension. Another way is to right-click the medium in the Name box on the Restore tab to access the Format and Re-tension options (plus other options for that particular medium). The Backup tool is opened by clicking the Start button, pointing to Programs, pointing to Accessories, pointing to System Tools, and clicking Backup. Formatting deletes existing information and automatically retensions a tape. Retensioning makes sure the tape starts from the beginning of the reel, so there is no slack that may cause lost data.

Once the tape is inserted and ready, you can perform a backup by using the Backup Wizard from the Welcome tab or by manually creating a backup from the Backup tab (see Figure 7-10). Each type of backup can be created with a job name so that you can perform the same backup over and over using that job name, or specify that name to schedule a backup job that is run unattended. Hands-on Project 7-7 enables you to practice making a backup.

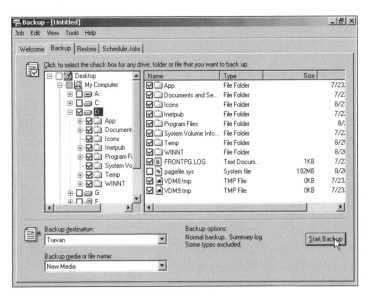

Figure 7-10 Manually starting a backup

Scheduling Backups

Windows 2000 Server includes a scheduling capability so that you can have the server automatically start backups after regular work hours or at a specific time of day. For example, you may schedule full backups to start at 7:00 p.m. after everyone has left work. An accounting office in an organization may perform a daily closing routine in which they stop processing by 4:20 p.m. and back up accounting files at 4:30 p.m. After the backups are complete, another process might start at 6:00 p.m., via the Windows 2000 Scheduled Tasks tool in the Control Panel, which closes out that day's activities and prepares accounting files for the next day.

The following general steps illustrate how to schedule a backup:

1. Click Start, point to Programs, point to Accessories, point to System Tools, then click Backup.

2. Select the drives and folders that you want to back up.

3. Click Start Backup.

4. Provide the backup job information such as the backup description, how to write on the media, and a label for the backup.

5. Click the Schedule button and click Yes.

6. Provide a filename in which to store the selection parameters for the backup job, and click Save.

7. Provide a password for the account from which the job will run, and confirm the password. Click OK.

8. Enter a job name.

9. Click the Properties button to specify the scheduling information, such as how often to run the backup, the start time, and the day or days of the week on which to run it. Figure 7-11 shows the display after you select Weekly in the Schedule Task box. Click OK and OK again.

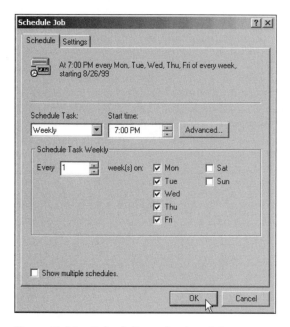

Figure 7-11   Scheduling a backup job

PERFORMING A RESTORE

Use the Backup tool to perform a restore from removable media. The Restore Wizard on the Welcome tab will step you through the process of a restore, or you can use the Restore tab. If you use the Restore tab, follow these steps:

1. Open the Backup tool and click the Restore tab.

2. Insert the medium from which to perform the restore, such as a tape or Zip disk.

3. In the left pane, double-click the medium from which to perform the restore, such as File (for a Zip drive, for example) or Travan (for a tape drive). In the right pane (or on the left pane under the medium) find the label of the backup that you want to restore, and double-click it.

4. Double-click down through the levels of the drives, folders, and subfolders to find what you want to restore. Place a checkmark in front of the drives, folders, and files that you want to restore.

5. In the *Restore files to* box, select a location to which to restore the files and folders. The options are to restore to the original location, to restore to an alternate location, or to restore to a single folder. The first two options retain the original folder structure as reflected on the backup medium. In the third option, restore to a single folder, the original folder structure is not retained, which means that the target folder will contain only files after the restore.

6. Click the Start Restore button.

7. Click Advanced on the Confirm Restore dialog box if you want to modify any of the restore options—for example, if you want to restore security information. Click OK if you decide to modify the advanced options.

8. Click OK to start the restore. Prior to starting, you may be prompted to supply the location, if you are restoring from a file.

9. Click Close and close the Backup tool.

CONFIGURING FOR PERFORMANCE

Besides properly setting up disk resources for fault tolerance and performance, you can immediately tune the server to improve performance. Three ways to tune the server are for application priority, for virtual memory, and to set memory to match the number of users on the server.

Configuring Application Performance

A Windows 2000 Server can be tuned to give the most processor priority to applications that are running in the foreground or to give foreground and background applications equal processor priority. Foreground applications are those you are likely to be running at the server console, such as the Backup tool. Background applications are those typically accessed by users, such as logon verification, printing services, and any other server services. In most cases you will tune the server to give equal processor access to both foreground and background processes, which is the default. Sometimes you may need to give foreground processes most of the processor's resources, for instance when you determine that a disk drive is failing and you want to back up its contents as fast as possible via the Backup tool at the console.

Application performance is configured through the Control Panel System icon. There are two settings that you can configure: (1) Applications, which gives priority to foreground applications, and (2) Background services, which gives equal processor time to all applications and services. Hands-on Project 7-8 gives you experience in tuning application performance.

Configuring Virtual Memory

Virtual memory is disk storage that Windows 2000 Server uses to expand the capacity of the physical RAM installed in the computer. When the currently running programs and processes exceed the RAM, they treat disk space allocated for virtual memory just as if it is real memory. The disadvantage of this is that memory activities performed through virtual memory are not as fast as those performed in RAM (although disk access and data transfer speeds can be quite fast). Virtual memory works through a technique called **paging**, whereby blocks of information, called pages, are moved from RAM into virtual memory on disk. On a Pentium computer, data is paged in blocks of 4 KB. For example, if the system is not presently using a 7 KB block of code, it divides the code block between two pages, each 4 KB in size (part of one page will not be completely full). Next, both pages are moved to virtual memory on disk until needed. When the processor calls for that code block, the pages are moved back into RAM.

Before virtual memory can be used, it must first be allocated for this purpose by tuning the operating system. The area of disk that is allocated for this purpose is called the **page file**. A default amount of virtual memory is always established when Windows 2000 Server is installed, but the amount should be checked by the administrator to ensure that it is not too large or too small.

Besides size, the location of the page file is important. Some tips for locating the page file are:

- Server performance is better if the page file is not placed on the boot partition of basic disks or the boot volume of dynamic disks.

- If there are multiple disks, performance can be improved by placing a page file on each disk (but avoid placing the page file on the boot partition or volume).

- In a mirrored set or volume, place the page file on the main disk, and not on the mirrored (backup) disk.

- Do not place the page file on a stripe set, striped volume, stripe set with parity, or RAID-5 volume.

The page file is called Pagefile.sys and can be viewed at the root level by using Windows Explorer or My Computer.

A general rule for sizing a page file is to start with the size recommended when you view the virtual memory settings via the Control Panel System icon, which is the amount of installed RAM times 1.5. For a server with 256 MB of RAM, the page file should be at least 384 MB (256 2 1.5). To set virtual memory, open the Control Panel, double-click the System icon, click the Advanced tab, click the Performance Options button, and click the Change button. Highlight the drive to contain the page file. Set the initial page file size to match your calculation for the size that is needed. Set the maximum size so it affords plenty of room for growth—twice the size of your initial page file setting. For example, if your initial setting is 384 MB, then consider setting the maximum size to 768 MB. Windows 2000 Server always starts at the initial size and only uses additional space as needed. Click the Set button to implement the change (see Figure 7-12).

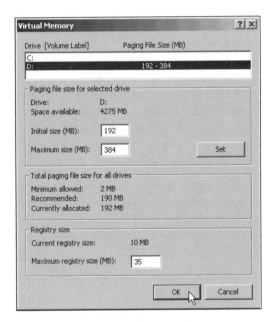

Figure 7-12 Configuring vitual memory

Also, there is a box to set the maximum size for the Registry file. As a general rule, the maximum Registry size is 18 to 25 percent of the initial page file size, which is about 70 MB for an initial page file size of 384 MB. Click OK to save the changes, and click OK twice more to leave the System Properties dialog box. Hands-on Project 7-8 gives you practice in tuning virtual memory.

Configuring Memory to Match the User Load

Memory is divided between server functions and network connectivity functions. The server functions include software applications, printing, and currently running services. Network connectivity is related to the number of user connections at a given time. Server functions use RAM and paging. The network connectivity only uses RAM. If the server performance is slow because memory is busy, the network memory parameters should be checked and tuned.

Network memory is adjusted from the Network and Dial-up Connections icon in the Control Panel (or on the Start button Settings menu). Open Network and Dial-up Connections, right-click Local Area Connection, and click Properties. Scroll the installed components list to find File and Printer Sharing for Microsoft Networks, and double-click that component to view the dialog box shown in Figure 7-13.

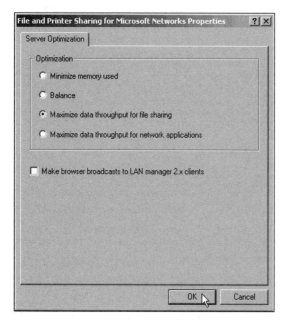

Figure 7-13   Adjusting memory allocation

The memory optimization settings are described in Table 7-2. For example, if a server has 120 users who regularly access Microsoft Access database files on the server, or who regularly install software from the server, the Maximize data throughput for file sharing option should be checked; or, if there are only 32 users on a small network, check the Balance radio button.

The memory settings shown in Table 7-2 are based primarily on how caching is handled compared to working sets. Caching involves storing often-used information, such as the contents of a file, in memory. A working set involves assigning physical memory to a process, for example to software application code. The *Minimize memory used* setting simply uses the minimum amount of memory for logged-on users. *Balance equally* divides memory use between caching and working sets. *Maximize data throughput for file sharing* gives caching most priority for use of available memory. *Maximize data throughput for network applications* gives working sets most memory and caching least memory.

Table 7-2   Configuring Server RAM

Optimizing Memory Settings	Purpose
Minimize memory used	Optimizes the memory used on servers with 10 or fewer simultaneous network users
Balance	Optimizes memory use for a small LAN with 64 or fewer users
Maximize data throughput for file sharing	Used for a large network with 64 users or more where file serving resources need more memory allocation to make the server efficient
Maximize data throughput for network applications	Used in servers that primarily handle network connections and to reduce paging activity when this affects server performance
Make browser broadcasts to LAN manager 2.x clients	Used for networks that have both Windows 2000 Server and Microsoft's early server operating system, LAN Manager

UPS Fault Tolerance

Disk drives, memory, and other key server components can sustain damage from power outages and fluctuations, such as brownouts. Also, the server may lose valuable data when a sudden power problem causes it to shut down without the opportunity to save data. A **UPS** (**uninterruptible power supply**) is the best fault tolerance method to prevent power problems from causing data loss and component damage.

There are two kinds of UPS systems commonly marketed: online and offline. Online UPS systems provide electrical power to equipment directly from their batteries. Their batteries are always charging from city power, until a power failure strikes. An offline UPS connects city power directly to the electrical equipment until it senses a sudden reduction in power, at which time it switches over to batteries. The advantage of an offline UPS is that it is less expensive than the online variety, and batteries often last longer. The disadvantage is that it may not switch to battery power in time to fully protect equipment during a sudden power failure. For this reason, many people prefer online systems for more guaranteed protection.

All UPS systems are designed to provide power for a limited time period, such as 10 to 20 minutes, so a decision can be made about how long the power failure will last and whether to shut down computers immediately. Of course, the amount of time the batteries can provide power depends on how much and what equipment is attached to the UPS. This is why most people attach only critical equipment to a UPS, such as computers and monitors, external disk arrays, and tape drives.

CAUTION
Some manufacturers recommend that laser printers not be plugged into a UPS, because those printers draw excessive power when turned on, risking damage to the UPS.

Most UPSs include circuitry to guard against power surges, which send so much power through electrical lines that it may damage motors, power supplies, or electronic components in equipment. Additional circuits may be present in offline UPSs to protect against power brownouts, or sags when not enough power is available. An online UPS normally regulates power to provide insurance for brownouts as well as outages. Also, many systems have protection for modem lines in case lightning strikes telephone lines. Another feature of modern UPS systems is the ability to communicate information to the computers they support, such as a warning that the power is out or that the UPS batteries are low.

Before connecting a server to a UPS, unpack the equipment and inspect it. Check to be sure a serial cable is included for communications with the server. Follow the manufacturer's directions for setting up the UPS. These directions may include, for example, inspecting the equipment, then shutting down the server, attaching the UPS serial cable to a serial communications port on the server, such as port 2 (COM2), plugging the UPS into the wall outlet, and plugging the server, monitor, and tape drive power cords into the UPS. Turn on the UPS and then power up the server.

The server and UPS communications options are set up in Windows 2000 Server from the Control Panel Power Options icon. After you open the Power Options tool, click the UPS tab to configure the communications for your particular UPS:

1. Click the Select button.

2. Use the Select manufacturer list box to select the UPS manufacturer, such as American Power Conversion.

3. Select the specific UPS model, such as the PowerStack, in the Select model list box.

4. In the *On port* box, specify the COM port to which the UPS is attached, such as COM2. Click Finish.

5. Click the Configure button in the Power Options Properties dialog box.

6. Configure the options that are appropriate to the UPS, which include how to send out notifications of a power failure, when to sound a critical alarm that the UPS is almost out of power, the ability to run a program just before the UPS is out of power, and if you want the computer and UPS to shut down just before the UPS is out of power. Click OK.

7. Click Apply.

8. Check the message at the bottom of the dialog box to make sure that the UPS is connected and communicating with the server. A large "X" in a red circle appears if it is not properly connected and communicating. If it does not, make sure that the serial cable is attached, ensure that you configured the same server port in Step 4 as is used for the cable, and make sure that the UPS is turned on.

9. Click OK and close the Control Panel.

CHAPTER SUMMARY

❑ Disk and removable storage management represents one of the most important advancements in Windows 2000 Server. The operating system provides two kinds of disk setup: basic and dynamic. Basic disks are backward-compatible to earlier operating systems, such as Windows NT Server, and provide rudimentary disk handling. Dynamic disks can be configured for more comprehensive disk management involving simple, spanned, striped, and RAID-5 volumes. Both basic and dynamic disks can be mounted to eliminate the need to identify them via a drive letter.

❑ Windows 2000 Server employs removable storage that includes tapes, CD-ROMs, CD-RWs, Zip, and Jaz drives. Removable storage is managed through libraries and media pools. Backups that are performed through the Windows 2000 Server Backup tool are one example of the automated use of media pools. Most server administrators back up their servers on a regular basis, using one or more of the backup techniques offered in Windows 2000 Server, such as the full or normal backup. Backups are a simple, but vital, form of insurance against lost data.

❑ After you set up a server, there are three immediate steps that you can take to tune performance. These include tuning how applications run, adjusting virtual memory, and tuning how memory is used for network connectivity. Finally, another important step to guarantee uninterrupted performance is to obtain and configure a UPS.

In the next chapter, you move from strictly working on the server to preparing both server and workstations for client access to the network.

KEY TERMS

active partition — The partition from which a computer boots.

basic disk — In Windows 2000, a partitioned disk that can have up to four partitions and that uses logical drive designations. This type of disk is compatible with MS-DOS, Windows 3.x, Windows 95, Windows 98, Windows NT, and Windows 2000.

boot partition — Holds the Windows 2000 Server \Winnt folder containing the system files.

defragmentation — A software process that rearranges data to fill in the empty spaces that develop on disks and make data easier to obtain.

disk fragmentation — A normal and gradual process in which files become spread throughout a disk, and empty pockets of space develop between files.

dynamic disk — In Windows 2000, a disk that does not use traditional partitioning, which means that there is no restriction to the number of volumes that can be set up on one disk or to the ability to extend volumes onto additional physical disks. Dynamic disks are only compatible with Windows 2000.

extended partition — A partition that is created from unpartitioned free disk space and is linked to a primary partition in order to increase the available disk space.

formatting — A process that prepares a hard disk partition for a specific file system.

full backup — A backup of an entire system, including all system files, programs, and data files.

home folder or **home directory** — A server folder that is associated with a user's account and that is a designated workspace for the user to store files.

incremental backup — A backup of new or changed files.

library — Removable storage media and the drive (or drives) used by the media.

master boot record (MBR) — Data created in the first sector of a disk, containing startup information and information about disk partitions.

media pool — A set of removable media in which the media are used for the same purpose and are managed in the same way, such as backup tapes for a Windows 2000 server.

mirrored volume — Two dynamic disks that are set up for RAID level 1 so that data on one disk is stored on a redundant disk.

mounted drive — A physical disk, CD-ROM, or Zip drive that appears as a folder and that is accessed through a path like any other folder.

page file — Disk space reserved for use when memory requirements exceed the available RAM.

paging — Moving blocks of information from RAM to virtual memory on disk.

partitioning — Blocking a group of tracks and sectors to be used by a particular file system, such as FAT or NTFS.

partition table — Table containing information about each partition on a disk, such as the type of partition, size, and location. Also, the partition table provides information to the computer about how to access the disk.

primary partition — Partition or portion of a hard disk that is bootable.

RAID-5 volume — Three or more dynamic disks that use RAID level 5 fault tolerance through disk striping and creating parity blocks for data recovery.

Registry — A database used to store information about the configuration, program setup, devices, drivers, and other data important to the setup of a computer running Windows 2000, Windows NT, Windows 98, or Windows 95.

robotic library — A library of removable media and drives in which multiple media, such as tapes, can be mounted and dismounted automatically.

simple volume — A portion of a disk or an entire disk that is set up as a dynamic disk.

spanned volume — Two or more Windows 2000 dynamic disks that are combined to appear as one disk.

stand-alone drive library — A library consisting of media and a drive, in which the media are mounted manually one at a time.

stripe set — Two or more basic disks set up so that files are spread in blocks across the disks.

striped volume — Two or more dynamic disks that use striping so that files are spread in blocks across the disks.

system partition — Partition that contains boot files, such as Boot.ini and Ntldr in Windows 2000 Server.

uninterruptible power supply (UPS) — A device built into electrical equipment or a separate device that provides immediate battery power to equipment during a power failure or brownout.

virtual memory — Disk space allocated to link with memory to temporarily hold data when there is not enough free RAM.

volume — A basic disk partition that has been formatted for a particular file system, a primary partition, a volume set, an extended volume, a stripe set, a stripe set with parity, or a mirror set. Or a dynamic disk that is set up as a simple volume, spanned volume, striped volume, RAID-5 volume, or mirrored volume.

volume set — Two or more formatted basic disk partitions (volumes) that are combined to look like one volume with a single drive letter.

REVIEW QUESTIONS

1. You notice that one of the servers in your organization seems to run slowly because there is heavy paging activity. What can you do to reduce the paging?

   a. Mount the page file on CD-ROM.

   b. Delete the page file and recreate it at half the size.

   c. Configure the server memory to maximize data throughput for network applications.

   d. Configure the server memory so it is balanced.

2. You want to set up two disks so they are mirrored, but there is no option to do this in the Disk Management snap-in. What is the problem?

   a. Windows 2000 no longer supports mirroring.

   b. You are working with basic disks and need to convert them to dynamic disks.

   c. You must stripe the disks first.

   d. The disks must contain over 2 GB to mirror them.

3. Which of the following are examples of libraries?

   a. robotic

   b. stand-alone

   c. synchronized

   d. all of the above

   e. only a and b

   f. only b and c

4. Your server has 512 MB of RAM, and your colleague who is also a server administrator wants to set the minimum page file size at 256 MB as a way to save on disk space. What is your reaction?

a. You agree that this is a good way to conserve disk space.

b. You do not agree because the page file size should be at minimum 1 GB for Windows 2000 Server.

c. You do not agree because the page file size should be at minimum 768 MB.

d. You agree, but recommend reducing the minimum even more to 125 MB.

5. Your organization is growing and becoming more dependent on its servers. One result is that tape backups now require about 2–3 hours to complete. Your boss is concerned about the after-work hours that you spend nursing the backups, waiting for each tape to finish and then inserting another until the backups are complete. What solution(s) might you suggest that are compatible with Windows 2000 Server?

a. Purchase a robotic tape unit to load tapes automatically.

b. Schedule the backups.

c. Only perform backups every other day.

d. all of the above

e. only a and b

f. only b and c

6. How much free space is needed on a basic disk to convert it to a dynamic disk?

a. 1 MB

b. 5 MB

c. 10 MB

d. none

7. Which of the following is(are) true about basic and dynamic disks?

a. Dynamic disks can be partitioned, but basic disks cannot.

b. Dynamic disks can be set up as spanned volumes.

c. Basic disks are formatted, but dynamic disks are not.

d. All of the above are true.

e. Only a and b are true.

f. Only a and c are true.

8. You want to set up a mounted volume on your Windows 2000 Server. As you go through the steps to mount the volume in the Disk Management snap-in, you find there is no option to mount the volume. What is the problem?

a. The disk containing the target folder for the mounted volume is formatted for FAT and not NTFS.

b. You did not first set up the target folder as a shared resource.

c. The target folder is not compressed.

d. Only a CD-ROM can be mounted, and you are trying to mount a dynamic disk.

9. You want to view the properties of the page file. Which of the following files would you right-click to view the properties?

a. Ntdetect

b. Pagefile.com

c. Pagefile.sys

d. Netcom.dat

10. You want to locate the media pool for the backups that you are running. Which tool provides this information about the media pool and enables you to manage it?

a. Disk Management

b. Removable Storage

c. System Tools

d. Backup

11. What is the dynamic disk called that contains the \Winnt folder?

a. boot folder

b. system partition

c. system disk

d. boot volume

12. Your server, which is set up for basic disks, will not boot. When you run an independent disk analysis tool from the disk manufacturer, it shows that the disk and the disk adapter are both working properly. What else might be the problem?

a. Windows 2000 is trying to boot too fast for that disk.

b. The disk is formatted as a simple volume and has lost it parity data.

c. The master boot record is damaged.

d. all of the above

e. only a and b

f. only a and c

13. You are new to an organization that is in the practice of throwing out tapes that contain old information but that are still usable. Which of the following might you suggest for this organization?

a. Create a free media pool for a managed way to cycle the tapes back into use.

b. Create an application media pool as a means to delete information on the tapes before they are thrown out.

c. Have server operators manually erase and retension the tapes to be used again.

d. Use a magnet to quickly initialize each tape so it can be reused.

14. As a consultant, you have been asked to improve the performance of a server that has a mirrored volume containing the \Winnt folder, a RAID-5 volume of seven physical disks, a simple volume labeled F:, and another simple volume labeled G:. When you check the location of the page file, you find one page file on the main disk of the mirrored volume. Would you make any changes?

a. The current setup is the ideal setup in this situation.

b. Add a page file to the RAID-5 volume.

c. Add a page file to each of the F: and G: volumes.

d. Remove the page file from the main disk in the mirrored volume and put it on the RAID-5 volume.

15. Virtual memory is an example of

a. allocating a section of RAM only for the operating system.

b. using disk space to supplement RAM.

c. using memory exclusively for network connectivity.

d. giving applications running on the server priority for RAM access.

16. Which of the following backup options are you most likely to use when you want to back up all files on a server?

a. copy

b. incremental

c. differential

d. normal

e. daily

17. How many partitions can you put on a dynamic disk?

a. 1

b. 2

c. 4

d. none

18. Your organization only has 12 users on the server. What setting would you use to configure memory use?

a. Balance

b. Maximize data throughput for file sharing

c. Maximize data throughput for network applications

d. Minimize memory used

7

19. You are setting up a server for a customer service organization that needs fast access to its data, but that is not as concerned about how fast information is updated on disk. The organization wants fault tolerance for data storage. Which of the following options would you recommend?

    a. a spanned volume

    b. a striped volume

    c. a RAID-5 volume

    d. a simple volume

20. In order to boot from a basic disk, which of the following must be true?

    a. It is a primary partition.

    b. It is an active partition.

    c. It is designated as drive C.

    d. all of the above

    e. only a and b

    f. only b and c

21. You are consulting for a small organization that has used their server for over two years without maintaining it, other than to replace a defective monitor. They are complaining that the server performance has gotten slower over the past several months. What would you do first to improve performance?

    a. Add RAM.

    b. Set memory to Make browser broadcasts to LAN manager 2.x clients.

    c. Increase the page file size by 300–500 MB.

    d. Defragment the disks.

22. You have created a RAID-5 volume that consists of seven 9-GB disks. How much disk space is usable to store files?

    a. all of the disk space

    b. 54 GB

    c. 62 GB

    d. 60 GB

23. Which of the following can be used in removable storage management?

    a. Jaz drive

    b. CD-ROM drive

    c. tape drive

    d. all of the above

    e. only a and b

    f. only b and c

24. You have set up a spanned volume, and one disk has failed. What are your alternatives?

    a. There is no problem because the other disks will take over.

    b. Use the Disk Management snap-in to start the parity repair tool.

    c. Replace the disk, repair the spanned volume, and perform a full restore.

    d. Use the Disk Management snap-in to make the remaining disks simple volumes, and then recover the data.

25. How many extended partitions can be on one basic disk?

    a. 1

    b. 2

    c. 4

    d. none

7

HANDS-ON PROJECTS

Project 7-1

In this hands-on activity you install the Disk Management and Disk Defragmenter snap-ins in the MMC. Next, you practice partitioning and formatting a basic disk.

To install the snap-ins:

1. Click **Start** and click **Run**. Enter **mmc** in the Open: box and click **OK**.

2. Maximize the Console windows, if necessary. Click the **Console** menu and click **Add/Remove Snap-in**.

3. Click the **Add** button and double-click **Disk Management**. Click **Local Computer** and click **Finish**.

4. Double-click **Disk Defragmenter**. Click **Close** and click **OK**.

5. Click the **Console** menu and click **Save As**. Enter **Disk.msc** as the name for this Console setup and click **Save**. Now you can access it in the future as Disk.msc from the Administrative tools menu or the MMC, so that you do not have to install the snap-ins again.

To partition and format a basic disk:

1. Double-click the **Disk Management** folder in the MMC tree.

2. Right-click an unallocated portion of disk space. Note that black is the default color that designates unallocated disk space.

3. Click **Create Partition**. Click **Next** in the Create Partition Wizard.

4. Click **Primary partition** and click **Next**.

5. Enter the amount of disk space to use, such as **8411 MB**. The Wizard provides information about the minimum and maximum amount of space that you can specify, on the basis of the total unallocated space (see Figure 7-14). Click **Next**.

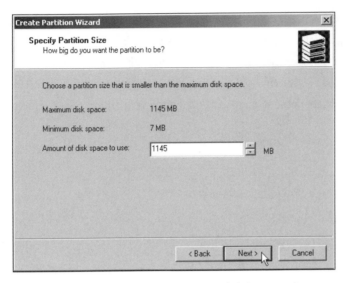

Figure 7-14   Specifying the amount of disk space for a new partition

6. Assign a drive letter, such as **D:** (or the next available drive letter). Click **Next**.

7. Click **Format this partition with the following settings:** Select the option to format using NTFS (but view the other options before you make your selection). Select **512** in the Allocation unit size: box (look at all of the options). Enter **Databases** as the volume label. Check the box to **Enable file and folder compression**. Click **Next**.

8. Use the scroll bar to review the settings you have specified. If you want to change any, click the Back button until you reach the appropriate dialog box. Record your observations about the options in this dialog box.

9. Click **Finish** when you are ready to create the partition and format it. (If you are just practicing and do not want to create the partition, click Cancel.)

10. Close the MMC.

Project 7-2

In this project, you practice marking a basic disk partition as the active partition (system partition) containing the boot files. The system that you use should have at least two partitions. If it does not, you can still view the option to mark a partition as active, but that option will be deactivated.

To mark the partition:

1. Click **Start** and click **Run**. Enter **mmc** in the Open: box and click **OK**.

2. Maximize the Console windows, if necessary.

3. Click **Console**, click **Open**, and double-click **Disk.msc**, which is the console file you created in Hands-on Project 7-1.

4. Notice the partitions available on the computer and record their sizes, file systems, and other information in your lab journal or in a word-processed document.

5. Find a partition that is not labeled as "(System)" and right-click it.

6. Notice the Mark Partition Active option on the shortcut menu. This is the option you would click to mark a partition as active. (Do not mark the partition active in this practice session, unless your instructor gives you permission.)

7. Click an empty portion of the Console window to close the shortcut menu, but leave the Console window open for projects that follow.

Project 7-3

In this hands-on activity, you practice changing the drive letter of an existing drive.

To change the drive letter:

1. Make sure that the Console window is open, with the Disk Management snap-in installed and open.

2. Right-click a drive, such as **C:** or **D:**, and click **Change Drive Letter and Path**.

3. Click the **Edit** button. What happens if you try to edit a boot or system partition or volume? Repeat Steps 2 and 3 for another volume if you right-clicked a boot or system volume in Step 2.

4. Click the **Assign drive letter:** radio button (if it is not selected by default), and view the drive letter options in the list box (see Figure 7-15). What drive letters are available on your computer?

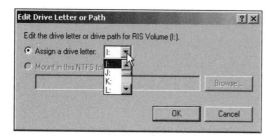

Figure 7-15   Changing the drive letter

5. Change the drive letter to a different letter than is already assigned, such as **G:**, and click **OK**.

6. What is the warning box that appears?

7. Click **Yes** if you have permission from your instructor to change the drive letter; if not, click **No** and click **Close**.

8. If you clicked Yes in Step 7, notice that the new drive letter is shown in the Disk Management snap-in.

Project 7-4

This Hands-on Project gives you the opportunity to create a simple volume for a dynamic disk. Before starting, the disk should be converted to a dynamic disk (see the section "Converting Disks," and follow those steps if it is not already converted).

To create the simple volume:

1. Make sure that the Console window is open, with the Disk Management snap-in is installed and open.
2. Right-click free space on a disk.
3. Click **Create Volume**. Click **Next** in the Create Volume Wizard.
4. Make sure the selection to create a Simple Volume is selected. Click **Next**.
5. Click **Next** in the Select Disks dialog box.
6. Click **Assign a drive letter** and use the default drive letter. Click **Next**.
7. Make sure the Format Volume dialog box is set for **NTFS**. Click **Next**.
8. Click **Finish**.
9. Click the **Action** menu and click **Rescan Disks**, if the volume is not displayed in the Disk Management snap-in.

Project 7-5

In this activity you practice analyzing a disk and then defragmenting it.

To analyze and defragment the disk:

1. Make sure that the Console window is open, with the Disk Defragmenter snap-in is installed.
2. Click **Disk Defragmenter** in the left pane.
3. Right-click a disk drive, such as drive **C**: and notice the options that are available. Make a note of these in your lab journal or a word-processed document. Click **Analyze**.
4. Does this disk need to be defragmented? If so, how much fragmentation exists (click the **View Report** button)?
5. Click **Defragment** in the Analysis Complete dialog box (even if it reports that you do not need to defragment).
6. What information is shown on the screen during the defragmenting process?
7. Click **View Report** in the Defragmentation Complete dialog box.
8. What information is shown in the report? Summarize the information in your lab journal or in a word-processed document.
9. Click **Close** to exit the report.

Project 7-6

In this project you create a mounted volume. In the first series of steps, you create a folder on an NTFS formatted volume or disk that will hold the mounted drive. After those steps, you mount the drive into the folder.

To create the mounted drive:

1. Open Windows Explorer or My Computer and click a main volume that is formatted for NTFS, such as drive **C:**.

2. Click the **File** menu, highlight **New**, and click **Folder**. Enter your initials appended to Mount for the folder name, for example MPMount. Press **Enter**.

3. Make sure that the Console window is open, with the Disk Management snap-in installed.

4. Right-click the disk drive you want to mount into the folder, and click **Change Letter and Drive Path**.

5. Click the existing drive letter for the drive, such as **D:** in the Name box, and click the **Add** button.

6. Click **Mount in this NTFS folder**.

7. Click the **Browse** button and locate the folder you created, then click that folder (for example, **MPMount**).

8. Click **OK** in the Browse for Drive Path dialog box.

9. Click **OK** in the Add New Drive Letter or Path dialog box (or click Cancel if you do not want to complete mounting the drive).

10. Go back to Windows Explorer or My Computer and find the mounted volume you created. What icon is used to represent it?

11. Right-click the mounted volume to examine its properties. Record your observations about the mounted volume's icon and properties in your lab journal or a word-processed document.

12. Close the mounted volume's properties dialog box and close Windows Explorer or My Computer.

Project 7-7

In this activity you practice backing up a disk drive. You will need a computer running Windows 2000 Server that is set up for a tape drive, and you will need a tape.

To practice a backup:

1. Insert a tape into the tape drive of the computer.

2. Click **Start**, point to **Programs**, point to **Accessories**, point to **System Tools**, and click **Backup**.

3. Click the **Backup** tab.

4. Check the box of a drive on the computer, such as drive **C:** or **D:**. Double-click that drive and notice which folders are checked for the backup. How would you back up only a portion of a drive, such as one or two folders? Record your observations in your lab journal or a word-processed document.

5. In the Backup destination box, select the backup medium that reflects the type of tape you are using, such as **Travan** or **4mm DAT**.

6. Click the **Start Backup** button.

7. Enter a description and label for the backup, such as **Set created 7/2/2000 at 10:00 AM** and **Media created 7/2/2000 at 10:00 AM**. If you are using a new tape or an old one that you can write over, click **Replace the data on the media with this backup**. If instead you want to retain data already on the tape, click **Append this backup to the media**.

8. Click the **Advanced** button.

9. Click **If possible, compress the backup data to save space**.

10. Click the **Backup Type** list box and view the options. Record the options in your lab journal or in a word-processed document, and note which dialog box enables you to access them. Select **Normal** as the option for this backup.

11. Click **OK**.

12. Click the **Start Backup** button (or you can click Cancel if you do not have a tape for practice). After you click the Start Backup button, you may see a dialog box with a warning that "There is no 'unused' media available," which means that the tape has been used previously. Click **Yes** if you see this warning.

13. Click **OK** when the backup is complete, and then close the Backup utility.

Project 7-8

In this project, you tune Windows 2000 server by setting the application response and changing the virtual memory allocation.

To tune the server:

1. Click **Start**, point to **Settings**, and click **Control Panel**.

2. Double-click the **System** icon and click the **Advanced** tab.

3. Click the **Performance Options** button.

4. Click **Applications**.

5. Click the **Change** button.

6. What is the current paging file size? Is it set at the recommended initial size? Is there a page file on more than one volume? Record your findings in a lab notebook or word-processed document.

7. Click drive **C:** or another drive containing a paging file.

8. Change the initial paging file size so that it is 10 MB over the current initial size, by entering this value in the Initial size (MB): box.

9. In the Maximum (MB): box, enter a value that is 10 MB over the currently entered size.

10. Click **Set**.

11. Click **OK** to exit the Virtual Memory dialog box, and click **OK** to leave the Performance Options dialog box.

12. Click **OK** to leave the System Properties dialog box.

CASE PROJECT

Aspen Consulting Project: Configuring Storage and Performance

Country Fresh Breads is a large bakery in Los Angeles that supplies baked goods to grocery and convenience stores. Their information technology group is implementing a new server with Windows 2000 Server that will be used to track sales and distribution data. Sales are handled over the telephone by customer representatives, who take weekly orders from grocery stores for bakery items to be delivered. Currently, Country Fresh Breads is using an aging UNIX server for the sales and distribution functions. The Country Fresh Breads customer representatives look up information when each store calls and then place the store's order via the computer. The disk response time on the UNIX server is relatively slow, and they are hoping to have faster look-up response on the new Windows 2000 server. The new server has a disk array containing eight 20 GB disks. Four of the disks are on one SCSI adapter, and four are on another SCSI adapter. The information technology group is contacting you to help in setting up the server. Their current need is to have you assist with the disk storage and in setting up backups.

1. What type of disk storage do you recommend that Country Fresh Breads use on this server: basic or dynamic disks? Why?

2. What fault tolerance do you recommend that they use, if any? If you do recommend fault tolerance, explain how to set it up.

3. The company wants to use one disk on this server for users' home folders. Explain how you would implement the disk for this purpose and what steps to follow in setting it up.

4. This server will have a CD-ROM jukebox that can hold up to five CD-ROMs, but Country Fresh Breads intends to make 15 CD-ROMs available for company-wide access. What Windows 2000 Server tool(s) can be used to track the CD-ROMs and notify operators to mount CD-ROMs as needed?

5. Explain how you would set up backup systems for the following purposes:

   ❑ Daily backups of the server

   ❑ Weekly backups of sales information contained in five folders to import into the accounting system on another server

   ❑ Yearly archiving of all sales data

6. The information technology group is not sure how to adjust the page file. Explain how to size the file, and provide instructions about what steps to use in the process.

OPTIONAL CASE PROJECTS FOR TEAMS

Team Case One

Mark Arnez is curious about how many ways there are to use mounted volumes in different kinds of situations. Form a team to develop a range of scenarios in which to use mounted volumes.

Team Case Two

Tape technologies are changing—the recent improvements in Travan technology are one example. Mark asks you to form a group to research the different kinds of tape technologies that are compatible with Windows 2000 Server. Which of these technologies can be used with libraries and media pools?

8

MANAGING ACCOUNTS AND CLIENT CONNECTIVITY

After reading this chapter and completing the exercises you will be able to:

♦ Establish account naming conventions

♦ Configure account security policies

♦ Create and manage accounts, including setting up a new account, configuring account properties, delegating account management, and renaming, disabling, and deleting an account

♦ Create local user profiles, roaming profiles, and mandatory profiles

♦ Configure client network operating systems to access Windows 2000 Server, and install client operating systems through Remote Installation Services

Clients are the reason for a server's existence. A server makes networking meaningful to clients because it gives clients access to all kinds of valuable resources such as files, databases, printers, Web information, and software. Providing client access to servers is the single largest reason for the worldwide explosive growth in networks. Windows 2000 Server is a particularly versatile server because it hosts a large range of clients from MS-DOS to Windows 2000 Professional to Macintosh and UNIX.

You have already started learning how to configure Windows 2000 Server for all types of clients by setting up protocols that include TCP/IP, NWLink, AppleTalk, NetBEUI, and DLC. In this chapter, you take the next step by learning how to establish a naming convention for accounts and how to configure account policies to help keep a network secure. You also learn to configure and manage accounts, including creating user profiles. Finally, you learn how to set up different client network operating systems to connect to Windows 2000 Server, and how to configure Windows 2000 Server for those clients.

SETTING UP ACCOUNT NAMING CONVENTIONS

Users access network servers and resources through accounts. Before establishing accounts, organizations set up account names based on the account user's actual name or function within the organization. For example, if the organization uses the users' actual names, it will adopt a particular naming convention, because it is clumsy to use the full names. Also, server storage for the full name is limited by the operating system. Some IBM mainframe operating systems limit the length of the username to eight characters. Windows 2000 Server limits user account names to 20 characters that include letters, numbers, and some symbols.

 Symbols that cannot be used in an account name in Windows 2000 Server are: [ ] ; : < > = , + / \ |. Also, each account name must be unique, so that there are no duplicates.

Some conventions for account names based on the user's actual name are as follows:

- Last name followed by the initial of the first name (PalmerM)
- First name initial followed by the last name (MPalmer)
- First name initial, middle initial, and last name (MJPalmer)

When an organization creates usernames by position or function, it often uses descriptive names. For example, the payroll office may use the names Paysuper (payroll supervisor), Payclerk (payroll clerk), and Payassist (payroll assistant). Another example is the names that schools give to accounts in student labs, such as Lab1, Lab2, Lab3, and so on. The advantage of naming accounts by function is that an account does not have to be purged when the account holder leaves or changes positions. The network administrator simply changes the account password, and gives it to the new person in that position. The advantage of having accounts based on the user's name is that it is easier to know who is logged on to a server (if the naming convention is well designed).

 In a large organization where computer systems and software are audited by independent financial auditors, the auditors often prefer to have accounts named for individual users. This provides the best audit tracking of who has made what changes to data.

ESTABLISHING ACCOUNT POLICIES

Account policies are security measures set up in a group policy that applies to all accounts or to all accounts in a container, such as a domain, when the Active Directory is installed (see Chapter 4). The account policy options affect two main areas, password security and account lockout. Another option is to use Kerberos security. There is no requirement to implement these security options, but most server administrators choose to use them. Many organizations like to have some guidelines to help computer users take advantage of computer security features to protect company information from people inside or outside the organization who could misuse it. Security features also protect the server and printer resources from malicious activities.

The first line of defense for Windows 2000 Server is password security, but it is only effective if users are taught to use it properly. Many users are careless about security, viewing it as an impediment to their work. They may tape passwords inside a desk drawer or use easily guessed passwords, such as the first name of a family member. Some users keep the same password for months or years, even though it may become known to several other people. Systems like Windows 2000 Server have built-in capabilities to help users become more conscious of maintaining passwords. One option is to set a password expiration period, requiring users to change passwords at regular intervals. Many organizations use this feature, for example requiring that users change their passwords every 45 to 90 days.

 TIP Server administrators should consider changing passwords every month for the Administrator account and other accounts that can access sensitive information.

8

Some organizations require that all passwords have a minimum length, such as six or seven characters. This requirement makes passwords more difficult to guess. Another option is to have the operating system "remember" passwords that have been used previously. For example, the system might be set to recall the last five passwords, preventing a user from repeating one of these. Password recollection forces the user to change to a different password instead of reusing the same one when a new one is set. Windows 2000 Server is capable of monitoring unsuccessful logon attempts, in case an intruder attempts to break into an account by trying various password combinations. The operating system can employ account lockout to lock out an account (including the true account owner) after a number of unsuccessful tries. The lockout can be set to release after a specified period of time or by intervention from the server administrator. For example, at one university, a part-time custodian who had keys to computer center staff offices attempted to access the Administrator accounts on servers at night. Account lockout prevented him from accessing those sensitive accounts until his surreptitious activities were discovered and stopped.

A common policy is to have lockout go into effect after five to ten unsuccessful logon attempts. Also, an administrator can set lockout to release after a designated time, such as 30 minutes. The 30 minutes creates enough delay to discourage intruders, while giving some leeway to a user who might have forgotten a recently changed password.

Kerberos security involves the use of tickets that are exchanged between the client who requests logon and network services access and the server or Active Directory that grants access. On a network that does not use the Active Directory, each standalone Windows 2000 server can be designated as a Kerberos key distribution center, which means that the server stores user accounts and passwords. When the Active Directory is used, then each domain controller is a key distribution center. When a user logs on, the client computer sends an account name and password to the key distribution center. The key distribution center responds by issuing a temporary ticket that grants the user access to the Kerberos ticket-granting service on a domain controller (or standalone server), which then grants a permanent ticket to that computer. The permanent ticket, called a **service ticket**, is good for the duration of a logon session (or for another period of time specified by the server administrator in the account polices) and enables the computer to access network services beginning with the Logon service. The permanent ticket contains information about the account that is used to identify the account to each network service it requests to use. You might think of a Kerberos ticket as similar to one you would purchase to enter a concert; the ticket is good for the duration of that event and for entry to refreshment and merchandise booths, but you must purchase a new ticket to attend a concert on another date.

Configuring account policies is accomplished through the MMC Group Policy snap-in. You can add the snap-in by using these steps:

1. Start MMC from the Start button, Run option, click the MMC Console menu, and click Add/Remove Snap-in.

2. In the Add/Remove Snap-in dialog box, click Add, scroll to Group Policy, and double-click it.

3. When the Select Group Policy Object Wizard starts, choose Local Computer, if you have not installed the Active Directory, and click Finish. If you have installed the Active Directory, click the Browse button, double-click Default Domain Policy, and click Finish.

4. Click Close and click OK.

The account policies are located in the Computer Configuration management category as part of the Windows Settings. For example, to access the domain-wide policies when the Active Directory is installed, in the left pane double-click Default Domain Policy, Computer Configuration, Windows Settings, Security Settings, and Account Policies, which will display the window shown in Figure 8-1.

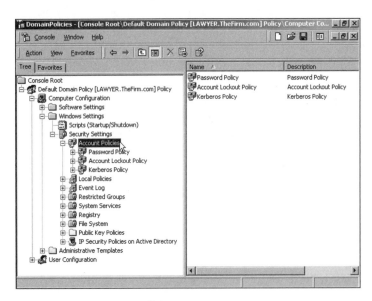

Figure 8-1   Account policies

Double-click Password Policy in the left or right pane to view the security options. To change an option, double-click that option and make the change in the dialog box that is displayed. The options are the following:

- *Enforce password history:* Enables you to require users to choose new passwords when they make a password change, because the system can remember the previously used passwords

- *Maximum password age:* Permits you to set the maximum time allowed until a password expires

- *Minimum password age:* Permits you to specify that a password must be used for a minimum amount of time before it can be changed

- *Minimum password length:* Enables you to require that passwords are a minimum length

- *Passwords must meet complexity requirements:* Enables you to create a filter of customized password requirements that each account password must follow

- *Store password using reversible encryption for all users in the domain:* Enables passwords to be stored in reversible encrypted format

Double-click Account Lockout Policy in the left pane to configure the account lockout parameters, which include:

- *Account lockout duration:* Permits you to specify in minutes how long the system will keep an account locked out after reaching the specified number of unsuccessful logon attempts

- *Account lockout threshold:* Enables you to set a limit to the number of unsuccessful attempts to log on to an account

- *Reset account lockout count after:* Enables you to specify the number of minutes between two consecutive unsuccessful logon attempts, to make sure that the account will not be locked out too soon

When the Active Directory is installed, the account policies include the option to configure Kerberos, which is the default authentication. If the Active Directory is not installed, Kerberos is not included in the account policies because the default authentication is through **Windows NT LAN Manager** (**NTLM**). NTLM is the authentication used by all versions of Windows NT Server prior to Windows 2000 Server. To configure Kerberos in the Active Directory, double-click Kerberos Policy in the left pane to access the following parameters:

- *Enforce user logon restrictions:* Turns on Kerberos security, which is the default

- *Maximum lifetime for a service ticket:* Determines the maximum amount of time in minutes that a service ticket can be used to continually access a particular service in one service session

- *Maximum lifetime for a user ticket:* Determines the maximum amount of time in hours that a ticket can be used in one continuous session for access to a computer or domain

- *Maximum lifetime for user ticket renewal:* Determines the maximum number of days that the same Kerberos ticket can be renewed each time a user logs on

- *Maximum tolerance for computer clock synchronization:* Determines how long in minutes a client will wait until synchronizing its clock with that of the server or Active Directory it is accessing

As is true for password and lockout policies, any of the Kerberos policy parameters can be included or excluded. Server and client operating systems that support Kerberos include Windows 2000 Server and Windows 2000 Professional. It can also be used in non-Windows 2000 operating systems that have the Directory Service Client software installed (described later in this chapter).

 TIP If getting users to log off when they go home at night is a problem, limit the *maximum lifetime for service ticket* or *maximum lifetime for user ticket* values to a certain number of hours, such as 10 or 12.

When you set up account policies, there is a difference between setting policies for a server that is in a domain and setting them for a server that is not. For a server that is not in a domain, you set policies for that local server only. In contrast, when the Active Directory is installed, you set policies for all computers that are members of the domain (try Hands-on Project 8-1).

You can, however, create organizational units (OUs) and create policies that are applicable to each OU and that may be different from the policies for the domain. For example, you may want to tighten security for a particular OU, such as a group of user accounts in which the users are performing highly secret research. In this case, you might tighten password security to require 10 characters for that group, whereas the domain security might require only six. If you create special security policies for particular OUs, then use the Security Templates MMC snap-in to create specially named templates for each OU, and then apply each template to a group policy that is applicable to its OU.

CREATING AND MANAGING ACCOUNTS

With the account policies established, the next step is to create accounts. Two accounts, Administrator and Guest, are set up when you install Windows 2000 Server. Accounts that are created when the Active Directory is not installed or that are on a standalone server that is not part of a domain are local user accounts and can only be used on that individual server. When accounts are created in the domain through the Active Directory, then those accounts can be used to access any domain server or resource.

New accounts are set up by first installing the MMC Local Users and Groups snap-in for servers that do not use the Active Directory. When the Active Directory is installed and the server is a domain controller, use the MMC Active Directory Users and Computers snap-in. Each new account is created by entering account information and password controls.

If you are using the Active Directory and are working on a DC, Windows 2000 Server will not allow you to install the Local Users and Groups snap-in, because you must use the Active Directory Users and Computers snap-in instead.

To create a local user account on a server that is not part of a domain:

1. Double-click Local Users and Groups in the MMC.

2. Click Users and then click the Action menu.

3. Click New User.

To create an account in the Active Directory:

1. Double-click the Active Directory Users and Computers snap-in in the left pane, and double-click the domain name.

2. Click Users in the left-pane tree.

3. Click the *Create a new user in the current container* button, which is an icon resembling a single person, on the button bar (see Figure 8-2).

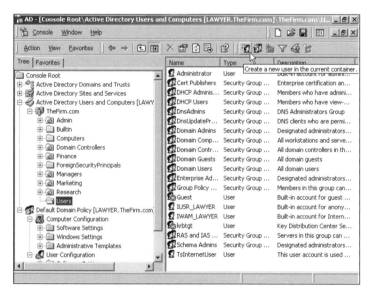

Figure 8-2   Creating a new user in a domain

Complete the name, user logon name, password, password confirmation, and optional parameters in the dialog boxes used to create a new account (one dialog box for a local user account and two dialog boxes for a domain account). For example, to create an account in the Active Directory, enter the first name, middle initial, and last name of the user and provide the user logon name (see Figure 8-3). The domain name is provided automatically, as is a pre-Windows-2000 logon name for pre-Windows-2000 clients. Click Next to go to the next screen.

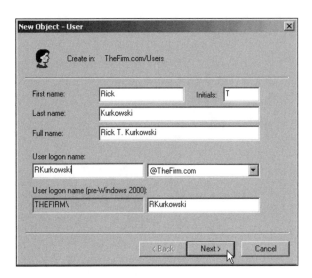

Figure 8-3   New user information

The next dialog box enables you to enter a password and confirm it for the account. Also, there are four parameters that enable you to control the account further. For example, the *User must change password at next logon* option forces users to enter a new password the first time they log on. This option is unnecessary for accounts used by the server administrator, but it is valuable for accounts created for others. Server administrators check this box when creating new accounts so that they will not know the passwords of account holders. Although the initial password is known, once it is given to the account holder, the administrator will not know the new password that the user is forced to enter at first logon.

Another option is to check *User cannot change password*, which means that only the network administrator can assign the password to an account. Under most circumstances, it is best for users to create their own confidential passwords, so they are the only ones using their accounts. Confidential passwords provide good security and ensure that if an account is audited, the activities audited are only those of the account holder. However, this option is used for special accounts, such as one that is used by the Windows 2000 Replicator for automatically copying files from one server to another server. Two other accounts for which the administrator may want to control the passwords are the Guest account and accounts used to access Internet Information Services.

The option *Password never expires* is used in some situations in which an account must always be accessed, even if no one remembers to change the password. That would be true for a utility account needed to run a program process. The password would be hard-coded into the program for the purpose of accessing the account to start the process. For example, you might create an account that automatically copies database files twice a day, which is done in client/server environments where one database is used for updating information throughout the day. A copy of the database is made, for example each morning and each afternoon, and is used for creating reports on the data. That way, heavy demand from large reports never slows down database updating, because reports are generated from the separate, copied database.

The *Account is disabled* option is used to stop activity on an account after the account holder leaves the organization. For example, if the payroll supervisor decides to go on a leave of absence for two months, the administrator might disable his or her account for that time period. That would secure the account until the supervisor's return. Figure 8-4 shows the New Object – User dialog box with the information entered for an account.

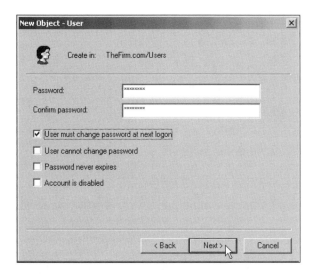

Figure 8-4   New user account parameters

After the parameters are entered, click Next to view a summary of the information you have entered, and then click Finish to create the account or click Back to reenter a parameter.

 If you are creating an account on a server on which the Active Directory is not installed, you would click Close instead of Finish after the parameters are entered, then double-click the newly created user account to access the account properties.

The next step is to double-click the account in the right pane, which displays user accounts and groups under Users, to further configure the properties associated with that account, as shown in Figure 8-5. (Try Hands-on Project 8-2 to create an account and to practice configuring account properties.)

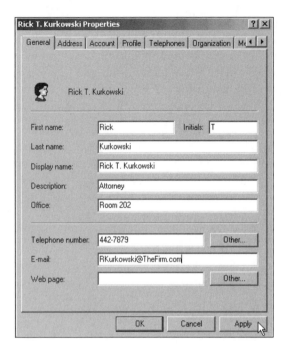

Figure 8-5 Account properties in the Active Directory

The account properties that you can set up are the following:

- *General tab:* Enables you to enter or modify personal information about the account holder that includes the first name, last name, name as it is displayed in the console, description of the user or account, office location, telephone number, e-mail address, and home page. There are also optional buttons to enter additional telephone numbers and Web page addresses for the account holder.

- *Address tab:* Used to provide information about the account holder's street address, Post Office box, city, state or province, postal code, and country or region.

- *Account tab:* Provides information about the logon name, domain name, account options such as requiring the user to change her or his password at next logon, and account expiration date, if one applies. For example, you can set an expiration date on an account when it is used by a temporary employee or when you know an employee's last day to work. There is also a button on this tab that enables you to set up an account so that the user cannot access the server at designated times, such as during backups and at times designated for system work on the server. For example, if your system work time is every Thursday evening from 8:00 to 10:00 p.m., you can reserve the server or domain so no one else can access it—or you may want to restrict accounts from accessing the server or domain over the weekend as a security measure when the office is closed. You do this by clicking the Logon Hours button on the Account tab. When the Logon Hours dialog box is displayed, block out the days and times when logon is denied, as in Figure 8-6. (Try Hands-on Project 8-2 to set server accessibility.)

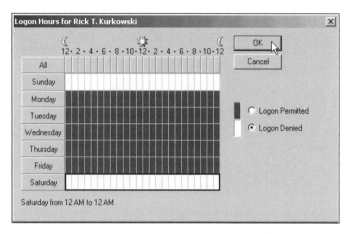

Figure 8-6   Controlling account access by the day of the week and time

The Log On To button on the Account tab enables you to limit where a user can log on to the server or domain. The Log On To option is a good security measure when you want to make sure certain accounts can only be accessed from designated workstations. For example, you might want to guard the Administrator account and your own account with administrator privileges so they are only accessible from the server, from a workstation in your office, and from your computer at home. At the same time, the employee who prepares the payroll in your organization may be required by the auditors to finalize the payroll from one computer only. For example, suppose that the payroll is finalized from the payroll clerk's workstation, which is assigned the computer name PAY. Click the option *The following computers*, enter PAY as the workstation's name, click the Add button, and click OK.

- *Profile tab:* Enables you to associate a particular profile with a user or set of users, such as a common desktop (profiles are discussed later in this chapter). This tab also is used to associate a logon script and a home folder (directory) with an account. When home folders are set up on a server, administrators often standardize the home folder of all users to a particular drive letter, such as H. To enter the home folder drive letter, click the Connect radio button and use the list box to select the drive letter. Enter the path to the home folder in the To box, for example \Users\Kurkowski. Each time the user logs on, an H drive will be shown in My Computer and in Explorer, with a path to the user's home folder on the server. If the home folder is on the user's computer, click the Local path option and enter the computer name and the path on the computer to be used as a home folder, such as \\Mycomputer\Mywork\, using the **Universal Naming Convention (UNC)**. The format for a UNC name is *servername*(or *computername*)*sharename**folder**file*. A **logon script** is a set of commands that automatically runs each time the user logs on to the server or domain. It is usually implemented as a DOS batch file, but it can also be an executable file. A summary of the commands is provided in Table 8-1.

Table 8-1 Windows 2000 Server Logon Script Commands

Script Command	Function
%Homepath%	Establishes the path to the user's home folder
%Homedrive%	Sets a drive letter for the system hard disk drive
%Username%	Specifies the user's logon name
%Userdomain%	Specifies the domain to which the user belongs
%OS%	Specifies the operating system being used
%Processor%	Specifies the type of processor
%Homeshare%	Specifies a home directory on a shared drive

- *Telephones tab:* Enables you to associate specific types of telephone contact numbers for an account holder, which include one or more numbers for home, pager, mobile, fax, and IP phones. You can also enter particular comments, such as "Call the pager number only between 5 p.m. and midnight."

- *Organization tab:* Provides a place to enter the account holder's title, department name, company name, and the name of the person who manages the account, if it is not the administrator. There is also a box that lists other accounts that are managed by this account.

- *Member Of:* Used to add the account to an existing group of users. Accounts that have the same security and access requirements can be assigned as members of a group. Security access then is set up for the group instead of for each account. User groupings can save a significant amount of time when there are tens or hundreds of accounts to manage. For example, if 42 accounts all need full access to a folder, it is easier to create a group, add each account to the group, and give the group full access. The more time-consuming method would be to set up access permissions on individual accounts, repeating the same steps 42 times. To place an account in a group, click the Add button on the Member Of tab and double-click the group among the list of groups displayed in the Select Groups dialog box (see Figure 8-7). You can add the account to one or more groups using this procedure and then click OK when you are finished (security groups are discussed in Chapter 9). The Set Primary Group button on the Member Of tab is used to designate a primary group membership for accounts that are accessed by a Macintosh or POSIX client. Windows 2000 Server requires these systems to log on as members of a **primary group**, which is a global security group (see Chapter 9) that can access any server in a domain. To set a primary group, first add the group, click it in the Member of box, and click Set Primary Group.

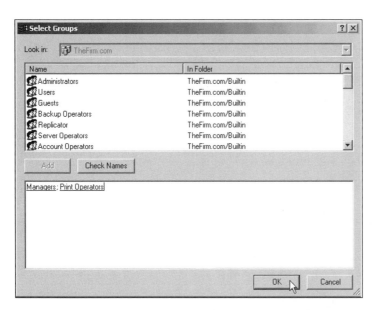

Figure 8-7   Adding an account to the Managers and Print Operators groups

- *Dial-in:* Permits you to control remote access to the domain or to an intranet, for example from dial-in modems. Remote access can be allowed, denied, or controlled through a policy (see Figure 8-8). To enable an account holder to access the server or domain from a home computer or while on the road, click Allow access. Also, set up **callback security** options for dial-in access so a server's modems can call back the accessing workstation after the initial request to log on is received. This enables the server to verify that the call is from a known location. The callback can be set from the workstation's modem or from a prearranged number used by the server. There are also options to verify by caller ID, to configure a static IP address for the remote computer, and to enable static routing. (Dial-in security is presented in detail in Chapter 12.)

- *Environment:* Enables you to configure the startup environment for clients that access Windows 2000 Server using terminal services, which means that the client simulates a terminal instead of acting as an independent workstation with its own CPU. The options include the ability to specify that a startup program be run and that client devices, such as disk drives and printers, be connected.

- *Sessions:* Used to configure session parameters for a client using terminal services, such as a session time limit, a limit on how long a session can be idle, what to do when a connection is broken, and how to reconnect.

- *Remote Control:* Enables you to set up remote control parameters for a client that uses terminal services. The remote control capability enables you to view and manipulate the client session while it is active, in order to troubleshoot problems.

- *Terminal Services Profile:* Used to set up a user profile for a client that uses terminal services.

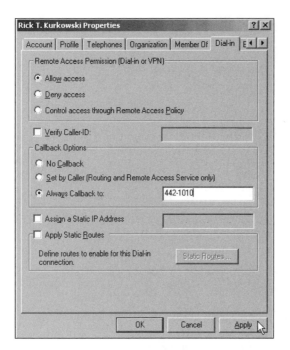

Figure 8-8   Configuring remote access

Creating an OU and Delegating Account Management

When you need to establish a group of accounts that have similar characteristics, for example for members of a particular department such as the payroll office, you have the option to create an OU (organizational unit) and place accounts in that container (but only if the Active Directory is installed). In this example, the OU might be called Payroll. You create the OU by clicking the domain in the left pane of the Active Directory Users and Computers console tree, clicking the *Create a new organizational unit in the current container* button on the button bar, entering the name of the OU (Payroll), and clicking OK. To create accounts in the OU, double-click the Payroll OU to open it in the console tree under the domain name, and click the *Create a new user in the current container* button on the button bar. Users are created as presented in the last section.

You also have the option to delegate management of accounts in the Payroll OU to a user or group. For example, you might delegate authority for creating new accounts in the Payroll Department to the payroll director. The steps that you use to delegate authority are as follows:

1. Right-click the OU, such as Payroll in our example, and click Delegate control.

2. When the Delegation of Control Wizard starts, click Next.

3. Click the Add button, double-click the user, group, or computer to which you want to delegate control. Add all of the users and groups that are appropriate. Click OK and click Next.

4. Make sure *Delegate the following common tasks* is selected, and then click the tasks that you are delegating, such as *Create, delete and manage user accounts* and *Reset passwords on user accounts*. Click Next. If instead you click *Create a custom task to delegate*, then you can customize how you want to delegate tasks by completing two additional dialog boxes for customizing object types and permissions. Click Next after completing each additional dialog box. The common delegated tasks are presented in Table 8-2.

5. Click Finish.

Table 8-2   Delegation of Control Options

Task	Description
Create, delete, and manage user accounts	Ability to fully set up and manage accounts
Reset passwords on user accounts	Ability to reset a member user's account password, should that user forget his or her password
Read all user information	Ability to access any information owned by the selected user accounts
Create, delete, and manage groups	Ability to set up and delete groups and modify group properties
Modify the membership of a group	Ability to add and delete members in a group
Manage Group Policy links	Ability to change the specified group policies or elements of a group policy

Account Maintenance

There are many options for maintaining an account after it has been created. One option is to double-click the account and change properties on the appropriate tabs, which has already been discussed. Also, there are maintenance shortcuts that you can access by right-clicking the account. The following sections describe shortcuts to maintenance activities that you are likely to perform frequently. If you have the Active Directory installed, these maintenance operations are performed using the Active Directory Users and Computers MMC snap-in; if the Active Directory is not installed, use the Local Users and Groups snap-in. If you are using the Active Directory Users and Computers snap-in, you will find accounts by locating the domain and then locating the Users or OU container under that domain. If there are many Active Directory OUs and levels of OUs, then you will need to look in each level until you find the account. Accounts in the Local Users and Groups snap-in are simply found under Users. If there are many OUs and levels of OUs, you can use the Find utility to locate an account. To use this utility:

1. Right-click the domain.

2. Click Find.

3. Enter the username (such as SGonzales), the account display name (such as Sarah Gonzales), or a portion of one of these (such as Gonzales).

4. Click Find Now.

Disabling, Enabling, and Renaming Accounts

When a user takes a leave of absence, for example for family leave, you have the option to disable his or her account. Your organization may also have the practice of disabling accounts when someone leaves and later renaming the account for that person's replacement (which is easier than deleting the account and creating a new one). To disable an account, right-click it and click Disable Account. Click OK when you see the informational dialog box that verifies you have disabled the account. The account icon will have an "x" in a red circle to show that it is disabled (see the Guest account shown earlier in Figure 8-2). No one can access the account until you enable it. To enable an account when the Active Directory is installed, right-click the account, click Enable Account, and click OK. If the Active Directory is not installed, right-click the account, click Properties, click the General tab, click Account is disabled, and click OK.

Renaming an account is nearly as easy as disabling and enabling one. To rename an account:

1. Right-click the account in the Active Directory Users and Computers snap-in and click Rename if the Active Directory is installed; if the Active Directory is not installed, right-click the account in the Local Users and Groups snap-in and click Rename.

2. In the highlighted box, enter the new name as you will see it in the Active Directory Users and Computers snap-in, for example renaming an account called Jason Brown to one called Sarah Gonzales.

3. Press Enter if the Active Directory is installed; if it is not installed, press Enter twice and provide the new name information in the General tab.

4. Complete the Rename User dialog box by entering the new full name, first name, last name, display name, user logon name, domain, and pre-Windows-2000 logon name (which is usually the same as the logon name and is used for naming via the UNC naming format).

5. Click OK. The renamed account will retain the same account properties, including access privileges and group memberships, as in the original account.

(Try Hands-on Project 8-2 to practice renaming and disabling an account.)

Moving an Account

When an employee moves from one department to another, for example from the payroll department to the budget office, you may need to move the account from one container to another—between OUs, for example. To move an account, right-click it and click Move. In the Move dialog box, double-click the domain to which to move the account, and the container, such as an OU or the Users container. Click OK and the account is moved by the Active Directory.

Deleting an Account

You can delete an account by right-clicking that account, clicking Delete, and clicking Yes to confirm the deletion (try Hands-on Project 8-2). When you delete an account, its globally unique identifier (GUID, see Chapter 4) is also deleted and will not be reused even if you create another account using the same name.

Resetting a Password

Sometimes users change their passwords or go several weeks without logging on—and forget their passwords. You do not have the option to look up a password, but you can reset it for the user. To reset a password, right-click the account, click Reset Password (or Set Password if the Active Directory is not installed), enter a new password, and confirm the password. When the Active Directory is installed, there is also a box that enables you to require that the user change his or her password as soon as he or she logs on. Checking the box enables you to force the user to change the password you set, so that you will not know the new password, which is often a requirement of auditors who scrutinize networks that handle financial information.

Account Auditing

Once accounts are set up, you can specify account **auditing** to track activity associated with those accounts. For example, some organizations need to track security changes to accounts, while others want to track failed logon attempts. In a college setting, security changes might be tracked on part-time students who work in sensitive administrative areas such as the registrar's office. Many server administrators track failed logon attempts for the Administrator account, to be sure an intruder is not attempting to access the server. Accounts that access an organization's financial information often are routinely audited to protect their users as well as the information they access. The events that can be audited are as follows:

- Logon and logoff activity
- Account modifications via management tools
- Accesses to files and objects (for files and folders set up to be audited)

Each listed activity is audited in terms of the success or failure of the event. For example, if logon attempts are audited, a record is made each time someone logs on to an account successfully or unsuccessfully.

CAUTION

Use auditing sparingly. Each audited event causes a record to be made in the Security event log. For example, if you audit all logon attempts of 200 domain accounts, the server log will quickly become loaded down just from auditing events and have fewer resources to perform other work.

Account auditing is configured as a group policy. For example, if your organization is required to set up account auditing for all accounts in a domain, first make sure that the default domain policy is set up as an MMC snap-in. In the MMC tree in the left pane, double-click Default

8

Domain Policy, double-click Computer Configuration, double-click Windows Settings, double-click Security Settings, double-click Local Policies, and click Audit Policy. In the right pane, double-click the policy you want to set up, such as Audit Account Logon events.

CUSTOMIZING CLIENT ACCESS WITH PROFILES

Client access to Windows 2000 Server can be customized through user and roaming profiles. A **local user profile** is automatically created at the local computer when you log on to an account for the first time, and the profile can be modified to consist of desktop settings that are customized for one or more clients who log on locally to the server. For example, if there are two server administrators and two backup operators who primarily run backups, you might want to create one profile for the administrators and a different one for the backup operators. That can be useful if each type of account needs to have certain program icons, startup programs, or some other prearranged desktop settings. Also, a user profile can be set up so it is downloaded to the client workstation each time a specific account is logged on. This is a **roaming profile**, which enables a user to start off with the same desktop setup, no matter which computer she or he uses in the office.

 Profiles are used in Microsoft operating systems to provide a consistent working environment for one or more users. A local user profile is a particular desktop setup that always starts in the same way and is stored on the local computer. A roaming profile is a desktop setup that starts in the same way from any computer used to access an account, including remote connections from home or on the road. A **hardware profile** provides a consistent hardware setup for a user at the server console, such as keyboard, display type, and other hardware components. Different hardware profiles are not used much in Windows 2000 Server, but are used more commonly in Windows 2000 Professional to facilitate portable computing.

In some circumstances, you need to set up profiles so that certain users cannot change their profiles. This is done by creating a **mandatory user profile** in which the user does not have permission to update the folder containing his or her profile. A mandatory user profile overrides the user's locally stored profile if it has been changed from the version stored on the server. To make a server profile (either local or roaming) mandatory, rename the user's Ntuser.dat file in the user's profile folder as Ntuser.man. The user's profile folder is found in \Documents and Settings*username*.

 If you do not assign a profile to a user's account, a default user profile is loaded by the server when the user logs on. Located in the \Documents and Settings\Default User folder, the default user profile is also loaded automatically when an account's assigned profile cannot be accessed. However, if a mandatory profile cannot be accessed for some reason, the user will not be able to log on because the default profile is not loaded in this situation.

An easy way to set up a profile is to first set up a generic account on the server or use the Guest account as a model with the desired desktop configuration, including desktop icons, shortcut folders, and programs in the Startup folder to start when the client workstation starts. Then copy the model to the \Documents and Settings\Default User folder, naming it Ntuser.dat. This step makes that profile the default for new users. You can also create a profile to use as a roaming profile for specific users. To create the roaming profile, set up a generic account and customize its desktop. For example, you might create an account called BUDGET for users in the budget office and customize its desktop. After you create that account, set up those users to access that profile by opening the Profile tab in each user's account properties and entering the path to that profile, as in Figure 8-9. You can also use the System icon (User Profiles tab) in the Control Panel to copy profiles from one account folder to another (try Hands-on Project 8-3).

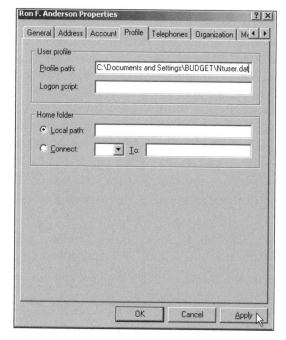

Figure 8-9   Setting a roaming profile in an account's properties

CONFIGURING CLIENT OPERATING SYSTEMS

After setting up accounts, it is also necessary to configure client computers to access those accounts. Many types of client operating systems can connect to Windows 2000 Server, including:

- MS-DOS
- Windows 3.1
- Windows for Workgroups
- Windows NT Workstation and Server
- Windows 2000 Professional
- Macintosh

- Windows 95
- Windows 98

- UNIX
- NetWare clients and servers

In general, when you configure a client operating system to connect, it is necessary to provide a way to identify the workstation to the network, by providing a name for the workstation and the domain it will join. Next, it is necessary to configure the protocol or protocols used to connect, such as TCP/IP, and to bind protocols to the NIC. Hands-on Projects 8-4, 8-5, and 8-6 give you practice in configuring the client operating systems you are most likely to encounter: Windows 3.11, Windows 95 and 98, and Windows NT 4.0. (Windows 2000 Professional is not included because you learned how to configure Windows 2000 operating systems in Chapter 6.)

Installing Active Directory Support for Non-Windows-2000 Clients

Microsoft offers the **Directory Service Client** (**DSClient**) software for Windows 95 and higher clients that connect to Windows 2000 Server. Directory Service Client does not provide the complete Active Directory Client features that are built into the Windows 2000 operating systems, but it does enable non-Windows-2000 clients to profit from two important capabilities: (1) the ability to use Kerberos authentication security, and (2) the ability to view information published in the Windows 2000 Active Directory, such as all network printers. To use DSClient, the client must have Internet Explorer 4.0 or higher and 10 MB of free disk space.

The DSClient program, Dsclient.exe, is located on the Windows 2000 Server CD-ROM in the folder \Clients\Win9x. To install the Directory Service Client software on a Windows 95 or Windows 98 client:

1. Copy DSClient.exe to a shared folder, such as one called DSClient, on a Windows 2000 server so that clients can access it over the network.

2. Log on to the domain from the client, such as Windows 98. Double-click Network Neighborhood on the client's desktop, find the host Windows 2000 server, double-click the server, and then double-click the shared folder containing DSClient.exe.

3. Double-click the DSClient.exe file and wait for the installation software components to be extracted into the client operating system.

4. The Directory Service Client Setup Wizard starts automatically. Click Next.

5. Click Next so that the Wizard can detect the system setup and copy the Directory Service Client files.

6. Click Finish and then click Yes to restart the client computer.

DSClient installs new features at the client, such as the ability to search the Active Directory for printers, even if the client does not know the specific name of a printer. To search for a printer using Windows 98 for example, click Start, point to Find, and click Printers (Printers is a new option added by the Directory Service Client).

Windows 95 also does not include the Distributed File System (Dfs; see Chapter 10) client software, while Windows 98 and Windows NT 4.0 do have the Dfs client software already installed. *When you install DSClient in Windows 95, it installs the Dfs client software along with the Directory Service Client software.* Dfs enables you to set up shared folders so that the client only needs to query the Dfs services for a hierarchy of shared folder locations, without first knowing which server contains the folder.

Setting Up Client Desktops Using Group Policy and Security Policy

In Windows NT 4.0 the desktop and other options viewed by clients can be customized by using the System Policy Editor as well as through user profiles. Windows 2000 Server uses group policies in place of the system policies, and system policies in Windows NT Server 4.0 are not migrated when you convert to Windows 2000 Server. However, it is possible to set up system polices in Windows 2000 Server that are compatible with Windows NT Server 4.0, if you have a domain with a mix of Windows NT and Windows 2000 servers, for instance.

Windows 2000 Server is installed with a default administrative template in group policies. For example, the default domain policy called System.adm can be configured to set up a consistent desktop in Windows 2000 Professional clients. Table 8-3 shows the administrative templates that are included with Windows 2000 Server to control client settings using group policy and using system policies.

8

 When you have an environment that contains non-Windows-2000 clients, you can also use Windows NT Server 4.0 compatible system policies that you set up using the Poledit.exe tool, located in the Windows 2000 Server \Winnt folder. This tool starts the System Policy Editor, which works in a similar manner to the equivalent tool in Windows NT Server 4.0. It is recommended that you implement group policies instead of system policies in Windows 2000, to take full advantage of the Active Directory and lower TCO.

Table 8-3   Administrative Templates Included with Windows 2000

Template	Purpose	Tool Used to Configure
Common.adm	Managing desktop settings that are common to Windows 95, 98, and NT	Poledit.exe
Ientres.adm	Default for managing Internet Explorer in Windows 2000 Professional clients	Group Policy snap-in or edit group policy by using the Active Directory Users and Computers tool
System.adm	Default for managing Windows 2000 Professional clients	Group Policy snap-in or edit group policy by using the Active Directory Users and Computers tool
Windows.adm	Managing Windows 95 and 98 clients	Poledit.exe
Winnt.adm	Managing Windows NT 4.0 clients	Poledit.exe

The Windows 2000 Server group policy settings offer a wide range of ways to configure the Windows 2000 Professional client desktop. Table 8-4 presents the components that you can manage using the default template, System.adm.

Table 8-4   Group Policy Components for Windows 2000 Clients

Component	Description
Windows Components	Controls access to installed software such as NetMeeting, Internet Explorer, MMC, Task Scheduler, and Windows Installer
Start Menu & Taskbar	Controls the ability to configure the Start menu and Taskbar, the ability to access program groups from the Start menu, and the ability to use Start menu options, including Run, Search, Settings, and Documents
Desktop	Controls access to desktop functions, including the icons for My Network Places, Internet Explorer, and the ability to configure the Active Desktop
Control Panel	Controls access to Control Panel functions such as Add/Remove Programs, Display, Printers, and Regional Settings, plus the ability to disable the Control Panel altogether
Network	Controls access to offline files and the ability to configure network access via Network and Dial-up Connections
System	Controls access to Logon/Logoff capabilities, scripts, Task Manager functions, Change Password, and other system functions

To configure Windows 2000 Professional client desktops in the default domain policy, for example:

1. Open the Active Directory Users and Computers tool.

2. Right-click the domain you want to configure, and click Properties.

3. Click the Group Policy tab.

4. Click Default Domain Policy and click Edit.

5. Double-click User Configuration and double-click Administrative Templates. (Keep in mind that System.adm is already installed by default.)

6. Double-click any of the component folders that you want to configure, as described in Table 8-4, such as Start Menu & Taskbar.

7. Double-click each of the entities that you want to configure, such as *remove common program groups from Start Menu*.

USING REMOTE INSTALLATION SERVICES

Remote Installation Services (RIS) enable you to install Windows 2000 Professional on client computers in environments that use the Active Directory. RIS can also be used to create boot disks from which to start a remote Windows 2000 Professional installation. RIS is one of the Windows 2000 Server options that enable you to reduce the cost (lower TCO, see Chapter 1) of managing a Windows 2000 network. When you install Windows 2000 Professional clients from a RIS server, you start by taking these steps:

1. Purchase licenses for the clients you wish to install.

2. Make sure the network that uses the Active Directory already has DHCP and DNS servers (see Chapters 3 and 13).

3. Install RIS on the Windows 2000 server that will become the RIS server.

4. Create a Windows 2000 Professional operating system image that will be copied to client computers. The image can be created from a Windows 2000 Professional CD-ROM or from an existing client running Windows 2000 Professional.

5. Create user accounts for the client computer users who will install Windows 2000 Professional.

Windows 2000 Professional is the only operating system that can be installed from a RIS server. This is different from Windows NT Server 4.0, which enables you to use the Network Client Administrator to remotely install MS-DOS, Windows 3.11, Windows 95, and Windows NT from a server. Unlike Windows 2000 Professional, none of these operating systems enables you to take full advantage of the lower TCO capabilities of Windows 2000 environments.

The client computer hardware for the RIS installation only needs to meet or exceed the minimum hardware requirements for Windows 2000 Professional, and does not have to match the hardware configuration of the RIS server. When you install Windows 2000 Professional on the client, the installation process uses Plug and Play to detect the unique hardware on the client, beginning with the NIC.

RIS uses an unattended answer file (a .sif image file) that you can customize for Windows 2000 Professional installations, for example to specify which file system to use. Also, if you are installing Windows 2000 Professional onto a client that already has a previously purchased copy of Windows 2000 Professional installed, you will need to modify the answer file for that installation so that it includes the product identification number of the retail version (see Chapter 5 for more information about the contents and syntax of an answer file). The product identification number is the key code that is located on the back of the CD-ROM jewel case. The answer file is located in the folder: \\Remoteinstall\Setup*language* [such as English]\Images\Win2000.pro\I386\Templates\Ristndrd.sif. When you modify the Ristndrd.sif answer file to include the product ID, use the following syntax under the [Userdata] section of the file:

```
ProductID = "nnnnn-nnn-nnnnnnn-nnnnn"
```

Plan to install RIS on a Windows 2000 server during your system maintenance time or when no users are logged on to the server, because it is necessary to reboot after the installation. To set up a Windows 2000 server as a RIS server:

1. Click Start, point to Settings, and click Control Panel.

2. Double-click Add/Remove Programs.

3. Click Add/Remove Windows Components.

4. Scroll the Components box until you find Remote Installation Services, and then check the box for that option. Notice the required disk space and total disk space available report at the bottom of the Windows Components Wizard dialog box, and make sure you have enough disk space before you continue.

5. Insert the Windows 2000 Server CD-ROM and click Next. (Provide the path to the \I386 folder on the CD-ROM, if requested.) Click Finish after all components are installed.

6. Click Yes to reboot the computer, first making sure that no one is logged on; or click No but plan to reboot the computer as soon as there is an opportunity to have all users logged off.

If the Active Directory is installed and there are DHCP and DNS servers on the network, you can configure the DHCP server to authorize only specific servers to provide RIS installations. This is a security feature that enables you to prevent unauthorized replication of Windows 2000 Professional and to limit the possibility of viruses. You authorize a RIS server through the DHCP MMC snap-in via the console Action menu, *Manage authorized servers* option.

Configuring RIS

After RIS is installed, you need to configure the services. For example, to configure RIS in a situation in which you use a Windows 2000 Professional CD-ROM for the image files (instead of a live Windows 2000 Professional workstation):

1. Open the Add/Remove Programs icon in the Control Panel, if it is not already open.

2. Notice that the *Set up services* box in the middle of the screen shows that you still need to configure RIS. Click the Configure button under Configure Remote Installation Services. The Remote Installation Services Setup Wizard starts. Click Next.

3. Specify the location for the folders used by RIS, such as D:\Remoteinstall. Make sure that you use a drive other than the one that holds the Windows 2000 Server operating system files (the \Winnt folder) and click Next.

4. Select whether or not to enable the option to have RIS immediately support client computers, and click Next.

5. Specify the path to the Windows 2000 Professional CD-ROM that contains the installation files, and click Next.

6. Enter a name for the folder that is to contain the Windows 2000 Professional installation files, such as Win2000.pro, and click Next.

7. Enter the "friendly" description (for users) of the installation image files, such as Microsoft Windows 2000 Professional. Also, enter help text that the installer will

see, such as, "Automatically installs Windows 2000 Professional without prompt-ing the user for input," which is the default text. Click Next.

8. Verify your installation selections and click Finish (or click Back to reconfigure a selection). The Wizard creates the installation folders, copies installation files, cre-ates the unattended answer file, and completes setting up and starting RIS.

9. Click Done.

You can modify the RIS configuration and set up advanced RIS capabilities by accessing the RIS server in the Active Directory Users and Computers tool. To modify these settings, open Active Directory Users and Computers and double-click the domain that contains the RIS server. Next, double-click Domain Controllers, if the server is a DC, or click Computers if it is a member computer. Right-click the RIS server, click Properties, and click the Remote Install tab. The tab contains three buttons:

- *Verify Server:* Verify that the installation files are fully intact.

- *Show Clients:* View RIS clients that are currently connected to the server.

- *Advanced Settings:* Set up a RIS client computer naming convention, specify the directory service location, and add, remove, or modify images.

On a network in which there is a computer naming convention or in which there are nam-ing conventions that vary by group, you may want to establish RIS computer naming con-ventions by domain or by OU. For example, in one domain the computer names may be set up to match each user's account name, while in another domain the computer names may be set up to enable customized naming. In another example, computer names may vary by OU so that those in the Customer Service OU are set up as the user's first initial followed by the last name and those in the Marketing OU are set up as the user's first name followed by her or his last initial. Hands-on Project 8-7 shows how to configure computer naming by Active Directory location.

Using RIS to Install Windows 2000 Professional on the Client Computer

The Windows 2000 Professional operating system files are installed on the client in one of two ways: by purchasing a client computer that has a Windows 2000 compatible remote-boot-enabled ROM or by creating a remote boot disk. Both support what Microsoft calls the **Preboot eXecution Environment** (**PXE**). PXE works with DHCP when the prospective client first boots and enables the client to request an IP address and a network connection to the RIS server. At the same time, the client is registered in the Active Directory with a computer name and a unique GUID (see Chapter 4). The steps that you use to create a remote boot disk are:

1. Insert a blank formatted floppy disk in the RIS server or in a Windows 2000 server or workstation that you can use to access the RIS server through the network.

2. Click Start, click Run, and enter the UNC path to the Rbfg.exe file, for exam-ple: D:\Remoteinstall\Admin\I386\Rbfg.exe. (If you run the file from another

computer used to access the RIS server, such as one running Windows 2000 Professional, enter the UNC path instead and make sure that the Remote install folder on the RIS server is shared.) Click OK.

3. Specify the drive on which to copy the files, such as drive A. There is an Adapter List button that enables you to check the adapters supported by the PXE process and Plug and Play detection at the client computer.

4. Click Create Disk.

5. Click Yes if you want to create another boot disk, or click No.

6. Click Close to exit the Windows 2000 Remote Boot Disk Generator.

CAUTION

The client should have a NIC that is listed on the Windows 2000 Professional HCL and that is supported by RIS. Also, if you experience boot problems, set up the computer's BIOS to use the NIC as the device from which to boot first.

When you boot the client computer using the remote-boot-enabled ROM or the remote boot disk, PXE launches the Client Installation Wizard. After the Wizard starts, press Enter and then provide the username, password, and domain name. Select the specific installation option from those listed in Table 8-5.

Table 8-5   Client Installation Wizard Options

Option	Description
Automatic Setup	Uses the unattended answer file to perform a complete Windows 2000 Professional installation without interactive input from the user
Custom Setup	Uses the unattended answer file to perform a Windows 2000 Professional installation, but enables the user to specify the computer name and location in the Active Directory
Restart	Enables the user to restart an installation that was previously interrupted (due to a power outage, for example, or that did not complete because of an installation problem)
Maintenance and Troubleshooting	Enables the user to troubleshoot an installation by using tools available through the Client Installation Wizard

Using Group Policies to Create Installation Groups

You can use group policies to create different installation options for different groups or containers, for example for different OUs or different domains. Before you link different installation options with different groups, first make sure that a group policy is in place for each container, and then modify the group policy. To associate a particular set of installation options with a container object:

1. Start the Active Directory Users and Computers tool.

2. Right-click the container you want to associate with particular RIS installation options, for example an OU or domain, and click Properties.

3. Click the Group Policy tab, click the group policy you want to modify under Group Policy Object Links, and click the Edit button.

4. In the left pane, click Windows Settings, which is located under User Configuration in the tree displayed for the group policy.

5. In the right pane, double-click Remote Installation Services.

6. In the right pane, double-click Choice Options.

7. Specify the type of user access for Automatic Setup, Custom Setup, Restart Setup, and Tools (see Figure 8-10).

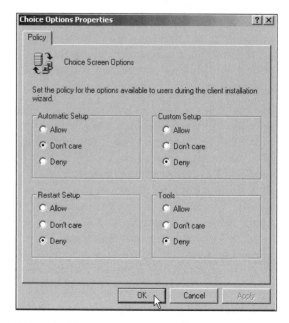

Figure 8-10   Setting RIS installation options through group policy

As Figure 8-10 shows, the policy options are Allow, Don't care, and Deny. Allow means that the designated capability can be used by client accounts that are defined in the container. Don't care is the default and means that the policy that applies to the parent container, such as the domain, applies to the current container, such as an OU in that domain. Deny means that the capability is not available to the group of users in the container.

Using RIS Troubleshooting Tools

Some third-party vendors offer troubleshooting and maintenance tools that can be used by administrators and users via the RIS server. A tool is installed by following the particular vendor's instructions. After tools are installed, you can view them by opening Active Directory Users and Computers, right-clicking the RIS server in the tree, clicking Properties, clicking the Remote Install tab, clicking the Advanced Settings button, and clicking the Tools tab. On the Tools tab you have three options. The Remove button is used to remove a particular tool from the unattended answer file, so that tool is not available to the user. The Properties button enables you to view the tool's properties and to modify the description of the tool that users will see. The Refresh button simply redisplays the RIS tool listing on the Tools tab.

CHAPTER SUMMARY

- ❏ Preparing a Windows 2000 server and domain for user access involves two essential steps: configuring user accounts and configuring individual client computers to access the network. Before you configure accounts, establish guidelines for account names. You may need to work with different groups, departments, or management bodies to develop naming guidelines that correspond to your organization's needs. Also, consult with members of your organization prior to establishing account security policies. Account security policies enable you to protect data and network resources through establishing password restrictions, account lockout security, and Kerberos security.

- ❏ After you have established naming guidelines and set up account policies, create accounts by using the Local Users and Groups snap-in for a standalone server that is not part of a domain, or by using the Active Directory Users and Computers snap-in when the Active Directory is in use. Account properties can be set up to provide information about an account holder that includes telephone numbers, address information, and Web page information. You can also control how the account accesses the domain, such as by limiting access via a specific computer. Other ways to manage access include creating profiles, configuring group policies, and setting up system policies. Client computers must each be configured to access the network so that they can log on to accounts. The configuration steps include installing and configuring protocols for operating systems such as Windows 3.11, Windows 95/98, Windows NT, and others.

- ❏ Remote Installation Services (RIS) is an option that enables you to install Windows 2000 Professional on multiple clients from a RIS server. RIS can greatly reduce the TCO of network management by automating the setup of clients.

In the next chapter, you learn how to manage server folders and groups, and you learn more about security options.

KEY TERMS

account lockout — A security measure that prohibits logging on to a Windows 2000 server account after a specified number of unsuccessful attempts.

auditing — Tracking the success or failure of events by recording selected types of events in an event log of a server or a workstation.

callback security — Used for remote communications verification; the remote server calls back the accessing workstation to verify that the access is from an authorized telephone number.

Directory Service Client (DSClient) — Microsoft software for Windows 95 and higher clients that connect to Windows 2000 Server that enables non-Windows-2000 clients to use Kerberos authentication security and to view information published in the Windows 2000 Active Directory, such as all network printers.

hardware profile — A consistent setup of hardware components associated with one or more user accounts.

local user profile — A desktop setup that is associated with one or more accounts to determine what startup programs are used, additional desktop icons, and other customizations. A user profile is local to the computer in which it is stored.

logon script — A file that contains a series of commands to run each time a user logs on to his or her account, such as a command to map a home drive.

mandatory user profile — A user profile set up by the server administrator that is loaded from the server to the client each time the user logs on; changes that the user makes to the profile are not saved.

Preboot eXecution Environment (PXE) — Services on a Windows 2000 remote-boot-enabled ROM or a remote boot disk that enable a prospective client to obtain an IP address and to connect to a RIS server in order to install Windows 2000 Professional.

primary group — A group designation used when setting up a Windows 2000 server account for workstations running Macintosh or POSIX. Windows 2000 Server requires that these systems be members of a global security group.

Remote Installation Services (RIS) — Services installed on a Windows 2000 Server that enable you to remotely install Windows 2000 Professional on one or more client computers.

roaming profile — Desktop settings that are associated with an account so that the same settings are employed no matter which computer is used to access the account (the profile is downloaded to the client).

service ticket — A Kerberos security key that gives a client access to specific services on a server or in a domain for a designated period of time.

Universal Naming Convention (UNC) — A naming convention that designates network servers, computers, and shared resources. The format for a UNC name is *Servername* [or *Computername*]*Sharename**Folder**File*.

Windows NT LAN Manager (NTLM) — An authentication protocol used in Windows NT Server 3.5, or 3.51, and 4.0 that is retained in Windows 2000 Server for backward compatibility with clients that cannot support Kerberos, such as MS-DOS and Windows 3.1x.

8

REVIEW QUESTIONS

1. You are the server administrator in the IT department of a community college. The financial auditors have just visited the college and have written up a concern that the Administrator account on the Windows 2000 server used for accounting can be accessed from anywhere on campus and even through remote dial-up access. How can you tighten security?

   a. Limit on-campus access to the Administrator account to the computer in your office.

   b. Rename the Administrator account to match your name.

   c. Set up the Administrator account Dial-in properties to use callback security.

   d. all of the above

   e. only b and c

   f. only a and c

2. The financial auditors mentioned in Question 1 also want to disable access to the server over the weekend to all users but you and the Accounting Department. How can this be done?

   a. Limit the logon hours in the account properties for all accounts that should not have access over the weekend.

   b. Put the server in hibernate mode during the weekends, except by special arrangements for Accounting Department members who provide you with advance notice.

   c. Use the account auditing feature in Windows 2000 to limit who can access accounting folders over the weekend.

   d. There is no way to limit access to meet this request.

3. Which of the following are examples of password policies that can be set up in group policies?

   a. Require that a password must be entered in the reverse order in which it is spelled.

   b. Require a minimum password length.

   c. Require that a password contain only proper names.

   d. all of the above

   e. only a and b

   f. only b and c

4. Mary Balsam is your organization's chief information officer and has specialized security access to resources in the domain. She is retiring on Friday, and the new CIO starts the next Friday. What is the easiest way to handle Mary's departure and set up an account for the new CIO?

   a. Delete Mary's account at the end of Friday and set up a new account for the incoming CIO on the following Friday.

   b. Create a copy of Mary's account for the new CIO and then delete Mary's account.

   c. Disable Mary's account at the end of Friday, and when the new CIO arrives, enable Mary's account and rename it for the new CIO.

   d. Create a new account for the incoming CIO and move it to a new domain.

5. Which of the following are account policies that you can set up for a domain?

   a. Kerberos

   b. account lockout

   c. password

   d. all of the above

   e. only a and þ

   f. only b and c

6. The board of directors for your organization wants the five department heads in the organization to set up and manage accounts for employees in each of their departments. How can you best help them accomplish this via the Active Directory?

   a. Give each department head administrator privileges.

   b. Create an OU for each department and delegate account management in each OU to the appropriate department head.

   c. Create a domain for each department and make the department head administrator for her or his domain.

   d. Show each department head how to take control of administrator privileges, because Windows 2000 Server requires this step in order to delegate these privileges.

7. Which of the following might be used in a logon script?

   a. homepath

   b. temppath

   c. homedrive

   d. all of the above

   e. only a and b

   f. only a and c

8. From where do you set an account to use a logon script?

   a. account properties

   b. account policies

   c. Kerberos policies

   d. domain setup properties

9. Which of the following clients would require an account in which a primary group is specified?

   a. Windows 3.1

   b. Windows 3.11

    c. Macintosh

    d. Windows 2000 Professional

10. Your organization requires that all Windows 2000 Professional users must use the same desktop setup and that there be an icon on the desktop that opens an inventory program. How can you set this up?

    a. Associate a mandatory profile with each of these users' accounts.

    b. Associate a local user profile with each of these users' accounts.

    c. Make sure the properties in each account are set to log on from a specific computer in each employee's office.

    d. There is no way to enforce use of the same desktop because users can configure and save any number of possibilities in Windows 2000 Professional.

11. As server administrator, how can you most easily make sure you do not know your users' passwords?

    a. Make each user an account administrator so that users must create their own accounts.

    b. When you set up an account, have the user come to your office at the same time and type in his or her password.

    c. Delegate password authority to each user.

    d. Check the box User must change password at next logon, when you create the account.

12. Which administrative template enables you to manage desktop settings for Windows 2000 Professional clients, and what tool do you use to set it up?

    a. Winnt.adm using the Group Policy MMC snap-in

    b. Common.adm using the Poledit.exe System Policy Editor

    c. Windows.adm using the Poledit.exe System Policy Editor

    d. System.adm using the Group Policy MMC snap-in

13. Ntuser.man is a:

    a. logon script

    b. mandatory profile

    c. home folder

    d. Administrator account profile

14. A Windows 2000 Server password can be up to _____ characters in length.

    a. 7

    b. 10

    c. 20

    d. 64

15. Which of the following enables you to copy an existing profile to an account's setup folder in Windows 2000 Server?

    a. Control Panel System icon

    b. Control Panel Network icon

    c. Active Directory Users and Computers MMC snap-in

    d. Local Computers and Users MMC snap-in

16. You have set up a Windows 95 client to access a Windows 2000 Server domain called Buffalo. When you log on from that client using the account name and password for the account that you created in the Windows 2000 Active Directory, you still do not see the computer as part of the domain. What might be the problem?

    a. You did not specify the domain name in the Windows 95 network setup.

    b. You did not enter a computer name in the Windows 95 network setup.

    c. You did not set up NetBEUI as a protocol in Windows 95, and this protocol must be used along with TCP/IP for Windows 95 connectivity to Windows 2000 Server.

    d. All of the above might be problems.

    e. Only a and b might be problems.

    f. Only a and c might be problems.

17. Which of the following is(are) true about setting up accounts in Windows 2000 Server?

    a. Accounts must be set up only in the Users container under the domain when the Active Directory is implemented.

    b. Accounts must have a password that is at least five characters long.

    c. Accounts can be set up so that the user cannot change the password.

    d. all of the above

    e. only a and b

    f. only b and c

18. When Kerberos is enabled in the Active Directory on a network that has 225 users, four domain controllers, and a member server, which of the following are key distribution centers?

    a. each client

    b. each domain controller

    c. only the domain controller that is set up first on the network

    d. only the member server

19. Which of the following models is(are) used for naming conventions?

    a. user's first two initials and last name

    b. user's position name in an organization

    c. user's function in an organization

    d. all of the above

    e. only a and c

    f. only b and c

20. Which of the following characters can be in a Windows 2000 Server account password?

    a. [

    b. >

    c. =

    d. none of the above

    e. only a and b

    f. only b and c

21. Which of the following can you perform on the *Member Of* tab in the properties of an account?

    a. adding the account to a group

    b. specifying the domain in which the account belongs, when the Active Directory is implemented

    c. providing telephone numbers associated with the account holder

    d. all of the above

    e. only a and b

    f. only a and c

22. Your network is set up to enable users to install Windows 2000 Professional from a RIS server. However, your boss has heard that another department is considering the implementation of a RIS server, but that it is lax on obtaining licenses. He wants to know if you can centralize installations only from your server in the IT department, as a way to ensure proper licensing. What is your reply?

    a. There is no way to prevent network users from installing Windows 2000 Professional from another department's RIS server.

    b. You can configure the network's DNS server so that it does not contain the IP addresses of other departments' servers.

    c. You can configure the network's Windows 2000 DHCP server so it only authorizes RIS installations from your RIS server.

    d. As network administrator, you can alter the Registries of all other RIS servers so that user connections time out before completing a full Windows 2000 Professional installation.

23. The president of your company has just changed his password and forgotten it. How can you help as the server administrator?

    a. Look up his password and give it to him.

    b. Reset his password, require that he change it as soon as he logs on, and give him the password that you reset.

   c. Rename the president's account and give him the new password you set up in the process.

   d. Delete and recreate the president's account and give him the new password you set up in the process.

24. You want to enable users in the Shipping OU to use RIS to install Windows 2000 Professional using only the Automatic Setup option. Also, you want users in the Accounting OU to use only the Custom Setup. What feature of Windows 2000 Server enables you to customize these RIS installation options?

   a. Group Policy

   b. Security Manager

   c. RIS Manager

   d. Active Directory Domains and Trusts

25. During your lunch hour, you have been deleting, copying, and reworking several profiles stored in Windows 2000 Server. After lunch, one of the users calls to report that she cannot log on to the domain, but she had no problems logging on just before going to lunch. What problem would you suspect first?

   a. You made an illegal change in a local user profile.

   b. You accidentally deleted her mandatory profile.

   c. You accidentally deleted her roaming profile.

   d. You forgot to unlock her account after working on its profile.

8

HANDS-ON PROJECTS

Project 8-1

This project enables you to practice setting account password and lockout policies in Windows 2000 Server when the Active Directory is already installed. You have the option to view the policies as they are currently set and to change the policies (with permission from your instructor).

To view and configure the policies:

1. Click the **Start** button, click **Run**, enter **mmc**, and click **OK**. Maximize the console windows, if necessary. Click the **Console** menu and click **Add/Remove Snap-in**.

2. In the Add/Remove Snap-in dialog box, click **Add**, scroll to **Group Policy** and double-click it.

3. When the Select Group Policy Object Wizard starts, click the **Browse** button, double-click **Default Domain Policy**, and click **Finish**. Click **Close** and click **OK**. Double-click **Default Domain Policy** in the left pane, double-click **Computer Configuration**, double-click **Windows Settings**, and click **Security Settings**. What options are displayed in the right window pane? Record your observations in a lab journal or in a word-processed document.

4. In the right pane, double-click **Account Policies**. What options are now displayed in the right window pane? Record your observations.

5. Double-click **Password Policy**. Notice and record the options in the right pane.

6. If you have permission from your instructor to change parameters, double-click **Enforce password history**. Make sure **Define this policy setting** is checked, enter **10** in the Passwords remembered box, and click **OK**. Next, double-click **Minimum password length** and make sure **Define this policy setting** is checked. Enter **7** in the characters box on the Security Policy Setting dialog box, and click **OK**. Notice that your changes are now reflected in the right pane.

7. Click **Account Lockout Policy** in the tree displayed in the left pane. Record the options available in the right pane.

8. If you have permission from your instructor to change parameters, double-click **Account lockout threshold**. Make sure **Define this policy setting** is checked, enter **5** in the invalid logon attempts box, and click **OK**. What parameters are dependent on this one? Click **OK** to automatically set those parameters. (Note that this box may not be displayed, if the other lockout parameters are already set.) Record the changes that are now reflected in the right pane.

9. Close the MMC and click **No**, if asked whether to save your console settings.

Project 8-2

In this project, you practice setting up an account, configuring it, renaming it, disabling it, and then deleting it. The Active Directory must already be installed to perform this project.

To set up the account:

1. Click the **Start** button, click **Run,** enter **mmc**, and click **OK**. Maximize the console windows, if necessary. Click the **Console** menu and click **Add/Remove Snap-in**. Click **Add** and double-click **Active Directory Users and Computers**. Click **Close** and click **OK**. What is another way to access the Active Directory Users and Computers tool, beginning from the Start button?

2. In the left pane, double-click **Active Directory Users and Computers** and click the domain name that is displayed under it. Record in your lab journal or in a word-processed document the options that are now shown in the right pane.

3. Double-click **Users** in the right pane. Are there any accounts already created? What objects are shown along with the accounts?

4. Click the **Action** menu or right-click **Users** in the left pane, click **New** and click **User**.

5. Enter your first name in the First name box, enter your middle initial (no period), and enter your last name, with **test** appended to it, in the Last name box, for example: **Palmertest**. Enter your initials, with **test** appended to them, in the User logon name box, for example: **MPTest**. What options are automatically completed for you? Record these in your lab journal or in a word-processed document. Click **Next**.

6. Enter a password, such as **Palmertest**, and enter the password confirmation. Click the box to select **User must change password at next logon**. Click **Next**.

7. Verify the information you have entered and click **Finish**.

To configure the account:

1. In the right pane, double-click the account you just created.

2. Notice the tabs that are displayed for the account properties and record them in your lab journal or in a word-processed document. If you are using a smaller monitor, and depending on its resolution settings, you may need to use the back and forward arrows to access all of the tabs.

3. Click the **General** tab, if it is not already displayed, and enter a description of the account, such as **Test account**.

4. Click the **Account** tab. What information is already completed on this tab?

5. Click the **Logon Hours** button. In the Logon Hours dialog box, point to the first shaded box on the left under 12 for the bottom row, which is Saturday. Drag the pointer to the rightmost box for Saturday (which is also under 12). Click **Logon Denied** and click **OK**.

6. Click the tabs you have not yet viewed to find out what information can be configured through each one. Record your observations about each tab.

7. Click **Apply** and click **OK**.

To rename the account:

1. In the right pane, right-click the account you just created.

2. Click **Rename** and enter your first two initials, a space, and **Rename**, for example: **MJ Rename**.

3. Press **Enter**.

4. Enter your first two initials in the First name box and enter **Rename** in the Last name box. Enter your first two initials and **Rename** in the Display Name box, for example: **MJ Rename**.

5. Click **OK**. Notice the new name as it is displayed in the right pane.

To disable the account:

1. In the right pane, right-click the account you created and renamed.

2. Click **Disable Account** and click **OK**.

3. Notice the appearance of the account in the right pane. How has the appearance changed?

To delete the account:

1. In the right pane, right-click the account you created, renamed, and disabled (make sure you select the correct account).

2. Click **Delete** and click **Yes**.

3. What has happened to the account in the right pane?

4. Close the MMC and click **No**, if asked to save your console settings.

8

Project 8-3

In this hands-on activity you configure a default user profile for accounts created in Windows 2000 Server. (Your instructor may prefer that you use a different account than Guest as the account in which to configure the default user profile. Also, the Guest account or any other account that you use will need access to log on locally.)

To configure the default profile:

1. Log on to the Guest account.

2. Click **Start**, point to **Settings**, and click **Control Panel**.

3. Double-click the **Display** icon and click the **Background** tab. Click the **Pattern** button and select a pattern such as **Boxes** or **Diamonds**. Click **OK**. What are some other desktop settings that you might configure to set up the default user profile? Record your suggestions in a lab journal or a word-processed document.

4. Click **Apply** and click **OK**.

5. Click the **Start** button, click **Shutdown**, and scroll the Shut Down Windows dialog box to select **Log off Guest**. Click **OK**.

6. Press **Ctrl+Alt+Del** and log on to the Administrator account or another account with Administrator privileges.

7. Click **Start**, point to **Settings**, click **Control Panel**, and double-click the **System** icon.

8. Click the **User Profiles** tab, click the **Guest** account (or another account as specified by your instructor), and click the **Copy To** button.

9. Click the **Browse** button, locate and then click the **Default User** or **All Users** sub-folder (depending on your setup) in the Documents and Settings folder, for example in **C:\Documents and Settings\Default User** or **C:\Documents and Settings\All User**. Click **OK** in the Browse for Folder dialog box.

10. Click **OK** in the Copy To dialog box and click **Yes** to confirm the copy (replace the current settings). Close the System Properties dialog box.

11. What happens to the display when you create a new account and log on to it? Record your findings. How can you make this a roaming profile?

Project 8-4

In this hands-on activity you configure Windows 3.11 to connect as a client to Windows 2000 Server.

To configure Windows 3.11:

1. After Windows 3.11 boots, open the **Main** program group in Program Manager.

2. Double-click the **Windows Setup** icon.

3. Click the **Option** menu and click **Change Network Settings**.

4. Click the **Networks** button in the Network Setup dialog box.

5. Click **Install Microsoft Windows Network:** and click **OK** (see Figure 8-11).

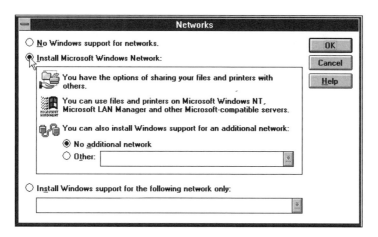

Figure 8-11   Configuring Windows 3.11

6. Click the **Drivers** button in the Network Setup dialog box, and click the **Add Protocol** button. Notice the protocol options and record them in your lab journal or in a word-processed document.

7. If you have the TCP/IP protocol on a disk from Microsoft or from the NIC vendor, click **Unlisted or Updated Protocol**, click **OK**, insert the disk in drive A, and click **OK**. If you do not have the TCP/IP protocol available, click **Microsoft NetBEUI** and click **OK**.

8. Click **Close** in the Network Drivers dialog box.

9. Click **OK** in the Network Setup dialog box.

10. Click **OK** to modify the System.ini file.

11. Click **Restart Windows** to reboot with the new network settings.

You can connect to a shared drive on Windows 2000 Server by opening File Manager from the Main program group and clicking the Connect Network Drive button. Another way to connect through File Manager is to click the Disk menu and click Connect Network Drive. The Connect Network Drive dialog box in Windows 3.11 contains an Always Browse option to enable you to browse domains, workgroups, and computers connected to the network. If this option is checked (which is the most likely condition), then Windows 3.11 may contend with Windows 2000 Server and Windows NT Server (and Windows NT Workstation and Windows 2000 Professional) computers as the Master Browser. A serious indication of this problem is seen when computers running Windows 95, Windows 98, Windows NT, and Windows 2000 experience problems in using Network Neighborhood or My Network Places, such as not seeing some or even all computers connected to the network. The solution is to modify the System.ini file in Windows 3.11 to have the line: MaintainServerList=no. As a Windows 2000 Server administrator, you can identify the contending Windows 3.11 system by checking the server System log for Master Browser contention (you will learn more about using the system log in Chapter 14).

Project 8-5

This project gives you an opportunity to practice setting up Windows 95 or Windows 98 as a client for Windows 2000 Server. Before you start, make sure that the computer you are setting up has a NIC already installed. Also, obtain a workgroup and domain name from your instructor and ask your instructor if the IP address is obtained automatically. If it is not, ask for an IP address and subnet mask (see Chapter 3).

To set up Windows 95 or 98 as a client:

1. Click **Start**, point to **Settings**, and click **Control Panel**.
2. Double-click the **Network** icon.
3. Click the **Identification** tab.
4. Enter a computer name, such as **Antelope** or your last and first name with 95 or 98 appended in the Computer name box, for example: **CandaleraJohn98**. Enter the workgroup name that you obtained from your instructor and enter a description, such as **John Candalera's computer** (see Figure 8-12).
5. Click the **Configuration** tab and click the **Add** button (see Figure 8-13).

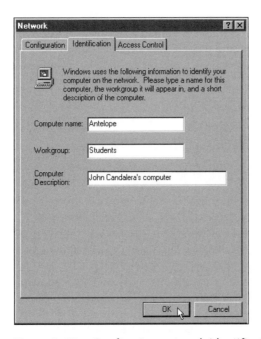

Figure 8-12   Configuring network identification in Windows 95 or 98

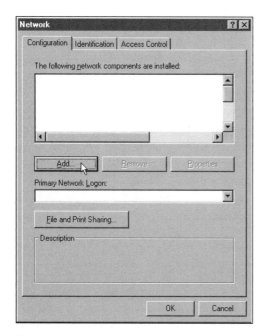

Figure 8-13   Configuring network connectivity in Windows 95 or 98

6. Double-click **Client** in the Select Network Component Type dialog box. What manufacturers are listed in the dialog box? Record your observations in your lab journal or in a word-processed document.

7. Click **Microsoft** in the Manufacturers: Select Network Clients box, click **Client for Microsoft Networks** in the Network Clients box, and click **OK**.

8. Back on the Configuration tab, click **Client for Microsoft Networks** and click the **Properties** button.

9. Click **Log on to Windows NT domain** and enter the domain name provided by your instructor in the Windows NT domain box. Also, click **Logon and restore network connections**. Click **OK**.

10. Again back on the Configuration tab, click the **Add** button on the Identification tab and double-click **Protocol**.

11. Click **Microsoft** in the Manufacturers box. Notice which protocols are available and record your observations. Click **TCP/IP** in the Network Protocols box and click **OK**.

12. On the Configuration tab, scroll to find **TCP/IP** → *network card name*, click that selection, and click **Properties**. Record the tabs that you see displayed. Click the IP Address tab, if it is not automatically displayed.

13. If your network uses DHCP (see Chapter 3), click **Obtain an IP address automatically**. If, instead, your instructor gave you an IP address and subnet mask to use, click **Specify an IP address** and enter the IP address and subnet mask (remember to advance from field to field by pressing the period key).

14. Click the **Bindings** tab and make sure that **Client for Microsoft Networks** is checked. If it is not, click that selection. Notice if there are other binding selections, and record your observation in your lab journal or in a word-processed document.

15. Click **OK** in the TCP/IP Properties dialog box.

16. Back on the Configuration tab, locate the computer's NIC in the scroll box, such as **3COM Fast EtherLink XL NIC**, and double-click it.

17. Click the Driver Type tab, if it is not already displayed. Make sure that the driver is **Enhanced mode (32 bit and 16 bit) NDIS driver**, and click that option if it is not already selected. Notice the other drivers that are available and record them in your lab journal or in a word-processed document.

18. Click **OK** in the Network dialog box and click **Yes** to restart the computer (make sure any open documents are saved first).

Project 8-6

This hands-on project gives you practice configuring Windows NT Workstation 4.0 as a Windows 2000 Server client. Before you start, make sure that the computer has an installed NIC and that you have an IP address and subnet mask, if these are not set through DHCP (consult your instructor). Also, you will need an account with Administrator privileges.

To configure Windows NT Workstation 4.0 as a client:

1. Log on to Windows NT 4.0 using your account and password.

2. Click **Start**, point to **Settings**, click **Control Panel**, and double-click the **Network** icon.

3. Click the **Identification** tab, if it is not already displayed (see Figure 8-14).

4. Click the **Change** button.

5. Enter the Computer Name, which is your last and first name concatenated along with NT, for example: **CandaleraJohnNT**, and click **OK** (Windows NT will check to make sure no other computer has the same name).

6. Click the **Change** button again. Click the **Domain** radio button.

7. Click **Create a Computer Account in the Domain** and enter the same account name and password that you used to log on to Windows NT Workstation. Note that this account must have been created earlier on the Windows 2000 Server domain controller. Click **OK** when you see the welcome dialog box.

8. Click the **Protocols** tab and click the **Add** button. Notice the protocols that you can install, and note them in your lab journal or in a word-processed document.

9. Click **TCP/IP protocol** and click **OK**.

10. Click **Yes** if your network uses DHCP, or click **No** if your instructor gave you an IP and subnet mask to use because there is no DHCP server.

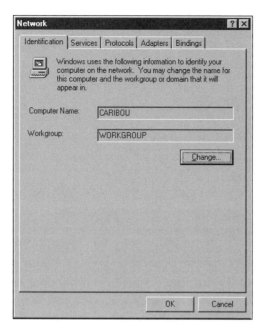

Figure 8-14   Configuring Windows NT 4.0

11. If asked for it, insert the Windows NT Workstation 4.0 CD-ROM and specify the path to the CD-ROM and \I386 folder, such as **D:\I386**, or obtain the installation files from the \I386 folder on your hard drive. Click **Continue**. If Remote Access Service (RAS) is installed, Windows NT will ask if you want to install TCP/IP for it; click **No** for this project exercise.

12. Click **Close** in the Network dialog box to bind the protocol to the NIC.

13. If you specified in Step 10 that you are not using DHCP, then the Microsoft TCP/IP dialog box appears. Make sure that **Specify an IP address** is selected, and enter the IP address and subnet mask obtained from your instructor (advance from field to field by pressing the period key).

14. Click **OK**.

15. Click **Yes** to restart the computer.

16. Click **OK** and click **Close**.

 Windows NT Server 4.0 is configured using the same steps as for Windows NT Workstation 4.0.

 ## Project 8-7

In this hands-on project, you practice configuring RIS computer naming conventions by domain. RIS should be installed and configured prior to trying this project. Log on as

Administrator or using Administrator privileges. Also, find out from your instructor the location and name of the RIS server in the Active Directory.

To configure computer naming:

1. Click **Start**, point to **Programs**, point to **Administrative Tools**, and click **Active Directory Users and Computers**.

2. Double-click the domain that contains the RIS server, and find the server's name in the Active Directory tree, for example under Domain Controllers or Computers.

3. Right-click the RIS server and click **Properties**. Click the **Remote Install** tab. Notice the options available on this tab and record your observations.

4. Click the **Advanced Settings** button. Record the names of the tabs that you see and note their functions.

5. Click the **New Clients** tab, if it is not already displayed, and then click the **Customize** button.

6. In the Format box, enter **%1First%Last**. This sets up the naming convention to be the user's first initial combined with the last name. Notice the other variables that are described in the Computer Account Generation box and record them along with examples of their use in your lab journal or in a word-processed document.

7. Click **OK**.

8. Click **The following directory service location** and then click **Browse**.

9. Double-click the domain for which you want to establish the computer naming convention and double-click **Computers** under the domain. Click **OK**.

10. Click **OK**.

11. Click **OK** and then close the Active Directory Users and Computers tool.

CASE PROJECT

Aspen Consulting Project: Configuring Clients

This week you are working with Stanley & Bernstein Associates, which is an architectural firm that designs high-rise apartments and lofts and specializes in building these structures in city locations that are experiencing renovation. The firm also designs professional buildings in suburban areas, such as office buildings for medical and dental professionals. Stanley & Bernstein employs 72 people, who are members of four company units: the architects unit, the graphics design unit, the business unit, and the computer and technology support unit. Each unit is managed by a supervisor, and the supervisors compose a management group along with the two managing partners, Martin Stanley and Sharon Bernstein. You have already installed two Windows 2000 servers on the firm's network, configured both for TCP/IP, installed the Active Directory, and created a domain called Buildit.

1. Before creating accounts for users, your first recommendation is to meet with the management group and to plan an account naming convention and account policies.

What factors will you discuss with the group to help them make decisions? Include the following in your discussion:

- Account naming guidelines
- Account password policies
- Account lockout policies
- Other account security measures

2. The management group wants to make sure that you train the computer and technology support unit on how to configure the Active Directory. For now, they ask you to develop a set of instructions showing how to set up password and lockout policies.

3. The computer and technology support unit is impressed by the instructions you developed in Assignment 2, and now they ask you to prepare general instructions showing how to set up an account.

4. Before the firm starts setting up accounts, the manager's group has decided to decentralize this function and have each unit's supervisor be responsible for account management. The computer and technology group has already provided the supervisors with the account setup instructions, but they want to know what other steps should be taken to delegate account setup to the supervisors.

5. The computer and technology group has decided to create roaming profiles for all users. How can they do this, and how does this plan affect the information you provided in Assignments 3 and 4?

6. The managers group will be the first to access the new servers, and each person in this group will have a workstation that runs Windows 2000 Professional; the plan is to eventually upgrade all users to have Windows 2000 Professional. Explain how to use RIS to install Windows 2000 Professional over the network instead of purchasing separate CD-ROMs for each installation. Also, the two managing partners have very sensitive accounts that they want to access only from the computers in their offices. Explain how to accommodate this need.

OPTIONAL CASE ASSIGNMENTS FOR TEAMS

Team Case One

Mark Arnez realizes that there are many advantages to using the Active Directory, but that it may not be appropriate for all types of organizations. He asks you to form a group and to develop a list of pros and cons for installing the Active Directory, considering the options available for setting up accounts, and for managing accounts, account policies, and security.

Team Case Two

Much has been in the news lately about productivity and the cost of doing business. Your firm is looking into the ways in which the use of profiles and group policies can lower the TCO of an organization. Form a group and develop two or three scenarios that illustrate how using profiles and group policies can reduce costs and increase users' productivity.

9

MANAGING GROUPS, FOLDERS, FILES, AND OBJECT SECURITY

After reading this chapter and completing the exercises you will be able to:

♦ Set up groups, including local, domain local, global, and universal groups, and convert Windows NT groups to Windows 2000 groups

♦ Manage objects, such as folders, through user rights, attributes, permissions, share permissions, auditing, and Web permissions

♦ Troubleshoot a security conflict

♦ Determine how creating, moving, and copying folders and files affect security

---

Windows 2000 Server contains many new features that enable it to excel in delivering file services—the services that your organization's clients use to access shared folders and files, such as documents, spreadsheets, databases, and software. Microsoft has significantly enhanced Windows 2000 Server to provide you with all kinds of ways to share resources while at the same time thoroughly securing them to match your organization's individual requirements. One of the best techniques for managing and securing shared resources, such as folders and files, is to use the different kinds of groups available in Windows 2000 Server. Complementing the use of groups are security measures that include an expanded range of rights and permissions. Windows 2000 Server also has a new option that enables you to use the **Encrypting File System (EFS)** to secure NTFS folders and files. EFS is a file encryption technique that guards information so that no one but the person who encrypts it can read it.

In this chapter you learn about the types of security groups offered through Windows 2000 Server and how to set up groups. You also learn how to use groups to manage object security, particularly folder and file security. In the process you learn about security descriptors that include user rights, attributes, permissions, auditing, and ownership. All of these tools enable you to offer folder and file resources to clients, while optimizing techniques to manage and secure those resources.

MANAGING SERVER RESOURCES AND SECURITY THROUGH GROUPS

There are three ways administrators can manage domain resources and user accounts:

- By individual user
- By resource
- By group

Managing by individual user is the most labor-intensive method. This requires customizing security access for each user account. In an organization of 20 users, creating and managing individual accounts is not unmanageable, but can be time-consuming. On a network of 200 users, managing resources by individual account quickly becomes a nightmare. Another way to manage network access is by resource. Assume that resources on a network are two file servers and one print server. One file server is for business applications and one is for scientific research applications. The business unit in the organization would have access to the business applications server and the print server. Scientists would have access to the science-related server and the print server. Some managerial people would have access to all resources. The problem with this security model is that managing access is still labor-intensive because it is customized by user and by resource.

The group management concept saves time by eliminating repetitive steps in managing user and resource access. Windows 2000 Server expands on the concept of groups from the one used in Windows NT Server. In Windows NT Server there are two types of groups: local groups that are used to manage resources on a single server or on servers in one domain, and global groups that are used to manage resources across multiple domains. With the introduction of the Active Directory, Windows 2000 Server expands the use of groups through the concept of **scope of influence** (or **scope**), which is the reach of a group for gaining access to resources in the Active Directory. When the Active Directory is not implemented, the scope of resources is limited to the standalone server, and only local groups are created. In contrast, the implementation of the Active Directory increases the scope from a local server or domain to all domains in a forest. (See Chapter 4 for a discussion of the different elements of the Active Directory.) The types of groups and their associated scopes are as follows:

- *Local:* Used on standalone servers that are not part of a domain. The scope of this type of group does not go beyond the local server on which it is defined.

- *Domain local:* Used when there is a single domain or used to manage resources in a particular domain so that global and universal groups can access those resources

- *Global:* Used to manage group accounts from the same domain so that those accounts can access resources in the same and in other domains

- *Universal:* Used to provide access to resources in any domain within a forest

All of these groups can be used for security or distribution groups (see Chapter 4). Security groups are used to enable access to resources on a standalone server or in the Active Directory. Distribution groups are used for e-mail or telephone lists, to provide quick, mass distribution of information. In this chapter, the focus is on security groups.

Implementing Local Groups

A **local security group** is used to manage resources on a standalone computer that is not part of a domain. For example, you might use a local group in a small office situation in which there are only a few users, for example 5, 15, or 30. Consider an office of mineral resource consultants in which there are 18 user accounts on the server. Four of these accounts are used by the founding partners of the consulting firm, who manage employee hiring, payroll, schedules, and general accounting. Seven accounts are for consultants who specialize in coal-bed methane extraction, and the seven remaining accounts belong to consultants who work with oil extraction. In this situation, the company may decide not to install the Active Directory, and divide these accounts into three local groups. One group would be called Managers and consist of the four founding partners. Another group would be called CBM for the coal-bed methane consultants, and the third group would be called Oil and used for the oil consultants. Each group would be given different security access based on the resources at the server, which would include access to folders and to printers.

Implementing Domain Local Groups

A **domain local security group** is used when the Active Directory is deployed. This type of group is typically used to manage resources in a domain and to give global groups from the same and other domains access to those resources. As shown in Table 9-1, a domain local group can contain members such as global groups, and it can be a member of access control lists (ACLs; see Chapter 4) and other domain local groups.

Table 9-1   Membership Capabilities of a Domain Local Group

Active Directory Objects That Can Be Members of a Domain Local Group	Active Directory Objects That a Domain Local Group Can Join as a Member
User accounts in the same domain	Access control lists for objects in the same domain, such as permissions to access a folder, shared folder, or printer
Domain local groups in the same domain	Domain local groups in the same domain
Global groups in any domain in a tree or forest (as long as there are transitive or two-way trust relationships maintained)	
Universal groups in any domain in a tree or forest (as long as there are transitive or two-way trust relationships maintained)	

The scope of a domain local group is the domain in which the group exists, but you can convert a domain local group to a universal group as long as the domain local group does not contain any other domain local groups. Also, to convert any group, the domain must be in native mode and not mixed mode. **Native mode** means there are only Windows 2000 Server domain controllers. **Mixed mode** consists of Windows NT 4.0 domain controllers (PDC and BDCs) and Windows 2000 Server domain controllers (DCs) and is typically used when an organization is in the process of converting from a Windows NT 4.0 Server environment to Windows 2000 Server.

> Mixed mode is the default for all domains unless you change it to native mode to reflect that there are no Windows NT 4.0 servers in the domain. Once you change from mixed to native mode you cannot change back. Try Hands-on Project 9-1 to practice changing from mixed to native mode.

Although a domain local group can contain any combination of accounts, plus local, global, and universal groups, *the typical purpose of a domain local group is to provide access to resources*, which means that you grant access to servers, folders, shared folders, and printers to a domain local group. Under most circumstances you should plan to put domain local groups in access control lists only, and the members of domain local groups should be mainly global groups. Generally, a domain local group does not contain accounts, because account management is more efficient when you handle it through global groups. Examples of using domain local groups with global groups are presented in the next section.

Implementing Global Groups

A **global security group** is intended to contain user accounts from a single domain and can also be set up as a member of a local group in the same or another domain (as long as the domain in which the global group is set up is trusted by the domain of the local group of which it becomes a member). This capability gives global groups a broader scope than domain local groups, because their members can access resources in other domains. Table 9-2 shows which Active Directory objects can be members of global groups and which objects global groups can join.

Table 9-2   Membership Capabilities of a Global Group

Active Directory Objects That Can Be Members of a Global Group	Active Directory Objects That a Global Group Can Join as a Member
User accounts from the domain in which the global group was created	Access control lists for objects in any domain in a forest (as long as a transitive trust is maintained between domains)
Other global groups that have been created in the same domain	Domain local groups in any domain in a forest
Levels of global groups, so that global groups can be nested to reflect the structure of organizational units (OUs) in a domain	Global groups in any domain in a forest
	Universal groups in a forest

Nesting global groups to reflect the structure of OUs means that global groups can be layered. For example, your organization might consist of an OU for management, an OU under the management OU for the Finance department, and an OU under the Finance department for the Budget office—resulting in three levels of OUs. Also, you might have a global group composed of the accounts of vice presidents in the management OU, a global group of accounts for supervisors in the Finance department OU, and a global group of all members of the Budget office in the budget OU. The global group membership can be set up to reflect the structure of OUs, as shown in Figure 9-1.

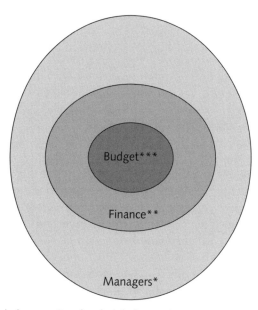

*Managers global group (top-level global group)
   Amber Richards
   Joe Scarpelli
   Kathy Brown
   Sam Rameriz
   **Finance global group (second-level global group)
      Martin LeDuc
      Sarah Humphrey
      Heather Shultz
      Sam Weisenberg
      Jason Lew
      ***Budget global group (third-level global group)
         Michele Gomez
         Kristin Beck
         Chris Doyle

Figure 9-1   Nested global groups

 TIP   Plan nesting of global groups carefully. You can convert a global group to a universal group at a later time, but only if it is not a member of another global group. Also, global groups can only be nested in native mode domains.

A global group can be converted to a universal group as long as it is not nested in another global group or in a universal group. In the example shown in Figure 9-1, the Finance and Budget global groups cannot be converted to universal groups because they already are members of the Managers and Finance groups, respectively.

A typical use for a global group is to build it with accounts that need access to resources in the same or in another domain and then to make the global group in one domain a member of a local group in the same or another domain. This model enables you to manage user accounts and their access to resources through one or more global groups, while reducing the complexity of managing accounts.

For example, consider a college that has a domain for students, a domain for faculty and staff, and a domain for research organizations that are associated with the college. The college's executive council, consisting of the college president and vice presidents, needs access to resources in all three domains. One way to enable the executive council to have access is to create a domain local group called LocalExec in each domain that provides the appropriate access to folders, files, and other resources. Next, create a GlobalExec global group in the faculty and staff domain that has the president's and vice presidents' user accounts as members (see Figure 9-2). These steps enable you to manage security for all of their accounts at one time from one global group. If the president or a vice president leaves to take another job, you simply delete (or disable) that person's account from the global group and later add an account (or rename and enable the old account) for her or his replacement. You also can manage access to resources in each domain one time through each domain local group, resulting in much less management work. If a new printer is added to a domain, for example, you can give the domain local group full privileges to the printer. (Try Hands-on Project 9-2 to practice setting up a domain local group and a global group.)

When the Active Directory structure becomes complex enough in a large organization so that many domains, trees, and forests are in use, global groups are used as members of universal groups to manage accounts, as described in the next section.

Implementing Universal Groups

In an Active Directory context in which there are multiple hierarchies of domains, trees, and forests, **universal security groups** provide a means to span domains and trees. These groups can have members and can join the Active Directory objects, as shown in Table 9-3.

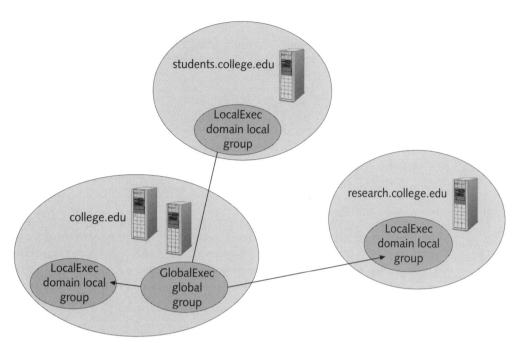

Figure 9-2   Managing security through domain local and global groups

Table 9-3   Membership Capabilities of a Universal Group

Active Directory Objects That Can Be Members of a Universal Group	Active Directory Objects That a Universal Group Can Join as a Member
Accounts from any domain in a forest	Access control lists for objects in any domain in a forest
Global groups from any domain in a forest	Any domain local group in a forest
Universal groups from any domain in a forest	Any universal group in a forest

A universal group can only be created in native mode (only Windows 2000 servers), not in mixed mode (a combination of Windows NT 4.0 and 2000 servers). Also, a universal group cannot be converted to a smaller scope, such as to a global or domain local group.

Universal groups are offered to provide an easy means to access any resource in a tree or among trees in a forest. If you carefully plan the use of universal groups, then you can manage security for single accounts with a minimum of effort. That planning is done in relation to the scope of access that is needed for a group of accounts. Here are some guidelines to help simplify how you plan to use groups:

- Use global groups to hold accounts as members—and keep the nesting of global groups to a minimum (or do not use nesting), to avoid confusion. Give accounts access to resources by making the global groups to which they belong members of domain local groups or universal groups or both.

- Use domain local groups to provide access to resources in a specific domain. Avoid placing accounts in domain local groups—but do make domain local groups members of ACLs for specific resources in the domain, such as shared folders and printers.

- Use universal groups to provide extensive access to resources, particularly when the Active Directory contains trees and forests, or to simplify access when there are multiple domains. *Make universal groups members of ACLs for objects in any domain, tree, or forest.* Manage user account access by placing accounts in global groups and joining global groups to domain local or universal groups, depending on which is most appropriate to the scope required for access.

 TIP If you attempt to create a new universal group, but find that the radio button in the Create New Object – (Group) dialog box is deactivated, this means that the domain is set up in mixed mode and you must convert the domain to native mode before you can create the group (see Hands-on Project 9-1).

In the example of setting up access for the executive council in a college that has three domains, an alternative is to create one universal group that has access to all resources in the three domains—create one global group containing the president and vice presidents, and make that global group a member of the universal group (see Figure 9-3). In this model there are only two groups to manage, compared to the model shown in Figure 9-2, in which there are four groups to manage.

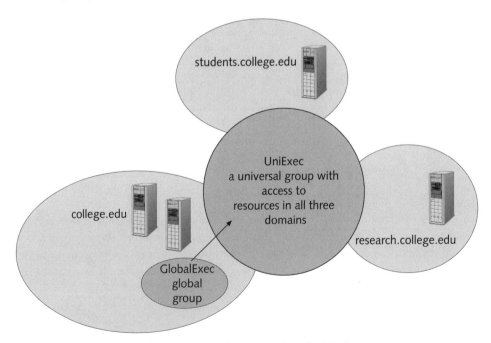

Figure 9-3 Managing security through universal and global groups

Creating Groups

Groups are created by using the Local Groups and Users tool when the Active Directory is not installed and by using the Active Directory Users and Computers tool when the Active Directory is installed. For example, to create a group using the Active Directory Users and Computers tool:

1. Click the container in which to create the group, such as the domain, the Users container (the default container of user accounts), or an OU within a domain.

2. Click the Action menu, point to New, and then click Group; or, click the *Create a new group in the current container* icon on the button bar.

3. Enter the name of the group in the Group name box (see Figure 9-4). A pre-Windows-2000 group name is also entered for use by Windows NT servers if you are running in mixed mode.

4. Click the group scope from the selections that are Domain local, Global, and Universal.

5. Click the group type, which is either Security or Distribution.

6. Click OK and verify that the group is displayed in the container you selected at the start.

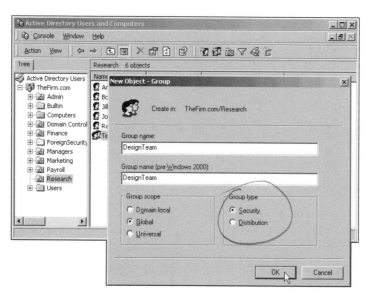

Figure 9-4   Creating a group

Each group has an associated set of properties that can be modified after the group is created, for example to add user accounts to the group or to make the group a member of another group. You can access the properties by double-clicking the group after you create it, for example in the Active Directory Users and Computers tool, where you will find the group under the container in which you created it. There are four tabs in the properties dialog box:

- *General:* Used to enter a description of the group, change the scope and type of group, and provide an e-mail address for a distribution group

- *Members:* Used to add members to a group, for example adding user accounts to a global group (click the Add button to add members; see Figure 9-5)

- *Member Of:* Used to make the group a member of another group (click the Add button to add the group to another group)

- *Managed By:* Used to establish an account or group that will manage the group, if the manager is other than the server administrator; also, the location, telephone number, and fax number of the manager can be provided

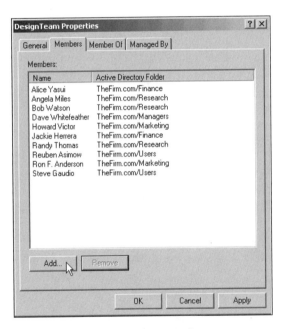

Figure 9-5 Adding group members

 The General tab enables you to change group scope, but only in the permitted direction. For example, you can change a global group into a universal group, but not into a domain local group. In this example, the domain local group will be deactivated so that you cannot select it. (Try Hands-on Project 9-3 to practice changing group scope.)

Converting Groups from Windows NT Server

When you upgrade Windows NT Server to Windows 2000 Server, the existing NT local groups on a primary domain controller are automatically converted to domain local groups, and the NT global groups are converted to global groups. If you continue to run in mixed mode because there are remaining Windows NT Server backup domain controllers, then the Windows NT servers recognize the converted groups as Windows NT local and global groups. A Windows NT server that does not run using Active Directory client software cannot recognize a universal group (see Chapter 8). With the Active Directory client installed, a Windows NT server treats a universal group as a Windows NT global group.

Default Windows 2000 Groups

Windows 2000 Server comes with several predefined domain local, global, and universal groups when the Active Directory is installed. For example, there is always a global Domain Administrators group called Domain Admins that starts by having the Administrator account as a member. The predefined groups can vary, depending on which services are installed. For instance, a domain local DHCP Administrators group is set up when you set up a DHCP server, and you will likely want to be sure that the Domain Adminis global group is a member. Table 9-4 shows many examples of the predefined Windows 2000 Server groups. When the Active Directory is installed, these groups are found in one of two containers in a domain tree, Builtin or Users.

The Builtin group contains local (on a standalone server) or domain local (in the Active Directory) groups that are used to help manage the server, such as Backup Operators. If you have used Windows NT 4.0, you will find that these are the same default groups created by that operating system.

Table 9-4   Windows 2000 Predefined Security Groups

Security Group	Scope	Active Directory Container Location/Default Members	Description
Account Operators	Built-in local [1]	Builtin	Used for administration of user accounts and groups
Administrators	Built-in local [1]	Builtin/Administrator account; Domain Admins and Enterprise Admins groups	Provides complete access to all local computer and/or domain resources
Backup Operators	Built-in local [1]	Builtin	Enables members to back up any folders and files on the computer
Cert Publishers	Global [1]	Users	Used to manage enterprise certification services for security
DHCP Administrators	Domain local	Users/Domain Admins group	Used to manage the DHCP server services (when DHCP server services are installed)

Table 9-4   Windows 2000 Predefined Security Groups (continued)

Security Group	Scope	Active Directory Container Location/Default Members	Description
DHCP Users	Domain local	Users	Enables users to access DHCP services when DHCP is enabled at the client (when DHCP server services are installed)
DNSAdmins	Domain local	Users	Used to manage the DNS server services (when DNS server services are installed)
DNSUpdateProxy	Global	Users	Enables each user access as an update proxy, so that a DHCP client can automatically update the DNS server information with its IP address
Domain Admins	Global [1]	Users/Administrator account	Used to manage resources in a domain
Domain Computers	Global [1]	Users	Used to manage all workstations and servers that join the domain
Domain Controllers	Global [1]	Users/all DC computers	Used to manage all domain controllers in a domain
Domain Guests	Global [1]	Users/Guest account	Used to manage all domain guest-type accounts, such as those for temporary employees
Domain Users	Global [1]	Users/all user accounts	Used to manage all domain user accounts
Enterprise Admins	Universal [1]	Users/Administrator account	Used to manage all resources in an enterprise
Everyone	Built-in local [1]	Does not appear in a container and cannot be deleted	Used to manage default access to local or domain resources; all user accounts are automatically members
Group Policy Creator Owners	Global [1]	Users/Administrator account	Enables members to manage group policy
Guests	Built-in local [1]	Builtin/Guest and IIS accounts, Domain Guests group	Used to manage guest accounts and to prevent access to install software or change system settings

Table 9-4   Windows 2000 Predefined Security Groups (continued)

Security Group	Scope	Active Directory Container Location/Default Members	Description
Pre-Windows-2000 Compatible Access	Built-in local [1]	Builtin/pre-Windows-2000 Everyone group	Used for backward compatibility to the Everyone group on Windows NT servers; limits access to read
Print Operators	Built-in local [1]	Builtin	Members can manage printers on the local computer or in the domain
RAS and IAS Servers	Domain local [1]	Users	Enables member servers to have access to remote access properties that are associated with user accounts, such as security properties
Replicator	Built-in local [1]	Builtin	Used with the Windows File Replication service to replicate designated folders and files
SchemaAdmins	Universal [1]	Users/Administrator account	Members have access to modify schema in the Active Directory
Server Operators	Built-in local [1]	Builtin	Used for common day-to-day server management tasks
Users	Built-in local [1]	Builtin/Domain Users group	Used to manage general user access, including the ability to be authenticated as a user and to communicate interactively

[1] The group scope cannot be changed

MANAGING OBJECTS AND OBJECT SECURITY

The purpose in creating groups is to help you to manage objects on a local server and in the Active Directory. The objects you will manage through groups include disk volumes, folders, files, printers, software, program processes, and network services. Each of these objects has an ACL to which you can add a group, such as a domain local group, so that an object can be managed as a shared resource.

Access to objects is controlled through common security techniques that include user rights, permissions, inherited rights and permissions, ownership, share permissions, and Web sharing. User rights enable an account or group to perform predefined tasks in the domain. The most basic right is the ability to access a server. More advanced rights give privileges to create accounts and manage server functions. There are two general categories of rights: privileges and logon rights. Privileges generally relate to the ability to manage server or Active Directory functions, and logon rights are related to how accounts, computers, and services are accessed. Table 9-5 shows the options included in each. Both types of rights are established through setting up the user rights group policy.

Table 9-5 Rights Security

Privileges	Logon Rights
Act as part of the operating system (a program process can gain security access as a user)	Access this computer from the network
Add workstations to a domain	Deny access to this computer from the network
Back up files and directories	Deny logon as a batch job
Bypass traverse checking (enables a user to move through a folder that the user has no permission to access, if it is on the route to one that she or he does have permission to access)	Deny logon as a service
Change the system time	Deny logon locally
Create a pagefile	Log on as a batch job
Create a token object (a process can create a security access token to use any local resource; normally should be reserved for administrators)	Log on as a service
Create permanent shared objects	Log on locally
Debug programs (can install and use a process debugger to trace problems; normally should be reserved for administrators)	
Enable computer and user accounts to be trusted for delegation	
Force shutdown from a remote system	
Generate security audits	
Increase quotas	
Increase scheduling priority	
Load and unload device drivers	
Lock pages in memory (included for backward compatibility with Windows NT and should not be used, because it degrades performance)	
Manage auditing and security log	
Modify firmware environment variables	

Table 9-5   Rights Security (continued)

Privileges	Logon Rights
Profile single process (can monitor nonsystem processes)	
Profile system performance (can monitor system processes)	
Remove computer from docking station	
Replace a process-level token (enables a process to replace a security token on one or more of its subprocesses)	
Restore files and directories	
Shut down the system	
Synchronize directory service data	
Take ownership of files or other objects	

The most efficient way to assign user rights is to assign them to groups instead of to individual user accounts. When user rights are assigned to a group, then all user accounts (or groups) that are members of that group inherit the user rights assigned to the group, making these **inherited rights**.

Permissions are associated with folders and files, controlling the way an account or group accesses information. For example, access can range from no permission to view files in a folder to full permission to add or change any files in the folder. User rights are a higher level of access than permissions. For instance, if the server administrator gives an account permission to access all software application files on the server but does not grant that account rights to access the server, the account cannot access the applications.

Share permissions are special permissions that apply to a particular shared object, such as a shared folder or printer. Share permissions do not offer as many options as user rights and regular permissions, in part because they are matched to the characteristics of the shared object, such as the ability to manage print jobs on a shared printer.

In general, rights, permissions, and share permissions are cumulative. This means that a user account, for example, has all of the rights and permissions of all of the groups to which it belongs. There are two primary exceptions to this rule: (1) a right or permission can be specifically denied and (2) the Administrators group always has the means to gain access to any resource. For example, if a user's account belongs to one group that has Full Control access to a folder and to another group that is denied access entirely, then that account will have no access.

Configuring Rights

You can configure rights as a group policy. You can start with configuring rights in the default group policy for a domain. If you need to customize rights for OUs in the domain, you can do that by setting up a group policy for specific OUs. A fast way to access the group policy for a domain or OU and to set user rights is as follows (also try Hands-on Project 9-4 to practice setting user rights in a group policy):

1. Open the Active Directory Users and Computers tool.

2. Right-click the domain or OU in the Console tree.

3. Click Properties and then click the Group Policy tab.

4. Click the group policy under Group Policy Object Links, and click Edit.

5. As necessary to expand the view in the tree, double-click Windows Settings under Computer Configuration, double-click Security Settings, and double-click Local Policies.

6. Double-click User Rights Assignment.

7. Double-click any of the policies in the right pane to configure it (see Figure 9-6).

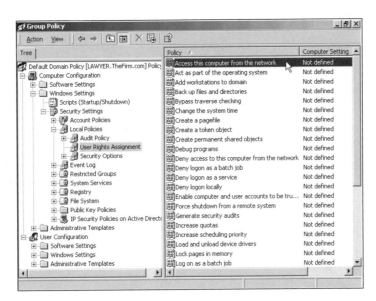

Figure 9-6   Configuring user rights as part of group policy

Configuring Folder and File Security

There are three types of security associated with Windows 2000 folders and files on a FAT-formatted drive: attributes, share permissions, and Web permissions. Folders and files on an NTFS-formatted drive have much tighter security because three additional measures are added: permissions, auditing, and ownership.

Always set up or check folder security before releasing a new server or folder on a server for public access.

Configuring Attributes

Use of **attributes** is retained in FAT and NTFS as a carryover from earlier DOS-based systems and to provide a partial migration path to convert files and directories from a Novell NetWare file server. DOS and NetWare systems use file attributes as a form of security and file management. Attributes are stored as header information with each folder and file, along with other characteristics, including volume label, designation as a subfolder, date of creation, and time of creation.

The folder and file attributes available in a FAT-formatted Windows 2000 Server disk are Read-only, Hidden, and Archive and are accessed from the General tab when you right-click a folder or file and click Properties (see Figure 9-7). If you check Read-only for a folder, the folder is read-only, but not the files in the folder. This means that the folder cannot be deleted or renamed from the Command Prompt. Also, it can only be deleted or renamed by a user belonging to the Administrators group. If an administrator attempts to delete or rename the folder, a warning message states that the folder is read-only and asks whether to proceed. Most Windows 2000 server administrators leave the read-only box blank and set the equivalent protection in permissions instead, because the read-only *permissions* apply to the folder and can be inherited by its files.

9

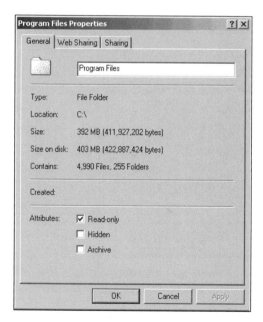

Figure 9-7   Attributes of a folder on a FAT-formatted disk

Folders can be marked as Hidden to prevent users from viewing their contents. For example, one college server administrator placed zip code verification software on a network, but kept the folder hidden while several users tested it. After testing was completed, the Hidden attribute was removed.

CAUTION

> The Hidden attribute can be defeated in Windows 95, Windows 98, Windows NT, and Windows 2000 by selecting the option to view hidden files and folders from the View or Tools menu (depending on the version of Windows) in Windows Explorer or My Computer.

The Archive attribute is checked to indicate that the folder or file needs to be backed up, because the folder or file is new or changed. Most network administrators ignore the folder Archive attribute, but instead rely on it for files. Files, but not folders, are automatically flagged to archive when they are changed. File server backup systems can be set to detect files with the Archive attribute, to ensure that those files are backed up (see Chapter 7). The backup system ensures that each file is saved, following the same folder or subfolder scheme as on the server.

An NTFS volume has the Read-only, Hidden, and Archive attributes plus the Index, Compress, and Encrypt attributes. The Read-only and Hidden attributes are on the General tab in an NTFS folder's or file's properties dialog box, and the other attributes, called extended attributes, are accessed by clicking the General tab's Advanced button (see Figure 9-8). When you make a change to one of the attributes in the Advanced Attributes dialog box in a folder's properties, you have the option to apply that change to only the folder and the files in that folder or to the folder, its files, and all subfolders and files within the folder (make sure you click the Apply button when you return to the General tab).

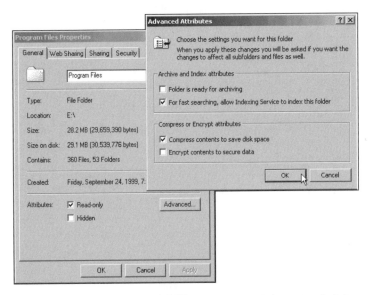

Figure 9-8 Attributes of a folder on an NTFS-formatted disk

The Index attribute is used to index the folder and file contents so that text, creation date, and other properties can be quickly searched in Windows 2000, using the Search button in My Computer or Windows Explorer.

The Index attribute relies on two preliminary steps in order to work. The first step is that the Indexing Service must already be installed as a Windows 2000 component (see Chapter 6). Also, the service should be set to start automatically after it is installed by clicking Start, pointing to Programs, pointing to Administrative Tools, clicking Computer Management, double-clicking Services and Applications in the left pane, clicking Services in the left pane, double-clicking Indexing Service in the right pane, and setting the Startup type box to Automatic.

A folder and its contents can be stored on the disk in compressed format, which is an option that enables you to save on the amount of disk space used for files, particularly in situations in which disk space is limited or for directories that are accessed infrequently, such as those used to store old fiscal year accounting data. Compression saves space, but it takes longer to access compressed information because each file must be decompressed before it is read.

If you are concerned about security and want to use the Encrypt attribute, do not compress files, because compressed files cannot be encrypted.

The Encrypt attribute protects folders and files so that only the user who encrypts the folder or file is able to read it. As administrator, you might use this option to protect certain system files or new software files that you are not yet ready to release for general use (try Hands-on Project 9-5 to encrypt the contents of a folder).

An encrypted folder or file uses Microsoft's Encrypting File System (EFS), which sets up a unique private encryption key that is associated with the user account that encrypted the folder or file. The file is protected from network intruders and situations in which a server or hard drive is stolen. When you move an encrypted file to another folder, that file remains encrypted, even if you also rename it. You can decrypt a folder or file by using Windows Explorer or My Computer to remove the Encrypt attribute and then applying the change. Folders and files can also be encrypted or decrypted by using the Command Prompt's *cipher* command. (Click Start, point to Programs, point to Accessories, and click Command Prompt. Type *cipher /?* in the Command Prompt window to view the command's switch options.)

Configuring Additional Security Options

Click the Security tab and use the Advanced button on an NTFS folder's properties dialog box to set up additional security that includes permissions, auditing, and ownership (see Figure 9-9). **Permissions** control access to the folder and its contents. **Auditing** enables the administrator to audit activities on a folder or file, such as the number of times the folder or file has been read or changed. **Ownership** designates the folder owner who has the ability to change permissions, share permissions, and Web sharing for that folder.

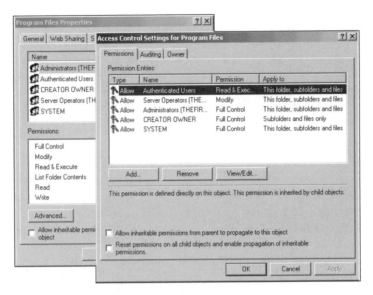

Figure 9-9 Configuring security options

 TIP Permissions can be set on individual files within a folder. However, managing these exceptions can become time-consuming and confusing. Instead, create a subfolder for exceptions, for easier management.

Many server administrators limit ownership to the Administrators as a group, except for a few situations. The folders typically owned by users include subfolders within their home folders and subfolders within publicly shared folders. Users can create and own subfolders within a folder where they have appropriate permissions.

Configuring Permissions

Use the Add and Remove buttons on the folder properties Security tab to change which groups and users have permissions for a folder. To add a group, for example, click Add, scroll to the group you want to add, double-click that group, click OK, and then select the permissions. Also, for groups and users that are already set up with permissions, you can modify the permissions by clicking the group and checking or removing checks in the Allow and Deny columns, as shown in Figure 9-10. However, if *Allow inheritable permissions from parent to propagate to object* is checked, then selected Allow and Deny boxes are shaded and cannot be changed until this option is unchecked. **Inherited permissions** are similar to inherited rights in that the same permissions on a parent object, such as a folder (or the root), apply to child objects, such as files and subfolders within the parent folder. Allowing permissions to propagate from the parent object means that the permissions used by a higher-level folder are inherited by the child objects that have this box checked. To remove the propagation of inheritable permissions, remove the check in the box and click Remove in the Security dialog box (see Figure 9-11); or, to set up permissions that are inherited from the parent, place a check in the box and click Copy.

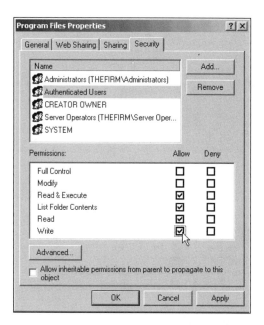

Figure 9-10   Configuring permissions by groups and users

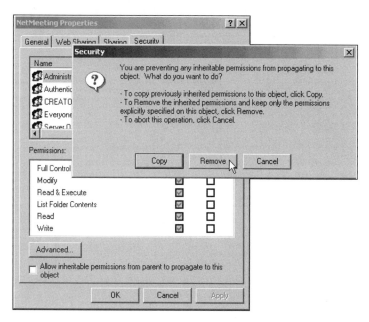

Figure 9-11   Configuring inherited permissions

Table 9-6 lists the folder and file permissions supported by NTFS.

Table 9-6   NTFS Folder and File Permissions

Permission	Description	Applies to
Full Control	Can read, add, delete, execute, and modify files plus change permissions and attributes, and take ownership	Folders and files
List Folder Contents	Can list (traverse) files in the folder or switch to a subfolder, view folder attributes and permissions, and execute files, but cannot view file contents	Folders only
Modify	Can read, add, delete, execute, and modify files, but cannot delete subfolders and their file contents, change permissions, or take ownership	Folders and files
Read	Can view file contents and view folder attributes and permissions, but cannot traverse folders or execute files	Folders and files
Read & Execute	Implies the capabilities of both List Folder Contents and Read (traverse folders, view file contents, view attributes and permissions, and execute files)	Folders and files
Write	Can create files, write data to files, appended data to files, create folders, delete files (but not subfolders and their files), and modify folder and file attributes	Folders and files

 If none of the Allow or Deny boxes is checked, then the associated group or user has no access to the folder (with the exception of a selected user who has access via a group). Also, when a new folder or file is created, it typically inherits permissions from the parent folder or from the root.

If you need to customize permissions, you have the option to set up special permissions for a particular group or user. For example, consider a situation in which you want to give a user account the equivalent of Full Control permissions, but without the ability to take ownership (leaving that permission to administrators only):

1. Open the folder properties dialog box by right-clicking the folder and clicking Properties.

2. Click the Security tab.

3. Click the user account in the Name text box or click Add, scroll to find the user account in the Select Users, Computers, or Groups dialog box, and double-click the account. Click OK.

4. Click the user account after adding it, and then click the Allow box for Full Control.

5. Click the Advanced button.

6. Scroll to and click the user account under the Permission Entries box, if the account is not already selected.

7. Click the View/Edit button.

8. Scroll to the bottom of the list of special permissions (see Figure 9-12) to find Take Ownership, and check the Deny box. Click OK.

9. Click OK. Click Yes if you see a warning box about using the Deny entry. Click OK again to leave the Properties dialog box.

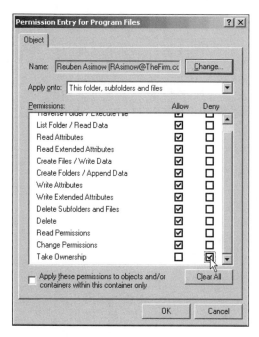

Figure 9-12   Configuring special permissions

The option at the bottom of the dialog box, *Apply these permissions to objects and/or containers within this container only*, enables you to designate that the special permissions apply to the current folder and its files only, and are not inherited by subfolders. You can fine-tune inheritance by using options in the *Apply onto* list box, which include applying the permissions strictly to:

- This folder only

- This folder, subfolders, and files

- This folder and subfolders

- This folder and files

- Subfolders and files only

- Subfolders only

- Files only

Table 9-7 summarizes the special permissions. Hands-on Project 9-6 enables you to practice setting up permissions and special permissions.

Table 9-7   NTFS Folder and File Special Permissions

Permission	Description	Applies to
Traverse Folder/ Execute File	Can list the contents of a folder and execute program files in that folder; keep in mind that all users are automatically granted this permission via the Everyone and Users groups, unless it is removed or denied by you	Folders (Traverse Folder) Files (Execute File)
List Folder/ Read Data	Can list the contents of folders and subfolders and read the contents of files	Folders (List Folder) Files (Read Data)
Read Attributes	Can view folder and file attributes (Read-only and Hidden)	Folders and files
Read Extended Attributes	Enables the viewing of extended attributes (Archive, Index, Compress, Encrypt)	Folders and files
Create Files/ Write Data	Can add new files to a folder and modify, append to, or write over file contents	Folders (Create Files) Files (Write Data)
Create Folders/ Append Data	Can add new folders and add new data at the end of files (but not delete, write over, or modify data)	Folders (Create Folders) Files (Append Data)
Write Attributes	Can add or remove the Read-only and Hidden attributes	Folders and files
Write Extended Attributes	Can add or remove the Archive, Index, Compress, and Encrypt attributes	Folders and files
Delete Subfolders and Files	Can delete subfolders and files (the following Delete permission is not required)	Folders and files
Delete	Can delete the specific subfolder or file to which this permission is attached	Folders and files
Read Permissions	Can view the permissions (ACL information) associated with a folder or file (but does not imply that you can change them)	Folders and files
Change Permissions	Can change the permissions associated with a folder or file	Folders and files
Take Ownership	Can take ownership of the folder or file (Read Permissions and Change Permissions automatically accompany this permission)	Folders and files

Microsoft provides guidelines for setting permissions, as follows:

- Protect the Winnt folder that contains operating system files on Windows 2000 servers and workstations, and its subfolders, from general users by allowing limited access, such as Read & Execute and List Folder Contents, or by just using the special permission to Traverse Folder/Execute File, but give the Administrators group Full Control access

- Protect server utility folders, such as those for backup software and network management, with access permissions only for Administrators, Server Operators, and Backup Operators

- Protect software application folders with Read & Execute and Write to enable users to run applications and write temporary files

- Create publicly used folders to have Modify access, so users have broad access except to take ownership, set permissions, and delete subfolders and their contents

- Provide users Full Control of their own home folders

- Remove the groups Everyone and Users from confidential folders, such as those used for personal mail, for sensitive files, or for software development projects

 Always err on the side of too much security. It is easier, in terms of human relations, to give users more permissions later than it is to take away permissions.

Configuring Auditing

Accessing folders and files can be tracked by setting up auditing. Some organizations choose to implement auditing on folders and files that involve financially sensitive information, such as those involving accounting and payroll. Other organizations monitor access to research or special marketing project information stored in folders and files. Windows 2000 Server NTFS folders and files enable you to audit a combination of any or all of the activities listed as special permissions in Table 9-7. When you set up auditing, the options for each type of access are to track successful and failed attempts, as shown in Figure 9-13. For example, consider a situation in which your organization's financial auditors specify that all accounting files in the Accounting folder must create an "audit trail" for each time a person who has access changes the contents of a file in the folder. Further, the only groups that have access to write to files are those in the Accounting and Administrator groups. You would set up auditing by configuring the folder's security to audit each successful type of write event, such as Create Files/Write Data and Create Folders/Append Data. For extra information, you might track permission, attribute, and ownership changes by monitoring successful attempts to Write Attributes, Write Extended Attributes, Change Permissions, and Take Ownership. Audited events are recorded in the Windows 2000 Security log that is accessed from the Event Viewer (see Chapter 16).

You can set up folder auditing through these steps:

1. Right-click the folder you want to audit, and click Properties.

2. Click the Security tab.

3. Click the Advanced button.

4. Click the Auditing tab in the Access Control Settings dialog box, and click Add.

5. Double-click the group you want to audit.

6. Check the Successful or Failed events that you want to audit, and click OK.

7. Click OK and click OK again to exit the Access Control Settings and the Properties dialog boxes.

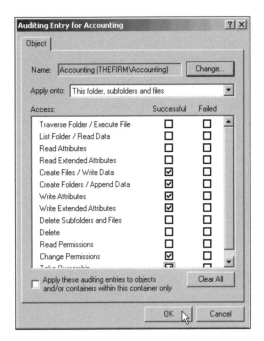

Figure 9-13   Configuring folder auditing

Troubleshooting Auditing

You cannot configure auditing for an object—an account or folder, for example—unless an auditing policy is already set up. If the policy is not set up, you will see an error message at Step 7, stating that the folder auditing cannot be configured. To configure an auditing policy that enables you to audit folder activity, start by modifying the group policy on a standalone server or the default domain policy on a server governed by the Active Directory. For example, you modify the default domain policy by using the following steps:

1. Open the Active Directory Users and Computers tool, and right-click the domain in which you want to modify the policy.

2. Click Properties and click the Group Policy tab.

3. Click Default Domain Policy and click Edit.

4. As necessary to expand the view in the tree, double-click Windows Settings under Computer Configuration, double-click Security Settings, and double-click Local Policies.

5. Double-click Audit Policy to view its options.

6. Double-click Audit object access.

7. Check Define these policy settings in the template, check Success, and check Failure. Click OK (see Figure 9-14).

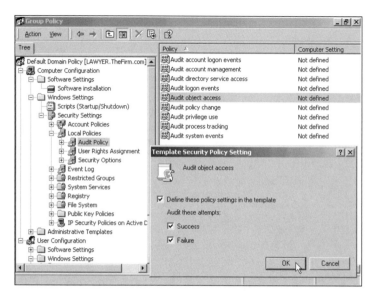

Figure 9-14   Configuring audit policy as part of the default domain policy

Also, if you are logged on but cannot configure auditing or view audited events in the Event viewer, check to make sure that you are logged on using an account that is a member of the Domain Admins group. Audit information is stored in the *system control access list,* which is a special security descriptor (list) that is associated with objects when auditing is turned on. Domain Admins have privileges to set up and modify the system control access list.

Configuring Ownership

With permissions and auditing set up, you may want to verify the ownership of a folder. Folders are first owned by the account that creates them, for example the Administrator account. Folder owners have the ability to change permissions for the folders they create. Also, ownership can be transferred only by having the Take Ownership special permission or Full Control Permission (which includes Take Ownership). These permissions enable a user to take control of a folder or file and become its owner. Taking ownership is the only way to shift control from one account to another. The Administrators group always has the ability to take control of any folder, regardless of the permissions, particularly because there are instances in which the server administrator needs to take ownership of a folder, such as when someone leaves an organization.

To take ownership of a folder, right-click the folder, click Properties, click the Security tab, click the Advanced button, and click the Owner tab. Select the account or group that will take ownership, such as the Administrators group, and click OK. Click OK again to exit the Properties dialog box.

Configuring Share Permissions to Share a Folder on the Network

Along with establishing permissions, auditing, and ownership, a folder can be set up as a shared folder for users to access over the network. To share a server folder, access the Sharing tab in the folder properties dialog box (right-click the folder and click Sharing). As Figure 9-15 shows, the Sharing tab has two main options: to share or to not share the folder. To share a folder so network users can access or map it, click the Share this folder button. Figure 9-15 shows the folder Public shared with the share name Public, for general sharing. The Maximum allowed button enables as many accesses as there are Windows 2000 Server client access licenses. The other option, Allow _____ Users, enables you to specify a limit to the number of simultaneous users. This is one way to ensure that the licensing restrictions for software are followed.

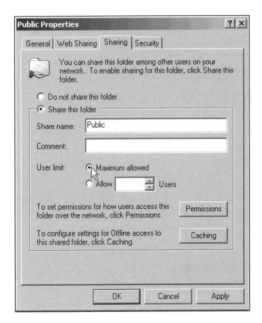

Figure 9-15   Configuring a shared folder

For example, suppose that you have an accounting software package in a folder and have only two licenses. In this case you would set the Allow _____ Users parameter to 2 so the license requirement is honored.

You can set permissions for the share from this tab by clicking the Permissions button. As explained earlier, share permissions for an object can differ from basic access permissions set through the Security tab, and the permissions are cumulative, with the exception of permissions that are denied. There are three share permissions that are associated with a folder:

- *Read:* Permits groups or users to read and execute files
- *Change:* Enables users to read, add, modify, execute, and delete files
- *Full Control:* Provides full access to the folder, including the ability to take control or change permissions

Before setting the share permissions, make sure you have selected the appropriate groups and users, for example by specifying the Everyone or Users groups for a publicly accessed folder. Use the Add button in the Permissions dialog box to set up additional groups, and the Remove button to delete a group's access to a shared folder. For example, you can remove a group by highlighting it in the list box in the Access Through Share Permissions dialog box and clicking Remove. To set the share permissions, highlight a group, and click the appropriate Allow and Deny boxes for the permissions.

The Caching button in Figure 9-15 enables you to set up a folder so that it can be accessed by a client even when the client computer is not connected to the network, for instance when the network connection is lost or when a user disconnects a laptop computer to take it home. Caching in this situation means that the folder is cached on the client computer's hard drive for continued access after losing the network connection, and that the folder location remains unchanged in Windows Explorer and My Computer. When the network connection is resumed, any cached files that have been modified can be synchronized with the network versions of the files. If two or more users attempt to synchronize a file, they have the option of choosing whose version to use or of saving both versions. A folder can be cached in three ways:

- *Automatic Caching for Documents:* Documents are cached without user intervention, which means that all files in the folder that are opened by the client are cached automatically.

- *Manual Caching for Documents:* Documents are cached only per the user's request per each document (the default option).

- *Automatic Caching of Programs:* Document and program files are automatically cached when opened, but their contents cannot be modified (which means that you must also set the shared folder permissions to Read).

 There is an option to hide a shared folder so that it does not appear on a browser list—in My Network Places in Windows 2000 or Network Neighborhood in Windows 98 or Windows NT, for example. To hide a share, place the $ sign just after its name. For instance, if the Share name text box contains the share name Budget, you can hide the share by entering Budget$. (This is an actual example of what one university does to discourage general scanning of a folder containing budget worksheets. However, department accounting technicians who know of the folder's existence can map it to help with budget planning.)

When you right-click on a folder to view its properties, the sharing option on the short-cut menu may be missing, or you may not see the Sharing tab. You can troubleshoot this problem by making sure that the Server service is started, and even if it is, you can restart it in case the service is hung (make sure no users are logged on if you restart it). To start or restart the Server service, click Start, point to Programs, point to Administrative Tools, and click Computer Management. Double-click Services and Applications, double-click Services, scroll to the Server service, and check for "Started" in the status column. Right-click the service; if it is stopped, click Start, and if it is already started, click Restart. After clicking Restart, a dialog box is displayed showing that other services will restart as well. Click Yes to restart the services.

To help guide you through the steps of creating a shared folder, Windows 2000 Server also offers the Shared Folder Wizard. To open the wizard, click the Start button, point to Programs, point to Administrative Tools, and click Configure Your Server. Next, click File Server on the menu in the left side of the screen and click the Start hyperlink to start the wizard. Try Hands-on Project 9-7 to set up a shared folder.

Web Sharing

Some folders and files stored in Windows 2000 Server may be intended for HTML or FTP access through a Web server (see Chapters 3 and 13). The Web server can be the same or a different Windows 2000 server from the one on which the folders and files reside. Use the following steps to set up a folder for Web sharing and to configure its Web sharing permissions:

1. Right-click the folder, click Properties, and click the Web Sharing tab.

2. Use the *Share on* box to specify the Default Web site or Administration Web Site on which the folder will be shared.

3. Click Share this folder.

4. Specify an alias for the folder, which enables clients to view it by a name other than the actual folder's name.

5. Check the appropriate access permissions from among the selections: Read, Write, Script source access, and Directory browsing (see Figure 9-16).

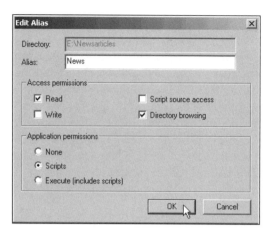

Figure 9-16   Entering Web sharing permissions

> 6. Check the application permissions from among the selections: None, Scripts, and Execute (includes scripts).
>
> 7. Click OK and click OK again to save your changes.

Tables 9-8 and 9-9 show the Web sharing application permissions and access permissions.

Table 9-8   Web Sharing Access Permissions

Access Permission	Description
Read	Enables clients to read and display the contents of folders and files via the Internet or an intranet
Write	Enables clients to modify the contents of folders and files; includes the ability to upload files through FTP
Script source access	Enables clients to view the contents of scripts containing commands to execute Web functions
Directory browsing	Enables clients to browse the folder and subfolders, for example for FTP access

Table 9-9   Web Sharing Application Permissions

Application Permission	Description
None	No access to execute a script or application
Scripts	Enables the client to run scripts to perform Web-based functions
Execute (includes scripts)	Enables clients to execute programs and scripts via the Internet or an intranet connection

9

TROUBLESHOOTING A SECURITY CONFLICT

Sometimes you will set up access for a user, but find that the user does not actually have the type of access you set up. Consider the example of Cleo Jackson, an English professor who maintains a shared subfolder called Assignments for his students from the account CJackson. Assignments is a subfolder under the parent folder English, which contains folders used by all English professors. CJackson needs to update files, copy in new files, and delete files. As Administrator, you have granted CJackson Modify access permissions to Assignments. However, you omitted the step of reviewing the groups to which CJackson belongs, such as the Paper group, which consists of Cleo Jackson and the student newspaper staff. The Paper group has been denied all access to the English folder and all of its subfolders. When Cleo Jackson attempts to copy a file to the Assignments folder, he receives an access denied message.

To troubleshoot the problem, you should review the folder permissions and share permissions for the CJackson account and for all of the groups to which CJackson belongs. In this case, because the Paper group is denied access, CJackson is also denied. The easiest solution is to remove CJackson from the Paper group and perhaps create a group of English professors, such as EngProfs, who all have access to the same resources as the Paper group.

This example also illustrates how you save both time and user aggravation when you carefully plan in advance the folder and group structures in light of the network and server security needs.

MOVING AND COPYING FILES AND FOLDERS

A common task is to move or copy files from one folder to another in the same volume or to a different volume. When a file is copied, the original file remains intact, and a copy is made in another folder. Moving a file causes it to be deleted from the original location and placed in a different folder on the same or on a different volume. Copying and moving work the same for a folder, but the entire folder contents (files and subfolders) is copied or moved. When a file or folder is created, copied, or moved, the file and folder permissions can be affected in the following ways (depending on how inheritance is set up in the target location):

- A newly created file inherits the permissions already set up in a folder.

- A file that is copied from one folder to another on the same volume inherits the permissions of the folder to which it is copied.

- A file or folder that is moved from one folder to another on the same volume takes with it the permissions it had in the original folder. For example, if the original folder had Read permissions for the Users domain local group and the folder to which it is transplanted has Modify permissions for Users, that file (or folder) will still only have Read permissions.

- A file or folder that is moved or copied to a folder on a different volume inherits the permissions of the folder to which it is moved or copied.

- A file or folder that is moved or copied from an NTFS volume to a folder in a FAT volume is not protected by NTFS permissions, but it does inherit share permissions if they are assigned to the FAT folder.

- A file or folder that is moved or copied from a FAT volume to a folder in an NTFS volume inherits the permissions already assigned in the NTFS folder.

Windows 2000 Server offers many ways to move and copy files and folders. You can use the right-click or left-click drag methods. Right-click the file or folder you want to copy or move, and while holding down the right mouse button, drag it into the folder to which you want it copied or moved. When you release the right mouse button, click Copy Here or Move Here on the shortcut menu. If you use the left mouse button to click and drag a file or folder, it moves or copies without presenting the shortcut menu. When you use the left mouse button, the file or folder is moved if the destination is on the same volume or disk; it is copied if the destination is on a different volume or disk. Another way to move and copy files and folders is to use the Cut, Copy, and Paste options in the Edit menu of My Computer and Windows Explorer.

 TIP If you discover you have moved or copied the wrong file or folder, immediately click the Undo button on the button bar in My Computer or Windows Explorer.

9

CHAPTER SUMMARY

❏ Windows 2000 Server groups offer a particularly effective way to manage user accounts and server resources such as access to specific servers, folders, and files. A Windows 2000 server that is used as a standalone computer has one type of management security group called a local group. When the Active Directory is implemented, three kinds of security groups exist: domain local, global, and universal. Your advance planning in terms of how to set up and use groups will be one of the most effective tools to save you time as administrator and to provide thorough security for your network.

❏ As you learned in Chapter 4, Windows 2000 Server objects are managed through an access control list that provides information about which user accounts and groups can access an object, such as a folder or file. There are many ways to control access, including user rights, inherited permissions, permissions, share permissions, Web permissions, auditing, and ownership. Managing access is a potentially complex process that is made easier by managing through groups and group membership rather than by managing individual accounts.

❏ Even when you manage access through groups, conflicts can occur that result in some users having too little access and other users having too much. One rule to use when you troubleshoot an access problem is to review the types of groups used and the group memberships, and to particularly look for situations in which a user belongs to one group that has access and another that is denied access. Also, as you create, copy, and move folders and files, make sure that you understand how access is inherited.

In the next chapter, you learn more about managing access to folders and files by setting up the Distributed File System. Also, you learn how to install and manage disk quotas and application software.

KEY TERMS

attribute — A characteristic associated with a folder or file used to help manage access and backups.

auditing — Tracking the success or failure of events associated with an object, such as writing to a file, and recording the audited events in an event log of a Windows 2000 server or workstation.

domain local security group — A group that is used to manage resources—shared folders and printers, for example—in its home domain, and that is primarily used to give global groups access to those resources.

Encrypting File System (EFS) — Set by an attribute of NTFS, this file system enables a user to encrypt the contents of a folder or a file so that it can only be accessed via private key code by the user who encrypted it. EFS adheres to the Data Encryption Standard's expanded version for data protection.

global security group — A group that typically contains user accounts from its home domain, and that is a member of domain local groups in the same or other domains, so as to give that global group's member accounts access to the resources defined to the domain local groups.

inherited permissions — Permissions of a parent object that also apply to child objects of the parent, for example to subfolders within a folder.

inherited rights — User rights that are assigned to a group and that automatically apply to all members of that group.

local security group — A group of user accounts that is used to manage resources on a standalone Windows 2000 server that is not part of a domain.

mixed mode — An Active Directory context in which there are both Windows NT 4.0 domain controllers (PDC and BDCs) and Windows 2000 Server domain controllers (DCs).

native mode — An Active Directory context in which there are only Windows 2000 Server domain controllers (DCs).

ownership — Having the privilege to change permissions and to fully manipulate an object. The account that creates an object, such as a folder or printer, initially has ownership.

permissions — In Windows 2000, privileges to access and manipulate resource objects, such as folders and printers; for example, privilege to read a file, or to create a new file.

scope of influence — The reach of a type of group, such as access to resources in a single domain or access to all resources in all domains in a forest (see domain local, global, and universal groups). (Another meaning for the term *scope* is the beginning through ending IP addresses defined in a DHCP server for use by DHCP clients; see Chapter 13.)

share permissions — Special permissions that apply to a particular shared object, such as a shared folder or printer.

universal security group — A group that is used to provide access to resources in any domain within a forest. A common implementation is to make global groups that contain accounts members of a universal group that has access to resources.

REVIEW QUESTIONS

1. Your college's president has several sensitive budget spreadsheets located in the Budgets subfolder under her home folder on a Windows 2000 server, and she wants to make sure that only she can read them. How can she set up security to be sure that only she can access and read those files?

   a. Use the Encrypting File System to protect the files in her Budgets subfolder.

   b. Set up the Users and Everyone groups to be denied access to the Budgets subfolder via all permissions.

   c. Set up the president's account password so it must be changed every week.

   d. Hide the Budgets subfolder by using the "$" character at the end.

2. You have set up a special Planning folder for the Promotions Planning Task force composed of members of the Marketing Department at your corporation. The folder is set up to give the Promo domain local group Full Control access permissions and Full Control share permissions. Also, you have a global group, called GlobalPromo, that contains only the members of the task force and is a member of the Promo group. However, after you set up the folder, no one in the GlobalPromo group can access it. Which of the following might explain why?

   a. You set up the Promo group to have Full Control access to the Planning folder, but denied ownership permission.

   b. You failed to set up automatic document caching for the Planning folder for the GlobalPromo group.

   c. You earlier made the GlobalMkt group a member of the Promo group, but also denied all permission access for GlobalMkt to the Planning folder when you set up the folder.

   d. all of the above

   e. only a and b

   f. only a and c

3. Last week you set up the AR folder for the Accounting Department as a shared folder and had members of that department successfully test their access to it. This morning several members of the Accounting Department report that they cannot access the folder. Also, one of your assistants is calling to report that he cannot set up a new shared folder on the server because there is no Sharing tab. What might be the problem?

   a. The Sharing service did not start properly on the server.

   b. The Server service did not start properly on the server.

   c. The Domain Local Policy Manager detected a sharing violation and turned off sharing.

   d. all of the above

   e. only a and b

   f. only b and c

9

4. You have an Active Directory structure that contains four domains. How might you plan to use groups in this situation?

   a. Use global groups to provide access to resources and domain local groups to contain user account members.

   b. Use only local groups to manage all access because you do not have enough domains to merit using universal groups.

   c. Use domain local groups and universal groups to manage resources and global groups to contain user account members.

   d. Use only universal groups because they are the best management technique when you have more than two domains.

5. Which of the following is not a Web sharing application permission?

   a. None

   b. Full Control

   c. Scripts

   d. Execute

6. You want to set up auditing on a sensitive folder. From where do you set it up?

   a. the Properties dialog box for that folder, using the Sharing tab

   b. the Control Panel, using the System icon

   c. the Active Directory Domains and Trusts tool

   d. the Properties dialog box for that folder, using the Security tab

7. When you attempt to set up auditing on a folder, you receive an error message indicating that you cannot set it up. What might be the cause of the problem?

   a. You have not enabled auditing an object as a group policy.

   b. The auditing service is not set to start automatically.

   c. You do not have the Active Directory installed.

   d. You are trying to set up auditing on a folder that is formatted for NTFS instead of FAT.

8. The CEO of your company is very angry because he lost important data while developing a critical spreadsheet for his board of directors meeting. He lost the data because his network connection was inadvertently cut by the construction firm hired to rewire parts of the network. How can you solve this problem so that it does not cause loss of data again?

   a. Hire a more careful construction company next time.

   b. Purchase a UPS for the CEO's computer.

   c. Set up certain folders, such as those used by the CEO, for caching.

   d. Use the folder Backup tool to automatically replicate certain folders at short intervals.

9. One way to reflect the organizational unit (OU) structure in a domain for security purposes is to

   a. create a universal group containing all members of all OUs.

   b. nest global groups to reflect the OU structure.

   c. use global groups to manage resources instead of domain local groups.

   d. make a local group for each OU's account composition.

10. You are making the first universal group, but find that the universal group option is deactivated. What is the problem?

   a. You must first install the Universal Grouping Service component in Windows 2000 Server.

   b. You have not first created any domain local groups.

   c. Universal groups can only hold user account members, and you are trying to use a domain local group as a member.

   d. You are running in mixed mode and must convert to native mode.

11. Martha was the accountant for your small company, but has now left, and you disabled her account. Unfortunately, her home folder on the server contains several vital accounting spreadsheets that one of the managing partners needs, but no one can access her home folder, including you as administrator. What is the best way to provide access to the information so that key company members can get to it?

   a. Enable the account, change the password, and give the password only to those who need it.

   b. Take ownership of Martha's home folder, change the permissions, and set up a share for those who need the information.

   c. Rename Martha's home folder, back it up, copy it into a publicly accessed shared folder, and hide that folder.

   d. Contact Martha to come back for a short time and distribute her data to those who need it.

12. With which of the following caching options should you set share permissions to Read?

   a. automatic caching of programs

   b. automatic caching for documents

   c. manual caching for documents

   d. none of the above because all must be set for Full Control access

13. One of the limitations of universal groups is that

   a. they cannot span domains.

   b. they cannot have global groups as members.

   c. they can only be used as distribution groups and not as security groups.

   d. none of the above is true.

   e. all of the above are true.

14. Which of the following are default global groups?

   a. Domain Guests

   b. Enterprise Admins

   c. Everyone

   d. all of the above

   e. only a and b

   f. only a and c

15. As administrator, you have set up a shared folder for the Inventory Department manager, and you ask him to take ownership and set up the permissions he wants. Later you receive a telephone call from him about a problem with a file in that folder. You log on to your account, which is a member of Domain Admins, and find that you cannot access the shared folder. Why not? (After all, you created it.)

   a. Even administrators cannot access files owned by another user.

   b. The problem with the file has spread to the entire folder, and the folder must be restored.

   c. The Inventory Department manager did not set up permissions access for the Builtin Administrators group or for Domain Admins.

   d. You must have ownership to access a folder through Domain Admins.

16. You are consulting for a doctor's office consisting of 18 networked workstations and one Windows 2000 server that is used to share folders. The office has a demo of a new medical database, but the licensing requires that not more than two people access it at the same time. How can you accommodate this requirement most easily?

   a. Set up the database in a hidden folder, because the access limit on a hidden folder is 2.

   b. Set up the database in a shared folder and set the user limit to 2.

   c. Set up the database in a shared folder, but change the permissions daily to a different combination of two people.

   d. Set up user rights to the server so that no more than two people can access the server at once.

17. The director of finance has called you into a planning meeting because your school has just determined that an accountant who quit four months ago embezzled $50,000 from the school. Besides setting permissions, the director wants to know other ways to help prevent this type of situation. What do you recommend?

   a. Deny access to log on locally to Windows 2000 servers.

   b. Establish an alert to the Administrators group whenever specific folders and files are accessed.

   c. Set up auditing on specific folders and files and regularly review the audit reports.

   d. Regularly remove the Archive attribute on specific folders so you can track how often they are accessed.

18. When you copy a file from a disk in drive A into an NTFS-formatted folder, what permissions are associated with the new file in the NTFS folder?

   a. The new file will not have any permissions set up.

   b. The new file will inherit the permissions set up for the NTFS folder.

   c. The new file can only be accessed by you, until you set up permissions.

   d. The new file will give the Users group Read permissions by default.

19. Access to Debug programs is an example of

   a. a special permission.

   b. an access permission.

   c. an attribute.

   d. a user right.

20. Which of the following are examples of extended attributes, and in which file system?

   a. Read only and Hidden in FAT

   b. Read only and Hidden in NTFS

   c. Archive and Compress in FAT

   d. Archive and Compress in NTFS

21. Yesterday your assistant was working with permissions and user rights, and today the Research group cannot access anything on your organization's Windows 2000 server. What might be the problem?

   a. He took away the permission for that group to access the TCP/IP driver.

   b. He removed or denied the user right for that group to access the server from the network.

   c. He removed ownership access to the \Public folder for the group.

   d. He changed the Full Control permissions to Read and Write on the shared drives the group accesses.

22. You have converted from mixed mode to native mode, but now want to convert back. How can you do that?

   a. Convert the mode in the Default Domain Policies.

   b. Convert using the Active Directory Domains and Trusts tool.

   c. Convert using the Active Directory Users and Computers tool.

   d. There is no tool that will enable you to convert back.

23. Which type of access control enables you to compress the contents of a folder?

   a. a permission

   b. a special permission

   c. a user right

   d. an attribute

   e. an auditing parameter

24. Your boss is a busy person and wants you to give him ownership of several folders so that he does not have to spend time on the task. As administrator, how do you accomplish transferring ownership?

   a. Simply give him Take Ownership permission, and he has ownership.

   b. Give him Full Control permissions and then transfer ownership to him.

   c. You can give him Take Ownership permission, but he must take ownership himself.

   d. Add him to the Domain Administrators group, and he automatically has ownership.

25. The Math Department head needs two files that you have in your folder, access to which is denied to anyone but you. What type of access will he have to the files after you simply move them to his folder?

   a. no access

   b. the access inherited from his folder

   c. ownership, but he must set his own permissions

   d. the Modify permissions

HANDS-ON PROJECTS

Project 9-1

This project gives you practice changing the mode (mixed to native) of a domain. You will need access to a domain controller and an account that has Administrator access for the domain. Also, check with your instructor about which domain to work on, and make absolutely sure you have permission to change modes before proceeding to Step 6 (otherwise you will simply view where to change modes).

To change the mode of a domain:

1. Start the MMC and make sure that the Active Directory Domains and Trusts snap-in is installed. If it is not, install it now.

2. Double-click **Active Directory Domains and Trusts**, and right-click the domain you want to work on.

3. Click **Properties**.

4. Make sure the General tab is displayed, and review its contents. Notice what other tabs are available, and click each one to briefly view its contents. Record your observations in a lab journal or in a word-processed document. Go back to the General tab.

5. What mode is currently set up? Is there a Change Mode button displayed on the tab? If it is not displayed, why not? If you have permission from your instructor to change modes and if the Change Mode button is displayed, go on to the next step. If not, click Cancel and close the MMC. Click No if you are asked to save the console settings.

6. Click the **Change Mode** button and click **Yes**.

7. Click **Apply** and notice the warning message that you must reboot for the change to take effect. Click **OK** to close the warning message.

8. Click **OK**, close the MMC, click **Yes** if asked to save your console settings, and shut down the domain controller (make sure no one is connected). Reboot.

9. Record and underscore an observation that you must reboot after changing modes, so you will have this information in the future.

Project 9-2

In this project, assume that you have been asked to set up groups to manage access for the managers in an Active Directory that has four domains. You will practice beginning the setup by creating a domain local group that will be used to manage resources and a global group of accounts. Last, you will add the global group to the domain local group. To complete the assignment, you will first need an environment in which the Active Directory is installed and two accounts that are already set up by your instructor. If your instructor asks you to set up your own accounts for practice, refer to Chapter 8 and create two accounts in which the usernames are built from your first initial, last name, and a unique number at the end, for example RBrown1 and RBrown2.

To set up the domain local group:

1. Install and use the **Active Directory Users and Computers** snap-in in the MMC, or click **Start**, point to **Programs**, point to **Administrative Tools**, and click **Active Directory Users and Computers**.

2. Double-click **Active Directory Users and Computers** in the tree, and click a domain, such as **TheFirm.com**.

3. Double-click **Users**. Notice what default groups are already created under Users, and record these in your lab journal or in a word-processed document.

4. Click the **Action** menu, point to **New**, and click **Group**. What defaults are already selected in the New Object – Group dialog box? Record your observations.

5. In the Group name box, enter **DomainMgrs** plus your initials, for example **DomainMgrsMJP**. What is the pre-Windows-2000 group name?

6. Click **Domain local** under Group scope, and click **Security** (if it is not already selected) under Group type.

7. Click **OK** and then look for the group you just created in the right pane within the Users container.

To create the global group and add it as a member of the local group:

1. Make sure that the Users container is still open.

2. Click the **Create a new group in the current container** icon on the button bar.

3. In the Group name box, enter **GlobalMgrs** plus your initials, for example **GlobalMgrsMJP**.

4. Click **Global** under Group scope, and click **Security** under Group type, if they are not already selected.

5. Click **OK** and then look for the group you just created in the right pane. Double-click the global group you created.

9

6. Click the **Members** tab. Are there any members already associated with the group?

7. Click the **Add** button. Scroll through the choices of members. Can you add only user accounts or are there other choices? Can you add the DomainMgrsXXX group that you created? Record your observations.

8. Scroll to find one of the accounts set up for this assignment, and double-click that account.

9. Scroll to find the second account set up for this assignment, and double-click it.

10. Make sure that both accounts are displayed in the bottom text box, and then click **OK**.

11. Click the **Members Of** tab and click **Add**.

12. Find the domain local group that you created, for example **DomainMgrsMJP**, and double-click it. This step adds the global group you created to the domain local group. Click **OK**.

13. Click **Apply** and click **OK** (or just OK to save your changes).

14. Double-click the domain local group, such as **DomainMgrsMJP**, and then click the **Members** tab. What members are shown? How would you remove a member and add another?

15. Click **Cancel**, but leave the Console display open.

16. Explain in your lab journal or in a word-processed document how to set up the necessary management groups in the other three domains. Also, note how you might perform the tasks in this assignment differently by using universal groups. Try the next assignment for ideas about using universal groups.

Project 9-3

In this hands-on activity, you will convert a domain local group to a universal group. (You must be working in a native mode domain to complete all of these steps.)

To convert the group:

1. Make sure that the Console is still open from Project 9-2 and also that the Users container is open.

2. Double-click the domain local group that you created in Project 9-2, for example **DomainMgrsMJP**.

3. Notice if any of the group scope selections are deactivated. If so, record which ones in your lab journal or in a word-processed document.

4. Click **Universal** under Group scope.

5. Click **OK**.

6. Double-click the group that you just converted, such as **DomainMgrsMJP**, and then click the **Members** tab. Did converting the group change the members? Record your observations.

7. Leave the Console window open for the next project.

Project 9-4

In this hands-on activity, you configure user rights in the default domain policy (group policy for the domain). You will set up the rights so that the domain local group that you converted to a universal group has access to the server over the network and to backup files and folders.

To configure the user rights:

1. Right-click the domain, such as **TheFirm.com**, in the Console tree under Active Directory Users and Computers.
2. Click **Properties** and then click the **Group Policy** tab.
3. If necessary, click **Default Domain Policy** under Group Policy Object Links, and click **Edit**.
4. As necessary to expand the view in the tree, double-click **Windows Settings** under Computer Configuration, double-click **Security Settings**, and double-click **Local Policies**.
5. Double-click **User Rights Assignment**. Notice the user rights that are available, and record some examples in your lab journal or in a word-processed document.
6. Double-click **Access this computer from the network** under the Policy column in the right pane.
7. Click **Define these policy settings** (if there is no check in the box), and then click **Add**.
8. Click the **Browse** button.
9. Find the domain local group that you made into a universal group in Hands-on Project 9-3, for example **DomainMgrsMJP**, and double-click it. Click **OK** in the Select users or Groups dialog box, click **OK** in the Add user or group dialog box, and click **OK** in the Security Policy Setting dialog box.
10. Under Policy in the right pane, double-click **Back up files and directories**.
11. Repeat Steps 7, 8, and 9.
12. How does the action you have just taken affect the users in the GlobalMgrs*XXX* group that you created in Hands-on Project 9-2?
13. Close the Group Policy window, and click **OK** in the domain properties dialog box.
14. Close the Active Directory Computers and Users console.

Project 9-5

In this project, you practice encrypting the contents of a folder, which enables you to use the Encrypting File System (EFS).

To encrypt a folder:

1. Use My Computer or Windows Explorer to create a new folder. For example, open **My Computer** on the desktop, double-click a local drive (NTFS formatted), such as drive **C**, click **File**, point to **New**, click **Folder**, and enter a folder name that is a combination of your last name and initials, for example **RLBrown**, and press **Enter**. Find a file to copy into the folder, such as a text or another file already in the root of drive C. To copy the file, right-click it, drag it to the folder you created, and click **Copy Here**.

2. Right-click your new folder—**RLBrown**, for example—and click **Properties**. Make sure that the **General** tab is displayed, and if it is not, then click it.

3. What attributes are already checked? Record your observations.

4. Click the **Advanced** button. Record which attributes are already checked in the Advanced Attributes dialog box.

5. Check **Encrypt contents to secure data**, and then click **OK**.

6. Click **Apply**.

7. Click **Apply changes to this folder, subfolders and files**, and click **OK**.

8. Click **OK**.

9. Note in your lab journal or in a word-processed document how you would verify that the file you copied into the folder is now encrypted. How would you decrypt the entire folder contents?

10. Decrypt the folder and leave it so that you can use it for the next project.

Project 9-6

In this project, you will practice setting up folder permissions and special permissions.

To set up permissions and special permissions:

1. Right-click the new folder you created in Project 9-5, click **Properties**, and then click the **Security** tab.

2. What users and groups already have permissions to access the folder, and what are the permissions?

3. Remove the check from **Allow inheritable permissions from parent to propagate to this object**, and click **Remove**. What access is available to the folder now?

4. Click **Add**.

5. Double-click **Users** and click **OK**. What permissions are automatically granted? Record your observations.

6. Click the **Allow** box for the **Write** permission.

7. Click the **Advanced** button. What options are available from the dialog box that is displayed?

8. Make sure that the **Users** group is highlighted in the Permissions Entries text box, or click Users if the group is not highlighted.

9. Click **View/Edit**. Notice and record the special permissions that are already set up.

10. Open the **Apply onto** list box and click **Subfolders and files** only.

11. Click the **Allow** box for the **Delete Subfolders and Files** special permission.

12. Click **OK**, and click **OK** again.

13. What permissions now show for the folder for the Users group? Why?

14. Use the **Add** button and give the Server Operators group Full Control.

15. Click **OK** to save your changes, and exit the Properties dialog box. Open the Properties dialog box again to check your work, and then close it.

Project 9-7

This Hands-on Project gives you practice configuring the folder you created in Hands-on Project 9-5 as a shared folder.

To configure the shared folder:

1. Right-click the new folder you created in Project 9-5, and click **Sharing**.
2. Click the **Share this folder** button on the Share tab. What share name is entered automatically?
3. Enter **Test share** as the comment.
4. Click the **Allow Users** button and enter **20** as the maximum number of clients who can simultaneously access this folder.
5. Click **Permissions**. Record the groups and access permissions that are displayed by default.
6. Click the **Everyone** group, if it is displayed, and click **Remove**.
7. Click the **Add** button.
8. Double-click **Server Operators** and click **OK**. Record the resulting access permissions that are available for a shared folder and the permissions that are now selected by default.
9. Click the **Allow** box for **Full Control**, and record how the permissions change. Click **OK**.
10. Click the **Caching** button, click **Allow caching of files in this shared folder** (if it is not already checked), and select **Automatic Caching for Documents** in the Setting box. Click **OK**.
11. Click **OK** to save your changes to the folder's properties and ACL.
12. Delete the folder you created by right-clicking it, clicking **Delete**, and clicking **Yes**. Click **Yes** again to the warning that others may be using files in the folder. Close My Computer or Windows Explorer.

9

CASE PROJECT

Aspen Consulting Project: Configuring Folder Management and Security

Mark Arnez has assigned you to work with a large restaurant called Feasters that specializes in serving giant meals. Feasters has a small network of 15 client workstations and one Windows 2000 server. Seven of the workstations are stationed throughout the restaurant and are used by the table servers to place customer orders. Five workstations are used by the owner and the business management staff, and three workstations are in the kitchen for the chef's staff. Feasters has hired you to set up the Windows 2000 server and to train two of the business management staff on its operation.

1. Feasters is at one location now, but they are negotiating to purchase four more restaurants to turn into new Feasters within one year. All of the new restaurants will be networked

into the main Windows 2000 server you are setting up at the first location. Explain how you would work with the current management staff to determine how to set up groups now that will enable them to be ready for the future. What natural groupings can you identify, and how would you implement them in terms of domain local, global, and universal groups?

2. The chef is very temperamental, and one of the guarantees that has been made is that no one but him will have access to the server folders that will contain his secret recipes. Using some or all of the following tools, explain how you would set up access and security on his folders.

- ☐ Groups

- ☐ User rights

- ☐ Attributes

- ☐ Permissions

3. The table servers need access to two shared folders that will enable them to place orders from any of the seven workstations available to them. Explain how you would set up security on their folders.

4. The two business management staff need training in how to set up shared folders with access permissions and share permission security. Develop a set of instructions to help them understand how to set these up.

5. Once all of the new restaurants are in operation, Feasters wants to have a Web site from which to advertise services and take reservations. As preparation, explain to the two business management staff how to set up and manage Web sharing.

6. The owner and management staff use portable computers to connect to the network. Is there a way for them to take files from certain folders to work on at home and then easily update their work on the server the next day? If so, how?

OPTIONAL CASE PROJECTS FOR TEAMS

Team Case One

Mark Arnez is aware that certain customers of Aspen Consulting seem to run into trouble when configuring permissions, share permissions, and Web-share permissions. He is asking you to form a team that will develop a general document that explains how to resolve common permission conflicts.

Team Case Two

Mark Arnez also wants to develop a comprehensive list of all of the ways in which group policies affect setup in a domain. Using the same group that you formed in Team Case One, develop a list of the ways in which group policies are used.

10

MANAGING DFS, DISK QUOTAS, AND SOFTWARE INSTALLATION

After reading this chapter and completing the exercises you will be able to:

♦ Design, configure, and manage the Distributed File System (Dfs) on a network

♦ Publish a shared folder and a Distributed File System shared folder in the Active Directory

♦ Enable and configure disk quotas

♦ Install and manage application software

♦ Edit and configure the Windows 2000 Server Registry

♦ Set up and use the Microsoft License Manager

Implementing servers with shared folders on a network sometimes translates into a steep learning curve for users as they attempt to determine how to find folders and files that they need to use. The learning curve increases with the number of server names to remember and the number of shared folders to access. Naming servers for their function has been one way to help users learn which server contains which resource. The Microsoft Distributed File System (Dfs) makes it even easier for users, because multiple shared folders and files located on multiple servers can be set up so that they appear under one folder on one server. Using the Distributed File System is a simple way to enable users to be immediately productive on a server network without the learning curve. Another reason for using the Distributed File System is to enable Windows 2000 Server file-sharing capabilities to match the distributed model of computing in enterprise networks, in which data and applications are spread throughout several server locations. The popularity of client/server applications has made distributed computing options essential in a server operating system.

In the sections that follow, you discover not only how to set up the Distributed File System on a network, but how to plan the setup before you implement it. Another part of setting up shared network folders and the Distributed File System is to use **disk quotas** to help you plan disk capacity and to ensure that users do not prematurely consume all of the disk capacity. You also learn how to install software on a server and how to edit the server Registry, which contains a wealth of hardware and software configuration information. Last, you learn about managing software licensing by using the License Manager.

CONFIGURING AND USING THE DISTRIBUTED FILE SYSTEM

The **Distributed File System** (**Dfs**) enables you to simplify access to the shared folders on a network by setting up folders to appear as if they are accessed from only one place. If the network, for example, has eight Windows 2000 servers that make a variety of shared folders available to network users, Dfs can be set up so that users do not have to know which server offers which shared folder. All of the folders can be set up to appear as though they are on one server and under one broad folder structure. Dfs also makes managing folder access easier for server administrators. Dfs is configured using the Distributed File System tool in the Administrative Tools menu (click Start, point to Programs, and point to Administrative Tools) or the Distributed File System MMC snap-in.

If Dfs is used in a domain, then shared folder contents can be replicated to one or more DCs or member servers, which means that if the original server goes offline, its shared folders are still available to users through the replica servers. Also, from the server administrator's perspective, he or she can update software in a shared folder without having to make the folder temporarily inaccessible during the update. Dfs offers the following advantages:

- Shared folders can be set up so that they appear in one hierarchy of folders, enabling users to save time when searching for information.

- NTFS access permissions fully apply to Dfs on NTFS-formatted volumes.

- Fault tolerance is an option by replicating shared folders on multiple servers, resulting in uninterrupted access for users.

- Access to shared folders can be distributed across many servers, resulting in the ability to perform **load balancing**, so that one server does not experience more load than others.

- Access to resources for Web-based Internet and intranet sites is improved.

- Vital shared folders on multiple computers can be backed up from one set of master folders.

 When you plan to use Dfs, strongly consider implementing it on a volume formatted with NTFS so that security capabilities such as access permissions, special permissions, and auditing can be used.

Besides enabling users to be more productive, Dfs also allows server administrators to be immediately more productive because Dfs reduces the number of calls to server administrators asking where to find a particular resource. Another advantage of Dfs in a domain is that folders can be replicated automatically or manually through Microsoft Replication Services (described later in this chapter). Shared folders in Dfs are copied to each designated replica computer, which yields two significant advantages: (1) important information is not lost when a disk drive on one server fails, and (2) users always have access to shared folders, even in the event of a disk failure.

In the pre-Dfs model of sharing, in Windows NT Server for instance, one or two servers might bear the brunt of most network activity because of heavy access to their shared folders. For example, consider a busy college network in which student registration information is housed in shared folders on one server. During registration that server is destined to experience extremely heavy access, delaying registration and causing students to wait in lines or be placed on hold when registering by telephone or through the Internet. If Dfs is implemented, the critical registration folders are replicated to multiple servers, causing access to be equally distributed among those servers. The result is faster registration and fewer headaches for students and the registrar's office. The same load-balancing features can be used to improve Web access by distributing the load among many servers. This is especially important, for example, to companies that rely on e-commerce for much of their business, because the companies can handle higher volumes of customer traffic and, at the same time, their customers are happier because they do not have to wait to transact business.

10

 TIP   In a mixed-mode domain that has a combination of Windows 2000 and Windows NT 4.0 servers, Dfs can be fully implemented on the Windows NT 4.0 servers as long as Service Pack 3 or above is installed.

Dfs Models

There are two models for implementing Dfs: standalone and domain-based. The standalone Dfs model offers more limited capabilities than the domain-based model. In the standalone model there is no Active Directory implementation to help manage the shared folders, and this model provides only a single or flat level share, which means that the main Dfs shared folder does not contain a hierarchy of other shared folders. Also, the standalone model does not have Dfs folders that are linked to other computers through a Dfs container that has a main root and a deep, multilevel hierarchical structure.

The domain-based model of Dfs has more features than the standalone approach. Most importantly, the domain-based model takes full advantage of the Active Directory and is available only to servers and workstations that are members of a domain. The domain-based model enables a deep root-based hierarchical arrangement of shared folders that is published in the Active Directory. Dfs shared folders in the domain-based model are replicated for fault tolerance and load balancing, whereas the standalone Dfs model does not implement these features.

Dfs Topology

The hierarchical structure of Dfs in the domain-based model is called the **Dfs topology**. There are three elements to the Dfs topology:

- The Dfs root
- The Dfs links
- Servers on which the Dfs shared folders are replicated as replica sets

A **Dfs root** is a main container in the Active Directory that holds links to shared folders that can be accessed from the root. The server that maintains the Dfs root is called the host server. When a network client views the shared folders in the Dfs root, all of the folders appear as though they were in one main folder on the Dfs root computer, even though the folders may actually reside on many different computers in the domain.

A **Dfs link** is a designated access path between the Dfs root and shared folders that are defined to the root. For example, a Dfs root might be set up to contain all shared research folders for a plant biology research group that has folders on four different servers. Those folders can be shared via links drawn from them to the Dfs root so that all of the folders appear as though they were available from one place through the published information in the Active Directory. Dfs links can also be made to another Dfs root on a different computer or to an entire shared volume on a server (see Figure 10-1).

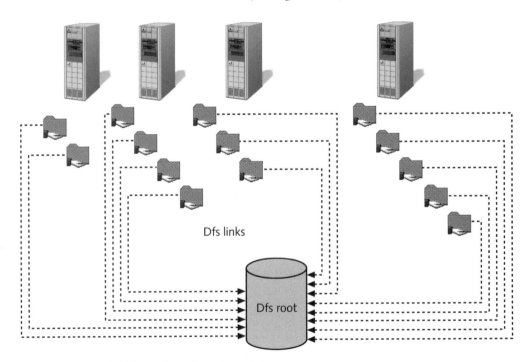

Figure 10-1   Dfs links in the Dfs root container

A **replica set** is a set of shared folders that is replicated or copied to one or more servers in a domain. In the plant biology example, the replica set would consist of all shared folders under the Dfs root that are designated to be replicated to other network servers. Part of this process establishes links to each server that participates in the replication. Another part of the process is to set up synchronization so that replication takes place among all servers at a specified interval, such as every 15 minutes.

Planning a Dfs Implementation

A Dfs implementation is most successful when it is well planned. There are several factors that Microsoft recommends you consider before installing and setting up Dfs:

- First, determine whether to use a standalone or domain-based model. On networks that deploy the Active Directory, the domain-based model provides the most options and enables you to manage the resulting network traffic. If you have a small network and have not deployed the Active Directory, then your only choice is to use the standalone model.

- Regardless of whether the standalone or domain-based model is used, place Dfs shared folders on disks that are formatted using NTFS, to ensure that there are strong security options.

- Consider using more than one Dfs root to reflect the particular needs of an organization. For example, in a college that has several divisions, such as arts and sciences, business, and engineering, there might be separate roots on different servers to reflect each division. Also there might be trees within a root for each department such as anthropology, art, biology, chemistry, English, physics, psychology, sociology, and so on, for the division of arts and sciences.

- Each time you manage Dfs through the MMC, save the console changes when you exit, so that they are available to you in your next management session.

- Set up a short cache timeout on folders with contents that change often.

- Determine the impact that Dfs will have on network traffic. If you determine there will be high-volume use of Dfs folders, consider using the domain-based model so that you can provide load balancing. Keep in mind that when you use load balancing in the domain-based model, Dfs is able to work with a DNS server to connect each user to the closest server providing Dfs services.

- When designing a domain-based model, create the first Dfs root and links to that root before creating additional Dfs roots.

- In the domain-based model, develop a synchronization schedule that will take into account the existing network traffic along different routes (segments) on which synchronization will occur. For example, synchronize more frequently on routes that have high-speed links, such as 100 Mbps, and less frequently on lower-speed routes that operate at 10 Mbps.

- Review all Dfs shared folders on a regular basis so that you can purge folders that are no longer in use.

10

Configuring the Standalone Dfs Model

The Distributed File System management tool can be accessed in two ways. One is to set it up as an MMC snap-in, and the other is to open it by clicking Start, pointing to Programs, pointing to Administrative Tools, and clicking Distributed File System. After the Distributed File System management tool is started:

1. Click the Action menu and click New Dfs Root to start the New Dfs Root Wizard.

2. Click Next.

3. Click Create a standalone Dfs root, and click Next (see Figure 10-2).

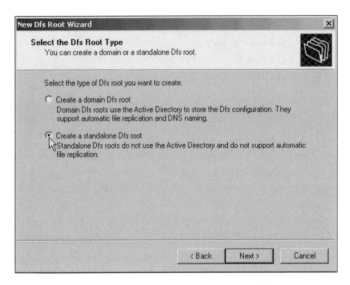

Figure 10-2   Specifying the standalone model

4. Enter the name of the server that will host the Dfs root and click Next.

5. Click Use an existing share, if you want to implement Dfs to use a shared direc-tory that is already created on the server. The text box provides a list of all of the possible selections. Otherwise, click Create a new share to set up Dfs from a shared directory that does not presently exist. If you are creating a new share, then provide the path to the share and the name of the share (see Figure 10-3). Click Next.

6. If creating a new share, click Yes to create the new folder, if it does not already exist.

7. The wizard assigns a unique name for the root folder, which is the same as the share name specified in Figure 10-3. Enter a comment to describe the share, and then click Next.

8. Review the information that has been entered, and click Finish; or click Back to go back and change information that is already entered.

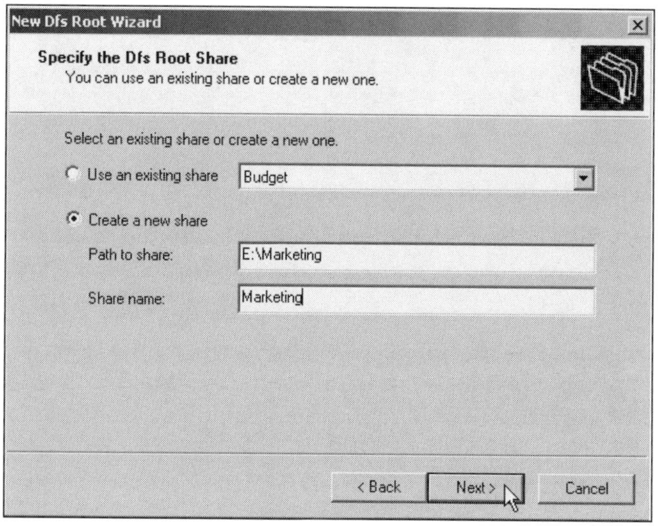

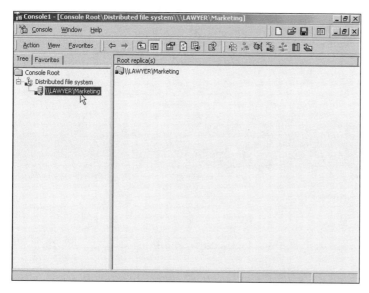

Figure 10-3   Creating a new Dfs share

After the standalone Dfs shared root folder is created, it is displayed in the Distributed File System console window, as shown in Figure 10-4. If you are using the MMC, make sure that you save the changes and provide a name for the console, so that you can easily view the Dfs shared folder the next time that you open the console. If the Dfs shared folder is not displayed the next time you access the MMC snap-in, because it was not saved, install the Distributed File System snap-in again. After the snap-in is installed, click Distributed File System under the Console Root, click the Action menu, click Display an Existing Dfs root, enter the server name and Dfs shared folder name, and click OK.

Figure 10-4   Viewing a new Dfs shared folder in the MMC console

If you attempt to create a standalone root on a server, and see the error message, "This server already hosts a Dfs root," this means that you cannot create an additional Dfs root on that server because one already exists, and a host server can have only one.

Configuring the Domain-based Dfs Model

Installing a domain-based Dfs root is similar to installing a standalone Dfs root, but there are some differences, such as specifying the domain in which the root resides. Use the following steps to set up a domain-based Dfs root:

1. Open the Distributed File System management tool as an MMC snap-in or from the Administrative Tools menu. If the Distributed File System snap-in is used, click Distributed file system under the Console Root.

2. Click the Action menu and click New Dfs root, or click the Create a new Dfs root icon on the button bar.

3. Click Next after the New Dfs Root Wizard starts.

4. Click Create a domain Dfs root.

5. Enter the name of the domain in which the root will reside (see Figure 10-5). Click Next.

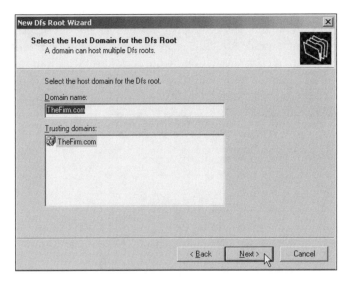

Figure 10-5 Entering the domain name

6. Enter the server name, or use the browse button to find the server and then click Next. The server name will be identified with the domain in which it resides.

7. Click the appropriate radio button to use an existing shared folder, or select the option to create a new shared folder. If you create a new shared folder, also provide

the path to the share and the share name (refer to Figure 10-3). Click Next. If you select Create a new share, click Yes to create the new folder for the share.

8. Enter the Dfs root name, or use the default already provided, which is the share name that you provided in the last step. Also, enter a comment to describe the root, and then click Next.

9. Examine the summary of information that you specified, and click Finish; or click Back to reenter information.

Try Hands-on Project 10-1 to practice setting up a new Dfs root.

Managing a Domain-based Dfs Root System

After the Dfs root system is set up, there are several tasks involved in managing the root, which can include:

- Deleting a Dfs root
- Adding and removing a Dfs link
- Adding root and link replica sets
- Configuring security
- Checking the status of a root or link

Each of these tasks is described in the following sections.

Deleting a Dfs Root

After a Dfs root is created, it is possible to delete it—when you want to configure it differently, for example. To delete a Dfs root:

1. Provide users with a warning that the root will be deleted, to make sure that no one is accessing the root when you delete it.

2. Open the Distributed File System management tool via the MMC or from the Administrative Tools menu.

3. Right-click the root that you want to delete under Distributed file system in the tree.

4. Click Delete Dfs Root.

5. Click Yes.

CAUTION

Keep in mind that when a domain-based Dfs root is deleted, so are the shared folder links to that root.

(You can practice deleting a Dfs root in Hands-on Project 10-3.)

Adding and Removing a Dfs Link

A link to a Dfs root can be established to a shared folder on the same computer as the root or to another computer that is a member of the domain. For example, there might be three servers that contain spreadsheets that should be placed under the Dfs root for easy access. To set up a link, follow these steps:

1. Open the Distributed File System management tool and right-click the root under the tree in the left pane.

2. Click New Dfs Link.

3. Enter a name that users will see (as a shared folder under the Dfs root folder) for the link (see Figure 10-6). Use the Browse button to find the computer and shared folder that you want to link to the Dfs root. Provide a comment to describe the link.

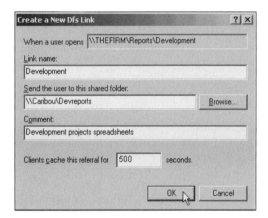

Figure 10-6   Creating a Dfs link

4. Establish the cache timeout (described in the following paragraph) in seconds for the link.

5. Click OK.

When you create a link, the first link automatically becomes the **master folder** for replication, which is the folder that contains the master copy replicated to the other links. It is listed in the right pane of the Distributed File System tool under the Replica(s) column. Also, the security, such as access permissions and auditing, that is already set up for the shared folder that becomes a link to a Dfs root is retained after the link is established. The **cache timeout** is the amount of time that a shared folder is retained in the client operating system's cache for fast access. A typical implementation for the timeout value is 300 seconds. Increase this amount by several hundred seconds, if you anticipate that the contents in the link will be changed often, and decrease the amount to 100 or 200 seconds if the contents will be changed less frequently.

TIP   The cache timeout can be adjusted after a Dfs link is created by right-clicking the link and resetting the cache timeout in the General tab.

A link is removed from the Dfs root by using the following steps:

1. Right-click the link in the left pane.

2. Click Remove Dfs Link.

3. Click Yes.

Hands-on Project 10-2 enables you to practice creating and deleting Dfs links.

Adding Dfs Root and Link Replicas

An entire Dfs root or specific Dfs links in a root can be replicated on servers other than the one that contains the master folder. The replication capability is what enables you to provide fault tolerance and to create load balancing. On a network in which there are multiple servers, replication can prove to be a vital service to provide uninterrupted access for users, in case the computer with the master folder is inaccessible. Load balancing also is vital as a way to provide users with faster service and better network performance by enabling users to access the nearest server containing the Dfs shared folders.

You can replicate the root and all of its links to shared folders to one or more computers other than the one that houses the original Dfs root and links. Any computer that contains a replica of the original root and links cannot already have any Dfs roots, because you can only create one root per computer. To create a replica of an entire root, first determine which domain controllers or member servers do not already contain a Dfs root. Next, right-click the Dfs root that you want to replicate using the Distributed File System management tool. Click New Root Replica, and use the New Dfs Root Wizard to provide the name of the server on which to place the replica, the path for the replica, and whether to manually or automatically synchronize the information between the master and the replica.

The replication is handled by the Windows 2000 File Replication service. If automatic synchronization is used, then the default synchronization interval is every 15 minutes. When manual synchronization is used instead of automatic, then new links must be manually built in each root replica by an administrator. Normally, you will set up to use automatic synchronization, but manual synchronization is an alternative if you do not want to fully replicate all links, for example. If you attempt to create a Dfs root replica on a server that already has a root, the New Dfs Root Wizard provides a message that one already exists on that computer. Also, if you try to create a Dfs root replica on a Windows NT 4.0 server, but receive an error message, check two possibilities: (1) Service Pack 3 or above is not installed on the Windows NT 4.0 server, or (2) you have previously converted the domain from mixed mode to native mode, and Windows NT 4.0 servers are no longer recognized as viable server members.

Depending on the domain and server Dfs architecture and planning, it may be desirable to replicate designated Dfs links. For example, you might set up link replication as a way to

10

load-balance access to specific folders on a busy network. Consider a business campus on which the accounting office is located several buildings away from the budget office. A Dfs link to shared accounting files might be replicated on servers that are located near the accounting department, while a link to shared budget files is replicated on a server located near the budget office. To set up replication of a designated link:

1. Right-click the Dfs link in the Distributed File System tool, and click New Replica.

2. Enter the computer name and shared folder on the computer to use for the replica, or use the browse button to locate the computer and shared folder in the domain. The computer name and shared folder are specified in UNC format.

3. Click Manual replication or Automatic replication, and then click OK (see Figure 10-7).

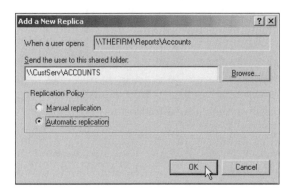

Figure 10-7   Adding a new replica for a Dfs link

4. If you selected Automatic replication in Step 3, set the replication policy, which enables you to change the master folder and to designate which replicas are enabled for automatic replication. Click OK.

5. The replica computer and folder path is added under the Replica(s) column in the Dfs tree for the designated link.

A Dfs root replica can be deleted by clicking the Dfs root, right-clicking the replica to be deleted under the Root replica(s) column, and then clicking Remove replica. Similarly, a replica of a Dfs link is deleted by clicking the Dfs link, right-clicking the link in the Replica(s) column, and clicking Remove replica.

After the first Dfs root or Dfs link replica is established, you can modify the replication policy for either one by right-clicking the Dfs root or link and clicking Replication Policy. The Replication Policy dialog box (see Figure 10-8) is used to enable or disable replication to a specific server and to set the master folder. Also, the cache timeout can be set on a Dfs root or link by right-clicking it in the Distributed Files System management tool and clicking Properties. Use the "Clients cache this referral for _____ seconds" parameter to set the timeout value (Hands-on Project 10-2 enables to you practice setting the cache timeout).

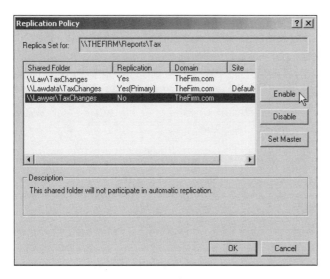

Figure 10-8   Configuring replication policy

Configuring the File Replication Service

Because automatic Dfs replication relies on the File Replication service, it is important to make sure that the service is started and that it is set to start automatically each time that the server is booted. The File Replication service is designed to synchronize the contents of folders between two or more Windows 2000 servers. The service consists of two broad functions within a single service. One function is to maintain information about each set of folders and associated servers to replicate, along with the process used to perform the replication. The second function is to establish connectivity between servers for the replication process.

When you configure Dfs replication, make sure that the File Replication service is configured. Click Start, point to Programs, point to Administrative Tools, and click Computer Management. Double-click Services and Applications in the left pane, and double-click Services in the right pane. Find the File Replication Service and make sure that the status is *Started* and that the Startup Type is *Automatic*. If you need to configure one or both of these settings, double-click File Replication service, set the Startup type box to Automatic, and click the Start button.

Configuring Security

The security on Dfs shared folders is inherited from the access and share permissions already established on those folders. Overall security for the Dfs root can be fine-tuned by applying permissions, auditing, and ownership parameters. The permissions to the contents of the Dfs root that can be allowed or denied to any user account, group, or computer are:

- *Full Control:* The ability to change permissions, take ownership, create, delete, modify, and manage Dfs shared folders and files; and the ability to delete trees and subtrees within the folder structure

- *Read:* The ability to list and read the contents of shared folders and files

- *Write:* The ability to modify the contents of shared folders and files

The security for a Dfs root is configured by right-clicking the root in the Distributed File System management tool, clicking Properties, and clicking the Security tab (if the Dfs root is located on an NTFS-formatted disk). The Security tab is nearly identical to the Security tab that is used for an ordinary folder. User accounts, groups, and computers are added by clicking the Add button and specifying the permissions (see Chapter 9).

Special permissions can be set up by clicking the Advanced button on the Security tab and then clicking View/Edit. The Advanced button on the Security tab also enables you to audit access to the Dfs root or to take ownership. Auditing works by monitoring successful and failed attempts to use any of the special permissions, such as successful attempts to list the root contents or failed attempts to delete the contents of the Dfs root. Auditing can be set by user account, group, and computer. Ownership of a Dfs root is taken via the Ownership tab.

Checking the Status of a Root or Link for Troubleshooting Connectivity

The most common problem associated with Dfs shared folders is that one or more Dfs links are inaccessible because a particular server is disconnected from the network or has failed. You can quickly check the status of a Dfs root, Dfs link, or replica by right-clicking it in the Replica(s) column of the Distributed File System management tool and then clicking Check Status. A Dfs root, link, or replica that is working and fully connected will have a green check mark in a white circle through its folder icon. One that is disconnected will have a white "x" in a red circle (see Figure 10-9) through its folder icon.

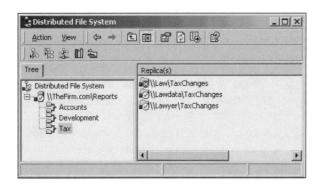

Figure 10-9   Checking the status of replicas in a link

PUBLISHING A SHARED FOLDER

When you set up regular shared folders or Dfs root folders, you can publish them in the Active Directory. It is not mandatory to publish them, but that provides yet another way to make them easy for users to find and access.

To publish a shared folder or a Dfs root:

1. Open the Active Directory Users and Computers tool.

2. Right-click the domain.

3. Point to New and click Shared Folder.

4. Enter the name for the published folder that users will see in the Active Directory.

5. Enter the path to the shared folder or Dfs root (see Figure 10-10), and click OK.

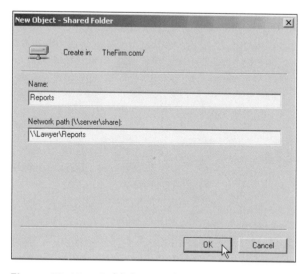

Figure 10-10   Publishing a shared folder

The domain objects displayed in the right pane for the domain in the Active Directory Users and Computers tool will now show a shared folder/drive icon. When you double-click the icon, you can enter a description of the shared folder or Dfs root, change the path (in case it is moved to another computer), and associate keywords that can be used to help identify its contents, so that when users search the Active Directory using those keywords, the published shared folder or Dfs root will be displayed. To associate keywords, double-click the folder, access the General tab, click the Keywords button, and enter the desired keywords for searches.

Windows 2000 Professional users can find the published folder by searching the Active Directory, using My Network Places, or the Start button, Search option (to search My Network Places). Windows 95, 98, and NT users also can employ the Directory Service Client (DSClient, see Chapter 8) software to search the Active Directory for the published folder.

CONFIGURING DISK QUOTAS

Another reason to set up shared folders and Dfs shared folders using NTFS-formatted volumes is to activate the ability to establish disk quotas. Using disk quotas has the following advantages:

- Prevents users from filling the disk capacity

- Encourages users to help manage disk space by deleting old files when they receive a warning that their quota limit is approaching

- Tracks disk capacity needs on a per-user basis for future planning
- Provides server administrators with information about when users are nearing or have reached their disk quotas

Disk quotas can be set on any local or shared volume. By simply enabling the disk quota feature on a volume, you can determine how much disk capacity is occupied by each user, without specifically setting quotas on those users. Another option is to set default quotas for all users, particularly on volumes that house user home folders. For example, many organizations establish a default quota of 10 to 100 MB per user on home folder volumes. The default quota prevents a few users from occupying disk space that is needed for all users. Disk quotas also can be established on a per-user basis, or special exceptions can be made for users who need additional space, such as a newspaper publishing group on a college campus that requires a large amount of space for text and graphics files.

 TIP Plan to establish disk quotas before offering shared and Dfs shared folders to network users. It is politically much easier to set quotas in the beginning than to set quotas after users have grown used to having no limits.

The general parameters that can be configured for disk quota management include:

- *Enable quota management:* Starts tracking disk quotas and sets up quota management
- *Deny disk space to users exceeding quota limit:* Prevents users from writing new information to disk after they have exceeded their quotas
- *Do not limit disk usage:* Tracks disk usage without establishing quotas on users, for example to gather statistics for disk-capacity planning
- *Limit disk space to:* Sets the default amount of disk space that users can use
- *Set warning level to:* Sets the default amount of disk space that users can occupy that will trigger a warning message to users that they are reaching their quota
- *Log event when a user exceeds their quota limit:* Causes an event to be entered in the System log to notify the administrator that the user has reached his or her quota
- *Log event when the user exceeds their warning level:* Causes an event to be entered in the System log to notify the administrator that the user is approaching his or her quota

To enable disk quotas, set up default disk quotas and warning levels, prevent users from exceeding their quotas, and receive notification when a user is approaching or has reached his or her quota on a volume (try Hands-on Project 10-4):

1. Open My Computer on the Windows 2000 Server desktop.
2. Right-click the volume on which to set the quotas, and click Properties.
3. Click the Quota tab.

4. Click Enable quota management. (If you later need to eliminate all disk quotas from a particular volume, you can do that by removing the check mark in front of Enable quota management.)

5. Click Deny disk space to users exceeding quota limit.

6. Click the radio button for Limit disk space to, and enter the limitation value, such as 100 MB.

7. Enter values in the Set warning level boxes, such as 90 and MB.

8. Place a check mark in front of Log event when a user exceeds their quota limit.

9. Place a check mark in front of Log event when a user exceeds their warning level.

10. Click OK (see Figure 10-11).

11. If you see a warning that you are about to enable the disk quota system, click OK.

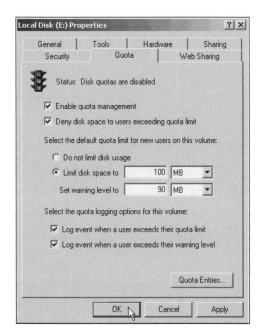

10

Figure 10-11   Setting default disk quotas

Disk quotas for specific user accounts that are exceptions to the default quotas are set by clicking the Quota Entries button on the dialog box shown in Figure 10-11. For example, to establish a disk quota for the account RKurkowski:

1. Click the Quota Entries button on the Quota tab.

2. Click the Quota menu and click New Quota Entry.

3. Double-click the RKurkowski account (which is listed by the full user name, account name, and domain) in the Select Users dialog box.

4. Click OK.

5. Click the radio button for Limit disk space to, and enter the disk space limitation, such as 200 MB.

6. Enter the value for Set warning level to, such as 150 MB.

7. Click OK (see Figure 10-12).

8. The Quota Entries dialog box is updated to reflect the quota for that account, so that you have an easy way to quickly view quotas on individual accounts and quota exceptions.

Figure 10-12   Setting a disk quota on a designated user account

The disk quota set on a particular account can be modified by clicking the Quota Entries button to open the Quota Entries dialog box. Double-click the account you want to modify, and then modify the disk quota parameters in the Quota Settings dialog box. To delete a quota associated with an account, right-click the account in the Quota Entries dialog box and click Delete, as in Figure 10-13. The disk quota associated with a particular user can change when ownership of files transfers from one owner to another. For example, consider Rick Kurkowski, who creates the Expenses.mdb database file that occupies 522 KB on a volume that contains a shared folder. After Rick creates Expenses.mdb, his available disk usage is decremented by 522 KB. When Rick's work assignment changes and Jason Brown takes ownership of Expenses.mdb, Rick's available disk usage goes up by 522 KB and Jason's is decremented by the same amount.

 TIP   You can view the disk quota limit and warning level set on any account and the amount of disk space used by an account by clicking the Quota Entries button, which opens the information in the Quota Entries dialog box.

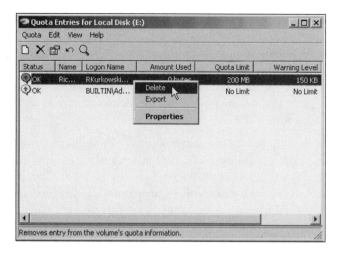

Figure 10-13   Deleting a disk quota on an account

When you enable disk quotas, but do not limit disk usage, you have the ability to gather information to plan disk capacity before setting up quotas. An easy way to use the information is to import the statistics on disk usage to a spreadsheet, database, or word-processed file (for example, into a Microsoft Word table). In general, the steps to accomplish this are:

1. Open the preformatted spreadsheet, database, or word-processed file that will hold the information, such as Microsoft Excel.

2. Right-click the volume on which you have collected disk usage information.

3. Click Properties and then click the Quota tab.

4. Click the Quota Entries button.

5. Click the Edit menu and click Select All to select all of the information to copy, or hold down the Ctrl key and click each entry that you want to copy.

6. Drag the information that you have selected into the spreadsheet, database, or word-processed file.

INSTALLING AND MANAGING APPLICATION SOFTWARE

There are several important issues to consider before installing application software for users to access or set up from a server. These include the following:

- Software licensing
- Network compatibility
- Temporary files
- Network performance
- Software testing
- Loading software from the network

Application software is licensed to the user as explained in the software licensing agreement. The server administrator should carefully read and follow the licensing agreement before loading software. Some companies offer site licensing for unlimited access to the software through the network. Others restrict software licensing to groupings, such as "5-packs" or "10-packs." Some come with license monitoring built into the software, whereas others rely on the server administrator to monitor use, for example by using the Microsoft License Manager or by placing a user access limit on a shared folder. **License monitoring** involves creating a mechanism to ensure that network users do not access software in numbers larger than the software license allows.

Some applications, such as desktop publishing programs, may not be designed to run from a network. In these cases, the best solution is to consult with the vendor about how to adapt the software for a network, if possible. The best advice is to check all applications to be certain they are network compatible. **Network-compatible programs** are designed for multiuser access, often with network capabilities such as options to send files through e-mail.

The network load generated by an application is another issue. Some database applications create high levels of traffic, particularly if the entire database is sent each time a user wishes to examine only a small amount of information. Database reporting tools, graphics, and computer-aided design programs also may generate high traffic. Traffic is not likely to be a problem on a small network, but it is important to closely monitor network activity associated with applications.

Some applications create temporary or backup files while the application is running. For example, Microsoft Word creates backup files so work can be restored after a power failure or computer problem. It is important to determine what extra files are needed to run an application and where to store them. For example, Word backup files can be directed to the user's home folder or to a local folder on the client through Word setup. Plan to teach software users how to deploy temporary and backup files created by software. Also, show users how to delete old temporary and backup files no longer needed.

Plan to test each software installation before releasing it to the users. You might test it from two or more special server accounts created for that purpose. Another way to test software is to first install and test it on a Windows 2000 Professional workstation and then port it to Windows 2000 Server, which is a common technique used by server and network administrators to determine that the software is working and that the permissions are correctly set.

Some applications, such as Microsoft Office, provide the option to install software application files from the network onto each client workstation. Another way is to install client software so application files are loaded from the server each time the application is run. The second way might take a few seconds longer to run the application, because the files are shipped over the network instead of loaded from the user's hard drive. The advantage is a significant savings in disk space on the workstation. A disadvantage is the extra network traffic created on a large network.

Installing Software Using Add/Remove Programs

The best way to install software on a server is to use the Add/Remove Programs icon in the Windows 2000 Server Control Panel. There are two important advantages in using the Add/Remove Programs utility:

- With this method, software configuration is stored in the Windows 2000 Registry. This makes software configuration easier, and configuration information can be updated to the emergency repair disk in case problems develop later.

- The Registry tracks the location of all files associated with software, such as program, initialization, and dynamic-link library (DLL) files. The Registry information makes it easier to remove all program pieces, if necessary.

Consider the installation of Microsoft Office. Before starting the setup, check the licensing information to be sure you have purchased enough licenses for the installation. To install Microsoft Office, insert the Microsoft Office CD-ROM in the server's CD-ROM drive, and then open Add/Remove Programs in the Control Panel. Click Add New Programs and then click CD or Floppy, as shown in Figure 10-14.

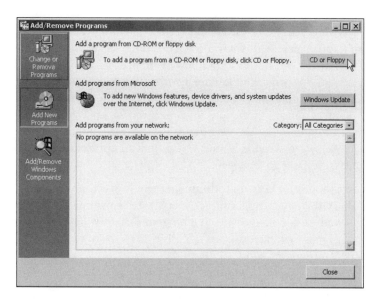

Figure 10-14   Installing application software

The Install Program Wizard takes over with a request to insert the setup disk in the floppy or CD-ROM drive. Click Next and then wait for the wizard to automatically detect the setup file (see Figure 10-15), or click the Browse button to provide the path to the setup file, such as the Microsoft Office setup program on the CD-ROM drive. With the correct path and installation program name entered, click Finish. Now started, the Microsoft Office setup program takes over providing different options to install the Office software. After the software is installed, create a shared folder such as Msoffice, and then create a link to the Dfs root for network users to access.

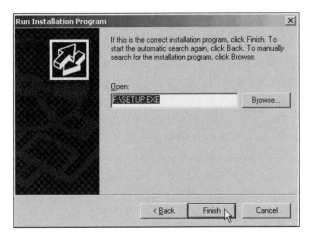

Figure 10-15   Providing the path to the setup program

Running Software Applications in User Mode

When a software application is run on Windows 2000 Server, it runs in **user mode**. This means it does not have direct access to the system kernel, operating system services, CPU, or hardware. Each application runs in its own memory address space, which is the extent to which it affects Windows 2000. The Windows 2000 kernel, consisting of operating system code and services, runs in the privileged **kernel mode**, which also is called the supervisor or protected mode. The operating system programs running in the kernel mode have access to hardware, CPU registers, and I/O functions. They also run in a protected area of memory that cannot be accessed by applications in user mode. If a software application needs to access hardware or an operating system service, it must go through an **application programming interface** (**API**) that serves as a go-between.

The advantage of user mode and kernel mode architecture is that the Windows 2000 operating system is not affected when an application experiences a run-time error or coding bug. Also, the operating system is not affected when a program hangs or has a problem handling memory. The disadvantage is that extensive use of APIs by a program can create system overhead due to the drain on memory and CPU resources.

When you run applications that use graphics, such as the OpenGL graphics screen savers mentioned in Chapter 6, these can put an extra load on a Windows 2000 server because graphics services run in kernel mode instead of user mode. The load is created when an application makes heavy use of the API that communicates between the kernel mode graphics services and the user mode graphics DLLs. Microsoft has developed a way to optimize memory for graphics communications between the kernel and user modes, but you still should watch the impact that graphics programs have on the server (see Chapter 14).

Using the Registry to Configure the Operating System Setup and Software

The Windows 2000 **Registry** is a very complex database containing all information the operating system needs about the entire server. For example, the initialization files used by earlier versions of Windows operating systems, including the critical System.ini and Win.ini files, are contained in the Registry. They also may exist as separate files, but this is only necessary for programs that are not designed for compatibility with the Registry, such as early MS-DOS and pre-Windows 95 programs. Some examples of data contained in the Registry are as follows:

- Information about all hardware components, including the CPU, disk drives, network interface cards, CD-ROM drives, and more

- Information about Windows 2000 services that are installed, which services they depend on, and the order in which they are started

- Data about user profiles and Windows 2000 Server group policies

- Data on the last current and last known setup used to boot the computer

- Configuration information about all software in use

- Software licensing information

- Control Panel parameter configurations

There is the option to use either of two editors to view the contents of the Registry: Regedit or Regedt32. Regedit is an earlier 16-bit version of the Registry editor and is preferred by some administrators because it has the most complete utility to search for keys, subkeys, values, data, and strings. A **key** is a category or division of information within the Registry. A single key may contain one or more lower-level keys called **subkeys**, just as a folder may contain several subfolders. A Registry **value** is a data parameter associated with a software or hardware characteristic under a key (or subkey). A Registry value consists of three parts—a name, the data type, and the configuration parameter—for example, ErrorControl:REG_DWORD:0 (ErrorControl is the name, REG_DWORD is the data type, and 0 is the parameter setting). In this value, the option to track errors is turned off if the parameter is 0, and error tracking is turned on if the value is 1. There are three data formats: DWORD is hexadecimal, string is text data, and binary is two hexadecimal values.

The Regedit editor window is very straightforward, with common menu utilities such as Registry, Edit, View, and Help. Regedt32 is a much fancier 32-bit editor with cascading windows and twice the number of menu bar options as Regedit. It has added options that manage Registry security, that sees information in expanded views, that sets up auditing to track who has accessed the Registry, and added keys or values, and that sets up access to the Registry in read-only mode to ensure against mistakes (try Hands-on Project 10-5 to practice using Regedt32).

10

TIP Neither Registry editor is automatically available from a menu or icon in Windows 2000 Server. Regedit is located in the Winnt folder, and Regedt32 is in the \Winnt\System32 folder. If you use one or both editors frequently, you will likely want to create a shortcut to access them. Otherwise, many administrators start them by using the Run option from the Start button.

The Registry data is stored in a top-down hierarchy with five root keys at the highest level:

- HKEY_LOCAL_MACHINE
- HKEY_CURRENT_USER
- HKEY_USERS
- HKEY_CLASSES_ROOT
- HKEY_CURRENT_CONFIG

A **root key**, also called a **subtree**, is a primary or highest-level category of data contained in the Registry. It might be compared to a main folder, such as the Winnt folder, which is at the root level of folders. All root keys start with HKEY to show they are the highest-level key.

HKEY_LOCAL_MACHINE

Under the HKEY_LOCAL_MACHINE root key is information on every hardware component in the server. This includes information about what drivers are loaded and their version levels, what IRQs (interrupt requests) are used, setup configurations, the BIOS version, and more. Figure 10-16 shows the Registry contents, using the Regedt32 editor to view the HKEY_LOCAL_MACHINE root key information about serial ports.

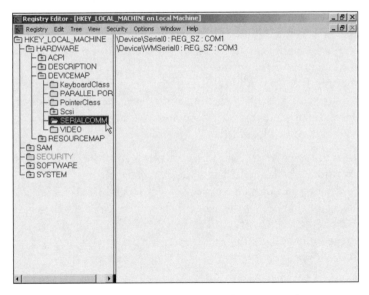

Figure 10-16   The HKEY_LOCAL_MACHINE root key

Under each root key are subkeys, which are HARDWARE, SAM, SECURITY, SOFTWARE, and SYSTEM for the root key in the figure. Each subkey may have subkeys under it, such as ACPI, DESCRIPTION, DEVICEMAP, and RESOURCEMAP under the HARDWARE subkey in Figure 10-16.

A few subkeys are stored as a set, called **hives**, because they hold related information. This is true for the SOFTWARE subkey, which holds information about installed software. You can make hardware configuration changes directly from the Registry, although this is not recommended (see the following Caution). For example, if Windows 2000 Server has incorrectly detected three serial ports, but only two are actually installed, you can delete one by using the Registry editor. For instance, to delete serial port 3, highlight the line in Figure 10-16, \Device\WMSerial0:REG_SZ:COM3, and then press Del, or open the Edit menu and click Delete.

CAUTION

Although it is possible to make hardware configuration changes directly from the Registry, this is a dangerous undertaking, because a wrong deletion may mean you cannot reboot your server into Windows 2000 Server. It is better to use other options first, such as the Control Panel. Make changes in the Registry only under the guidance of a Microsoft technical note or a Microsoft support person.

10

HKEY_CURRENT_USER

The HKEY_CURRENT_USER key contains information about the desktop setup for the account presently logged on to the server console. It contains data on color combinations, font sizes and type, the keyboard layout, the Taskbar, clock configuration, and nearly any setup action you have made on the desktop. For example, if you want to change the environment parameter governing where temporary files are stored for applications, you can do it from here. The new path is set by clicking the Environment subkey under the HKEY_CURRENT_USER root key and changing the path shown as the value in the right pane. The sounds associated with a given event can be set by clicking the path \HKEY_CURRENT_USER\AppEvents\EventLabels and then changing the sound value for a particular event, such as the event to close a window, which is a single value in the Close subkey (\HKEY_CURRENT_USER\AppEvents\EventLabels\Close).

Another example is to change a program that runs in association with a particular file extension. For example, click the following path: \HKEY_CURRENT_USER\Software \Microsoft\Windows NT\CurrentVersion\Extensions (Figure 10-17; notice there are so many subkeys that not all of the path fits into a single screen display). If the Notepad program is associated with files ending in .txt, you can make a change to have Wordpad start instead. To do this you would change the value, "txt:REG_SZ:notepad.exe ^.txt" to "txt:REG_SZ:write.exe ^.txt," because Write.exe is the file that starts the Wordpad application.

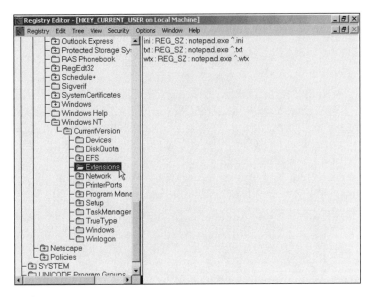

Figure 10-17   Changing Registry data for file associations

HKEY_USERS

The HKEY_USERS root key contains all of the user profiles kept on the server for all users. Each profile is listed under this root key. Within each user profile there is information identical to that viewed within the HKEY_CURRENT_USER root key. The profile used when you are logged on is one of the profiles stored under HKEY_USERS. You can make the same changes just examined, by finding the subkey for your profile and making the changes here instead of under the HKEY_CURRENT_USER root key.

HKEY_CLASSES_ROOT

The HKEY_CLASSES_ROOT key holds data to associate file extensions with programs. This is a more extensive list than the one viewed under HKEY_CURRENT_USER. Associations exist for executable files, text files, graphics files, clipboard files, audio files, and many more. These associations are used as defaults for all users who log on to Windows 2000 Server, whereas the associations in HKEY_CURRENT_USER and HKEY_USER are those that have been customized for a given user profile.

HKEY_CURRENT_CONFIG

The last root key, HKEY_CURRENT_CONFIG, has information about the current hardware profile. It holds information about the monitor type, keyboard, mouse, and other hardware characteristics for the current profile. On most servers, there is only one default hardware profile set up. Two or more profiles could be used, but this is more common for a portable computer running Windows 2000 Professional that is used with and without a docking station. One profile would have the keyboard and monitor used when on the road, and another would have a larger keyboard and monitor used when the computer is docked.

SETTING UP AND USING THE LICENSE MANAGER

Microsoft includes a licensing monitor tool called the License Manager in Windows 2000 Server. The License Manager works for Microsoft products, such as Windows 2000 Server, and for the Microsoft BackOffice products, such as Microsoft Exchange Server for e-mail, Internet Information Services for Internet connectivity, Systems Management Server to help manage network workstations and software, and SQL Server for large databases.

The License Manager is equipped to monitor licensing on a per seat or per server basis (see Chapter 5). Per seat licensing means that there needs to be a license to run a software application for the computer on which that software is loaded, no matter whether the executable files are loaded over the network from the server or from a folder on that workstation's hard disk. If there are 72 computers on a network that need to run a program, such as Microsoft Word, then there must be 72 licenses. The per server licensing approach places the licensing burden on the server instead of on the workstation. In the per server method, there only need to be enough licenses for the maximum number of client workstations that use a software application at a given time. For example, in per-seat licensing, the highest number of people who use Microsoft Word simultaneously might be 22, even though there are 72 total workstations connected to the network. In this case, only 22 Microsoft Word licenses are needed for that server. When you purchase software licenses, make sure you understand what type of licensing you are getting, and set up the license monitoring to match the type of license you have. Costs for per seat licenses are often different from costs for per server licenses. Also, some software vendors license only to a specific computer and have no per seat or per server arrangement, making that software difficult to employ in a network environment. Always read the license information or check with the software vendor to make sure you understand the licensing stipulations.

Besides tracking the per seat and per server license privilege, the License Manager is used to add new licenses or to delete licenses. Also, it can replicate licensing to other Windows 2000 servers in a domain. Thus if you have 1000 licenses for a BackOffice product and 15 Windows 2000 servers, the License Manager can spread the licenses across all servers or workstations (depending on the licensing mode). The License Manager does not stop use of software when the number of users exceeds the number of licenses, it only keeps statistics on use and provides information when there is a need to purchase more licenses. However, it does have the capability to revoke a software license for a user or to limit licensing for a particular server.

The first step in setting up the License Manager is to make sure the License Logging Service is enabled and set to automatically start when the server is booted. The procedure to do that is the same as for configuring the File Replication Service discussed earlier, except that you look for the License Logging Service in the list of services.

The next step is to open the Administrative Tools menu and click Licensing. Click the License menu and then New License. The New Client Access License dialog box opens, as shown in Figure 10-18, from which you can add new licenses as you purchase them (try Hands-on Project 10-6).

Figure 10-18 Adding new licenses

To view the software that is installed, click the View menu in the License Manager, and click Products View. The installed products are listed with information about the per-seat and per-server allocation of the licenses, plus the maximum license use that has been reached. Other information is available as well, such as the purchase history. To view the license usage statistics, click the View menu in the License Manager and then click Clients, which shows the licensed and unlicensed usage.

CHAPTER SUMMARY

❑ Using the Distributed File System (Dfs) enables both you and your users to be more productive. For users, Dfs means that they can more easily find and access important shared folders. For you, Dfs simplifies the management of shared folders, particularly when you manage multiple servers. Dfs can be implemented using the standalone or domain model. When Dfs is implemented in a domain, it can be used to provide fault tolerance, load balancing, and a single place from which to back up critical files.

❑ Disk quotas are an important feature for any type of server, whether standalone or in a domain. Before disk quotas, it was possible for the rapid accumulation of files, particularly temporary and unused files, to occupy huge amounts of disk space. By enabling disk quotas, you can accomplish two important tasks: (1) obtain statistics for disk capacity planning and (2) place limits on the amount of disk space that individual users can occupy. Disk quotas can be used in a positive sense to help users learn how to clean up unused files, make more disk space available for all purposes, and save money on disk resources.

❑ The Add/Remove Programs tool in the Control Panel is provided to help you manage software installations, easily upgrade software, and easily remove software. Add/Remove Programs works with the Registry to configure software and track software elements. When you install software, there may be times when it is necessary to edit the Registry as a way to tune a particular software or hardware feature.

❑ When you install software, plan to use the Microsoft License Manager to help track the available licenses and determine when more licenses must be purchased.

The next chapter focuses on managing local and network printing resources in Windows 2000 Server. Network printing services are yet another resource that is especially popular among users.

KEY TERMS

application program interface (**API**) — Functions or programming features in a system that programmers can use for network links, links to messaging services, or interfaces to other systems.

cache timeout — The amount of time that a Dfs shared folder is retained in the client operating system's cache for fast access.

Dfs link — A path that is established between a shared folder in a domain and a Dfs root.

Dfs root — The main Active Directory container that holds Dfs links to shared folders in a domain.

Dfs topology — Applies to a domain-based Dfs model and encompasses the Dfs root, Dfs links to the root, and servers on which the Dfs structure is replicated.

disk quota — Allocating a specific amount of disk space to a user or application, with the ability to ensure that the user or application cannot use more disk space than is specified in the allocation.

Distributed File System (**Dfs**) — A system that enables folders shared from multiple computers to appear as though they exist in one centralized hierarchy of folders instead of on many different computers.

hive — A set of related Registry keys and subkeys stored as a file.

kernel mode — Protected environment in which the Windows 2000 operating system kernel runs, consisting of a protected memory area and privileges to directly execute system services, access the CPU, run I/O operations, and conduct other basic operating system functions.

key — A category of information contained in the Windows 2000 Registry, such as hardware or software.

license monitoring — A process used on network servers to be certain the number of software licenses in use does not exceed the number for which the network is authorized.

load balancing — On a single server, distributing resources across multiple server disk drives and paths for better server response; on multiple network servers, distributing resources across two or more servers for better server and network performance.

master folder — The main folder that provides master files and folders for a Dfs root or link when replication is enabled.

network-compatible program — Software that can operate in a multiuser environment using network or e-mail communication APIs.

Registry — A database used to store information about the configuration, program setup, devices, drivers, and other data important to the setup of a computer running Windows 2000, Windows NT, Windows 98, or Windows 95.

replica set — A grouping of shared folders in a Dfs root that are replicated or copied to all servers that participate in Dfs replication. When changes are made to Dfs shared folders, all of the participating servers are automatically or manually synchronized so that they have the same copy.

root key — Also called a subtree, the highest category of data contained in the Registry. There are five root keys.

subkey — A key within a Registry key, similar to a subfolder under a folder.

10

subtree — Same as root key.

user mode — A special operating mode in Windows 2000 used for running programs in a memory area kept separate from that used by the kernel and in which the program cannot access the kernel or operating system services except through an API.

value — A data parameter in the Registry stored as a value in decimal, binary, or text format.

REVIEW QUESTIONS

1. The computer planning committee at your company is working to project Windows 2000 Server disk capacity needs for the next two years, as part of the computer equipment budgeting process. Because you are part of the committee, they ask you if there is any way to gather statistics on present disk use over a three-month period to help in making projections. How can you obtain the statistics that they want?

   a. Turn on disk auditing for each user's account, and compile the audit reports.

   b. Set default disk quotas to a low number, and gather statistics based on the resulting reports that users are out of disk space.

   c. Enable disk quotas, and after three months copy the disk quota statistics into a spreadsheet.

   d. There is no easy way to gather the statistics except to ask all employees to calculate the space they use.

2. Which of the following are Dfs models that you can set up in Windows 2000 Server?

   a. standalone

   b. transitive

   c. domain-based

   d. all of the above

   e. only a and b

   f. only a and c

3. You have set up Dfs replication among four servers, but none of the shared folders is being replicated automatically. What might you do to solve the problem?

   a. Make sure that the Dfs replicate permission box is checked for Allow in the Dfs root.

   b. Make sure that you have set up automatic replication and not manual replication.

   c. Use the Computer Management tool to determine if the File Replication service is started.

   d. All of the above may be a source of the problem.

   e. Only a and b are possibilities.

   f. Only b and c are possibilities.

4. You need to uninstall a display monitor driver in Windows 2000 Server so that you can set up a new monitor and driver. Which is the safest way to uninstall the driver?

a. Use the Device Manager.

b. Use Regedit to delete the driver in the Registry's HKEY_LOCAL_MACHINE root key.

c. Use Regdt32 to delete the driver in the Registry's HKEY_LOCAL_MACHINE root key.

d. Use the Add/Remove Programs icon in the Control Panel.

5. Your assistant is attempting to set up a second Dfs root on a server, but the New Dfs Root Wizard will not let him proceed. What is the problem?

a. He did not reboot the server after creating the first Dfs root.

b. The first Dfs root must contain at least two Dfs links before a second Dfs root can be set up.

c. He did not rescan the disks after creating the first Dfs root.

d. Only one Dfs root can be created on a server.

6. It is the end of the fiscal year, and your boss has money still budgeted to purchase additional licenses for users to access your Windows 2000 server. Unfortunately, he has waited until the last minute and needs the information by this afternoon. How can you quickly assess present use of licenses?

a. Check the Server service properties, which can show the number of times users have been prevented from logging on as a result of a shortage of licenses.

b. Check the statistics in the License Manager.

c. Check the connection statistics available through the Network and Dial-up Connections tool.

d. There is no way to gather the information on short notice because you must first set up license quotas on each volume.

7. You currently have shared folders set up on seven Windows 2000 servers, which are in different locations and on different subnets of your organization. Network traffic on two of those subnets is very intense each afternoon. What can you do to balance the load?

a. Move all of the shared folders to the server on the subnet with the least traffic.

b. Decrease the cache timeout for each shared folder.

c. Set up all of the folders via Dfs and use replication.

d. Set up all of the folders via Dfs and then set the speed of the Dfs links to 100 Mbps for those on the traffic-intense subnets.

10

8. Which of the following is (are) true about permissions used on a Dfs root?

    a. There is no Full Control permission, because only the server Administrator can have the equivalent access.

    b. Special permissions can be set up to customize access.

    c. Dfs permissions must be set up for each Dfs link.

    d. All of the above are true.

    e. Only a and b are true.

    f. Only a and c are true.

9. The chief financial officer of your organization is very opposed to your accessing Microsoft Excel and other application programs on the same server that has the organization's accounting and payroll files, because she believes that if Excel hangs it will make the server inaccessible when she is in the middle of updating a file. What might you say to alleviate her worries?

    a. Explain that application software like Excel runs in user mode.

    b. Explain that application software like Excel runs in kernel mode.

    c. Agree to manually allocate a separate RAM location for the applications that you run.

    d. Set your own disk quota to *Deny disk space to users exceeding quota limit*, so that if you go over your quota it will not affect anyone else's server access.

10. Which of the following can contain hives?

    a. a Dfs link

    b. the Registry

    c. a Dfs root

    d. software licensing groups

11. The management in your organization wants to limit all employees to 7 MB of disk space, on each volume which they can use to store files in shared folders and in home folders. What is the best way to accomplish this?

    a. Set up a default disk quota of 7 MB on each shared volume.

    b. Set up a disk quota for each user via the Active Directory Users and Computers tool.

    c. Set up a disk quota of 7 MB for each user account on each volume.

    d. It is not possible to set up disk quotas of 7 MB, because quotas are set in 2 MB increments.

12. Which of the following are part of the Dfs topology when Dfs is set up in a domain?

    a. roots

    b. replica sets

    c. links

    d. all of the above

e. only a and b

f. only a and c

13. It is better to implement Dfs folder sharing on:

   a. FAT-formatted disks because it is faster using FAT

   b. a domain controller instead of a member server because DNS servers give domain controllers higher priority

   c. NTFS-formatted disks because of better security

   d. standalone servers, which enable a deeper folder/subfolder tree structure

14. Sara and Richard each have a disk quota of 2 MB. Recently Sara has taken ownership of an 800 KB database file previously owned by Richard. How does this action affect their disk quotas?

   a. When ownership of a file is transferred, that file is exempt from the disk quota allotment.

   b. The disk quotas of Sara and Richard are unchanged.

   c. Sara's disk quota is now 2.8 MB, but Richard's stays the same.

   d. Sara has 800 KB less space out of the 2 MB quota, and Richard has 800 KB more.

15. ErrorControl:REG_DWORD:0 is an example of:

   a. a Dfs root

   b. a Registry key

   c. a Registry value

   d. a Dfs script command

16. You set up the Dfs root so that the domain local Users group is allowed Read permissions only. The Docs shared folder that is part of the Dfs setup allows the same group Modify permissions. What permissions does the Users group have for that folder within Dfs?

   a. Read

   b. no permissions, because there is a permission conflict

   c. Modify

   d. Full Control, but without the ability to take ownership

17. You have installed a 32-bit Windows application in Windows 2000 Server that includes many .dll and other files, some of which have been copied to the \Winnt\System32 folder. Today you need to remove that application. How do you remove it?

   a. Delete the desktop icon that starts the application.

   b. Delete the folder that contains the application, and use My Computer to search for its related .dll files and delete those as well.

   c. Delete the .exe file that starts the application.

   d. Use the Add/Remove Programs tool in the Control Panel.

10

18. You have received from an Internet newsgroup a technical alert advising you to change a Registry parameter in all user profiles in Windows 2000 Server. What are you likely to edit in the Registry?

    a. the HKEY_USERS root key

    b. the SYSTEM subkey

    c. the HKEY_CLASSES_ROOT root key

    d. the SOFTWARE subkey

19. Which of the following can be set up in the Dfs root properties?

    a. auditing

    b. taking ownership

    c. permissions

    d. all of the above

    e. only a and c

    f. only b and c

20. How can you delete a Dfs link?

    a. Right-click the link in the Distributed File System management tool, and click Remove Dfs link.

    b. Deactivate the Dfs link and then delete it in the Distributed File System management tool.

    c. Delete its root and then delete the link in the Distributed File System management tool.

    d. To ensure data security, you cannot delete a link after it is created.

21. It is 3:00 p.m. on a Friday afternoon, and several people are calling in a panic to report that they do not see several shared folders on the main server, which you know is home to their Dfs root. What is the first step that you should take?

    a. Restart the File Replication service.

    b. Run to the machine room and make sure that the main server is booted and working normally.

    c. Use the Distributed File System management tool to check the status of the root and of the links in question.

    d. Use the Dfs tool to restart the Dfs root and to rescan its links.

22. Which of the following are maintenance tasks that you can perform on your Dfs system of shared folders?

    a. Regularly check for folders that are no longer in use and that should be deleted.

    b. Periodically check the cache timeout values to make sure that they are appropriate to how particular folders are used.

    c. Use My Computer to periodically move folders from high-impact servers to those with a lower impact, and then establish new links.

    d. all of the above

    e. only a and b

    f. only a and c

23. The lead research scientist in your company needs to work over the weekend to prepare information for a lecture she is presenting on Monday. She does not know how close she is to reaching her disk quota and is calling you to find out. How can you determine where she stands?

    a. There is no way to determine where she stands, but you can increase her quota to make sure there is no problem.

    b. Check the Quota Entries dialog box in the properties of the shared disk volume that she uses.

    c. Open the Command Prompt window and use the Quota command along with her account name to find out.

    d. Use the Distributed File System management tool to query quotas.

24. Your boss has been reading about companies that are lax in making sure that they have enough licenses for the software that they use. You already know that you have enough Windows 2000 Server licenses, but you are not sure about licenses for SQL Server and Exchange Server. How can you find out if use has exceeded the number of licenses for these products?

    a. Check in the License Manager.

    b. Check the Registry, which can track the number of times the license limit has been exceeded.

    c. Look for license alerts displayed by the Registry at the server's console.

    d. Create a license monitor filter to capture the names of accounts that exceed license limitations.

25. Which of the following would you find in the Registry?

    a. keys

    b. subtrees

    c. root keys

    d. all of the above

    e. only a and b

    f. only a and c

10

HANDS-ON PROJECTS

Project 10-1

Suppose that the financial auditors are visiting your organization and you have decided to organize Dfs shared folders for all spreadsheets that they must view. In this project you practice creating a Dfs root using the domain-based model. The server on which you create the root must have no other Dfs root, and the Active Directory must already be installed. Also, before you start, check with your instructor about which drive path to use for the Dfs root.

To create a Dfs root:

1. Click **Start**, point to **Programs**, point to **Administrative Tools**, and click **Distributed File System**.
2. Click **Distributed File System** in the console tree.
3. Click the **Action** menu, click **New Dfs root**, and click **Next** after the New Dfs Root Wizard starts.
4. Click **Create a domain Dfs root**, if it is not already selected. Click **Next**.
5. Make sure the domain name is displayed in the Domain name box, or use a different domain per your instructor's permission. What other information is displayed in the dialog box? Click **Next**.
6. Click the **Browse** button to find the server. What information is displayed in the Find Computers window that can help you locate a server, such as a domain controller? Double-click the server on which the Dfs root will reside, and then click **Next**.
7. Click **Create a new share**. Enter the path specified by your instructor, such as **D:\Spreadsheets**, and enter **Spreadsheets** as the share name. Click **Next**. Click **Yes** to confirm that you want to create a new folder.
8. Use the default Dfs root name, **Spreadsheets**, and enter the comment **Sales history spreadsheets**. Click **Next**.
9. Examine the summary of information that you specified. How might you reenter information if you find that you made a mistake in earlier steps? Record the summary information in your lab journal or in a word-processed document. Click **Finish**.
10. Look for the new root in the console tree under Distributed file system.
11. Leave the console tree open for the next project.

Project 10-2

In this project, you practice creating, customizing, and then deleting a Dfs link in preparation for the auditors. Before you start, obtain the name and location of a shared folder from your instructor (or create a shared folder on the server from which you are working, and use that folder for this project).

To create the new Dfs link:

1. Right-click the **Spreadsheets** root under the tree in the left pane.
2. Click **New Dfs Link**.

3. Enter **Projects** in the Link name box. What happens in the *When a user opens* text box as you enter the link name? Click **Browse** to find the computer and shared folder that you obtained from your instructor (or that you created in advance for this project). Provide a comment to describe the link, such as **Project costs**.

4. Enter **2000** in the Clients cache this referral for _____ seconds box.

5. Click **OK**. (If you get an error message, make sure that the account you are using has access to the shared folder for the link, that you have a good network connection, and that the computer with the shared folder is compatible with Dfs.)

6. In the left pane, click the link you created, if it is not already highlighted. What information is displayed under the Replica(s) column in the right pane? Record your observations in your lab journal or in a word-processed document.

Assume that the contents of the link you created will not change often and that you need to customize the cache timeout.

To customize the cache timeout for a Dfs link:

1. Right-click the link you created, and click **Properties**.

2. Make sure the **General** tab is displayed.

3. Notice the value already set in the Clients cache this referral for _____ seconds parameter and record your observation in your lab journal or in a word-processed document.

4. Enter **500** as the new cache timeout value.

5. Click **OK**.

When the auditors are finished with this particular link, you delete it in an effort to keep unneeded links from proliferating.

To remove the Dfs link that you just created:

1. Right-click the link that you created in the left pane.

2. Click **Remove Dfs Link**.

3. Click **Yes**.

4. Note in your lab journal or in a word-processed document if there is a way to recover the link, such as from the Recycle Bin or by clicking an Undo button.

Project 10-3

In this hands-on activity assume that the financial auditors in your organization will need to access the Dfs root link, but your boss wants you to make sure they cannot write to any of the folders. Finally, you will delete the Dfs root that you created in Project 10-1, after the auditors are finished examining the information.

To set up security:

1. Right-click the **Spreadsheets** root that you created in Project 10-1.

2. Record the options that you see in your lab journal or in a word-processed document.

3. Click **Properties**.

4. What tabs are displayed in the Properties dialog box? What is the purpose of each tab?

5. Click the **Security** tab.

6. How do the options on this tab compare with those that you would find on a regular Windows 2000 Server folder? What groups are already assigned permissions for the Dfs root?

7. Click **Authenticated Users** and notice what permissions this group has.

8. Click the **Add** button.

9. Double-click the **Guests** group (or another group that is not already listed in Step 6), and click **OK**.

10. What permissions are automatically given to the Guests group (or other group that you used in Step 9)?

11. Click the **Deny** box for the **Write** permission. Click **Apply** and then click **Yes**.

12. Practice removing the Guests group by clicking that group and then clicking **Remove**. Click **OK**.

To delete the Dfs root:

1. Right-click the **Spreadsheets** root that you created in Project 10-1.

2. Click **Delete Dfs Root**.

3. Click **Yes** to confirm the deletion.

4. Close the Distributed File System console.

Project 10-4

The main disk on your server contains user home folders, and you discover that users are rapidly occupying vital disk space. In this project you set up default disk quotas on that NTFS volume.

To configure the default disk quotas:

1. Open **My Computer** and right-click an NTFS formatted volume, such as drive **C**.

2. Click **Properties** and then click the **Quota** tab. If the Quota tab is not displayed, what does this mean?

3. Click **Enable quota management** if it is not already selected.

4. Click **Deny disk space to users exceeding quota limit** if it is not already selected.

5. Click **Limit disk space to** and enter **20** in the first box, then select **MB** in the box next to it.

6. Enter **18** and **MB** as the warning level.

7. Click **Log event when a user exceeds their quota limit**.

8. Leave the box blank for **Log event when a user exceeds their warning level** (to reduce the number of event log entries).

9. Click the **Quota Entries** button to view quota entries. How would you set 2 MB as the disk quota limit for the Guest account?

10. Close the Quota Entries dialog box, and then click **OK**. Click **Yes** if you are asked to enable the quota system.

Project 10-5

In this project you view where Control Panel settings are stored in the Registry and practice using the Regedt32 editor.

To view the Control Panel settings:

1. Click **Start**, click **Run**, and enter **regedt32** in the Open box. Click **OK**.

2. Click the **Options** menu and place a checkmark in front of **Read Only Mode** to make sure that you cannot inadvertently change the Registry contents during this project.

3. Access the **HKEY_CURRENT_USER** window and double-click **Control Panel**.

4. What Control Panel subkeys do you see? Record your observations in your lab journal or in a word-processed document.

5. Double-click **Accessibility**. What are the subkeys displayed?

6. Click **MouseKeys** to view the values set for that subkey.

7. Click two or three other subkeys to view their values.

8. Click a value and then click the **Edit** menu to view how to modify a value, delete a value, or add a new one (but absolutely do not make any changes).

9. Close the Registry editor.

Project 10-6

In this activity you view which products are installed via the License Manager, and then you add 10 new Windows 2000 Server licenses that your organization has purchased.

To use the License Manager:

1. Click **Start**, point to **Programs**, point to **Administrative Tools**, and click **Licensing**.

2. Click the **View** menu and then click **Products View**.

3. Notice the products that are installed under the Product column. Also notice the number of licenses. The last column, Per Server Reached, shows the maximum number of users who have used the licenses at a given time. Record your observations.

4. Click **Windows Server** under the Product column.

5. Click the **License** menu and then click **New License**.

6. Make sure **Windows Server** is selected in the Product scroll box.

7. Enter **10** in the Quantity box.

8. Click the radio button for the License mode, Per Seat or Per Server (unless this is already selected by default).

10

9. Add the comment **New licenses for student lab**.

10. Click **OK**. If a licensing agreement message is displayed, check the box to indicate that you agree with the licensing terms and then click **OK**. Close the License Manager.

CASE PROJECT

Aspen Consulting Project: Configuring Dfs, Disk Quotas, and Licensing

Precision Digital is a company that makes compact discs for digital use, such as CD-ROMs, CD-Rs, and CD-RWs. They design, manufacture, sell, and research discs entirely for computer-related digital applications. Precision Digital has employees located in four buildings, and there is a Windows 2000 server in each building. All servers are in one domain. One building houses the administrative and business offices, one is used for research teams, and the other two are used to manufacture discs. Precision Digital's server administrator has just resigned, and they are in the process of hiring a new one. In the interim, they have hired you through Aspen Consulting to help work on several special projects.

1. Each server contains from 10 to 20 shared folders that are accessed by various users throughout the company. The problem is that users are still very confused about which folders are on which servers. As a result, they waste a lot of time trying to find the information that they need. Precision Digital asks you to help them develop a way to make the folders easier to find and access. Explain to Precision Digital's administrative team how Dfs works and how it can be of value in their situation. Suggest a very general Dfs folder structure that they might implement.

2. After you make your presentation about Dfs, the human resources director at Precision Digital calls to let you know that they have hired a new server administrator, but the new administrator has only worked with other server operating systems, not with Windows 2000. Prepare an explanation for the new administrator about how to set up Dfs in a domain.

3. While you are training the new administrator, you receive a call from a research team leader that one of the volumes on the server used by the research groups is full. Your first recommendation is to have users delete old and temporary files on that volume. The team leader mentions that none of the company's servers is set up to limit the amount of disk space that a user might occupy. Discuss how the company can set limits on disk usage and how it can better plan disk capacity in the future.

4. One of your projects is to install Microsoft Office on the server used by the administrative offices. Explain in general terms how to install the software. Also, prepare a checklist for the new administrator about the steps to take before installing new software on a server.

5. The previous administrator purchased 20 new licenses for the administrative server. Explain how to install the licenses. Also, explain how to view the current license usage statistics.

OPTIONAL CASE PROJECTS FOR TEAMS

Team Case One

Because Dfs can be of vital importance to organizations, Mark Arnez is concerned about developing a table with steps or a flowchart for troubleshooting Dfs. He asks you to form a group to develop a complete set of troubleshooting steps.

Team Case Two

Setting disk quotas has two dimensions: political and technical. Mark Arnez asks you to form a group to explore both elements for setting up disk quotas. Create a report in which the first section deals with how to prepare users in an organization for the implementation of disk quotas. In the second section, explain different scenarios for setting up disk quotas, such as scenarios involving default quotas, individual user account quotas, and gathering information about disk use before setting quotas.

10

11

INSTALLING AND MANAGING PRINTERS

After reading this chapter and completing the exercises you will be able to:

♦ Explain and apply the fundamentals of Windows 2000 Server printing

♦ Install local, network, and Internet printing services in Windows 2000 Server

♦ Configure printing services for all types of needs

♦ Manage printers and print services

♦ Solve common printing problems

Network printing is one of the most used resources on any network, because the word-processing, database, computer graphics, and other work performed by users often ends with a printed document as the final product. Printed materials are used for important meetings, presentations, information analysis, and a huge realm of other activities. Because printing is so important, it is also a major source of frustration to users when it does not work well. Fortunately, Windows 2000 Server networks have simplified printing and made it more reliable. Windows 2000 print services are much easier to set up and manage than those in many other server network operating systems that require you to know how to use an army of tools. In Windows 2000 Server, most of the setup and management work is performed from one place, the Printers folder.

In this chapter you learn the basics of how Windows 2000 Server printing works on a local computer, a network, or the Internet. You learn how to set up local, network, and Internet printing services for all kinds of uses, and how to manage them. You also learn to solve problems when printing does not go as planned, for instance when one printer fails and you want to transfer its workload to another printer.

An Overview of Windows 2000 Printing

The network printing process on Windows 2000 Server LANs begins when a client workstation user decides to print a file. For example, in a law firm, a Microsoft Word user prints a file, which goes to the printer designated in the user's Printer Setup configuration within Word. The Printer Setup may direct the printout to the user's local printer or to a network printer available through a printer share for which the user has permission. A shared printer can be a workstation sharing a printer, a printer attached to the file server, or a printer attached to a print server device. The workstation that initially generates the print job is the network **print client**, and the computer offering the printer share is the network **print server**.

A shared printer is an object, like a folder, that is made available to network users for print services. Microsoft also includes faxes as **print device** objects that can be treated in the same way as printers. The print device is offered from a server, workstation, or print server device. Several manufacturers make print server devices that connect directly to the network without the need of an attached computer. These devices eliminate dependence on a computer, which may be shut off or inconveniently located. Some print server devices are small boxes that connect to the network at one end of the box and to one or more printers at the other. Another kind of print server is a card that is mounted inside the printer, with a network port similar to a NIC on the card. One of the most commonly used print server cards is Hewlett-Packard's JetDirect card, used in many laser printers for network printing. Figure 11-1 shows examples of print server devices.

Figure 11-1   Print server devices

When the printout goes to a printer share, it is temporarily spooled in specially designated disk storage and held until it is sent to be printed. **Spooling** frees the server CPU to handle other processing requests in addition to print requests.

Print jobs are usually printed in the same order as received, unless an administrator or printer operator (with appropriate permissions) changes the order because of a high-priority situation. The server administrator can disable spooling, but this is rare because it defeats the value of background print services, which free server and client resources for other tasks.

When its turn comes, the print file is sent to the printer along with formatting instructions. The formatting instructions are provided by a **printer driver** that holds configuration information for the given printer. The formatting and configuration information includes instructions to reset the printer before starting, information about printing fonts, and special printer control codes.

The printer driver resides on the computer offering the printer services (for local and network print jobs) and also can reside on the workstation client sending the print job. For example, when you send a print job to be printed on a Windows 2000 server print share, your printout is formatted using the printer driver at your workstation and then further interpreted by print services software on the print server. The printer driver is either contained on the Windows 2000 Server CD-ROM or obtained from the printer manufacturer.

When the user selects the option to use a printer share, the document to be printed is formatted for the driver on that share. The printer can start printing the file as soon as the first page is received, or it can be instructed to print the file only when all pages have been received. The advantage of printing immediately, rather than waiting for the entire print file to be spooled, is that printing starts sooner. The disadvantage is that in offices where there are constant print requests, a pause at a workstation sending a print job may result in another job printing pages in the middle of the first job. If this is a problem, it is better to have the printer share wait until the entire file is spooled. This instruction is set at the shared printer. Figure 11-2 shows a summary of printing stages.

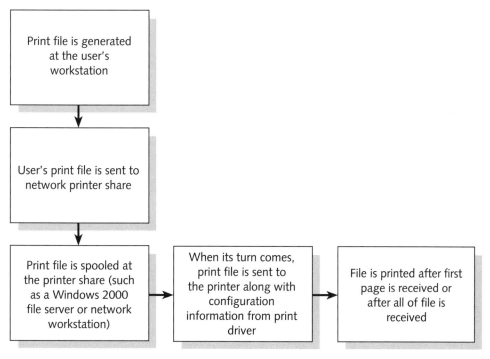

Figure 11-2   Printing stages

How Network Printing Works

In technical terms, both the network print client and the network print server run specific processes to finally deliver a print job to a printer. The first stage in the process is when the software application at the client generates a print file. As it creates the print file, the application communicates with the Windows **graphics device interface (GDI)**. The GDI integrates information about the print file—such as word-processing codes for fonts, colors, and embedded graphics objects—with information obtained from the printer driver installed at the client for the target printer, in a process that Microsoft calls rendering. When the GDI is finished, the print file is formatted with control codes to implement the special graphics, font, and color characteristics of the file. At the same time, the software application places the print file in the client's spooler by writing the file, called the **spool file**, to a subfolder used for spooling. In the Windows 95, 98, NT, and 2000 operating systems, a **spooler** is a group of DLLs, information files, and programs that processes print jobs for printing. Spool files are kept in the \Winnt\system32\spool\printers folder in Windows 2000 Server.

CAUTION
Large print files cannot be processed if there is inadequate disk space on which to store spooled files. Make sure clients and the server have sufficient disk space to handle the largest print requests, particularly for huge graphics and color files that are targeted for a color printer or plotter.

The remote print provider at the client makes a remote procedure call to the network print server to which the print file is targeted, such as a Windows 2000 server. If the print server is responding and ready to accept the print file, the remote printer transmits that file from the client's spooler folder to the Server service on Windows 2000 Server.

The network print server uses four processes to receive and process a print file: router, print provider, print processor, and print monitor. The router, print provider, and print processor all are pieces of the network print server's spooler. Once it is contacted by the remote print provider on the print client, the Server service calls its router, the Print Spooler service. The router directs the print file to the print provider, which stores it in a spool file until it can be sent to the printer. While the file is spooled, the print provider works with the print processor to ensure that the file is formatted to use the right data type, such as TEXT or RAW. When the spool file is fully formatted for transmission to the printer, the print monitor pulls it from the spooler's disk storage and sends it off to the printer.

How Internet Printing Works

When a print job is processed over the Internet or an intranet, the Internet Information Services (IIS) must be installed and running in Windows 2000 Server (see Chapter 13), and the client must connect to the Windows 2000 Server IIS using a Web browser, such as Internet Explorer 4 or higher. The print process on the client is nearly the same as for network printing, with a couple of exceptions. One exception is that it is the browser that sends the print file to the GDI instead of a software application such as Word. Another exception is that the remote print provider at the client makes a remote procedure call to the IIS on the Windows 2000 Server. The remote procedure call is made through the HTTP protocol (see Chapter 3), which transports another protocol, called the **Internet Printing Protocol (IPP)**. The IPP encapsulates the remote procedure call and print process information and is transported in HTTP just as a human passenger is transported inside a bus along a highway. The IIS sends the IPP encapsulated information to its HTTP print server, which is composed of the files contained in the folder \Program Files\Common Files\Microsoft SharedWeb Server Extensions\40\Isapi. The HTTP print server works with the regular Windows 2000 spooler services—the print provider, print processor, and print monitor processes—to prepare the print file for transmission to the target printer.

Print Job Data Types

Each print processor is designed to work with a specific data type. A **data type** is the way in which information is formatted and presented in the print file. Some data types involve minimal data formatting for printing, and others involve more extensive formatting. Different data types are used to accommodate printing from different kinds of clients, and they consists of the following:

- RAW
- RAW with FF appended
- RAW with FF auto
- TEXT
- Enhanced metafile (EMF)
- PSCRIPT1

A print file formatted as the RAW data type is often used for files sent from MS-DOS, Windows 3.x, and UNIX clients. It is also the default setting for a PostScript printer (discussed later in this chapter). A RAW print file is intended to be printed by the print server with no additional formatting. In the data type RAW with FF appended, the FF is a form-feed code placed at the end of the print file. Some non-Windows and older 16-bit Windows software do not place a form feed at the end of a print file. The form feed is used to make sure the last page of the file is printed. When RAW with FF appended is designated, the print code for a form feed is written by the Windows 2000 Server print processor as the last thing in the print file. RAW with FF auto means that the print processor checks the print file for a form feed as the last character set, before appending a form feed at the end. If there already is a form feed, it does not add anything to the file.

 Prior to the ability to insert a form feed in the print file, many users found it necessary to press the form feed button on a printer or to send another print job to print the last page.

The TEXT data type is used for printing text files formatted according to the ANSI standard that uses values between 0 and 255 to represent characters, numbers, and symbols. You would use the TEXT data type for printing many types of MS-DOS print files, such as text files printed from older word processors or MS-DOS text editors such as EDLIN.

Windows 95, 98, NT, and 2000 clients use the enhanced metafile (EMF) data type. This is the data type that is created when a print file is prepared by the GDI at the client. EMF print files offer a distinct advantage in Windows operating system environments because they are very portable from computer to computer. The RAW, TEXT, and EMF data types are handled by the Windows 2000 *WinPrint* print processor and can be configured when you configure a printer (try Hands-on Project 11-1).

The PSCRIPT1 data type is intended for Macintosh clients that print on a Windows 2000 print server. The print processor uses this data type to translate a PostScript coded print file into one that can be printed on a non-PostScript printer. Using the PSCRIPT1 data type, the Windows 2000 print processor builds a bitmap file, which is again reformatted to be printed on the target printer. If you use this data type, keep in mind that bitmap files can be very large, requiring extra disk space for the spooler. The PSCRIPT1 data type is offered through the *SFMPSPRT* print processor when you configure a printer.

Windows 2000 Print Monitors

Microsoft provides a range of print monitors with Windows 2000 Server. The print monitors, located in the folder \Winnt\system32, are used to do local printing and to print using specialized print servers such as those from Hewlett-Packard, Macintosh, and others. **Local printing** refers to printing on the same computer to which print devices are attached. When you install a local or network printer in Windows 2000 Server, configure the port to which the printer is connected so that it uses one of the print monitors provided through Windows 2000 Server.

The local print monitor is the file Localmon.dll, which handles print jobs sent to a local physical port on the server, such as an LPT or COM port, and is set up by using the *Local Port* option in the printer configuration. (try Hands-on Project 11-2 to practice configuring the local port option). It also sends print jobs to a file, if you specify *FILE* as the port. When a print job is sent to FILE, there is a prompt to supply a filename.

The combination of Ipmontr.dll and Tcpmon.dll files is used for TCP/IP-based printers that are connected to the network through print server cards or print servers, as shown in Figure 11-1. When you configure a printer to use a *Standard TCP/IP Port*, these are the print monitors that are used.

The line printer (LPR) print monitor consists of two files, Lprmon.dll and Lpr.exe, and is used when you configure a printer for an LPR port. This is employed for transmitting files by means of the Microsoft TCP/IP Printing service for printers connected to a UNIX, DEC VAX, or IBM mainframe computer or from these computers as clients to printers attached to Windows 2000 servers. To use this, you first need to install the TCP/IP protocol in Windows 2000 Server and Print Services for UNIX (part of the Other Network File and Print Services that is a Windows component installed through Add/Remove Programs in the Control Panel). Also, to use LPR, there must be a line printer daemon (LPD) server. The LPD server can be a UNIX computer, an MVS (IBM mainframe) computer with TCP/IP, a computer running Windows NT or 2000, or a print server device such as a Hewlett-Packard JetDirect card in a Hewlett-Packard printer. If you create an LPR port on the server, you will need to provide the IP address of the LPD server.

> **TIP** LPR is not one of the regular options provided in the port setup, but Lprmon.dll and Lpr.exe are included with Windows 2000 Server. Use the New Port Type option on the Port tab in the printer properties to implement it. LPR combined with an LPD server provides a way to integrate printing on a mainframe, such as an IBM mainframe running open MVS, with network printers. Through it you can use Windows 98 or Windows 2000 Professional, for example, to print a mainframe file to a network printer. Also, when using LPR, you may need to experiment with using either RAW or TEXT as the data type, depending on the software used at the client.

As mentioned in the previous paragraphs, there are several ways to send print jobs to a Hewlett-Packard printer containing a JetDirect print server card, such as using a standard TCP/IP print setup or using LPR when communication with host mainframe computers is involved. Some older HP printers, such as the HP 4Si, and even newer printers may have older JetDirect cards that do not support TCP/IP communications. For these older cards, Hewlett-Packard provides print handling software that employs the option to use the DLC protocol (see Chapter 3). Windows 2000 Server offers a DLC-compatible print monitor, called Hpmon.dll, which even comes with a help file, called Hpmon.hlp, to help you set up a JetDirect card. Both print monitor and help file are located in the folder \Winnt\system32. If you choose to use this monitor, make sure you also install the Microsoft DLC protocol, because Hpmon.dll only works through DLC. Hpmon.dll is set up by using the *Hewlett-Packard Network Port* configuration option.

11

> **TIP** If you are working on a Microsoft network in which computers cannot send printouts to an HP printer connected to the network through a print server card, determine if the print share is set up to use Hpmon.dll. If it is, each workstation client that needs to use the printer must have DLC installed.

Apple LaserWriter printers and print servers can be used on a Microsoft network by implementing the Macintosh print monitor, Sfmmon.dll. This monitor uses the AppleTalk protocol (see Chapter 3), which means that the Services for Macintosh must be installed on Windows 2000 Server and on clients, such as Windows 2000 Professional or Windows 98. Also, Apple LaserWriters are PostScript printers, requiring that the client and print server software use a LaserWriter driver and that the Windows 2000 Server print server services be set up to use a PostScript separator page (discussed later in this chapter). Use the *AppleTalk Printing Devices Port* configuration to employ Sfmmon.dll for LaserWriter printers.

Macintosh computers can be in groupings of computers called AppleTalk zones. When you set up the AppleTalk Printing Devices Port configuration, the setup automatically detects zones.

Many newer printers use **bidirectional printing**, which means that print communications are transported both ways on the cable at the same time. The bidirectional capability is accomplished using the printer job language (PJL) print monitor, Pjlmon.dll. It makes two-way communications between the printer and the print server possible and enables the print server to automatically obtain information about the printer. Windows 2000 Server uses this monitor when you configure a printer port to enable bidirectional printing.

Printers connected to computers running early versions of NetWare (before version 5) and using IPX/SPX communications (see Chapter 3) can be set up to use Windows 2000 Server as a print server by using two steps in addition to configuring them as network printers in Windows 2000: (1) install NWLink on Windows 2000 Server and on the clients that will access the printers, and (2) install Client Services for NetWare on Windows 2000 Server.

Finally, printers that connect to a USB port on a Windows 2000 Server use the Usbmon.dll print monitor, which is automatically configured when you install and set up the printer driver.

Table 11-1 summarizes the print monitors and their associated files.

Table 11-1   Windows 2000 Server Print Monitors

Print Monitor	File(s)
Local	Localmon.dll
Standard TCP/IP printing	Ipmontr.dll and Tcpmon.dll
Line printer (LPR)	Lprmon.dll and Lpr.exe
Hewlett-Packard older JetDirect cards	Hpmon.dll
Macintosh	Sfmmon.dll
Printer job language (PJL) for bidirectional printers	Pjlmon.dll
USB printer ports	Usbmon.dll

INSTALLING LOCAL AND SHARED PRINTERS

On a Microsoft network, any server or workstation running Windows 2000 Server, Windows 2000 Professional, or Windows NT, 98, or 95 can host a shared printer for others to use through network connectivity. In Windows 2000 Server, you configure a printer that is attached to the server computer as a local printer and then enable it as a shared printer. When you share a printer, the Windows 2000 server becomes a print server. Figure 11-3 is a simplified representation of how shared printers are connected to a network, including printers connected to servers, workstations, and print server devices.

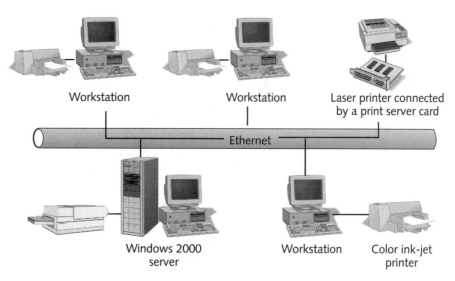

Figure 11-3   Shared network printers

Setting up a printer in Windows 2000 can follow three routes, as described in this section. One is to allow the Add/Remove Hardware Wizard to detect and set up a new printer. A second is to use the Add Printer Wizard, but to yield control to the Add/Remove Hardware Wizard. Both of these routes use Plug and Play detection and do not enable you to customize the printer setup during installation, which means you must do that later through configuring the printer's properties. If you do not use Plug and Play detection, or the printer is not detected through Plug and Play, you have more opportunity to customize the printer setup as you install it.

When you first connect a printer to a Windows 2000 server, it is recommended that you shut down the server, connect and power on the printer, and then reboot the server. Shutting down the server helps to ensure that you do not damage the port used to connect the printer (unless you are using a USB port). When the server reboots and you log on as Administrator (or with Administrator privileges), Windows 2000 Server will automatically install the printer entirely, or it will start the Found New Hardware Wizard (the same as the Add/Remove Hardware Wizard). The level of automatic detection will depend on the printer model, the printer driver, and the printer's implementation of Plug and Play. If Windows 2000 Server starts the Found New Hardware Wizard, click Next to view the screen in Figure 11-4.

11

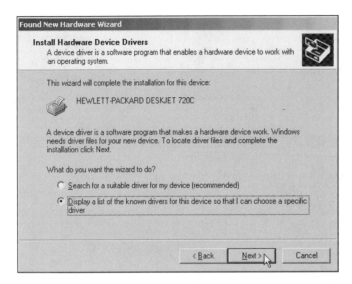

Figure 11-4   Add/Remove Hardware Wizard detecting the printer

Decide whether to have Windows 2000 Server search for a driver or display a list of drivers. For example, if you want to install the most current driver from a floppy disk or CD-ROM provided by the manufacturer, click *Display a list of the known drivers for this device so that I can choose a specific driver* and click Next. Click the Have Disk button, insert the floppy disk or CD-ROM containing the driver, provide the path to the floppy disk or CD-ROM, and click OK (the manufacturer's setup may ask you to provide additional information about the printer). Click Next, if the Wizard shows a dialog box specifying that it will install the default settings for the printer. Click Finish.

After the Add/Remove Hardware Wizard is finished, open the Printers folder to view the printer you installed and other printers installed previously. The Printers folder also contains the Add Printer Wizard, which provides another way to install a new printer. There are several ways to open the Printers folder. One is to open the Control Panel and click the Printers folder. The Printers folder also is available by clicking the Start button and pointing to Settings. Another way to manage a printer or to start a local printer installation is by clicking Start, clicking Programs, clicking Administrative Tools, clicking Configure Your Server, and clicking Print Server. Once the Printers folder is open, you can modify a printer's configuration by right-clicking that printer and clicking Properties.

CAUTION

When you use the Add/Remove Hardware Wizard to detect and install a printer, the Wizard enables printer sharing by default. Immediately check and modify the security settings in the printer's properties to make sure they are appropriate.

If you connect a printer without shutting down the server, or if the Add/Remove Hardware Wizard does not automatically detect the printer, open the Printers folder and double-click the Add Printer icon to start the Add Printer Wizard, and then click Next. The Add Printer Wizard starts, as shown in Figure 11-5. There are two radio buttons on the dialog box, one for setting up a printer connected to the server and one for setting up a printer already shared on the network. The Local printer option configures a printer directly connected to the Windows 2000 server. [The Network printer option sets up a shared printer from another computer on the network that the Windows 2000 Server can both print and manage (discussed later in this chapter)]. Click the Local printer radio button and check the option to *Automatically detect and install my Plug and Play printer*, then click Next. If the printer is detected by the Plug and Play service, the Add Printer Wizard will automatically start the Add/Remove Hardware Wizard to install the printer. When the Add/Remove Hardware Wizard finishes, it returns control to the Add Printer Wizard, which provides an option to print a test page. Click Yes to print the test page, and click Finish.

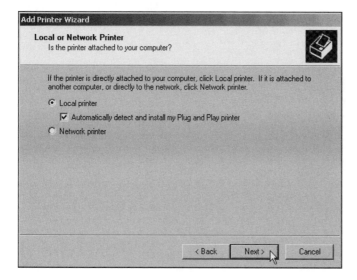

Figure 11-5   Setting up a local printer

 If Windows 2000 Server is not able to detect a printer through Plug and Play, use the Administrative Tools Computer Management tool to make sure that the Plug and Play service is started and that the service is not disabled (see Chapter 6).

If the printer is not automatically detected, you can set it up manually by clicking Next in the dialog box that reports that Windows could not detect the printer. The next screen is used to select the printer port to which the printer is attached. There are options to use parallel ports LPT1, LPT2, or LPT3, and serial ports COM1 through COM4. Also, there is an option to direct print jobs to a file, rather than to print them. This option might be useful for capturing print output to send later to a fax or to store in a file for use by a graphics program. The *Create*

a new port radio button is used to add a particular print monitor from the choices already described: AppleTalk Printing Devices, Hewlett-Packard Network Port, Local Port, and Standard TCP/IP Port.

If you do not specify a print monitor, the Wizard installs both Local Port (Localmon.dll) and Standard TCP/IP Port (Ipmontr.dll and Tcpmon.dll). Click Next after you configure the port information.

The Add Printer Wizard requests information about the printer manufacturer and the printer model, as shown in Figure 11-6. In the Manufacturers and Printers selection boxes, scroll to the manufacturer and printer model. With both selected, click Next or insert the printer driver disk supplied by the manufacturer into drive A (or use the Windows 2000 Server CD-ROM), and click Have Disk.

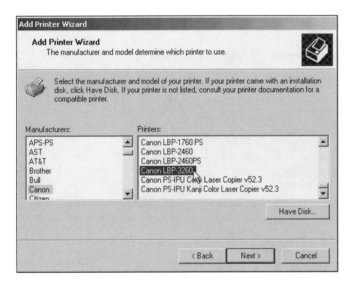

Figure 11-6 Entering the type of printer

If you click Have Disk, enter the path, such as D:\, to the driver disk in the *Copy manufacturer's files from* box in the Install From Disk dialog box. Click OK and wait briefly for the Wizard to load the driver to the server.

After the driver is loaded, you need to enter a name for the printer and to decide whether or not to set it up as a shared printer. You also need to provide a name for the printer share. The printer name will appear as an icon in the Printers folder, while the share name is what users will see when they access the printer from the network. Many server administrators use the same name for both, simplifying management of the printer by eliminating confusion from having two names for one printer. As a rule, a printer and a printer share name are easiest to manage and use if some basic guidelines are followed, such as:

- Compose names that are easily understood and spelled by those who will use the printer.

- Include a room number, floor, or workstation name to help identify where the printer is located.

- Include descriptive information about the printer, such as the type, manufacturer, or model.

For example, if the server name is Lawyer and the printer is a Hewlett-Packard DeskJet color printer, the name and share name might be Lawyer_Deskjetc. Or if the printer is located in the Administration Building and is a laser printer, you might call it Admin_Laser. Develop a printer-naming scheme for your organization from the beginning of the server installation. It is hard on users if you change names after a printer has been in use, because your users will have to reinstall those network printers at their workstations.

CAUTION

On networks in which there are MS-DOS workstations, it may be necessary to limit printer share names to eight characters or fewer, since this is the maximum MS-DOS can decipher.

Enter the printer name in the Printer Name box, select whether you want this printer to be used as the default for print jobs that originate at the server, and then click Next. On the screen that follows, click the Shared radio button if you want to share the printer on the network. If the printer is to be shared, enter the printer share name in the *Share as* box (see Figure 11-7). Click Next and click Yes to confirm the name, if it is over eight characters and there are no MS-DOS clients. If there are MS-DOS clients, click Back and enter a name that is eight characters or fewer.

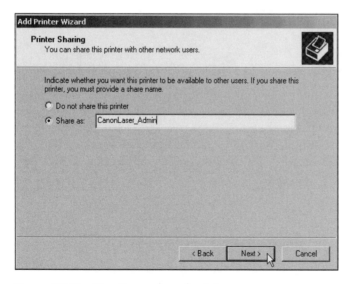

Figure 11-7   Creating a shared printer

If you choose to make this a shared printer, enter the location of the printer and a comment to describe the printer—both of which are used to provide users with information about the printer—and click Next. Click Yes (recommended) to print a test page, as a way to check that the setup is working, and then click Next. Review the setup information and click Finish (see Figure 11-8), or click Back to change a parameter. If you selected to print a test page verify it and click OK in the next dialog box, or if there is a problem, click the Troubleshoot button, which displays remedies via the Print Troubleshooter. To use the Print Troubleshooter, click the description of the problem and then click Next. Also, you can confirm that a shared printer is available on the network by checking for it in My Network Places. (Try Hands-on Project 11-3 to install a local printer, share it, and practice using the Print Troubleshooter.)

Figure 11-8   Printer setup summary

CONFIGURING LOCAL AND SHARED PRINTERS AFTER INSTALLATION

The setup information that you specify while stepping through the Add/Remove Hardware Wizard or the Add Printer Wizard can be modified and further tuned by accessing the Properties dialog box for a printer. Printer properties are available by opening the Printers folder, right-clicking the printer you want to modify, and clicking Properties. You can manage the following functions associated with a printer from the tabs in the Properties dialog box:

- General printer information
- Printer sharing
- Printer port setup
- Printer scheduling and advanced options
- Security
- Device settings

These are the main printer properties available after a printer is installed. Other properties and tabs may be available, depending on the printer and its driver, such as a Color Management and Services tab for printers that support color printing.

General Printer Specifications

The title bar and top portion of the General tab show the name of the printer (see Figure 11-9). The Location and Comment boxes are used to store special notes about the printer that can help distinguish it from other printers, particularly for the sake of users if the printer is shared on the network. Below the Comment box is the printer model name, and under that is an area that describes features of the printer, such as its speed and resolution. The Printing Preferences button is used to specify additional information about printing, such as whether to use portrait or landscape printing as the default and the default paper source, if the printer supports special trays and sheet or envelope feeders. Also, the Print Test Page button enables you to print a test page as a way to verify that the printer is working.

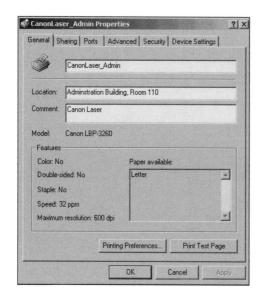

Figure 11-9 Printer Properties General tab

Sharing Printers

The Sharing tab is used to enable or disable a printer for sharing, as well as to specify the name of the share (see Figure 11-10). You can use this if you decide to set up a printer for sharing after you have configured it in the Add Printer Wizard or to turn off sharing if the printer is configured using the Add/Remove Hardware Wizard. Click *Not shared* to turn off sharing, or click *Shared as* to turn it on. If you enable sharing, provide a name for the shared printer and check *List in the Directory* to publish the printer through the Active Directory. When you publish a printer, Windows 2000 Professional clients and other client operating systems that have the Directory Service Client software installed (see Chapter 8) can easily find it and other network printers by clicking Start, Search, or Find (depending on the operating system), and For Printers or Printers (depending on the operating system).

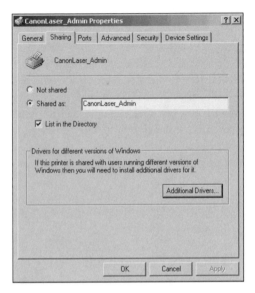

Figure 11-10   Configuring printer sharing

 TIP   Another way to publish a printer in the Active Directory is to open the Active Directory Users and Computers tool, right-click the domain, click New, click Printer, and enter the UNC path to the shared printer.

The group policy to allow printers to be published should be enabled by default. However, make sure it is enabled by opening the Group Policy MMC or by editing the group policy using the Active Directory Users and Computers tool. To edit the policy, open the Group Policy MMC, for example for the Default Domain Policy when the Active Directory is installed. Double-click Computer Configuration, double-click Administrative Templates, and double-click Printers. Double-click *Allow printers to be published,* click Enabled, and click OK. Also, if you want to make sure the Windows 2000 server can use printers over the Internet or through an intranet, double-click *Web-based printing* and make sure it is enabled.

The Additional Drivers button on a printer's properties Sharing tab (refer to Figure 11-10) is used to add new types of clients, if there are clients who will access the shared printer from computers running non–Windows 2000 operating systems. For example, if there are Windows 98 clients and Windows NT 4.0 clients, click the Additional Drivers button and check the boxes for these operating systems. When you check these boxes, the client does not need to already have a printer driver for the shared printer, because it can instead use the driver already provided by the Windows 2000 print server for the client's operating system. A client can load the driver by finding the shared printer in the Active Directory listing, My Computer, or My Network Places and selecting the option to install or connect (depending on the operating system).

 TIP There are two philosophies about loading the printer driver from the server to the client. On the positive side, loading the driver in this way saves users work because they do not have to find their operating system installation disks to load a printer driver. Also, this practice helps ensure that all clients are using the same driver version, which reduces your individual client support work. On the negative side, if the server administrator does not regularly update printer drivers at the server, then after several months these drivers may be out of date. In the latter case, it is better to leave additional operating systems unchecked to force new users to load more recent drivers from their own operating system disks or from the manufacturer.

Port Specifications

The Ports tab has options to specify which server port, such as LPT1, is used for the printer, and options to set up bidirectional printing and printer pooling (see Figure 11-11). Bidirectional printing is used with printers that have bidirectional capability. A bidirectional printer can engage in two-way communications with the print server and with software applications. These allow the printer driver to determine how much memory is installed in the printer, or if it is equipped with PostScript print capability. The printer also may be equipped with the ability to communicate that it is out of paper in a particular drawer or that it has a paper jam.

11

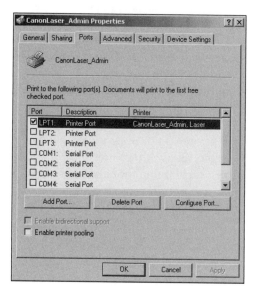

Figure 11-11   Configuring printer ports

> TIP   Before you connect a printer, consult the manual to determine whether the printer is bidi-rectional. If so, the printer requires a special bidirectional cable labeled as an IEEE 1284 cable, and the printer port may need to be designated as bidirectional in the computer's BIOS setup program. Check both of these contingencies if you have a bidirectional printer, but the bidirectional box is deactivated on the Ports tab.

Printer pooling involves configuring two or more identical printers with one print server setup. For example, you might connect three identical laser printers (except for port access) to one parallel port and two serial ports on a Windows 2000 server. On the Ports tab, check the *Enable printer pooling* box, and then check all of the ports to which printers are attached, such as LPT1, COM2, and COM3.

All of the printers in a pool must be identical so that they use the same printer driver and handle print files in the same way. The advantage of having a printer pool is that the Windows 2000 print monitor can send print files to any of the three printers (or however many you set up). If two of the printers are busy, it can send an incoming file to the third printer. Printer pooling can significantly increase the print volume in a busy office, without the need to configure network printing for different kinds of printers. Hands-on Project 11-4 gives you practice installing pooled printers.

> TIP   It is wise to locate pooled printers in close physical proximity, because users are not able to tell to which pooled printer a print job may be sent.

The Add Port button enables you to add a new port, such as a new print monitor or a fax port. Click this button if you need to configure any of the print monitors for specialized printing needs, already described in the section "Windows 2000 Print Monitors." The options are: AppleTalk Printing Devices, Hewlett-Packard Network Port, Local Port, and Standard TCP/IP Port. The Delete Port button is used to remove a port option from the list of ports. The Configure Port button is used to tune the configuration parameters that are appropriate to the type of port. On an LPT port, click the Configure Port button to check the port timeout setting. This setting is the amount of time the server will continue to try sending a print file to a printer, while the printer is not responding. The default setting is normally 90 seconds. Consider increasing the setting to 120 seconds or more if you are installing a printer to handle large print files, such as files for combined graphics and color printing. On a COM port, the Configure Port button is used to set the serial port speed in bits per second, the data bits, parity, stop bits, and flow control.

Printer Scheduling and Advanced Options

The Advanced tab allows you to have the printer available at all times or to limit the time to a range of hours (see Figure 11-12). To have the printer available at all times, click *Always available*; to limit printer use to only certain times, click *Available from* and enter the range of times when the printer can be used, such as from 8:00 AM to 10:00 PM.

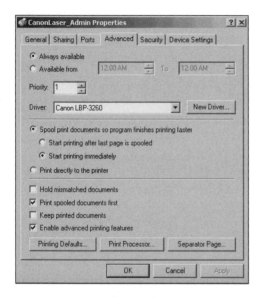

Figure 11-12   Advanced printer properties

You can set the priority higher to give a particular printer or printer pool priority over other printers attached to the server, which applies only if there are two or more printer icons set up in the Printers folder. The priority can be set from 1 to 99. For example, if the server is managing several printer shares, one may be set for higher priority because it prints payroll checks or is used by the company president.

> **TIP**   Printer scheduling can be useful when there is one printer and two printer objects (shares) for that printer. One object can be set up for immediate printing, and the other can be used for long print jobs that are not immediately needed. The object for the longer jobs that can wait might be set up so those print jobs are scheduled to print between 6:00 PM and midnight. Another way to handle the longer jobs is to pause that printer object and resume printing when the printer has a light load, such as at noon or during slow times of the day (for information about pausing a printer, see the section "Controlling the Status of Printing").

The Advanced tab provides the option to use spooled printing or to bypass the spooler and send print files directly to the printer. It works best to spool print jobs so they are printed on a first-come, first-served basis and to enable background printing so the CPU can work on other tasks. Printing directly to the printer is not recommended, unless there is an emergency need to focus all resources on a specific printout. Print spooling also helps ensure that jobs are printed together, so a long Word document is not interrupted by a one-page print job. Without spooling, such an interruption can happen if the one-page job is ready to print at the time the Word job is pausing to read the disk. The spool option is selected by default, with the instruction to start printing before all the pages are spooled. This is an appropriate option in a small office in which most print files are not resource-intensive and there is infrequent contention for printers, reducing the odds of intermixing printouts.

> If there is a problem with pages intermixing from printouts, in a busy office, for example, click the option to *Start printing after last page is spooled*.

The *Hold mismatched documents* option causes the system to compare the setup of the printer to the setup in the document. For example, if the printer is set up in a print share as a Hewlett-Packard 5Si and the document is formatted for a plotter, the print job is placed on hold. The job does not print until the document is released by the user, a member of the Print Operators or Server Operators group, or an administrator.

> The Hold mismatched documents option is a good way to save paper in a heterogeneous situation, such as a student lab, where users have very different formatted print jobs. One mismatch situation can use hundreds of pages printing one character per page.

The option to *Print spooled documents first* enables jobs that have completed spooling to be printed, no matter what their priority. Where there is high-volume printing, this speeds the process by reducing the wait for long print jobs to spool. The *Keep printed documents* option retains documents in the spooler after they have printed, which enables the network administrator to re-create a printout damaged by a printer jam or other problem. For example, if a large number of paychecks are printing and a printer problem strikes in the middle of the printout, this critical option makes it possible to reprint the damaged checks. However, this option should be accompanied by a maintenance schedule to delete documents no longer needed. *Enable advanced printing features* is an option that permits you to make use of special features associated with a particular printer, such as the ability to print booklets or to vary the order in which pages are printed—back to front, for example.

The Printing Defaults button enables you to specify default settings for print jobs, unless they are overridden by control codes in the print file. These can include the print layout, page print order (front to back), and paper source, depending on the printer.

Use the Print Processor button to specify one of the print processors and data types discussed earlier in this chapter, for example using the WinPrint print processor and the EMF data type for Windows-based clients, or the SFMPSPRT print processor and the PSCRIPT1 data type for PostScript printing.

The Separator Page button is used to place a blank page at the beginning of each printed document. This helps designate the end of one printout and the beginning of another, so that printouts do not get mixed together, or so that someone does not take the wrong print-out in a medium or large office setting in which many people share the same printer. Another advantage to using a separator page is that it sends control codes to the printer to make sure that special formatting set for the last printout is reset prior to the next one. In small offices, a separator page may not be needed, because print formatting may not vary, and users can quickly identify their own printouts. Windows 2000 Server has four separator page files from which to choose, located in the \Winnt\System32 folder:

- *Sysprint.sep:* Used with PostScript-only printers and prints a separator page at the beginning of each document

- *Sysprtj.sep:* Used in the same way as Sysprint.sep, but for documents printed in the Japanese language

- *Pcl.sep:* Used to print a Printer Control Language (PCL) separator page on a printer that handles PCL and PostScript

- *Pscript.sep:* Used to print a PostScript separator page on a printer that handles PCL and PostScript

Most non-PostScript laser printers use a version of the **Printer Control Language (PCL)**, which was developed by Hewlett-Packard.

You can create a customized separator page file by using one of the four default files, adding your own control codes, and saving the file with a different name. Table 11-2 lists the control codes you can use.

Consider the cost of paper before you set up separator pages. If you set up a separator page for each document, and each user also specifies a banner page from the client, the resulting paper costs quickly mount in an office. For example, depending on the setup, there will be one or more extra pages printed per document, turning a one-page original document into two, three, or more printed pages. Many offices sharing a printer simply decide to forgo separator and banner pages, because each person knows what he or she printed anyway.

Table 11-2 Separator Page Customization Codes

Control Code	Result
\	Indicates that the file is a separator page file and must be the first character in the first line of the file
\B\M	Double-width block printing until turned off by \U
\B\S	Single-width block printing until turned off by \U
\D	Includes the date and time of the print job
\E	End of file marker, or can be used to begin a new separator page when there are more than one
\F*path*	Prints a text file located in the *path* designation
\H*nn*	Sends the printer control code *nn* to the printer, but you need to read the printer documentation to find out what control codes can be used
\I	Includes the ID or job number of the print job
\L*mno*	Continuously prints one or more characters as specified, such as *mno*, until the next control code is found in the separator file
\N	Includes the name of the person who sent the print file
\n	Skips *n* lines to enable formatting the separator page
\U	Stops single- or double-wide block printing

Configuring Security

As an object, a shared printer can be set up to use security features such as share permissions, auditing, and ownership. To configure security for a printer, you must have Manage Printer permissions for that printer. Click the Security tab to set up printer share permissions (see Figure 11-13). Usually, the default share permissions are set up so that the Everyone group is granted Print permissions, the Administrators, Print Operators, and Server Operators all have permissions, and the Owner has Manage Documents permissions. Click an existing group to modify its permissions, and use the Add button to add new groups or the Remove button to delete a group from accessing the printer. Table 11-3 lists the printer share permissions that can be set (try Hands-on Project 11-5 to practice setting printer permissions and auditing).

Table 11-3   Printer Share Permissions

Share Permission	Access Capability
Print	Users can connect to the shared printer, send print jobs, and manage their own print requests (such as to pause, restart, resume, or cancel a print job).
Manage Documents	Users can connect to the shared printer, send print jobs, and manage any print job sent (including jobs sent by other users).
Manage Printers	Users have complete access to a printer share, including the ability to change permissions, turn off sharing, configure printer properties, and delete the share.

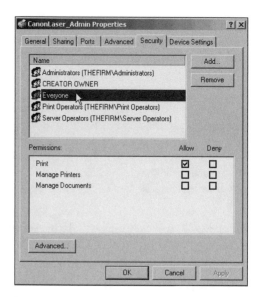

Figure 11-13   Configuring security

By clicking the Advanced button on the Security tab you can:

- Set up special printer permissions for a specific group or user (click the Permissions tab, click the group or user, and click View/Edit)

- Add or remove a group or user for security access or denial (click the Permissions tab)

- Set up printer auditing (click the Auditing tab)

- Take ownership of a printer (click the Owner tab)

Special permissions enable you to fine-tune shared printer permissions, for instance to configure a group that has Manage Printers permission so that group can perform all functions except taking ownership. Any user account or group can be set up for auditing, by clicking the Auditing tab and the Add button. Before you set up printer auditing, make sure that there is a group policy or default domain policy that enables object auditing on the basis of successful and failed activity attempts. For a shared printer you can track successful or failed attempts to:

- Print jobs
- Manage printers
- Manage documents
- Read printer share permissions
- Change printer share permissions
- Take ownership of the printer

As is true of most objects that can have permissions or share permissions, the available special permissions are the same as the events that can be audited.

If you are not certain what security and group policies are set on a broad scale for a server, an OU, or a domain, use the Security Configuration and Analysis MMC snap-in to analyze the security of a particular group policy, so you can review what is set up and what is not (see Chapter 16). For example, to determine the security set for the default domain policy, load and start the snap-in, create a database for the default domain policy, right-click Security Configuration and Analysis in the tree, and click Analyze Computer Now.

Ownership of a printer created on a Windows 2000 server is usually held by Administrators, because ownership is first given to the account that set up the printer. The Owner tab enables anyone with Manage Printers permissions to take ownership.

Configuring Device Settings

The Device Settings tab enables you to specify printer settings such as printer trays, memory, paper size, and fonts (see Figure 11-14). For example, in many cases, if you have a multiple-tray printer you will leave the paper tray assignment on Auto Select and let the software application at the client specify the printer tray. However, if your organization uses special forms such as paychecks, you can specify use of a designated paper tray when checks are printing.

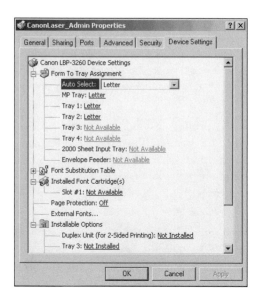

Figure 11-14   Configuring printer device settings

The printer memory is usually automatically detected in bidirectional printers, but if it is not, you can specify the amount of memory in the *Printer Memory* option under Installable Options. In the client operating systems, such as Windows 2000 Professional or Windows 98, the workstation printer setup also can have information about how much memory is installed in a shared printer.

 Make sure the memory reported in the device settings matches the memory installed in the printer, because this enables the print server to offload more work to the printer, improving the speed at which print jobs are completed, as well as server performance. Most other settings are better left to the software at the client end to handle. For example, a client printing in Microsoft Word can specify font and paper tray instructions inside the document and by using the Printer Setup.

Allocating Virtual Memory for PostScript Printers

PostScript printers sometimes slow down when printing files containing several fonts and font sizes. A **PostScript printer** is one that has special firmware or cartridges to print using a **page-description language** (**PDL**). PDL printing instructions are performed through PostScript programming code that produces extremely high-quality printing with extensive font options. Windows 2000 Server includes an option to make virtual memory available to a PostScript printer, to circumvent the purchase of extra RAM for that printer. The virtual memory is not part of the paging file that you tune to enhance the server performance. Instead, it is a separate allocation of disk space for PostScript printing.

Virtual memory is a useful way to extend memory capabilities, but keep in mind that disk access speeds (5 milliseconds or less) are slower than RAM access speeds (70 nanoseconds). Virtual memory can help server and printer performance, but it is still no match for the performance boost provided by adding additional RAM to a server for server activities and to a printer for printing fonts, graphics, and colors.

To set up virtual memory for a PostScript printer, first use the Add/Remove Hardware Wizard or the Add Printer Wizard to install the printer. Next, open the Printers folder and right-click the new icon for the PostScript printer. Click Properties and the Device Settings tab. Click Available PostScript Memory and enter the virtual memory size in KB. Consider setting the virtual memory at 1000 KB or more.

A file called Testps.txt is available from Microsoft with recommendations on what memory settings should be used with specific PostScript printers. The virtual memory option is available only for PostScript printers because of their high memory requirements, and is used for storing and managing fonts.

Configuring a Nonlocal Printer or an Internet Printer

There are times when you want to enable a Windows 2000 server to connect to a printer that is not directly connected to one of its ports, for example a printer shared from a workstation, another server, the Internet, or an intranet, or one that is connected to the network through a print server card or device (see Figure 11-1). You can connect to a network printer by using the Add Printer Wizard:

1. Start the Add Printer Wizard, click Next, and then click the Network printer radio button (see Figure 11-5). Make sure the checkmark is removed from *Automatically detect and install my Plug and Play printer* and click Next.

2. The Locate Your Printer dialog box is displayed, with options to: (1) *Find a printer in the Directory* (for Active Directory installations), (2) *Type the printer name, or click Next to browse for a printer*, or (3) *Connect to a printer on the Internet or on your intranet*. Click the appropriate option and click Next. If you specified that you want to find a printer in the Directory, the Find Printers dialog box is started. If you click *Type the printer name, or click Next to browse for a printer* without entering a printer name, a browse box is displayed showing domains and workgroups on Microsoft Networks; it also has the option to browse NetWare-compatible networks (if TCP/IP or NWLink is installed). If you choose *connect to a printer on the Internet or on your intranet*, then you need to provide the URL before clicking Next.

3. Click Yes to print a test page, and then click Next.

4. Click Finish.

When the remote printer is installed on a domain controller, you can change the properties of the shared printer you just installed, even though you are not logged on to its host computer. This means you can manage any remote shared network printer, even though it is not connected to a port on the server. For example, open the Printers folder and right-click the remote printer you installed. Click the Properties option and make any changes you desire. This capability is very useful when you manage a large network with network printers located in distant buildings. If you need to change the print processor used by a shared printer that is a block away, you can do so without leaving your office.

Configuring a Printer by Identifying Its IP and MAC Addresses

Network printers on TCP/IP networks that have internal print server cards or externally attached print servers can be set up through Windows 2000 Server by identifying them through their IP and MAC (Media Access Control, see Chapter 3) addresses. You do this by configuring the Standard TCP/IP Port option (Ipmontr.dll and Tcpmon.dll) and specifying the address of the print server. For example, to install one of these types of printers using an IP address:

1. Be sure that the printer is turned on and that its print server card or external print server box is connected to the network (and has power, if required).

2. Start the Add Printer Wizard and click Next.

3. Install the printer as a local printer, but uncheck the option to *Automatically detect and install my Plug and Play printer*. Click Next.

4. In the Select the Printer Port window, click Create a new port.

5. Open the Type list box and select Standard TCP/IP Port, as in Figure 11-15 (note that you also can install non-IP print servers using the other options, such as Hewlett-Packard Network Port, Local Port, and AppleTalk Printing Devices). Click Next.

6. Click Next after the Add Standard TCP/IP Printer Port Wizard starts.

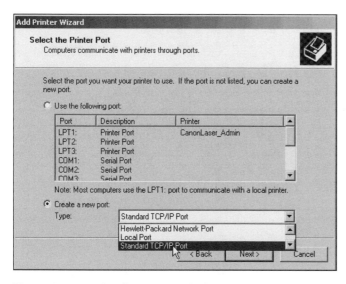

Figure 11-15   Configuring a TCP/IP port

7. Enter the IP address. The Wizard automatically enters a port name on the basis of the IP address, such as IP_129.70.10.7. Click Next. The Add Standard TCP/IP Printer Port Wizard will find the print server to which the printer is attached, by using the IP address and by automatically determining the print server's MAC address from the ARP (Address Resolution Protocol, see Chapter 3). If the printer or print server to which it is attached is not turned on or connected to the network, the Wizard will ask you to troubleshoot the problem before proceeding.

8. Click the Standard radio button under the device type and select the print server model in the list box, or click the Custom radio button and the Settings button to perform a custom setup. Click Next and in the following dialog box click Finish.

If the printer is connected to a mainframe, UNIX, or other host computer and you also must use LPR for enterprise network print services, then select the custom setup. Also, if you want to monitor the print server using the SNMP network monitoring protocol (see Chapters 3 and 15), and you have determined that the print server supports that protocol, use the custom setup to enable SNMP.

9. Back in the Add Printer Wizard, select the printer manufacturer and model, and then click Next.

10. Provide a printer name and choose whether or not to make this the default printer. Click Next.

11. Select the option to share the printer, provide a share name, and click Next.

12. Enter the location of the printer and a descriptive comment about the printer. Click Next.

13. Click Yes to print a test page, and then click Next.

14. Click Finish and click OK if the test page printed, or click Troubleshoot to find help.

15. The printer's Properties dialog box has a new port listed, which has the port name you provided and the description Standard TCP/IP Port (see Figure 11-16). You can change the IP address and other configuration information by clicking the port and then clicking the Configure Port button.

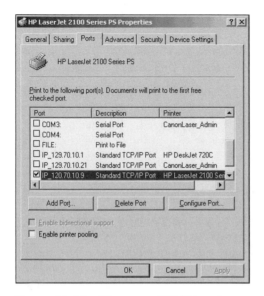

Figure 11-16   The new TCP/IP port

Try Hands-on Project 11-6 to practice setting up a printer through IP addressing.

If you have to replace a print server device and assign a new IP address in its setup, or if you want to turn on SNMP, use the Configure Port button, as described in Step 15.

11

MANAGING PRINT JOBS

In the time after a print job is sent and before it is fully transmitted to the printer, there are several options for managing that job. Users with Print permissions can print and manage their own jobs. Also members of the Printer Operators, Server Operators, and Administrators groups can manage the jobs of others through the Manage Documents and Manage Printers permissions. The printer and print jobs management tool is accessed by opening the Printers folder and clicking the icon for the printer you want to manage. The following options are available to users with Print permissions:

- Send print jobs to the printer
- Pause, resume, and restart their own print jobs
- Delete or cancel their own print jobs

Print Operators, Server Operators, and other groups having only Manage Documents permissions can:

- Send print jobs to the printer

- Pause, resume, and restart any user's print jobs

- Delete or cancel any user's print jobs

Administrators, Print Operators, Server Operators, and any other groups having Manage Printers permissions can do all of the same things as those with Manage Documents permissions, but they also can change the status of the printer, for example to start and stop sharing, set printer properties, take ownership, change permissions, and set the default printer for the Windows 2000 server.

Controlling the Status of Printing

Printer control and setup information for a particular printer is associated with that printer's icon in the Printers folder. For example, if you have two printers installed, HPLaser_Rm20 and InkJet_Rm8, there is a set of properties and printer control information for each printer. If you want to pause a print job on the HPLaser_Rm20 printer, you need to double-click its icon in the Printers folder, and if you want to delete a print job on the InkJet_Rm8 printer, you need to double-click its icon.

 If you work frequently at the console of a server, consider setting its default printer to the selection that suits your needs. For example, if you print most to a laser printer called HPLaser_Rm20, then make it the default printer for local printing on the server. You can do that by double-clicking its icon, clicking the Printer menu, and checkmarking Set As Default Printer (see Figure 11-17). After it is set as the default, the printer icon has a check mark next to it (try Hands-on Project 11-3).

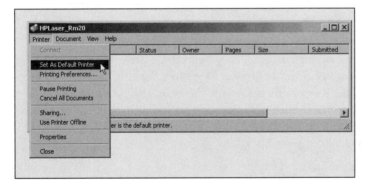

Figure 11-17   Designating a default printer

Sometimes you need to pause a printer to fix a problem, for example to reattach a loose cable or to power the printer off and on to reset it. You can pause printing to that printer by double-clicking its icon in the Printers folder, clicking the Printer menu, and checkmarking Pause Printing. Remember that you need to uncheck Pause Printing before print jobs can continue printing. The Pause Printing capability is particularly important if a user sends an improperly formatted document to the printer, for example a PostScript-formatted document to a non-PostScript printer. If you do not have Hold mismatched documents enabled, the printer may print tens or hundreds of pages with a single control code on each page. By pausing printing, you have time to identify and delete the document before too much paper is used. (Try Hands-on Project 11-7 to practice pausing a printer.)

Also, you connect or attempt to reconnect a network printer by clicking the Connect option on the Printer menu. If you checkmark the Use Printer Offline option in the Printer menu, then users can view a network printer on their computers even when their computers are disconnected from the network, such as when a laptop is undocked. When the computer is reconnected to the network, the print job is sent to the shared network printer. The Printer menu also has a Properties option to access that printer's properties and a Sharing option, which allows you to turn printer sharing on or off.

Controlling Specific Print Jobs

You can pause, resume, restart, or view the properties of one or more documents in the print queue of a printer. A **print queue** is like a stack of print jobs, with the first job submitted at the top of the stack and the last job submitted at the bottom, and all of the jobs waiting to be sent from the spooler to the printer.

To pause a print job, open the Printers folder and double-click the icon for the target printer. The resulting window shows a list of jobs to be printed, the status of each job, the owner, the number of pages to be printed, the size of the print file, and when the print job was submitted. Click the document you want to pause, click the Document menu, and then click Pause. That print job will stop printing until you highlight the document and click Resume or Restart on the Document menu. Resume starts printing at the point in the document where the printing was paused. Restart prints from the beginning of the document. Keep in mind that portions or all of a document may already have been sent to the printer's memory. You only pause from the portion that is left in the print server's spooler. If the printer has a large amount of memory, such as 1, 2, or more megabytes, you may not be able to pause a document before it is loaded into the printer's memory.

You also can use the Document menu to cancel a print job. First click the job in the status window, click the Document menu, and click Cancel (try Hands-on Project 11-7).

Jobs print in the order they are received, unless the administrator changes their priority. Jobs come in with a priority of 1, but can be assigned a priority as high as 99. For example, if you work for a university, the president may need to quickly print a last-minute report before going to a meeting with the trustees. You can give the president a 99 priority by clicking her print job in the window listing the print jobs. Next click the Document menu, Properties, and the General tab. The Priority box is in the middle of the General

11

tab. Move the priority bar from Lowest (1) to Highest (99), and click OK. (Learn where to set print priority in Hands-on Project 11-7.)

You also can use the General tab to set a time for selected jobs to print on a printer. For example, if the server is very busy during the day, you can ease the load by setting jobs to print at a certain time of day, such as from noon to 1 PM If you do schedule printing, plan to notify the users of that printer in advance. The General tab also shows the size of a print file, the owner, the data type used, the print processor used, and when the job was submitted.

Moving Print Jobs

Sometimes a printer can malfunction at the worst time, such as when your organization is working to meet a deadline for a project and is printing hundreds of pages for multiple copies of a report. In this or similar situations, you can move the unfinished print jobs to another shared printer that is working. You do this in one of two ways: (1) by moving the jobs to another port already configured, for multiple or pooled printers already connected to a print server, for example, or (2) by adding a new port on the broken printer's setup that points to the working printer, then specifying the path to that printer.

For example, consider a situation in which printer Pub_5Si, which is connected to LPT1, is broken, but Pub_4Si, which is connected to LPT2 on the same Windows 2000 server, is working. To move the print jobs, open the Printers folder, right-click Pub_5Si, click Properties, and click the Ports tab. Click LPT2, which also shows that Pub_4Si is connected to it, and click OK.

In another situation, printer Laser_Rm1, which is directly connected to the Admin server, is broken, but Laser_Rm5, a printer that is connected to the Accounts server in another room, is working (assume that both printers use the printer name for the share name too). To move the print jobs, open the Printers folder, right-click the Laser_Rm1 icon, and click Properties. Click the Ports tab and the Add Port button. Click Local Port in the Printer Ports dialog box, and click the New Port button. Enter the UNC path to the working printer, for instance \\Accounts\Laser_Rm5, and click OK. Click Close in the Printer Ports dialog box, and Apply and Close in the Laser_Rm1 dialog box (try Hands-on Project 11-2 to transfer a print job).

 If you cannot redirect printer jobs, the most likely cause is that you do not have Manage Printers permissions on the two printers.

SOLVING A COMMON PRINTING PROBLEM

One common printing problem occurs when the Windows 2000 Print Spooler service experiences a temporary problem, gets out of synchronization, or hangs. Because the spooler contains several complex pieces, it is a source of printer problems. The result is that print jobs are not processed until the problem is solved. If a print job is not going through, and you determine that the printer(s) are not paused and that the cable connection is good, then stop and restart the Print Spooler service. You do this by clicking Start, pointing to Programs, pointing to Administrative Tools, clicking Computer Management, and clicking Services and Applications in the tree. Double-click Services and scroll to Print Spooler. Check the status column to determine if it is started, and make sure that it is set to start automatically. If it is not started, if it is not set to start automatically, or if you need to stop and restart the spooler, double-click Print Spooler. To start the service, click Start. If you need to set it to start automatically, set this option in the Startup type box; to stop and restart the service, click Stop and then click Start. Make sure that the service status is Started and that the startup type is Automatic. Click OK.

Warn users before you stop and restart the Print Spooler service, because queued print jobs will be deleted.

Because the Print Spooler service is dependent on the Remote Procedure Call (RPC) service, check to make sure that the Remote Procedure Call service is also started and set to start automatically. Further, make sure that the Server service is working, if you have spooler problems.

11

CHAPTER SUMMARY

❑ As with most computer operating systems, you can connect one or more printers to a computer running Windows 2000 Server. Also, a Windows 2000 server can be turned into a print server to enable network users to send documents to printers connected to it and to printers connected to other computers and print servers on a network. Before you configure a Windows 2000 server as a print server, make sure that you understand how network and Internet printing works, including how to use print monitors and data types.

❑ A new printer can be installed using the Add/Remove Hardware Wizard, the Add Printer Wizard, or a combination of both tools. After a printer is installed, you can modify its properties to match particular printing needs, in literally dozens of ways, from setting defaults for documents that do not use much printer formatting to holding print jobs that have inappropriate formatting for a particular printer. Security can be set on a shared printer to control access, audit printer activity, and set ownership of the printer.

❑ After a printer is installed and configured, there are options to manage the printer, such as pausing it or canceling all print jobs in its queue. Also, documents can be managed by stopping and restarting them, resetting the printing priority, and canceling one or more documents.

In the next chapter, you learn how to set up and manage remote access to a Windows 2000 server network, and how to configure a virtual private network.

Key Terms

bidirectional printing — Ability of a parallel printer to conduct two-way communication between the printer and the computer, for example to provide out-of-paper information; also bidirectional printing supports Plug and Play and enables an operating system to query a printer about its capabilities.

data type — Way in which information is formatted in a print file.

graphics device interface (GDI) — An interface on a Windows network print client that works with a local software application, such as Microsoft Word, and a local printer driver to format a file to be sent to a local printer or a network print server.

Internet Printing Protocol (IPP) — A protocol that is encapsulated in HTTP and that is used to print files over the Internet.

local printing — Printing on the same computer to which print devices are attached.

page-description language (PDL) — Printing instructions involving a programming code that produces extremely high-quality printing with extensive font options.

PostScript printer — A printer that has special firmware or cartridges to print using a page-description language (PDL).

print client — Client computer that generates a print job.

print device — A device, such as a printer or fax, that uses the Spooler services in Windows 2000 Server.

print queue — A stack or line-up of print jobs, with the first job submitted at the top of the stack, the last job submitted at the bottom, and all of the jobs waiting to be sent from the spooler to the printer.

print server — Network computer or server device that connects printers to the network for sharing and that receives and processes print requests from print clients.

Printer Control Language (PCL) — A printer language used by non-PostScript Hewlett-Packard and compatible laser printers.

printer driver — A file containing information needed to control a specific printer, implementing customized printer control codes, font, and style information.

printer pooling — Linking two or more identical printers with one printer setup or printer share.

spool file — A print file written to disk until it can be transmitted to a printer.

spooler — In the Windows 95, 98, NT, and 2000 environment, a group of DLLs, information files, and programs that processes print jobs for printing.

spooling — A process working in the background to enable several print files to go to a single printer. Each file is placed in temporary storage until its turn comes to be printed.

REVIEW QUESTIONS

1. Someone in your office often sends documents formatted for PostScript to the office's PCL printer, causing it to print page after page of garbage and waste paper. How can you best solve this problem?

   a. Determine who is sending the documents and take away his or her permissions to use the printer.

   b. Configure the printer to hold mismatched documents.

   c. Use printer pooling, but make the second printer a PostScript printer.

   d. Configure the printer to use a different type of separator page for PostScript and PCL print jobs.

2. You have a Hewlett-Packard 4Si printer that contains an older JetDirect card. When you set it up in Windows 2000 Server, you are unable to print to it, even though you have set up the Hpmon.dll print monitor. Which of the following should you check?

   a. that the data type is TEXT

   b. that the port timeout value is decreased to 20

   c. that the server and clients are configured to use the DLC protocol

   d. all of the above

   e. only a and b

   f. only a and c

3. Your boss is on the way to a meeting and needs to print a five-page document in a hurry. Unfortunately, there are 22 documents ahead of his. What can you do to help?

   a. Cancel the documents that are ahead of his, but reschedule them to print later.

   b. Pause and restart the printer to clear the queue, and then resubmit his document.

   c. Stop and restart the print queue, and then resubmit his document.

   d. Give his document a priority of 99.

4. Which of the following is not a shared printer permission?

   a. Full Control

   b. Manage Printers

   c. Manage Documents

   d. Print

5. The power supply in one of your shared printers has burned out. You plan to purchase an identical printer, but not for two weeks. Which of the following enables you to prevent users from trying to use that printer?

   a. Disable the printer sharing.

   b. Change permissions so that no one but you can access the printer.

   c. Set up auditing on the Everyone group, using the failure option.

   d. all of the above

11

    e. only a and b

    f. only b and c

6. You are setting up an Intel Netport Express print server that is connected to a network and to a laser printer that is shared on the network. The print server communicates using TCP/IP. How can you set up the print server in Windows 2000 Server by identifying it through its IP address?

    a. Set it up as a Standard TCP/IP Port.

    b. Set it up as a Hewlett-Packard Network Port, because it works like a JetDirect card.

    c. Use the Active Directory Users and Computers tool to set it up through the IP address.

    d. You cannot manage this type of print server through Windows 2000 Server.

7. How do you restart a printer after you have paused it?

    a. Click Restart in the Document menu.

    b. Click Restart in the Printer menu.

    c. Remove the checkmark from Pause Printer in the Printer menu.

    d. Click Connect in the Printer menu.

8. Your office can only afford one printer. The problem is that some people occupy the printer by sending 100-page print jobs that do not need to print immediately. What solution can you use to solve this problem?

    a. Frequently monitor the print queue and pause the long print jobs until near the end of the workday.

    b. Develop a voluntary system so that users with jobs over 50 pages print only during the lunch hour or after 5 P.M.

    c. Change permissions for users who send long print jobs from Print to Limited Print, and then set the limited print jobs to 25 pages or fewer.

    d. Set up two printer objects for one printer, but implement one object for long print jobs and schedule it to print after the workday or overnight.

9. You have purchased a bidirectional laser printer and have verified that the cable connection between the printer and your Windows 2000 server is intact. However, when you configure the printer, the bidirectional box on the Ports tab is deactivated. What should you check?

    a. Open the Device Manager, find the printer, and double-click it to make sure it is connected.

    b. Check to make sure you are using an IEEE 1284 cable.

    c. Check the BIOS setup in the computer to make sure that bidirectional is enabled for the port to which the printer is attached.

    d. all of the above

    e. only a and b

    f. only b and c

10. You are in a meeting to troubleshoot a problem with printing checks for your organization, which has 500 employees. Last night, the printer jammed when checks were printing, and the payroll office spent hours resetting the payroll program to print only certain checks that were damaged. How can you prevent such drastic time loss next time, so the payroll office can go home earlier?

    a. Configure that printer to *Keep printed documents* just before printing the paychecks.

    b. Configure that printer to *Print directly to the printer* just before printing the paychecks.

    c. Schedule paychecks to print at night so there is more time to deal with this problem.

    d. Set the printer to print from Tray 2, because Tray 1 is more likely to cause jams.

11. In the meeting described in Question 10, the payroll manager asks what you would do if paychecks were printing and the printer failed completely. What is your answer?

    a. Use the Windows 2000 Server CD-ROM to reinstall all of the spooler components.

    b. Use the Ports tab for that printer to redirect the check printing to a printer that is working.

    c. Power down the server and reboot it, in case some of its services are not working properly.

    d. Allocate more virtual memory to the printer, in case there is a memory conflict with another process.

12. The _____ integrates information in a print file with a printer driver to prepare a print job for printing.

    a. spooler monitor

    b. data type

    c. graphics device interface (GDI)

    d. Spoolmon.dll file

13. During the last month before closing the books at the fiscal year-end, the Accounting Office prints reams of reports. It is vital that each printed report have the date and time it was printed. How can you accommodate this need?

    a. Activate the Date/Time parameter on the Advanced tab in the properties of the network printers used by the Accounting Office.

    b. Use the scheduling capability of the properties of the network printers so that reports are only scheduled to be printed on certain dates.

    c. Enable use of a separator page and edit the page's parameters to add the /D option.

    d. Use the Date Stamp capability of NTFS to stamp the date on the first page of each report.

11

14. You power off your company's server, attach a new ink-jet printer, and reboot. After the server reboots, it does not detect the new printer. What is most likely to be the problem?

    a. The printer is bidirectional and cannot be automatically detected.

    b. You must first start the Add/Remove Hardware Wizard to automatically detect new hardware.

    c. You must first PING ink-jet printers to detect them.

    d. The Plug and Play service is disabled.

15. A user is calling you to report that he sent a print job to the printer at least four hours ago and it still has not printed. How can you verify the exact time when the job was submitted, to help in your analysis of the problem?

    a. Check the properties of the print job.

    b. Check the properties of the printer.

    c. Check the printer's Advanced tab.

    d. That information is not available.

16. Several IBM mainframe computers send print jobs to a shared printer connected to your Windows 2000 server. One problem you have noticed is that the last page of the print job is never printed. What would you do?

    a. Use a PostScript separator page.

    b. Edit the Registry and change the printer share to UNIX Enabled.

    c. Use the SFMPSRT print processor.

    d. Set the data type to RAW [FF appended].

17. You have set up a shared printer on the server, but Sandra Hanson gets an access denied message when she attempts to use the printer. Sandra belongs to two global groups, Managers and Sales, which are members of the domain local groups Managers and Marketing, respectively. Which of the following might be a problem?

    a. You have granted print permissions to the global groups, but not to the domain local groups.

    b. The Managers domain local group is denied Print permissions.

    c. You have granted print permissions to the domain local groups, but not to the global groups.

    d. The Sales global group must also be a member of the Print Operators group.

18. You are setting up auditing via the Security tab on a printer, but you see a message that auditing is not turned on. Your server is a standalone server. What should you do?

    a. Install the Windows Auditing component.

    b. You cannot use auditing on a standalone server.

    c. Turn on auditing in the local group policy.

    d. Turn on auditing for the entire Printers folder.

19. Which document printing option commences a print job from where it left off?

    a. Resume

    b. Reset

    c. Restart

    d. Renew

20. The warehouse for your company has one network printer on its Windows 2000 server, and that printer is always busy printing fulfillment orders. What can you do to help printing go faster?

    a. Increase the port timeout value.

    b. Purchase an identical printer and use pooled printing.

    c. Use a separator page with the /S14400 option to set the printer port speed at 14,000 bps.

    d. Use the compressed printing option.

21. Your Windows 2000 server is a print server for five printers. One of those printers handles the majority of critical print jobs that should print as soon as possible. What should you do?

    a. Attach that printer to LPT1, which is the port with the highest priority on a computer.

    b. Attach that printer to COM1, which is the faster port on a computer.

    c. Assign each printer on the print server a priority from 1 to 5, giving the printer with the critical jobs a priority of 5.

    d. Purchase and set up another server and attach only the critical printer to that server.

22. The Payroll Department has one network printer, called PAY, that is used only to print checks. The printer is always loaded with checks, but kept in a locked room. What other steps would you take to secure this printer?

    a. Set the permissions so that only the Payroll Department can access the printer.

    b. Audit the Everyone group for successful printing to that printer.

    c. Have the Payroll Department take ownership of the printer.

    d. all of the above

    e. only a and b

    f. only a and c

23. You have set up a printer that has two trays. Tray 1 holds letter-sized paper and Tray 2 holds envelopes. Also, you have just added 16 MB of memory so that the printer now has 32 MB. From which tab in the printer's properties do you specify these particular properties?

    a. General

    b. Advanced

11

      c. Device Settings

      d. Ports

24. You are setting up a Windows 2000 Server printer to receive print jobs from an IBM mainframe. You set up LPR printing in Windows 2000 Server. What other component must be set up?

      a. virtual memory for the printer

      b. an LPD server

      c. the SNMP protocol

      d. Client Service for NetWare

25. You want to configure Windows 2000 to use a printer that is connected through the Internet. How is this possible?

      a. Use the Add Printer Wizard and select to install a network printer.

      b. Use the Add Printer Wizard and select to install a local printer.

      c. Set up the printer first and then configure the Ports tab for Local Port, providing the IP address of the Internet printer.

      d. For reasons of security, you can only configure Windows 2000 Professional for Internet printing, and not Windows 2000 Server.

HANDS-ON PROJECTS

Project 11-1

In this project you practice changing the data type to accommodate UNIX and mainframe clients that print to a printer connected to Windows 2000 Server. Assume that you have been experiencing garbled printouts using the TEXT setup and a problem with getting the first page to print. To solve the problem, you change the data type to RAW with FF appended. To practice, you need a printer that is already set up in Windows 2000 Server.

To change the data type:

1. Click **Start**, point to **Settings**, and click **Printers**.

2. Right-click the printer that you want to configure, and click **Properties**.

3. Click the **Advanced** tab and click the **Print Processor** button.

4. What print processors and data types are listed? Record your results in your lab journal or in a word-processed document.

5. Click **WinPrint** and click **RAW [FF appended]**.

6. Click **OK**.

7. What are some other parameters that you can set on the Advanced tab? Record several of these in your lab journal or in a word-processed document.

8. Click **Apply** and then **OK**. Leave the Printers folder open for the projects that follow.

Project 11-2

In this project, assume that you have a small network in which there is a printer connected to the server that has failed and an identical printer shared by a workstation on the network that is working. You practice configuring the print monitor associated with the Local Port option and at the same time learn how to transfer print jobs to the other printer. You will need a printer set up in Windows 2000 Server. Obtain from your instructor the name of a workstation (or server) that has a shared printer.

To configure the print monitor and transfer print jobs:

1. Right-click the same printer that you used in Hands-on Project 11-1, and click **Properties**.

2. Click the **Ports** tab.

3. What port is already set up? Record your observation.

4. Click the **Add Port** button.

5. What port types are available? Record your observations.

6. Click **Local Port** and then click the **New Port** button. Enter the UNC name of the workstation and printer provided by your instructor, such as \\Lab1\HPLaser, and click **OK**. (Note, if your server has two printers connected you can also enter the server name and the name of the other printer.)

7. Click **Close**.

8. Is the new port added to the list of ports? What is the Port name and description?

9. Click **Close**.

11

Project 11-3

This Hands-on Project gives you experience manually setting up a local printer and sharing it on a network. You also practice using the Microsoft Troubleshooter for printers. Although it is helpful, you do not need to have a printer connected to a Windows 2000 server to complete this project.

To set up a printer:

1. If the Printers folder is closed, click **Start**, point to **Settings**, and click **Printers**. Are there any printers already installed? If so, what are they? Which one is set up as the default printer for this server? Record this information for later use.

2. Double-click **Add Printer** and then click **Next**.

3. Click **Local printer** and remove the check mark from **Automatically detect and install my Plug and Play printer**, if this option is checked. Click **Next**.

4. What port selections are available? Record your observations in your lab journal or in a word-processed document.

5. Click an unused port, such as LPT2 or COM2; or, if there is a printer attached to your computer, select the port to which it is connected. Click **Next**.

6. How many printer manufacturers are represented in the Manufacturers list, and who are they? Select a manufacturer, such as HP, and a printer model, such as HP LaserJet 6L; or if there is a printer connected to your computer, select that printer's manufacturer and model. Click **Next**.

If you select a printer manufacturer and model that is already installed via another printer icon in the Printers folder, a dialog box appears that asks if you want to keep the existing driver or use a new one. If you see this dialog box, click Keep existing driver (recommended), and then click Next.

7. Enter a printer name, such as **HPLaser_Rm2**. Click **Yes**, so that this printer is the default. Click **Next**.

8. Make sure the Share as radio button is selected, and enter the share name, for example **HPLaser_Rm2.** Click **Next**.

9. Enter a location for the printer, such as Room 2, and enter a comment, such as **HP LaserJet 6L printer for all users**. Click **Next**.

10. Click **Yes** to print a test page, regardless of whether there is a printer connected to your computer (so you can access the Print Troubleshooter).

11. Review the information you have entered for the printer configuration, and click **Finish**.

12. When the test information box is displayed, click **Troubleshoot** to view the troubleshooting information.

13. Click **My network server printer won't print**, and click **Next**.

14. Read the troubleshooting information and then click **No, I can't establish a basic network connection**. Click **Next**.

15. Read the troubleshooting information and assume that the problem is that the printer driver is corrupted. Click **To remove and reinstall your default printer**. Since you are just practicing using the Troubleshooter, do not reinstall the printer. Click **Yes I can print from my program** and then click **Next**. How would you go back to find more troubleshooting information?

16. Close the Troubleshooter, but leave the Printers folder open. What printer is now shown as the default? How do you know it is the default printer? If you set up to use a printer that is not connected, click Cancel to the warning that a test page did not print.

To set the default printer back as originally set (refer to step 1 in the first set of steps in this project—if there was an original default):

1. Right-click the printer that was originally set as the default.

2. Click **Set as Default Printer**.

3. Has that printer's icon changed?

Project 11-4

Assume that your office will have heavy printing traffic to the printer you set up in Hands-on Project 11-3. To solve the traffic load, you decide to attach an identical printer to an available communications port and configure the print server for pooling (you do not need another printer to practice setting up pooling).

To configure printer pooling:

1. Right-click the printer that you installed in Hands-on Project 11-3.
2. Click **Properties**.
3. Click the **Ports** tab.
4. Click **Enable printer pooling**.
5. Click **COM3:** or another port that is not in use.
6. Click **Apply**. How has that port's printer assignment changed? Record your observations.
7. How could you print a test page?
8. Click **OK**.

Project 11-5

You need to set up security on the pooled printers installed in Hands-on Projects 11-3 and 11-4. Your boss asks you to remove the Everyone group from access to the printers, but to add Domain Users, which is a domain local group that has specific global groups as members. He also wants you to set up auditing of failed printing attempts for the Domain Users group.

To set up printer security:

1. Right-click the printer that you installed in Hands-on Project 11-3, and click **Properties**.
2. Click the **Security** tab. What security is set up already? Record your observations.
3. Click the **Everyone** group and click **Remove**. Is the Name box updated to reflect the change?
4. Click the **Add** button.
5. Scroll to find **Domain Users** and double-click that selection. Click **OK**.
6. What permissions are given to this group by default?
7. Make sure that the **Allow** box for Print is checked.
8. Click the **Advanced** button.
9. Click the **Auditing** tab.
10. Click **Add**, then find and double-click **Domain Users**.
11. List the contents of the Apply onto box and record the options. Make sure **This printer and documents** is selected.

12. Click the **Failed** box for Print and click **OK**.

13. What information now appears in the Auditing Entries box?

14. Click **OK**. If there is a message that auditing is not turned on as a group policy, how would you turn it on? Also, click **OK** if you see a message that auditing is not turned on.

15. Click **OK**.

Project 11-6

In this activity you set up a JetDirect print server so you can manage it through Windows 2000 Server. If you do not have a printer with a JetDirect card, you can still use this project for practice. Obtain an IP address from your instructor before starting.

To set up the JetDirect print server:

1. Double-click **Add Printer** and click **Next**.

2. Click **Local printer** and remove the check mark from **Automatically detect and install my Plug and Play printer**, if it is checked. Click **Next**.

3. Click **Create a new port** in the Select the Printer Port window, and select **Standard TCP/IP Port** in the Type box. Click **Next**. Click **Next** again when the Add Standard TCP/IP Printer Port Wizard starts.

4. Enter the IP address provided by your instructor, such as 129.88.1.15. What happens to the Port Name box as you enter the IP address? By what other means can you identify the printer, besides by IP address? Record your findings. Click **Next**. If there is no print server connected, the next window will report that it cannot be found on the network. Ignore the message, if you are practicing without an actual print server.

5. Make sure that the **Standard** radio button is selected under the device type, and select **Hewlett Packard Jet Direct** in the list box. Click **Next**. Is the device configured for SNMP? Click **Finish**.

6. When you return to the Add Printer Wizard, select the printer manufacturer, such as HP, and model, such as HP LaserJet 5Si, and then click **Next**.

7. Enter a printer name, such as HPLaser_Rm3, and click **No**. Click **Next**.

8. Make sure that **Share as** is selected and enter the share name **HPLaser_Rm3**. Click **Next**.

9. Enter **Room 3** as the location, and enter **HP LaserJet 5Si printer in Room 3** as the comment. Click **Next**.

10. Click **Yes** to print a test page, if you are working with a live printer; otherwise click **No**. Click **Next**.

11. Click **Finish** and click **OK** if the test page printed, or click **Troubleshoot** to find help.

12. How would you verify that the printer port has been created?

Project 11-7

Assume that the printer you created in Hands-on Project 11-3 is printing sheet after sheet of garbled printing, and you need to pause printing to that printer until you can cancel the print job. This project enables you to simulate pausing the printer and deleting a document.

To pause a printer, cancel a document, and resume printing:

1. Double-click the printer that you installed in Hands-on Project 11-3.

2. Click the **Printer** menu and click **Pause Printing**. Has the title bar of the printer window changed, and if so how?

3. Using a word processor or Notepad, create a document that contains only one or two words, such as Test. Send the document to the printer that you have paused.

4. When the document appears in the printer window, click it.

5. Click the **Document** menu. What options are available to you to control a print job? Click the **Properties** option. How would you reset the priority of this print job from the General tab? Click the **Cancel** button to close the Properties dialog box.

6. Right-click the document that you sent to the printer, and click **Cancel**.

7. Click the **Printer** menu and click **Pause Printing** to remove the check mark.

8. Has the title bar of the printer window changed?

9. Close the printer window.

If your instructor asks you to delete the printer that you created in Hands-on Project 11-3, right-click the printer and click Delete. Confirm the deletion by clicking Yes.

11

CASE PROJECT

Aspen Consulting Project: Configuring Network Printing

Modular Furnishings manufactures steel and wood furniture products for offices and computer rooms. The manufacturing building has three servers, one that is used for manufacturing, one that tracks inventory, and one that handles product distribution. Because each server is in a central location for its associated function, the company has purchased two identical printers to connect to each server. There also are four printers that attach to the network by means of print server cards. Modular Furnishings has hired you to advise them on the setup of the printers.

1. The manufacturing building has two people who are assigned to manage the printers for the entire building. Modular Furnishings asks you to explain how to set up the printers that are attached to the servers and the printers that have their own print server cards. Develop a general instruction set that they can refer to when setting up a printer. As you develop your instructions, keep in mind that all of the workstations that access the printers are running Windows 98. Also, two of the printers that are

connected to the print server cards are PostScript only. All other printers are PCL only. The network is TCP/IP-based.

2. Explain what permissions should be granted to the two people who will be setting up and managing the printers, and explain how to set up the permissions.

3. The people who are assigned to manage the printers ask for your recommendations on whether to manage all of the printers from one server, from two servers, or from all three. What questions would you ask to help you make recommendations? In general, are all of these options possible? Explain your answers.

4. The inventory process uses a just-in-time (JIT) technique that requires constant printing of tags for each inventory item, and it is anticipated that both of the printers on the inventory server will be continuously busy. How do you recommend setting up the printers for this situation? Create an addendum to your answer in Assignment 1 to explain the specifics of how to implement your recommendation. Also, does your answer to this question affect your response to Assignment 2?

5. The management of the manufacturing unit wants to track all successful and failed printed distribution invoices created from the distribution server. Explain how this can be accomplished.

6. The two printer coordinators have some extra questions about the following:

   □ Is there a way to set up large print jobs so that they only print after 7:00 PM, when most employees have gone home?

   □ How can a printer be stopped from printing while it is being maintained?

   □ Is there a way to retain print files so that they can be reprinted? If so, how are they deleted when no longer needed?

   Prepare a document to answer their questions.

7. Printouts from the printers connected to the manufacturing server often have pages from other printouts mixed in. How can you solve this problem?

OPTIONAL CASE PROJECTS FOR TEAMS

Team Case One

Mark Arnez is curious about the range of Windows 2000 Server printing capabilities. He asks you to form a team to compile as complete a list as possible that explains all of the printing features and options supported in Windows 2000 Server.

Team Case Two

Mark Arnez wants you to form a small group of consultants to develop a troubleshooting flow chart for printing problems that might occur in Windows 2000 Server. Use the Print Troubleshooter and other resources to develop a complete flow chart.

12

REMOTE ACCESS AND VIRTUAL PRIVATE NETWORKS

After reading this chapter and completing the exercises you will be able to:

♦ Explain how remote access and virtual private network (VPN) services work

♦ Explain how to implement remote access communications devices and protocols

♦ Configure remote access services, security, dial-up connectivity, and client access

♦ Configure VPN services, security, dial-up connectivity, and client access

♦ Troubleshoot remote access, VPN services, and client connectivity

---

For millions of computer users who telecommute from home or while traveling, the ability to remotely connect to a network directly affects how they do business. People who telecommute represent one of the fastest growing populations of network users, which is fueling dramatic changes in telecommunications as well as in the capabilities of desktop, laptop, and notebook computers. The client computers used in remote communication connect through a wide range of options, consisting of plain telephone lines, high-speed dedicated lines, cable TV, and satellite communications. Windows 2000 Server comes equipped with Remote Access Server services and virtual private network (VPN) services, which give clients remote access using nearly all conceivable options.

In this chapter you learn how to install, configure, and troubleshoot Windows 2000 Remote Access and VPN server services. You learn to set up security to protect the network that is accessed remotely and to protect the client, and you learn how to set up remote access using simple dial-up modem lines and more complex high-speed communications lines.

HOW REMOTE ACCESS WORKS

There are several ways to remotely access a server on a network. If you use public telephone lines to dial in to your local Internet service provider (ISP), you have already experienced one method of remote access. That method requires that you have a computer with a modem, a computer operating system, and an Internet browser such as Microsoft Internet Explorer. The servers you access may be UNIX, Windows 2000, or other servers that offer a special interface like the Microsoft Internet Information Services (IIS). The files and information that you access are strictly controlled by the capabilities of the interface on the server and the Internet site manager or "Webmaster."

Before widespread use of the Internet, many people accessed their organization's network by dialing into a network workstation running remote access software, such as pcANYWHERE or Carbon Copy. That workstation is left running most of the time so that a single user can dial in to it from a remote computer, such as one at home (see Figure 12-1). The remote computer takes control of the network computer that is left turned on and accesses hosts, servers, or software available through the network. When this method was first used, access was frustrating because modems were slow, and someone might inadvertently turn off the computer connected to the network. Failing to leave the network workstation turned on is still a problem, and there are limitations because the mouse on the network workstation cannot be accessed by the user over the telephone connection.

Another way to set up remote communication is to configure TCP/IP, Telnet (a terminal emulator), and FTP (for file transfer) at the network workstation and leave the workstation turned on. The remote workstation that accesses the network workstation has the same elements configured, and obtains or sends files through FTP. This method also has disadvantages because it is complex to set up, has limited GUI support and enables access to the remote workstation only, and many people fail to set a password because the software is hard to use. Also, there still is the problem that the network workstation may not be left turned on or that a power failure will shut it down.

In the early 1990s Novell improved on remote access technology by introducing the NetWare Access Server (NAS). The original concept of NAS was to make one computer connected to the network act as many workstations in the same unit. For example, a network computer running NAS might contain five modem cards, enabling that number of users to dial in. On that system each user would have a specific portion of the computer to use, including CPU and hard disk space, with the NAS acting like five small computers in one.

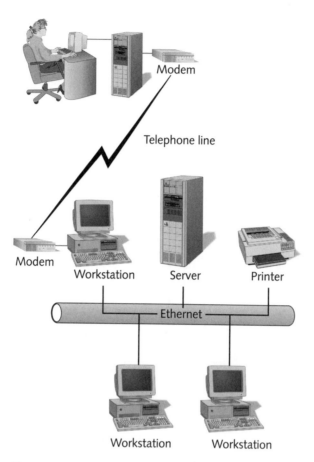

Modem

Telephone line

Modem
Workstation   Server   Printer

Ethernet

Workstation   Workstation

12

Figure 12-1   Remotely accessing a workstation on a network

Microsoft dramatically improved network access in Windows NT Server—and now in Windows 2000 Server—by enabling a server to double as a remote access server. A computer running Windows 2000 Server can have **Remote Access Services** (**RAS**) installed to turn it into a RAS server capable of handling hundreds of simultaneous connections (see Figure 12-2). The Windows 2000 server performs its normal functions as a server, but serves remote access needs at the same time. A user dials in to the RAS server, providing her or his Windows 2000 Server account name and password, accessing a standalone Windows 2000 server or multiple servers and resources, if the Active Directory is installed. Another way for a client to access the RAS server is through the Internet or an intranet, using specialized tunneling protocols (discussed later in this chapter). If NWLink is set up at the user's workstation and NetWare Client Service is set up in the RAS server, that user also can provide a password to log on to one or more NetWare servers through a Windows 2000 server set up as a RAS server.

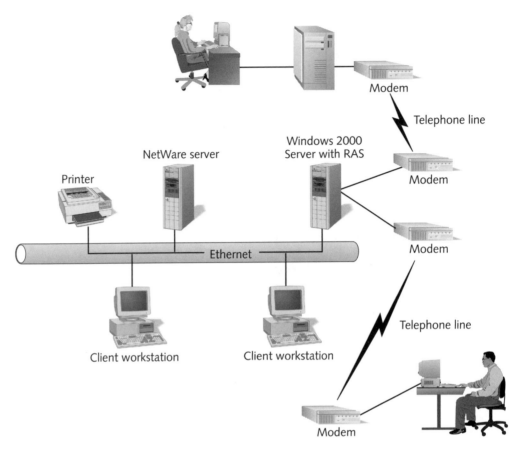

Figure 12-2   Remotely accessing a network through Microsoft RAS

HOW VIRTUAL PRIVATE NETWORKS WORK

A **virtual private network** (**VPN**) is an intranet (see Chapters 1 and 3) that is designed for restricted access by specific clients who can be identified in a combination ways: by user account, by IP address, and by subnet address. For example, you might set up a VPN for students at a college so that only authorized students have access to the VPN to look up their academic progress reports and financial information. Another example is to set up a VPN for managers and supervisors in a company to enable them to view confidential sales and accounting information. Many VPNs are accessed remotely by connecting remote networks through routers and by connecting remote VPN clients through dial-up and high-speed communications lines. Some companies are also finding that they can save money on connections by setting up VPNs over the Internet and using World Wide Web communications (see Chapter 13). This is a common use of a Microsoft VPN server in which the server is also configured as a Web server, or connects remote network connections to a Web server. The user accesses the server by starting her or his Web browser and then connecting to the combined Microsoft VPN and Web server over the Internet. Although it is transported over the Internet, the connection is protected from other Internet traffic, because the VPN/Web server sets up a special communications tunnel within the Internet. An organization can save thousands of dollars in modems and other connection equipment and still enable several hundred remote users to access their network through one or two Internet communications lines.

A Windows 2000 server can be set up as a VPN server by implementing Routing and Remote Access Services and then limiting who can access the server by setting up remote access policies that limit access to only those clients on certain subnets, only those who have certain IP addresses, only those who have certain user accounts, or a combination of these. In the example of the company VPN for managers and supervisors, you might install VPN services on a server that is connected to the subnet 177.28.19, which is used by the company CEO and managers. Access to the VPN server would be limited to only the users on that subnet (users whose IP addresses begin with 177.28.19). Also, the supervisors and some managers, who are scattered throughout different locations and who are on different subnets, can be granted access by authorizing their individual IP addresses, such as 177.28.23.10, 177.28.44.129, and so on. A tunnel can even be set up to a Web server on another subnet, such as 177.28.7. When the CEO, managers, and supervisors are at home or in a remote location, they access the VPN server by connecting through the Internet or through a telecommunications line. You might compare setting up a VPN to creating a private tunnel through a network or the Internet, and telecommunications links for each member client. Clients can access the tunnel from many different locations, but they first must have authorization to enter the tunnel. The particular VPN server that they need to reach is at the end of the tunnel. One network or the Internet can have hundreds of these special tunnels to different locations, and every access to every tunnel is carefully protected (through security protocols) for members only. Figure 12-3 illustrates the architecture of a VPN. In this instance, the Windows 2000 server is also set up to act as a VPN server that authorizes incoming remote clients for access through routers on a network and through two high-speed WAN links: T-carrier and frame relay. A **T-carrier** link is a WAN link that supports different levels of high-speed computing through lines that supply multiple communications channels. The most common versions are T-1 for communications up to 1.544 Mbps, and T-3 for communications up to 44.736 Mbps. **Frame relay** is a high-speed WAN communications technology that uses switched channels for communications that range from 56 Kbps to 45 Mbps. The combined VPN server acts like a network guardian for those who access the network remotely.

12

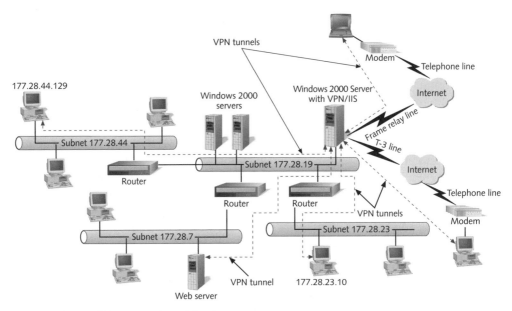

Figure 12-3   VPN network architecture

USING MICROSOFT REMOTE ACCESS SERVICES

A Windows 2000 server that is also a RAS server offers secure, flexible remote access into that server and to other Windows 2000, Windows NT, and NetWare servers on a network. A computer with one or more modems and the Windows 2000 Server or Windows 2000 Professional operating system can be set up for RAS, because RAS is included with the operating system. Windows 2000 Professional is a limited RAS server because it can handle only one caller at a time. Windows 2000 Server enables up to 256 dial-in remote callers and a nearly unlimited number (depending on the hardware) of Internet-based clients to con-nect at the same time. A RAS server offers remote connectivity to the following client oper-ating systems:

- MS-DOS
- Windows 3.1 and 3.11 (Windows for Workgroups)
- Windows NT (all versions)
- Windows 95
- Windows 98
- Windows 2000 Server and Professional

Not only is it designed to work with many kinds of clients, but a RAS server also supports the following types of connections:

- Asynchronous modems (such as the modem you may already use in your PC)
- Synchronous modems through an access server
- Null modem communications
- Regular dial-up telephone lines
- Leased telecommunication lines, such as T-carrier
- ISDN lines (and digital modems)
- X.25 lines
- DSL lines
- Frame relay lines

Integrated Services Digital Network (**ISDN**) is a standard for delivering data services over specialized digital telephone lines using 64 Kbps channels. The channels are combined to offer different types of services, for example, an ISDN basic rate interface consists of three channels. Two are 64 Kbps channels for data, voice, and graphics transmissions. The third channel is a 16 Kbps channel used for communications signaling. Many United States telecommunications companies offer ISDN, which is often used for industrial-strength Internet connectivity. **X.25** is an older WAN communications method originally used to transmit data over telecommunications lines at speeds up to 64 Kbps, but upgraded in 1992 to provide speeds up to 2.048 Mbps. X.25 is more commonly used in Europe and other countries than in the United States or Canada.

One of the most common ways to connect is by using asynchronous modems and dial-up telephone lines, which in many areas offer 56 Kbps connectivity through regular modems. In some areas, telecommunications companies offer **digital subscriber line** (**DSL**) technology over regular telephone lines that enable upstream (sending from the client) communications that are as fast as 2.048 Mbps and downstream (receiving at the client) communications at up to 60 Mbps. As you plan what services to use, purchase modems and communications adapters (such as those for ISDN, DSL, and X.25) listed in the hardware compatibility list (HCL, see Chapter 2).

Microsoft RAS provides support for the standardized modem driver, **Universal Modem Driver**, used by recently developed modems. It also contains support for the **Telephone Application Programming Interface** (**TAPI**). TAPI is an interface for line device functions, such as automatic dialing, call holding, call receiving, call hang-up, and call forwarding. **Line devices** are communications equipment such as modems, ISDN adapters, X.25 adapters, and fax cards that directly connect to a telecommunications line.

Besides supporting different types of modems and communications equipment, Windows 2000 RAS is compatible with the following network transport and remote communications protocols:

- NetBEUI
- TCP/IP
- NWLink
- PPP
- PPTP
- L2TP

12

Implementing Remote Communications Devices

Improvements in remote access have involved dramatic improvements in remote communications devices such as modems. Modems are a key piece in making remote access possible and worthwhile. The term **modem** is a shortened version of the full name, modulator/demodulator. This device converts a computer's outgoing digital signal to an analog signal that can be transmitted over a telephone line. It also converts the incoming analog signal to a digital signal that the computer can understand. A modem is attached to a computer in one of two ways: internally or externally. An internal modem is installed inside the computer, using an empty expansion slot on the main board. An external modem is a separate device that connects to a serial or USB port on the computer. An external modem is attached by using a cable that is designed for modem communications and that matches the serial port or USB connector on the computer. The most commonly used type of modem is asynchronous, which means that each unit of information is communicated using a special signal or data bit to show the start and end of a unit during transmission. Synchronous modems are less commonly used and employ a clocking technique to indicate the start and end of a communications unit.

The modem data transfer rate is measured in **bits per second** (**bps**). Dial-up telephone line modems are currently capable of up to 56 Kbps rates, and are soon expected to reach over 100 Kbps. Cable TV modems transmit at a much higher rate, depending on the modem and the cable TV company. For example, one vendor's modem transmits at up to 30 Mbps for upstream (sending) communications and at up to 15 Mbps for downstream (receiving).

CAUTION

Cable TV RAS communications are not recommended at this writing because there can be security problems that enable other cable subscribers to intercept your communications.

When a computer is connected to a modem, the data transfer speed is the **data terminal equipment** (**DTE**), communications rate. A workstation client and the RAS server are both examples of DTE because they prepare data to be transmitted. The modem is called the **data communications equipment** (**DCE**), and its speed is the DCE communications rate. The computer's port setup for the modem (DTE rate) should be the same or higher than the DCE rate of the modem. For example, if you have a 56 Kbps modem, select a maximum speed of 57600 (the closest setting) in Windows 2000 Server when you configure the computer for that modem. (You can view how a modem and its computer port are set up in Hands-on Project 12-1.)

CAUTION

Sometimes modems will not communicate because of how they are set up. For example, an older 14.4 Kbps modem on a client will not be able to establish communications with a newer 56 Kbps modem, if the 56 Kbps modem is not set up to negotiate down to a slower speed. Also, when telephone lines are very noisy, some modems attempt to step down to a slower speed for data compression. If one of the communicating modems does not have data compression capability or cannot automatically step down to a slower speed, they may not be able to establish a link-up. Keep these cautions in mind when you set up network modems and work with users to solve modem communication problems.

ISDN requires using a **terminal adapter** (**TA**) to connect a computer to an ISDN line. A TA also is called a digital modem, even though it is not truly a modulator/demodulator, because it uses digital instead of analog technology. ISDN digital TAs are available for about the same cost as a high-quality asynchronous modem, but with higher data transfer capabilities, such as 128 Kbps or faster. If you connect using X.25 or DSL, then you will need a specialized X.25 or DSL adapter to install in the computer. (T-carrier and frame relay are typically connected by using an access server or a router that forwards communications to the Windows RAS or VPN server.)

Use the Add/Remove Hardware Wizard to install regular telephone modems, DSL adapters, ISDN TAs, or X.25 adapters. Also, use the Network and Dial-up Connections tool to create a specialized connection for each type of device (see the section titled "Configuring a Dial-up Connection for a RAS Server").

12

TIP One advantage when using ISDN is that it is possible to link multiple lines or communications channels as though they were one, for example linking two 64 Kbps channels into one 128 Kbps link, called an **aggregate link**. Windows 2000 Server can configure aggregate links by using Multilink, which is described later in this chapter.

If you need to provide remote access by setting up more than two modems or by offering several different access options, such as a combination of regular analog modems, ISDN, and X.25 lines, consider using an access server. An **access server** is a device that connects directly to a network at one end and that offers combinations of communications options for connecting to outside telecommunications lines. An access server can be equipped with one or more TAs, X.25 adapters, and modems. For example, one access server might contain 16 modem connections (sometimes called a modem bank), two ISDN connections through the appropriate types of adapters, and one T-1 connection. Some modular access servers can have nearly 70 modems and are equipped with redundant power supplies for fault tolerance. Further, many access servers include specialized software to work with a Windows 2000 server over a network to provide connectivity for RAS clients and for Web server clients. Figure 12-4 illustrates an access server.

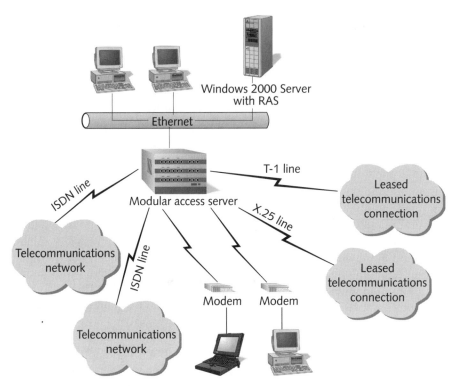

Figure 12-4   Using an access server

Implementing Remote Access Protocols

Two protocols are used most frequently in remote communications: SLIP and PPP. **Serial Line Internet Protocol** (**SLIP**) was originally designed for UNIX environments for point-to-point communications among computers, servers, and hosts using TCP/IP. SLIP is an older remote communications protocol with more overhead (larger packet header and more network traffic) than PPP. Compressed Serial Line Internet Protocol (CSLIP) is a newer version of SLIP that compresses header information in each packet sent across a remote link. CSLIP, now usually referred to as SLIP, reduces the overhead of a connection so that it is less than that of PPP, by decreasing the header size and thus increasing the speed of communications. However, the header still must be decompressed at the receiving end. The original SLIP and the newer SLIP (CSLIP) are limited in that they do not support network connection authentication to prevent someone from intercepting a communication. They also do not support automatic negotiation of the network connection through multiple network connection layers at the same time. Another disadvantage of both versions of SLIP is that they are intended only for asynchronous communications, such as through a modem-to-modem type of connection.

Point-to-Point Protocol (**PPP**) is used more commonly than either version of SLIP for remote communications because it has lower overhead and more capability. PPP supports more network protocols, such as IPX/SPX, NetBEUI, and TCP/IP. It can automatically negotiate communications with several network communications layers at once, and it supports connection authentication. PPP is supplemented by the newer **Point-to-Point Tunneling Protocol (PPTP)**, which enables remote communications to RAS and a VPN through the Internet or an intranet. Through PPTP, a company manager can access a report housed on that company's in-house intranet by dialing in to the Internet from a remote location. Microsoft VPN networks also use **Layer Two Tunneling Protocol (L2TP)**, which works similarly to PPTP. Both protocols encapsulate PPP and create special tunnels within a network or over the Internet that reflect intranets and VPNs. Unlike PPTP, L2TP uses an additional network communications standard, called Layer Two Forwarding, that enables forwarding on the basis of MAC addressing (device address, see Chapter 3) in addition to IP addressing. PPP, PPTP, and L2TP all support the security measures described later in this chapter.

As you think about protocols encapsulating protocols, consider the process of shipping a computer in the mail. The computer is packaged in protective styrofoam, and then sealed in a box. In the same way, TCP/IP (and other network protocols, such as NWLink) is encapsulated in PPP to be shipped over a remote network, and then PPP is encapsulated in PPTP or L2TP for shipment over the Internet, an intranet, or a VPN.

PPP and PPTP both support synchronous and asynchronous communications, enabling connectivity through modems, dial-up and high-speed leased telecommunication lines, DSL lines, ISDN, and X.25 lines. On the client side, PPP is available in Windows 95, Windows 98, all versions of Windows NT, and all versions of Windows 2000. *When a Windows 2000 server is also configured as a RAS server, supports PPP and its associated protocols, but not SLIP.* PPP configuration is well suited on networks in which users perform remote access through computers running Windows 95, 98, NT, or 2000. Table 12-1 compares SLIP to PPP.

12

Windows NT Server 4.0 supports either SLIP or PPP when configured as a RAS server. If you convert Windows NT Server 4.0, set up with RAS and using SLIP, to Windows 2000 Server, plan to convert the RAS implementation and all RAS clients to use PPP.

Table 12-1 SLIP and PPP Compared

Feature	SLIP	PPP
Network protocol support	TCP/IP	TCP/IP, IPX/SPX, and NetBEUI
Asynchronous communications support	Yes	Yes
Synchronous communications support	No	Yes
Simultaneous network configuration negotiation and automatic connection with multiple levels of the OSI model between the communicating nodes	No	Yes
Support for connection authentication to guard against eavesdroppers	No	Yes

CONFIGURING RAS

There are several essential steps to configuring RAS communications on a Windows 2000 Server network:

- Configuring a Microsoft 2000 server as a network's RAS server, including configuring the right protocols to provide RAS access through dial-up connectivity
- Configuring a DHCP Relay Agent for TCP/IP communications
- Configuring RAS security
- Configuring a dial-up and remote connection
- Configuring RAS on client workstations

Configuring a RAS Server

There are two components to making a Windows 2000 server double as a RAS server. You already have learned the first component, which is to implement a way to connect multiple modems to a network. On a very small network you may need to install only one or two modems directly into an existing networked computer running Microsoft 2000 Server. For a larger network, you can install an access server with enough modems, ISDN, and other types of connections for the type of communications required by users.

CAUTION

Choose an access server that is designed to be compatible with Microsoft 2000 Server. A compatible access server will include software and drivers that can be used to coordinate communications between the Windows 2000 server and the access server, including IP routing capabilities.

The second component is to install the software needed to turn the Windows 2000 server into a RAS server. (As for most other administrative functions, you must be logged on as Administrator or with Administrator privileges.) You install RAS using the Routing and Remote Access tool, which is opened from the Administrative Tools menu or as an MMC snap-in. For example, to start the tool from the Administrative Tools menu, click Start, point to Programs, point to Administrative Tools, and click Routing and Remote Access. After the tool is started:

1. Click Routing and Remote Access in the tree, if it is not already selected, click the Action menu, and click Add Server.

2. The Add Server dialog box enables you to install routing and RAS capabilities on the local server or on another Windows 2000 server connected to the network or in the domain. Also, there is a Browse button that enables you to search for another server on which to install the services. For example, click *This computer* to install routing and RAS on the local server, and then click OK.

3. Under the tree, right-click the computer and click Configure and Enable Routing and Remote Access (see Figure 12-5).

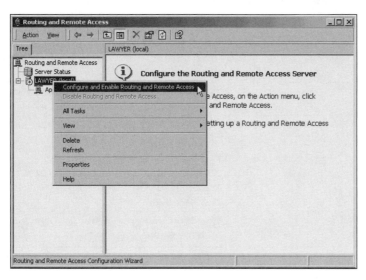

Figure 12-5   Configuring routing and RAS

4. Click Next after the Routing and Remote Access Server Setup Wizard starts.

5. There are five options (see Figure 12-6 and Table 12-2) from which to select. Click *Remote access server* to make this a RAS server, and then click Next.

6. If a screen displays asking you to choose between creating a basic or advanced remote access server, select set up an advanced remote access server.

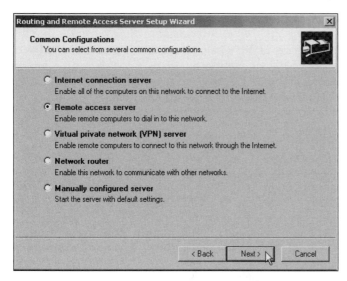

Figure 12-6   Selecting the option to install RAS

12

Table 12-2 Routing and Remote Access Options

Option	Description
Internet connection server	Use this option so that networked computers in addition to the server can connect to the Internet, which is especially useful in a small office environment in which all users need Internet access, but there is only one dial-up, ISDN, or other outside line to an ISP.
Remote access server	Use this option to set up remote access services to the network through the Windows 2000 server.
Virtual private network (VPN) server	Use this option when you have an intranet (VPN) that you want users to be able to access through a remote connection or the Internet.
Network router	Use this option to have Windows 2000 Server function as a router on the network—directing traffic to other networks or subnetworks.
Manually configure the server	Use this option when you want to customize the routing and remote access capabilities.

7. The protocols that are already installed on the server are displayed. Click Yes to use all of the protocols listed, or click No if you need to add protocols to the list for support through RAS. Click Next. (If you clicked No, then click Next and click Finish on the next screen to end the Wizard, install the additional protocols, and restart the Wizard.)

8. If you clicked Yes and AppleTalk is among the supported protocols, the Wizard displays a dialog box to enable AppleTalk clients to access the RAS server through the Guest account.

CAUTION

> If you enable AppleTalk access, you cannot set a password for the Guest account. This means you should carefully check what resources are available through the Guest account, because they can be accessed by anyone, including intruders. If the Macintosh clients support IP (such as MAC OS 8.5 and higher), consider using IP instead of AppleTalk to access the RAS server.

9. If TCP/IP is one of the installed protocols, then the Wizard displays a dialog box with two options (see Figure 12-7), to use DHCP to automatically assign IP addresses for clients who access the network through RAS or for you to manually specify a range of IP addresses. If you choose to specify a range of addresses, a specialized dialog box is displayed in which to enter the range; make sure that none of the addresses in the range is already in use by any network client. Also, if you have Internet access and use an ISP, consult your ISP about what range is acceptable and will not interfere with other Internet sites. Click Next after you make your selection.

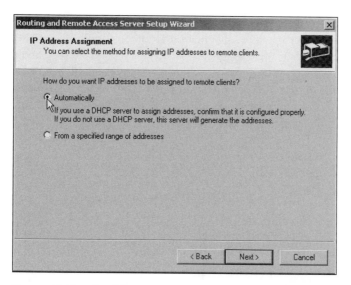

Figure 12-7   IP address assignment options

10. In the Managing Multiple and Remote Access Servers dialog box, you have the option to make this or another RAS server a **Remote Authentication Dial-in User Service (RADIUS)** server. A RADIUS server is used when you plan to set up two or more RAS servers and want to standardize access policies and authentication. If you have only a standalone server or plan to have only one RAS server, click No and then click Next. If you plan to set up additional RAS servers, for example in a domain, click Yes. Clicking Yes and then Next displays another dialog box on which to specify one RADIUS server to coordinate authentication and to keep track of remote dial-in statistics for all RAS servers. You can also specify an alternate RADIUS server as a backup and a password to enable the RAS server to access the RADIUS server. Further, if you click Yes, you should also later install the **Internet Authentication Service (IAS)** through the Add/Remove Programs utility. IAS enables you to establish security (discussed later in this chapter) for RAS dial-in access.

11. Click Finish. (If you configured to use DHCP for IP address assignment, also click OK in the information message that you must configure the RAS server as a DHCP Relay Agent.)

If you selected to automatically assign IP addresses and are using DHCP, configure the DHCP Relay Agent so that it contains the IP address of the RAS server. A **DHCP Relay Agent** broadcasts IP configuration information between the DHCP server and the client acquiring an address, when they are on different networks.

Try Hands-on Project 12-2 to set up a RAS server.

After the RAS server is set up, you can further configure it from the Routing and Remote Access tool by right-clicking the RAS server in the tree and clicking Properties (see Figure 12-8). For example, the Properties dialog box has a tab for each protocol that you have configured, and each protocol's tab is used to enable or disable that protocol for remote access. Also, the IP tab is used to specify how IP addresses are assigned (DHCP or a manually specified range). The IPX tab is used to specify how IPX network numbers are assigned (for access to older NetWare servers), and the NetBEUI tab is used to specify whether NetBEUI use applies only to the RAS server or to the entire network. Also, there is a General tab on which you can configure Windows 2000 Server to function as a router for the LAN or for the LAN and for dial-in client connections. The Security tab is used to configure security and authentication methods, which you will explore later in this chapter. The PPP tab is used to configure PPP options, such as aggregating ISDN connections (also discussed later in this chapter). Last, there is a tab to configure event logging, such as access errors and warnings or errors using the PPP protocol.

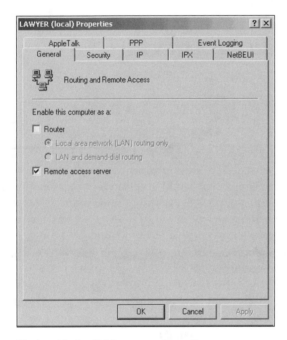

Figure 12-8   RAS server properties

Configuring a DHCP Agent

When a RAS server is configured so that the IP addresses of RAS dial-in clients are obtained automatically, then the RAS server must be designated as a DHCP Relay Agent. Use the following steps to configure a DHCP Relay Agent:

1. Open the Routing and Remote Access tool.

2. Double-click the RAS server in the tree.

3. Click IP Routing in the tree.

4. Right-click DHCP Relay Agent in the IP Routing pane, and click Properties.

5. Enter the IP address of the RAS server and click Add.

6. Click OK.

You can further configure the DHCP Relay Agent by specifying the maximum number of routers, called the hop count, that an IP configuration broadcast can pass through between the client, RAS server, and DHCP server. Click DHCP Relay Agent under the tree, right-click the interface, such as Internal, and then click Properties. Make sure that the Relay DHCP packets box is checked, and then specify the *Hop-count threshold*. For example, consider a situation in which each client must go through one router to reach the RAS server, and the RAS server must go through one router to reach the DHCP server. In this example, the threshold should be set at 2 or 3 if the server is configured as a router (try Hands-on Project 12-3).

Configuring Multilink and Bandwidth Allocation Protocol

A RAS server can be configured to support **Multilink** (also called **Multilink PPP**). Multilink is used to combine or aggregate two or more communications channels so they appear as one large channel. For example, Multilink can combine two 64 Kbps ISDN channels and one 16 Kbps signaling channel in the *basic rate interface* service to appear as one 144 Kbps channel; or, multiple 64 Kbps *primary rate interface* channels and one 64 Kbps signaling channel are aggregated into 1.536 Mbps. Another example is combining two 56 Kbps modems into an aggregate speed of 112 Kbps. The limitation of using Multilink is that it must be implemented in the client as well as in the server, so that the client can take full advantage of the aggregated links. Thus if you use Multilink to aggregate two 56 Kbps modems for one 112 Kbps link at the server, the client, such as Windows 2000 Professional, must have a communications link set up using Multilink to aggregate two 56 Kbps modems.

Multilink can be used with **Bandwidth Allocation Protocol (BAP)** to ensure that a client's connection has enough speed or bandwidth for a particular application. BAP helps ensure that the amount of bandwidth increases to the maximum for the aggregated channels as needed, and reciprocally contracts as the need becomes less. For example, consider a connection in which the remote client begins by accessing a relatively low-bandwidth application such as e-mail over an aggregated link of two 56 Kbps modems. BAP might determine that only 56 Kbps is needed for the application. However, when the client accesses a voice and video presentation in a multimedia application, such as a chemistry lesson or a movie clip, BAP can increase the bandwidth to the full aggregated speed of 112 Kbps by adding the line to the second modem for the duration of the multimedia presentation. BAP matches bandwidth utilization to the need, so that unused bandwidth can be given to another client whenever possible. Besides adding a line for use by a client, BAP can hang up a line so that another client can use it.

To configure Multilink and BAP, right-click the RAS server in the Routing and Remote Access tool, click Properties, and then click the PPP tab (see Figure 12-9). Check the *Multilink connections* option to enable Multilink, and check *Dynamic bandwidth control using BAP or BACP* to use BAP or BACP. (**BACP** is the **Bandwidth Allocation Control Protocol**, which selects a preferred client when two or more clients vie for the same bandwidth.)

12

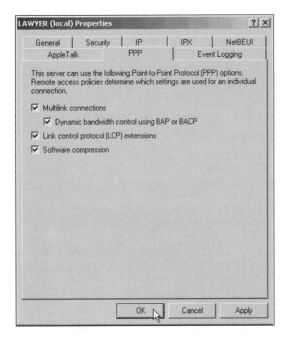

Figure 12-9   Configuring Multilink and BAP

The option to use Link control protocol (LCP) extensions should also be checked when you want to use callback security (discussed later in this chapter). Also, check the *Software compression* option to compress data over a remote link for faster transport. This option enables the use of the Microsoft Point-to-Point Compression Protocol (try Hands-on Project 12-4).

Configuring Security and RAS Options Through a RAS Policy and Profile

When a user accesses a RAS server through his or her account, that access is protected by the account access security that already applies, for example through a group policy or the default domain policy. Thus, if account lockout is set up in a group policy, the same account lockout settings apply when a RAS user enters her or his account name and password. Besides the security policies already in place, you can set up RAS security through several other techniques, which include creating user account dial-in security, setting remote access group policies, and establishing security through protocols.

The first step to take is to set up dial-in security at the user account, which enables you to employ callback security. (Recall from Chapter 8 that callback security entails having the RAS server call back the workstation that is requesting access.) This security is set on each user's Windows 2000 server or domain account. For example, the remote workstation client calls into the RAS server to access a particular Windows 2000 server user account. With callback security set up, the server calls back the remote computer to verify its telephone number, in order to discourage a hacker from trying to access the server. The callback options available in Windows 2000 Server are the following:

- *No Callback*, which means the server allows access on the first call attempt
- *Set By Caller*, so that the number used for the callback is provided by the remote computer
- *Always Callback to*, so the number to call back is already permanently entered into Windows 2000

To set up callback security on a particular user account, double-click the account and set the dial-in security in the account's properties (try Hands-on Project 12-5). For example, if the Active Directory is installed:

1. Open the Active Directory Users and Computers tool.

2. If necessary to display the objects under it, double-click the domain in which the account resides, and then double-click the container holding the account, such as Users.

3. Right-click the account on which you want to set up dial-in security, and click Properties.

4. Depending on how Windows 2000 automatically adjusts to your screen's resolution and capabilities, the next screen shows all user Properties tabs or displays double arrows from which to view the tabs (see Figure 12-10). Access the Dial-in tab by clicking it in the display of tabs or by using the double arrows and then clicking to open the tab.

12

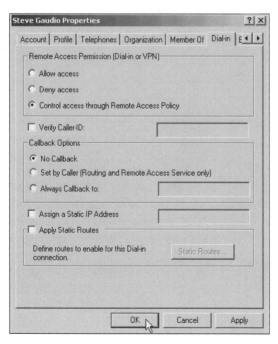

Figure 12-10   Configuring dial-in security for a user account

5. Click the Allow access radio button or click Control access through Remote Access Policy (remote access policies are described later in this section).

6. Click Verify Caller-ID and provide the user's telephone number, if that user and your organization have Caller ID and the user will always use the same number to dial in remotely.

7. Select the callback option (enter a telephone number to call back if you select *Always Callback to*).

8. Select whether to define a static IP address that will always apply to anyone who dials in remotely to that account and whether to use static routing (or leave the boxes blank to enable DHCP and IAS to determine an IP address and routing).

9. Click OK.

Some Dial-in parameters are deactivated (grayed-out) if you are operating in mixed mode instead of native mode (see Chapter 9). These parameters include Control Access through Remote Access Policy, Verify Caller-ID, Assign a Static IP Address, and Apply Static Routes.

When you decide to set up remote access policies for dial-in RAS or VPN servers (see the section "Configuring a VPN Server"), first install IAS (Internet Authentication Service) to enable you to centrally manage one or more RAS servers. IAS is installed by following these steps:

1. Open the Control Panel and double-click Add/Remove Programs.

2. Click Add/Remove Windows Components. If the Windows Components Wizard dialog box is not automatically started, click the Components button to start it.

3. When the Windows Components Wizard starts, scroll to find Networking Services and then double-click that option.

4. Make sure the box for Internet Authentication Service is checked (along with any other services you want to add), and click OK.

5. Click Next.

6. Click Finish.

7. Close the Add/Remove Programs window and the Control Panels.

If you have only one RAS or VPN server, you can set the remote access policies on a single server by using the Routing and Remote Access Tool, double-clicking the server, and double-clicking *Allow access if dial-in permission is enabled*. Then complete the parameters, which are the same as those described next for IAS member servers coordinated by RADIUS.

After IAS is installed, add participating RAS and VPN servers by opening the Internet Authentication Service, which is accessed by clicking Start, pointing to Programs, pointing to Administrative Tools, and clicking Internet Authentication Service. To add a server, right-click Clients under Internet Authentication Service in the tree and click New Client. Provide the name of the client server, and click Next. Provide the IP address of the server, select RADIUS Standard for the Client-Vendor, provide a secret RADIUS password in the

Shared secret box, confirm the password, and click Finish. Use the Remote Access Policies object in the tree to configure several types of security that include (but are not limited to):

- Granting dial-in access, if dial-in access is also granted on a user's account
- Specifying dial-in constraints, such as the hours and days when RAS can be accessed
- Setting IP address assignment rules
- Setting authentication
- Setting encryption
- Allowing Multilink connections

To begin configuring security, click Remote Access Policies in the tree and double-click *Allow access if dial-in permission is enabled*, to display the dialog box in Figure 12-11. The name of the policy is displayed in the Policy name box, enabling you to create one or more policies with unique names. By default the name is "Allow access if dial-in permission is enabled." Below the Policy name box is another box that enables you to set the time of day and day of the week restrictions on when a user can access RAS servers. To change these settings, double-click the default that is already highlighted, click the Grant or Deny radio buttons, use your pointing device to mark the desired times and days, and click OK. Click the Add button to set up additional access attributes, such as a particular telephone number that must be used by an account, or to specify that the user must belong to a particular predefined group, such as RAS Users. Finally, click the Grant remote access permission radio button to enable users to access the RAS and VPN servers on the basis of conditions you set up in the *Specify conditions to match* box (try Hands-on Project 12-6).

12

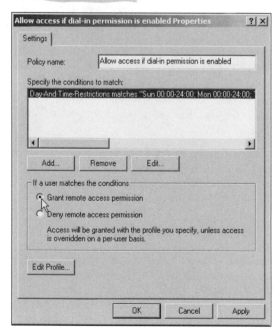

Figure 12-11 Granting remote access as a RAS policy

TIP One way to manage users' access to RAS and VPN servers is to set up only specific user accounts to grant dial-in access or to control access through the remote access policies (see Figure 12-10). If you control access through the remote access policies, consider fine-tuning the management of user account access by creating groups. For example, create a universal or domain local group that has access to one or more RAS or VPN servers, and create a global group of the user accounts that you want to have the access. Make the global group a member of the universal or domain local group. Next, open the Remote Access Policies object under the RAS or VPN server, click the Add button (see Figure 12-11), double-click Windows-Groups, click Add, double-click the universal or domain local group you created, click OK, and click OK twice.

To configure the profile and security associated with the remote access policies, click the Edit Profile button to view the dialog box shown in Figure 12-12. The options for each tab are summarized in Table 12-3. The tabs that particularly affect security are the Authentication and the Encryption tabs. The Authentication tab enables you to set up security through protocols that work with PPP, which are:

- **Extensible Authentication Protocol** (**EAP**): EAP is used for clients who access RAS through special devices such as smart cards, token cards, and others that use certificate authentication. If you click this option, then Certificate Services should be installed so that you can configure them for a particular device or certificate type. Certificate Services is installed as a Windows component by using the Control Panel Add/Remove Programs tool.

- **Challenge Handshake Authentication Protocol** (**CHAP**): CHAP requires encrypted authentication between the server and the client, but uses a generic form of password encryption, which enables UNIX computers and other non-Microsoft operating systems to connect to a RAS server.

- **CHAP with Microsoft extensions** (**MS-CHAP**): MS-CHAP and MS-CHAP v2 are set as the defaults when you install a RAS server, which means that clients must use MS-CHAP with PPP. MS-CHAP is a version of CHAP that uses a challenge-and-response form of authentication along with encryption. Windows 95, 98, NT, and 2000 support MS-CHAP.

- **CHAP with Microsoft extensions version 2** (**MS-CHAP v2**): Developed especially for VPNs, MS-CHAP v2 provides better authentication than MS-CHAP, because it requires the server and the client to authenticate mutually. It also provides more sophisticated encryption by using a different encryption key for receiving than for sending. Windows 2000 clients support MS-CHAP v2 and clients such as Windows 95 and Windows 98 can be updated to support this protocol. VPNs attempt to use MS-CHAP v2 with a client and then use MS-CHAP if the client does not support version 2.

- **Password Authentication Protocol** (**PAP**): PAP can perform authentication, but does not require it, which means that operating systems without password encryption capabilities, such as MS-DOS, are able to connect to RAS.

- **Shiva Password Authentication Protocol** (**SPAP**): SPAP provides PAP services for remote access clients, network equipment, and network management software manufactured by the Shiva Corporation, which is owned by Intel Corporation.

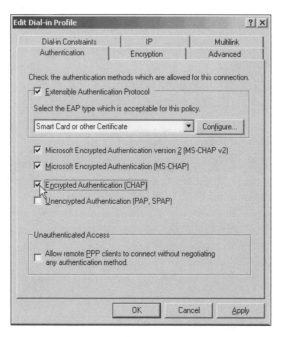

Figure 12-12   Configuring authentication

12

You can use one or a combination of these authentication protocols, and if you use a combination, then the RAS server will negotiate with the client until it finds an authentication method that will work. Also, there is an option to enable clients to connect without negotiating any form of authentication, which is *Allow remote PPP clients to connect without negotiating any authentication method.*

The Encryption tab contains four data encryption options. The data encryption options specify the types of data encryption, which include IPSec and **Microsoft Point-to-Point Encryption** (**MPPE**). IPSec is described in Chapter 4, and MPPE is a starting-to-ending-point encryption technique that uses special encryption keys varying in length from 40 to 128 bits. As is true for authentication protocols, you can select to use one or a combination of encryption options to match what the client is using. The encryption options are:

- *No Encryption:* Enables clients to connect and not employ data encryption

- *Basic:* Enables clients using 40-bit encryption key MPPE (available in Windows operating systems sold throughout the world) or IPSec

- *Strong:* Enables clients using 56-bit encryption key MPPE or IPSec

Expect Microsoft to soon include a "strongest" option for 128-bit encryption using MPPE via an upgrade or service pack.

IPSec requires that you first configure IPSec as a TCP/IP property on the RAS server (using the Network Dial-up and Connections tool, see Chapters 4 and 6). MPPE requires that the client have MS-CHAP, MS-CHAP v2, or EAP authentication support. Also, if only No Encryption is checked, then encryption is not used with any client, regardless of the client's capabilities.

Table 12-3   Dial-in and VPN Remote Access Policies Tabs

Tab	Description
Advanced	Used to designate connection attributes, such as RADIUS, frame types, AppleTalk zones, special filters, and many others
Authentication	Used to select the type or types of authentication methods, such as EAP, CHAP, MS-CHAP, MS-CHAP v2, PAP, and SPAP (or no authentication)
Dial-in Constraints	Used to set dial-in limitations, such as times of the day and days of the week when the RAS servers can be accessed, amount of time a connection can be idle before it is disconnected, maximum session time, dial-in number, and media through which to dial in (such as ISDN, X.25, modem, and fax)
Encryption	Used to designate encryption levels: no encryption, basic, strong
IP	Used to define how TCP/IP dial-in clients obtain an IP address—for example, by using the server user account settings—and to set up packet filters to limit which IP addresses can access the RAS servers
Multilink	Used to enable Multilink connections, when RAS is set up for Multilink, and to specify Multilink BAP settings

Configuring a Dial-up Connection for a RAS Server

After RAS is installed and configured, create one or more ways for the RAS server to connect to the network so it can be accessed by clients. Besides the Local Area Connection that you set up when installing Windows 2000 Server, you can also create other connections to match your particular connectivity needs, by configuring a dial-up connection to a private network or ISP through a phone line, for example, or by enabling clients to connect through a telecommunications line or the Internet. You create any of these connections by opening the Network and Dial-up Connections tool. For example, if you want to connect through a modem and dial-up telephone line:

1. Open the Network and Dial-up Connections tool.

2. Double-click Make New Connection, and click Next.

3. Click Dial-up to private network (see Figure 12-13), and click Next.

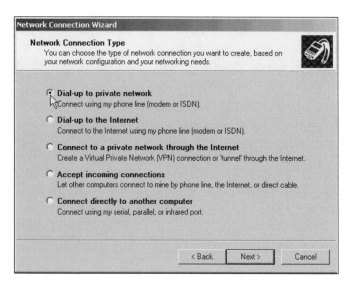

Figure 12-13   Creating a new connection

4. Enter the telephone number of the private network to which to connect, and click Next.

5. Click *For all users* so that other users can connect through this connection, and click Next.

6. If this is a small office and several users connect through a server connected to the Internet, click *Enable Internet Connection Sharing for this connection*, and click Next. Click Yes to the warning about changing the IP address, if you selected to use Internet connection sharing. Click Next.

7. Enter a name for the connection and click Finish.

Configuring Clients to Connect to RAS through Dial-up Access

Common RAS clients include Windows 95, 98, NT, and 2000. You have already learned how to install RAS in Windows 2000 and to set up a dial-up connection. To access a RAS server from the other operating systems, you must also install RAS and configure a dial-up connection on those clients. Hands-on Project 12-7 gives you practice installing RAS in Windows NT 4.0. To install RAS and dial-up connectivity in Windows 95 or 98, use the following general three-stage process:

1. Install the dial-up networking software.

   a. Open the Control Panel.

   b. Double-click the Add/Remove Programs icon.

   c. Click the Windows Setup tab.

   d. Click the Communications box and then the Details button.

    e. Click the Dial-up Networking box and click OK.

    f. Click OK.

    g. If requested, insert the Windows 95 or 98 CD-ROM and provide the drive and path to the operating system files.

    h. Click OK when the installation is completed, and if requested, click Yes to reboot.

2. Create and configure the dial-up networking connection:

    a. Double-click My Computer.

    b. Double-click the Dial-up Networking folder. If the Make New Connection Wizard does not start automatically, double-click the Make New Connection icon.

    c. The wizard will detect the modem installed at the workstation.

    d. Check the modem information to verify that it is correct. Enter a name to identify the dial-up connection (in the *Type a name for the computer you are dialing* box), and click Next.

    e. Enter the area code, telephone number, and country code of the RAS server, and click Next.

    f. Click Finish.

    g. An icon for the dial-up connection is created in the Dial-up Networking folder in My Computer; open the Dial-up Networking folder.

    h. Right-click the newly created icon, and click Properties.

    i. Click the Server Type button in Windows 95 (early version) or the Server Types tab in the later version of Windows 95 and in Windows 98.

    j. Specify PPP as the protocol for the dial-up server.

    k. Click the appropriate Advanced options, such as "Log on to network".

    l. Select the appropriate protocol, such as TCP/IP.

    m. Click the TCP/IP Settings button and enter the appropriate IP addresses for the workstation and the RAS server.

    n. Click OK three times in the early version of Windows 95 or twice in the later version of Windows 95 or in Windows 98 to save your changes.

3. Establish networking settings.

    a. Open the Control Panel and double-click the Network icon.

    b. Click the Configuration tab, highlight Dial-up Adapter, and click the Properties button.

    c. On the Driver Type tab, select Enhanced mode (32-bit or 16-bit) NDIS driver.

    d. Click the Bindings tab and checkmark the desired protocol, such as TCP/IP.

e. In the Advanced tab, select the appropriate properties, and click OK to return to the Configuration tab.

f. Select each protocol associated with the dial-up adapter (one at a time), such as TCP/IP —> Dial-up Adapter, and click Properties.

g. Check to make sure the properties match the need for the dial-up service.

h. If TCP/IP —> Dial-Up Adapter is used, make sure the necessary IP address information is provided for its properties.

i. Click OK when you are finished entering the properties.

j. Click OK in the Network dialog box. Insert the installation CD-ROM; if requested, and also restart the computer, if requested.

CONFIGURING A VPN

A Windows 2000 server can be configured as a VPN server for access through the Internet, through routers, and through telecommunications lines, such as frame relay. The general steps for setting up a VPN server are as follows:

1. Create a network connection to an ISP, a public network, or a private network by installing a WAN adapter in the server, such as an ISDN TA, or by connecting through an access server or router that goes to a WAN connection. Set up WAN access addressing as instructed by your WAN or Internet service provider.

2. Install the Routing and Remote Access Service and configure it as a virtual private network (VPN) server.

3. Establish the remote access policies and profile, including setting up EAP authentication.

4. Configure the number of PPTP and L2TP ports.

Creating a Network Connection to the ISP

The specific methods for configuring the connection to the WAN will vary, depending on whether you use a WAN adapter, an access server, or a router to connect. For example, the general steps if you are using a WAN adapter are as follows (each step may vary, depending on the equipment and manufacturer):

1. Begin by installing the WAN adapter in an appropriate expansion slot in the server.

2. Use the Add/Remove Hardware Wizard to configure the WAN adapter (see Chapter 6).

3. Use the Network and Dial-up Connections tool to create a connection to the WAN network, as described in the section "Configuring a Dial-up Connection for a RAS Server."

4. Use the Network and Dial-up Connections tool to configure Internet and local area network connections for TCP/IP according to your ISP's instructions (to configure the IP address and subnet mask, see Chapter 6).

12

If you are using an access server, follow these general steps (which may vary depending on the manufacturer's specific instructions):

1. Use the Network and Dial-up Connections tool to create a VPN connection to an access server or a router, as described in the section "Configuring a Dial-up Connection for a RAS Server."

2. Use the Network and Dial-up Connections tool to configure the VPN and local area network connections for TCP/IP according to your ISP's instructions (to configure the IP address and subnet mask, see Chapter 6).

Installing a VPN Server

To install and configure a VPN server, begin by opening the Routing and Remote Access tool as an MMC snap-in or from the Administrative Tools menu, by clicking Start, pointing to Programs, pointing to Administrative Tools, and clicking Routing and Remote Access. Then:

1. Click the Action menu and click Add Server.

2. The Add Server dialog box enables you to install routing and VPN capabilities on the local server or on another Windows 2000 server connected to the network or in the domain. For example, click *This computer* to install routing and VPN on the local server, and then click OK.

 Before you select a server, keep in mind that routing and remote access services, such as RAS, should not already be set up on that server if you want to perform a fresh installation.

3. Under the tree, right-click the computer and click Configure and Enable Routing and Remote Access.

4. Click Next after the Routing and Remote Access Server Setup Wizard starts.

5. Click *Virtual private network (VPN) server* and click Next.

6. The protocols that are already installed on the server are displayed. Click Yes to use all of the protocols listed, or click No if you need to add protocols to the list to support through the VPN server. Click Next. If you clicked No, click Next and then click Finish on the next screen to end the Wizard, install the additional protocols, and restart the Wizard.

7. If you clicked Yes and AppleTalk is among the supported protocols, the Wizard displays a dialog box to enable AppleTalk clients to access the VPN server through the Guest account. Decide whether to enable AppleTalk access, and click Next.

8. Select the method to access the WAN network or the Internet. For example, if access is through a WAN adapter, click that adapter in the Internet connection box, and then click Next.

9. Decide whether to use DHCP or IP address assignment or to assign a static range of addresses. For example, if you decide to assign a static range, click *From a specified range of addresses* as the means to assign IP addresses, and click Next. Click the New button and then enter the range of IP addresses that can be used (see Figure 12-14). Click OK and click Next. If you choose to use DHCP instead of a static range, configure the DHCP Relay Agent, as already described in the section "Configuring a DHCP Agent" (but click the new VPN server instead of a RAS server).

 Keep in mind that the upper limit of addresses that can be assigned to a static pool is 253.

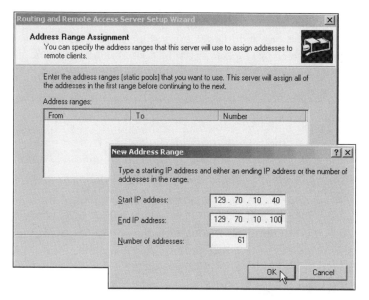

Figure 12-14   Providing a range of addresses for a VPN server

10. Specify whether this will be a RADIUS server, and click Next.

11. Click Finish.

Configuring VPN Server Properties, a VPN Policy, and a VPN Profile

You can further configure a VPN server in the same way as for RAS, by configuring its properties, remote access policies, and profile. After the VPN server installation is complete, right-click the server in the tree and click Properties to configure the server properties. Make certain that the VPN server is configured as a router (see Figure 12-8) by checkmarking the Router box and then clicking *LAN and demand-dial routing*. The other tabs in the Properties dialog box enable you to modify the configuration, for example by using the IP tab to add or remove static IP addresses from the address pool. If you are using Multilink, configure the Multilink connectivity by clicking the PPP tab (refer to Figure 12-9).

After you examine and configure the VPN server properties, set up the remote access policies and profile. If you are managing multiple VPN and RAS servers, install a RADIUS server and install IAS, as previously explained in this chapter. Set the remote access policies and profile in IAS. If there is only one VPN server, double-click the server to display the objects in the tree under it (if they are not already displayed). Next, click *Remote Access Policies* under the server, and double-click *Allow access if dial-in permission is enabled* to view the policy settings (see Figure 12-11). The remote policy settings are identical to those already discussed for a RAS server. Make sure that either *Grant remote access permission* or *Deny remote access permission* is selected to match, the conditions you establish, such as the day and time access to the VPN server.

> As previously described for managing RAS and VPN access, consider controlling access by creating groups and granting group access by clicking the Add button on the screen shown in Figure 12-11 and clicking Windows-Groups to select the group or groups to have access.

Edit the remote access profile by clicking the Edit Profile button in the *Allow access if dial-in permission is enabled* Properties dialog box (refer to Figure 12-11). The profile options are nearly identical to those that apply to a RAS server (refer to Figure 12-12). Make sure that the EAP box is checked when you configure security, because many users will access the VPN server through routers.

Also, click the Encryption tab and set the types of encryption, which include No Encryption, Basic, and Strong. Click the Multilink tab if you are set up to use Multilink, which enables you to configure the same Multilink and BAP settings already described for a RAS server.

Configure the Number of Ports

Consult with your WAN provider on the number of ports that are available through your WAN connection. Once you have this information, configure the number of WAN ports in the VPN server. To configure the number of ports, right-click Ports in the tree under the server and click Properties. Double-click WAN Miniport (PPTP) and set the appropriate number of ports (see Figure 12-15). Also, double-click WAN Miniport (L2TP) and configure the same number of ports.

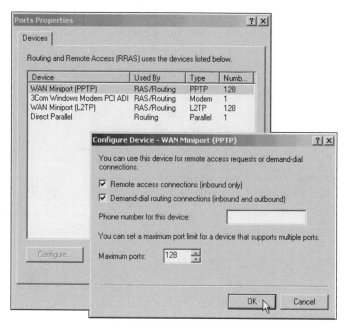

Figure 12-15 Configuring the number of ports

TROUBLESHOOTING RAS AND VPN INSTALLATIONS

12

Troubleshooting a RAS or VPN server communications problem can be divided into hardware and software troubleshooting tips.

Hardware Solutions

If no one can connect to the RAS or VPN server, try these hardware solutions:

- Use the Add/Remove Hardware tool or Device Manager to make sure modems and WAN adapters are working properly. Also, use the Device Manager to make sure that a modem or WAN adapter has no resource conflicts. If there is a conflict, fix it immediately.

- Use the Network and Dial-up Connections tool to test modem dial-up connections and VPN WAN connections. To test a connection, open the tool and click the connection you want to test.

- If you are using an access server, make sure it is properly connected to the network and to the telecommunications and WAN lines. Also, make sure it has power.

- If you are using one or more internal or external modems connected to the server, make sure the telephone line(s) is (are) connected to the modem(s) and to the wall outlet(s).

- For external modems, make sure the modem cable is properly attached, that you are using the right kind of cable (do not use a null modem cable), and that the modem has power.

- For internal modems, make sure they have a good connection inside the computer. Reseat internal modem cards, if necessary.

- Test the telephone wall connection and cable by temporarily attaching a telephone to the cable instead of the modem and making a call.

Software Solutions

Try the following software solutions if no one can access the RAS or VPN server:

- Use the Computer Management tool to make sure the Remote Access Auto Connection Manager and the Remote Access Connection Manager services are started.

- Make sure that a RAS or VPN server is enabled. To check, right-click the server in the Routing and Remote Access tool and make sure that the Remote Access Server box is checkmarked on the General tab (for a RAS or VPN server).

- Use the Ports option under the RAS or VPN server name to check the status of configured ports. Check to determine if all ports are being used. Double-click a port to view its connection statistics and information, if you think there might be a problem with a specific port.

- If TCP/IP connectivity is used, make sure that the IP parameters are correctly configured, for providing an address pool for a VPN server, for example. If IP configuration depends on DHCP, make sure that the DHCP server is working on the network and that you have configured a DHCP Relay Agent (with the correct hop-count threshold).

- If you are using a RADIUS server, make sure that it is connected and working properly and that IAS is installed.

- If you have configured a remote access policy, check to be sure that it is consistent with the users' access needs. For example, users may not be able to access a RAS or VPN server because the server is set to prevent access at certain times, or because certain users are not in a group that has access to the server.

If only certain clients but not all are having connection problems, try these solutions:

- Check the dial-up networking setup on the clients.

- Make sure the clients are using the same communications protocol as the server, for example PPP, and that they are using an authentication and encryption method that is supported by the RAS or VPN server.

- Make sure that each client has a server account and that each knows the correct account name and password. Also, make sure that accounts have the necessary rights and permissions to access files and folders on the server.

- If you manage access to a RAS or VPN server by using groups, make sure that each user account that needs access is in the appropriate group.

- Make sure the client accounts have been granted dial-up access capability and have the correct callback setup.

- For a dial-up RAS connection, determine if the clients' modems are compatible with the modems on the RAS server.

Monitoring User Connections

A monitoring capability is available to view user accounts that are in session on a RAS or VPN server. Monitoring connections can help you to develop an understanding of the average user load and aid in diagnosing problems. For example, a common problem on popular RAS servers, particularly in college and university settings, is that some users cannot connect because all ports are frequently busy, indicating that you may need to add more connectivity or another server. Also, you can use the tool to diagnose telephone or communications line problems in situations in which a certain port is never active. To access the tool, open the Routing and Remote Access tool, click the RAS or VPN server under the tree to view its child objects, and then click Remote Access Client(s). The right pane enables you to view the names of users who are connected, the duration of each connection, and the number of ports used by each connection.

CHAPTER SUMMARY

12

- ❑ A Windows 2000 server configured for RAS enables clients to remotely dial in to a server or a network of servers. Similarly, a Windows 2000 server configured as a VPN server enables clients to remotely access a private network that works like a members-only tunnel through a larger network. VPNs provide added security for remote communications and increase performance through router-based networks.

- ❑ Remote access to a Windows 2000 server network can be through regular dial-up telephone lines, special high-speed lines, Internet connections, and routers. Remote traffic over telephone lines is transported through the Point-to-Point Protocol (PPP). Traffic through the Internet or through a VPN is transported via the Point-to-Point Tunneling Protocol (PPTP) and the Layer Two Transport Protocol (L2TP).

- ❑ When you set up a RAS or VPN you can manage one or multiple servers through remote access policies and profiles. Creating a RADIUS server and implementing IAS enable you to manage two or more RAS and VPN servers through coordinated remote access policies. Remote access policies and profiles are used to establish how a server is available to users and to set up security.

In the next chapter, you learn more about network interoperability, for example setting up a Web server, connecting to a Novell NetWare server, and setting up terminal services. You also learn more about Windows 2000 DCHP and DNS.

KEY TERMS

access server — A device that connects several different types of communications devices and telecommunication lines to a network, providing network routing for these types of communications.

aggregate link — Linking two or more communications channels, such as ISDN channels, so that they appear as one channel, but with the combined speed of all channels in the aggregate.

Bandwidth Allocation Control Protocol (BACP) — Similar to BAP, but is able to select a preferred client when two or more clients vie for the same bandwidth.

Bandwidth Allocation Protocol (BAP) — A protocol that works with Multilink in Windows 2000 Server to enable the bandwidth or speed of a remote connection to be allocated on the basis of the needs of an application, with the maximum allocation equal to the maximum speed of all channels aggregated via Multilink.

bits per second (bps) — Number of binary bits (0s or 1s) sent in one second, a measure used to gauge network, modem, and telecommunications speeds.

Challenge Handshake Authentication Protocol (CHAP) — An encrypted handshake protocol designed for standard IP- or PPP-based exchange of passwords. It provides a reasonably secure, standard, cross-platform method for sender and receiver to negotiate a connection.

CHAP with Microsoft extensions (MS-CHAP) — A Microsoft-enhanced version of CHAP that can negotiate encryption levels and that uses the highly secure RSA RC4 encryption algorithm to encrypt communications between client and host.

CHAP with Microsoft extensions version 2 (MS-CHAP v2) — An enhancement of MS-CHAP that provides better authentication and data encryption and that is especially well suited for VPNs.

data communications equipment (DCE) — A device that converts data from a DTE, such as a computer, to be transmitted over a telecommunications line.

data terminal equipment (DTE) — A computer or computing device that prepares data to be transmitted over a telecommunications line to which it attaches by using a DCE, such as a modem.

DHCP Relay Agent — A server, such as a RAS or VPN server, or computer that broadcasts IP configuration information between the DHCP server on a network and the client acquiring an address.

digital subscriber line (DSL) — A technology that uses advanced modulation technologies on regular telephone lines for high-speed networking at speeds of up to 60 Mbps between subscribers and a telecommunications company.

Extensible Authentication Protocol (EAP) — An authentication protocol employed by network clients that use special security devices such as smart cards, token cards, and others that use certificate authentication.

frame relay — A WAN communications technology that relies on packet switching and virtual connection techniques to transmit at from 56 Kbps to 45 Mbps.

Integrated Services Digital Network (ISDN) — A telecommunications standard for delivering data services over digital telephone lines with a current practical limit of 1.536 Mbps and a theoretical limit of 622 Mbps.

Internet Authentication Service (IAS) — Used to establish and maintain security for RAS, Internet, and VPN dial-in access, and can be employed with RADIUS. IAS can use certificates to authenticate client access.

Layer Two Tunneling Protocol (L2TP) — A protocol that transports PPP over a VPN, an intranet, or the Internet. L2TP works similarly to PPTP, but unlike PPTP, L2TP uses an additional network communications standard, called Layer Two Forwarding, that enables forwarding on the basis of MAC addressing.

line device — A DCE, such as a modem or ISDN adapter, that connects to a telecommunications line.

Microsoft Point-to-Point Encryption (MPPE) — A starting-to-ending-point encryption technique that uses special encryption keys varying in length from 40 to 128 bits.

modem — A modulator/demodulator that converts a transmitted digital signal to an analog signal for a telephone line. It also converts a received analog signal to a digital signal for use by a computer.

Multilink or **Multilink PPP** — A capability of RAS to aggregate multiple data streams into one logical network connection for the purpose of using more than one modem, ISDN channel, or other communications line in a single logical connection.

Password Authentication Protocol (PAP) — A nonencrypted plaintext password authentication protocol. This represents the lowest level of security for exchanging passwords via PPP or TCP/IP. Shiva PAP (SPAP) is a version that is used for authenticating remote access devices and network equipment manufactured by Shiva (now part of Intel Corporation).

Point-to-Point Protocol (PPP) — A widely used remote communications protocol that supports IPX/SPX, NetBEUI, and TCP/IP for point-to-point communication (for example, between a remote PC and a Windows 2000 server on a network).

Point-to-Point Tunneling Protocol (PPTP) — A remote communications protocol that enables connectivity to a network through the Internet and connectivity through intranets and VPNs.

Remote Access Services (RAS) — Microsoft software services that enable off-site workstations to access a Windows 2000 server through telecommunications lines, the Internet, or intranets.

Remote Authentication Dial-In User Service (RADIUS) — A protocol and service set up on one RAS or VPN server, for example in a domain, when there are multiple RAS or VPN servers to coordinate authentication and to keep track of remote dial-in statistics for all RAS and VPN servers.

Serial Line Internet Protocol (SLIP) — An older remote communications protocol that is used by UNIX computers. The modern compressed SLIP (CSLIP) version uses header compression to reduce communications overhead.

Shiva Password Authentication Protocol (SPAP) — See Password Authentication Protocol.

12

T-carrier — A dedicated leased telephone line that can be used for data communications over multiple channels for speeds of up to 44.736 Mbps.

Telephone Application Programming Interface (TAPI) — An interface for communications line devices (such as modems) that provides line device functions, such as call holding, call receiving, call hang-up, and call forwarding.

terminal adapter (TA) — Popularly called a digital modem, links a computer or a fax to an ISDN line.

Universal Modem Driver — A modem driver standard used on recently developed modems.

virtual private network (VPN) — A private network that is like a tunnel through a larger network—such as the Internet, an enterprise network, or both—that is restricted to designated member clients only.

X.25 — An older packet-switching protocol for connecting remote networks at speeds up to 2.048 Mbps.

REVIEW QUESTIONS

1. One of your users is trying to connect to a RAS server, but is not able to make the connection. All ports and communications devices at the server end are working. The user, who is running Windows NT 4.0 Workstation, has checked his modem and telephone system, and all are working. Which of the following might be the problem?

   a. The user's modem has a top speed of 33.3 Kbps, and the RAS server modem cannot step down from 56 Kbps.

   b. The user's account is denied dial-in access in the account's properties.

   c. The user's dial-up connectivity is set to use SLIP:Internet.

   d. all of the above

   e. only a and b

   f. only b and c

2. You have installed a RAS server to obtain IP addresses from a DHCP server that is connected to the network. No error messages were displayed during the installation, but for some reason, IP addresses are not being automatically assigned to RAS clients. What step might you have omitted?

   a. configuring a DHCP relay agent

   b. configuring a "hard-coded" IP address at each client

   c. disabling IPX, which creates routing problems with TCP/IP

   d. all of the above

   e. only a and b

   f. only b and c

3. Your assistant set up RAS to use AppleTalk. Now it seems that all kinds of users have figured out how to access a wide range of network resources without having an account. What would you check first?

a. that AppleTalk is only enabled for zone 1

b. that the DHCP server is online

c. that the Guest account's rights and permissions security are carefully limited

d. that the DNS server is properly communicating with the DHCP server

4. You are converting a RAS server that runs Windows NT Server 4.0 to Windows 2000 Server. The server you are converting is set up to use SLIP. Which of the following steps should you complete when upgrading the RAS server to Windows 2000 Server?

a. Convert to use CSLIP as the remote communications protocol and make sure clients are also set up to use CSLIP.

b. Convert to use PPP as the remote communications protocol and make sure clients are also set up to use PPP.

c. Replace the modems in the server with ISDN adapters, because Windows 2000 RAS no longer supports asynchronous modem connections.

d. all of the above

e. only a and c

f. only b and c

5. Your network is located in Philadelphia, but five employees in your organization telecommute from a shared office that is in Washington, D.C. Each of the telecommuters has her or his own telephone line and dedicated number. How can you set up security so that the RAS server verifies each user by her or his telephone number?

a. Set up callback security on each user's account so that only a specific number is called back.

b. Assign a static IP address to each of the five users and set up a telephone number in the RAS server that is assigned to each IP address.

c. Control RAS server access through a remote access policy that contains a list of telephone numbers that the server can call back.

d. You cannot set up verification on the basis of a specific telephone number, only by area code.

6. About half of your RAS server's clients use smart cards. What authentication protocol must you configure for them?

a. Password Authentication Protocol (PAP)

b. Extensible Authentication Protocol (EAP)

c. Shiva Password Authentication Protocol (SPAP)

d. CHAP with Microsoft extensions (MS-CHAP)

12

7. When you set up Routing and Remote Access services, which of the following is not an option?

    a. to install a RAS server

    b. to install a VPN server

    c. to install an Internet connection server

    d. to install a telephone switching system for remote callers

8. You have two modems installed in a server for RAS communications. Both are 56 Kbps modems and both telecommunications lines are capable of 56 Kbps communication, but right now users on only one line can transmit at 56 Kbps. Connections to the other line are never over 14.4 Kbps. What should you check to troubleshoot the problem?

    a. Make sure that the port speed on the slower line is set at 56 Kbps or higher.

    b. Check to determine if the slower line has a RAS speed filter set up in the remote access policies.

    c. Connect the modem to the telephone line by using a faster telephone cable.

    d. If a telephone is connected through an output jack to the slower modem, disconnect the cable to the telephone, because it creates extra resistance.

9. How can you best configure authentication for a VPN server?

    a. through a modem's or WAN adapter's properties

    b. by using the CSLIP protocol

    c. by creating remote access policies and a profile

    d. by setting RAS and VPN user access rights through the Active Directory Users and Computers tool

10. Which of the following protocols can be transported by PPP?

    a. NWLink

    b. NetBEUI

    c. TCP/IP

    d. all of the above

    e. only a and c

    f. only b and c

11. Your organization is setting up five VPN servers and wants to establish one set of remote access policies and one place from which to coordinate all of the VPN servers. How is this possible?

    a. Make one of the VPN servers a RADIUS server.

    b. Establish one VPN global group that is enabled to access all of the VPN servers.

    c. Add a RAS server as a lead domain controller.

    d. Each VPN server will automatically coordinate with all other VPN servers.

12. After you set up a VPN server and test it over a WAN link, you see a message that says it is unable to transport via L2TP (Layer Two Tunneling Protocol). What should you check first to diagnose this problem?

    a. Make sure that you have enabled L2TP ports and specified the number of L2TP ports to match the number of ports available over the WAN connection.

    b. Disable PPTP because it is conflicting with L2TP communications.

    c. Make sure that the VPN server is configured to transport NetBEUI as well as TCP/IP, because L2TP is a special Microsoft network routing protocol.

    d. This message is normal because you have set up a T-1 WAN link, and T-1 does not enable use of L2TP.

13. You want to set up a RAS server that enables users to dial in through a group of 12 modems or through an ISDN line. What might you use in addition to the RAS server to provide these dial-in links?

    a. a bridge

    b. an access server

    c. a port expander

    d. several dedicated computers that have free expansion slots

14. You need to take your VPN server offline for some maintenance. Is there a way that you can disable access to the server for a short time?

    a. Use the remote access policies to change the hours that the server is available, so that it cannot be accessed when you want it offline.

    b. Remove the check mark in the Remote access server box in the server's properties for the time that you want to make the server unavailable.

    c. Use the *Disconnect users from network* feature in the server's properties for the time that you want to make the server unavailable.

    d. all of the above

    e. only a and b

    f. only b and c

15. The computer committee at your business has been discussing setting up a VPN that includes remote access through high-speed communications lines. The committee has already contacted the local telephone company and found that they can connect using T-1, T-3, and frame relay. Also, they have found that they can connect remote networks using any of these links attached to routers. Which of these is compatible with a Windows 2000 VPN server?

    a. T-1 and T-3 are compatible, but frame relay and routers are not.

    b. T-3 and frame relay are compatible, but T-1 and routers are not.

    c. Only frame relay with routers is compatible.

    d. T-1, T-3, frame relay, and routers all are compatible.

    e. None of the options is compatible, because a VPN server can only connect through an ISDN line.

12

16. Your VPN server is configured to enable Multilink as a way to enable the aggregation of frame relay channels when users need more bandwidth—for example, for multimedia applications. However, when a user connects, the server does not seem to adjust for the amount of bandwidth needed by a user. How can you fix the problem?

    a. Restrict Multilink to increments to 56 Kbps per port.

    b. Configure the VPN server to limit the maximum number of ports to 1.

    c. Configure the VPN server to dynamically use the Bandwidth Allocation Protocol (BAP) along with Multilink.

    d. all of the above

    e. only a and c

    f. only a and b

17. You have set up a VPN server to connect to another network through a router. The server handles incoming traffic through the router properly, but does not seem to reliably route outgoing traffic. Where might you look to solve this problem?

    a. Make sure that no internal routing interfaces are configured.

    b. Make sure that the VPN server is enabled as a router.

    c. Enable the VPN server to double as a RAS server, because RAS servers are able to route.

    d. Set up the VPN server to use the Layer 4 routing protocol.

18. What tool(s) can be used to help you diagnose a resource conflict between a WAN adapter and another device in a RAS or VPN server?

    a. Device Manager

    b. Routing and Remote Access tool

    c. Active Directory Domains and Trusts tool

    d. all of the above

    e. only a and c

    f. only b and c

19. You have set up a VPN server so that remote clients can access Windows 2000 servers on a network that uses only TCP/IP and on which the VPN connection is through the Internet. When a client accesses that VPN server from home by connecting through an Internet connection, what protocol(s) is that client using?

    a. TCP/IP

    b. PPTP

    c. PPP

    d. all of the above

    e. only a and c

    f. only b and c

20. Which of the following tools enables you to monitor client connections to a RAS or VPN server?

    a. Active Directory Users and Computers tool

    b. Routing and Remote Access tool

    c. Security MMC snap-in

    d. IP Routing tool

21. All of your RAS server clients are configured to use 56-bit encryption key MPPE, but when you use a network analyzer it appears that none of the communications is actually encrypted. Which of the following might be the problem?

    a. The remote access policies profile is set only for *No Encryption* and should instead be set for *Strong*.

    b. The remote access policies profile must be set for *Basic* encryption.

    c. The RAS server is not set up to use EAP authentication.

    d. Multilink must be configured in order for clients to use 128-bit encryption key MPPE.

22. You are planning to connect your RAS server to an ISDN line. What type of line device or adapter must you purchase for the server?

    a. asynchronous modem

    b. X.25 adapter

    c. terminal adapter

    d. synchronous modem

23. On your TCP/IP network, each VPN client must go through two routers to reach the VPN server, and the VPN server must go through one router to communicate with a DHCP server. If the VPN server is set up to use DHCP, what should the hop-count threshold be when you configure the DHCP Relay Agent at the VPN server? (Remember that a VPN server is also configured as a router.)

    a. 1

    b. 2

    c. 3

    d. 4

24. Which of the following can be Windows 2000 RAS server clients?

    a. Windows NT 3.51

    b. Windows 95

    c. Windows 3.11

    d. all of the above

    e. none of the above

    f. only a and b

12

25. You have set up a RAS server that is to be accessed by clients running Windows 2000 Professional and a few clients still running MS-DOS. What authentication should you configure for the RAS server?

a. Password Authentication Protocol (PAP)

b. Challenge Handshake Authentication Protocol (CHAP)

c. CHAP with Microsoft extensions version 2 (MS-CHAP v2)

d. all of the above

e. only a and b

f. only a and c

HANDS-ON PROJECTS

Project 12-1

In this project you practice optimizing RAS communications by making sure that the speed set for a serial communications port matches the capabilities of a modem connected to that port on a RAS server. Assume that the modem can transmit at 56 Kbps. You also practice using the Hardware Troubleshooter, in case there is a connection problem. You will need a computer running Windows 2000 Server or Windows 2000 Professional, with a modem installed.

To check the serial port's setup and use the Hardware Troubleshooter:

1. Click **Start**, point to **Programs**, point to **Administrative Tools,** and click **Computer Management**.

2. Click **Device Manager** in the tree.

3. Double-click **Modems** in the right pane, and then double-click the modem attached to the computer, for example **3Com Windows Modem PCI ADI**.

4. Click the **General** tab, if necessary. Is the modem working properly? Record your findings in your lab journal or in a word-processed document.

5. Click the **Troubleshooter** button to view how to access troubleshooting advice for situations in which the modem and port are not working. Record which of the options address modem problems. How would you solve a situation in which the modem is not detected? Close the Hardware Troubleshooter.

6. Click the **Modem** tab. To what port is the modem attached? What is the setting for the Maximum Port Speed?

7. If the Maximum Port Speed is less than 56 Kbps, change it by clicking the list arrow and selecting **57600** or **115200**.

8. Click the **Advanced** tab and click the **Change Default Preferences** button.

9. How can you use this button to change parameters such as data bits, parity, stop bits, and enabling data compression? Record how you might use these capabilities to resolve problems in which users' modems fail to communicate with the modem in the server.

10. Click **Cancel**.

11. Click **OK** and then close the Computer Management tool.

The tabs and options associated with a particular modem can vary, depending on the modem driver. Examine all of the tabs and use the appropriate options for your particular modem.

Project 12-2

In this project, you practice installing RAS to make a Windows 2000 Server a RAS server. The Windows 2000 server that you use might not already be set up as a RAS or VPN server. If it is, open the Routing and Access tool as described in Step 1, right-click the server under the tree, and click Delete to remove it.

To install RAS:

1. Click **Start**, point to **Programs**, point to **Administrative Tools**, and click **Routing and Remote Access**.

2. Right-click **Routing and Remote Access** in the tree and then **Add Server**.

3. Click **This computer**, if necessary. How would you install RAS on another network server or another server in a domain? Record your observations. Click OK.

4. In the left-pane tree, right-click the computer and then click **Configure and Enable Routing and Remote Access**.

5. Click **Next**.

6. What options can be installed through this wizard? Record your observations.

7. Click **Remote access server** and click **Next**.

8. What protocols are displayed? How would you add a protocol that is not on the list? Click **Yes** and then click **Next**.

9. If AppleTalk is installed, checkmark the box to enable AppleTalk clients to access the Guest account. What precautions should you take in this situation?

10. If TCP/IP is installed, click **Automatically** in the IP Address Assignment dialog box, if necessary. What is the other option, and what would happen if you specified that option? Click **Next**.

11. Click **No**, if necessary, so that this server is not set up as a RADIUS server and then click Next. What is the advantage of using a RADIUS server? What additional service should you set up for security management?

12. Click **Finish**. What message is displayed, if you specified use of DHCP? Click **Yes** if you see an informational message. Leave the Routing and Remote Access tool open for the next project.

Project 12-3

Because you set up RAS to use DHCP in Hands-on Project 12-2, you now need to set up a DHCP Relay Agent.

To set up a DHCP Relay Agent:

1. Make sure the Routing and Remote Access tool is open, and if not, open it.

2. Double-click the RAS server in the tree, for example **Lawyer**, if the child objects are not already displayed under it.

3. What child objects are displayed in the tree under the RAS server? Click each object to quickly review what it does, and record your observations in your lab journal or in a word-processed document.

4. Click **IP Routing** in the tree, if necessary, to view objects under it.

5. Click **General**, if necessary, under IP Routing in the tree. How would you determine the IP address of the local connection for the RAS server?

6. Right-click **DHCP Relay Agent** under IP Routing in the tree, and click **Properties**.

7. Enter the IP address of the RAS server, for example **129.70.10.1**, and click **Add**.

8. Click **OK**.

9. Click **DHCP Relay Agent** under IP Routing in the tree, and then double-click the interface, such as **Internal**, in the right pane. How would you set the hop-count threshold? Click **Cancel**. Leave the Routing and Remote Access tool open for the next project.

Project 12-4

Assume that you are using a T-3 connection to a RAS or VPN server and you want the ability to enable clients to use Multilink. This project enables you to view where to set up Multilink.

To view the Multilink configuration options:

1. Right-click the RAS server that you created in Hands-on Project 12-2, and click **Properties**.

2. What tabs are displayed? Click each tab and record your general observations of its purpose.

3. Click the **PPP** tab.

4. What options are available for configuring Multilink? Which option would you check to enable use of callback security?

5. Click **Cancel**. Leave the Routing and Remote Access tool open.

Project 12-5

In this activity, you practice setting dial-in security on a user's account. Before you begin, create a practice account or use an account that is specified by your instructor. (This project assumes that the Active Directory is installed.)

To set dial-in security:

1. Open the Active Directory Users and Computers tool, and double-click the domain to display the child objects under it in the tree.

2. Click the container in which the account is located, such as **Users**.

3. Double-click the account you created or that is specified by your instructor.

4. Click the **Dial-in** tab (depending on the resolution of your monitor, you may need to click the right arrow to view the tab before you can click it).

5. Click **Control access through Remote Access Policy** (or if it is deactivated because you are in mixed mode, click a different option). What other options are available for remote access permission?

6. Click **Set by Caller (Routing and Remote Access Service only)**.

7. How would you assign a static IP address for a client that dials in remotely?

8. Click **OK** and then close the Active Directory Users and Computers tool.

Project 12-6

In this project, you set up remote access policies and edit the profile of the RAS server you created in Hands-on Project 12-2.

12

To set up the remote access policies and edit the profile:

1. Make sure the Routing and Remote Access tool is open, and if it is not, open it.

2. Double-click the RAS server in the tree, for example **Lawyer**, if necessary to display the child objects under the server.

3. Click **Remote Access Policies** in the tree.

4. Double-click **Allow access if dial-in permission is enabled** in the right pane.

5. Double-click the **Day-And-Time Restrictions matches** parameter in the *Specify conditions to match* box.

6. Drag the pointer to select all of the times of day boxes in the row for Sunday (the top row), and click **Denied**. What happens to the boxes?

7. Drag the pointer to select all of the times of day boxes in the row for Saturday (the bottom row), and click **Denied**.

8. Click **OK**.

9. Check the **Grant remote access permission** radio button.

10. Click the **Edit Profile** button.

11. Click the **Authentication** tab. What protocols are selected by default? Record your observations. Which protocol would you check to enable the use of smart cards?

12. Click the **Encryption** tab. What selections are already made? Record your observations. Also, make sure that **No Encryption**, **Basic**, and **Strong** are all check marked, and if not, check them.

13. Click the **Dial-in Constraints** tab. How would you disconnect users who have had no activity for over 15 minutes?

14. Click **OK**. Click **No** if an information box appears to display Help information because you have changed authentication methods.

15. Click **OK**. Close the Routing and Remote Access tool.

 If IAS were installed, you could follow nearly the same steps to configure remote access policies for multiple servers.

Project 12-7

In this project, you install RAS in Windows NT Workstation 4.0 so that it can access a RAS server as a client. You will need the Windows NT Workstation CD-ROM, and the computer should already have a modem installed.

To install RAS in Windows NT Workstation 4.0:

1. Log on as Administrator or using an account with Administrator privileges.

2. Click **Start**, point to **Settings**, and click the **Control Panel**

3. Double-click the **Network** icon, and click the **Services** tab. Click **Add**, select the **Remote Access Service**, and click **OK**.

4. Insert the Windows NT Workstation CD-ROM, provide the path to the CD-ROM drive, and click **Continue**. (If the Windows NT Workstation auto run program starts, close its window.) The RAS setup will automatically detect the modem or it will display the Add RAS Device dialog box, from which you can click Install Modem to start the Install New Modem Wizard.

5. In the Remote Access Setup dialog box, highlight the modem and click the **Configure** button. Set the port to **Dial out only** or to **Dial out and Receive calls**. For example, the modem needs to be able to receive calls if the RAS server at work is set up to call back the user as a security measure to ensure that a known user is requesting access.

6. Click **OK** in the Configure Port Usage dialog box, and click **Continue** in the Remote Access Setup dialog box.

7. Click **OK** in each box to enable client access to network servers using specific protocols (depending on which protocols are installed on the RAS server). For example, click OK in the RAS Server TCP/IP Configuration dialog box.

8. Windows NT Workstation should automatically configure bindings for the remote access. If there is no message that it is configuring bindings, click the Bindings tab on the Network dialog box to initiate the Bindings configuration.

9. Click **Close** in the Network dialog box and remove the Windows NT Workstation CD-ROM. Save any open work and click the option to restart the computer.

To set the dial-up configuration:

1. Double-click **My Computer** and then double-click the **Dial-Up Networking** icon.

2. Click **New** in the Dial-Up Networking dialog box.

3. Enter **RAS** as the name for the automated dial-up connection, and click **Next**.

4. Checkmark **Send my plain text password if that's the only way to connect.** The plaintext password is the password for the user's account on the RAS server. Leave the other boxes blank, and click **Next**.

5. Enter the telephone number of the line attached to the computer's modem in the Phone number text box in the Phone number dialog box. Do not click the box for telephony dialing properties, because the line is a basic telephone line and does not require specialized information. Click **Next**.

6. Click **Finish** in the last dialog box to complete the installation wizard.

7. Back in the Dial-up Networking dialog box, select the connection you just made as the Phonebook entry to dial, click the **More** button, and click **Edit entry and modem properties**.

8. Click the **Server** tab and make sure **PPP:Windows NT, Windows 95 Plus, and Internet** is selected in the Dial-up server type box. Click **OK**.

9. Click **Close** in the Dial-up Networking dialog box.

12

CASE PROJECT

Aspen Consulting Project: Setting Up RAS and VPN Servers

The International Wheat Association is a nonprofit association of wheat growers, researchers, and bakers that provides a wide range of information about growing, processing, and using wheat and wheat-based products. The association is located in Toronto and has member groups throughout the world. One of the International Wheat Association's most popular services is maintaining a database of research information for all members. The database has been on a Windows NT 4.0 RAS server, but the association has hired you to help them convert this vital service to a new Windows 2000 server set up as a RAS server.

1. In your first meeting with those who manage the research database and the association's small IT staff, you are asked to describe the general issues involved in converting the Windows NT RAS server to a Windows 2000 RAS server. Explain the issues involved and begin preparing a planning paper for the conversion.

2. As you are working on your planning paper, you realize that it provides a good opportunity to introduce other planning issues. Include in the paper issues that will affect the use of the RAS server, which are:

   ❑ Remote access protocols

   ❑ IP addressing

   ❑ Remote access policies

   ❑ Authentication

   ❑ Encryption

   ❑ Multilink connectivity

3. The Windows NT RAS server is currently connected to the outside world through two basic-rate interface ISDN adapters. The association's management would like to dramatically increase connectivity so that over 50 remote clients can access the RAS server at one time. Discuss other connectivity options that are available to them through Windows 2000 RAS capabilities.

4. The IT staff of four people wants you to train them in how to manage the RAS server after it is installed. Provide a preliminary training paper that discusses the tools available to them for configuring, managing, monitoring, and troubleshooting the server.

5. The association's research group has received funding from management to set up a VPN server that can be remotely accessed over the Internet by top-level researchers all over the world. Explain any special configuration and setup steps that the IT staff needs to be aware of for the VPN server setup.

OPTIONAL CASE PROJECTS FOR TEAMS

Team Case One

Mark Arnez asks you to form a group to research dedicated RAS and access servers that are available from computer and network vendors. Form a team to use the Internet and any other means to research and describe these devices and their capabilities. Create a document that can be a resource for other consultants.

Team Case Two

Keep your team together, because Mark is now asking you to prepare a document that describes different ways that organizations can use RAS and VPN servers for business, research, and educational purposes.

13

MANAGING INTERNET AND
NETWORK INTEROPERABILITY

> **After reading this chapter and completing the exercises you will be able to:**
>
> ♦ Install and configure a Web server and a Media Services server
>
> ♦ Install and configure DNS and WINS servers
>
> ♦ Install and configure a DHCP server
>
> ♦ Install and configure a terminal server
>
> ♦ Configure a Telnet server
>
> ♦ Install and configure a NetWare gateway

Microsoft Windows 2000 Server is capable of providing a large range of specialized connectivity services, including Web services, operating as DNS/WINS or DHCP servers, and functioning as terminal or Telnet servers. Operating as a Web server is one of the most popular functions for a Windows 2000 server, because Web servers are used all over the world for e-mail communications, selling goods and services, disseminating information, advancing scientific research, and a wide range of other uses. DNS/WINS and DHCP servers provide vital behind-the-scenes functions on networks by translating computer names to IP addresses and by automatically assigning IP addresses. Terminal servers enable companies to save money by using low-cost computers with minimal operating system functions to access the resources of a Windows 2000 server. Configuring Windows 2000 Server as a Telnet server is a way to enable clients without Windows operating systems to access a server. Also, Windows 2000 Server can be configured as a NetWare gateway to enable users to access a NetWare server's directories and printers without directly connecting to NetWare as a client.

In this chapter, you first learn how to set up Windows 2000 Server to operate as a Web server. Next, you learn how to set up DNS, WINS, and DHCP servers. Finally, you learn how to configure terminal services, a Telnet server, and a NetWare gateway.

To configure any of these services you must have Administrator privileges.

MICROSOFT INTERNET INFORMATION SERVICES

Microsoft **Internet Information Services** (**IIS**) is a component included on the Windows 2000 Server CD-ROM that enables you to offer a complete Web site from a Windows 2000 server. Your Web site might fulfill any number of functions. On a college campus you might use it to enable applicants to apply for admission, or to allow currently enrolled students to view their progress toward completing degree requirements. Many companies use their Web sites for multiple purposes such as to announce new products, provide product support, take product orders, and advertise job openings. Another use is providing training to company employees on using software such as an inventory or order entry system.

IIS benchmarks prove that these services are fast, and the software design enables the use of extensions to link other software applications to an IIS server, such as a distributed client/server system that implements Web-based features. One reason why IIS services are fast and can be integrated with other programs is the built-in **Internet Server Application Programming Interface** (**ISAPI**). ISAPI is a group of DLL (dynamic-link library) files that are applications and filters. The application files enable developers to link customized programs into IIS and to speed up program execution. IIS filters are used to automatically trigger programs, such as a Microsoft Access database lookup or a security program that authorizes user access to specific Web functions. The IIS component contains two critical services for a Web site: World Wide Web and FTP. The World Wide Web (Web or WWW) is a series of file servers with software such as Microsoft IIS that make HTML and other Web documents available for workstations. HTML files are read by Internet, intranet, and VPN users with the help of client software called a **Web browser**, such as Netscape Communicator and Microsoft Internet Explorer. FTP is a TCP/IP-based application protocol that handles file transfers over a network (see Chapter 3). Also, there are additional services that you can install to make an IIS server function as an e-mail server using the Simple Mail Transfer Protocol (SMTP, see Chapter 3) and as a **Network News Transfer Protocol** (**NNTP**) server. An SMTP server acts as an Internet gateway in partnership with e-mail services, such as Microsoft Exchange, to accept incoming e-mail from the Internet and forward it to the recipient. It also forwards outgoing e-mail from a network's e-mail service to the Internet. NNTP is used over TCP/IP-based networks by NNTP servers to transfer news and informational messages to client subscribers who compose "newsgroups."

There are several reasons why Windows 2000 Server makes a good candidate as a Web server. One reason is that the Windows 2000 Server privileged-mode architecture (see Chapter 1) and fault-tolerance capabilities (see Chapter 7) make it a reliable server platform. Another reason is that Windows 2000 Server is compatible with small databases, such as Microsoft Access, and large databases, such as SQL Server and Oracle. Also, users can log directly into a database through the IIS **Open Database Connectivity** (**ODBC**) drivers. ODBC is a set of rules developed by Microsoft for accessing databases and providing a standard doorway to database data. This makes IIS very compatible with Web-based client/server applications. IIS also is compatible with MPPE security (see Chapter 12), IPSec, and the **Secure Sockets Layer (SSL)** encryption technique (Chapter 4). SSL is a dual-key encryption standard for communication between a server and a client and is also used by Internet Explorer. IIS enables security control on the basis of username and password, IP address, and folder and file access controls.

Installing a Web Server

There are several requirements for installing and using IIS:

- Windows 2000 Server installed on the computer to host IIS

- TCP/IP installed on the IIS host

- Access to an Internet service provider (ISP)—ask the ISP for your IP address, subnet mask, and default gateway IP address

- Sufficient disk space for IIS and for Web site files (the required space depends on the number of Web files that you publish)

- Disk storage formatted for NTFS (IIS can run on FAT, but NTFS has better performance and security)

- A method for resolving computer and domain names to IP addresses, such as DNS and WINS

You can install IIS when you install Windows 2000 Server, which is the default installation method. When the Windows 2000 Server Setup displays the list of components that can be installed, IIS is automatically checked as one of those components (see Chapter 5). If you do not install IIS during the Windows 2000 installation, you can install it later by using the Control Panel Add/Remove Programs icon. After you open the icon, click Add/Remove Windows Components, click the Components button (if necessary) to start the Windows Components Wizard, and select the option to install Internet Information Services in the Windows Components dialog box (try Hands-on Project 13-1). Another way to install IIS and to configure the IIS services is to:

1. Click Start, point to Programs, point to Administrative Tools, and click Configure Your Server.

2. Click the Web/Media Server hyperlink in the menu on the left side of the window, and then click Web Server.

3. Click the Start hyperlink to access the Windows Components dialog box.

4. Scroll to Internet Information Services (IIS) and double-click that option.

5. Make sure all of the services that you want to install are checked in the Internet Information Services (IIS) dialog box (see Figure 13-1 and Table 13-1). Click any box to place a check in it or to remove a check. Click any of the service names to view a description of it. Double-click service names that have their own subcomponents from which to select, and check the subcomponents that you want to install. Click OK on all dialog boxes that you have opened and configured, until you return to the Windows Components Wizard dialog box.

13

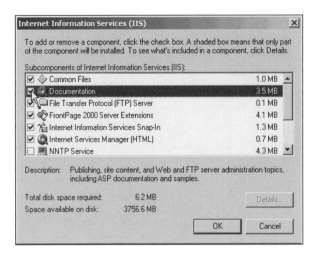

Figure 13-1 Specifying Internet Information Services components

    6. Click Next.

    7. Insert the Windows 2000 Server CD-ROM, specify the path to the CD-ROM drive and the \I386 folder, and click OK.

    8. Click Finish.

    9. Close the Add/Remove Programs tool, if it remains open.

Table 13-1 Internet Information Services Components

IIS Component Option	Purpose
Common Files	Files needed for general IIS functions that must be installed, but should not be installed without installing other services
Documentation	Documentation for publishing to and managing Web and FTP sites
File Transfer Protocol (FTP) Server	Used to set up FTP server services for Internet, intranet, and virtual private network (VPN) file transfers between the Windows 2000 server and a client
FrontPage 2000 Server Extensions	Used to work with Microsoft FrontPage and Visual InterDev for creating and publishing Web materials developed through those tools (both tools are purchased separately)
Internet Information Services Snap-In	Installs an MMC snap-in that is used to manage an IIS server
Internet Services Manager (HTML)	Sets up a browser-based tool to manage an IIS server that is in HTML format
NNTP Service	Enables an IIS server to function as a Network News Transfer Protocol server to provide newsgroups and news messages to client subscribers

Table 13-1   Internet Information Services Components (continued)

IIS Component Option	Purpose
SMTP Service	Enables an IIS server to function as a Simple Mail Transfer Protocol server (see Chapter 3) to distribute SMTP-formatted e-mail messages on a network or through the Internet
Visual InterDev RAD Remote Deployment Support	Used to remotely deploy (on another server) applications developed through the Microsoft Visual InterDev Rapid Applications Development (RAD) tool
World Wide Web Server	Enables the IIS server to function as a Web server on the Internet, via an intranet, or through a VPN

 TIP When you install IIS, it sets up the services you selected so that they start automatically each time the server is booted. Some services, such as the SMTP service, can be checked using the Computer Management tool. Other services are optimized to run as part of the Iissrv.exe program that runs in the background. You can view this program by using Windows 2000 Task Manager (review Hands-on Project 1-7 in Chapter 1). If you experience problems, use both the Task Manager and the Computer Management tool to check that the Iissrv.exe and IIS services are started.

After IIS is installed, click the Next button in the Windows 2000 Configure Your Server window to further configure IIS. In the next window (see Figure 13-2), you have the option to create a virtual directory in which to store HTML and other documents to publish on the Web site. Two other options in the window are to click *Manage* to start administering the IIS Web server and to click *Learn more* to view IIS documentation. Creating a virtual directory and managing the server are described in the next sections.

13

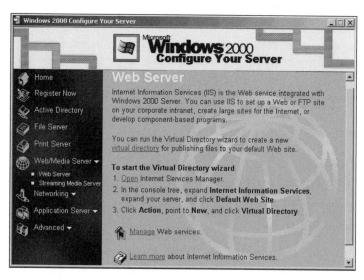

Figure 13-2   Configuring an IIS Web server

Creating a Virtual Directory

A **virtual directory** is really an actual folder on an IIS Web server that is also associated with a **Uniform Resource Locator** (**URL**) so that it can be accessed over the Internet, an intranet, or a VPN. The reason for creating a virtual directory is to provide an easy way for multiple users to publish on the Web site, by modifying and uploading files to the virtual directory. A URL is a special addressing format used to find particular Web locations. When you set up a virtual directory, you give it an alias, which is a name to identify it to a Web browser. The URL format for accessing a file in a virtual directory entails providing the server name, the virtual directory alias, and the filename, for example: \\Lawyer\Webpub\Mypage.html. In this example, Lawyer is the server name, Webpub is the alias of the virtual directory, and Mypage.html is the file.

To create a virtual directory, access the Internet Information Services management tool by clicking the Open hyperlink shown in Figure 13-2 or by clicking Start, pointing to Programs, pointing to Administrative Tools, and clicking Internet Services Manager. Double-click the Web server in the tree, right-click Default Web site in the tree, point to New, click Virtual Directory, and use the wizard to create the virtual directory (try Hands-on Project 13-2). When you create a virtual directory, you can choose the security options you want to apply, shown in Table 13-2.

Table 13-2 Virtual Directory Security Options

Security Option	Purpose
Browse	Enables users to browse the contents of the virtual directory
Execute	Enables users to execute programs and scripts
Read	Enables users to open files in the virtual directory
Run scripts	Enables users to run command scripts
Write	Enables users to add new files to the virtual directory and to modify the contents of existing files

After a virtual directory is created, you can modify its properties in the Internet Information Services tool by clicking Default Web Site in the tree under the server, right-clicking the virtual directory's alias, such as WebPub, and then clicking Properties (see Figure 13-3). Table 13-3 presents a general description of the properties that can be configured for a virtual directory.

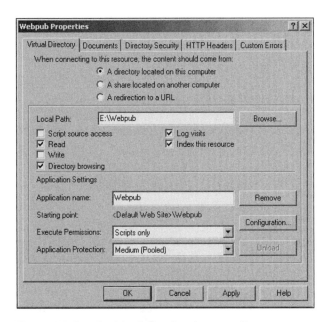

Figure 13-3   A virtual directory's properties

Table 13-3   Virtual Directory Properties Tabs

Properties Tab	Purpose
Virtual Directory	Used to specify general properties that include the computer on which the physical folder is located, the local path, security, and application settings
Documents	Used to define a default Web page and to specify a footer for Web documents
Directory Security	Used to fine-tune security, including whether to allow anonymous access, to set IP address restrictions and restrictions on domain names that can access the site, and to require secure communications through certificates
HTTP Headers	Used to set an expiration date on the directory contents, to set properties of headers that are returned to the client's browser, to set content ratings (such as for content limited to adults), and to specify Multipurpose Internet Mail Extensions (MIME)
Custom Errors	Used to set up error messages that are displayed in a client's browser when specific errors occur

The physical folder properties, including permissions, share permissions, and Web sharing permissions (see Chapter 9), can also be modified by right-clicking the folder and choosing properties in Windows Explorer or My Computer when you are directly logged on to the server.

Managing and Configuring an IIS Web Server

After it is installed, you can manage a Web server using the Internet Information Services tool, also called the Internet Services Manager, described in the previous section. You can access the tool in several ways. One way is to click the *Manage* hyperlink in the Windows 2000 Configure

Your Server window shown in Figure 13-2. Two other ways are to use the Internet Information Services MMC snap-in or to click Start, point to Programs, point to Administrative Tools, and click Internet Services Manager.

The Internet Information Services tool enables you to manage the following types of IIS components (depending on which components you have installed):

- Default Web site
- Administration Web site
- FTP site
- SMTP virtual server
- NNTP virtual server

The Default Web site component is used to manage WWW services offered through an IIS server. The Administration Web site enables you to manage multiple IIS servers from one administrative Web server. FTP site is for managing FTP services offered through an IIS server. The SMTP and NNTP virtual server components are used to manage Internet e-mail and newsgroup services on an IIS server. To manage any of these components, open the Internet Information Services tool and double-click the IIS server in the tree under Internet Information Services (see Figure 13-4). Next, click the component under the tree, for example Default Web Site.

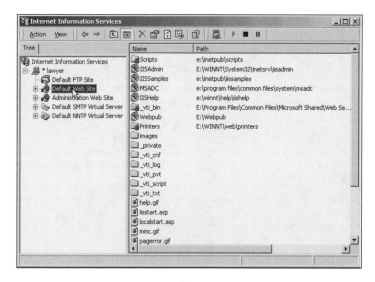

Figure 13-4   Managing a Web site

 TIP   There are many parameters that you can configure for a Web site, but the best advice is to start by configuring the basic properties, for example configuring performance to match the number of users, and configuring security.

To configure an IIS Web server, open the Internet Information Services tool and double-click Internet Information Services in the tree to display the name of the Web server. Double-click the server in the tree, right-click Default Web Site in the tree (or in the right pane), and click Properties. Click the Web Site tab, if it is not displayed already, and begin configuring properties (see Figure 13-5). For example, make sure that the IP address for the Web site is specified in the IP Address box. You can make one Web site appear as several different sites by clicking the Advanced button and configuring additional IP addresses. Optimize the Web site by clicking the Limited To radio button and setting a limit on the number of connections, to match or exceed the traffic that you anticipate for the server, for example 100 simultaneous connections for a small site or 500 for a medium-sized site.

Figure 13-5   Configuring Web site properties

Click the Performance tab and configure the Web site for the number of users (or "hits") who access the site on a given day. The options are: Fewer than 10,000, Fewer than 100,000, and More than 100,000. Next, click the Directory Security tab to establish security. Click the Edit button on the tab to specify if anonymous access is allowed (access in which the user does not have to provide identification). Also, specify the type of authentication, from the following choices:

- *Basic authentication (password is sent in clear text):* Used for clients who cannot send an encrypted password

- *Digest authentication:* Used to transmit a hashed security communication, and not a password, between the Web server and the client. A hashed value is created by using a mathematical formula to create a random value.

- *Integrated Windows authentication:* Uses a secret code prepared by a cryptographic formula between the client and the Web server to authenticate the client, instead of using a password.

Two other options to create secure communications are to set IP restrictions and to secure communications through the use of certificates. The next section discusses how to set up IP restrictions when the Web server is designed to be a VPN server (see Chapter 12).

Table 13-4 presents a summary of the Web site Properties tabs.

Table 13-4   Default Web Site Properties Tabs

Properties Tab	Purpose
Web Site	Used to configure IP addressing, number of connections, connection time-out, and activity logging
Operators	Used to specify which user accounts and groups have privileges to manage the Web server
Performance	Used to optimize performance on the basis of daily hits, bandwidth, and CPU/process utilization
ISAPI Filters	Used to set up Internet Server Application Programming Interface (ISAPI) filters, which are used to provide special instructions on how to handle specific HTTP requests
Home Directory	Specifies the location of the main folder in which Web programs and processes are stored (which is usually \\server\inetpub\wwwroot) and enables you to set security on that folder
Documents	Defines a default Web page for the Web site and enables you to specify a footer for Web documents
Directory Security	Used to set up security for a Web site, including whether to allow anonymous access, authentication methods, IP address and domain restrictions, and use of certificate security
HTTP Headers	Used to set an expiration date on the directory contents, to set properties of headers that are returned to the client's browser, to set content ratings (for example, for content limited to adults), and to specify Multipurpose Internet Mail Extensions (MIME)
Custom Errors	Used to set up error messages that are displayed in a client's browser when specific errors occur while accessing the Web server
Server Extensions	Used to establish security and controls for publishing documents using FrontPage

Configuring IP and Domain Security Access for Intranets/VPNs

You can limit access to a Web server by setting restrictions on which IP addresses, which subnet mask, and which domains can access the server. You would set these restrictions when you create a combined Web and VPN server, for example. In this instance, you can set up the VPN server access to be controlled through the physical WAN or router connection; you can limit access even further by setting up restrictions on which individuals and groups can access the server through IP address restrictions and by restricting access to only certain domains. For example, consider a VPN server configured for access to Web services in which you want to limit access to only those users on subnets 177.28.19 and 177.28.23. Also, you want to grant 10 other users access on the basis of their unique IP addresses. You can restrict the access to the Web services by opening the Internet Information Services management tool, double-clicking the Web server in the tree, right-clicking Default Web Site, and clicking Properties. Click the Directory Security tab and the Edit button for access by IP addresses. Deny access to all computers, except those in the groups 177.28.19 and 177.28.23 and the 10 single computers that you specify by IP address (see Figure 13-6). Try Hands-on Project 13-3 to practice restricting a Web site for use on a VPN.

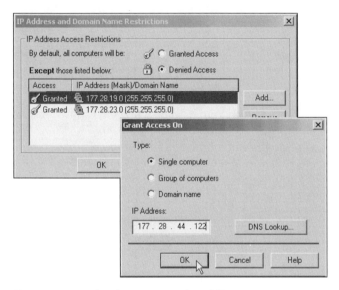

Figure 13-6   Configuring restricted IP access

Troubleshooting a Web Server

Occasionally a Web server used for a Web site, intranet, or VPN can experience problems—for example, users cannot connect to the server, or the server is not enabling e-mail to be sent. Table 13-5 illustrates possible problems and their solutions.

Table 13-5   Troubleshooting IIS

Problem	Solution(s)
The Web server is not responding.	1. Use the Network and Dial-up Connections tool to make sure that the server's connection to the network or Internet is enabled. 2. Use the Task Manager to make sure that the Iissrv.exe program is working. 3. Right-click the Web server in the IIS management tool and click Restart IIS to restart the IIS service. 4. Use the Computer Management tool to make sure that the Server and Workstation services are started and set to start automatically.
No one can access the Web server, but the server is booted and its network and Internet connections are enabled.	1. Make sure there is a WINS server on the network and that it is functioning. 2. Make sure that the DNS server(s) is(are) connected and working on the network. 3. Use a Web browser from different computers and locations to test the connection and determine if the problem is due to a network segment location, the Internet connection, or a specific client that cannot access the server.
Clients can connect to the Web server, but cannot access its contents.	1. Make sure that the authentication and encryption set at the server match the authentication and encryption properties that the client computers can support. 2. Check the Web sharing permissions on Web folders to make sure that they enable the appropriate client access, such as permission to read files and run scripts (try using the IIS Permissions Wizard for help, or check the folders' properties). 3. Make sure that no NTFS permissions on Web folders are set to Deny. 4. Make sure that the \Inetpub\wwwroot folder is intact and contains all of the necessary HTML files (open the IIS management tool, right-click Default Web Site, and click Open).
FTP to the Web server does not work.	1. Make sure that the File Transfer Protocol (FTP) Server service is installed as a Windows component through the Add/Remove Programs tool. 2. Grant the appropriate permissions on folders used for FTP, including the ability to write for those who upload documents to the server. 3. Use the Computer Management tool to make sure that the FTP Publishing Service is started and set to start automatically.

Table 13-5   Troubleshooting IIS (continued)

Problem	Solution(s)
E-mail is not going through the Web server.	1. Make sure that the SMTP service is installed as a Windows component through the Add/Remove Programs tool. 2. Use the Computer Management tool to make sure that the Simple Mail Transfer Protocol service is started and set to start automatically.
Newsgroups are not supported on the Web server.	1. Make sure that the NNTP service is installed as a Windows component through the Add/Remove Programs tool. 2. Make sure that there are virtual directories set up for newsgroups and that the permissions are appropriately set for users to access, for example permissions to browse and read. 3. Use the Current Sessions tool in the IIS management tool to determine if users are connecting to the service.
Users cannot publish using FrontPage.	1. Make sure that the FrontPage 2000 Server Extensions are installed as a Windows component through the Add/Remove Programs tool. 2. Encourage users to upgrade to FrontPage 2000 for best compatibility.

INSTALLING WINDOWS MEDIA SERVICES

When multimedia applications are played in **streaming** mode, the audio and video begin playing as soon as received, without waiting for the entire file to be received at the client. A Windows 2000 Server can be set up to provide streaming media services by installing the Windows Media Services component. The Windows Media Services component is separate from the Internet Information Services component and can be installed after you install IIS. Media services enable you to serve voice and video multimedia applications from a Web server—for example, an audio/video lesson demonstrating a hazardous chemistry experiment that is too dangerous for students to try in a lab on their own. When you install Microsoft Windows Media Services, you must also install the Windows Media Services Administrator, which is used to manage the services. Hands-on Project 13-4 enables you to practice using the Add/Remove Programs tool in the Control Panel to install the media services and administrator.

To use the media services, determine if your applications are capable of unicasting or multicasting, as described in Chapter 3 (multicasting is more efficient). You can configure the server for either type of transmission by using the Windows Media Services Administrator. Open the Windows Media Services Administrator from the Administrative Tools menu (try Hands-on Project 13-4), and click Configure Server for instructions about how to configure the server for a specific type of application (see Figure 13-7).

13

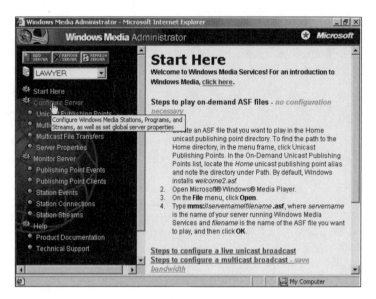

Figure 13-7   Windows Media Services Administrator

INSTALLING MICROSOFT DNS SERVER

One of the requirements for running IIS is to have a domain name resolution service available to it, such as Domain Name Service (DNS) or Windows Internet Naming Service (WINS) (see Chapters 3 and 4). If there is not a DNS server on your network, you will need to install Microsoft DNS Server, WINS, or both. **DNS Server** is a Microsoft service that resolves IP addresses to computer names, such as resolving 129.77.1.10 to the computer name Brown; it also resolves computer names to IP addresses. WINS is used with DNS Server to resolve IP addresses and computer names on networks in which NetBIOS applications are still in use, including NetBIOS computer names for pre-Windows 2000 clients, such as Windows 95, 98, and NT (see Chapter 3).

When you implement the Active Directory, it also requires at least one DNS server and will prompt you to automatically install the Microsoft DNS service, if a DNS server is not already present on the network. If you use the Active Directory and have two or more domain controllers (DCs), plan to set up Microsoft DNS services on at least two of the DCs, because the multimaster replication model (see Chapter 4) enables you to replicate DNS information on each DC. The advantage of replicating DNS information is that if one DC that hosts DNS services fails, another DC is available to provide uninterrupted DNS services for the network. This is especially critical on a network that provides Internet access and Web-based SMTP e-mail services.

Microsoft DNS Server is installed from the Control Panel Add/Remove Programs icon, using the following steps:

1. Click Start, point to Settings, and click Control Panel.

2. Double-click Add/Remove Programs.

3. Click Add/Remove Windows Components. If the Windows Components Wizard dialog box is not automatically started, click the Components button to start it.

4. Double-click Networking Services to view the individual components that can be installed and to check Domain Name System (DNS), as in Figure 13-8. Click OK in the Networking Services dialog box.

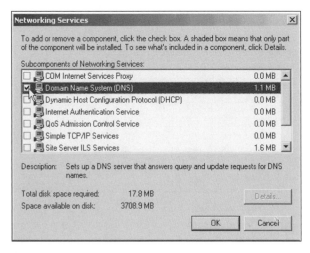

Figure 13-8   Installing Microsoft DNS

5. Click Next in the Windows Components Wizard dialog box.

6. If requested, insert the Windows 2000 Server CD-ROM, specify the path to the CD-ROM drive and the \I386 folder, and click OK.

7. Click Finish.

 Microsoft recommends that DNS servers have a static IP address (one that is manually configured, not automatically assigned by DHCP; see Chapters 3 and 6). Also, before installing DNS on a server when the Active Directory is in use on a network, make sure that the server is a DC, or promote it to be a DC if it is not. Use the Dcpromo tool to promote a member server to a DC by clicking Start, clicking Run, entering *dcpromo*, and clicking OK. When you use Dcpromo, the program will inform you whether the computer is a DC. *If the computer is already a DC, click Cancel when the Active Directory Installation Wizard starts, because if you continue, the wizard will remove the Active Directory setup on that computer.*

After you install DNS Server, it is necessary to configure it through the DNS management tool, which can be accessed from the DNS MMC snap-in or by clicking Start, pointing to Programs, pointing to Administrative Tools, and clicking DNS. Use the DNS Manager to create two primary zones of DNS information. One zone, called the **forward lookup zone**, holds host name records, called address records, to map a computer name to the IP address. Each IP-based server and client should have a host record so that it can be found through DNS. For example, if the DNS server name is Lawyer, with the IP address 129.70.10.1, then the forward lookup zone maps Lawyer to 129.70.10.1. In IP version 4, a host record is called a **host address (A) resource record**. Figure 13-9 shows the forward lookup zone host records as shown in the DNS management tool. When you install DNS on a DC in a domain, a forward lookup zone is automatically created for the domain, with the DNS server record already entered. You must enter the records of other hosts or configure DHCP to automatically update the DNS forward lookup zone each time it assigns an IP address.

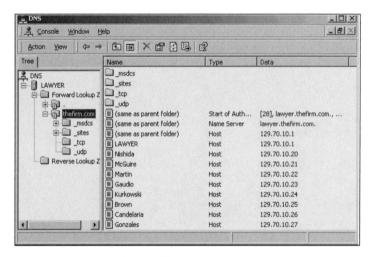

Figure 13-9 DNS forward lookup zone

At this writing, IP version 4 is a 32-bit address (4 octets) and is used in most places. IP version 6 (IPv6) is under development and consists of a 128-bit address. An IPv6 record is called an IPv6 host address (AAAA) resource record. Windows 2000 Server DNS is compatible with both types of host records.

Depending on the domain structure and Internet connectivity, a DNS server can have several forward lookup zones, but there should be at least one for the parent domain, such as *thefirm.com*. On the Internet, this is called a second-level domain name because it is constructed from "thefirm" and "com." The first level is the root, which indicates the type of Internet site, such as "com," which denotes that this is a company and not an educational institution (edu), for example.

Another zone, called the **reverse lookup zone**, holds the **pointer (PTR) resource record**, which contains the IP-address-to-host name. The reverse lookup zone is not as commonly used as the forward lookup zone, but can be important to create for those instances when a network communication requires associating an IP address to a computer name, such as for monitoring a network using IP address information. Because it is used less commonly, the reverse lookup zone is not automatically created when DNS is installed. To create the reverse lookup zone:

1. Open the DNS management tool, and double-click the DNS server in the tree, if the child objects under it are not displayed.

2. Click Reverse Lookup Zone to select it, click the Action menu, and click New Zone.

3. Click Next after the New Zone Wizard starts.

4. If the Active Directory is installed, click *Active Directory Integrated* for the type of zone to create. This option integrates storage of DNS information with the Active Directory and enables you to replicate DNS information among DCs. If the Active Directory is not installed (or if you do not want to integrate DNS data with the Active Directory—which is not recommended), click Standard primary, which puts the data into a text file. Click Next.

5. Enter the network ID of the reverse lookup zone (which is the first two or three octets that identify the network, depending on the subnet mask that you use). This information is used to build the "in-addr.arpa" reverse lookup zone name. For example, if your zone network address is 129.70, then the in-addr-arpa reverse lookup zone is named 70.129.in-addr.arpa. The Wizard automatically builds the in-addr-arpa name format when you enter the network address (see Figure 13-10). Click Next. If the wizard asks whether to create a new file or use an existing file, select to create a new file and then click Next.

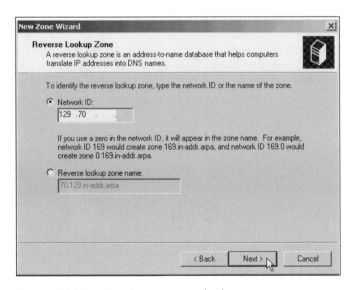

Figure 13-10   Creating a reverse lookup zone

6. Review the information you have entered, and click Finish.

7. If you are using subnets, you can create a folder for each one under the parent reverse lookup zone by right-clicking the new zone, such as 129.70.x.x Subnet, clicking New Domain, and entering the subnet value, such as 10 (for subnet 129.77.10). Click OK, and repeat this step for each subnet. Figure 13-11 illustrates the way the new subfolder is displayed in the DNS management tool.

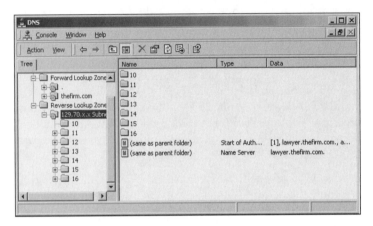

Figure 13-11 Reverse lookup zone subfolders for subnets

After the two primary zones are created, it is necessary to populate each zone with records, to enable forward and reverse address translations. If DHCP is set up to work with DNS, it will automatically populate the zones. You also have the option of manually entering records for servers and clients. For example, to enter a forward lookup zone host address (A) resource record using the DNS management tool, double-click the DNS computer and Forward Lookup Zones in the tree. Right-click the domain name, click New Host, enter the host name and IP address, and check *Create associated pointer (PTR) record* to automatically create the reverse zone record (see Figure 13-12). To manually create a reverse lookup zone record in the tree under the DNS server, double-click Reverse Lookup Zones and double-click to display the appropriate subfolder for the computer's subnet. Right-click the subfolder representing the subnet, click New Pointer, and enter the IP address and host name (see Figure 13-13). Try Hands-on Project 13-5 to practice creating forward and reverse lookup zone records.

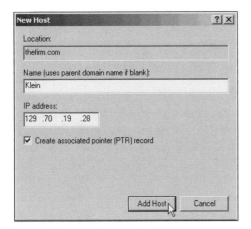

Figure 13-12   Creating a host address (A) resource record

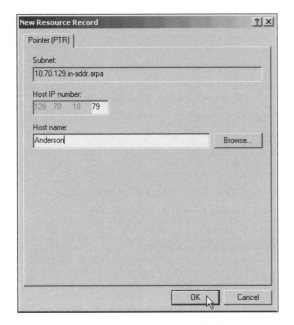

Figure 13-13   Creating a PTR record

The forward lookup zone is used more frequently than the reverse lookup zone, because net-work hosts (servers and clients) are most commonly identified by their computer names. For instance, when you want to access a shared folder or a Web server, you usually do so by using the computer's name or the Web server's domain identification, not the IP address. For another example, when you access Microsoft's Web site at *microsoft.com*, the DNS servers at that site use the forward lookup zone to link the domain name with the appropriate Web server by IP address.

If DNS is installed, but is not resolving names, or does not seem to be working, check to make sure that the DNS Server and DNS Client services are both started and set to start automatically on the DNS server.

To check that the DNS Server and DNS Client Services are started, click Start, point to Programs, point to Administrative Tools, and click Computer Management (or right-click My Computer and click Manage). Double-click Services and Applications in the console tree, and click Services. Scroll to view the DNS Client and DNS Server services, and then check the status and startup type information for both. If you need to start one or both services, double-click the service and click the Start button. Also, make sure that the Startup type box is set to Automatic. The DNS Server service is dependent on the NT LM Security Support Provider and the Remote Procedure Call (RPC) services, so make sure both of these services also are started and set to start automatically.

INSTALLING MICROSOFT WINS

WINS is used to register NetBIOS computer names and map them to IP addresses for pre-Windows 2000 servers and clients. WINS automatically registers network clients that use NetBIOS and builds a database that other network clients can query in order to locate a computer. For example, if there is a Windows 95 network computer called Eggplant that offers a shared folder for other network clients, those other clients can query WINS to find Eggplant. WINS also makes it possible for NetBIOS-named computers to send and receive SMTP e-mail over the Internet.

The steps for installing WINS are nearly the same as for installing DNS, using the Add/Remove Programs tool in the Control Panel. The difference is that when you select which network service to install, you choose Windows Internet Name Service (WINS), as follows:

1. Open Add/Remove Programs in the Control Panel.

2. Click Add/Remove Windows Components. If the Windows Components Wizard dialog box is not automatically started, click the Components button to start it.

3. Double-click Networking Services, and check Windows Internet Name Service (WINS). Click OK in the Networking Services dialog box.

4. Click Next in the Windows Components Wizard dialog box.

5. If requested, insert the Windows 2000 Server CD-ROM, specify the path to the CD-ROM drive and the \I386 folder, and click OK.

6. Click Finish.

Plan to use the default configuration for WINS after it is installed. If you need to manage WINS, you can access the WINS management tool as an MMC snap-in or from the Administrative Tools menu. For example, you can use this tool to import a special database of computers to register, or to set up replication with other WINS servers in a domain.

INSTALLING MICROSOFT **DHCP**

The Dynamic Host Configuration Protocol (DHCP, see Chapter 3) is a protocol in the TCP/IP suite that is used along with DHCP services to detect the presence of a new network client and assign an IP address to that client. When you set up a Windows 95, 98, NT, or 2000 client to automatically obtain an IP address, the client contacts a DHCP server to obtain an address. The DHCP server has a preassigned range of IP addresses that it can give to new clients. Each address is assigned for a specific period of time, such as eight hours, two weeks, a month, or a year. A range of contiguous addresses is called the **scope**. A single Microsoft DHCP server can support the following:

- Dynamic configuration of DNS server forward and reverse lookup zone records
- Up to 1000 different scopes
- Up to 10,000 DHCP clients

A Windows 2000 server can be configured as a DHCP server using Microsoft DHCP services. When you set up a Microsoft DHCP server, you have the option of setting it up to automatically enter forward and reverse lookup zone records in a Microsoft DNS server. The DHCP server automatically updates the DNS server at the time it assigns an IP address. Using dynamic DNS updates can significantly save time in creating DNS lookup zone records.

Multiple scopes are supported in a single Microsoft DHCP server, because it is often necessary to assign different address ranges, such as one range that is 129.70.10.1 to 129.70.10.122 and another that is 129.70.20.10 to 129.70.20.78. As this example illustrates, you can assign address ranges to reflect the network subnet structure or other network divisions.

13

CAUTION
If your network has Internet connectivity, make sure you obtain IP address ranges from your Internet service provider, so that you use addresses that are specifically assigned to your organization and recognized as valid by the Internet community.

DHCP is installed using the Control Panel Add/Remove Programs tool as a networking service in the Windows components. To install DHCP:

1. Open Add/Remove Programs in the Control Panel.
2. Click Add/Remove Windows Components. If the Windows Components Wizard dialog box is not automatically started, click the Components button to start it.
3. Double-click Networking Services, and check Dynamic Host Configuration Protocol (DHCP). Click OK in the Networking Services dialog box.
4. Click Next in the Windows Components Wizard dialog box.
5. If requested, insert the Windows 2000 Server CD-ROM, specify the path to the CD-ROM drive and the \I386 folder, and click OK.
6. Click Finish.

Configuring a DHCP Server

After DHCP is installed, it is necessary to set up one or more scopes and to authorize the DHCP server. The process of authorizing the server is a security precaution to make sure that IP addresses are only assigned by DHCP servers that are managed by network and server administrators. The security is needed because it is critical that IP address assignment be carefully managed to ensure that only valid IP addresses are used and that there is no possibility that duplicate IP addresses can be assigned. DHCP servers that are not authorized are prevented from running on a network. A third step that is not required, but that saves time in managing DNS, is to configure the DHCP server and its clients to automatically update DNS records.

 TIP   Only DCs and member servers can be authorized as DHCP servers when the Active Directory is in use on the network. If the Active Directory is not implemented, a stand-alone server can be authorized.

Managing a DHCP server is accomplished through the DHCP management tool, which is accessed as an MMC snap-in or by clicking Start, pointing to Programs, pointing to Administrative Tools, and clicking DHCP. To start the New Scope Wizard, open the DHCP management tool, double-click DHCP, right-click the DHCP server, click New Scope, and complete the steps presented by the wizard (try Hands-on Project 13-6). Figure 13-14 illustrates how to enter an address range via the wizard.

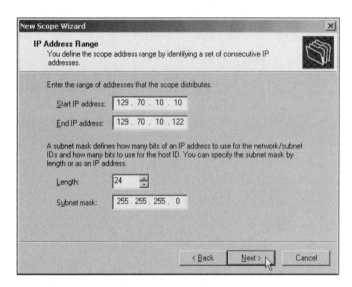

Figure 13-14   Creating a scope

TIP Set the duration of a lease on the basis of the type of connection. For desktop computers that are connected on a more permanent basis, set leases to expire after a longer period, such as from three days to a couple of weeks. Particularly, use a longer lease period on medium-and large-sized networks in which you have a large number of IP addresses that can be used. For laptop and portable computers that are less permanent on the network, set leases to expire after the duration of the communication session, such as 8–24 hours.

To authorize a DHCP server in the Active Directory via the DHCP management tool after you create a scope (you must be logged on as Administrator or as an Enterprise Administrator):

1. Right-click the server as you did when creating the scope.

2. Click Authorize on the menu.

When it is installed, a DHCP server is automatically configured to register IP addresses at the DNS servers, but you must also provide the DNS servers' IP addresses when you configure each scope. You can make sure that automatic DNS registration is set up on the DHCP server by right-clicking the server in the DHCP management tool and then clicking Properties. Click the DNS tab to check its setup (see Figure 13-15). The *Automatically update DHCP client information in DNS* box should be checked. If all clients are running Windows 2000 operating systems, and you want the clients to update the DNS server records, check the radio button to *Update DNS only if DHCP client requests.* Windows 2000 clients can automatically communicate with the DNS server to perform their own updates. If some clients are running Windows 95, 98, or NT, then click the radio button to *Always update DNS*, which means that the DHCP server takes the responsibility to update the DNS server's records every time a client obtains the IP address. Also, make sure that *Discard forward (name-to-address) lookups when lease expires* is checked, so that the DHCP server alerts the DNS server to delete a record each time a lease is up. If some clients are running Windows 95, 98, or NT, also check *Enable updates for DNS clients that do not support dynamic update*.

13

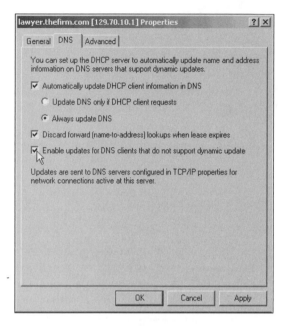

Figure 13-15 Configuring automatic DNS registration

Troubleshooting DHCP

When you set up a DHCP server, it is possible for problems to occur. Some possible problems include, among others: (1) the server is stopped or not working, (2) it is creating extra network traffic, and (3) it is not automatically registering with DNS servers. Table 13-6 presents several typical problems and their resolutions.

Table 13-6 Troubleshooting a DHCP Server

Problem	Solution(s)
The DHCP server will not start.	1. Use the Computer Management tool to make sure that the DHCP Client and DHCP Server services are started and set to start automatically. If the DHCP Server service will not start, make sure that the Remote Procedure Call (RPC) and the Security Accounts Manager services are already started, because the DHCP Server service depends on both. 2. Make sure that the DHCP server is authorized.

Table 13-6   Troubleshooting a DHCP Server (continued)

Problem	Solution(s)
The DHCP server creates extra or excessive network traffic.	Increase the lease period in each scope, so there is less traffic caused by allocating new leases when the old ones expire.
The DNS lookup zone records are not automatically updated.	1. Make sure that DNS servers and IP addresses are set up in each DHCP scope. 2. Make sure that the DHCP server's properties are set up to automatically update the DNS server. Also, have the DHCP server do the updating, instead of clients, when there are pre-Windows 2000 server clients. Last, enable DNS updating for clients that do not dynamically support it.
One of the leased IP addresses is conflicting with a permanent IP address assigned to a computer, such as a server.	Exclude that IP address from the scope.
Your network has a large number of portable and laptop computers and is in short supply of IP addresses.	Reduce the lease duration so that leases expire sooner and can be reassigned.
The System log is reporting Jet database error messages.	The DHCP database is corrupted. Have users log off from the DHCP server, and disable the server's connection (use the Network and Dial-up Connections tool). Use the DHCP management tool to reconcile the scopes (right-click the server and click Reconcile All Scopes). Another option is to open the Command Prompt window and use the Jetpack.exe program to repair the database. A third option is to use the Nesh.exe command to dump the database and then reinitialize it.
The DHCP server is not responding.	Use the Network and Dial-up Connections tool to make sure that the server is connected to the network.

13

CONNECTING THROUGH TERMINAL SERVICES

Besides using Windows 2000 as a Web, DNS, or DHCP server, you can also use it as a terminal server. A **terminal server** enables clients to run services and software applications on the Windows 2000 server instead of at the client, which means that nearly any type of operating system can access Windows 2000. The Windows 2000 Terminal Services are used for three broad purposes: to support thin clients, to centralize program access, and to remotely administer Windows 2000 servers. One of the main reasons for using a terminal server is to enable **thin clients**—such as specialized PCs that have minimal Windows-based operating systems—to access a Windows 2000 server, so that most CPU-intense operations (creating a spreadsheet for example) are performed on the server. Some examples of thin client computers are Hewlett-Packard's Netstation, Maxspeed's MaxTerm, Neoware's NeoStation, and Wyse Technologies'

Winterm terminals. These function similarly to a basic **terminal** that has no CPU and that accesses a mainframe computer to perform all program execution and processing on the mainframe. Thin client network implementations are generally used to save money and reduce training and support requirements. Also, they are used for portable field or hand-held remote devices, such as remote hotel reservation terminals and inventory counting devices. Thin client computers typically cost hundreds of dollars less than full-featured PCs, and because the operating system is simpler it is easier to train users. Thin client field devices can be made inexpensively and tailored for a particular use, such as taking inventory in warehouses.

The second reason for using a terminal server is to centralize control of the way programs are used. Some organizations need to maintain tight control over certain program applications, such as sensitive financial applications, top-secret program development, word-processed documents, and spreadsheets. For example, a network equipment company that invents a switch that is 100 times faster than any other on the market can use a terminal server to closely guard access to design documents and programs. These are stored and modified only on the server, which can be configured to provide a high level of security.

 TIP If you plan to set up a terminal server for clients to run programs in multiple sessions, consider the CPU and RAM needs in advance. Use a server that has a fast CPU, such as a Pentium III or faster. Also, populate the server with ample RAM (see Chapter 2 for server selection).

The third reason for using a terminal server is to allow a server administrator to remotely access management tools, such as Active Directory Users and Computers, the Computer Management tool, the DNS tool, and others that appear in the Administrative Tools menu or as MMC snap-ins. Remote access enables a server administrator to manage one or more servers from her or his workstation on the same network, or to dial in from home or while traveling.

Windows 2000 Terminal Services support not only thin clients, but other types of client operating systems, including MS-DOS, Windows 3.x, Windows 95, Windows 98, Windows NT, Windows 2000, UNIX, UNIX-based X-terminals, and Macintosh. There are four main components that enable terminal server connectivity, which are shown in Table 13-7.

Table 13-7 Terminal Services Components

Component	Description
Windows 2000 multi-user terminal services	These services enable multiple users to simultaneously access and run standard Windows-based applications on a Windows 2000 server.
Terminal Server Client	This client software runs on Windows 3.11, Windows 95, Windows 98, Windows NT 3.51, Windows NT 4.0, and Windows 2000 to enable the client to run the Windows graphical user interface, which looks like a regular 32-bit version of Windows.

Table 13-7 Terminal Services Components (continued)

Component	Description
Remote Display Protocol (RDP)	This protocol is used for specialized network communications between the client and the server running terminal services. RDP follows the International Telecommunications Union (ITU) T.120 standard to enable multiple communications channels over a single line.
Terminal services administration tools	These tools are used to manage terminal services.

CAUTION

Before you implement terminal services on a Windows 2000 server, determine in advance if you want that server to be able to cache files at the client for offline access, because offline access is not compatible with terminal services and must be turned off.

Installing Terminal Services

Before you install terminal services, determine if you want the server to function as an application server to clients or as a remote administration server for server administrators, because the installation cannot be set up for both on a single server. When you install the terminal services, you have the option of configuring the server as an application server or a remote administration server at the time it is installed. The only way to change the configuration to the other mode is to reinstall the terminal services. Also, if you plan to set up an application server, then one Windows 2000 server must also be configured as a terminal services licensing server.

Windows 2000 terminal services are installed using the Add/Remove Programs tool in the Control Panel. To install terminal services:

1. Open Add/Remove Programs in the Control Panel.

2. Click Add/Remove Windows Components. If the Windows Components Wizard dialog box is not automatically started, click the Components button to start it.

3. Check the box in front of Terminal Services and make sure that the box is not gray, since a gray box means that not all components are installed. If the box is gray, double-click Terminal Services, check all of the subcomponents, and click OK in the Terminal Services dialog box.

4. If this is the first or only Windows 2000 server configured as a terminal server, also click Terminal Services Licensing in order to license clients to use terminal services.

5. Click Next in the Windows Components Wizard dialog box.

6. Select whether this server is to be a remote administration server for server administrators or an application server (see Figure 13-16). Click Next.

13

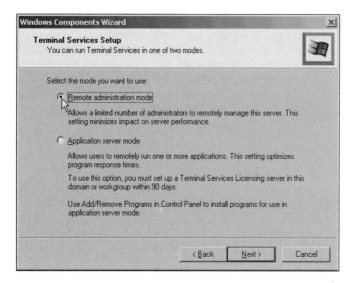

Figure 13-16   Selecting the function of a terminal server

7. If in Step 6 you selected to configure for the application server mode, two dialog boxes are displayed next. The first enables you to specify the security level for access to software applications. You can either use permissions that are compatible with Windows 2000 security or permissions that are less secure for compatibility with some older software applications. The second dialog box shows applications that are currently installed, such as Microsoft Office, and that may need to be reinstalled to function using Terminal Services.

8. If in Step 4 you selected to install Terminal Services Licensing, in the next dialog box click *Your entire enterprise*, if this server is to be used to manage licenses for all clients in an enterprise; click *Your domain or workgroup*, if this server is to be used to manage licensing only for clients in a domain or on a standalone server. Also, select the folder location for the license database. Click Next.

9. If requested, insert the Windows 2000 Server CD-ROM, specify the path to the CD-ROM drive and the \I386 folder, and click OK.

10. Click Finish.

11. Select the option to restart the server to enable the new services to go into effect.

Managing Terminal Services

After the terminal services are installed, three management tools are available in Windows 2000 Server: Terminal Services Client Administrator, Terminal Services Configuration, and Terminal Services Manager. When you install the Terminal Services Licensing component, a fourth tool also is available, Terminal Services Licensing. Table 13-8 lists these tools, including a description of their functions and how to access them.

Table 13-8 Terminal Services Management Tools

Management Tool	Function	Tool Location
Terminal Services Client Creator	Used to make floppy installation disks for clients	Administrative Tools menu
Terminal Services Configuration	Used to configure terminal server settings and connections	Administrative Tools menu and an MMC snap-in
Terminal Services Licensing	Used to administer client licenses for terminal servers in an enterprise or in a single domain	Administrative Tools menu
Terminal Services Manager	Used to control and monitor clients that are connected to terminal services on one or more servers	Administrative Tools menu

Configuring Terminal Services

Begin by using the Terminal Services Configuration tool to configure the remote connection properties. Only one connection is configured for each NIC in the server, which is used to handle multiple clients. For example, click Start, point to Programs, point to Administrative Tools, and click Terminal Services Configuration. Double-click Terminal Services Configuration, if necessary, to view the Connections and Server Settings folders in the tree. Click Connections to view the connection set up during installation. If you have more than one NIC, you can create another connection by right-clicking Connections and clicking Create New Connection. To manage the properties of a connection, double-click the connection in the right pane, such as RDP-Tcp. Figure 13-17 shows the connection Properties dialog box and Table 13-9 describes the capabilities of each tab.

One property that should be checked from the start is permission security (try Hands-on Project 13-7). If the terminal server is used by server administrators for remote administration, make sure that access is set up only for the appropriate administrators group, such as Administrators or Domain Admins. If the terminal server is configured as an application server, first use the Active Directory Users and Computers tool or the Local Users and Groups tool (on a standalone server) to create one or more groups of users who will have access to the terminal server. Then use the Terminal Services Configuration tool to set up the permissions.

13

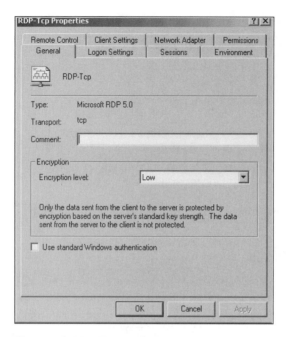

Figure 13-17   Terminal service connection properties

Table 13-9   Terminal Services Components

Tab	Description
General	Used to set up encryption and authentication
Logon Settings	Used to determine how the client logs on, by using information provided by the client or by using a preset logon account setup
Sessions	Used to establish timeout settings and the way clients can reconnect to the server if a session is interrupted
Environment	Enables you to establish a program that runs automatically when the client logs on, and to enable or disable client wallpaper for faster server response
Remote Control	Enables you to remotely control a client or to observe a client's session while that session is active, for example to watch the user's key and mouse strokes to help diagnose a problem without having to go to the client's site
Client Settings	Enables you to configure client connection settings such as whether to use client settings, connect to client drives, or connect to a default printer; also mapping features can be enabled or disabled, such as printer and printer port mapping, clipboard mapping, drive mapping, and audio mapping
Network Adapter	Enables you to specify a NIC to use and to control the number of simultaneous connections
Permissions	Used to set up access permissions by user and by group

Click the Permissions tab to view the defaults that are configured. The Allow and Deny permissions include:

- *Full Control:* Enables access that includes query, set information, reset server, remote control, logon, logoff, message, connect, disconnect, and virtual channel use

- *User Access:* Enables access to query, connect, and send messages

- *Guest Access:* Enables access to logon

Another property that should be checked is the implementation of encryption and authentication. Click the General tab to check these properties. Authentication can be set to use either no authentication or standard Windows authentication when the clients are Windows 95, 98, NT, or 2000. The encryption options are:

- *Low:* Data sent from the client to the server is encrypted.

- *Medium:* Data sent from the client to the server and from the server to the client are encrypted using the default server encryption.

- *High:* Data sent from the client to the server and from the server to the client are encrypted using the highest encryption level at the server.

Configuring a Terminal Services Client

You can configure a client to access a terminal server by making an installation disk using the Terminal Services Client Creator tool, which is started from the Administrative Tools menu. Before you start, format four floppy disks for Windows 3.11, or two disks for Windows 95 or higher and for UNIX systems. Once you start the Terminal Services Client Creator tool, the Create Installation Disk dialog box is displayed (see Figure 13-18). Select the option that fits the client, such as *Terminal Services for 32-bit x86 windows* if the client is running Windows 98. Insert the first disk, and click OK to begin making the disk set. Click OK again to confirm that you want to start making the disks (Hands-on Project 13-7 enables you to practice making installation disks).

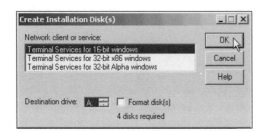

Figure 13-18   Creating a terminal services installation disk

To install the terminal server client software on the floppy disks, for instance on a computer running Windows 95 or Windows 98, insert the first disk in the computer. Click Start, click Run, and enter *a:\setup* in the Open box. Click OK to start the Setup program, which installs the software and creates a program group of the programs used to access the terminal server.

Configuring Licensing

When you set up a terminal server as an application server, you must activate the server and configure licensing by using the Terminal Services Licensing tool (make sure the Terminal Services Licensing component is installed at the same time that you install the Terminal Services component). To open the tool, click Start, point to Programs, point to Administrative Tools, and click Terminal Services Licensing. Double-click *All servers* in the tree to display the servers that offer terminal services. To activate a server, right-click the server in the tree and click *Activate Server*. When the Licensing Wizard starts, click Next and complete the instructions for contacting Microsoft to activate the licenses. There are four ways to contact Microsoft: Internet, World Wide Web, Fax, and Telephone.

 If the Terminal Services Manager fails to start properly for a terminal server that is configured as an application server, or if users are unable to connect to the server, check to make sure that you have activated the server using the Terminal Services Licensing tool.

Installing Applications

When you configure a terminal server to function in the applications server mode, applications are installed to be compatible with this mode. For this reason, you may need to reinstall some applications, as noted by the Windows Components Wizard when you install Terminal Services. Use the Control Panel Add/Remove Programs tool to install new applications after the Terminal Services are installed, and use the same tool to uninstall and reinstall programs that were installed prior to setting up the server for Terminal Services.

 On a terminal server, software applications are installed only via the install mode, which is automatically invoked when you install applications by clicking Add/Remove Programs in the Control Panel, clicking the Add New Programs button, and clicking the CD or Floppy button to start the program installation. You should not install programs by using the Start menu and Run Option or by double-clicking the installation program from Windows Explorer or My Computer.

Running Windows 16-bit programs, which is accomplished through the virtual DOS machine and Windows on Windows (WOW, see Chapter 1), is not recommended when Windows 2000 Server is set up as a terminal server for applications. When users run 16-bit programs, the CPU can support only 60% of the total number of simultaneous connections that can be supported when only 32-bit programs are run. Also, the amount of RAM used per each 16-bit program is 50% more. MS-DOS programs should not be run at all, because of their high use of CPU resources.

Monitoring Terminal Services

Open the Terminal Services Manager to monitor live sessions and processes. By using the Terminal Services Manager you can:

- View status information about a session
- Connect to view a session or disconnect from one
- Log off a user's session
- Reset a user's session
- Send a message
- End a process
- Control a session remotely

To use any of these features on a user's session, click Start, point to Programs, point to Administrative Tools, and click Terminal Services Manager. Click the name of the server in the console tree. The right-hand pane displays three tabs: Users, Sessions, and Processes. The Users tab identifies user accounts that are connected and shows the sessions they have in progress. The Sessions tab lists sessions first and then the users who are engaged in those sessions. The Processes tab shows the processes currently in use in Windows 2000 Server.

To perform any function on a user's connection, click the Users tab and right-click the connection. The shortcut menu displays the following options: Connect, Disconnect, Send Message, Remote Control, Reset, and Status. For example, to view the status of a connection, right-click that connection and click Status. If you want to watch a user's session while that user is in action, right-click the user and click Connect. When you are finished watching the session, right-click the user again and click Disconnect. Or, if you want to take over the session (for example, to show the user how to do a particular task), right-click the user and click Remote Control.

13

 In Chapter 14, you learn how to use the System Monitor to monitor terminal services.

Troubleshooting Terminal Services

Sometimes users experience problems while using terminal services, such as connecting to the terminal server or logging off because their session is hung. Table 13-10 presents troubleshooting ideas for terminal servers and clients.

Table 13-10   Troubleshooting a Terminal Server

Problem	Solution(s)
The client cannot log on.	1. Make sure that the encryption and authentication set at the server match what the client is capable of handling. 2. Have the client user manually enter her or his username and password instead of relying on the automatic connection. 3. For network connections, make sure that the client is configured to use the same protocol as the server, such as TCP/IP. For dial-up connections, make sure that the client's dial-up connection is using PPP and the same protocol as the server, such as TCP/IP.
The terminal server is not configured to run applications.	Use the Add/Remove Programs tool to uninstall terminal services, and then reinstall using the option to configure as an application server.
The terminal server is not configured as a remote administration server.	Use the Add/Remove Programs tool to uninstall terminal servers, and then reinstall using the option to set up as a remote administration server.
A user's session is hung or the user cannot log off.	Open the Terminal Services Manager, right-click the user, and click Log Off.
You need to send a message to a user.	Open the Terminal Services Manager, right-click the user, click Send Message, enter the message, and click OK.
A user cannot run a program correctly.	The program is likely to have been installed before terminal services were installed. Remove the program and reinstall it.
No one can access the terminal server.	The server is disconnected or is not active. Open Terminal Services Manager, right-click the server, and click Connect to connect the server. Use the Terminal Services Licensing tool to activate server licenses.

CONFIGURING A TELNET SERVER

Another way for clients to access resources on a Windows 2000 server is to use Telnet. Telnet is particularly useful for non–Windows clients such as IBM AS/400, some versions of UNIX, and others that support Telnet but that cannot access a Windows 2000 server as a terminal services client. As you learned in Chapter 3, Telnet is part of the TCP/IP application suite that enables a client to act as a terminal to access a server. Telnet is a technology that is almost as old as TCP/IP and is a TCP/IP application used to set up one computer as a network host and other computers as clients. Instead of running Windows-based terminal services, the client runs TCP/IP-based Telnet and accesses the Windows 2000 server, which is set up as a Telnet server instead of a Microsoft terminal server. The access is accomplished in a character-based mode and requires two elements: the Telnet Server service running on Windows 2000 Server, and Microsoft Telnet client or some other version of Telnet on the client computer. Also, the server and client must be configured for TCP/IP prior to running either Telnet Server or the client software. When a user telnets to a server, he or she must have a user account and supply the account name and password. Telnet can use NTLM authentication (see NT LAN Manager in Chapters 4 and 7) to protect access to the server, but you must first turn on NTLM from the client (by entering the *NTLM* command in Telnet, if the client supports NTLM). Once connected, the user can execute programs and processes on the server for which that user has permissions. Telnet Server supports up to 63 clients.

The Windows 2000 Server Telnet Server service is started in one of two ways (on a server that is already configured to use TCP/IP). To use the first way:

1. Open the Computer Management tool and double-click Services and Applications.

2. Click Services under the tree.

3. Scroll the right-hand pane to find Telnet, right-click the service, and click Properties.

4. Click the Start button to start the service. If you plan to have the service running all of the time, set the Startup type box to Automatic. Click OK.

The second way to start the service is to open the Command Prompt window, enter *net start tlntsvr*, and press Enter.

The client computer must have Telnet installed—Windows 2000 Telnet client, for example. The Windows 2000 Telnet client is started from the Command Prompt window. To find out about Telnet commands, enter *telnet /?* in the Command Prompt window; to connect to a server, enter *telnet* and the name of the host computer, such as *telnet Lawyer*. To disconnect from a server, enter *exit* (or *quit* on some systems). When a Windows 2000 user starts Telnet and connects to the server, he or she views a command prompt window that is very similar to the same window on the client, but that window is actually on the server. On other systems, such as UNIX, Telnet may simply consist of command-line operations without a full-screen command window.

13

Windows 2000 Server out of the box is licensed to use only two simultaneous Telnet connections. More licenses are available when you purchase the add-on pack for Microsoft Windows Services for UNIX.

There are several different versions of Telnet client software. Make sure that users who telnet into a Telnet server check to make sure that they have set a password on the client side, or else intruders can telnet into their computers.

INSTALLING A NETWARE GATEWAY

On a network that combines use of NetWare servers and Windows 2000 servers, you may need to create a way for users to access a NetWare server through a Windows 2000 server that acts as a gateway. This is accomplished by installing **Gateway Service for NetWare**

(**GSNW**) in a Windows 2000 server. Used in this context, *gateway* means that the server acts as a go-between for Windows-based workstations and a NetWare file server. The workstations do not need to be NetWare clients, because they access the directories and files through the gateway, which appears to them as just another shared Windows 2000 server folder.

To install Gateway Service for NetWare, use the following general steps:

1. Create an account on the NetWare server for the Windows 2000 server to access (using SYSCON or NWADMIN). The appropriate directory and file attributes and access rights or group membership should be granted to the account, as determined by which directories and files will be made available for the users. For example, the NetWare account might be granted Read and File Scan access rights, which enable users to read files, run programs, and view file and subdirectory names.

2. Create a group on the NetWare server called NTGATEWAY, which has access rights to the files and directories that need to be used.

3. Make the NetWare user account a member of the NTGATEWAY group.

There are two places from which to control access to NetWare resources offered by a gateway. You can set up security through the access rights on the NetWare server, or you can set up security using share permissions on the Windows 2000 server. If you set up security in both places, keep in mind that the Windows 2000 server's gateway access is first restricted by the NetWare access rights and that user access is next restricted by the Windows 2000 Server share permissions.

4. Create a corresponding account on the Windows 2000 server.

5. Make sure that the appropriate protocol is installed in Windows 2000 Server for connecting to the NetWare server, such as NWLink or TCP/IP (see Chapters 3 and 6).

6. Install Gateway Service for NetWare on the Windows 2000 server by opening the Network and Dial-up Connections tool, right-clicking Local Area Connection, clicking Properties, and clicking the Install button. Double-click Client and then double-click Gateway (and Client) Services for NetWare.

7. If you see the Select NetWare Logon dialog box to designate a preferred NetWare server, you can enter that information now or configure it later as described in the next paragraphs. If you configure it now, enter the name of the Preferred Server and its associated information and then click OK. Or, click Cancel and then Yes, if you choose to configure the information later.

8. Click Yes to restart the Windows 2000 server.

After the Gateway (and Client) Services for NetWare are loaded, a new GSNW icon is added to the Control Panel. The GSNW icon enables you to configure the gateway, for instance establishing a path to the NetWare server directories that will be offered as shared directories to clients. The steps for configuring the gateway are as follows:

1. Open the GSNW icon on the Control Panel, and click the Gateway button.

2. Click Enable Gateway.

3. Enter the NetWare account name, password, and password confirmation.

4. Click Add to create a shared folder.

5. Enter the share name, path to the NetWare server, drive, and user limit.

6. Click OK.

7. Set the share permissions.

8. Click OK.

9. Close the GSNW utility.

You can create multiple shared folders to different NetWare drives or directories by using the Add button and specifying a different share name, network path, and drive letter each time. When you configure the gateway, you have the option of specifying a preferred server or a default tree and context. A preferred server is the NetWare server that the gateway accesses by default, and that authenticates the logon. The tree and context option is used when the NetWare environment supports NetWare Directory Services, and it refers to the user account object and directory tree that are set by default.

When you install Gateway Service for NetWare, there also is an option to set default options for print queues that are accessed through the gateway. The print options are as follows:

- Add a form feed to each printout to make sure the last page prints

- Send a notification to users when a job has printed

- Print a banner page with each print job

There also is an option to run a login script on the NetWare server each time the gateway account logs on. The login script is a text script similar to Windows 2000 Server's logon script, containing commands that automatically run, such as specifying the operating system, account name, and other information. The preferred server, tree and context, print, and login script options are set from the Gateway Service for NetWare dialog box that appears when you first open the GSNW icon.

> **TIP**
> If you are troubleshooting a problem with connecting through Gateway Service for NetWare, start by using the *net* command to make sure that the service is working. Open the Command Prompt window, type *net view /network:nw*, press Enter, and look for a list of NetWare servers. If you see servers displayed, the gateway is working. If you do not see a list of NetWare servers, enter *net start "gateway service for netware"* in the Command Prompt window, and then use the *net* command to list the NetWare servers.

13

After Gateway Service for NetWare is installed, you can connect to NetWare print queues (the same as Windows 2000 Server shared printers) by using the Add Printer Wizard. To connect to NetWare printers for sharing on a Windows 2000 Server network:

1. Click Start, point to Settings, and click the Printers folder.

2. Double-click Add Printer, and click Next after the wizard starts.

3. Click Network printer and click Next.

4. Click *Type the printer name*, and enter the name of the NetWare printer in UNC format (*server**printer* in the Name box). Click Next.

5. Click Yes to print a test page, and click Next.

6. Click Finish.

7. Right-click the newly added printer in the Printers folder, click Sharing, and set up the printer to be shared. Also, if the Active Directory is installed, use the Active Directory Users and Computers tool to publish the printer (see Chapter 11).

CHAPTER SUMMARY

❑ A Windows 2000 server can be turned into a Web server through the installation of Internet Information Services (IIS). IIS comes with a range of tools that enables you to configure it for Internet Web access, to act as a media server, as an intranet server, and as a Web-based server for a VPN.

❑ Three other options for configuring a Windows 2000 server are as a DNS server to provide computer name and IP address resolution for a network, as a WINS server for NetBIOS-name-to-IP-address resolution, or as a DHCP server to lease IP addresses to network hosts.

❑ Providing terminal services is yet another function that a Windows 2000 server can perform. Terminal services involve using one of two modes: to enable remote access for server administrators to manage network servers, and to enable clients, such as thin clients, to run applications on the server.

❑ For clients that cannot use Windows 2000 terminal services, there is also the option to set up a Windows 2000 server as a Telnet server. Telnet is part of the TCP/IP application suite and is used to enable clients to emulate terminals on a computer set up as a Telnet server.

❑ Interoperability is important for enterprise networks that include Novell NetWare servers. Windows 2000 Server can be configured as a gateway to NetWare so that NetWare resources, such as directories and printers, appear as shared Windows 2000 Server resources.

In the next chapter, you learn how to monitor Windows 2000 Server, which is a first step in learning to pinpoint and diagnose problem areas, such as the need to add more RAM. You also learn how to tune and optimize server services and server performance.

KEY TERMS

DNS Server — A Microsoft service that resolves computer names to IP addresses, for example, resolving the computer name Brown to IP address 129.77.1.10, and that resolves IP addresses to computer names.

forward lookup zone — A DNS zone or table that maps computer names to IP addresses.

Gateway Service for NetWare (GSNW) — A service included with Windows NT and Windows 2000 Server that provides connectivity to NetWare resources for Windows NT and Windows 2000 servers and their clients, with the Windows NT or Windows 2000 server acting as a gateway.

host address (A) resource record — A record in a DNS forward lookup zone that consists of a computer name correlated to an IP version 4 address.

Internet Information Services (IIS) — A Microsoft Windows 2000 Server component that provides Internet Web, FTP, mail, newsgroup, and other services, and particularly the ability to set up a Web server.

Internet Server Application Programming Interface (ISAPI) — A group of dynamic-link library (DLL) files that consists of applications and filters to enable user-customized programs to interface with IIS and to trigger particular programs, such as a specialized security check or a database lookup.

Network News Transfer Protocol (NNTP) — A TCP/IP-based protocol used by NNTP servers to transfer news and informational messages to client subscribers who compose "newsgroups."

Open Database Connectivity (ODBC) — A set of rules developed by Microsoft for accessing databases and providing a standard doorway to database data.

pointer (PTR) resource record — A record in a DNS reverse lookup zone that consists of an IP (version 4 or 6) address correlated to a computer name.

reverse lookup zone — A DNS server zone or table that maps IP addresses to computer names.

scope — A range of IP addresses that a DHCP server can assign to clients.

Secure Sockets Layer (SSL) — A dual-key encryption standard for communication between an Internet server and a client.

streaming — Playing a multimedia audio, video, or combined file received over a network before the entire file is received at the client.

terminal — A device that consists of a monitor and keyboard, used to communicate with host computers that run the programs. The terminal does not have a processor to use for running programs locally.

terminal server — A server configured to offer terminal services so that clients can run applications on the server, which is similar to having clients respond as terminals.

thin client — A specialized personal computer or terminal device that has a minimal Windows-based operating system. A thin client is designed to connect to a host computer that does most or all of the processing. The thin client is mainly responsible for providing a graphical user interface and network connectivity.

13

Uniform Resource Locator (URL) — An addressing format used to find an Internet Web site or page.

virtual directory — A URL-formatted address that provides an Internet location (virtual location) for an actual folder on a Web server that is used to publish Web documents.

Web browser — Software that uses HTTP to locate and communicate with Web sites and that interprets HTML documents, video, and sound to give the user a sound and video GUI presentation of the HTML document contents.

REVIEW QUESTIONS

1. Your company has set up a Web server to publish special promotions that have expiration dates. The marketing group is asking you if IIS has features to help with causing promotional Web files to expire after a certain number of days. How might this be possible?

   a. Configure the Operators default Web site properties to issue an alert to Web operators when files need to be deleted.

   b. Set up multiple Web publishing folders containing information that expires at the same time. Manually delete a folder on its expiration date.

   c. Create a Web-based spreadsheet showing when promotions expire and what files need to be deleted. Delete the files on the basis of the spreadsheet each morning.

   d. Configure the HTTP Headers default Web site properties to expire documents.

2. Your Web server users are calling to complain that FTP does not work, because they cannot use it to download files. How might you troubleshoot this problem?

   a. Check the permissions on FTP folders for those users.

   b. Install Media Services, which are required for FTP activity on an IIS server.

   c. Make sure that the FTP Publishing service is started.

   d. all of the above

   e. only a and b

   f. only a and c

3. You have set up a Web server, and now your users are asking for a better way to publish their Web pages than to hand-carry them to your office for you to install on the server. Which of the following will make you and them more productive?

   a. Create one or more virtual directories.

   b. Install Web services on all of their client computers and make pointers from the Web server to the clients.

   c. Configure Dfs for Web-only publishing.

   d. There is no more efficient way for users to publish Web pages.

4. You are in a planning meeting to set up a new network that will have Internet access, one Windows 2000 Web server, and four Windows 2000 servers for general file and printing access. Many of the clients are still using Windows 95 and NetBIOS applications. The organization for which you are planning has decided to implement the Active Directory. Which of the following should they include in their planning?

a. Make at least two of the Windows 2000 servers domain controllers (DCs).

b. Make at least two of the Windows 2000 servers DNS servers.

c. Make at least one of the Windows 2000 servers a WINS server.

d. all of the above

e. only a and b

f. only b and c

5. You are planning to implement a Web server that will also handle Internet e-mail services in conjunction with Microsoft Exchange service. Which of the following services enables you to transport e-mail over the Internet?

a. SMTP

b. NNTP

c. FTP

d. PPTP

6. You have configured DHCP to automatically update DNS servers, but the problem is that old leases are sometimes not removed or updated in the DNS servers. This is causing some mismatched IP resolutions. What can you do to solve the problem?

a. This problem is most common on large networks, and you must disable automatic updating.

b. This problem is caused by using TCP with IP on the network, and you must convert DNS servers to instead use UDP with IP.

c. You need to configure DHCP to discard lookup records when their leases expire.

d. You need to set leases so that they don't expire for a longer period of time.

7. You are the server administrator for a company and are on call several evenings a week to handle problems that may occur. Unfortunately, you live about 40 minutes from work and often have to go in to work in the evenings for tasks that only take a couple of minutes. How can you make your life easier by accessing administrative programs from home?

a. Configure a terminal server as an application server.

b. Configure a terminal server as a remote administration server.

c. Configure a terminal server as a thin client.

d. Unfortunately, there is no way to administer Windows 2000 servers from home.

13

8. Which of the following are IIS components that can be installed in Windows 2000 Server?

   a. Visual InterDev RAD Remote Deployment Support

   b. Common Files

   c. NNTP Service

   d. all of the above

   e. only a and b

   f. only a and c

9. One of your terminal services clients on a Windows 2000 server is having trouble with a client/server program that he runs. How might you help diagnose the problem?

   a. Lengthen the session timeout.

   b. Observe his keystrokes by connecting to view his session.

   c. Observe the applications he is using through the Command Prompt *Window* command.

   d. Restart the client/server program at the server.

10. One of your colleagues who works for another company is testing a Microsoft IIS Web server, but is concerned because there isn't better file security, such as the ability to designate one folder for read access to one group and another folder for read and write access by another group. What would you suggest?

    a. Use folder and file attributes for security.

    b. Configure the drive containing the Web files for NTFS, because as it now stands he has configured it for FAT, which has less security.

    c. Set up a VPN to configure security for general Web server access.

    d. all of the above

    e. only a and c

    f. only b and c

11. When you create a DNS server, what type of record will you most likely find in a reverse lookup zone?

    a. pointer resource record

    b. IPv6 host address (AAAA) resource record

    c. host address (A) resource record

    d. reverse host (R) resource record

12. Which of the following is(are) installed through the Add/Remove Programs tool as a Windows software component?

    a. IIS

    b. DHCP

    c. Terminal Services

d. all of the above

e. only a and b

f. only a and c

13. You have installed a counter on your e-commerce Web site and determined that it handles about 22,000 to 40,000 hits a day. This is a lot of traffic, and the Web site seems sluggish. Which of the following should you try first?

   a. Install more RAM.

   b. Set the foreground applications to get the most CPU time.

   c. Tune the Web server performance parameter from fewer than 10,000 hits to fewer than 100,000 hits.

   d. Decrease the page file size to reduce the amount of disk writing.

14. How can you make a client installation disk for a Terminal Services Windows 3.11 client?

   a. Use the Active Directory Users and Computers tool.

   b. Use the Terminal Services Client Creator tool.

   c. Use the Terminal Services Configuration tool.

   d. Terminal Services does not support Windows 3.11.

15. You have set up a Web server and now the management in your company wants to use it for multimedia training presentations. You have installed media services to prepare the server for this purpose. However, when you access a training film from the server at your workstation, it seems to take an unbearably long time to load before it starts playing. What should you do?

   a. Set up to use the streaming mode.

   b. Only purchase multimedia presentations that employ unicasting.

   c. Configure to use strongest encryption for fastest network access of multimedia.

   d. Make sure that no training file is larger than 1 MB, because this is a limitation for media services.

13

16. You have set up a TCP/IP-based Windows 2000 terminal server, and a user calls because she is trying to use the service for the first time by dialing in from home, but is not succeeding. What should she check?

   a. that her home computer is configured for TCP/IP

   b. that her home computer is set for full duplex

   c. that her home computer is configured for PPP

   d. all of the above

   e. only a and b

   f. only a and c

17. You are setting up a DHCP scope in which all of the clients are portable computers. For how long should you establish leases?

    a. one to two months

    b. seven days

    c. three to four days

    d. 8 to 24 hours

18. You have set up a Web server, created a virtual directory, and established the appropriate permissions for Web folders. After you release the server to users so that they can publish their own documents, many report some incompatibilities with using Microsoft FrontPage. Which of the following might be the problem?

    a. A special FrontPage FP permission must be assigned to the Web folders in which clients publish.

    b. The Web server IP address configuration tab has a FrontPage Extensions parameter that must be enabled so that it will authorize uploading FrontPage files from a client.

    c. FrontPage 2000 Server Extensions are not loaded as an IIS component.

    d. all of the above

    e. only a and c

    f. only b and c

19. Your network consists of 20 Windows 2000 servers and one older NetWare server that is using IPX/SPX communications. There are about 40 people who periodically access the NetWare server, but only at the rate of about four or five people at a time. What is the best way to access the NetWare server?

    a. Configure all clients to use RSVP to periodically reserve time on the NetWare server.

    b. Install Gateway Service for NetWare on one of the Windows 2000 servers for the clients to access.

    c. Configure the NetWare and Windows 2000 servers to use NetBEUI for common access.

    d. Use Windows 2000 Server terminal services for clients to access the NetWare server.

20. Your boss has worked on computer systems that support the use of a hashing algorithm for security, and she prefers this method. Can IIS Web security be configured for this security method?

    a. yes, by configuring it to use integrated Windows authentication

    b. yes, by configuring it to use basic authentication

    c. yes, by configuring it to use digest authentication

    d. A Web server does not support hashing for authentication.

21. When you are planning the installation of a DNS server, which of the following is(are) important to include in your planning?

    a. The DNS server should have a static IP address, not one assigned by DHCP.

    b. The DNS server should have an IP address that ends in "1," such as 129.70.88.1, because it must be the first server seen on the network.

    c. The DNS server must also be a DC.

    d. all of the above

    e. only a and b

    f. only a and c

22. Users are not able to access your Web server, and when you try it from your office, you cannot access it either. Which of the following might you do?

    a. Use the Internet Information Server management tool to restart IIS.

    b. Make sure that the Server service is started and running.

    c. Take the WINS server offline, because WINS can interfere with network access to IIS.

    d. all of the above

    e. only a and b

    f. only a and c

23. Which of the following are permissions used for Terminal Services?

    a. Full Control

    b. Write

    c. Execute

    d. all of the above

    e. only a and b

    f. only b and c

13

24. The Research group in your organization is setting up a Web server for a VPN that must have very restricted access. In a committee meeting, they ask you to list methods that can be used to restrict access. Which of the following is(are) possible?

    a. Restrict access by individual user IP address.

    b. Restrict access by IP subnet.

    c. Restrict access by domain.

    d. all of the above

    e. only a and b

    f. only b and c

25. You have installed Terminal Services, and several clients have called to say that Microsoft Word is not working properly. What should you do to solve the problem?

    a. Increase the channel bandwidth, because Microsoft Word requires more bandwidth.

    b. Reinstall Microsoft Word, because it was installed prior to installing Terminal Services.

    c. Increase the Terminal Services buffer used at those clients.

    d. all of the above

    e. only a and b

    f. only b and c

HANDS-ON PROJECTS

Project 13-1

In this project, you install Internet Information Services to set up a Web and FTP site.

To install IIS:

1. Click **Start**, point to **Settings**, and click **Control Panel**.

2. Double-click **Add/Remove Programs**, and click **Add/Remove Windows Components** (you may need to click the **Components** button next).

3. Find and then double-click **Internet Information Services (IIS)** in the Windows Component Wizard dialog box. What services are checked by default? Note these in your lab journal or in a word-processed document.

4. Make sure the following services are checked: **Common Files, Documentation, File Transfer Protocol Server (FTP), FrontPage 2000 Server Extensions, Internet Information Services Snap-in, Internet Services Manager (HTML),** and **World Wide Web Server**. Click **OK**.

5. Make sure that the box for **Internet Information Services (IIS)** is checked and has a gray background (the gray background in the box means that not all possible IIS services will be installed, only the ones you have checked in Step 4). Click **Next**.

6. If requested, insert the Windows 2000 Server CD-ROM and click **OK**. Also, if requested, provide the path to the CD-ROM and the \I386 folder. Click **OK**.

7. Click **Finish**.

8. Close the Add/Remove Programs tool, if it is still open.

Project 13-2

In this project, you set up a virtual directory from which to publish documents for the IIS Web server that you set up in Hands-on Project 13-1. Before you start, create a folder called Web Documents with your initials at the end of the folder name, for example Web DocumentsMJP.

To create a virtual directory:

1. Click **Start**, point to **Programs**, point to **Administrative Tools**, and click **Internet Services Manager**.

2. In the tree, click the name of the server on which you installed IIS in Hands-on Project 13-1, for example **Lawyer**.

3. Right-click **Default Web Site** in the right pane, point to **New**, and click **Virtual Directory** (Figure 13-19).

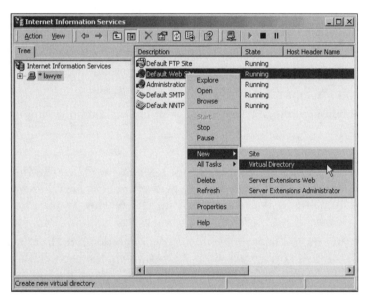

Figure 13-19   Creating a virtual directory

4. Click **Next** after the Virtual Directory Creation Wizard starts.

5. Enter an alias for the virtual directory, which users will employ to access it—for example, Webdocs plus your initials at the end, like this: **WebdocsMJP**. Click **Next**.

6. Enter the path to the actual folder you created before starting this assignment, for example **C:\Web DocumentsMJP**. Click **Next**.

7. What security options are available for you to set? What options would you need to set to enable users to copy HTML documents to the virtual directory? Similarly, how would you provide to users access only to read, browse, and view the source code for scripts? Record your observations in your lab journal or in a word-processed document.

8. Make sure that the options for **Read** and **Run Scripts** are checked; check these options if they are not selected. Also, check **Browse**. Click **Next** after you have configured the security options.

9 Click **Finish**.

10. How would you use the Internet Information Services tool to view the properties of the new virtual directory? Record your answer. Leave the Internet Information Services tool open for the next project.

Project 13-3

Assume that the Web site that you installed and configured in Hands-on Projects 13-1 and 13-2 is to be used for a VPN. You want to restrict access to users on the subnet 122.44.5 and to five users whose IP addresses are 122.44.10.22, 189.80.17.252, 189.80.19.40, 122.44.34.8, and 122.44.15.142.

To set up the IP restrictions:

1. Display the Web server, such as Lawyer, in the tree, and display its child objects to include Default Web Site.

2. Right-click **Default Web Site** and click **Properties**.

3. Click the **Directory Security** tab.

4. Click the **Edit** button in the IP address and domain name restrictions area of the tab.

5. Click **Denied Access** so that no IP addresses but those that you specify can access the Web site.

6. Click the **Add** button and click **Single computer**. How would you find an IP address, if you did not know it in advance? Record your observation. Enter the IP address **122.44.10.22** and click **OK** (refer to Figure 13-6). How would you enter the other four IP addresses? Enter each of the other addresses.

7. Back in the IP Address and Domain Name Restrictions dialog box, click the **Add** button and click **Group of computers**. Enter **122.44.5.0** for the network ID and **255.255.255.0** for the subnet mask, and then click **OK**. How would you enter additional subnets?

8. How would you restrict access to a domain? Record your answer.

9. Click **OK** to close the IP Address and Domain Name Restrictions dialog box, and click **OK** again.

Project 13-4

In this project, you learn how to install Windows Media Services and the Windows Media Services Administrator. An IIS Web server must already be installed before you begin.

To install Windows Media Services and the Administrator:

1. Click **Start**, point to **Settings**, and click **Control Panel**.

2. Double-click **Add/Remove Programs**, and click **Add/Remove Windows Components** (you may need to click the **Components** button next).

3. Find and then double-click **Windows Media Services** in the Windows Component Wizard dialog box.

4. Check the box for **Windows Media Services**. What happens to the **Windows Media Service Admin** box? Click **OK**.

5. Back in the Windows Components Wizard box, click **Next**.

6. If requested, insert the Windows 2000 Server CD-ROM and click **OK**. Also, if requested, provide the path to the CD-ROM and the \I386 folder. Click **OK**.

7. Click **Finish**.

8. Close the Add/Remove Programs tool, if it is still open.

9. Open the newly installed Windows Media Services Administrator by clicking **Start**, pointing to **Programs**, pointing to **Administrative Tools**, and clicking **Windows Media**. How would you determine if there is an equivalent MMC snap-in? Record whether there is a snap-in.

10. Notice the configuration options in the left pane, and note the options in your lab journal or in a word-processed document. What options are available to find out more about Windows Media Services?

11. Close the Windows Media Services Administrator.

Project 13-5

In this activity, you practice using the DNS management tool to create a record in the forward lookup zone. Also, you check for subfolders in the reverse lookup zone. Before you start, obtain from your instructor the name of a computer to add and its IP address. DNS should be previously installed on the computer that you use for practice.

To create a forward lookup zone record:

1. Click **Start**, point to **Programs**, point to **Administrative Tools**, and click **DNS**.

2. In the tree, double-click **DNS**, double-click the computer name of the DNS server, double-click **Forward Lookup Zone**, and double-click the domain, such as **thefirm.com**.

3. In your lab journal or in a word-processed document, note the entries that you see in the right-hand pane for hosts. What is the entry for the DNS server?

4. Display the domain in the tree, if it is not already displayed, by double-clicking **DNS**, the DNS computer name, and the domain name.

5. Right-click the domain, such as **thefirm.com**, and click **New Host**.

6. Enter the name of the host computer, such as **Caribou**, and its IP address, such as **129.70.10.50** in the New Host dialog box.

7. Check the box to **Create associated pointer (PTR) record** (refer to Figure 13-12).

8. Click **Add Host** and click **OK** to confirm the creation of the new record.

9. Click **Done**.

13

To explore the reverse lookup zone:

1. Double-click **Reverse Lookup Zone** to display its child objects.

2. What reverse lookup zones exist for the DNS server?

3. How would you create a new zone?

4. Double-click a zone to display the folders under it for subnets. How would you create a new folder?

5. Double-click one of the folders, such as **10**.

6. What entries exist in the folder? Record the entries in your lab journal or in a word-processed document.

7. Right-click a folder and click **New Pointer**. What information do you need to enter to create a PTR record? Click **Cancel**.

8. Close the DNS management tool.

Project 13-6

In this project, you practice configuring a scope in DHCP and authorizing the server. The DHCP network services Windows component should be installed before you begin. Also, obtain the address or computer name of a DNS server from your instructor (your instructor may further want to provide you with a range of addresses for the scope and an address to exclude from the scope, but if not, use the addresses suggested in the project).

To configure DHCP:

1. Log on as Administrator or as a member of Enterprise Administrators.

2. Click **Start**, point to **Programs**, point to **Administrative Tools**, and click **DHCP**.

3. Double-click **DHCP** in the tree, if the DHCP server name is not already displayed.

4. Right-click the DHCP server, such as **lawyer.thefirm.com [129.70.10.1]**, and click **New Scope**.

5. Click **Next** after the New Scope Wizard starts.

6. Enter a name for the scope to make it easy to identify as you maintain it—for example, **Manufacturing**—and enter a description for the scope, such as **Manufacturing building subnet**. Click **Next**.

7. Enter the start and end IP addresses, such as **129.70.19.51** and **129.70.19.99**. Further, enter the subnet mask, such as **255.255.255.0**, and then click the entry area in the Length box. What happens when you click the box? Click **Next**.

8. Enter the address **129.70.19.70** in the Start IP address box, and click **Add**. What happens after you click Add? Do you need to enter an ending address? Record your observations. Click **Next**.

9. What is the default lease time? For what types of situations would this default be appropriate? Record your answers. Change the default lease time to **4** days. Click **Next**.

10. Click **Yes, I want to configure these options now**, and click **Next**.

11. What information would you enter in the next dialog box, and why would you enter it? Click **Next**.

12. Enter the parent domain in which DNS name resolution will occur, such as **thefirm.com**. Enter the name of the DNS server obtained from your instructor, and click **Resolve**, or enter the DNS server's IP address. Click **Add**. How would you enter more than one DNS server? Click **Next**.

13. What information can you enter in the next dialog box, and why would you enter it? Click **Next**.

14. Click **Yes, I want to activate this scope now**, and then click **Next**.

15. Click **Cancel**, or if you have permission from your instructor to create the scope, click **Finish**.

To authorize a DHCP server:

1. Right-click the DHCP server, such as **lawyer.thefirm.com [129.70.10.1]**.

2. Click **Authorize**.

3. Does the status column change? If so, what does it say? Record your observations.

4. If the status column does not change, right-click the DHCP server, and click **Refresh**.

5. Right-click the server again, and click **Properties**.

6. Click the **DNS** tab. Is the server set up to update DNS lookup records? Will the default setup enable Windows 98 clients to update the DNS lookup records? Click **Cancel**.

7. Close the DHCP management tool.

Project 13-7

In this project, you set Terminal Services security in Windows 2000, and you create an installation disk for a Windows 98 client. Terminal Services should already be installed on the computer running Windows 2000 Server, and you will need to have two blank, formatted floppy disks.

To set the Terminal Services security:

1. Click **Start**, point to **Programs**, point to **Administrative Tools**, and click **Terminal Services Configuration**.

2. In the tree, double-click **Terminal Services Configuration**, if the Connections and Server Setting folders are not displayed.

3. Click **Connections**. What connections are displayed in the right-hand pane? Record your observations.

4. Double-click the connection, such as **RDP-Tcp**.

5. Click the **General** tab, if it is not displayed. What encryption level is set?

6. Click the arrow to list the options in the Encryption level box. What options do you see? Record your observations. Select **Medium**.

7. Check the box **Use standard Windows authentication**.

8. Click the **Permissions** tab.

9. Make sure the **Allow** boxes are checked for **Full Control**, **User Access**, and **Guest Account** for the **Administrators** group. How would you add a group and give it permissions?

10. Click **OK** and close the Terminal Services Configuration tool.

To create a client installation disk for Windows 98:

1. Click **Start**, point to **Programs**, point to **Administrative Tools**, and click **Terminal Services Client Creator**.

2. Click **Terminal Services for 32-bit x86 windows**. Make sure that the destination drive is A:, and click **OK**.

3. Insert the first floppy disk and click **OK**.

4. When you are prompted, remove the first disk, insert the second disk, and click **OK**.

5. Click **OK** after the files are copied to the second disk. What would you do next to install the software in Windows 98?

CASE PROJECTS

Aspen Consulting Project: Configuring Interoperability

Brighton Community College is designing and implementing a new network that primarily consists of Windows 2000 servers. They have purchased 10 server computers that will run Windows 2000 Server. The campus will have Internet access and will offer a Web server on the Internet. They also plan to set up DNS and DHCP servers for the network. Currently, they have a small network that has two older NetWare servers running NetWare version 4.1. The college has hired you to work with their IT Department to plan and implement the new network.

1. Develop a document explaining to the IT Department how to plan the implementation of the Web, DNS, and DHCP servers. In that document, address the following issues, as well as others that you think are important:

   ❑ In what order should the Web, DNS, and DHCP services be implemented for network use? Should all of these services be implemented on one server or on different servers?

   ❑ What setup elements should be planned in advance, such as DHCP scopes, DNS lookup zones, and Web services? What factors should go into their planning?

   ❑ What security issues should be addressed in the setup of these services?

2. The IT Department needs training in how to deploy a Web and FTP server. Create a general training document that explains the following:

   ❑ How to install a Web and FTP server

   ❑ How to set up a virtual directory

   ❑ How to configure the Web server

3. The IT Department has now set up a Web and FTP server, but no one is able to access it. Work through different troubleshooting steps that they can follow to identify the problem.

4. The IT Department has set up a DNS server, but it has no reverse lookup zone. This prompts several questions about DNS setup:

   ❑ What is the purpose of a reverse lookup zone, and how can it be set up?

   ❑ Can more than one DNS server be configured when the Active Directory is deployed, and if so, what is the advantage?

   ❑ Can DHCP be configured to automatically update DNS records, and if so, how?

5. The IT Department has installed DHCP and configured it, but for some reason it is not communicating on the network. What troubleshooting steps should it try in order to solve the problem?

6. The computer room in which the Windows 2000 servers are located is down the hall from the IT offices. How can the IT Department configure terminal services so that it can remotely administer the servers without going to the computer room? How can it set security to make sure that only the IT Department can access the servers?

7. Once all of the Windows 2000 servers are set up, the IT Department wants to set up access to directories on the NetWare servers so that NetWare access appears like any other shared Windows 2000 folder. How can it set up this type of access to the NetWare servers?

OPTIONAL CASE PROJECTS FOR TEAMS

13

Team Case One

Many of the Aspen consultants are not sure about all of the ways that Windows 2000 Server Terminal Services can be deployed to benefit an organization. Form a team and document four scenarios in which to use terminal services.

Team Case Two

Multimedia applications are growing in use via Web-based servers. Mark Arnez asks you to form a team to research three different kinds of multimedia Web applications and how to deploy them using Windows 2000 Server IIS.

14

SERVER MONITORING AND OPTIMIZATION

After reading this chapter and completing the exercises you will be able to:

- ◆ Establish monitoring benchmarks
- ◆ Monitor server services, logged-on users, and server functions
- ◆ Use Task Manager to monitor processes and performance data
- ◆ Use the System Monitor to monitor page file, memory, processor, disk, and other critical server performance functions and to tune these functions as needed
- ◆ Set up performance logs and alerts for monitoring
- ◆ Identify key system elements to monitor for problems

Monitoring a server can mean the difference between being caught off guard when a problem strikes, and anticipating and correcting an impending problem before the users notice. For example, a failing disk adapter may be diagnosed and replaced before it fails. In another situation, you may implement a popular new application that requires more server memory than anticipated, a potential problem that you can monitor and correct before users realize there is a problem. Server monitoring enables you to be proactive in maintaining fast server response, and it gives you the tools to quickly find and resolve problems after they strike.

In this chapter, you learn about the Windows 2000 Server services that keep everyday functions going and how to monitor those services. You also learn to use the Task Manager to monitor the server and help you optimize its performance. The System Monitor is the most powerful monitoring tool, which you learn to use in a multitude of ways for tracking system performance and determining how to optimize server functions. You also learn how to create logs for storing performance information and how to set up alerts to warn you of a problem as soon as it occurs.

MONITORING THE SERVER

Server monitoring accomplishes several purposes. One reason to monitor is to become familiar with your server's performance so you know how to interpret a problem. It may be difficult to diagnose a problem or determine if there is a resource shortage unless you first know what performance is typical for your server. Other reasons to monitor are to prevent problems before they occur and to diagnose existing problems to resolve them. Monitoring enables you to pinpoint problems and identify solutions, for example by tracking disk errors and replacing a hard disk before it fails. Table 14-1 shows some typical performance areas that play a significant role in a server's response and that can be monitored through the tools included with Windows 2000 Server.

Table 14-1   Server Activities to Monitor

Monitoring Area	Factors Causing the Problem
Server services	Hung or stopped service, or one using a high percentage of CPU resources
Logged-on users	Number of users logged on and types of resources they are accessing
Software	Server resources used by software packages
Paging	Page file sizing and performance
RAM	Memory shortage or damaged memory
CPU	CPU utilization and performance
Hard disk	Disk performance, capacity, and errors
Caching	Cache allocation and performance

Establishing Server Benchmarks

The most important way to get to know your server is to use monitoring tools to establish normal server performance characteristics. This is a process that involves establishing benchmarks. **Benchmarks**, or baselines, provide a basis for comparing data collected during problem situations with data showing normal performance conditions. This creates a way to diagnose problems and identify components that need to be upgraded. Benchmarks are acquired in the following ways:

- By generating statistics about CPU, disk, memory, and I/O with no users on the system, to establish a baseline for comparison to more active periods. Keep spreadsheets or databases and print performance charts of this information.

- By using performance monitoring to establish slow, average, and peak periods. Keep records on these periods.

- By gathering performance statistics each time a new software application is installed, on slow, average, and peak periods during its use.

- By establishing benchmarks to track growth in the use of servers, such as increases in users, increases in software, and increases in the average amount of time users are on the system.

The best way to get a feel for a server's performance is to gather benchmarks and then to frequently monitor server performance after you have the benchmark data. Performance indicators can be confusing at first, so the more time you spend observing them, the better you'll understand them. For example, viewing the CPU utilization on a server the first few times does not tell you much, but viewing it over a period of two or three months, noting slow and peak periods, helps you develop knowledge about how CPU demand varies for that server.

Using Windows 2000 Server Services

Windows 2000 Server automatically starts a range of system services that run in the background as the server is running and that should be monitored periodically. Many are default services that are automatically installed when you first install Windows 2000 Server. Other services can be installed or added when you install additional Windows components from the Windows 2000 Server CD-ROM (such as DNS services) or from independent software sources. Some are automatically started when the server boots, and others are started manually as needed. There are several default services that provide for messaging, logging, scheduling, server, and printer activities. If the server is having performance problems, you have the option to check the services and determine if one is stopped or possibly hung. You also have the option to stop an unused service to ease the server load. The default services that are automatically started are summarized in Table 14-2.

Table 14-2   Windows 2000 Server Default Services

Service	Description
Alerter	Sends notification of alerts or problems on the server to users designated by the network administrator
Computer Browser	Keeps a listing of computers and domain resources to be accessed (see the Note following this table)
EventLog	Enables server events to be logged for later review or diagnosis, in case problems occur
File Replication Service	Replicates the Active Directory elements on multiple domain controllers, when the Active Directory is installed
Intersite Messaging	Transfers messages between different Windows 2000 Server sites
IPSEC Policy Agent	Enables IPSec security and management
Kerberos Key Distribution Center	Enables Kerberos authentication and enables the server as a center from which to issue Kerberos security keys and tickets
Licensing Logging Service	Enables the monitoring of server licensing and other licensing
Logical Disk Manager	Monitors for disk problems, such as a disk that is nearly full
Messenger	Handles messages sent for administrative purposes
Net Logon	Maintains logon services such as verifying users who are logging on to the server or a domain
Plug and Play	Enables automatic detection and installation of new hardware devices or devices that have changed

14

Table 14-2   Windows 2000 Server Default Services (continued)

Service	Description
Print Spooler	Enables print spooling
Protected Storage	Enables data and services to be stored and protected by using private key authentication
Remote Procedure Call (RPC)	Provides remote procedure call services
Remote Procedure Call (RPC) Locator	Used in communications with clients using remote procedure calls to locate available programs to run
Remote Registry Service	Enables the Registry to be managed remotely
Removable Storage	Enables management of removable storage media, such as tapes, CD-RWs, and Zip and Jaz drives
RunAs Service	Used to run programs via an account that is different from the one currently logged on, such as running a program as Administrator from a computer logged on to another user's account (so that an Administrator does not have to log off a user).
Security Accounts Manager	Keeps information about user accounts and their related security setup
Server	A critical service that supports shared objects, logon services, print services, and remote procedure calls
System Event Notification	Enables the detection and reporting of important system events, such as a hardware or network problem
Task Scheduler	Used to start a program at a specified time and works with the software Task Scheduler
TCP/IP NetBIOS Helper Service	Activated when TCP/IP is installed and used to enable NetBIOS name resolution and NetBIOS network transport
Uninterruptible Power Supply	Used with a UPS to coordinate supplying power to the server during power failures
Windows Time	Enables updating the clock
Workstation	Enables network communications and access by clients over the network

Computers on a network can be viewed within Windows 2000 by means of the Computer Browser service. The service is used by tools such as My Computer, the MMC, and others to view computers. Any Windows 3.1, 3.11, 95, 98, NT, or 2000 computer configured for network access is a part of the Browser system. A Windows 2000 server is selected through the Computer Browser service to be the **master browser**, keeping the main list of logged-on computers, while the other browsers play a support role, such as that of **backup browsers**, which maintain a copy of the list in case the master browser is offline. There are also potential browsers that can be promoted to backup browsers, if more are needed, and nonbrowsers, which are computers that do not maintain a list. The Server and Workstation services depend upon the Computer Browser service.

TIP If a LAN Manager client is attached to the network, it will not receive a browse list from Windows 2000 Server or Windows NT Server, unless the server is configured to send the list. To configure Windows 2000 Server, open the Network and Dial-up Connections tool, right-click Local Area Connection, click Properties, double-click File and Printer Sharing for Microsoft Networks, and click Make browser broadcasts to LAN manager 2.x clients (see Chapter 7). (To configure Windows NT Server 4.0 for LAN Manager 2.x browser broadcasts, open the Control Panel, double-click the Network icon, and click the Services tab.)

Monitoring Server Services

As you have already learned in earlier chapters, Windows 2000 Server services can be viewed and managed from the Computer Management tool, which is opened from the Administrative Tools menu (click Start, point to Programs, point to Administrative Tools, and click Computer Management). Two other ways to manage services are from the Administrative Tools menu Services option or by using the MMC Services snap-in. For example, if you open Services from the Administrative Tools menu, a console window opens, as shown in Figure 14-1. Services are displayed in the right pane of the window, which contains five columns. The Name column shows services listed alphabetically. A short description of each service is provided in the Description column. The Status column indicates the condition of the service as follows:

- *Started* shows that the service is running.

- *Paused* means that the service is started, but is on hold to the users.

- A blank means that the service is halted or has not been started.

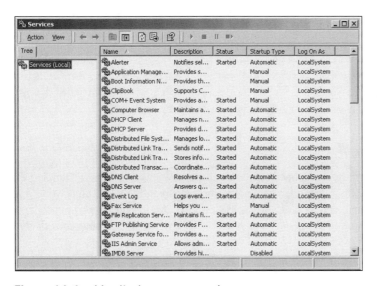

Figure 14-1   Monitoring server services

14

The Startup Type column shows how a service is started. Most services are started automatically when the server is booted. Some services are started manually because they may not be needed until a given time. In Figure 14-1, the ClipBook service is not currently running and is set to start manually when needed by the administrator. The ClipBook service is used to enable remote users to access ClipBook contents on the server. The Log On As column shows information about where the service is running, such as on the local computer system, which is usually the case, or from a specialized area, as with a program service that runs through the Administrator account.

> When you use the Services MMC snap-in, you can monitor services on another Windows 2000 or NT server, or even on a computer running Windows 2000 Professional or Windows NT Workstation. To access another computer's services, start MMC, click Console, click Add/Remove Snap-in, click Add, double-click Services, click Another computer, specify the computer's name or click Browse to find it, click Finish, click Close, and then click OK.

When you experience a problem on a server that is associated with a service, check the status of the service to make sure that it is started or set to start automatically. You can start, stop, pause, resume, or restart a service by right-clicking it and clicking any of these options. For example, occasionally a service does not start properly when the server is booted or hangs while the server is running, such as the Print Spooler service. The Services tool provides a way to monitor this situation. Even if the Print Spooler shows that it is started and you determine that you want to restart it, right-click the service and click Restart.

In another example, consider a message at the server that the Server service is suspended because of a problem, and you cannot log on to the server from the workstation in your office. When you log on to the server console as Administrator, the logon process takes four minutes, and when you click the Printers folder for a shared printer, the folder hangs for a minute and aborts with a message that the Server service is suspended. One way to address the problem is to open the Services tool to view the currently started services and to check the Server service to see if it is stopped or paused. If it is stopped or paused, you can start it by right-clicking the Server service and clicking Start.

> Use the stop option carefully, because some services are linked to others. Stopping one service will stop the others that depend on it. For instance, stopping the Workstation service affects the Alerter, Computer Browser, Distributed File System, Messenger, Net Logon, and Remote Procedure Call services. The system gives you a warning when other services are affected by stopping a particular service.

You can check dependencies by double-clicking a service and clicking the Dependencies tab (see Figure 14-2). (Try starting and stopping a service, as well as viewing its dependencies, in Hands-on Project 14-1.)

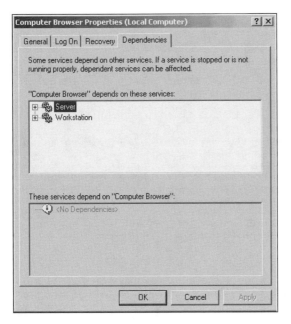

Figure 14-2   Service properties

Many services are linked to the Server and Workstation services, including logged-on users. If it is necessary to stop one of these services—for example, to diagnose a problem—give the users advance warning or stop it after work hours.

14

Pausing a service takes it offline to be used only by Administrators or Server Operators. For example, if the ClipBook service is sending error messages to users, you can pause the service so it is only available to the Administrator for testing until the problem is resolved. A paused service is restarted by right-clicking it and clicking Restart.

Another way to manage a service is to double-click it to view that service's properties (see Figure 14-2). For example, you can set a service to start automatically by double-clicking the service, accessing the General tab, and setting the Startup Type box to automatic. The function of each properties tab is presented in Table 14-3.

Table 14-3   Services Properties Tabs

Properties Tab	Description
General	Displays general information about the service, enables you to determine whether to start the service automatically, start it manually, or disable it; you can also start, stop, pause, and resume services
Log On	Enables you to specify the account that the service uses to log on, which is normally the local system account
Recovery	Enables you to specify how the computer will respond if the service fails, for example by automatically restarting the service
Dependencies	Displays the services that depend on a particular service and the services on which a particular service depends

Monitoring Logged-on Users and Resource Use

Network administrators frequently monitor the number of users who are accessing a server, for several reasons. One is to develop an indication of how many users are typically logged on at given points in time, which provides information about normal user load. Also, if a problem develops and the server needs to be shut down, the administrator can determine when the shutdown will have the least impact. Another reason is to be aware of security or misuse problems, such as an account that is in use when the owner is not at his or her workstation. On large networks, it is a good idea to frequently check the number of users on a server. An especially popular server may need to be upgraded as more users log on for extended periods.

To view logged-on users, start the Computer Management tool from the Administrative Tools menu, double-click objects in the tree as necessary to view Computer Management (Local), System Tools, Shared Folders, and Sessions. Click Sessions. The right-hand pane shows the users who are connected with active sessions, the operating system used at the client, the number of files each user has open, the connected time, the idle time, and whether the user is logged on as a guest. Depending on how it is connected, a single client may have two or more connections, such as a network connection for the computer and a connection for the user account. If you need to close a user's session—for example, if the session is hung and stays active after the user has logged off—right-click the user and click Close Session.

You can also view information about which shared folders are being accessed by users when you click Shares instead of Sessions in the console under Shared Folders (see Figure 14-3). The *# Client Redirections* column shows the number of clients using shares. Notice in Figure 14-3 that some shares, such as C$ and print$, are set up by default as hidden ($ after the share name hides the share on the network). The print$ share enables you to view the number of clients currently using the server as a print server. You can stop sharing by right-clicking any shared file and clicking Stop Sharing. Also, you can view which files are in use by clicking Open Files under Shared Folders. The right-hand pane shows the named pipes, number of open files, file locks, and permissions mode, such as Read+Write. The open file information shows if a file is in use. A **file lock** means that no one else can update a specified file, and **named pipes** are open communication links between two processes on the server or between the server and a client. This information is useful, for example, if one user has a file in use and another user cannot update the file because it is locked. You can check the lock information and inform the user who wants to update that the file is already in use by someone else. Or, if you need to close the connection that has the file locked, so that the second user can perform an update, right-click the connection you want to close and click Close Open File (try Hands-on Project 14-2).

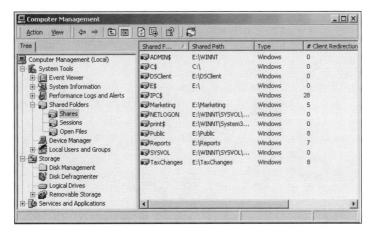

Figure 14-3   Shared resources

MONITORING APPLICATIONS WITH TASK MANAGER

Not all software applications are designed equally. Some have an extremely inefficient design that places unnecessary demand on the server. For example, an application may generate excessive network traffic by transporting more data than it needs between the server and the client. Another source of demand is reports that run against a database, requiring the system to read all of the records in the database instead of the limited few needed for each report. An inefficient program is often signaled by high CPU, memory, or disk utilization each time the program runs.

CAUTION

Some applications advertised to be client/server based are not truly designed according to these standards and can be inefficient when using server and network resources. For example, client/server design is intended to efficiently spread the workload between server and clients, but some applications place excessive work on the server or use poor database design at the server. Check on actual performance before you buy.

14

You can use Task Manager to view applications running on the server by pressing Ctrl+Alt+Del while logged on as Administrator or with Administrative privileges. After pressing this key combination, you will see the following options:

- *Lock Computer:* Secures the Windows 2000 Server console from access

- *Change Password:* Used to change the password of the account currently logged on

- *Log Off:* Logs off the account that is currently logged on

- *Task Manager:* Used to view information about tasks and services currently running

- *Shut Down:* Shuts down the server

- *Cancel:* Returns to the Windows 2000 desktop

 An alternate way to start Task Manager is to right-click an open space on the taskbar and click Task Manager.

Click the Task Manager button, which displays a dialog box with three tabs: Applications, Processes, and Performance. The Applications tab, shown in Figure 14-4, displays all of the software applications running from the server console, including 16-bit applications. Any of the applications can be stopped by highlighting it and clicking the End Task button. If an application is hung (no longer responding to user input), you can press End Task to release more resources for the server. The Switch To button brings the highlighted application to the front so you can work in it, and the New Task button enables you to start another application at the console, using the Run option, which is the same option that you would access from the Start button. The status bar at the bottom of the screen shows information about the total number of processes, the CPU usage, and minimum/maximum available memory. For example, in Figure 14-4, there are 46 total processes running, using 6% of the CPU and 159060K out of 310304K total memory. As used in the context of the Task Manager, a **process** is an executable program or one or more executable programs that run from a main program. For example, when you click Help from the Microsoft Excel menu bar, the Winhlp32.exe process runs along with Excel.exe.

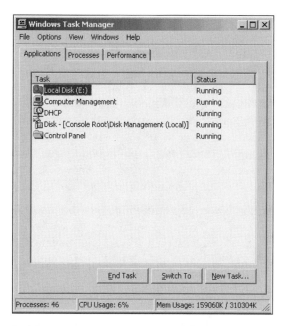

Figure 14-4   Monitoring started tasks

 TIP As you will learn as you monitor a server, even if CPU utilization goes to 100% this is not a cause for immediate concern, because it may mean that a process is simply using the CPU very efficiently. However, if utilization frequently stays at 100% for several minutes instead of several seconds, this is cause for concern and may indicate a software or hardware problem.

If you right-click a task or highlight a task and right-click the heading in the Task column or Status column, several options appear in a shortcut menu, as follows:

- *Switch To:* Takes you into the highlighted program

- *Bring to Front:* Maximizes and brings the highlighted program to the front, but leaves you in the Task Manager

- *Minimize:* Causes the program to be minimized

- *Maximize:* Causes the program to be maximized, but leaves you in the Task Manager

- *End Task:* Stops the highlighted program

- *Go To Process:* Takes you to the Processes tab and highlights the process associated with the program

The Processes tab lists the processes in use by all running applications. If you need to stop a process, you can stop it from this screen by highlighting it and clicking End Process. Also, the Processes tab shows information about each started process, as summarized in Table 14-4.

14

.The Processes tab lists the processes in use by all running applications. When a process is started or while it is running, it may start other processes, all of which compose the **process tree**. The additional processes in the process tree are displayed on the Processes tab so that they are indented under a main process. For example, when you start a 16-bit process, such as one called Image.exe in Windows 2000 Server, that causes two other processes to start, the virtual DOS machine (Ntvdm.exe, see Chapter 1) and Windows on Windows (Wowexec.exe). Because Image.exe is a 16-bit process, it must directly start Ntvdm.exe, which is a 32-bit process started by Windows 2000 Server in order to run a 16-bit process within it. Also, Image.exe indirectly starts Wowexec.exe ,which simulates a 16-bit window in Windows 2000. All three processes compose the process tree, and the Processes tab shows Ntvdm.exe as the main process, with image.exe and Wowexec.exe running under it.

If you need to stop a process, you can stop it from the Processes tab by highlighting the process and clicking End Process. To stop all direct and indirect processes in a process tree, right-click the main process (the one above the indented processes in the tab) and click End Process Tree. Also, the Processes tab shows information about each started process, as summarized in Table 14-4.

Table 14-4 Task Manager Information on Processes

Process Information	Description
Image Name	The process name, such as winword.exe for Microsoft Word
PID	The process identifier (PID), which is an identification number assigned to the process so the operating system can track information on it
CPU	The percentage of the CPU resources used by the process
CPU Time	The amount of CPU time used by that process from the time the process started
Mem Usage	The amount of memory the process is using

 TIP Table 14-4 lists only the default information that is displayed on the Processes tab. You can change the display to view other information, such as page faults, base priority class, and threads (all described later in this chapter) by clicking the View Menu and then clicking Select Columns.

For example, if you suspect that a program is causing a bottleneck at the CPU, go to the Applications tab, right-click the program, and click Go To Process, which identifies the program's process on the Processes tab. Next, look in the CPU and CPU Time columns to see how much of the CPU that program's process is using. Also, check the figure in the Mem Usage column to see if the program is causing a memory bottleneck. If the program is using too many resources, such as 90% of the CPU, consider stopping it and discontinuing its use until you know the source of the problem.

Also, you can increase the priority of a process (or processes) in the list so that it has more CPU priority than what is set as its default. Suppose, for example, that you want to increase the priority for Windows Explorer, which is process Explorer.exe. To start, right-click

Explorer.exe, displaying a shortcut menu in which you can end the process, end the process tree (end that process and all subprocesses associated with it), or reset the priority. Click Set Priority to reset the priority (see Figure 14-5).

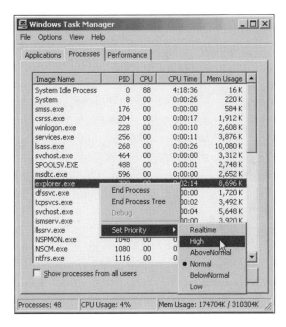

Figure 14-5   Resetting a process priority

Normally, the priority at which a process runs is set in the program code of the application, which is called the **base priority class**. If the base priority class is not set by the program, a normal (average) priority is set by the Windows 2000 Server operating system. The server administrator always has the option to set a different base priority. As shown in Figure 14-5, the administrator can change the priority to any of six options: Low, BelowNormal, Normal, AboveNormal, High, or Realtime. You might think of these processes as being on a continuum, with Normal as the midpoint, which is 0. Low is -2, BelowNormal is -1, AboveNormal is +1, or High is +2. Realtime is given an extra advantage at +15. For example, a Low priority means that if a process is waiting in a queue—for example, for processor time, disk access, or memory access—all processes with a higher priority will go first. The same is true for BelowNormal, except that processes with this priority will run before those set at Low, and so on. (Try Hands-on Project 14-3 to practice resetting a priority and stopping a task.)

Use the Realtime priority with great caution. If assigned to a process, that process may completely take over the server, preventing work by any other processes. For instance, you might want to assign a Realtime priority when you detect a disk drive that is about to fail and you want to give all resources over to the backup process so you can back up files before the disk fails.

14

The Performance tab shows vital CPU and memory performance information through bar charts, line graphs, and performance statistics (see Figure 14-6). The CPU Usage and MEM Usage bars show the current use of CPU and memory. To the right of each bar is a graph showing the immediate history statistics. The bottom of the Performance tab shows more detailed statistics, such as those for handles and threads, which are described in Table 14-5. A **handle** is a resource, such as a file, used by a program and having its own identification so the program is able to access it. **Threads** are blocks of code within a program.

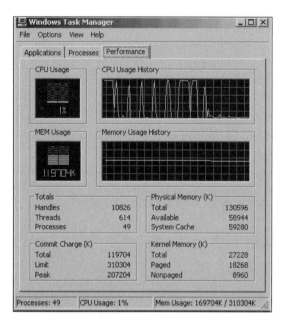

Figure 14-6 Performance data

Notice that in Figure 14-6 the Physical Memory Total is 130596K, but the Commit Charge Total is only 119704K, which is the setting for the initial page size. Also, notice that the Commit Charge Peak for this monitoring session is 207204K, which shows that the initial page size has already been exceeded. As discussed in Chapter 7, the initial page file size should be equal to 1.5 times the amount of installed RAM. Thus, the performance statistics show that the page file size may be set too low at under 195894K (130596 * 1.5) and that the server administrator may need to tune the virtual memory for this server. The page file is tuned by opening the Control Panel System icon, then clicking the Advanced tab, clicking the Performance Options button, and clicking the Change button.

Table 14-5   Task Manager Performance Statistics

Statistic	Description
Handles	The number of objects in use by all processes, such as open files
Threads	The number of code blocks in use, in which one program or process may be running one or more code blocks at a time
Processes	The number of processes that are active or sitting idle
Physical Memory Total	The amount of RAM installed in the computer
Physical Memory Available	The amount of RAM available to be used
System Memory File Cache	The amount of RAM used for file caching
Commit Charge Total	The size of virtual memory currently in use
Commit Charge Limit	The maximum virtual (disk) memory that can be allocated
Commit Charge Peak	The maximum virtual memory that has been used during the current Task Manager monitoring session
Kernel Memory Total	The amount of memory used by the operating system
Kernel Memory Paged	The amount of virtual memory used by the operating system
Kernel Memory Nonpaged	The amount of RAM memory used by the operating system

USING SYSTEM MONITOR

The most vital tool used to help detect and fix any problems on a Windows 2000 server is **System Monitor**. System Monitor is like a window into the inner workings of just about every aspect of the server, such as hard disks, memory, the processor, disk caching, a started process, and the page file. For example, you might monitor memory and page to determine if you have fully tuned the page file for satisfactory performance and to determine if you have adequate RAM for the server load.

System Monitor is opened from the Administrative Tools menu by clicking Performance to view the console screen, which offers two main choices. System Monitor is the top selection in the tree, and Performance Logs and Alerts (discussed later in this chapter) is the other option. Make sure that System Monitor is selected in the tree to view the screen as shown in Figure 14-7. The screen is in the chart mode, showing a grid that you use for graphing activities on the server. To begin tracking, you must select one or more objects to monitor. A System Monitor object may be memory, the processor, or another part of the computer. Table 14-6 lists the main computer system objects that can be monitored (in the next chapter, network objects are presented). Other objects are added as you add server services. For example, when you install IIS, more objects are added to monitor Internet Information Services, the HTTP Service, and FTP Server activity.

14

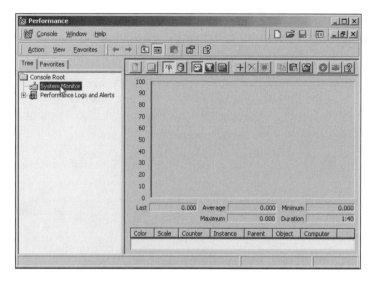

Figure 14-7   System Monitor

Table 14-6   System Monitor Objects

Object	Description
Active Server Pages	Monitors client requests, transactions, and sessions at the server
Browser	Tracks the activity of the browser service that enables My Network Places to communicate and exchange information with other computers on the network, for example tracking duplicate master browsers
Cache	Supplies performance information on data caching
Distributed Transaction Coordinator	Monitors distributed transactions processed through the server
Job Object	Monitors CPU, kernel mode, and user mode activity for a job object (a group of processes that are handled as one entity)
Job Object Details	Monitors detailed information about a job object, such as I/O activity, paging activity, and working set activity
Memory	Provides information about RAM use, such as percent of memory in use, amount of memory available to processes, caching, and paging
Objects	Tracks the activities of special objects, such as started processes and started threads
Paging File	Supplies data on page file performance, such as current usage and peak usage
Process	Supplies performance data on a specific process that is running
Processor	Tracks demands on the processor such as the percent in use, the number of requests from hardware components, percent in use by users, and the percent in use by the operating system

Table 14-6   System Monitor Objects (continued)

Object	Description
Redirector	Monitors network connection information, such as folder access requests from other computers on the network and information about workstations presently connected
Server	Tracks information about the Server service, such as number of bytes sent out and received, logon errors, and logged-off sessions
Server Work Queues	Provides information about active threads, bytes received from clients and sent to clients, length of the CPU's work queue, and rate at which the server is reading and writing data
System	Monitors file access, system calls, operating system activities, processes handled by the server, and processor queue length
Telephony	Monitors activity to telecommunications lines connected to the server
Thread	Tracks a specific thread running within a process, such as the processor time used by the thread

For each object, there are one or more counters that can be monitored. A **counter** is an indicator of a quantity of the object that can be measured in some unit, such as percent, rate per second, or peak value, depending on what is appropriate to the object. For example, the % Processor Time counter for the Processor object measures the percentage of processor time that is in use by non-idle processes. Pages/sec is an example of a counter for the Memory object that measures the number of pages written to or read from virtual memory per second. The processor is one of the common objects to monitor when a workstation or server is slow. Table 14-7 gives examples of some of the most frequently used counters for the Processor object (try Hands-on Project 14-4 to view objects and counters).

Table 14-7   Sample Processor Counters in System Monitor

Counter	Description
% DPC Time	Processor time used for deferred procedure calls, for example for hardware devices
% Interrupt Time	Time spent on hardware interrupts by the CPU
% Privileged Time	Time spent by the CPU for system activities in privileged mode, which is used for the operating system
% Processor Time	Time the CPU is busy on all non-idle activities
% User Time	Time spent by the CPU in user mode running software applications and system programs
Interrupts/sec	Number of device interrupts per second

Sometimes there are instances associated with a counter. An **instance** exists when there are different elements to monitor, such as individual processes when you use the Process object, or when a process contains multiple threads or runs subprocesses under it for the Thread object. Other examples are when there are two or more disks or multiple processors to monitor. In many cases, each instance is identified by a unique number for ease of monitoring.

System Monitor Options

System Monitor offers several buttons from which to operate it and to set up the display options. After the tool is opened, click the Add button (represented by a plus sign) on the button bar just above the tracking window (refer to Figure 14-7), to access the dialog box from which to select objects to monitor, counters, and instances (described in more detail in the following sections). You can monitor one or more objects at a time as a way to get a better understanding of how particular objects interact, for example by monitoring both memory and the processor. Also, you can monitor the same object using different combinations of counters. You stop monitoring by clicking the Delete button (represented by an X) on the button bar.

When you monitor objects, you can use one of three modes: chart, histogram, or report. A chart is a running line graph of the object that shows distinct peaks and valleys. For example, when you use the chart mode and monitor for different objects, each object is represented by a line with a unique color, such as red or green. A histogram is a running bar chart that shows each object as a bar in a different color. The report mode simply provides numbers on a screen, which you can capture to put in a report. Each of these options is set from a button on the button bar just above the tracking window, and the buttons are titled: View Chart, View Histogram, and View Report. You can change the view mode at any time by clicking the appropriate button. Figure 14-8 illustrates the use of the chart mode to monitor several counters.

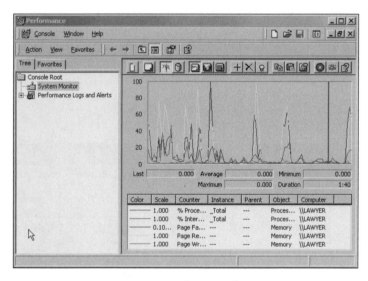

Figure 14-8   System Monitor chart mode

The System Monitor can also be set up to run from inside Microsoft Word so that you can create visual reports and print them using Word (or send them through e-mail). To run System Monitor in Word (see Figure 14-9):

1. Start Microsoft Word (Word 97 or higher).

2. Click the View menu, highlight Toolbars, and click Control Toolbox.

3. Click More Controls (the icon with the hammer and ruler).

4. Scroll to find System Monitor Control, and click that option.

5. Adjust the size of the figure display and move it to the desired location in the document.

6. Click the Exit button.

7. Use the options in System Monitor as you would normally, for example to select counters, objects, and instances and to select the monitor mode, such as charting (see the next section).

8. Use the Word commands in a normal fashion to format the document, save it, and print it.

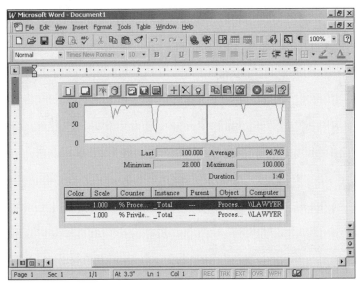

Figure 14-9   Running System Monitor inside Microsoft Word

14

Monitoring Page File and Memory Performance

To monitor the server's page file performance (recall that a page file is disk space reserved for use when memory requirements exceed the available RAM), click the Add button (plus sign) to bring up the Add Counters dialog box, in which you can select the computer and the objects to monitor. At the top of the box, select the computer to monitor by clicking either *Use local computer counters* for the local computer or *Select counters from computer* and then selecting the computer to monitor, which can be the local computer or another computer on the network. You can also specify the UNC for a computer, such as \\Lawyer (the \\ indicates a workstation or server). The server from which you start System Monitor is already inserted as the default computer. This is a powerful option for a server administrator, because it means you can monitor other network servers or workstations from one place. Many network administrators monitor a server from System Monitor in their Windows 2000 Professional workstation.

After selecting the computer to monitor, go to the Performance object list box and click the list arrow to select an object to monitor—such as Memory, in this example, to monitor paging. Make sure *Select counters from list* is selected, and for the counter, select Pages Input/sec (see Figure 14-10). This counter measures the number of virtual memory pages read back into memory per second. If you have a question about an object and counter combination, click the Explain button to view a description in a separate dialog box. After selecting the counter, click the Add button to start monitoring. While still in the Add Counters dialog box, select the options to monitor the object Memory and the counter Pages Output/sec, which shows the number of pages written to the page file each second. Also, select to monitor the % Usage and % Usage Peak counters for the Paging File object, to show the amount in use and the peak usage. The Paging File object also has instances that allow you to monitor a page file on a specific disk, if you use more than one page file or monitor all page files at once. Click Total as the instance, so that you monitor all page files at once. When you finish, click Close to view the four objects charted at the same time.

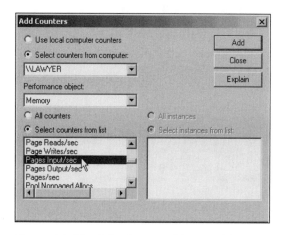

Figure 14-10   Selecting an object and its counter

Gather data for a short time before checking on the progress of System Monitor. Each object and counter combination is charted using a different color, so that one can be separated from the other. For instance, % Usage might be red, % Usage Peak might be green, while Pages Input/sec is blue, and Pages Output/sec is yellow (see Figure 14-11, which is not shown in color). The counters are shown at the bottom of the screen with a key to indicate the graphing color for each one. When you click one of these counters, the status bar just above the counters shows the following for that counter:

- *Last*—the current value of the monitored activity
- *Average*—the average value of the monitored activity for the elapsed time
- *Maximum*—the maximum value of the activity over the elapsed time
- *Minimum*—the minimum value of the activity over the elapsed time
- *Duration*—the amount of time to complete a full graph of the activity

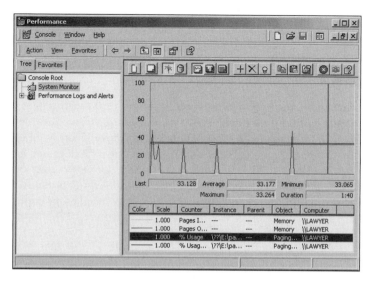

Figure 14-11   Monitoring page file performance

In Figure 14-11, the charting shows that paging looks good. The % Usage and the % Usage Peak are not over 40% at any point in time. But, some of the peaks for the Pages Input/sec are a concern. To follow up in this situation you might close the two paging-related counters, Pages Input/sec and Pages Output/sec by clicking each, one at a time, in the bottom of the screen, then clicking the Delete button.

In this example, you would further monitor the two counters for the Paging File object, % Usage and % Usage Peak, at a later time. You can save these settings and start and stop monitoring at different times. To save the settings, right-click the Copy Properties button, click Save As, and enter a file in which to store them. The next time you start System Monitor, open the file that you saved, copy its contents, and click the Paste Counter List button in System Monitor.

Assume that you have periodically monitored the Paging File counters % Usage and % Usage Peak over a period of a few days and find that the % Usage is almost always over 90% and that the % Usage Peak goes up to 100%. In addition, you monitor the Memory counter, Page Faults/sec, and continue checking the results. A **hard page fault** occurs when a program does not have enough physical memory to execute a given function. If there are frequently over five hard page faults per second, this is another strong indication of a memory bottleneck. In this situation, the combination of statistics indicates the need to add memory to the server.

Another situation resulting in a page fault occurs when two processes share the same 4 MB block of paged data. One process may read the block from disk into memory, just before the other process is about to do the same. The second process is unable to access the paged block, because it is in use. A page fault is also caused when there is not enough RAM to be shared by virtual memory and caching. All of these page fault problems are monitored by using Memory as the object and Page Faults/sec as the counter. One way to reduce page faults and improve performance is to increase RAM. This is especially important if database systems

14

such as Microsoft SQL Server or Oracle are installed, which are designed to share memory blocks when there is limited RAM.

CAUTION

A page fault in a kernel (operating system) process may occur if a reference to a page location is lost or corrupted. If this happens, the Windows 2000 system may crash with a Stop message. The error may be caused by a small power fluctuation, a damaged memory module, or a corrupted operating system file. Try rebooting to determine if the error recurs. If it does not, it was most likely caused by a transient situation, such as a power fluctuation. If it persists, test the computer's memory and replace damaged memory modules, or contact a Microsoft technician for information on how to read a crash dump to determine what process is linked to the crash.

Table 14-8 provides a summary of tips for monitoring and tuning memory and paging.

Table 14-8   Using System Monitor Objects and Counters to Monitor Memory and Paging

Object: Counter	Explanation
Memory: Available Bytes	Measures the bytes of memory available for use on the system. Microsoft recommends that this value be 4096 KB or higher. If values stay at or below this, your system will benefit from additional RAM. This figure is also available on the Task Manager Performance tab.
Memory: Cache Faults/sec	Measures the number of times the page file is called from disk or relocated in memory. Higher values indicate potential performance problems. (Higher values will be about double baseline values or more, on a lightly loaded system.) Remedy this by adding more memory; in this case, L2 cache (see Chapter 2) is better than adding main RAM.
Memory: Page Faults/sec	Returns a count of the average number of page faults per second for the current processor. Page faults occur whenever memory pages must be called from disk, which explains how memory overload can manifest as excessive disk activity. If the value is frequently over 5, or more than double that in a light-load baseline, consider adding more RAM.
Memory: Pages Input/sec Memory: Pages Output/sec	These counters measure the number of virtual memory pages read into (Input/sec) and out of (Output/sec) memory per second. If their total is frequently over 20, this shows a need to add RAM. By using both counters you can assess demands on memory and paging at once. Pages Input/sec translates into page faults. Pages Output/sec shows demand on memory, and when this value is frequently over 15–20, this indicates a need to add RAM.

Table 14-8   Using System Monitor Objects and Counters to Monitor Memory
and Paging (continued)

Object: Counter	Explanation
Memory: Pages/sec	Tracks the number of pages written to or read from disk by the Virtual Memory Manager plus paging traffic for the system cache. If this value is more than double the light-load baseline, or if it is typically over 20, it indicates a need for additional RAM.
Paging File: % Usage Paging File: % Usage Peak	Both show how much of the page file is currently occupied. Neither object/counter should frequently exceed 99% but look at this information in relation to Memory:Pages Input/sec, Memory:Pages Output/sec, and Memory:Available Bytes. If the values are frequently over 99%, increase the page file size.
Server: Pool Paged Peak	Shows the most that the server has used in terms of virtual memory. This should be at least 1.5 times the size of RAM in the server.

Interaction Between Software and Memory Use

Software applications sometimes use the server's RAM very inefficiently, causing performance problems. Inefficient use of memory occurs for at least two reasons: poor program design and failure to return memory to the server after a process is complete.

Consider a program that needs to obtain four different data values from a database table. An inefficient program loads the database table, extracts the first value, and works on that value, going through the same process four times and therefore loading the entire table four times. A significant amount of memory is used each time the table is loaded. A more efficient way to design the program and use memory is to create in advance a view of the table that will include only the type of data that program accesses, such as the four data values. When the program needs the data, it loads only the view, which is a technique that uses much less memory than loading the entire table. The four data values are then extracted from the view at the same time, instead of in four different cycles. This design enables the program to access and work on the data faster, using much less memory and less processor time than the inefficient way of writing the program.

Another way in which programs use memory inefficiently is by **leaking memory**, which means that the application fails to release memory when it is no longer needed. This is a very common problem that has a cumulative impact, because the program may go through several cycles in which it repeatedly accesses blocks of memory that are not released. The result is that the page file continually grows, resulting in slower and slower server performance.

Adding RAM or increasing the page file size to combat the inefficiency of a program is not likely to address the server's performance problem. A better solution is to identify the program and redesign it or purchase one that is more efficient. System Monitor is an effective tool for identifying an inefficient program. In System Monitor, track the Process object and the counters, Page File Bytes and Page Faults/sec, for each process that you suspect is causing a problem. All of the currently running processes are listed in the instances list in System Monitor's Add Counters dialog box (see Figure 14-12). As you select processes to monitor,

14

also add Total as an instance to monitor the combined page faults for all processes. A high rate of page faults for one process is a strong indicator that there is a problem with that process.

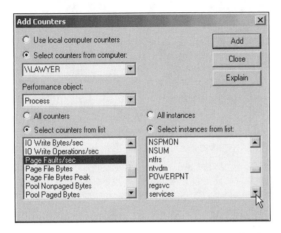

Figure 14-12   Using System Monitor to find an inefficient program process

Table 14-9 provides general tips for monitoring the relationship between software and memory.

Table 14-9   Using System Monitor Objects and Counters to Monitor Software Use of Memory

Object: Counter	Explanation
Process: Page Faults/sec	Measures the number of page faults for all threads in a process. Compare the number of page faults to the total amount of bytes for that process stored in the page file (Process:Page File Bytes). If the number of page faults is high and the number of bytes continues to grow, suspect a problem with leaking memory.
Process: Page File Bytes	Measures the number of bytes stored by a process in the page file. If this number continues to grow excessively as the program is running, suspect a problem with leaking memory.

Monitoring the Processor and Locating Processor Bottlenecks

Besides monitoring the processor in Task Manager, you can also use System Monitor, for example for diagnosing processor overload. There are three important components to studying the processor load:

- The percent of time the processor is in use
- The length of the queue containing processes waiting to run
- The frequency of interrupt requests from hardware

System Monitor has processor counters to measure each type of processor load. Start monitoring the processor load by selecting Processor as the object and % Processor Time as the counter. This counter measures how much the processor is in use at the present time. It is normal for the processor use to fluctuate between 50% to 100%. If the processor constantly remains at a high percentage, such as between 90% to 100%, this is an indicator that there is a problem.

When processor use is high, it is time to collect additional data by monitoring the number of processes waiting in line for their turn on the processor. Use the Processor Queue Length counter for the System object to determine if there is a queue of waiting processes. If the processor is often at 100%, but there are no processes waiting in the queue, the processor is handling the load. If four or five processes are always in line, this suggests that it is time to consider a faster processor.

 TIP You can monitor the same information about processor queue length by monitoring the Server Work Queues object and the Queue Length counter.

Before deciding that you need to purchase a new processor, make sure the processor load is not due to a malfunctioning hardware component, such as a NIC or disk adapter. When you monitor the processor load, add two additional counters, % Interrupt Time and Interrupts/sec, for the Processor object. A high frequency of interrupts per second, such as over 1000, is an indication that there is a problem with a hardware component. Also, frequently high % Interrupt Time, such as over 80%, is another indication of a hardware problem. These counters do not locate the component, but they do show that the overload problem is unlikely to be solved by a new processor. If you encounter a high level of hardware interrupts, check the system log (refer to Chapter 16) for information about hardware problems. Practice monitoring the processor in Hands-on Project 14-5.

14

 TIP Collect benchmarks on the level of hardware interrupts, so as to have comparative data for diagnosing problems later.

You can fine-tune your analysis of possible processor bottlenecks that are not related to a hardware problem by monitoring several additional objects and counters. For example, check for one or more processes that may be causing the load by monitoring two object:counter combinations: the Processor: % Processor Time and the Process: % Processor Time. You can select by name different processes to monitor as an instance. Also, in case the processor load is due to priorities set for certain processes, monitor the Process object using the Priority Base counter for each process (selected as the instance) that may be set too high. This method enables you to determine the exact priority of any process. If the bottleneck is due to a priority that is set too high, the solution to the bottleneck may be as simple as lowering the priority.

You can also use Task Manager to view all base priority class settings by accessing the Processes tab, clicking the View menu, clicking Select Columns, and clicking Base Priority.

When you determine that a bottleneck is focused on one process and that its priority is not set too high, monitor the threads used by that process by using the Thread object and % Processor Time as the counter. Each thread is displayed as an instance that you can select. For example, if the process FastBK looks like the culprit and has eight threads, monitor each thread from FastBK/1 to FastBK/8.

Sometimes the processor bottleneck is due to multiple processes running on the server. In this situation, determine how many threads within each process that are placing a load on the processor. For example, if the processes use an average of two or three threads, then the processing load is likely to be alleviated by upgrading to a faster processor. However, if the combined processes are using a high number of threads on average, such as 6 to 8 threads, then implementing a faster processor may not provide enough performance enhancement to solve the bottleneck. In this situation, it is necessary to upgrade to a multiple processor (SMP) computer, on which the processing load is equalized across processors. Table 14–10 gives tips on monitoring and tuning processor use.

Table 14-10   Using Objects and Counters to Monitor a Processor

Object: Counter	Explanation
Process: Priority Base	Measures the priority base of a selected process. This enables you to determine if one process is causing a processor bottleneck because its priority is set too high.
Processor: % Interrupt Time	Measures the amount of the processor's time that is used to service hardware requests from devices such as the NIC, disk and CD-ROM drives, and serial and parallel peripherals. A high rate of interrupts when compared to your baseline statistics indicates a possible hardware problem, such as a malfunctioning disk controller or NIC.
Processor: % Processor Time	Measures the percentage of time since System Monitor started that the CPU is busy handling nonidle threads. Sustained values of 80–85% or higher indicate a heavily loaded machine; consistent readings of 95% or higher may indicate a machine that needs to have its load reduced, or its capabilities increased (with a new machine, a motherboard upgrade, or a faster CPU).
Processor: Interrupts/sec	Measures the average number of times per second that the CPU is interrupted by devices requesting immediate processing. Network traffic and system clock activity establish a kind of background count with which this number should be compared. Problem levels occur when a malfunctioning device begins to generate spurious interrupts, or when excessive network traffic overwhelms a network adapter. In both cases, this will usually create a count that's five times, or greater, that of a lightly loaded baseline situation.

Table 14-10   Using Objects and Counters to Monitor a Processor (continued)

Object: Counter	Explanation
Server Work Queues: Queue Length	Indicates the number of items in a single processor's work queue. Frequent situations in which the queue length is over 4 indicate that the processor is experiencing a bottleneck.
System: Processor Queue Length	Measures the number of execution threads waiting for access to a CPU. If this value is frequently over 4 on a single CPU, it indicates a need to distribute this machine's load across other machines, or the need to increase its capabilities, usually by adding an additional CPU (where possible) or by upgrading the machine or the motherboard. When the value is over 2 per each CPU on multiple-processor systems, you should consider adding processors or increasing the processor speed.
Thread: % Processor Time	Measures the load on the processor due to threads running in processes. If 2 to 3 threads, on average, are running per each process, consider upgrading to a faster processor. If 6 to 8 threads are running, on average, per each process, consider upgrading the number of processors by using an SMP computer.

Monitoring Disk Performance and Disk Tuning

Before using System Monitor to study hard disk performance, it is necessary to install the Disk Performance Statistics Driver, which includes counters for disk monitoring. The driver is installed by running the program Diskperf, which is located in the \Winnt\System32 folder. Figure 14-13 shows the installation screen for the driver, which can be installed from the Command Prompt window or from the Start button, Run option. After the driver is installed, or after you change the driver configuration, the server needs to be rebooted. The parameters for Diskperf are as follows (try Hands-on Project 14-6):

- *Diskperf:* Indicates if the driver is installed and if the counters are started
- *Diskperf −y:* Installs the driver and the complete set of disk performance counters
- *Diskperf −yd:* Installs the driver and counters to work for physical drives
- *Diskperf −yv:* Installs the driver and counters to work for logical drives
- *Diskperf −n:* Deactivates the counters
- *Diskperf −nd:* Deactivates the counters only for physical drives
- *Diskperf −nv:* Deactivates the counters only for logical drives
- *Diskperf \\server:* Sets up the counters on the specified computer
- *Diskperf /?:* Displays the Diskperf parameter settings

14

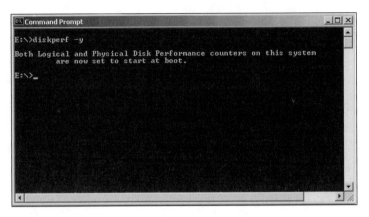

Figure 14-13   Running Diskperf

After the Diskperf counters are loaded and you reboot the system, two new objects and their associated counters are available in System Monitor: LogicalDisk and PhysicalDisk. Use LogicalDisk to observe activity on a set of disks, such as a striped volume. Use PhysicalDisk if you want to monitor a specific disk, such as disk 0 in a set of five disks. Watch at least two counters, % Disk Time and Current Disk Queue Length. The first counter shows the amount of activity on a disk, and the second shows the number of waiting requests to access the disk. If one disk frequently is busy at the 100% level, information on the number of waiting requests helps to diagnose the problem. If there are 0 to 1 requests normally in the queue, the disk load is acceptable. If the queue generally has 2 or more requests, it is time to move some files from the overloaded disk to one less busy.

The best way to determine which files to move is to understand what applications and data are on the server and how they are used. If all of the server disks are constantly busy, it may be necessary to purchase disks with more spindles or to add additional data paths. (A spindle is a rod attached to the center of a hard disk platter and to a motor used to rotate the rod and disk.)

TIP   Individual drives typically have one spindle, and RAID drives have multiple spindles within the disk array. A RAID array is a good investment for growing servers because of the combined performance and redundancy features.

Another source of disk activity is the page file. Monitor the Memory counter Pages/sec and the PhysicalDisk counter % Disk Time simultaneously. This shows the paging activity in relationship to the activity on the disk. Sometimes the disk data transfer rate, which is measured by the PhysicalDisk counter Disk Bytes/sec, also is a problem. Use all three counters to track page file activity and how fast the page file is written to disk. This gives you a good idea of the page file activity and the disk speed at the same time, particularly since the page file is a very large file. Also, experiment with the disk transfer rate by copying a large file from floppy drive A to the hard disk you are monitoring. Another option is to monitor the transfer rate when a large number of records are written to a database on the disk. If page file activity is a problem, consider increasing RAM or implementing a page file on more than one disk. If paging activity is low, but the transfer rate is slow for large files, such as the page file or a database file, consider upgrading to faster disks.

A visible indication that a disk may be a bottleneck is that its LED is lighting constantly and you can hear the disk busily reading and writing data. There are three general reasons why a disk is busy. One reason is simply that it is experiencing heavy sustained use. Heavy use is not an automatic indication that there is a problem, if the disk is handling the load. If the Current Disk Queue Length and Avg. Disk Queue Length generally stay in the 1 to 2 range, the disk is handling the load, even though you may see its lights on frequently. If the queue length is often in the 3 and over range, then you need to explore more about the problem, which leads to the other reasons why a disk is busy.

Another reason why a disk may appear as a bottleneck is that there is really a memory shortage causing disk activity because of heavy use by the page file. Use the techniques you have learned to monitor memory, paging, and file system cache to determine if there is a memory shortage. Also, monitor the following to check the link between paging and disk activity:

- The Memory object and Pages/sec counter

- The LogicalDisk object and the counters % Disk Time, Avg. Disk Queue Length, Avg. Disk Read Queue Length, and Avg. Disk Write Queue Length

Four additional reasons why one or more disks are busy or are a source of bottlenecks are:

- Fragmentation

- Disk fault tolerance method

- Location of files

- Disk speed

Perhaps the most common reason for a disk bottleneck is that one or more disks are heavily fragmented. You can easily address this problem by running the Disk Defragmenter, as explained in Chapter 7.

14

If you have configured disk storage RAID-5 volumes, the bottleneck may be linked to more active disk writing than you initially estimated. RAID-5 disks are able to read data faster than they can write it, because they must take time to calculate and write parity and fault tolerance data with each write operation. You can compare read to write activity by using the following System Monitor measures:

- For read activity, monitor the LogicalDisk and PhysicalDisk counters Avg. Disk Bytes/Read and Avg. Disk sec/Read.

- For write activity, monitor the LogicalDisk and PhysicalDisk counters Avg. Disk Bytes/Write and Avg. Disk sec/Write.

The Avg. Disk Bytes/Write and Avg. Disk Bytes/Read counters measure the average number of bytes transferred to or from the disk per each read or write activity. The Avg. Disksec/Read and Avg. Disksec/Write counters show the average number of seconds it takes to perform the disk read or write activity. If the disk write activity is much more frequent than read activity and the users report delays in their work, consider using disk mirroring or duplexing instead of stripe sets with parity or RAID-5 volumes.

On disks that employ no fault tolerance measures or that are mirrored, the location of disk files can be important to diagnosing a bottleneck. Frequent visual inspection may show that one set of mirrored volumes is busier than another set. Suppose you have two sets of mirrored volumes, disk sets 0 and 1, and your visual inspections indicate that disk set 0 is often busy, but disk set 1 is not. You can study the discrepancy further by monitoring on both disks using the LogicalDisk counters % Disk Time, Avg. Disk Queue Length, Avg. Disk Read Queue Length, and Avg. Disk Write Queue Length. If you find, for example, that disk set 0 is nearly always busier than disk set 1, consider moving files. This tuning requires knowledge of the files and their purpose. For example, disk set 0 may contain a set of Microsoft Access databases that are used constantly, while disk set 1 has only sparse data. In this situation, you can spread the load of the databases between the two disks (consulting first with the users).

In some situations, a hard disk simply may have a slow transfer rate and may need to be upgraded, particularly if it is an older disk. As discussed earlier, measure the disk transfer rate by monitoring the PhysicalDisk counter Disk Bytes/sec along with % Disk Time. Set up a test by transferring large files to that disk or by developing a large query of a database. The disk performance is related to the data transfer rate of the disk adapter and controller, and the disk access time is the speed of the disk in accessing data. It can be very worthwhile to replace old disk technology with newer disks that use high-speed SCSI adapters and that have fast disk access times (see Chapter 2). Table 14-11 presents a summary of tips for monitoring and tuning disk performance.

Table 14-11   Using System Monitor Objects and Counters to Monitor Disk Performance

Object: Counter	Explanation
LogicalDisk: % Disk Time	Measures the percentage of time that a disk is busy with Read or Write requests. If this level is sustained at 80% or greater, redistribute files to spread the load across multiple logical drives. Also check the corresponding PhysicalDisk counter.
LogicalDisk: Avg. Disk Bytes/Read and LogicalDisk: Avg. Disk Bytes/Write	Used together, these provide a way to compare disk read to disk write activity, as a way to determine if you need to modify a currently established fault-tolerance method or add disk spindles.
LogicalDisk: Avg. Disk Bytes/Transfer	Measures the average number of bytes transferred between memory and disk during Read and Write operations. If the value is at or near 4 KB, this might mean excessive paging activity on that drive. A larger number indicates more efficient transfers than a smaller one, so watch for declines from the baseline as well.
LogicalDisk: Avg. Disk Queue Length and LogicalDisk: Current Disk Queue Length	These objects/counters indicate how many system requests are waiting for disk access. If the queue length is greater than 2 for any logical drive, consider redistributing the load across multiple logical disks, or if this is not possible, upgrade the disk subsystem. Also check the corresponding PhysicalDisk counters. Monitor these counters with Avg. Disk Read Queue Length and Avg. Disk Write Queue Length for more detailed statistics.

Table 14-11   Using System Monitor Objects and Counters to Monitor Disk Performance (continued)

Object: Counter	Explanation
PhysicalDisk: Avg. Disk Queue Length and PhysicalDisk: Current Disk Queue Length	These objects/counters track activity per hard disk, but provide much the same kind of information that the logical disk counters do. However, the problem threshold for physical disks is different than it is for logical ones. For physical disks, the threshold is between 1.5 and 2 times the number of spindles on the hard drive. For ordinary drives, this is the same as for logical disks. But for RAID arrays (which Windows 2000 treats as a single drive) the number is equal to 1.5 to 2 times the number of drives in the array. Monitor these counters with Avg. Disk Read Queue Length and Avg. Disk Write Queue Length for more detailed statistics.
PhysicalDisk: % Disk Time	Measures the percentage of time that a hard drive is kept busy handling Read or Write requests. The sustained average should not exceed 90%, but even if sustained averages are high, this value is not worrisome unless the corresponding queue length numbers are in the danger zone as well.
PhysicalDisk: Avg. Disk Bytes/Read and PhysicalDisk: Avg. Disk Bytes/Write	Used together, these provide a way to compare disk read to disk write activity, as a way to determine if you need to modify a currently established fault-tolerance method or add disk spindles.
PhysicalDisk: Avg. Disk Bytes/Transfer	Measures the average number of bytes transferred by Read or Write requests between the drive and memory. Here, smaller values are more worrisome than larger ones, because they can indicate inefficient use of drives and drive space. If a small value is caused by inefficient applications, try increasing file sizes. If it is caused by paging activity, an increase in RAM or cache memory is a good idea.
PhysicalDisk: Disk Bytes/sec	Tracks the number of bytes read from and written to disk each second. Use this object/counter combination to study the transfer rate of a disk to determine if you need to purchase a faster disk drive.

14

Monitoring Terminal Services

When you install terminal services on a server, you can monitor two objects through System Monitor: Terminal Services and Terminal Services Session. The Terminal Services object enables you to monitor active sessions, inactive sessions, and total sessions. The Terminal Services Session object enables you to view selected sessions or all sessions and to determine how they affect the server load—for example, by selecting Terminal Services Session as the object, selecting % Processor Time as the counter, and clicking to view all instances, as in Figure 14-14.

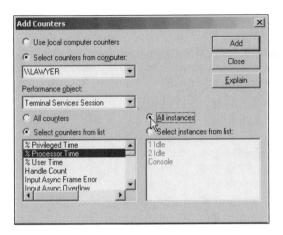

Figure 14-14   Monitoring terminal services

Monitoring File System Cache

Windows 2000 Server uses a portion of RAM for file system cache as a way to enhance a server's performance. **Cache** is employed by computer systems to store frequently used data in quickly accessed storage, such as memory. In Windows 2000 Server, file system cache operates as an intermediary between disk operations and an application that requests data. When the application requests data, the operating system first checks cache and then checks disk storage to locate the data.

In Windows 2000 Server, the operating system attempts to store both program code and data that have a high probability of being accessed, including code and data that have been used most recently, in the file system cache. In some cases, if the operating system determines that records in a particular file are likely to be accessed, it may cache the entire file.

When working with file systems, Windows 2000 does not truly load data into cache, but instead creates maps or pointers to the disk location of data. The pointers enable the system to quickly access data without engaging in a search process to obtain its disk location and then load the data. The cache pointers are kept in RAM only, relieving the stress on page file resources.

The success of file system caching is measured through cache hits and misses. A *cache hit* is an instance in which an application goes to cache and there is a pointer to the disk location of the data the application needs. A *cache miss* occurs when there is no pointer and a disk search process is used to find the data location. A low cache miss rate means that low disk I/O activity has been used to obtain data, because there was less searching to find the data. When the operating system determines there is no longer a need to store certain information in file system cache, it performs a *flush* to make that cache area available for the next cached information.

File system cache performance is influenced by the way in which an application obtains data and by the way data is stored in a file. The best performance results when an application accesses data sequentially and when data is stored sequentially in a file and on disk, because it is not necessary to jump to different disk locations for data. A program's caching efficiency can be measured through System Monitor by watching the Cache object and the Copy Read Hits % counter. Microsoft recommends that this counter should be in the 80-90% range.

The Windows 2000 Server operating system controls the amount of RAM that is allocated to file system cache. Also, the amount allocated is determined by the amount of RAM in the server. For example, if there is 64 MB of RAM, the amount allocated to cache is likely to be about 10–15 MB, and for 128 MB RAM, cache will be around 30–40 MB. The Performance tab in Task Manager (refer to Figure 14-6) shows the amount of RAM allocated for file system cache.

Too little file system cache equates to a system bottleneck, particularly on servers in which software applications make extensive use of the cache. There are only limited ways to tune the cache on a server. The best way to tune cache is to install more memory. A second option is to increase the priority given to file system cache in memory, as you learned in Chapter 7. To increase the priority, open Network and Dial-up Connections, right-click Local Area Connection, and click Properties. Scroll the installed components list to find File and Printer Sharing for Microsoft Networks, and double-click that component to view memory tuning options. Click *Maximize data throughput for file sharing* to give a higher priority to file system caching, so more RAM is allocated by the operating system for this purpose (see Figure 14-15). If, instead, you click *Maximize data throughput for network applications*, priority (RAM space) is taken away from file system cache and used for working sets.

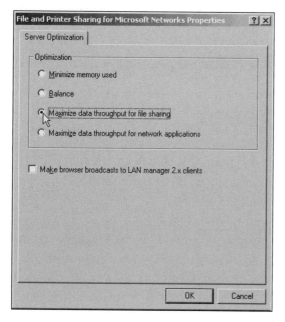

Figure 14-15 Tuning file system cache

14

A **working set** is the amount of RAM allocated to a running process. Thus, when you tune the server you need to determine if you need more RAM allocated to file system cache or more to running processes. One way is to use System Monitor to study cache needs for memory, compared to working set needs. To make a comparison, first monitor cache using the following at the same time: (1) Cache as the object and Copy Read Hits % as the counter, (2) Memory as the object and Available Bytes as the counter, and (3) Process as the object, Page Faults/sec as the counter, and Total as the instance. Next, monitor the working set activity by using at the same time: (1) Process as the object and the counters Working Set and Page Faults/sec, and (2) Memory as the object and Available Bytes as the counter. As a general rule, if the server is used most to run applications and access data files, consider tuning it to give priority to cache. If the server is mostly used to run processes, tune it for working sets. Table 14-12 presents tips for monitoring and tuning file system cache.

Table 14-12   Using System Monitor Objects and Counters to Monitor File System Cache

Object: Counter	Explanation
Cache: Copy Read Hits %	Tracks the file system cache access and should be in the range of 80–90%. If it is lower than this range, make sure the server is tuned to *Maximize data throughput for file sharing* or add more RAM.
Memory: Available Bytes	Measures the amount of RAM that can be used by processes
Process: Page Faults/sec	Measures the number of page faults for a process. Monitor the page faults of all processes by using Total as the instance.
Process: Working Set	Tracks the amount of RAM currently allocated to a process. Monitor using Total as the instance to determine how much RAM is allocated to all processes.

USING PERFORMANCE LOGS AND ALERTS

Performance logs and alerts work as partners with System Monitor. **Performance logs** are used to track performance data over a given period of time, and **alerts** are used to warn you of problems when they occur. There are two kinds of performance logs: counter logs and trace logs. A counter log traces information on System Monitor objects that you configure, taking a snapshot at intervals that you determine, such as every 15 seconds. Trace logs monitor particular events that you specify, so that the log contains only those instances when the events occur, for example creating a trace to record each time there is disk input/output activity or when there is an Active Directory Kerberos security event. After a log is created, you can open it from System Monitor to view its contents. You can also create a log in a format that can be imported into a spreadsheet, for example into Excel. Table 14-13 shows the file formats that are available.

Table 14-13   Counter Log File Formats

Format	Description
Text file – CSV (.csv extension)	Used to export data into a spreadsheet that employs comma delimiters after data lines
Text file – TSV (.tsv extension)	Used to export data into a spreadsheet that employs tab delimiters after data lines
Binary File (.blg extension)	Used when you want to stop and start performance recording
Binary Circular File (.blg extension)	Used when you want to record information for an extended time and automatically restart at the beginning of the file

In general, the steps to create a counter log are to open the Performance tool from the Administrative Tools menu, double-click Performance Logs and Alerts to display the objects under it in the tree, right-click Counter Logs, and click New Log Settings (see Figure 14-16). Enter a name for the log, click the Add button, and complete setting up the monitoring parameters in the Select Counters dialog box, which is similar to the Add Counters dialog box used in System Monitor setup. Try Hands-on Project 14-7 to set up a counter log.

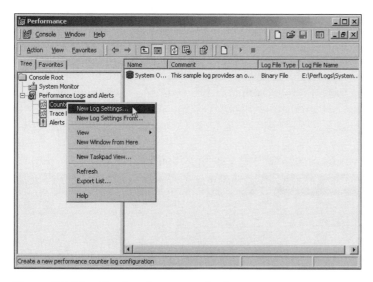

Figure 14-16   Configuring a counter log

TIP   Counter logs can occupy a significant amount of disk space and can slow system performance. Microsoft recommends that you take a snapshot at 15-second intervals or more frequently, if you plan to monitor for 4 hours or less. If you plan to monitor for over 4 hours, increase the interval. For example, if you monitor for 8 hours, take a snapshot at about every 5 minutes or so. Also, adjust the log file size so that it is large enough to hold the information sampled for a specified period of time.

14

If you need to manually stop the log before the specified stop time, right-click the log in the right-hand pane of the Performance tool, and then click Stop. You can restart the log by right-clicking it, and then clicking Start. Also, you can start a new logging session, for example, each morning, by right-clicking the log and then clicking Start. To add more objects and counters to monitor, right-click the log, click Properties, and then access the General tab. Click Add to use more objects and counters or click Remove to delete ones you do not want. Also, each new generation of a log (for instance if you start a log every morning for a week) is automatically labeled according to your specifications, which are set on the Log Files tab. Or, you can use the default, which is to end the saved log file from each recording session with an incremented number in the form "*nnnnnn*," such as 000001 for the first session, 000002 for next session, and so on.

Trace logs are useful when you do not want to continuously monitor performance, but want to document each instance of a particular event over a period of time. This is especially helpful in finding intermittent problems, such as excessive load on the server or network at certain times of the day or on certain days of the week. The elements that you can monitor in a trace log are more limited than those available to a counter log. Table 14-14 shows the trace log elements that can be monitored by the type of element. There are two types of elements: system provider and non-system-provider. The system provider elements are system processes, such as starting processes or performing disk operations. Non-system-processes are those handled by entities such as the Active Directory or local security provider. Also, there are only two file types available for trace logs: circular trace file and sequential trace file (both have a .etl extension). A circular trace file is used when you want the system to automatically overwrite data from the beginning of the file, when the file's capacity is exceeded. A sequential trace file is one in which the file is automatically closed when it is filled, and the system starts a new file. Hands-on Project 14-8 shows how to configure a trace log.

Table 14-14   Trace Log Elements That Can Be Monitored

System Process Elements to Monitor	Nonsystem Process Elements to Monitor
Process creations/deletions	Active Directory: Kerberos
Thread creations/deletions	Active Directory: SAM
Disk input/output	Active Directory: NetLogon
Network TCP/IP	Local Security Authority (LSA)
Page faults	Windows NT Active Directory Service
File details	

An alert gives you immediate warning when a problem occurs. For example, you may want Windows 2000 Server to send you an alert each time that the CPU is at 100% utilization. Each alert is sent to specific accounts, such as to the accounts belonging to the Administrators domain local group. To configure an alert to track 100% CPU use, for example:

1. Open the Performance tool from the Administrative Tools menu.

2. Double-click Performance Logs and Alerts to display the objects under it in the tree.

3. Right-click Alerts and click New Alert Settings.

4. Enter a name for the alert and click OK.

5. Click Add.

6. Select the option to monitor the Processor as the object, % Processor Time as the counter, and select the instance, such as Total, to monitor all processors. Click Add and then click Close. Click OK if a warning is displayed that you must set the alert limit.

7. Make sure that the object and counter are highlighted, and then enter Over in the *Alert when the value is* box. Enter 99 in the *Limit box*.

8. Set the interval at which the system should check for this event, such as every 5 or 10 seconds.

9. Click the Action tab. Check *Log an entry in the application event log*, if it is not already checked. Check *Send a network message to* and specify your account name or a group, such as Domain Admins. There also are options to start a performance log or to run a program when the event occurs.

10. Click OK.

11. Click Alerts in the tree, and then right-click the Alert that you created and click Properties, if you want to modify any of the parameters that you configured.

CAUTION

System Monitor, performance logging, and alert monitoring have been enhanced in Windows 2000 to use less CPU and memory resources, but they do occupy some resources. Use these tools only when you need them so that you do not regularly affect server performance with monitoring activities.

14

CHAPTER SUMMARY

❏ The best preventive medicine for keeping server performance at its peak is to develop solid monitoring techniques. The first step in the monitoring process is to create a set of benchmarks so you have a way to compare normal performance to situations in which there are performance, hardware, or software problems. Benchmarks enable you to quickly identify and address problem areas as they develop.

❏ Server services are often the first place administrators go to monitor Windows 2000 Server, because so many critical functions rely on these services working smoothly. Other areas to monitor are the users who are logged on and the resources they access, such as shared folders.

❏ One of the easiest-to-use monitoring tools is Task Manager. Through it you can stop applications that are hung, tune processes, and keep track of memory and CPU use. Tuning a process can be an inexpensive and effective way to improve server performance.

❐ System Monitor is a versatile and widely used Windows 2000 Server monitoring tool. It enables you to monitor key server components such as processor, disk, and memory performance. There are hundreds of System Monitor configurations to track and diagnose almost every type of server problem. Performance logs and alerts employ System Monitor capabilities to enable you to track information in logs for later reference and to receive instantaneous notification of when there is a problem.

In the next chapter, you learn how to implement and use network monitoring tools to help in tuning network performance and diagnosing problems.

KEY TERMS

alert — Provides a warning of a specific Windows 2000 Server system or network event. The warning is sent to designated users.

backup browser — A computer in a domain or workgroup that maintains a static list of domain/workgroup resources to provide to clients browsing the network. The backup browser periodically receives updates to the browse list from the master browser.

base priority class — The initial priority assigned to a program process or thread in the program code by Windows 2000 when the program is started.

benchmark — A measurement standard for hardware or software used to establish performance baselines under varying loads or circumstances. Also called a baseline.

cache — Storage used by a computer system to house frequently used data in quickly accessed storage, such as memory.

counter — Used by System Monitor, this is a measurement technique for an object, for example, for measuring the processor performance by percentage in use.

file lock — Flagging a file so that it cannot be updated by more than one user at a time, giving the first user to access it the ability to perform an update.

handle — A resource, such as a file, used by a program that has its own identification so the program is able to access it.

hard page fault — When a program does not have enough physical memory to execute a given function and must obtain information from disk.

instance — Used by System Monitor, when there are two or more types of elements to monitor, such as two or more threads or disk drives.

leaking memory — Failing to return memory for general use after a process is finished using a specific memory block.

master browser — On a Microsoft network, the computer designated to keep the main list of logged-on computers.

named pipes — A communications link between two processes, which may be local to the server or remote, for example, between the server and a workstation.

performance log — Tracks system and network performance information in a log that can be viewed later or imported into a spreadsheet, such as Microsoft Excel.

process — An executable program that is currently running, such as Microsoft Word. A process may launch additional processes that are linked to it, such as a Help process to view documentation or a search process to find a file.

process tree — All of the processes that run directly or indirectly in association with an original process.

System Monitor — The Windows 2000 utility used to track system or application objects. For each object type there are one or more counters that can be logged for later analysis, or tracked in real time for immediate system monitoring.

thread — A block of program code executing within a running process. One process may launch one or more threads.

working set — Amount of RAM allocated to a running process.

REVIEW QUESTIONS

1. Your advertising firm is expecting a new client to visit in about 15 minutes. In preparation, you have been printing out reports and graphics for the meeting, but the print process has been going slowly because the server is so busy. What can you do to best help ensure that the printouts are finished in time?

   a. Log all other users off, even if there is not time to give them sufficient notification.

   b. Increase the priority of the print spooler process to AboveNormal or High.

   c. Decrease the priority of all processes, except the spooler process to Low.

   d. Quickly increase the page file size by 1–2 MB to handle the printouts.

2. You are about to back up a Windows 2000 server in a small office and everyone has gone home for the evening. However, you notice through a window in a locked office that a computer is still logged on and seems to have a file open. How can you log off that computer from the server?

   a. Use the System Tools option in the Computer Management console.

   b. Use the Services and Applications option in the Computer Management console.

   c. Right-click that user's account in Local Users and Groups and access the General tab.

   d. Right-click that user's account in Local Users and Groups and click Log Off.

3. You are using the System Monitor Memory object and the Available Bytes counter to monitor memory. Which of the following results would be an indication that you need to add more RAM?

   a. frequent values between 7 and 10 MB

   b. frequent values of 3 MB or lower

   c. frequent values of 1 to 2 MB

   d. all of the above

   e. only a and b

   f. only b and c

14

4. Your Windows 2000 server is running slowly, and you suspect there is a program or program process that is causing the problem because you just installed eight new programs on it which are run by you on the server and by clients using terminal services. Which of the following tools enable you to monitor for the problem?

   a. Task Manager using the Processes tab

   b. System Monitor using the Process object

   c. Computer Management tool using the Services option

   d. all of the above

   e. only a and b

   f. only b and c

5. Which of the following modes can you use in System Monitor for displaying tracked data?

   a. histogram

   b. chart

   c. report

   d. all of the above

   e. only a and b

   f. only b and c

6. Several of your Windows 2000 Server clients are running Windows 3.11 and may be contending as master browsers. How can you monitor possible contention?

   a. Monitor the processes in Task Manager.

   b. Use the System Monitor Browser object.

   c. Monitor the number of user connections and the resources they are employing.

   d. Monitor for excessive cache hits.

7. While you are directly logged on to a Windows 2000 server using Internet Explorer, you discover that the program is not responding to any keystrokes you make, including your attempts to close the program. When you go to another window, all functions are normal. How can you close Internet Explorer?

   a. Use the Services tool to stop and restart the Explorer service.

   b. Use the Computer Management tool to stop and restart the Browser service.

   c. Use the Performance snap-in to set the priority of the Explorer.exe program to 0.

   d. Use Task Manager to end the Internet Explorer task.

8. You are receiving calls from users saying that they cannot log on to a Windows 2000 server over the network. You know that the server has a reliable NIC and network connection and that it is running without apparent problems. Which service should you check as one place to start working on the problem?

   a. Workstation

   b. System Event Notification

   c. Plug and Play

   d. RunAs

9. Through monitoring with System Monitor, you have located a program that is slowing server response because it is leaking memory. What is the best solution?

   a. Have the vendor fix the program or purchase another one that does not leak memory.

   b. Add more RAM.

   c. Install a faster processor.

   d. Increase the page file size.

10. You want to tune file caching on your server, but before you do, you decide to monitor file caching. Which of the following monitoring tools will help provide the performance information you need before tuning the server?

   a. System Monitor, using the Processor object and % Processor counter

   b. Task Manager, using the Performance tab

   c. System Monitor, using the Cache object and Copy Read Hits % counter

   d. all of the above

   e. only a and c

   f. only b and c

11. You are gathering system performance statistics, using the counter log, so that you can compile them into a spreadsheet to present to the Computer Resources Committee in your organization. What file type can you employ to store the data using tab delimiters for importing into a spreadsheet?

   a. text file format, using the .csv extension

   b. binary circular file format, using the .blg extension

   c. binary file format, using the .blg extension

   d. text file format, using the .tsv extension

12. You have assigned your assistant to monitor paging on the server to determine if more RAM is needed. In the absence of baselines, what number of page faults per second should she look for that would indicate it may be time to add RAM?

   a. more than 5

   b. 3 to 4

   c. 2 to 3

   d. 1 to 2

14

13. You work for a company that has servers distributed in different locations throughout a business building. How can you monitor, start, and stop server services from a Windows 2000 server located next to your office, so that you do not have to walk all over the building?

    a. Use System Monitor.

    b. Use the MMC Performance snap-in.

    c. Use the MMC Services snap-in.

    d. Services cannot be monitored on another server, except by using terminal services.

14. Which of the following may be solutions to relieving a processor bottleneck?

    a. Lower the priority of a particular process.

    b. Replace mirrored volumes with RAID-5 volumes as a way to reduce the number of CPU calls from adapters.

    c. Locate a possible hardware problem in which the device constantly accesses the processor.

    d. all of the above

    e. none of the above

    f. only a and b

    g. only a and c

15. While practicing, your assistant changed the priority of Windows Explorer, and now the server response for all users is extremely slow. What priority did he most likely set?

    a. High

    b. Normal

    c. Realtime

    d. Low

16. In Question 15, if you did not already know the process for which the priority was changed, which tool could you use to determine the process?

    a. Task Manager Performance tab

    b. Task Manager Processes tab

    c. System Monitor, using the Process object

    d. all of the above

    e. only a and b

    f. only b and c

17. Your boss has been using System Monitor to exclusively track the Processor object and % Processor time on a single CPU server. She does not have much time to monitor, but has decided that it is time to purchase a faster CPU because % Processor time occasionally reaches 85 to 100%. What is your advice?

    a. You agree that it is time to purchase a new CPU.

    b. You recommend adding more RAM instead.

c. You recommend rebooting the server immediately, because this is a sign of CPU leakage.

d. You recommend doing nothing, because this only indicates efficient use of the CPU by some programs and services.

18. One of your server administrator colleagues in another company is struggling to understand the data produced by System Monitor. The servers and network at that company have been in place for about 5 months, but he has been too busy setting up clients to gather information about server performance. Now he does not know how to interpret the information so as to determine in what areas performance is normal and in what areas it is not. What should he have done in advance?

a. Gather server and network benchmarks.

b. Started the System Monitor from day one and left it running continuously to gather data on the 10 most critical monitor objects.

c. Run a trace log at least two full days a week, every week, monitoring system provider events.

d. all of the above

e. only a and c

f. only b and c

19. You want to stop the Remote Procedure Call service, but are not sure what other services depend on it. How can you most easily find out?

a. View the properties for the Remote Procedure Call service in the Services tool and access the Dependencies tab.

b. Open the Services Dependencies object in the tree of the Services tool.

c. Stop the services that you think it might depend on and look for the error messages.

d. Look in the System Information option under the console tree in the Computer Management tool.

14

20. You want to set up a counter log to track system activity over a 12-hour period on two processor-based counters and one memory counter. What adjustments should you make when you set up the counter log?

a. Set the log file size large enough to hold this much information.

b. Only track system provider events for those objects.

c. Set the sampling interval relatively high, for example, once every 10 or 20 minutes.

d. all of the above

e. only a and b

f. only a and c

21. Which of the following is not an object that you might monitor in the System Monitor?

a. Job Object

b. Distributed Transaction Coordinator

c. Network Connection Linker

d. Server Work Queues

22. The vice president of marketing is calling you because he is trying to update an Excel spreadsheet that is shared from a Windows 2000 server. On the phone he is concerned because when he enters new data, there is a message that the file cannot be updated. Which of the following might cause this problem and what tool can you use to find the cause?

    a. The share is hidden, which means it cannot be updated. Use the Computer Management tool to check.

    b. The file is locked by another user. Use the Computer Management tool to check if this is the case.

    c. The Excel.exe process priority is set too low, at BelowNormal, which means updates are not processed. Use Task Manager to change the process's priority.

    d. all of the above

    e. only a and b

    f. only a and c

23. Your assistant wants to monitor the number of clients actively using a Windows 2000 terminal server. How can this be accomplished using System Monitor?

    a. Monitor the Server object

    b. Monitor the Terminal Services object

    c. Monitor the Browser object

    d. Terminal Services clients can only be monitored using the Terminal Services Manager, which is not part of System Monitor.

24. Which of the following System Monitor objects would you monitor to study paging activity on a server?

    a. Paging File

    b. Memory

    c. Server

    d. all of the above

    e. only a and b

    f. only a and c

25. Which of the following should you monitor when watching for a processor bottleneck in Windows 2000 Server?

    a. The length of the queue that holds processes waiting to access the CPU.

    b. The typical number of interrupt requests from hardware devices.

    c. The percentage of time in which the processor is engaged in non-idle processes.

    d. all of the above

    e. none of the above

    f. only a and b

    g. only a and c

HANDS-ON PROJECTS

Project 14-1

In this project you practice monitoring, starting, and stopping a service. You also view the service's dependencies.

To monitor the service, manage it, and view its dependencies:

1. Click **Start**, point to **Programs**, point to **Administrative Tools**, and click **Services**.
2. Scroll the right-hand pane to view the services that are installed and then find the ClipBook service.
3. What is the status and Startup Type of the service? Record your observations in your lab journal or in a word-processed document.
4. Double-click the **ClipBook** service.
5. If the service is not started, click the **Start** button, or if it is started, click the **Stop** button.
6. If you started the service, now click the **Stop** button, or if you stopped it, click the **Start** button.
7. How would you change the startup type? Record your observations.
8. Click each tab to view what it does and note your observations.
9. When you click the Dependencies tab, what services are dependent on the ClipBook service? On what services does the ClipBook service depend? Record your observations.
10. Click **OK** and then close the Services tool.

Project 14-2

In this project, you practice viewing the users who are connected to a Windows 2000 server and determining which files are locked.

To view the user connections:

1. Right-click **My Computer** on the desktop and click **Manage**.
2. Double-click **Shared Folders** under System Tools in the tree.
3. Click **Sessions** in the tree.
4. How many users are connected to the server? How many of those users have open files? Record your observations.
5. Click **Open Files** in the tree.
6. Are there locked files? If so, record some examples of files that are locked.
7. Record how you would view the shares that are set up on a server and the number of clients connected to each share.
8. Close the **Computer Management** tool.

14

Project 14-3

In this activity you set a process's priority and stop a task. To perform this activity, open Control Panel and then My Computer before starting.

To set the priority and stop a task:

1. Press **Ctrl+Alt+Del**.

2. Click the **Task Manager** button in the Windows 2000 Security dialog box.

3. Click the **Applications** tab, if it is not already displayed. What applications are currently running?

4. Right-click **My Computer** and then click **Go To Process**. (This takes you to the Processes tab.)

5. Right-click the **explorer.exe** process.

6. Click **Set Priority** and then click **AboveNormal**. Click **Yes** in the Task Manager Warning dialog box. What might happen if you clicked Realtime instead of AboveNormal? Record your answer.

7. Click the **Applications** tab.

8. Click **Control Panel** and then the **End Task** button. What happens to Control Panel? Record your observation.

9. Close Task Manager.

Project 14-4

This project gives you an opportunity to practice viewing objects, counters, and instances in System Monitor.

To view System Monitor objects, counters, and instances:

1. Click **Start**, point to **Programs**, point to **Administrative Tools**, and click **Performance**.

2. Double-click **Console Root** to view System Monitor, if it is not displayed.

3. Click **System Monitor**.

4. What is displayed in the right-hand pane?

5. Click the **Add** button (a plus sign) in the button bar in the right-hand pane.

6. What computer is selected by default for monitoring? How would you monitor activity on a different computer? Record your observations.

7. Click the down arrow in the Performance object box. Scroll through the options and record some of them in your lab journal or in a word-processed document.

8. Select the default, which is **Processor**. Make sure that the **Select counters from list** radio button is selected. Scroll to view the counters associated with the Processor object. What instances are available?

9. Next, click **Server** as the object. How many counters and instances are associated with this object?

10. Click **Process** as the object. How many counters and instances are associated with the Process object?

11. Observe two more objects and their associated counters and instances.

12. Click **Close** in the Add Counters dialog box, but leave the Performance console open for the next assignments.

Project 14-5

In this project, you use System Monitor to check for processor bottlenecks, such as the processor's ability to handle the server load and possible problems caused by hardware.

To check for processor bottlenecks:

1. Make sure that the Performance console is already open; if not, open it to display System Monitor.

2. Click the **Add** button in the button bar to add counters.

3. If it is not already selected, click **Select counters from computer** and make sure that the computer you are using is selected.

4. Make sure that **Processor** is selected in the Performance object box.

5. Make sure that **Select counters from list** is selected and click **% Processor Time**. Leave **Total** as the default for instances. What information does this counter provide for the Processor object? How would you find out, if you didn't know? Record your observations.

6. Click **Add**.

7. Click **% Interrupt Time** as the counter and leave **Total** as the instance. Click **Add**.

8. Scroll the counters list and click **Interrupts/sec**. Leave **Total** as the instance and click **Add**. How do the % Interrupt Time and Interrupts/sec counters help in diagnosing a processor bottleneck?

9. In the Performance object box, select **System**.

10. Scroll the counters list and click **Processor Queue Length**. Are there any instances? Click **Add**. What information does this object and counter combination provide in monitoring for a processor bottleneck?

11. Click **Close**.

12. Monitor the system for several minutes to determine if there are any processor problems. Record any problems that you diagnose using System Monitor. How would you change the view mode from a chart to a histogram? How would you add another object to monitor? Record your observations.

13. In the bottom portion of the right-hand pane, click each counter, one at a time, and click the **Delete** button (an X) on the button bar. (Leave the Performance console open for Hands-on Projects 14-7 and 14-8.)

14

Project 14-6

In this activity, you check on whether the Diskperf driver is installed and the System Monitor disk counters are activated:

To check on Diskperf's status:

1. Make sure you are logged on as Administrator or with Administrator privileges.

2. Click **Start**, point to **Programs**, point to **Accessories**, and click **Command Prompt**.

3. In the Command Prompt window, type **diskperf**.

4. What message is displayed in the first line after the command? What other information is provided? Record your results.

5. How would you start Diskperf to set up counters only for physical drives?

6. Type **exit** and press **Enter** to close the Command Prompt window.

Project 14-7

This project gives you practice in creating a counter log. Consider a situation in which you want to monitor paging and memory for a typical workday to help determine if you need to adjust the page file size or to add more RAM.

To set up a counter log for monitoring performance over a period of 8 hours:

1. Make sure that the Performance console is already open, and if not, open it to display Performance Logs and Alerts.

2. Double-click **Performance Logs and Alerts** to display the objects under it in the tree.

3. Right-click **Counter Logs** and click **New Log Settings** (refer to Figure 14-16).

4. Enter **Mem** and your initials, such as **MemMJP**, as a name for the log and then click **OK**.

5. Click the **Add** button.

6. Compare the options that you see to those you can use in System Monitor and record your observations.

7. Click **Use local computer counters**.

8. Choose the performance object, **Paging File**, select **% Usage** as the counter, and then select **_Total** as the instance. Click **Add**.

9. Choose the object, **Paging File**, select **% Usage Peak** as the counter, and then select **_Total** as the instance. Click **Add**.

10. Choose the object **Memory**, select **Page Faults/sec** as the counter. Are there any instances from which to select? Click **Add**.

11. Click **Close**.

12. Set the Interval box to **5** and the Units box to **minutes**.

13. Click **OK**.

14. Click **Yes** to create the folder for the log in which to record the information, if a folder has not already been created.

15. Click **Counter Logs** in the tree. There will be a green disk icon in front of the log name in the right-hand pane that shows the log is active and gathering data. Right-click the log, click **Properties**, and then click the **Schedule** tab.

16. In the Start log section of the dialog box, make sure that **At** is clicked and set the start time and date to match the current time and date.

17. Next, in the Stop log section, click **After** and enter **8** in the After box and **hours** in the Units box.

18. Click the **Log Files** tab. List the options for the Log file type and record them. (Note that any of the file formats can be converted to another format by using the Save As option when you right-click the log in the right-hand pane.)

19. Click **OK**. How would you view the log's contents?

20. After the log has run for a few minutes, right-click it and then click **Delete**.

Project 14-8

In this project, you set up a trace log to monitor each time a page fault occurs. Because this type of monitoring requires extra system resources, you will only set it up to monitor for 30 minutes.

To create a trace log of page faults:

1. Make sure that the Performance console is already open, and if not, open it to display Performance Logs and Alerts. Make sure that Trace Logs is displayed under it in the tree.

2. Right-click **Trace Logs** and then click **New Log Settings**.

3. Enter **CPU** and your initials as the log name, such as **CPUMJP**. Click **OK**. (If no folder has previously been created for log files, click OK to create the folder.)

4. On the General tab, click **Events logged by system provider** and make sure that only **Process creations/deletions** and **Page faults** are checked. Notice the name and location of the log file, which is where you can access it later to obtain its contents. Record this information.

5. Click the **Schedule** tab.

6. If it is not already selected, click the **Manually (using the shortcut menu)** radio button to start the log manually.

7. In the Stop log area, click **After**, and set the After box to **30** and the Units box to **minutes**.

8. Click **OK**. (Click **Yes** if you are asked to create the \Perf Logs folder.)

9. Click **Trace logs** in the tree and find the log you created in the right pane. What color is the icon that represents the log? Right-click the log and make sure that the Start option is deactivated, which means that it is already started. If it is not started, click **Start**.

10. Instead of waiting for 30 minutes, manually stop the log file after about 10 minutes, by right-clicking the log name, such as CPUMJP, in the right-hand pane and then clicking **Stop**. How would you restart the log?

11. Close the Performance console.

14

CASE PROJECTS

Aspen Consulting Project: Server Monitoring

Funds Unlimited is a firm that nonprofit organizations hire to help plan fundraising strategies and projects. The firm handles clients such as colleges, universities, charitable organizations, and others. They have two Windows 2000 servers that provide networked services to 80 consultants, managers, and staff members. The servers and network have been in use for about one year and now there seem to be some performance problems that Funds Unlimited wants to address. They have hired you to work with four staff members who administer the servers.

1. Funds Unlimited has never taken the time to gather server performance benchmarks. Develop a plan for gathering benchmarks that will help them monitor the server, perform regular tuning maintenance, and diagnose problems.

2. The server administrators are very unfamiliar with the basic server monitoring tools. Prepare a brief description of each of the following tools, including how to access each tool:

   ❑ Services MMC snap-in

   ❑ Computer Management tool and the Shared Folders option

   ❑ Task Manager

   ❑ System Monitor

   ❑ Performance logs and alerts

3. While you are on-site, one of the programs that is running on the server stops responding. Explain how to close the program. While you are closing the program, also explain to the server administrators how to set the priority on a process, including any precautions you have to take when doing this.

4. Funds Unlimited has recently implemented a new client/server system in which a large database is kept on one of the servers and the program files are on the other server. The database server experiences frequent slowdowns throughout the day, but no one has kept track of specific instances. The management is discussing whether to purchase a faster CPU or an SMP computer to speed up access to the database server. Explain how they might gather information about the server's performance before making a decision to upgrade the server. In particular, address how they might do the following:

   ❑ Monitor the number of users

   ❑ Monitor the processor

   ❑ Monitor memory and paging

   ❑ Monitor processes used by the client/server system

   ❑ Monitor disk response

5. Explain how to set up a counter log to assist with the monitoring that you described in Assignment 4. Also, explain how they might set up alerts to help in gathering information.

OPTIONAL CASE PROJECTS FOR TEAMS

Team Case One

There are many ways to analyze memory, paging, and processor interaction on a Windows 2000 server. Mark Arnez asks you to form a group to develop a set of guidelines that can be used to learn when to add more RAM to a server and when to upgrade the processor.

Team Case Two

Mark Arnez asks your same team to work on a document that shows how to develop a plan for establishing server benchmarks in an organization. Develop two models as examples of how to develop benchmarks. For one model, use a small office that has one server and that uses mainly word-processing, spreadsheet, and small database applications. In the second model, use a larger business in which there are 10–40 servers, many of which are running databases, client/server software, multimedia software, and graphics/publishing software.

14

15

NETWORK MONITORING AND TUNING

> **After reading this chapter and completing the exercises you will be able to:**
> ♦ Establish network benchmarks
> ♦ Install Network Monitor Driver
> ♦ Install, configure, and use Network Monitor, including setting up filters and triggers
> ♦ Install and configure the SNMP service
> ♦ Use System Monitor to monitor a network
> ♦ Troubleshoot and tune a network

Monitoring a network is as important as monitoring servers on the network. Network monitoring enables you, as an administrator, to quickly identify and fix problems and to determine when to upgrade a network to match growing needs. One important reason to gather network benchmarks and to monitor the network on an ongoing basis is so that you can differentiate between problems created by servers and workstations and those created by network difficulties. If administrators do not regularly monitor a network, it might be possible, for example, to mistakenly upgrade hubs or routers when the real problems are with servers or workstations, such as overloaded servers or slow NICs.

In this chapter, you learn how to use Network Monitor and System Monitor to identify network problems and differentiate them from server or workstation problems. You learn how to establish network benchmarks and how to monitor networks in different ways, as well as how to install network monitoring utility software such as Network Monitor, Network Monitor Driver, and the SNMP service. All of these tools will prove to be critical to you, particularly as your servers and the network grow more complex.

NETWORK MONITORING

Networks can be very dynamic in terms of changing patterns of communication. One minute a network may be running smoothly with no delays, and the next minute there are network slowdowns. Regularly monitoring your network is vital, because there are many factors that can influence network performance. For example, a network may experience slow traffic because of a defective cable or hub. Another source of problems can be a malfunctioning NIC on a server or workstation that creates bottlenecks by endlessly sending broadcasts over the network. In some cases, a server NIC may be performing normally, but may be too slow for the number of clients it must handle. Similarly, the network may be working normally, but appear to be slow because of a server that has a slow processor that causes network clients to wait in line.

Another reason why network activity changes is that client activity changes on the basis of times of the day and days of the week. For example, a segment of a college's network in the administration building may experience intense activity at certain times such as when the college is preparing its annual budget or working to finalize the payroll. A small architectural firm may experience heavy network activity when architects are completing large graphics files to submit to one or more clients.

Because networks are so dynamic, the best way you can prepare for and resolve problems is to monitor the network. Network monitoring is also more meaningful when you establish network benchmarks, so that you have a way to determine what network conditions are normal and what conditions indicate problems or the need to expand or upgrade the network. To establish network benchmarks, consider monitoring for the following:

- Slow, average, and peak network activity in relation to the work patterns at your organization

- Network activity that is related to specific protocols, such as TCP/IP and IPX/SPX

- Network activity that is related to specific servers and host computers

- Network activity that is related to specific workstations

- Network activity on individual subnets or portions of a larger network

- Network traffic related to WAN transmissions

- Network traffic created by particular software, such as client/server and multimedia applications

Plan to use your network benchmarks, along with the server benchmarks discussed in Chapter 14, as critical tools in helping you to tune the network and servers for optimum performance, as well as to quickly identify problems. For example, these benchmarks will help you determine if a slowdown reported by users is caused by a problem at a server or by a network problem, such as a broken network hub or switch.

Windows 2000 Server Network Monitoring

There are four key network management and monitoring tools available in Windows 2000 Server:

- Network Monitor Driver
- Network Monitor
- SNMP service
- System Monitor

Network Monitor Driver enables server and workstation NICs to capture network performance statistics that are used by the Network Monitor and System Monitor tools. The SNMP service is used with specialized network monitoring systems to gather wide-ranging network data and to manage network devices. All of these tools are explained in the sections that follow.

Using Network Monitor Driver

Network Monitor Driver is a protocol that works along with Network Monitor to enable you to monitor a network. **Network Monitor** is a Microsoft tool that captures and distills network performance information. When you install Network Monitor Driver on a server or workstation, it enables that computer's NIC to collect statistics about network performance, such as the number of packets sent and received at that computer. When Network Monitor Driver is installed, it links up with Microsoft's NDIS (Network Driver Interface Specification, see Chapter 3) on the computer in what is called the **local-only mode**, which captures and views only the contents of frames and packets sent to and transmitted from the local computer. This is in contrast to the **promiscuous mode** used by some network monitors and devices, in which the contents of all frames and packets are captured for possible viewing. With Network Monitor Driver loaded, the NIC gathers information about protocol traffic and network utilization, and data concerning broadcasts, unicasts, and multicasts. **Broadcasts** are transmissions sent to all locations of a network, for example, when a server or workstation sends a periodic broadcast that it is connected and working. A **unicast** transmission (see Chapter 3) involves sending one copy of each packet to each targeted destination. Thus, if eight workstations are requesting a multimedia application from a server, the server sends eight copies of each packet, one copy for each workstation—a transmission method that can generate considerable network traffic. **Multicasts** enable a multimedia server to make one transmission to a group of designated computers, which means that if eight computers request a multimedia application, only one packet is sent per transmission to the eight computers as a group.

A Windows 2000 workstation or server running Microsoft analysis software, such as Network Monitor or System Monitor, can connect to the computer running Network Monitor Driver and use that computer's NIC to capture data for analysis. Even computers remotely connected through RAS can be turned into network data collection stations. Figure 15-1

15

illustrates a computer running Windows 2000 Server, with Network Monitor and Network Monitor Driver loaded, obtaining data from a computer running Windows 2000 Professional in another location on the same network and from a computer running Windows 2000 Professional that is connected to a branch network and that has dialed into the main network through a RAS connection. Both computers running Windows 2000 Professional have Network Monitor Driver installed and the server that has Network Monitor can gather network performance data via the NICs on those computers.

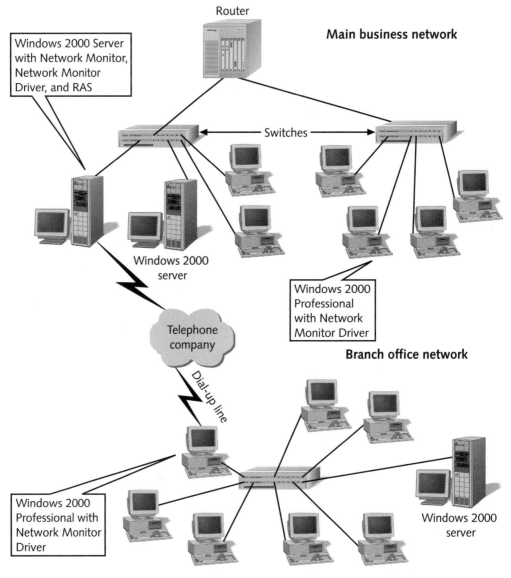

Figure 15-1   Using Network Monitor Driver to gather network performance information on two separate networks

TIP Windows 2000 Server comes with a version of Network Monitor Driver that works only on computers running Windows 2000 (Professional, Server, Advanced Server, and Datacenter). If you want to use other workstations as network data collection agents, such as those running Windows 95, Windows 98, or Windows NT, then it is necessary to purchase Microsoft Systems Management Server, which includes versions of Network Monitor Driver for these operating systems.

Network Monitor Driver is installed in Windows 2000 Server by using the Network and Dial-up Connections tool. Click Start, point to Settings, click Network and Dial-up Connections, right-click Local Area Connection, click Properties, click Install, double-click Protocol, and double-click Network Monitor Driver (see Figure 15-2). The Network Monitor Driver installation does not also install Network Monitor, which is installed separately as described later in this chapter. Try Hands-on Project 15-1 to install Network Monitor Driver.

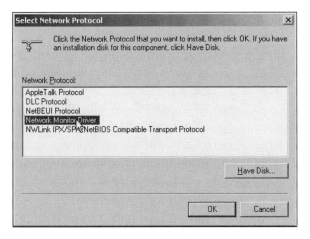

Figure 15-2   Installing Network Monitor Driver

USING NETWORK MONITOR

Network Monitor is included with the Windows 2000 Server CD-ROM and uses Network Monitor Driver to monitor the network from the server's NIC. When Network Monitor is installed, it enables you to monitor a full range of network activity and to check for possible problems. Network Monitor tracks information such as the following:

- Percent network utilization

- Frames and bytes transported per second

- Network station statistics

- Statistics captured during a given time period

- Transmissions per second information

- Information about broadcast, unicast, and multicast transmissions

- NIC statistics

- Error data

- Addresses of network stations

- Network computers running Network Monitor and Network Monitor Driver

When you run Network Monitor to monitor traffic across a network, Network Monitor Driver detects many forms of network traffic and captures packets and frames for analysis and reporting by Network Monitor. Since it operates in the local-only mode, only the contents of packets and frames sent to and from the server can be viewed. However, all packets and frames that pass through the server's NIC are monitored (although not all contents are viewed) so that it is possible to determine basic information about the network, such as the amount of traffic, the types of packets, and the source and destination addresses of computers transmitting data.

 The version of Network Monitor that is included on the Windows 2000 Server CD-ROM is only designed to capture data at the server's NIC. Consider purchasing Microsoft Systems Management Server, which comes with a version of Network Monitor that can connect to and monitor activity from a NIC on any network computer that has Network Monitor Driver installed.

The general steps for installing Network Monitor are as follows (try Hands-on Project 15-2):

1. Open the Control Panel Add/Remove Programs tool.

2. Click Add/Remove Windows Components. If the Windows Components Wizard dialog box is not automatically started, click the Components button to start it.

3. Double-click Management and Monitoring Tools in the Windows Components Wizard dialog box.

4. Check Network Monitor Tools (see Figure 15-3) and click OK.

5. Click Next.

6. If requested, insert the Windows 2000 Server CD-ROM and click OK. (If a second dialog box is displayed, provide the path to the \I386 folder on the CD-ROM and click OK again.)

7. Click Finish.

8. Close the Add/Remove Programs window.

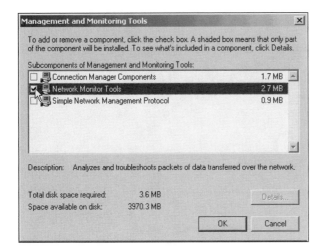

Figure 15-3   Installing Network Monitor tools

The steps for starting Network Monitor are as follows:

1. Click Start, point to Programs, point to Administrative Tools, and click Network Monitor.

2. Click OK if there is an information box that reminds you to select the network to monitor or to use the local area network as the default, and then click the network you want to monitor in the *Select a network* dialog box.

3. Maximize one or both Network Monitor screens, if the display is not maximized.

4. Click the Start Capture button on the button bar to start capturing network performance data.

5. View the data displayed on the screen, such as % Network Utilization or the Network Statistics (see Figure 15-4).

6. Use the scroll bars in each of the four windows to view the information they offer.

7. If you want to pause capturing data, click the Pause button on the button bar, and click it again later to resume capturing. When you are finished, click the Stop Capture button on the button bar.

8. Close Network Monitor.

9. If the Save File dialog box is displayed, click Yes if you want to save the captured data in a file, or click No if you do not want to save the data. If you click Yes, specify the filename in which to save the captured data, and then click Save.

15

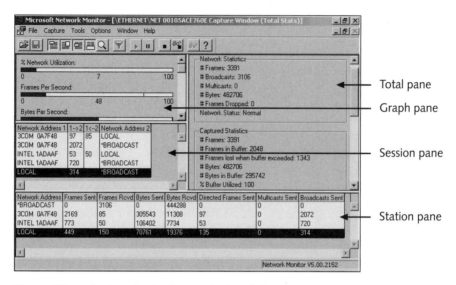

Figure 15-4   Network Monitor capturing data

> **CAUTION**
>
> Both Network Monitor and System Monitor create a load on the CPU of the computer where they are running. When you implement these as a server administrator, plan to run them on a limited basis from a server, so that time spent gathering the data does not interfere with the server's other activities. Some server and network administrators run Windows 2000 Professional on their personal workstation and gather network data from there, using the workstation's NIC, or by briefly attaching to a server's NIC.

Network Monitor can be customized to present many different pictures of network activity, because it displays four panes of data and because **filters** (explained in the next section) can be set to collect specific types of information. The four panes (see Figure 15-4) and the information that they record are presented in Table 15-1. Filters can be built based on addresses, protocols, and properties. For example, you might create a filter to capture only information about IP activity or only IPX transmissions. You can choose to capture data for a short or long period of time.

Table 15-1   Network Monitor Panes

Pane	Information Provided in the Pane
Graph	Provides horizontal bar graphs of the following: % Network Utilization, Frames Per Second, Bytes Per Second, Broadcasts Per Second, and Multicasts Per Second
Total	Provides total statistics about network activity that originates from or that is sent to the computer (station) that is using Network Monitor and includes many statistics in each of the following categories: Network Statistics, Capture Statistics, Per Second Statistics, Network Card (MAC) Statistics, and Network Card (MAC) Error Statistics

Table 15-1   Network Monitor Panes (continued)

Pane	Information Provided in the Pane
Session	Provides statistics about traffic from other computers on the network, including the MAC (device) address of each computer's NIC (see Chapters 2 and 3) and data about the number of frames sent from and received by each computer
Station	Provides total statistics on all communicating network stations, including: Network (device) address of each communicating computer, Frames Sent, Frames Received, Bytes Sent, Bytes Received, Directed Frames Sent, Multicasts Sent, and Broadcasts Sent

The Session and Station panes only display up to 100 sessions at once. If your network has over 100 connected devices, you must view the devices 100 at a time by clicking the Capture menu and clicking Clear Statistics.

After you have captured a specific amount of data, you can view all of the captured information as a line-by-line report of each captured event by clicking the Stop and View Capture button on the button bar to display the screen shown in Figure 15-5.

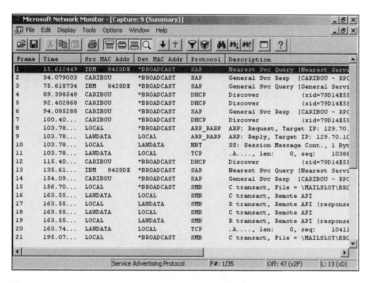

Figure 15-5   Viewing capture summary data

Table 15-2 lists the information provided in the capture summary.